LANGUAGE

Social Psychological Perspectives

Other Pergamon Titles of Interest

B Babington Smith & B Farrell
Training in Small Groups

H Giles & B Saint Jacques
Language and Ethnic Relations

L Hersov *et al*
Language and Language Disorders in Childhood

M Morris
Saying and Meaning in Puerto Rico

L Strickland
Soviet and Western Perspectives in Social Psychology

L Tamir
Communication and the Aging Process

T Taylor
Linguistic Theory and Structural Stylistics

A Related Journal

LANGUAGE & COMMUNICATION
An Interdisciplinary Journal

Editor: ROY HARRIS, *University of Oxford*

The primary aim of this new journal is to fill the need for a publicational forum devoted to the discussion of topics and issues in communication which are of interdisciplinary significance. It will publish contributions from researchers in all fields relevant to the study of verbal and non-verbal communication.

Emphasis will be placed on the implications of current research for establishing common theoretical frameworks within which findings from different areas of study may be accommodated and interrelated.

By focusing attention on the many ways in which language is integrated with other forms of interactional behaviour it is intended to explore ways of developing a science of communications which is not restricted by existing disciplinary boundaries.

Free specimen copy available on request.

LANGUAGE

Social Psychological Perspectives

Selected papers from the first International
Conference on Social Psychology and Language held
at the University of Bristol, England
July 1979

Edited by

HOWARD GILES, W PETER ROBINSON

and

PHILIP M SMITH

University of Bristol, England

PERGAMON PRESS

Oxford · New York · Toronto · Sydney · Paris · Frankfurt

U.K.	Pergamon Press Ltd., Headington Hill Hall, Oxford OX3 0BW, England
U.S.A.	Pergamon Press Inc., Maxwell House, Fairview Park, Elmsford, New York 10523, U.S.A.
CANADA	Pergamon of Canada, Suite 104, 150 Consumers Road, Willowdale, Ontario M2J 1P9, Canada
AUSTRALIA	Pergamon Press (Aust.) Pty. Ltd., P.O. Box 544, Potts Point, N.S.W. 2011, Australia
FRANCE	Pergamon Press SARL, 24 rue des Ecoles, 75240 Paris, Cedex 05, France
FEDERAL REPUBLIC OF GERMANY	Pergamon Press GmbH, 6242 Kronberg-Taunus, Hammerweg 6, Federal Republic of Germany

First edition 1980

British Library Cataloguing in Publication Data

International Conference on Social Psychology and Language, 1st. University of Bristol, 1979
Language.
1. Psycholinguistics - Congresses
2. Social psychology - Congresses
I. Title
II. Giles, Howard
III. Robinson, William Peter   IV. Smith, Philip M
301.2'1   P37   80-40714
ISBN 0-08-024696-6

P
37
.I53
1979

In order to make this volume available as economically and as rapidly as possible the authors' typescripts have been reproduced in their original forms. This method has its typographical limitations but it is hoped that they in no way distract the reader.

Printed in Great Britain by A. Wheaton & Co. Ltd., Exeter

To Anne Mallitte
in appreciation

Contents

Preface

In the 1970s a substantial number of social psychologists emerged, who individually and independently had begun active research into topics across a wide range of issues in the intersect of language and social behaviour. This work was marked by a distinctive methodological character, which became increasingly interesting to those from other disciplines, but it did not cohere conceptually into a unified social psychological paradigm.

We therefore decided that the end of the decade would offer a suitable occasion for bringing together as many such research workers as we could under the aegis of the first International Conference on Social Psychology and Language. This would enable scholars from within and without social psychology to recognise the importance and potential of that perspective and to familiarise each other with their theoretical, methodological and empirical concerns and achievements. There was no subtle implication that there is a single, best social psychological perspective; the title of this volume acknowledges a diversity of legitimate enterprises. The lack of an established view was revealed in the letters of the many puzzled enquirers who wrote to us prior to the conference wondering what the conference was to be about. In the hope that a conference would bring greater thrust and coherence to our endeavours we organised this conference at the University of Bristol, from July 16th to 20th, 1979, under the auspices of the Social Psychology Section of the British Psychological Society.

The task of selecting the topics to be represented at the conference caused us considerable concern. We wished the symposia to reflect the wide variety of social and communicative processes extant. We knew there were many viable alternative ways of categorising these. We were aware that we would be persuading people to convene the symposia. With such considerations in mind we chose nine topics: language acquisition; interpersonal communication; language and sex roles; language and social class; language and ethnicity; language and attitudes; language, personality, emotion and psychopathology; temporal aspects of speech; bilingualism, multilingualism and code switching. We were extremely fortunate in attracting eminent scholars, who had themselves worried constructively about the "whys" of sociolinguistic and communicative phenomena and made significant contributions to theory as well as to empirical knowledge: Catherine Snow, Charles Berger, Cheris Kramerae, Norbert Dittmar, Donald Taylor, Ellen Bouchard

Ryan, Klaus Scherer, Aron Siegman, Stanley Feldstein and Carole Scotton.   Each
generously agreed to scrutinise papers submitted and to encourage contributions
that would provide a balanced coverage of problems within a symposium topic, and
each convenor duly made these difficult selections.   At the conference they
personally introduced and chaired the delivery of these papers and ensuing discussion, in some cases also acting as discussants.   Their considerable contribution to the conference must be gratefully acknowledged.

Given the overwhelming number of acceptable submissions and the limitations of
time, we felt obliged to supplement the original symposia in two ways: additional
sessions of triads on language acquisition, interpersonal communication, language
and sex roles, humour and communication skills and two further symposia of strong
contemporary interest on second language learning and language and the law, the
latter especially convened by Brenda Danet.   This left us regretfully rejecting
further papers submitted, simply because they did not fit into the temporal or
classificatory framework of the conference.   We had similarly to restrict attendance to some 270 participants because accommodation was limited.   Those who came
did so from the five corners of the earth and represented in various strengths
each of the communication, linguistic and social sciences.

We were particularly grateful to the four speakers who gave invited addresses to
the conference: Wallace Lambert, Michael Argyle, Susan Ervin-Tripp, and Walt
Wolfram.   Robert Farr very kindly set the conference in its historical context.

The conference was assessed by most of the participants to have been a great
success.   Certainly there was a gratifying flow of grateful letters to the
organisers, expressing satisfaction with both the intellectual and social aspects
of the conference.   The cooperative goodwill expressed towards the intellectual
offerings of the conference extended to the extra-mural and informal, and we
should like to acknowledge our debt not only to the guest speakers, symposium
convenors and paper givers, but to the administrative and social helpers as well:
to Jitendra Thakerar for exercising his never-exhausted energies in organising
social events and to Mike Huggins and his Company for their exciting review; to
Mike Huggins and his Team in their administrative roles, to Alma Foster for
typing the abstracts, and to Anne Mallitte.   Anne painstakingly and patiently
shepherded us through the event from its inception through to the publication of
the proceedings, which she typed.

Not all the papers read are incorporated in this volume.   Spatial constraints
precluded the inclusion of papers outside those of the original nine symposia and
the guest speakers.   Some of these will be published elsewhere in collections
edited by Paul Werth (Conversation, speech and discourse, Croom Helm) and Peter
Robinson (Communication in development, Academic Press).   Since these collections
allowed greater space to authors one exchange was made: Allen Grimshaw's extended
paper will appear in Paul Werth's collection while Rolf Hänni's paper has been
moved to this volume.   For various reasons a small number of the symposium contributions were not received as papers to be published.   In the light of with-
drawals and other difficulties Norbert Dittmar decided that the symposium on
language and social class could not be in the published proceedings.   All contributors had to abide by strict limits to the length of their presentations, and it
is possible that some readers would wish for more specific details and arguments
than the authors were able to include.   Brenda Danet offered an overview of the
symposium on language and the law, and the editors have written a Prologue to set
the scene and an Epilogue to comment on the conference papers and to suggest
possible priorities for the future.   Hopefully the richness of the volume in
other respects will compensate for any excessive brevity.

The papers presented are varied in their points of departure, offering a balance of theoretical and empirical contributions, and within the latter a mixture of laboratory experiments and naturalistic studies.   A number of papers were written by persons who would not see themselves as social psychologists, but who appreci- ate the importance that social psychological processes have for our understanding of the complexities and dynamics of language behaviour.   We hope that this variety will inspire readers from all disciplines to delve deeper into the subject matter of this embryonic and rapidly growing field.   In this sense, we trust that we can continue to reflect Lambert's appraisal that "ingenuity, vitality, and concern have become the hallmarks of the field" (p. 415).

April 1980   The Editors
                                                                     University of Bristol

Social Psychological Perspectives on Language: Prologue

H. Giles*, P. M. Smith* and W. P. Robinson**

*Department of Psychology, University of Bristol, 8-10 Berkeley Square,
Bristol BS8 1HH, U.K.
**School of Education, University of Bristol, 35 Berkeley Square,
Bristol BS8 1JA, U.K.

Despite the existence of a number of studies prior to the 1960s on social aspects
of language use, the study of language behaviour in its social context only really
emerged as a distinct field with its own label, "sociolinguistics", about the
mid-1960s.   In part, it developed as a reaction to the asocial linguistics and
psycholinguistics prevalent at that time which was attempting to provide understandings of language use without due concern for the context of situation in
which it was spoken;   it was as if context was considered a static given.   Yet,
as a result of its strong empirical activities (e.g. Fishman 1970;   Gumperz and
Hymes 1972;   Labov 1970;   for a recent review, see Hudson 1980), sociolinguistics
has acquired such momentum over a ten year period that it is almost unthinkable
for scholars of contemporary language use to think of themselves as anything
other than sociolinguists, whatever their particular research interests.
Sociolinguistics developed as a multidisciplinary endeavour by receiving strong
inputs from sociology and social anthropology as well as from linguistics itself;
hence its distinguishable sub-branches (e.g. sociology of language, secular
linguistics, ethnography of speaking), some of which are more sociologically-
oriented, whilst others are more linguistically-oriented in their approach
(Trudgill 1978).

Although the discipline as a whole has provided an array of interesting findings
in a relatively short period of time, particularly with respect to how, when and
where we change which features of our speech, a dissatisfaction (perhaps paralleled in other social sciences, certainly interestingly so in social psychology)
with the state-of-the-art was discernible by the mid-1970s.   Certain of these
worries, which we have discussed in more detail elsewhere (Giles, Hewstone and
St. Clair, in press;   Smith, Giles and Hewstone 1980), were fuelled in the main
by social psychologists although other language scientists (e.g. Scotton and Ury
1977) also voiced strong reservations.   First, sociolinguistics
had been relatively taxonomic and descriptive rather than explanatory in its
emphasis.   Second, sociolinguistic accounts of language variation had been couched
primarily in terms of associations between the use of specific speech features and
membership of apsychological social entities (large-scale, socio-demographic groupings, for example).   Such an approach was clearly incapable of contributing to the
idea that language behaviours (including the often sociolinguistically neglected
body movements, gestures, facial expressions and gaze patterns) are significantly
determined by the ways in which speakers construe themselves and the situation
rather than by the classifications of category of membership imposed by researchers
from without.   As argued by Giles, Hewstone and St. Clair (in press):

> ... objectively describing a social situation <u>as</u> 'a formal interview on
> a serious topic with a 90-year-old Black woman' will have little pre-
> dictive value concerning her likely speech patterns if she herself de-
> fines the interview informally, considers the subject matter irrelevant
> and trivial, feels "White" and 50-years of age.

The third and related concern was that sociolinguistics had tended to separate
language from definitions of society and social situations.   Traditional sociolinguistics cannot cope systematically with the idea that language behaviour, far
from being the passive automatic reflection of an underlying social reality, is
the product of individuals who are actively engaged in the construction of social
reality who perhaps, as often as not, use language to create and manage situations
and impressions.   As Smith, Giles and Hewstone (1980, p.285) have pointed out:

> ... our assignment of an interlocutor to a certain SES or ethnic
> category, or our definition of a social situation as informal or
> technical, can on many occasions be based exclusively on our inter-
> pretations of the other's speech.   To exclude language <u>a priori</u>
> from a definition of social variables is to run the risk of
> employing concepts that are impoverished from the perspective of
> participants and observers of interaction.

Although some sociolinguists have acknowledged the importance of these problems
(e.g. Labov 1969; Sankoff 1972) and have alluded to the mediating influence of
social psychological constructs such as attitudes, motivations, identities and
intentions in determining language behaviours, this does not seem to have
resulted in a widespread change in the way that sociolinguistics is practised or
interpreted.

With a few exceptions, for example Brown (1965) on power and solidarity in forms
of address, Gardner and Lambert (1972) on attitudes in second language learning,
and Argyle (1975) on processes of nonverbal communication, social psychology has
made little theoretical impact on sociolinguistics, as it appears in journals and
texts.   Given that language behaviour was central to <u>initial</u> developments in
social psychology (see Farr) and that much individual <u>social</u> behaviour (supposedly
the "meat" of social psychology) involves language and its use, this could be considered a surprising state of affairs.   Contemporary social psychology could be
defined, by elaborating the approach outlined by Allport (1968) with a European
addendum (cf Israel and Tajfel 1972) as the study of the ways in which the
thoughts, feelings, and behaviours of others are influenced by the actual,
imagined and implied presence of others and by the sociostructural forces operating in society.   Hence, language behaviour, in addition to being a product of
people who are influenced by others, is also one of the means by which we can
exert influence.   Armed, therefore, with a belief and commitment to the idea
that their particular theories and methodologies could at least help to ameliorate
the situation in sociolinguistics and to weld it with important work being conducted in relative isolation by other communication scientists, the latter half of
the 1970s (in particular) has witnessed a sudden flourish in books on language
behaviour written by social psychologists (e.g. Robinson 1972; Giles and Powesland 1975; Markova 1978; Giles and St. Clair 1979; Scherer and Giles 1979; St.
Clair and Giles 1980).   The present volume is in many ways a manifestation and
celebration of the arrival of a social psychological perspective (or set of perspectives) which has now been recognised indisputably as an important and substantive approach to understanding the complexities and dynamics of language behaviour.

The distinctive contributions of a social psychological perspective on language
may lie in its ability to integrate the study of the system and resources of

language with the study of social behaviour more generally, and in the potential
for social psychological theory and method to shed light on the alternating roles
of language variables as explicit and consciously-manipulated sources of influence
on the one hand (see Berger, Kramarae), and as passive indices of influence on the
other.   Before elaborating further on the possible character of a social psychological perspective, it may well be useful to provide a summary introduction of
papers in this volume.

Although it is impossible to do justice in this brief overview to the wealth and
complexity of the data and ideas reported, it is possible to separate the contributions which further our understanding of the encoding aspects of language behaviour from those which are primarily concerned with decoding; admittedly some
papers attend to both processes.   In line with Argyle's definition of the social
psychology of language as "the study of the use of language and sequences of
utterances in social situations" (p. 397), many of the papers which focus upon encoding have been concerned with the plasticity of language behaviour in different
contexts, whether or not they are under some form of conscious control (Berger).
For instance, language behaviour and communicational effectiveness have been
found to be dependent on the social relationships between interactants in terms of
their age (Berko-Gleason; Ervin-Tripp; Gormly and colleagues), ethnicity (Drake;
Lambert; Platt, pp. 171-177; Taylor and Royer), social class (Scherer and colleagues);
sex (Fishman; Leet-Pellegrini; Pedersen), social roles (Berko-Gleason; Engle;
Ervin-Tripp), professional roles (Danet; Hinnenkamp), perceived warmth (Siegman
and Crown), aggressiveness (Scherer, Helfrich and Scherer), familiarity (Duchan;
Leudar), particular speech patterns (Cappella; Kendall; Krause; Wolfram).   In
addition, authors have been at pains to point out that other aspects of context
also influence language behaviour such as the topic of conversation (Brown, pp.
237-245; Platt, pp. 345-351), task complexity (Pedersen), perceived functional
goals (Argyle; Dabbs; Fishman) and the sociostructural context in which the
interaction takes place (Clément; Hinnenkamp; Taylor).   Many contributors have
of course varied more than one of these contextual attributes within the same
design.

The complexity of this encoding process is further highlighted in four ways.
First, there are often elaborate, and sometimes conflicting social norms prescrib-
ing language behaviour (Bourhis and Genesee; McKirnan and Hamayan), thereby
confronting speakers with a complex decision-making process (Platt, pp. 171-177).
Ultimately perhaps some aspects of this may be described post hoc in terms of a
set of formal situational rules making up a probabilistic grammar (Clarke, Ellgring
and Wagner).   Second, on some occasions, the situation may be so weakly defined
that appropriate norms and language behaviour have to be negotiated by means of a
complex set of interrelated maxims (Scotton, pp. 359-365).   Third, language behaviour is not only determined by situational features alone (or "external pulls"
as Scherer calls them) but also by "internal pushes" such as speakers' psycho-
physiological and clinical states (Brown, pp. 237-245; Ellgring, Wagner and
Scherer; Leudar; Wallbott and Scherer) and the desire to self-present in a particular way so as to elicit a particular desired reaction from listeners (Scherer,
Helfrich and Scherer).   Fourth, language behaviour adapts creatively not only to
changing demands within the duration of a single encounter (Argyle; Siegman and
Crown) including the processes of mutual influence (Howe; Johnson; Wells) and
previous situational influence (Hänni), but also to the changing demands of the
same relationship across different encounters (Kendall) as well as to socio-
historical changes between different sections of society (Drake; Taylor).

However, as mentioned previously, language behaviour also operates as an independent variable determining the operation of social processes.   How does it operate
in the decoding processes?   Investigations show that particular linguistic features and language styles adopted by speakers may affect seriously recipients'
understanding of their messages (MacKay) and their behavioural reactions to it

(Sebastian and colleagues), its effectiveness in anticipated compliance (Bradac and colleagues, pp.71-76) as well as their assessments of the speakers' intents (Danet; Grayshon), emotional and psychopathological states (Brown, pp.237-245; Wallbott and Scherer), social identities (Drake; Smith) and their perceived psychological attributes (Brown, pp.293-300 ; Sebastian and colleagues). Moreover, these different language features can be shown to affect speakers' presumed effectiveness in certain important applied contexts including the employment (Kalin, Rayko and Love), legal and bureaucratic (Danet; Hinnenkamp), educational (Lambert) and clinical (Wallbott and Scherer) domains. Among the speech variables shown to have important social consequences are language choice (Bourhis and Genesee), accent (Kalin, Rayko and Love; Sebastian and colleagues), jargons and slang (Danet; Drake; Wober), speech rate (Brown, pp.293-300), fundamental frequency (Scherer, Helfrich and Scherer; Wallbott and Scherer) and lexical diversity (Bradac, Courtright and Bowers). Coming more or less full circle, contextual and sociostructural variables (Roberts and Williams; Smith and Bailey) not only influence the decoding process in terms of socially evaluating speakers' language styles but also can provide essential shared meaning for comprehending and re-acting appropriately to the utterances themselves (Argyle; Ervin-Tripp).

The topics just surveyed closely resemble those considered in other branches of sociolinguistics. This is bound to be the case since most of the authors repre-sented in this volume owe historical debts to one or another of the research fields subsumed by contemporary sociolinguistics. While we are optimistic that this similarity of concern will continue to bode well for the cross-fertilisation of our disciplines, an ever-widening gap appears to yawn between the sources of theoretical inspiration and methodological precedents informing sociolinguistic practice and those upon which social psychologists draw; let us précis some of the theoretical and methodological preoccupations of contemporary social psychology.

Most currently prominent theories in social psychology are concerned with how in-dividuals search for understanding of the behaviour of others and the situations in which they find themselves and how this understanding serves to guide be-haviours. In essence the focus is upon understanding the <u>cognitive organisation which mediates</u> between a person's perception of the situation and his or her be-havioural reactions. Of particular relevance to the social psychologist inter-ested in language are questions as to how and why speech and nonverbal behaviours are dependent upon cognitive organisation in adults. How and why has this organisation developed? At the same time, however, the behaviour of others stimulates inferences about their social category memberships and attitudes, their motivations and views of the situation, inferences which are organised in terms of their own expectancies, values systems, past experiences, etc.. In short, language is also an independent source of input for cognitive organisation. While we have no grand theory of cognitive organisation to guide our explorations into language behaviour we do have a wide variety of heuristic models and empiri-cal generalisations which have provided social psychologists with insights into (non-linguistic) social behaviours. For instance, causal attribution theory proposes that when we observe behaviour of others we attribute motives and in-tentions to it. Different theoretical perspectives on this principle (e.g. Harvey, Ickes and Kidd 1978) attempt to make explicit the conditions under which people attribute this behaviour to stable <u>internal</u> dispositions of the indivi-duals concerned or to certain transient <u>external</u>, situational factors operating on them at the time. Developments of these ideas might enable us to understand <u>why</u> certain cooperative language strategies such as code switching or convergence of styles would be viewed positively by listeners in some contexts but not in others; we might also be able to predict the conditions under which certain groups' speech patterns (e.g. those of women, working class and ethnic minority speakers) would be seen as reflecting their cognitive and/or communicative com-petences rather than as responses to the situational constraints as they perceive

them.   The usefulness of attribution theory for understanding social issues of
language has been well articulated by Berger and Calabrese (1975), Lind and O'Barr
(1979) and more recently Hewstone (in press),(see also Taylor).   Middle range
social psychological theories can elucidate processes underlying encoding as well
as decoding of language behaviour.   For instance, social identity theory proposes
that we desire to belong to social categories which afford us a positive group
identity;   the theory attempts to make explicit the conditions under which group
members will search for, or even create, dimensions along which they are positively differentiated from relevant outgroups (Tajfel 1978).   Such a theory enables
us to explain why some groups maintain their own languages, dialects and styles,
while others lose them and assimilate towards the speech patterns of a more
powerful group (Cherry;   Drake;   Taylor;   Giles 1979);   it also indicates under
which conditions people in bilingual contexts will actively resist learning an
outgroup's tongue to the extent of native-like proficiency (Clément;   Lambert).

One important feature of this volume is that contributors are highlighting not
only the foregoing two processes but also social psychological constraints
and theories of cognitive organisation.   In encoding, language behaviour is
treated as being mediated by processes of perceived goal structures (Argyle),
perceived power relationships (Cherry;   Bradac and colleagues, pp. 71-76;
Ervin-Tripp;   Leet-Pellegrini;   Pedersen;   Scotton, pp.359-365), social identification (Drake;   Lambert;   Smith;   Taylor), social comparison (Drake;   Taylor),
social norms (Ellgring and colleagues;   McKirnan and Hamayan), arousal (Cappella;
Clément;   Krause;   Scherer and colleagues), self-presentation (Scherer and
colleagues), group polarization (Taylor and Royer), solving communicational problems (Duchan;   Fishman;   Kendall) and cognitive monitoring (Berger;   Engle;
Hänni;   Johnson;   Siegman and Crown;   Wells). Such are the aspects of cognitive
organisation highlighted.   Decoding of language behaviour is likewise referred
to mediating processes of violation of role expectancies (Bradac and colleagues,
pp. 71-76), causal attributions (Danet;   Grayshon;   Taylor), attitudes and
identities (Clément;   Harrison;   Hinnenkamp;   Lambert;   Wober), arousal
(Sebastian and colleagues;   Wallbott and Scherer), social identification (Kalin
and colleagues;   Smith) and behavioural control (Bradac and colleagues, pp.217-
221).   In addition, for both encoding and decoding, attention is given to the
ways in which individuals' cognitive representations and organisation of perceived sociostructural forces operating in society mediate the production and
reception of language behaviour (Clément;   Hinnenkamp;   Roberts and Williams).

An important tool of social psychologists has been the experimental method,
although there have been critics of it within the discipline (e.g. Harré and
Secord 1972;   see however Turner, in press).   Such a procedure is of course
extremely useful in its potential for replication and rigorous control of extra-
neous variables as well as in its capacity to allow more exact specifications of
the conditions under which certain language patterns are emitted, and the types
of responses people afford particular language behaviours in specific contexts.
This is a methodological feature almost unique to psychology among the social
sciences and it is used by the majority of empirical investigations reported in
this volume.

In addition social psychology has techniques for measuring complex psychological
dispositions (e.g. ideologies, personality) for attitudes by means of traditional
Likert-type scales, semantic differentials and Thurstone/Guttman scales (see for
example Bradac and colleagues, pp. 71-76;   Bradac and colleages, pp. 217-221;
Bourhis and Genesee;   Brown, pp.293-300;   Dabbs;   Jose and colleagues;   MacKay;
Smith;   Taylor and Royer), and more recently it has developed the capacity to
explore the ways in which individuals construe or cognitively organise a situation.   We refer here particularly to multidimensional scaling, a technique which
simultaneously enables informants to reveal their cognitive organisation, while

retaining the methodological rigour of other more limiting tools (Taylor 1976;
Wish and Kaplan 1977; Forgas 1979; Giles, Llado, McKirnan and Taylor 1979).
With this and related techniques it has been possible to discover the conceptual
structures implicitly used by people in their coding both of interpersonal
communication and of identity profiles of members of different social categories
(Argyle; Bradac and colleagues, pp. 71-76;   Lambert; Wiemann and Krueger).

We have stressed the value of a social psychological approach to language and
this emphasis might be interpreted as pointing to actual and potential conflicts
between this orientation and other sociolinguistic pursuits grounded in sociology,
social anthropology and linguistics.   Obviously, we recognise the validity and
importance of these approaches.   Sometimes they focus on different phenomena,
but when we all focus upon the same ones they provide different levels of explanation from our own.   Interdisciplinary "wars" usually evolve from trying to go
beyond one's brief.   As social psychologists we are not equipped to offer
biological, anthropological, sociological, historical or linguistic explanations
for the similarities and differences we observe; it would of course be lamentable
if we were totally ignorant of them.   This is of course not to say we cannot
examine - as already stated - how these non-psychological issues are cognitively
organised by individuals.   However we can imagine a caricature of academics
from different disciplines looking for common problems to research and then
arguing at length about priorities of perspectives as candidates for investigation.
This risk may be as perilous as a single-minded pursuit of the social psychology
of language.   Let us each to our own enterprise, cooperating and learning
wherever possible, rather than wasting time on arguments about relative validity
or value.

In sum then, social psychological perspectives on language provide contemporary
sociolinguistics with useful complements in terms of (i) existing methodology
and important theoretical contributions of the middle-range; (ii) focussing
upon the manner in which language and social parameters interact as independent
and dependent variables; (iii) and relating this more specifically to how
individuals construe their interactions over the course of an encounter through
processes of cognitive organisation.   In this manner, we may be able to broaden
the explanatory scope of sociolinguistics and harden the socio component of this
multidisciplinary endeavour.   In the Epilogue, we will address ourselves to the
current state of the art and the methodological and theoretical priorities for
the future.

References

Allport, G. W. Historical background of modern social psychology, in G. Lindzey
    and E. Aronson (Eds.) Handbook of social psychology (Volume 1). Reading,
    Mass.: Addison-Wesley, 1968
Argyle, M. Bodily communication.   London: Methuen, 1975
Berger, C. R. and Calabrese, R. J. Some explorations in initial interaction and
    beyond: toward a developmental theory up into personal communication.
    Human Communication Research, 1975, 1, 99-112
Brown, R. Social psychology.   London: Collier-Macmillan, 1965
Fishman, J. A. Sociolinguistics: a brief introduction.   Rowley, Mass.: Newbury
    House, 1970
Forgas, J. P. Multidimensional scaling: a discovery method in social psychology,
    in G. P. Ginsburg (Ed.) Emerging strategies in social psychology. London:
    Wiley, 1979
Gardner, R. C. and Lambert, W. E. Attitudes and motivation in second-language
    learning. Rowley, Mass.: Newbury House, 1972
Giles, H. Ethnicity markers in speech, in K. Scherer and H. Giles (Eds.)
    Social markers in speech.   Cambridge: Cambridge University Press, 1979

Giles, H., Hewstone, M. and St. Clair, R. Speech as an independent and dependent variable of social situations: an introduction and new theoretical framework, in H. Giles and R. St. Clair (Eds.) The social psychological significance of speech. Hillsdale, New Jersey: Erlbaum (in press)

Giles, H., Llado, N., McKirnan, D. and Taylor, D. M. Social identity in Puerto Rico. International Journal of Psychology, 1979, 14, 185-201

Giles, H. and Powesland, P. F. Speech style and social evaluation. London: Academic Press, 1975

Giles, H. and St. Clair, R. Language and social psychology. Oxford: Blackwell, 1979

Gumperz, J. J. and Hymes, D. Directions in sociolinguistics: the ethnography of communication. New York: Holt, Rinehart and Winston, 1972

Harré, R. and Secord, P. The explanation of social behaviour. Oxford: Blackwell, 1972

Harvey, J. H., Ickes, W. and Kidd, R. F. New directions in attribution theory. Vol. 2. Hillsdale, New Jersey: Erlbaum, 1978

Hewstone, M. Attribution processes and the social psychology of language, in J. Jaspars, F. Fincham and M. Hewstone (Eds.) Attribution theory: essays and experiments. London: Academic Press (in press)

Hudson, R. Sociolinguistics. Cambridge: Cambridge University Press, 1980

Israel, J. and Tajfel, H. The contexts of social psychology. London: Academic Press, 1972

Labov, W. The logic of nonstandard English. Georgetown University Monographs on Language and Linguistics, 1969, 22, 1-31

Labov, W. The study of language in its social context. Studium Générale, 1970, 23, 66-84

Lind, E. A. and O'Barr, W. M. Social significance of speech in the courtroom, in H. Giles and R. St. Clair (Eds.) Language and social psychology. Oxford: Blackwell, 1979

Markova, I. Language in its social context. London: Wiley, 1978

Robinson, W. P. Language and social behaviour. Harmondsworth: Penguin, 1972

Sankoff, G. Language use in multilingual societies: some alternative approaches, in J. B. Pride and J. Holmes (Eds.) Sociolinguistics. Harmondsworth: Penguin, 1972

Scherer, K. and Giles, H. Social markers in speech. Cambridge: Cambridge University Press, 1979

Scotton, C. M. and Ury, W. Bilingual strategies: the social functions of code-switching. International Journal of the Sociology of Language, 1977, 13, 5-20

Smith, P. M., Giles, H. and Hewstone, M. Sociolinguistics: a social psychological perspective, in R. St. Clair and H. Giles (Eds.) Social and psychological contexts of language. Hillsdale, New Jersey: Erlbaum, 1980

St. Clair, R. and Giles, H. Social and psychological contexts of language. Hillsdale, New Jersey: Erlbaum, 1980

Tajfel, H. Differentiation between social groups: studies in intergroup behaviour. London: Academic Press, 1978

Taylor, D. M. Ethnic identity: some cross-cultural comparisons, in J. W. Berry and J. W. Lomer (Eds.) Applied cross-cultural psychology. Amsterdam: Severs and Zeitlinger, 1976

Trudgill, P. Introduction: sociolinguistics and sociolinguistics, in P. Trudgill (Ed.) Sociolinguistic patterns in British English. Edward Arnold: London 1978

Turner, J. C. Some considerations in generalising experimental social psychology, in G. M. Stephenson and J. H. Davis (Eds.) Progress in applied social psychology, Vol. 1. London: Wiley (in press)

Wish, M. and Kaplan, S. J. Toward an implicit theory of communication. Sociometry, 1977, 40, 234-246

Language Acquisition: Introduction

The Editors

Recent approaches to the study of language development in young children differ in two important ways from the dominating psycholinguistic perspective of the late 1960s (McNeill 1970). In the first place the conception of language has broadened from concerns with competence in syntax to interest in communicative skills across a range of language functions. As lists of functions have been expanded to include social activities (Dore 1978; Halliday 1975; Robinson 1972; Wells 1975), so inquiries have begun into the child's sociolinguistic competence. The analysis of Johnson extends the age range studied earlier in respect of contingent queries, a device for encounter regulation and management. Berko-Gleason's examination of routines and politeness formulae is starkly social, politeness being a cultural phenomenon par excellence. She links the differential behaviour of boys and girls to possible differential treatment and modelling by parents.

The second change in orientation has been towards an interest in input-output relationships. At a crude empirical level we can simply ask what variation in input is associated with what variation in output, but as we begin to resurrect or construct explanations that relate internal processes to products, theories of learning and tests of explanations for children's development should come to reassume their proper place.

A concern with differences between fathers and mothers in their interactions with children is the main focus of Engle's exposure of variability: she shows that fathers as well as mothers need to be included in studies of input to and treatment of children. Howe directs attention to rates of semantic development and seeks to relate these to different types of parent-child conversation; the data are consistent with her suggestion that interactions requiring the child to take an active role in the conversation facilitate development. Wells, with a larger number of children and more complicated arrays of speech variables for both child and parent shows that speech addressed to fast developing children is both quantitatively and qualitatively different from that addressed to slow developers. Such useful sets of empirical associations are ripe for explanations.

References

Dore, J. Variation in pre-school children's conversational performances, in K. E. Nelson (Ed.) Children's language, Vol. 1, New York: Gardner Press, 1978
Halliday, M. A. K. Learning how to mean. London: Arnold, 1975
McNeill, D. The acquisition of language. New York: Harper, Row, 1970

Robinson, W. P. <u>Language and social behaviour.</u>   Harmondsworth: Penguin, 1972
Wells, C. G. <u>Coding manual for the description of child speech.</u>   Bristol:
        University of Bristol, 1975

Contingent Queries: The First Chapter[1]

C. E. Johnson

*Division of Audiology and Speech Sciences, Faculty of Medicine, University of
British Columbia, Vancouver, B.C. V6T1W5, Canada*

ABSTRACT

The present study reports the development of contingent queries in eight children –
a girl and a boy at each six month age interval from 1;6 to 3;0 in relation to
question acquisition in general and the development of other discourse skills.
Overall results support Garvey's finding that contingent queries are used frequently and successfully by young children, and provide a counter-example to Corsaro's
(1977) observation that three children, 2;6-5, rarely produced them.   Data from
six audio- and video-taped play sessions over $2\frac{1}{2}$ months for each child indicate
that the earliest CQs are specific requests for confirmation (Garvey's taxonomy),
appearing by 1;6.   This supports Garvey's suggestion that this discourse unit
seems to play an important role in child-caregiver interaction from the earliest
stages of language learning, providing the child with immediate feedback on the
intelligibility of his own utterances as well as a means of checking his understanding of adult utterances.   The non-specific request for repetition appears
as "hm?" by 2;0 and the request for specification is first used at about 3;0.
Requests for elaboration were not used by these children.   The data suggest an
extension of Garvey's taxonomy, which does not account for the "insincere" contingent query as a turn filler.

Key words

Child development; speech; contingent query; request; clarification; conversation

INTRODUCTION

Catherine Garvey (1977) has described the unsolicited Contingent Query (CQ) as a
dependent speech act which satisfies the conditions for the independent speech act
Request for Information except that it occurs within the domain of another speech[2]
act, the force of which remains in effect during the contingency sequence.   In

---

1. This research was supported in part by Medical Research Council of Canada Grant
   No. M.A.4217 to Dr. J. H. V. Gilbert
2. Garvey also discusses solicited contingent queries, where an utterance such as
   "Know what?" has the elicitation of the partner's "What?" as its sole intended
   perlocutionary effect.   These have a slightly different set of conditions and
   will not be discussed in this paper.

this sequence the Hearer must clarify some aspect of the situation in order to respond appropriately to the dominant speech act.   The sequence consists of three
steps: an utterance which provokes the query, the query itself, and a response to
the query.   This is illustrated in the preschool conversation in Example 1, taken
from Garvey (p.73).[3]

1.   Y: "Look it.   We found a parrot in our house."

                                                X: "A what?"

     Y: "A parrot.   A bird."

                                                X: "Wow!"

The final utterance in this example illustrates the subordinate nature of the contingent query; once the clarification has been effected, the conversational partner must respond to the dominant speech act.   We can also see, as Garvey has observed, how the "CQ module is truly embedded in the sense that, if it were removed,
the dominant act and the response would remain intact and well formed" (p.69).
Gail Jefferson (1972) has described a similar phenomenon as "a side-sequence within
an ongoing sequence" (p.294) and William Corsaro (1977) has called the same object
a clarification request, "an interrogative which calls for the clarification, confirmation or repetition of the preceding utterance of a co-interactant, ... employed as a device to keep interaction running smoothly" (p.185).

By appealing to the relations among the three components of the CQ sequence, Garvey
has determined that the query has a selectivity function with respect to the utterance that provokes it, referring to the whole utterance, a specific part of it, or
something not there at all; it has a determining function with respect to the response that follows, specifying the form it should take.   Various combinations of
these two functions yield a taxonomy of CQ types, described and illustrated in
Figure 1.   It is noteworthy that Garvey has claimed additional complexity for
Types 5 and 6 - perhaps due to their reference to factors not explicitly included
in the utterance queried - and limited her study to the four "simpler" types.

Garvey coded videotaped play sessions of same-age dyads from a group of 48 children
ranging in age from 2:10 to 5:7, for the first four CQ types.   The results led her
to conclude that, by 3 to $3\frac{1}{2}$ years, the children formed and used CQ components and
sequence structure - and so maintained and regulated discourse - frequently, highly
successfully, and according to adult rules.   The significance of these results is
that they indicate some sophisticated knowledge about both rules of discourse and
the structure of individual utterances.   While Garvey has speculated that the CQ
sequence is learned even earlier, playing an important role in the language learning that follows, the age range of her subjects did not allow her to document this
or describe the development of this competence; the first chapter of the story of
children's contingent queries is missing.   Questions I would like to raise with
respect to under-threes deal with when CQs are learned, whether they fit Garvey's
taxonomy, whether some types are learned before others, how their occurrence relates to their success-rate in regulating discourse, and how they develop in relation to independent requests for information.

---

3. Where a particular speaker is not identified, I will follow Garvey's convention
   of designating the originator of the CQ as X and the conversational partner as
   Y.   Where it is relevant to indicate intonation, I will use her convention of
   ↗ for rising and ↘ for falling phrase final contour.

1. nonspecific request for repetition (NRR)	Y: This is a nice place X: What? ↗ Y: This is a nice place
2. specific request for repetition (SRR)	Y: Look at it. We found a parrot in our house X: A what? ↗ Y: A parrot. A bird
3. specific request for confirmation (SRC)	Y: Then you're not scared. If you're not a scaredy-cat X: Scaredy-cat? ↗ Y: Uh-huh
4. specific request for specification (SRS)	Y: Look at that little mirror up there X: Where? ↘ Y: Up there (pointing)
5. potential request for elaboration (PRE)	Y: I hear a noise X: Where? ↘ Y: Outside
6. potential request for confirmation (PRC)	Y: I hear a noise X: Where? ↘ Outside? ↗ Y: Yes

Note: Examples for types 1-4 are from preschool conversations cited by
       Garvey.   Types 5 and 6 are illustrated by her hypothetical
       examples.

Fig. 1   Garvey's (1977) Taxonomy for Unsolicited Contingent
         Queries

METHOD

Subjects

The subjects for this study, which is part of a more general study of the development of questions, were eight children ranging in age from one-and-a-half to three
years, with one girl and one boy at each six-month age interval.   They were all
first-born, normal, middle-class children from families where only English was
spoken.

Data collection

The children were each video and audio taped for six half-hour sessions at biweekly
intervals over a period of two-and-a-half months.   These sessions, consisting of
spontaneous mother-child interaction centred around toys I had provided, were
taped in a living room setting in a T.V. studio by two cameramen, coordinated from
a control room by a third cameraman.   Studio lighting was used, and a grid of suspended microphones produced a soundtrack on the video tape.   In addition, I hand-
held a parabolic microphone connected to an Ampex tape recorder to obtain an inde-

pendent high fidelity sound recording.

Transcription and coding

All adult and child utterances were transcribed from the audio tapes - played back on a Revox tape recorder with headphones - with English orthography.   All child request utterances were identified and transcribed with IPA.   Contingent queries from five play sessions for each child were identified and coded into the categories listed in Figure 1.   Responses to the queries were coded (following Garvey) as expected-predicted replies (ER) if they followed the model presented in Figure 1, as other relevant responses (OR), or as no response (NR).   The OR category included paraphrases, repetitions, elaborations and demonstrations responsive to the query but not determined by the form of the query.   The NR category included responses that were relevant to the conversation or activity but did not reply to the query per se.   A query answered with either an ER or an OR was counted as successful.

RESULTS AND DISCUSSION

The number and types of contingent queries produced by each child are presented in Table 1.

TABLE 1   Frequency of contingent queries, by type, produced by each child

Child	Age Range	Syntactic Stage Range *	CQ Type**				Total CQ's
			NRR	SRC	SRS	PRE	
1. Benjamin	1;5:11-1;8:17	<I	—	10	—	—	10
2. Pieta	1;7: 7-1;8:17	<I	—	11	—	—	11
3. Graham	2;2:18-2;4:20	I-III	126	39	1	4	170
4. Chloe	2;2:24-2;5:13	I- II	6	1	—	—	7
5. Darcy	2;5: 6-2;7:29	II-III	2	16	1	2	21
6. Jane	2;6:28-2;8:30	III- V	81	15	10	—	106
7. Lindsay	3;0: 6-3;2: 8	IV- V	16	11	2	5	35
8. Anthony	3;1: 9-3;3: 4	III- V	50	35	17	12	104

 * Brown's stages as defined by MLU

** CQ types as shown in Figure 1.   None of the children produced any examples of type SRR and only the oldest child produced one example of type PRC.   These types are not tabulated.

While the specific request for confirmation was the first CQ to appear, it was very infrequent, accounting for less than 1% of Benjamin and Pieta's utterances and about 7% of their interrogatives.   Only a few sequences, such as Example 2, were convincing instances of this type.   Others, e.g. Example 3, were treated like non-specific requests for specification, while still others seemed like little more than echoes of the mothers' utterances and elicited almost no expected responses. These queries all took the form of a single word with rising intonation.

(Examples 2 and 3 from Benjamin (1;5:30))

2. M: "And there's a bee.   They say bzz, bzz, zzz."

                                                    B: "Bee?↗ "

   M: "A bee."

                                                    B: "Bee.↘ "

3. C: "Ben, can you put the cups together?"

                                                    B: "Cup?↗ "

   C: "Those cups.   Can you put them one
       inside the other?"

It appears that these youngest children have begun to use contingent verbalizations
to regulate discourse, but in nonspecific ways.   Garvey's taxonomy is too highly
specified to describe what the children knew about CQs at this developmental stage.

Another look at Table 1 tells us that the children in this sample were using the
nonspecific request for repetition by age 2;2, Brown's Stage I.   Once this request,
encoded as "hm?" in almost all instances, came into use, it was the most frequent
CQ for five of the six children.   The nonspecific "hm?" presents some special problems.   While "hm?" was always coded as a nonspecific request for repetition, the
verbal or nonverbal context did not always support this interpretation.   This is
illustrated in Examples 4, 5 and 6.

(Examples 4-6 from Jane (2;8:16))

4. M: "Oh, I think there's a bit over here."

                                      J: "Hm? ↗   Right here?↗ "

5. M: "I'm going to make a fence all the
        way around this house."

                                      J: "Huh? ↗   Where?↘
                                                     Where?↘ "

   M: "I'm making a fence that goes around
        the house."

6. M: "D'you have any tea?

                                      J: "Hm? I'm not going to buy
                                            some."

In none of these examples did Jane really require a repetition.   In each case
there was enough time following Jane's utterance of "hm?" for a response to have
occurred; when none was forthcoming, she was able to make her verbalization more
specific, uttering a specific request for confirmation in Example 4 and a specific
request for specification in Example 5.   Note that the falling intonation in
Example 5 distinguishes this use of "where?" from its equally plausible use as a
specific request for repetition.   In Example 6 Jane's second utterance was an
appropriate response to the mother's dominant speech act, indicating that the preceding "hm?" was not a sincere request for repetition.   In other instances, the
doubtful "hm?" was not followed by a second CQ; when her mother made suggestions
Jane sometimes responded with her contingent "hm?" while nonverbally behaving in
accordance with the suggestion.   Similar equivocal queries were produced by Graham
and Anthony.

Such instances raise the question of what the child actually has in mind while uttering "hm?" in seemingly appropriate, as well as in these more questionable, circumstances.   Ervin-Tripp (1978) discussing repetition as a characteristic of adults'
speech to children, has suggested that "repetition reduces semantic density" (p.366).

If children can to some extent control this helpful redundancy of semantic (and syntactic) information, they do indeed possess a powerful tool to aid their learning of language.   If a child has understood the general import of an incoming message, he or she might still legitimately request a repetition to have one more chance to pick up a tricky syntactic or semantic detail.   Corsaro has suggested that "hm?" and its variants are clarification markers which, along with different kinds of repetitions, are used when the Hearer does not hear or understand properly, or to mark or fill a turn in interaction.   This latter function might well account for Example 6 and Jane's query accompaniment to her informed action.

Even if children start using "hm?" to indicate willingness to be good conversationalists - and in some cases continue to do so - their mothers' consistency in responding to this utterance as a request for repetition might, as Ryan (1974) has pointed out, teach them what they conventionally mean, thus providing the mechanism for eliciting useful redundancy.   However, that mothers do not always interpret "hm?" as a request for repetition can be seen from the 25% rate of expected responses for this category and is illustrated by Example 7.

7. Jane (2;8:2)

    M: "The dollies ... they're called puppets.   J: "dolly ↘ "

                                                             J: "Hm?↗ "

    M: "They're puppets.   J: "Hm?↗ "

    M: "See, you put your hand in ...   J: "Hm?↗ "

    M: "Remember, we've got the owl at home?   J: "Hm?↗ "

    M: "Hello Jane!"   J: (laughs)

Here, Jane's patient mother saw, after one repetition, that some other type of clarification was called for, and proceeded to try to clarify by analogy and demonstration.   In other examples she responded to Jane's "hm?" as if it were a request for specification or confirmation.

Examples 4, 5 and 6, provoke still more speculation.   One possibility is that in each case the child is using "hm?" to gain the time necessary to formulate a more specific response or query.   Perhaps the crux of the matter is actually the non-specific/specific distinction.   Another look at Figure 1 reveals that the request for repetition, always realised as "hm?" or "what?", is the only CQ type designated nonspecific.   While Garvey has defined this as a relation that holds between the first two components of the CQ sequence, it is possible that - early in the ontogeny of the CQ - a nonspecific relation also holds between the query and its response, only later differentiating into particular determining functions.   This interpretation is supported by the mothers' responses, which were not highly constrained by the determining function of the non-specific request for repetition (or, for the youngest children, the specific request for confirmation).   It may also be significant that none of the children produced any specific requests for repetition.   Development from general to specific is well documented in other aspects of language acquisition.   That more general categories perseverate when specific ones have come into use was attested by Anne Carter (1975) in her study of the development of sensorimotor morphemes and can also be heard in children's use of the primitive "ʔə̃ʔə̃ʔə̃" long after more sophisticated request forms have been mastered.

Requests for confirmation produced by the oldest six children fit this category in a more standard way than did most queries from Benjamin and Pieta.   The small number of specific requests for specification and potential requests for elabora-

tion suggests that these might develop later than the other types.   These took
the form of wh-questions, most of them requesting specification of a location, although all of Lindsay's and seven of Anthony's requests for elaboration asked
"why?".   Bloom, Rocissano and Hood (1977) reported that, for the four children in
their study,

> Using the information in a prior utterance to ask a Wh-question,
> that is, asking a question that is linguistically contingent,
> appears to have been more difficult than producing a linguistically
> contingent statement, or asking a noncontingent question.   While
> Wh-questions occurred in the children's speech at Stage 2, they were
> not linguistically contingent until after Stage 2 (pp.538-9)[4].

This observation is supported in my sample by Chloe, who at Stage III produced
very few wh-questions, none of them contingent.   The observation receives mixed
commentary from Graham and Darcy, who produced contingent wh-questions by Stage
III, but not contingent wh-words that were not also uttered noncontingently.
If Bloom and colleagues mean that any given wh-words will be used noncontingently
first, their observation is countered by Lindsay and Anthony, who both used "why?"
contingently but did not use it as a dominant speech act.   This is one more aspect of _why_ that sets it off from other wh-questions.

Except for Jane, all of the children who produced specific requests for specification produced similar potential requests for elaboration.   Compare Example 8
(SRS) and Example 9 (PRE).

(Examples from Anthony (3;3:4))

8.   M: "Why don't you tell Carolyn where you
            were yesterday?"

                                                    A: "Where? ↘ "

9.   M: "We saw a big long train with three
            engines."

                                                    A: "Where? ↘ "

The children did not seem to be troubled by the fact that one of these types is
contingent on a constituent in the previous utterance, the other on a constituent
that might have occurred but did not.   It is not clear from these data that
Garvey's distinctions between specific and potential, specification and elaboration, are useful in developmental terms;   they do not predict or describe the
developmental data in this small study.

The number of CQ's, and the frequency with which they occur in any child's speech,
are not predicted by age or syntactic stage.   The three children who did the most
contingent querying represent three age groups and cross stages I-V.   Chloe, who
produced the fewest CQ's - less than 1% of her total utterances - had by far the
greatest success rate (100%) and the highest percentage of expected responses
(86%).   Graham, Jane and Anthony, who each produced more than 100 CQ's, representing 7-9% of their total utterances and about a third of their interrogatives,
received expected responses 19-48% of the time and had a success rate of 57-72%.

---

4. Bloom and colleagues' definition of linguistic contingency as "speech that expanded the verb relation of the prior adult utterance with added or replaced
   constituents within a clause" (p.521) overlaps with Garvey's definition only
   in the case of contingent wh-questions.

Thus it does not seem to be the case that the frequent use of CQ's depends heavily on their success in eliciting the responses determined by their forms. All of the mothers in the study initiated CQ sequences with their children, but I have not determined the frequency or types of these queries and cannot report how these correlate with the children's usage. The children's interactive styles may play a part in the explanation of the frequency facts. If this is the case, we might ask how the children who do not use CQ's keep their conversations going and manipulate their partners into repeating and clarifying selected parts of the discourse.

TABLE 2   Adult responses to the children's contingent queries

CQ Type	Response Type			Success Rate
	ER** %	OR %	NR %	%
NRR*	25	37	38	62
SRC	53	16	31	69
SRS	42	35	23	77
PRE	44	13	44	57
				(66% overall)

* Types described in Figure 1

** ER = expected response;   OR = other relevant response;   NR = no response

The responses to, and success rate of, each type of CQ are presented in Table 2. This table reveals that the CQ's of the children in this study were not, overall, as successful as those in Garvey's study (80-85%). This might be a function of the mother-child as opposed to her child-child condition; a child might take another's CQ at face value and feel obligated to respond appropriately, while the mothers in this study often seemed to use situational cues to override the force of their children's queries. It might also be related to the ages of the children in this study, which overlapped only the youngest group observed by Garvey. The most interesting number in Table 2 is the 25% expected responses for the nonspecific request for repetition. This might represent the failure of the determining relation discussed earlier or the mothers' lack of belief in the sincerity of these queries (which itself may be related to this failure).

CONCLUSIONS

Garvey's speculation that CQ's are learned before the age of three was supported by the data from this study. The types of knowledge that Garvey proposed as necessary for producing CQ's - turn allotment rules, obligations of the respective participants to respond to the dominant and subordinate speech acts, and ability (in the case of specific CQ's) to identify appropriately a particular constituent of the dominant speech act - do not all underlie the earliest CQ's. That children have been well-schooled in turn taking from their earliest months (see Snow 1977, for example) is obvious in their earliest CQ's. CQ's might be learned early because of this very fact; the predictable discourse structure in which the queries would be explained. This would also be in accordance with evidence from Gove (1971), Ninio and Bruner (1978) and Steffensen (1978) that noncontingent questions may be learned in this way, as well as Keenan, Schieffelin and Platt's (1978) notion that questions are used to check attention and indicate immediate concerns.

The other aspects of underlying competence described by Garvey appear to develop gradually over the age range represented in this study. Ervin-Tripp (1978) has described the development of conversational cohesion for about the same age range, citing (relevant to this study) an increase in both relevance and explicitness of replies. Bloom, Rocissano and Hood (1977) also reported an increase in relevance (topical contingency) over the period of their study. The CQ, an example of conversational relevance, occurred to at least some degree by about one-and-a-half years, increasing considerably thereafter, though not predictably in terms of age, syntactic stage, or success rate. Explicitness, represented by contingent requests for specification and elaboration, also increased over this age range. These results can thus be offered as other examples of the areas described by Ervin-Tripp and Bloom, Rocissano and Hood, further information about the developmental history of conversational ability.

REFERENCES

Bloom, L., Rocissano, L. and Hood, L. Adult-child discourse: developmental interaction between information processing and linguistic knowledge. Cognitive Psychology, 1977, 8, 521-552

Carter, A. The transformation of sensorimotor morphemes into words: a case study of the development of 'here' and 'there'. Papers and Reports in Child Language Development, Stanford University, 1975, 10, 31-47

Corsaro, W. A. The clarification request as a feature of adult interactive styles with young children. Language in Society, 1977, 6, 183-207

Ervin-Tripp, S. Some features of early child-adult dialogues. Language in Society, 1978, 7, 357-373

Garvey, C. The contingent query: a dependent act in conversation, in M. Lewis and L. Rosenblum (Eds.) Interaction, conversation and the development of language. New York: Wiley, 1977, 63-93

Gove, A. F. Development of interaction skills in a one-year-old child. Word, 1971, 27, 170-178

Jefferson, G. Side sequences, in D. S. Sudnow (Ed.) Studies in social interaction. New York: The Free Press, 1972, 294-338

Keenan, E. O., Schieffelin, B. and Platt, M. Questions of immediate concern, in E. Goody (Ed.) Questions and politeness. Cambridge: The University Press, 1978, 44-55

Ninio, A. and Bruner, J. The achievement and antecedents of labelling. Journal of Child Language, 1978, 5, 1-15

Ryan, J. Early language development: toward a communicational analysis, in M. P. Richards (Ed.) The integration of the child into a social world. London: Cambridge University Press, 1974, 185-213

Snow, C. E. The development of conversation between mothers and babies. Journal of Child Language, 1977, 4, 1-22

Steffensen, M. S. Satisfying inquisitive adults: some simple methods of answering yes/no questions. Journal of Child Language, 1978, 5, 221-236

The Acquisition of Social Speech Routines and Politeness Formulas[1]

J. B. Gleason

Department of Psychology, Boston University, 64 Cummington Street, Boston, Massachusetts 02215, U.S.A.

ABSTRACT

Interest in children's emerging communicative competence has recently led to the study of the acquisition of the social and interactive components of language. Children must learn to use language appropriately in many different interpersonal situations. The acquisition of routines (e.g. bye bye, greetings, thanks and even rare formulae like trick or treat) is an important part of linguistic socialisation. Moreover, parents explicitly teach routines and prompt their children to produce them.

This paper examines the ways in which parents socialise their children in the use of a number of such routines. Parents and children were observed in naturalistic settings for the study of some routines, and a laboratory setting was used for others. In the laboratory, 22 pre-school children interacted separately with their fathers and mothers in a situation designed to elicit politeness routines. Principal aims of the study included determining if some routines are more obligatory than others, as well as finding out if there were any sex differences either in the behaviour of fathers and mothers or in the ways that boys and girls were treated.

Results indicate that while boys and girls are treated similarly, their parents provide different models for them, with mothers producing more polite speech than fathers. Parents themselves use a remarkably consistent prompting formula in attempting to elicit routines from their children, and thank you is the routine most likely to be insisted upon. The significance of the study is related to questions of how children acquire communicative competence as well as to broader questions relating to how children are socialised as bearers of particular sex roles and members of particular societies.

Key words

Communicative competence; interaction; politeness routines; child development; sex differences; parent differences

INTRODUCTION

The current literature on children's language acquisition is beset with a number of controversies. One particular area of contention is related to the question of what, if any, impact the structure and content of adult language to children has on

---

1. This research was supported by Grant BNS 75-21909 A01 from the National Science Foundation.

subsequent language acquisition by those children.   Some researchers have argued
that adult input language has little effect on the acquisition of syntax (Newport,
Gleitman and Gleitman 1975), while others (Nelson 1976) have shown that when
adults consistently recast or reformulate sentences in particular ways, the structures used by the adults appear in the children's speech earlier than might otherwise be expected.   The emphasis in many of these studies has been on the acquisition of grammar, particularly syntax.   Almost no research has examined the relationship between adults' phonological input to children and children's phonological development, although, of course, phonological modifications have been documented.   Finally, despite a burgeoning interest in developmental sociolinguistics, very little attention has been concentrated on the ways in which adults may
influence children's learning of the social and interactive components of language.

The controversy over whether children acquire language essentially by themselves
or are taught language by adults has, of course, been differentially supported by
conflicting theoretical models.   Psycholinguistic-innatist models support a
view that exposure to adult language suffices to provide the child with a data
base from which to formulate linguistic hypotheses without further adult intervention.   The various learning theories, on the other hand, assume that adults actively teach language to children, either through reinforcement of successive approximations of the target language, or through modelling and the encouragement of imitation.   There is, however, no reason to assume that only one model can account
for all of language acquisition, especially when we consider that earlier notions
of linguistic competence have been broadened to include a much wider range of
skills, and we now want to explain how children acquire communicative competence
(Hymes 1971).   The goal is to describe how children acquire the social rules for
language use as well as the more traditional linguistic subsystems.   It seems
likely that acquiring some parts of the language, like syntax, may depend primarily on the child's own linguistic and cognitive capacities, while the acquisition
of other aspects of language may be more dependent on the kinds of explicit
teaching, modelling or more subtle emphases provided by adults.

The best kind of language acquisition model we can put forward should take into
account the specialised cognitive and linguistic capacities the child brings to
the task, the special kind of linguistic environment provided by adults, and the
interaction between the two.   Based on our current knowledge, it is fairly easy
to say that specialised linguistic input makes language acquisition easier, although there are those who would argue with even that statement.   A somewhat
stronger claim, and one that has certainly not been proven, is that specialised
input makes language learning possible.   Support for this kind of claim comes
from the fact that all languages appear to have special registers for talking to
children, that many features of those registers are not optional (that is, all
speakers provide some modifications), and that there is no strong evidence that
children can learn to speak the language from mere exposure to what adults say to
one another.   There are no documented cases, for instance, of children who have
learned to speak solely from watching television or listening to the radio.

While some parts of language may be acquired by children with little obvious help
from adults, the acquisition of social speech and politeness routines is a singu-
larly social activity, one in which adults take an active, even energetic, part.

In the past several years, our research group has undertaken the study of the acquisition of routines by children.   I use the term routines loosely to refer to
formulaic, ritualised speech that children must learn to produce on particular
social occasions, such expressions as "Trick or treat" on Hallowe'en, "Hi" as a
greeting, "Thanks", "Goodbye", "I'm sorry", "God bless you" when someone sneezes,
the pledge to the flag, and so on.   Such routines are distinguished by the fact
that they may have no intrinsic meaning, or their meaning may be opaque or at odds
with the actual feelings of the speaker: the child who is forced to say "Thank

you" for a birthday present she hates, for instance, clearly does not feel thankful.

The use of routines entails cognitive activity, but it requires a different sort
of cognition from what is required in order to produce appropriate referential
speech; and children's use of either referential speech or routines is monitored
in quite different ways by adults.   Referential speech for the young child generally involves such things as mapping a report about an inner state onto language,
or conveying an observation about the world: "I want a drink of water", or "The
kitty is on the table".   Adults, as Brown and Hanlon (1970) pointed out, are concerned primarily with the truth value of such children's utterances.   They are
liable to say: "You don't want a drink of water.   You just had a drink of water.
Now go to sleep", or "That's not a kitty, it's a raccoon".   With routines, the
situation is quite otherwise.   The kind of cognition required by the child involves the ability to recognise a particular social situation and apply the appropriate formula.   Adults are not concerned with the truth value of the routine,
only with its performance, and are happy if their child says "Thank you" when
given a gift.   When a child says "Thank you", adults do not say things like,
"You're not thankful. You already have a toy like that at home".   Such statements strike us as brutally rude.   Children are expected early on to learn to
say the polite thing, regardless of the mismatch between their feelings and the
words.   Here, the primary match is between the social situation and the formula,
rather than between the inner state and the words.   The fact that we recognise
that there are thanks we mean and thanks we say but do not mean is reflected in
expressions like "heartfelt thanks".   Since adults are particularly concerned
that their children produce routines at the right times, it is not surprising
that the acquisition of routines by children involves very specific kinds of adult
behaviour.

Routines can be studied naturalistically and in the laboratory.   We chose to
study the American Hallowe'en ritual in the field, and the politeness formulas
"Hi", "Thanks" and "Goodbye" were studied in the laboratory.   Details of both
studies are available elsewhere (Gleason and Weintraub 1976; Gleason and Greif
1979).

TRICK OR TREAT

The Hallowe'en study was particularly difficult to conduct because it is a study
that can be carried out during a period of only about four hours a year.   It is
rather like studying eclipses of the sun in this respect.   Only on Hallowe'en
evening do costumed children go from door to door in American communities, ringing
the bell and asking for candy by saying "Trick or treat".   (There may be regional
variations of this routine, and it has certainly varied over time.   One informant
reports, for instance, that in Bronxville, New York, during the 1930s children
said, "Anything for Hallowe'en?")   In our Hallowe'en study we tape recorded this
ritual on three successive Hallowe'ens in two different households.   We also
followed a pair of five year olds and their mothers from door to door and recorded
these children, their mothers, and the candy-giving householders.   In all, we
collected data on 115 children.   Our only intervention was to stop the children
as they left after receiving their candy and ask them their ages.

The typical Hallowe'en scenario (Gleason and Weintraub 1976, p.132) is as follows:

1. The child rings the bell; 2. Adult opens the door; 3. Child says, "Trick or
treat"; 4. Adult answers with part of some adult routine like "Come on in", or
"Oh, my goodness", and gives the child candy; 5. Child says "Thank you", and
turns to go; 6. Adult says "Goodbye", and the child, leaving, says "Goodbye".

The children's portion of the Hallowe'en routine contains three basic utterances: "Trick or treat", when the door is opened; "Thank you", on receiving the treat (candy); and "Goodbye", on leaving. Both "Thank you" and "Goodbye" are, of course, common politeness formulas. We examined the children's production of these utterances, and found that by and large the age of the child predicted what would be produced. Children younger than three simply rang the bell and stood silently with their bags opened expectantly. Children aged four to five said only "Trick or treat" and "Thank you"; and children over 11 said "Goodbye" as well.

It is difficult to explain why enacting this once-a-year ritual in this way is so important, but adults accompanying young children from door to door, who typically remained on the sidewalk while the children went up to ring the doorbell, urged the children to say "Trick or treat" and checked with them when they returned: the mothers of the five year-olds we followed frequently said such things as "Don't forget to say 'Trick or treat' and 'Thank you'", and we frequently heard parents call out "Thank you" themselves when their child was given the candy. This adult pressure appears to be fairly successful, since the incidence of "Thank yous" among the children rose from 21% in the group under six years of age to 88% in the group consisting of those over 11. We were struck by the emphasis on "Thanks" and by the fact that adults consistently used the word <u>say</u> in attempting to elicit the routines from children: "What do you say?" "Say 'Thank you'", etc.

HI, THANKS AND GOODBYE

We had the opportunity to study two of the foregoing routines, "Thank you" and "Goodbye", as well as the greeting "Hi", or "Hello" in the laboratory. As part of an ongoing videotaped study of parent-child interaction we saw 22 children between the ages of two and five on two occasions each, once with his or her father and once with the mother. The parent and child first engaged in some structured play for about a half hour. At what appeared to be the end of the session, an assistant entered the room with a gift for the child, which she presented according to a script designed to elicit the three routines. It went essentially as follows:

> "Hi. I'm _____. Hi, (child's name)". (pause to wait for response). "Here's a gift for you for today's visit".(pause to wait for response). Some unstructured conversation. Then, turning to go, "Goodbye, (child's name)". (pause to wait for response).

By structuring the interaction in this way we could look very closely at some of the things that the Hallowe'en study had only touched on, and we could make some direct comparisons of male and female behaviour that were previously impossible, since there was no way to control for sex in the naturalistic study, while we had equal numbers of boys and girls, fathers and mothers in the laboratory.

Specifically, analyses were aimed at answering the following questions:

1. Are some routines more likely to be produced by children than others?

2. What happens when children fail to produce a politeness formula?

3. Are there sex differences among children, either in the way they produce routines or in the way they are treated by parents; for instance do parents insist on more polite behaviour from girls?

4. Do mothers and fathers themselves differ, either in the way they treat children or in the kinds of models they provide? We had noted, for instance, in the Hallowe'en study that some parents called out "Thank you" when their child received the candy, and

the laboratory provided the opportunity to compare mothers and
fathers likelihood of behaving in this fashion.

Results indicated that these children, all of whom were five or younger, were not
very likely to produce these routines of their own accord.   In the Hallowe'en
study 21% of the children under six said "Thank you".   Here only 7% did.   The
figures were almost identical with "Goodbye":   26% for children under six at Hallow-
e'en and 25% in the laboratory.   And 27% of the laboratory sample said an unpromp-
ted "Hi".   Thus "Thanks" was the least likely routine to be produced spontaneously
by children.

Prompting by parents was the rule rather than the exception.   If the child did not
say the right thing, the parent frequently prompted her or him.   Prompts overwhelmingly took the form of "Say 'Thank you'" or "What do you say?"   In fact, the
word say appeared in 95% of parent prompts.   Only one child in the study produced
no routines and was never prompted by either parent.   The prompts were not evenly
distributed among the routines.   If the child did not say "Hi" or "Goodbye", the
parent prompted about 30% of the time.   But parents prompted children who failed
to say "Thank you" over 50% of the time.   "Thank you" is therefore least likely
to be produced spontaneously and most likely to be prompted.   We also looked at
what happened after the child was prompted for each routine, and, here again there
were differences.   Children who had not said "Hi" and then were prompted to do so
subsequently said "Hi" 44% of the time.   Eighty two percent of children said
"Goodbye" after being prompted, and 86% said "Thank you" when told to do so.
Some parents also prompted several times for thanks, while this was not typically
the case with the other routines.   "Thank you" thus emerges as a politeness formula with little likelihood of spontaneous production by young children and a very
great likelihood of being insisted on by adults, after which children consistently
comply.

When we looked for sex differences among children, only one emerged, and that was
that a much higher percentage of boys than girls said "Hi" to the project assistant when she entered: 41% to 18%, a difference that was statistically significant.
This difference in greeting behaviour may be related to the fact that girls are
frequently shyer than boys, and it may also be an early reflection of the pressure
that society puts on males to provide greetings.   In our society at least, males
greeting other males are required to shake hands and speak, and they are expected
to stand up when greeting females.   The ritual is not so obligatory for females.
Otherwise, boys and girls were equally likely to say "Thank you" and "Goodbye",
and parents prompted girls and boys with equal frequency.   While the children
ranged in age from about two and a half to five, there was no observable increase
in politeness with age, and parents used the same sorts of prompts with younger and
older children.   By and large, our earlier hypothesis that parents may be more
insistent that girls produce polite phrases was disconfirmed.

The parents' speech, on the other hand, did show a differential use of politeness
markers.   The parents themselves had the opportunity to greet the assistant when
she entered, and some of them also thanked her themselves when the child received
the gift.   Finally, they, too, could say "Goodbye" when she left.   Equal numbers
of fathers and mothers, essentially the entire sample, (41 out of 44, 20 mothers
and 21 fathers) said "Hi" or "Hello".   Mothers were much more likely to thank the
assistant themselves for the child's gift, and to say "Goodbye": of the 15 parents
who thanked the assistant,   11 were mothers, and of 18 parents who said "Goodbye",
13 were mothers.   These differences were statistically significant.   (For "Thank
you" $X^2 = 4.95$, p < .05 and for "Goodbye" $X^2 = 6.00$, p < .02).   Thus, while girls
and boys were treated in similar fashion by parents, the parents themselves provided quite different models of politeness behaviour, with mothers showing more
politeness in the use of two of the three routines studied here.   The study thus
confirms speculation that women are more polite than men, and indicates a mechanism

whereby young children learn sex-appropriate speech patterns: modelling, or imitation of the parental model stands out as the likely candidate, rather than
differential reinforcement or any other different treatment of girls and boys.

CONCLUSIONS

Research on the social and interactive aspects of language has shown us one thing
very clearly: parents explicitly teach children some parts of the language. The
fact that essentially all of the children we saw were prompted to produce the politeness markers we studied is good evidence of the importance of social speech
and of the regular patterns employed by parents in imparting these routines. The
parents we saw were drilling their children in the use of "Hi", "Thanks", and
"Goodbye": "What do you say? Thank you". Just as earlier we had noted that
children on Hallowe'en said "Trick or treat" without any idea of what the expression might mean, we found here that children produced politeness routines without
any discussion of their meaning or any evidence that they knew what thanks were
supposed to mean; they never varied the forms, for instance, or expressed their
appreciation in any other words. It was also clear that "Thanks" was the most
obligatory of these routines. (It is interesting to note that "You're welcome"
as a second member of this routine is certainly less obligatory and may have quite
different regional distribution. It appears to be much more prevalent in the
United States than in Britain, for instance.)

While parents obviously emphasise the use of politeness markers, their doing so
reflects a greater social truth. A recent letter to a newspaper advice column
begins: "Dear Ann Landers: I'm so hurt I'm in tears as I write this letter. Why
would a person who has been a friend of yours for years pass you on the street and
not speak?" The letter is signed "Too crushed to see things clearly". Failure
to say "Hi", "Thanks" and "Goodbye" at the appropriate moments is not just a breach
of etiquette; it is a gross social error that can result in disastrous interpersonal consequences. Social speech slips by almost unnoticed when it is there, but
its absence is noted immediately, and unless there is some obvious excuse, like
physical disability, the person who omits politeness formulas is judged very harsh-
ly. Ann Landers, for instance, suggested to the letter writer that perhaps her
friend needed to wear glasses and was too vain to wear them.

The importance of social speech was emphasised recently in a seminar we held at the
Rhode Island School for the Deaf. Dr. Blackwell, the director, pointed out that
as a result of some of our work on routines they had instituted a programme involving deaf children and their parents. The parents were taught to teach their children routines. The results were two-fold: first, the parents found that routines
were easy to teach, probably because of their lack of deeper meaning, and second,
as soon as the children learned the routines the parents felt much happier with
them because they had become almost overnight much more socially acceptable individuals. On reflection, it seems likely that a child who says nothing but "Hi",
"Thanks", and "Goodbye" at the appropriate moment when out in public would strike
strangers as a quiet but exceptionally well mannered individual.

Young children do not appear to be motivated to acquire politeness routines;
adults by and large have to force them into producing them. By contrast, there
is a great deal of evidence that children are strongly motivated to acquire other
kinds of language. In the various accounts of early language acquisition that
have been put together in order to show linguistic universals in the one and two
word stage, the only routine that appears is the "Hi" of greeting, typically referred to as serving the function of notice. Many infants not only say "Hi" when
they notice people or inanimate objects, they have also discovered that if they say
"Hi" to an adult the adult will invariably say "Hi" back, and this is a game that
can be repeated ad nauseam, at least so far as the adult is concerned. The in-

fant, of course, has made an interesting sociolinguistic discovery: adults' responses are so strong that no matter how many times you say "Hi" to them they will
say "Hi" right back.   Somewhat older children play a game with one another in
which on parting the object is to see who will say the last "Goodbye".

"Hi", "Thanks" and "Goodbye" are just some of the routines that children must learn.
Parents are active teachers, as are other adults.   We have seen, for instance,
flight attendants on airplanes who insisted that children travelling alone say
"Please" when asking for a deck of cards, and "I'm sorry" when they stepped on someone's toe.

The families that we studied in the laboratory also allowed us to make tape recordings of their dinner table conversations.   These rich data will provide us with
additional information on routines and social speech.   The next formula to be
studied will be "Please": we might title the study "What's the magic word?"

REFERENCES

Brown, R. and Hanlon, C. Derivational complexity and order of acquisition in
        child speech, in J. R. Hayes (Ed.) Cognition and the development of
        language.   New York: Wiley, 1970
Gleason, J. Berko and Weintraub, S. The acquistion of routines in child language.
        Language in Society, 1976, 86, 616-626
Gleason, J. Berko and Greif, E. Blank. Hi, thanks and goodbye.   Paper presented
        at The Stanford Child Language Research Forum, April 1979
Hymes, D. Competence and performance in linguistic theory, in R. Huxley and E.
        Ingram (Eds.) Language acquisition: models and methods.   London: Academic
        Press, 1971
Nelson, K. E. Facilitating children's syntax acquisition.   Developmental Psycho-
        logy, 1976, 13, 101-107
Newport, E. L., Gleitman, L. R. and Gleitman, H.   A study of mothers' speech and
        child language acquisition.   Paper presented at The Seventh Annual Child
        Language Research Forum, Stanford, April 1975

Language and Play: A Comparative Analysis of Parental Initiatives[1]

M. Engle

School of Education, Harvard University, Cambridge, Massachusetts 02138, U.S.A.

ABSTRACT

To test whether there are interactional differences in the play of mothers and fathers with their two and three year old children, the language of parents and children during free play was examined. The variable, initiative, is proposed to analyse the playing styles. An initiative, defined as an utterance or set of utterances used to direct attention to a new activity or a new variation of an on-going activity, can have either a specific or non-specific intent.

It was found that fathers use significantly more of the directive specific initiatives than the mothers, e.g. "Let's build a truck!"; mothers use a higher percentage of the less directive non-specific initiatives than the fathers, e.g. "What would you like to play with now?" The younger children use fewer initiatives with their fathers than with their mothers. The older children show no difference. The results are interpreted in the light of the parents' complementary roles. Fathers, being less concerned about the children's immediate desires, introduce new ideas and new ways of playing with toys. Mothers have a playing style suited to the integration of new ideas. The older children are more able to handle their fathers' style of play.

Key words

Language acquisition; play; mother-child interaction; father-child interaction; parents

INTRODUCTION

Although the parent-child free play situation has been the setting for numerous language acquisition studies, rarely has the play been the focus of the analysis. The studies that examine parental language differences (Gleason 1975; Engle 1979; Rondal 1978; Weintraub 1978) have often remarked on the apparent differences in

---

1. The author is very grateful to Elissa Newport, Marilyn Shatz and Uta Frith for helpful conversations during the early stages of this paper. Robert Engle provided much appreciated statistical assistance. Inquiries may be sent to 412 Vincente Way, La Jolla, California 92037.

the interaction styles of mothers and fathers.   Actual analysis of these styles is
lacking.

Gleason (1975) reported a story telling situation in which the fathers were more
concerned with telling a good story (whether or not the child appeared to understand it) than the mothers who spent the time interacting with the child, asking
questions, and making sure that the meanings were clear.   During the evening meal,
Rondal (1978) observed that fathers tended to ask their young children more about
the day's activities: the mothers helped their children learn the names of objects on the table.

Engle (1979) in a cross-sectional study of two- and three-year-old children and
their parents in a home free play situation, observed that both parents seemed to
enjoy playing with their child and played quite avidly during the interactions.
The fathers, in contrast to the mothers, tended to look at the toys independently
and played with them whether or not the child appeared particularly interested.
Parallel play was a common feature of father-child play.   In addition, the fathers
were very project oriented, starting and finishing various constructions.   They
often included the child in the play but nevertheless, the fathers appeared to control the interaction quite closely.

In contrast, the mothers adopted a style that seemed to give some of the control to
the child.   They often waited until the child initiated play and then expanded
on the child's choice.   If the child did not choose, the mothers asked for a
choice.   Parallel play occurred rarely and when a mother attempted to set it up,
it was halted very quickly. This more nurturant style of interaction which progressed at the child's pace was also reflected in the cross-age analysis of the
mother-child language used during the play.   The mothers of the three-year-olds
had significantly higher MLU and Propositional Complexity scores and used significantly fewer imitations and deictic utterances than the mothers of the two-year-
olds.   The child to mother speech exhibited exactly the same pattern.

The fathers' language, on the other hand, showed none of the above changes.   The
fathers of the two-year-olds used a higher percentage of imperatives and questions
than did the fathers of the older children.   In addition, the fathers of the three-
year-olds used significantly more stock expressions than any other group of parent
speakers.   None of the changes in the children's speech to their mothers other
than MLU was carried over into speech with their fathers.   Neither were the
changes in the fathers' speech reflected in the children's speech to their fathers.

From both the language and observational data it seemed that the mothers were more
responsive to their children and that the fathers were more directive.   This paper
explored that hypothesis by looking directly at the language used in specific play
sequences to determine whether those apparently different styles were, in fact,
there.

One way to examine playing style differences would be to look at how the play interactions began and how they were continued.   Who started the play and what was said
in the process?   Who changed the focus of the ongoing play activity and how was it
accomplished?   To answer these questions an analysis was undertaken of each play
sequence.   Those utterances that initiated the play sequences were examined for
their directive content.   These New Initiatives, as they were named, were divided
into one of two categories depending upon whether they made a specific suggestion
or whether they asked for a suggestion.   The former were described as specific
and the latter as non-specific.   "Let's make a truck" was a specific New Initiative: "What shall we play with now?" would have been called a non-specific New

Initiative.

Often when a play sequence was initiated, the initial goal was either met or changed during the play.   A suggestion was made by either speaker that redirected
the ongoing activity in a way that was not originally planned.   These sequences
were called Continuation Initiatives and they too could have either a specific or
non-specific intent.

The purpose of this study was to distinguish between the types of New and Continuation Initiatives to determine whether the hypothesised role differences in play
could be found in the language used during the interaction episodes.   If so, then
we would expect that the fathers would use a higher number of specific initiatives
than the mothers.   Conversely, the mothers should have a higher percentage of
non-specific initiatives than the fathers.

METHOD

Subjects

Four two-year-old children and their parents and four three-year-old children and
their parents were the subjects for this study.   All the children were first-born
and male.   All the parents were college educated.   The fathers held traditional
professional type jobs which required them to be away from home during the day-
time hours.   Three of the mothers worked part-time away from home: the remaining
mothers did not work.   All of the mothers considered themselves as the child's
primary caretaker.

The mean age of the two-year-olds was 24.1 months with a range from 22 to 25.5
months.   The three-year-olds ranged from 37 to 43 months with a mean of 40.25
months.

Apparatus

The verbal interactions between the parent and child formed the data for this experiment.   A Sony TC-92 Solid State tape recorder with an omni-directional microphone was used to record the interactions.   At the same time, the experimenter
sat quietly taking context notes.

The experimenter brought the same assortment of toys to each session.   These included Lego Preschool Blocks, hand puppet cards, a Tonka car carrier truck, a bag
of plastic animals, an elephant hand puppet and Funtastic, a plastic construction
toy.

Procedure

The data analysed in this experiment are a part of a larger data collection effort
(see Engle 1979).   For the free play segment, which occurred first in all interactions, the parents were given the toys and asked to play with the child as they
would normally for 20 minutes.

The mother-child and father-child interactions were taped in the families' homes on
different days.   The order of the interactions gathered within families was counter balanced.   All the sessions were taped during times that the parent would
ordinarily be spending with the child in a play type activity.   The parent not
being taped could neither see nor hear the interaction.

Coding

The complete 20 minute parent-child play interaction was analysed for the presence
of initiatives.   To do this the transcripts were divided into play sequence segments.   These were delineated by the initial intent of the activity and the prolonging or redirecting of that activity.   Each activity began with one or a
series of New Initiatives.   The prolonging or redirecting - which was accomplished
through the addition of new elements or the recombination of existing elements -
began with one or a series of Continuation Initiatives.   Making an airplane out
of Lego was one new activity.   Adding a runway for the plane was a continuation.

An initiative was defined as an utterance or set of utterances that were used to
direct attention to a new activity or a new variation on an ongoing activity.
These utterances could be made by either speaker.   In addition, the initiatives
could be one of two types: either specific or non-specific.   These delineations
referred to the directive content of the initiatives: did the initiative contain
a specific suggestion or did it request a suggestion?   Requests for permanent information such as colours, origin of dinosaurs, etc. were counted as specific.
Examples of the coding categories follow.

New Initiatives-specific: "I'm going to make a truck".   "I'll make a bat race
car".   "Let's make a dog."   "What colour is this?" (as the start of a naming
sequence).   "Why don't you make a chimney?"

New Initiatives-non-specific: "Do you want to do anything with these little ones
right here?"   "What else can we make with that?" (referring to Funtastic pieces).
"Do you want to look at any of the other toys over here?"

Continuation Initiatives-specific: "Why don't you give me a man there? I'll put
the man on the truck".   "Want to make it this way?   Let's change it over like
this".   "You wanna drive your truck (now that it is made)?"   "Off!   Take it
off!"

Continuation Initiatives-non-specific: "Whall we put something else on the truck?
What else shall we put on the truck?"   "Okay, now what do you want to put on next?"

Statistical Analysis

Tallies of the numbers of specific and non-specific New Initiatives and Continuation Initiatives were made for each speaker within each play interaction.   The
total number of specific initiatives and non-specific initiatives was also computed.

The variable analysed by a 2-way mixed model analysis of variance was the percentage of all New and Continuation Initiatives which were specific.   Naturally
whenever the percentage of specific initiatives was higher then the percentage of
non-specific initiatives was lower.   Since the children made no non-specific
initiatives, their raw scores were used directly.

The two factors in the analysis of variance were Age, either of the child speaker
or the parent of that aged child and Sex, either of the parent or the child speaking to that sex of parent.   The speakers were either mothers, fathers, children
speaking to mothers, or children speaking to fathers.

Whenever the analysis of variance showed overall significance, cell means were compared using Duncan's Multiple Range Test (Edwards 1968).

RESULTS

As predicted the mothers used a significantly higher percentage of initiatives,

both New and Continuation, that were non-specific than the fathers.   The fathers
used significantly more specific initiatives, both New and Continuation, than the
mothers.   These differences were maintained in both age groups.   There was no
difference in the total number of initiatives used by the mothers or the fathers
either within or across age groups.

The two-year-olds differentiated their use of specific initiatives with the
parents.   They directed twice as many to their mothers as to their fathers.   No
differences were found in the total number of specific initiatives employed by the
three-year-olds with their mothers or fathers.

TABLE 1   Proportions of parents' specific initiatives

Speakers	New Initiatives	Continuation Initiatives	Total
Fathers of 2-year-olds	.848	.886	.856
Mothers of 2-year-olds	.656	.755	.715
Fathers of 3-year-olds	.833	.938	.907
Mothers of 3-year-olds	.649	.677	.653
F statistic for Sex difference, df = 1;6	12.03*	14.98**	11.66*

* p = < .025, ** p < .01

Table 1 illustrates the parents' results.   The fathers of the two-year-olds used
significantly more specific initiatives across all three categories than did the
mothers.   The same result was repeated for the parents of the three-year-olds.
The F statistic for the Sex difference variable was significant in all three categories.   Additionally, Duncan test results on the cell means were all significant
(p < .05) for sex differences within the age groups.

The total number of specific initiatives was analysed for the children.   The Duncan test performed on the significant Age X Sex interaction (F 1,6 = 8.0, p < .05)
revealed that the two-year-old child to mother mean of 15 initiatives was significantly greater than the two-year-old child to father mean of 7.5.   Furthermore,
the three-year-olds used significantly more initiatives with their fathers
(X^2= 13.5) than the two-year-olds.   The child to mother mean for the three-year-
olds was 11.0.

DISCUSSION

The results suggest that the fathers were more directive with their sons than the
mothers.   Conversely, the mothers encouraged their sons to give direction to the
play more often than the fathers.   What are the consequences of these differences?

The fathers, by being less concerned about the children's immediate desires, introduced new ideas and new ways of playing with toys to the children.   Because they
were willing to play on their own and make their own constructions, etc. the
fathers exhibited through their own example the inherent possibilities in the activities.

Mothers took a different view of the play interaction.   They very rarely played
separately from their children but instead encouraged them to develop the activity
as they could.   Mothers asked their children for suggestions both at the start of
the activity and during its progress into other variations.   Playing provided an
opportunity for the mothers to help their children learn how to choose.   Play with

the mother may not have been as exciting as play with the father: but it was
comfortable.

These roles are very complementary. No doubt, they did not work as directly as
suggested: mothers did bring in new ideas and fathers were nurturant. Nevertheless, the data do support the notion that the fathers were a good source of new
information for the children and that the mothers had a playing style suited to
the integration of those new ideas that the children wished to pursue.

The two-year-olds initiated twice as many activities and their continuations while
playing with their mothers than with their fathers. Possibly they were responding
to their mothers' higher use of non-specific initiatives. If this were solely the
case, then the pattern should have held in the play of the three-year-olds. Instead, the older children used the same number of initiatives with their mothers as
with their fathers. These means were quite close to those of the younger children
in play with their mothers. An age and development interaction may be at work.
The younger children seemed somewhat overwhelmed by their fathers' approach.
There were numerous instances in the transcripts where the fathers were engaged in
activities that appeared to hold little, if any, interest for the children. The
mothers of these children used an approach that brought out their most active performance. The older children had more skills as a function of their age and development and may have found their fathers' ideas less incomprehensible. By
three they could understand their fathers' play better and they had plenty of practice in making suggestions from playing with their mothers. These children made
specific initiatives in concert with or in contrast to their fathers'. The older
children seemed to share their fathers' fun more fully. (See Clarke-Stewart 1978
for another instance of this phenomenon).

The differences in how the parents approached the free play task ran along the
same lines. The fathers made remarks to their children such as "It's like having
a birthday" or "It's just like Christmas" and then, at the end of the playtime,
they thanked me for bringing such good toys for them to play with. The mothers
did not allow themselves such pleasures. The mothers who wanted to finish an
activity that particularly interested them but no longer engaged their child had
a difficult time allowing themselves to do so - generally, they did not.
Helping children learn how to play is a serious business.

REFERENCES

Clarke-Stewart, A. K. And Daddy makes three: the father's impact on mother and
        young child. Child Development, 1978, 49, 466-478
Edwards, A. Experimental design in psychological research. New York: Holt,
        Rinehart and Winston, 1968, 3rd edition
Engle, M. Do fathers speak motherese? An analysis of the language environments
        of young children. Manuscript submitted for publication 1979.
Gleason, J. B. Fathers and other strangers: men's speech to young children, in
        D. Dato (Ed.) Developmental psycholinguistics: theory and applications.
        Washington, D.C.: Georgetown University Press, 1975
Rondal, J. A. Fathers' speech and mothers' speech in early language development.
        Paper presented at the First International Congress for the Study of Child
        Language, Tokyo, August 1978
Weintraub, S. Parents' speech to children: some situational and sex differences.
        Unpublished Ph.D. dissertation, Boston University, 1978.

Mother-Child Conversation and Semantic Development

C. J. Howe

Department of Psychology, University of Strathclyde,
Turnbull Building, 155 George Street, Glasgow G1 1RD, U.K.

ABSTRACT

Twenty four mother-child pairs were videotaped while playing in their homes on two occasions during the child's second year. Conversations held by these mother-child pairs were analysed and related to measures of syntactic and semantic development. The mother-child pairs produced three styles of conversation which were closely associated with rate of semantic development. It is argued that these results imply a new interpretation of how mother-child conversation influences semantic development. This interpretation involves attributing motivational as well as informational properties to mother-child conversation.

Key words

Child development; mother-child interaction; conversation types; requests; initiation

INTRODUCTION

Fifteen years ago it was widely believed that explaining language development entailed crediting children with innate predispositions. More recently, this notion has been challenged on the grounds that children move in particularly facilitative linguistic environments. Evidence that assistance comes from maternal speech has already been published. As Snow's (1977) summary shows, this speech is slow, clear, well-structured and just slightly more complex than the child's speech. There is now growing suspicion that assistance comes also from mother-child conversation. However, this suspicion currently rests on case studies like those reported by Lieven (1978). There are no adequately sampled studies showing that mother-child conversations have common characteristics at given levels of language development let alone that these common characteristics facilitate language development. Consequently, this paper will report a study which attempted to investigate the relation between conversation and developmental level using a sizeable sample of mother-child pairs. Far from discovering common, facilitative characteristics, the study found mother-child conversations varying in character and probable helpfulness.

METHOD

Subjects

The study involved 24 mother-child pairs recruited by advertisement when the children were aged about 18 months. Twelve children were boys and twelve were girls. Thirteen had fathers with professional occupations and eleven had fathers with manual occupations. Seven were only children, seven were the youngest of two, four were the oldest of two, four were the youngest of three, and two were twins.

Procedure

The mother-child pairs were recorded in their homes on two occasions, once when the children were aged 20 to 22 months and again when they were aged 23 to 25 months.   They were recorded on videotape while playing for 20 minutes with their own toys and for 20 minutes with specially provided toys.   Videotape was used because neither the children's speech nor their conversations could have been coded without non-vocal information.   Toys were used because the children had spent long and similar periods (about 33% of the total) playing with toys during 4-hour observations prior to the study.   Toys were provided to make the recordings enjoyable, to ensure that experimenter and equipment were not the only novelties, and to encourage the children to stay within range of the equipment. The toys were equally familiar to all children and were always presented in the same order.   The mothers were encouraged to act normally, and the recordings were preceded by warm-up periods.

Transcription

The tapes were replayed for transcription immediately after recording.   Taking mother and child separately, changes in actions and objects were noted hieroglyphically on paper which was being propelled at constant speed across a pad. Vocalizations were noted using dashes since they were being re-recorded on audiotape.   They were transcribed from the audiotapes using English words or syllables and inserted on the non-vocal transcripts as indicated by the dashes.   It was usually obvious who was talking but doubtful cases were resolved from the videotapes.   The tapes varied in speaker intelligibility and background noise.   The mean percentages of intelligible utterances were 95% for the children and 98% for the mothers.   Ten months after the final recording, extracts from 10 recordings were re-transcribed.   The percentage agreement between this and the original transcription was 92% for the speech and 84% for the speech and non-vocal behaviour.

Coding

The next problem was locating mother-child conversations.   Conversations consisted of speaker exchanges which fulfilled three conditions: firstly, successive speakers must address each other using gazes or names.   The exchange in (1) which like all numbered examples is taken from the videotapes is not conversational because the first speaker does not address the second:

(1) (Mother watches Lucy brushing doll's hair): Mother: "Everybody's got hair, haven't they?"   (Robert points to me); Robert: "That got hair".

Secondly, first speakers must request information using wh-questions or provide information using yes/no-questions or statements.   The exchange in (2) is not conversational because the first speaker directs behaviour rather than requests or provides information: (2) (Mother watches Ursula posting shapes): Mother: "Pop it in"; Ursula: "Can't".

Finally, second speakers must reply.   The exchange in (3) is not conversational because the second speaker does not reply: (3) (Mother points to picture; Nicola rocks doll): Mother: "What's this, Nicola?"   (Nicola turns to mother); Nicola: "Baby asleep".

Second speakers can reply to requests for information as in (4) by providing or declining to provide the information: (4) (Sally stares at me); Sally: "Mummy, what is that?"   Mother: "That's a camera".

They can reply to provisions of information as in (5) by evaluating or correcting
the information: (5) (Mother and Oliver play with animals); Mother: "There's a
penguin sitting on top"; Oliver: "Penguin".

If they fulfil these "minimal" requirements, they can make "extended" replies as
in (6) by requesting or providing new information about the same subject or the
same information about a new subject: (6) (Yvonne feeds doll); Yvonne: "Poor
dolly's hungry"; Mother: "Yes, I should think so. She's been in her box all
night".

Locating exchanges which fulfilled these requirements was not altogether straightforward since gazes, names, wh-questions, yes/no-questions and statements can be
used for purposes other than addressing and requesting or providing information.
Although an examination of the non-vocal transcripts resolved most ambiguities,
there were inherently unclear cases from both mothers and children which were
arbitrarily but consistently treated as conversational.

The aim was not simply to describe mother-child conversation but also to relate
it to language development. The previous discussion suggests that mastery of
speech forms for requesting and providing information will be most relevant to
mother-child conversation. Brown's (1973) review indicates that these forms
undergo syntactic and semantic development. Syntactically, they develop through
gradually introducing copulas, auxiliaries, inflections and subject pronouns.
Semantically, they initially focus on naming objects with nouns chosen from a
small set. Gradually, the repertoire of nouns expands and features other than
names like properties, locations and actions appear. Occasionally, several features like properties plus names and actions plus locations are mentioned in
single remarks. Accordingly, the children's mastery of forms for requesting and
providing information was assessed using syntactic and semantic measures. The
measures utilised remarks which were not replies and seemed from their form and
non-vocal context to request or provide information. They include:
1) the percentage which contained copulas or auxiliaries,
2) the percentage which were about object names but mentioned new names,
3) the percentage which mentioned features other than names,
4) the precentage which mentioned more than one feature.

The use of percentages compensated for overall talkativeness. The exclusion of
replies meant that language development was assessed partially independently of
conversation.

RESULTS

The analysis continued by separating conversational exchanges initiated by
mothers' remarks from conversational exchanges initiated by children's. The
percentages of mother-initiated exchanges beginning with requests rather than provisions of information and ending with extended rather than minimal replies were
calculated for every mother-child pair in both recordings. The equivalent percentages of child-initiated exchanges were also calculated. Inspection of these
percentages revealed considerable heterogeneity within both recordings in mother-
initiated exchanges beginning with requests and child-initiated exchanges ending
with extended replies. Five mother-child pairs produced markedly fewer of the
former; another eight mother-child pairs produced markedly fewer of the latter.
There was more homogeneity in mother-initiated exchanges ending with extended
replies and child-initiated exchanges beginning with requests both being generally
avoided.

Thus, the mother-child pairs fell into three groups whose mean percentage of
different exchanges are shown in Table 1 together with the results of comparing

them on t-tests.

TABLE 1.   Mean percentages of different exchanges

		Mother-Initiated Exchanges		Child-Initiated Exchanges	
		% Beginning with Requests	% Ending with Extended Replies	% Beginning with Requests	% Ending with Extended Replies
Group I	(R1)*	11	9	2	34
(n = 5)	(R2)	25	8	6	32
Group II	(R1)	54	2	6	5
(n = 8)	(R2)	44	9	12	21
Group III	(R1)	52	12	4	28
(n = 11)	(R2)	40	14	8	28

	Statistically Significant Differences ($p<0.05$)			
	% Beginning with Requests	% Ending with Extended Replies	% Beginning with Requests	% Ending with Extended Replies
Across Groups/	I(R1)< II(R1) I(R1)<III(R1)	II(R1)<III(R2) –	– –	II(R1)< I(R1) II(R1)<III(R1)
Within Recordings	I(R2)< II(R2) I(R2)<III(R2)	– –	– –	II(R2)< I(R2) II(R2)<III(R2)
Within Groups/	–	II(R1)< II(R2)	–	II(R2)< II(R2)
Across Recordings	–	–	–	–

* (R1) = First recording;   (R2) = Second recording

Group I produced conversations like (7) where mother-initiated exchanges rarely began with requests or ended with extended replies and child-initiated exchanges rarely began with requests but frequently ended with extended replies: (7) (Mother and Oliver play with animals); Mother: "Look, a little monkey"; Oliver: "Monkey"; Mother: "Yes, he's trying to drive the lorry, isn't he?" Oliver: "Drive. Drive". Mother: "Drive, uhm"; Oliver: "Drive".

Group II produced conversations like (8) where mother-initiated exchanges often began with requests but rarely ended with extended replies and child-initiated exchanges rarely began with requests or ended with extended replies: (8) (Mother shows Ian another car); Mother: "What colour's that one?" Ian: "Yellow"; Mother: "It's a yellow one. What colour's this one?" Ian: "Yellow"; Mother: "No, it's red"; Ian: "It yellow".

Group III produced conversations like (9) where mother-initiated exchanges frequently began with requests but rarely ended with extended replies and child-initiated exchanges rarely began with requests but frequently ended with extended replies: (9) (Mother and Kevin look at pictures); Mother: "And what are those?" Kevin: "Shells"; Mother: "Shells, yes. You've got some shells, haven't you? What's that?" Kevin: "Milk"; Mother: "Milk, yes"; Kevin: "Milk".

To see how these variations related to language development, the mean scores which the children in the three groups obtained on the four measures were computed. These means and the results of comparing them on t-tests are shown in Table 2.

As Table 2 shows, there were no significant differences in the first recording.
In the second recording, all children had advanced, but the children in Group III
were ahead of the children in Group I on all semantic measures.   They were ahead
of the children in Group II on the syntactic measure and two semantic measures.
The children in Group II were ahead of the children in Group I on the first semantic measure.

TABLE 2.   Mean scores on measures of language development

		% Remarks with Copulas and Auxiliaries	% Different Names in Remarks about Names	% Remarks about Non-names	% Remarks about Several Features
Group I	(R1)	3	24	22	6
	(R2)	9	29	41	10
Group II	(R1)	2	30	26	5
	(R2)	3	43	32	15
Group III	(R1)	3	30	20	5
	(R2)	11	46	50	24

Statistically Significant Differences Across Groups Within Recordings (p<0.05)

% Remarks with Copulas and Auxiliaries	% Different Names in Remarks about Names	% Remarks about Non-names	% Remarks about Several Features
II(R2)<III(R2)	I(R2)< II(R2) I(R2)<III(R2)	I(R2)<III(R2) II(R2)<III(R2)	I(R2)<III(R2) II(R2)<III(R2)

DISCUSSION

These results show that variations in conversation could not have resulted from
variations in language development.   The three groups had emerged by the first recording when the children did not differ developmentally.   However, variations
in language development could have resulted from variations in conversation, and
the present section will discuss this possibility.   Since semantic differences
were particularly clear-cut, we can ask whether variations in conversation could
explain why the children in Group III were ahead of the children in Group I on all
semantic measures and ahead of the children in Group II on two semantic measures.
The only conversational difference between the children in Groups I and III was
mother-initiated exchanges beginning with requests;   the children in Group III experienced proportionately more of them.   However, in replying to maternal requests
the children in Group III were actively providing new information whereas in replying to maternal provisions the children in Group I were passively acknowledging
old information.   The relatively active conversational roles of the children in
Group III may have motivated informational or semantic development in a manner
not achieved by the relatively passive conversational roles of the children in
Group I.

While this accounts for the differences between the children in Groups I and III,
it does not account for the differences between the children in Groups II and III.
Despite experiencing similar percentages of mother-initiated exchanges beginning
with requests, the children in Group II were slower than the children in Group III
at introducing features other than names and mentioning several features in single
remarks.   However, this becomes more comprehensible on realising that all mother-
child pairs produced child-initiated exchanges which normally began with remarks

about object names.   Hence, the children in Group II were restricted to evaluative
and corrective feedback on names since they received predominantly minimal replies.
This would presumably help them expand their repertoire of names but do little for
other aspects of semantic development.   The children in Group III on the other
hand not only received evaluative and corrective feedback, but also received extended replies which by definition would have usually been about features other
than names.   As about 50% of extended replies were embedded in minimal replies as
in (10), these children would also have seen that several features can be mentioned
in single remarks: (10) (Nicola picks nose): Nicola: "Nose": Mother: "Blocked-
up nose".
Hence the children in Group III received feedback which was arguably helpful for
all aspects of semantic development.

However, the effects of mother- and child-initiated exchanges cannot be independent.
After all, the children in Group I received as many extended replies as the children in Group III but developed more slowly.   Rather, any effect of child-initiated exchanges must be constrained by mother-initiated exchanges.   Specifically,
mother-initiated exchanges must influence motivation for semantic development.
Given high motivation, children will wish to learn from maternal replies and will
be influenced by percentages of minimal and extended replies.   Clearly, this
model departs quite radically from previous attempts to argue a facilitative role
for mother-child conversation.   It proposes that mother-initiated exchanges have
motivational value.   Previous attempts have only considered their informational
value focussing, of course, on exchanges where children use imitation to make
evaluative replies.   The present model also proposes that the beneficial effects
of extended replies are dependent on other phenomena whereas writers like Cross
(1978) have implied the opposite.   However, the model must at present be treated
as tentative given the non-experimental nature of the study.   If it is eventually
supported experimentally, it will not only lead to revised ideas about how mother-
child conversation helps language development.   It will also give a partially
affirmative answer to the question underlying the present study: mother-child
conversation can help language development, but some children are helped more than
others.

REFERENCES

Brown, R. A first language: the early stages. London: George Allen and Unwin
     Ltd., 1973
Cross, T. G. Mother's speech and its association with rate of linguistic develop-
     ment in young children, in N. Waterson and C. Snow (Eds.) The development
     of communication.   Chichester: John Wiley and Sons, 1978
Lieven, E. V. M. Conversations between mothers and young children: individual
     differences and their possible implications for the study of language learn-
     ing, in N. Waterson and C. Snow (Eds.) The development of communication.
     Chichester: John Wiley and Sons, 1978
Snow, C. E. Mothers' speech research: from input to interaction, in C. E. Snow
     and C. A. Ferguson (Eds.) Talking to children: language input and acquisi-
     tion.   Cambridge: Cambridge University Press, 1977.

Adjustments in Adult-Child Conversation: Some Effects of Interaction[1]

G. Wells

The Research Unit, University of Bristol School of Education, 19 Berkeley Square, Bristol BS8 1JA, U.K.

ABSTRACT

The adoption of a distinguishable register by adults when talking to young children has now been clearly established. However, it is not clear, firstly, whether all children have equal experience of adult speech which is finely adjusted to their level of communication ability nor, secondly, whether any of the observed adjustments in adult speech are facilitative of children's linguistic development. In the study reported here, these questions have been investigated as part of the Bristol longitudinal study of the language development of a representative sample of children. Time-based samples of spontaneous interaction show that the speech addressed to fast developers is both quantitatively and qualitatively different from that addressed to slow developers. However, although this seems to suggest that the caretakers of fast developers provide a linguistic environment that facilitates accelerated development, it is argued that this environment is created through interaction to which the children themselves contribute significantly.

Key words

Language development; adult input; linguistic interaction

INTRODUCTION AND METHOD

That adults systematically modify their speech when talking to young children is now well attested. However, although this register would seem to be functionally adapted to the needs of the language learner, it still has to be established: a) which, if any, of its features are facilitative of the child's linguistic development, and b) whether its occurrence is the result of quite fine adjustments to the communicative abilities of the particular child with whom the adult is interacting or merely a generalised response to linguistic immaturity. The results of studies addressed to these issues so far have been inconclusive, either because the samples investigated were socially and/or developmentally homogeneous, or because individual differences between parents in their degree of adjustment were confounded with differences related to the children's developmental level. In addition, in most of the studies reported, the situations in which recordings were made - sessions in which parents played with their children in the presence of a research-

---

1. This research is funded by the Social Science Research Council. The help of Sally Barnes and David Satterly in analysing the data is gratefully acknowledged.

er/observer – are likely to have yielded unrepresentative samples of adult-child
interaction.   In addition to these methodological difficulties, however, there
are also serious theoretical difficulties associated with the investigation of interaction, as will become clear in what follows.   The present investigation does
not claim to provide any final answers, therefore; however it does offer a somewhat different perspective, which it is hoped will help to clarify some of the
issues involved.

The data to be presented here were derived from recordings made as part of the
Bristol longitudinal study of language development, and were not collected specifically for this investigation.   A sample of 128 children, selected to represent
the population in terms of sex, season of birth and class of family background,
were observed at 3 monthly intervals over a period of $2\frac{1}{4}$ years, each observation
including a recording of the child's spontaneous verbal interaction at home, obtained by means of a radio microphone controlled by a preset timing device to
take 24 90-second samples at approximately 20 minute intervals between 9 a.m. and
6 p.m.   In this way, a wide range of contexts was sampled and, because no observer was present there can be considerable confidence that the recordings provide
a valid and representative sample of each child's experience of linguistic interaction.   Contextual information was obtained by replaying the recording to the
parents in the evening and asking them to recall, in as much detail as possible,
the activities and participants involved in each sample.   For the present investigation, a representative sub-sample of 33 children was selected from the younger
age-group, each of whom was first observed at the age of 15 months.

The first aim was to establish which features of the adult speech addressed to the
children were most strongly associated with the children's rate of development.
To this end, the children were initially equated for developmental level by selecting the recording for each child at which the Mean Length of his Structured Utterances was as close as possible to 1.5 morphemes.   From the child's speech on this
occasion the following developmental indices were also calculated: Mean Length
of the five Longest Utterances, the number of semantic clause-types used by that
occasion (Semantic Range), the number of optional semantic distinctions encoded
(Semantic Complexity), the average number of Verbs per Utterance and the number
of inter-personal functions used by that occasion (Pragmatic Range) (cf Wells 1978
for details).   Scores on the same indices were also obtained for each child on a
second occasion nine months later.   An assessment of each child's progress during
the nine months was then made by calculating the difference between his actual
score and his predicted score on the second occasion (residual gain score) for
each of the five indices.

All adult speech addressed to the children at the first observation was then
coded with respect to five broad groupings of categories:

1.   Formal Features.   Mean Length of Structured Utterances (MLUS) was calculated
      and a Difference between Adult's and Child's MLUS obtained for each child.
      Three further summary measures of the form of adult speech were obtained:
      Average Number of Utterances per Turn, Average Number of Propositions per
      Utterance and Percentage of Incomplete Utterances.   Each adult utterance
      was also coded for Mood (Declarative, Imperative, Polar Interrogative, Wh-
      Interrogative, Moodless) and the proportional distribution expressed as a
      percentage.

2.   Discourse Functions.   Six basic discourse function categories were employed:
      Request, Question, Inform, Answer, Acknowledge and Expressive.   Requests
      were further sub-categorised as Direct or Indirect with a distinction being
      made within the former between those concerned with Safety and Welfare and
      all others.   Questions were sub-categorised as requesting deictic/naming

information (Indicate), other types of information (Comment), Display of knowledge or competence, or Text-Contingent Query, and Informs as either Indicate or Comment (Wells, Montgomery and MacLure 1979). Two other categories, Offer and Accept/Refuse, were initially included, but instances were so rare that these were later omitted from the analysis. Otherwise, all utterances were assigned uniquely to one of these categories, with the exception of those utterances that both acknowledged the previous utterance and realised one of the other functions in addition.

3. Topic Incorporation. Each structured adult utterance was classified with respect to its relation, if any, to the child's previous utterance or current activity: Imitation, Expansion or Extension. Extensions were further sub-categorised as relating to the Topic Noun Phrase of the child's previous utterance, as Contrasting with that utterance, as relating to the child's Current Activity or extending his utterance in some other way. Utterances that were not related to the child's utterance or activity were classified as Unrelated (with further sub-categories: Stock Utterance, Sequence Initiating or other); Repetitions of Previous Adult Utterances (with sub-categories: Full or Part Repetition, Paraphrase or other); or Extensions of Previous Adult Utterances.

4. Locus of Reference. The state or event referred to in each structured adult utterance was classified firstly according to the participants involved: Child, Adult, Joint Activity or Third Party; and according to its temporal relation to the time of speaking: perceptually Present, Past, Future or 'Abstract'. Proportional frequencies in each category were then expressed as percentages.

5. An additional feature of this investigation, made possible by the time-based method of speech sampling, was the inclusion of an estimate of the actual amount of speech both produced by, and addressed to, the child. Since this probably fluctuates considerably from day to day, it was considered that a more reliable estimate would be obtained by taking the mean of three recordings, centring around Observation 1. For this, as for all the measures of adult speech, frequencies were based on 18 90-second samples, three samples being selected at random from each sequence of four, after samples in which the child was out of range of the radio-receiver had been excluded.

RESULTS AND DISCUSSION

Two forms of analysis were carried out: a) each adult speech variable was submitted to simple product-moment correlation analysis with each of the child residual gain scores and with the Amount of Child Speech and Child Age at Observation 1; b) having ranked the children according to their residual gain-scores on each index, each child's ranks were summed to give an overall ranking of amount of progress made in the nine months between Observations 1 and 2. Two groups, each of 9 children, at the top and bottom of the overall rank order were then identified as 'Faster' and 'Slower' developers, and comparisons were made between the mean scores of each group and the sample mean on each adult variable, and the Mann-Whitney U Test used to test the significance of·the difference in the distributions of the scores in the two groups. The results are shown in Tables 1A and 1B. However, because of the limitations of space, only those findings which are most suggestive for further investigation will be commented on here.

Perhaps the most interesting concerns the very large variation across the sample as a whole on the amount of speech actually produced. Whilst the amount of adult speech received by the child is clearly associated with his rate of progress,

TABLE 1A Adult speech variables at Observation 1

	Amount of Adult Speech	MLU (Structured)	Difference Ad.-Ch. MLU	Utterance/ Turn	Proposition/ Utterance	%Incomplete Utterances	%Declarative	%Imperative	%Polar Int.	%Wh-Int.	%Moodless	Direct Request (Safety & Welf.)	Direct Request (Other)	Indirect Request	Question (Indicate)	Question (Comment)	Question (Display)	Text-Contingent Query	Inform (Indicate)	Inform (Comment)	Answer Question	Acknowledge	Expressive
A. Child Progress Obs.1 - Obs.2																							
MLU (Longest)	.45**	.29	.43*	.55**	.19	.01	-.02	.09	.17	-.18	-.04	.49**	.10	.24	-.01	.09	.13	.05	.32	.20	-.03	.21	.54**
Semantic Range	.19	.27	.38*	.52**	.03	.12	-.24	.06	.37*	-.21	-.06	.27	-.02	.06	-.12	-.12	-.01	-.13	-.10	-.03	-.05	.14	.22
Semantic Complexity	.35*	.14	.25	.36*	.06	.09	-.15	.16	.26	-.34	.05	.40*	.03	.14	-.08	-.14	-.12	-.06	.22	-.14	.09	.23	.40*
Verbs/Utterance	.46**	.16	.19	.35*	.02	-.04	.02	.04	.25	-.15	-.12	.40*	.25	.33	.08	.23	.04	.12	.24	.29	.14	.20	.44*
Pragmatic Range	.25	.06	.18	.20	.11	.21	-.36*	0	.37*	-.06	.15	.27	.09	-.02	.17	.27	.13	-.03	.07	.07	-.06	.14	.21
Child at Obs.1																							
Amount of Speech	.69**	.13	.13	.07	.11	.01	-.09	-.13	.32	.05	0	.16	.47**	.54**	.40*	.56**	.38*	.41*	.41*	.57**	.30	.45**	.46**
Age	.07	.29	.23	-.15	-.20	-.32	-.05	.03	.06	.19	-.18	.08	.09	.02	.02	.12	-.05	.02	-.01	.18	-.07	.06	-.12
B. Group Comparisons																							
Whole Sample Mean	105.2	4.34	2.62	1.27	1.13	17.8	25.3	25.2	11.5	9.1	28.7	8.9	12.1	2.4	2.1	8.9	4.2	6.0	5.9	12.9	1.2	19.5	6.0
Standard Deviation	69.4	0.72	0.63	0.13	0.06	8.9	7.4	9.8	5.4	5.5	8.2	8.3	9.3	2.6	2.5	6.8	6.4	5.8	8.2	11.7	2.0	19.0	5.3
Faster Group Mean	127.1	4.51	2.94	1.39	1.12	19.6	24.6	27.0	12.8	6.4	29.3	16.5	12.3	3.6	1.4	9.1	3.8	7.3	8.2	13.4	1.3	19.5	10.3
Standard Deviation	85.6	1.11	0.79	0.13	0.08	6.7	8.2	6.3	4.9	3.1	4.9	11.4	10.8	3.2	1.6	4.4	6.8	7.4	11.4	12.7	1.7	23.1	7.2
Slower Group Mean	72.7	4.05	2.31	1.20	1.11	16.3	28.4	25.7	8.8	10.1	26.7	7.4	9.2	2.1	1.8	5.1	3.0	6.0	4.0	9.9	1.1	12.1	3.3
Standard Deviation	30.6	0.66	0.64	0.11	0.04	11.7	7.9	12.7	5.4	7.0	10.5	4.0	7.5	2.3	2.3	4.0	4.9	5.5	3.7	7.9	1.6	7.7	2.7
Faster vs. Slower (Sig. level)	.01	-	-	-	-	-	-	-	-	-	-	.01	-	-	-	.025	-	-	-	-	-	-	.025

Mood

Discourse Function

TABLE 1B   Adult speech variables at Observation 1 continued

	Imitation	Expansion	Imitation & Expansion	Extend Child (Topic NP)	Extend Child (Child Act.)	Extend Child (Contrast)	Extend Child (Other)	Total Extend	Extend & Expansion	Unrelated (Stock Utt.)	Unrelated (Initiating)	Total Unrelated	Adult Repetition (Full or Part)	Adult Repetition (Paraphrase)	Total Adult Repetition	Extend Adult	%Joint Activity	%Third Party	%Time Non-present
					Topic Incorporation													*Locus of Reference*	
A. Child Progress Obs.1 - Obs.2																			
MLU (Longest)	.46**	.38*	.46**	.42*	.55*	.54*	.36	.47*	.47*	.49*	.07	.32	.11	.45**	.27	.06	.28	-.17	-.04
Semantic Range	.13	.20	.17	.31	.24	.21	.03	.15	.16	.15	-.09	.04	-.01	.25	.06	.04	.49**	-.28	-.06
Semantic Complexity	.33	.21	.31	.33	.35*	.36*	.27	.34	.33	.27	.04	.19	.10	.20	.17	.06	.30	-.18	.01
Verbs/Utterance	.27	.38	.34	.47**	.34	.47**	.29	.37*	.39*	.34	.29	.40*	.20	.44*	.32	.18	.13	.07	-.07
Pragmatic Range	.25	.08	.20	.17	.20	.12	.11	.16	.16	.27	.11	.24	.13	.06	.15	.15	.42*	-.24	-.06
Child at Obs.1																			
Amount of Speech	.44*	.42*	.47*	.47*	.24	.31	.55**	.51*	.52**	.47**	.34	.60**	.51**	.42*	.60**	.56**	-.09	.35*	.10
Age	-.22	-.17	-.22	-.02	-.19	.06	-.05	-.09	-.11	.01	.36*	.22	.12	-.05	.08	.10	.02	-.01	.28
B. Group Comparisons																			
Whole Sample Mean	5.8	3.0	8.8	3.3	6.3	3.7	15.6	25.3	28.3	7.8	9.4	23.4	8.6	2.7	13.6	13.3	3.3	21.8	7.6
Standard Deviation	6.7	4.4	10.3	4.0	6.6	3.1	14.1	22.3	25.7	7.3	7.7	14.7	7.4	3.4	10.1	10.7	3.1	10.9	4.7
Faster Group Mean	8.8	5.2	14.1	5.6	12.0	6.1	20.8	38.5	43.7	12.2	9.7	27.6	9.1	5.3	16.5	11.4	4.4	18.8	7.1
Standard Deviation	9.9	7.3	15.8	5.2	9.1	2.5	21.4	33.5	39.1	10.3	6.3	16.5	4.6	5.0	10.1	8.3	2.5	13.9	4.1
Slower Group Mean	3.8	1.4	5.2	1.6	4.0	2.8	12.3	17.9	19.3	5.0	8.6	18.4	6.0	1.7	9.8	9.3	1.3	23.1	8.7
Standard Deviation	3.1	1.2	3.5	1.3	4.5	2.4	8.7	12.6	12.8	3.8	5.5	9.0	4.6	2.1	7.0	6.0	1.8	10.4	5.9
Faster vs. Slower (Sig. level)	-	-	-	.01	.025	.01	-	-	-	-	-	-	-	.01	-	-	.01	-	-

the faster group being significantly more likely to receive more than the slower
group (p < .01), the relationship is not straightforward.   On the one hand, within-group differences are in all cases greater than between-group differences, as is
indicated by the very substantial within-group variance and by the small number of
variables on which between-group differences achieve a level of statistical significance.   On the other hand, even when the effect of amount of adult speech is
partialled out, few of the significant correlations between adult variables and
child gain scores disappear and some actually increase.   It appears, therefore,
that whilst fast developers tend to have the simple advantage of receiving more
adult speech, they also receive speech which is qualitatively different from that
addressed to slower developers in certain important respects.

It has been variously suggested (Cross 1977; Wells 1974) that the ideal situation
for the language learner is to receive utterances which encode what is currently
the focus of inter-subjective attention, particularly where such utterances incorporate and extend matter previously contributed to the ongoing discourse by the
child.   This is strongly confirmed by the significant correlations between gain in
the length and semantic/syntactic complexity of the child's utterances and the frequency of adult Extending utterances, particularly those incorporating the topic
NP of his utterance, relating to his activity or contrasting with his previous utterance.   Still further confirmation is provided by the fact that the faster group
differs significantly from the slower group in receiving more of each of these
types of extending utterance.

The fact that Expansions are found to be less significantly associated with progress than in previous studies is probably more a function of their generally low
frequency of occurrence than of their unimportance.   However it is suggested that
previous reports of a much higher proportional incidence of Expansions, and of
their significance, may have been misleading: in our observations expansions only
occur with any frequency when a stranger is present - a situation which has occurred in other studies when a researcher has been present during the collection of
data.

A further indication of the importance of adult speech which is closely related to
the field of inter-subjective attention is to be seen in the significant association between reference to Joint Activity and the two progress variables concerned
with range of meanings expressed.   It is noticeable that, although the absolute
frequency of such utterances is small, this is one of the variables on which the
faster group differs significantly from the slower group (p < .01).

The findings concerning Discourse Functions are less expected.   Whilst functions
concerned with the requesting and giving of information might have been expected to
be associated with progress in language learning, this does not prove to be the
case.   On the other hand, it is precisely those functions that seem least likely
to introduce new material - Requests designed to control the child in the interests
of safety and welfare, and Expressives - which are associated with progress.   In
both cases, the difference between the faster and slower developers is significant
at the 1 per cent level.   However, although such utterances are typically unrelated to what the child has just said, they do frequently occur in response to what
he is doing, if only, in the case of the Requests, to tell him not to!

With respect to the formal features, the present investigation is generally in accord with previous studies in not finding significant associations between the
length and syntactic complexity of adult speech and children's rate of progress
(cf. Cross 1977, 1978; Newport and colleagues 1977).   The significant association
between frequency of Polar Interrogatives and range of meanings expressed is therefore at first sight surprising.   However, inspection of the data shows that such
interrogatives occur predominantly as the realisation of questions about the child's

intentions, feelings and opinions and are thus strongly associated with the establishment and maintenance of intersubjectivity.

However, of all the adult variables investigated, it is Mean Number of Utterances per Turn which is most significantly associated with all the measures of progress, even though the absolute size of the difference between the two groups on this variable is small.   The explanation is found to lie in the fact that many multi-utterance turns, when following a preceding child utterance, consist of an acknowledgement of that utterance, frequently realised as an imitation, followed by some form of extension - both of which types of utterance are found to be independently associated with accelerated progress.

Taken together than, these results lend support to the hypothesis that there are qualitative aspects of adult speech to children which are facilitative of the children's development, and this is found to hold relatively independently of socio-economic status and of the child's position in the family.

The second hypothesis concerning 'fine-tuning' cannot be tested directly on the data presented here, as the effect of controlling for stage of development at Observation 1 is to restrict the variance on the child variables to a minimum. However, the significant correlations between many of the adult speech variables and the amount of child speech at Observation 1 makes it clear that there are other differences amongst the children besides level of development that contribute to the patterns of interaction from which those adult input variables are derived that have been found to be associated with rate of progress.   To take just one example, the frequency with which an adult produces an utterance which extends a topic proposed by the child is necessarily dependent on the frequency with which the child proposes a topic to be extended and, as can be seen, this varies very considerably from child to child, independently of the stage of development reached.

In a related study involving many of the same children, Ellis and Wells (1980) found that, of all the adult speech variables considered, it was those derived from the formal characteristics of utterances, such as length and complexity, that showed the strongest evidence of fine adjustment to the children's linguistic level;   yet these are not the features of the register that are most closely associated with children's differential rate of development.   On the other hand, relative frequencies of variables concerning discourse functions and locus of reference, found to be facilitative here, remained relatively constant over the period studied by Ellis and Wells.

It appears, therefore, that the formal features of the specialised register used when adults interact with young children do show quite close adjustment to the communicative abilities of the children concerned, and such adjustments can appropriately be described as 'fine-tuning'.   However, insofar as there is variation in the children's experience of linguistic interaction which can be interpreted as differentially facilitative of development, this emerges from the actual topics proposed and from the way in which they are collaboratively negotiated and to this both child and adult contribute in varying proportions.   To ask who is responsible for creating a facilitating linguistic environment, therefore, is to misunderstand the nature of interaction: as with the problem of the chicken and the egg, the question is inappropriately conceived.

REFERENCES

Cross, T. G. Mothers' speech adjustments: the contribution of selected child
     listener variables, in C. Snow and C. Ferguson (Eds.) Talking to children.
     Cambridge: Cambridge University Press, 1977

Cross, T. G. Mothers' speech and its association with rate of linguistic develop-
        ment in young children, in C. Snow and N. Waterson (Eds.) The development
        of communication. New York: Wiley, 1978

Ellis, R. and Wells, C. G. Enabling factors in adult-child discourse. First
        Language, 1980, 1.

Newport, E. L., Gleitman, H. and Gleitman, L. R. Mother I'd rather do it myself:
        some effects and non-effects of maternal speech style, in C. Snow and
        C. Ferguson (Eds.) Talking to children. Cambridge: Cambridge University
        Press, 1977

Wells, C. G. Learning to code experience through language. Journal of Child
        Language, 1974, 1, 243-269

Wells, C. G. What makes for successful language development? in R. Campbell
        and P. Smith (Eds.) Recent advances in the psychology of language. New
        York: Plenum Publishing Company, 1978

Wells, C. G., Montgomery, M. M. and MacLure, M. Adult-child discourse: outline
        of a model of analysis. Journal of Pragmatics, 1979, 3, 337-380

Self-Consciousness and the Study of Interpersonal Interaction: Approaches and Issues

C. R. Berger

*Department of Communication Studies, School of Speech, Northwestern University,
1822 Sheridan Road, Evanston, Illinois 60201, U.S.A.*

In a very real sense, the persons who make up this symposium capture the interdisciplinary spirit of this conference.   The areas of communication, linguistics,
sociolinguistics and social psychology are represented in this symposium by one
or more researchers.   While the bringing together of a heterogeneous group of
researchers is likely to produce considerable excitement in terms of cross-
fertilization of ideas, it does make the task of making relative comparisons
among papers difficult.   Thus, rather than overview and critique each paper
individually, I will outline a particular problem associated with the study of
conversation and interpersonal interaction and show how this problem impacts
upon each of the studies presented in the symposium.   The problem to be addressed
here concerns the role of self-consciousness in social interaction.

Thought and Talk: Excuse me, but have I been talking to myself?

The core of my concern can be nicely illustrated by an incident involving three
of our graduate students who were eating lunch one day in the university cafeteria.
A woman who was a total stranger to all three students sat down in a vacant chair
beside one of them and after a moment asked, "Have I been talking to myself?".
Further conversation with the woman revealed that she was indeed serious in her
request for information about her verbal behaviour!   The woman had just finished
taking her qualifying examinations and was apparently quite concerned about her
performance on them.   Although this fact can be invoked to explain her rather
strange "opening move" in the conversation, the important point of the incident
is that the woman entertained the possibility that her speech was not under conscious control.   This obviously extreme example serves to introduce the proposition that a considerable proportion of everyday interaction is carried out at
rather low levels of consciousness and that theories and perspectives which are
based upon the assumption that high levels of volition, planning, rehearsal, and
cognitive effort precede the production of speech in most everyday interactions,
are likely to have severely restricted boundary or scope conditions.

The idea that in everyday life social actors may have relatively low levels of
self-awareness is not a new one.   Cooley (1922) cogently observed:

> It is true, however, that the attempt to describe the social self
> and to analyze the mental processes that enter into it almost un-
> avoidably makes it appear more reflective and 'self-conscious'
> than it usually is ...   Many people whose behavior shows that

their idea of themselves is largely caught from persons they
are with, are yet quite innocent of any intentional posing;
it is a matter of subconscious impulse or mere suggestion. (p.209)

Cooley's position not only argues that social actors frequently have low levels
of self-awareness in interaction situations, but also indicates that those who
study social behaviour may inadvertently attribute too much awareness to those
actors who are the objects of study. More recently, Turk (1974) has contended
that in diffuse social relationships, such as those which characterize a considerable portion of family interaction, interaction goals may not be clear to
the participants themselves or to those who observe their interactions. Turk
relies partially on psychoanalytic theory to make the case that interaction goals
may be unknowable. He does point out that in specific relationships, e.g. the
relationship between a salesperson and a customer, interaction goals are likely
to be clear and knowable.

In addition to the general observations cited above, there are several ongoing programmes of research which bear directly upon the issues of self-consciousness
and self-awareness in social interaction situations. First, Duval and
Wicklund's (1972) theory of objective self-awareness posits two discrete states
of consciousness. When persons focus their attention on themselves as objects,
they are said to be objectively self-aware. When persons focus their attention
outward, they are said to be subjectively self-aware. According to the theory,
objective self-awareness is essentially a noxious state because self-scrutiny
reveals intrapsychic discrepancies between one's idea and actual self-concepts;
however, Wicklund (1975) has pointed out that sometimes objective self-awareness
may not prove to be an uncomfortable state. Objective self-awareness is generated experimentally by having persons view themselves in mirrors, listen to tape
recording of themselves, and watch themselves on video tape. Various experiments have shown that in the objectively self-aware state persons use more first
person pronouns in their speech (Davis & Brock, 1975), lower their self-evalu-
ations (Duval & Wicklund, 1972), exit more quickly from a room when given the
chance (Duval & Wicklund, 1972) and show greater attitude change under some conditions (Insko, Worchel, Songer & Arnold, 1973).

While objective self-awareness theory and research emphasize the local environmental conditions which give rise to increased self-awareness, there are two strands
of research which view self-awareness as a personality characteristic. Snyder
(1974) developed an instrument to measure the construct of self-monitoring.
According to Snyder, high self-monitors are persons who are better able to contιʊl
their self-presentations and are more likely to use the behavioural cues provided
by others as guides for their own conduct. Snyder (1974) found actors to have
higher levels of self-monitoring than college students and mental patients to
have exceptionally low levels of self-monitoring. In addition, high self-monitors were better able to enact various emotional states than low self-monitors.
Ickes and Barnes (1977) reported that dyads composed of one high self-monitor
and one low self-monitor experienced more conversational disruptions than dyads
composed of the three other combinations of high and low self-monitors. In
this study, high self-monitors reported higher levels of self-consciousness when
paired with low self-monitors. Another trait approach to self-consciousness is
represented by the work of Fenigstein, Scheier and Buss (1975). These investigators differentiate between private self-consciousness and public self-consciousness. Private self-consciousness is viewed by these authors as a trait akin to
introversion in which attention is focussed upon the self alone. Public self-
consciousness is seen as a form of self-focused attention which derives from a
concern for others' evaluations of the self. This conception is rooted in the
social behaviourism of Mead (1934).

Finally, working from the context of artificial intelligence, Abelson (1976) and Schank and Abelson (1977) have argued that for repeated sequences of behaviour persons develop <u>scripts</u> which enable them to understand and respond to the situation in which they find themselves.   Abelson (1976) defines a script as, "a coherent sequence of events expected by the individual, involving him either as a participant or as an observer". (p.33).   Langer (1978) has employed the notion of scripts to support the proposition that when persons' behaviours are script based, their levels of awareness concerning their behaviours are low.   She cites numerous studies which support this proposition.   She further argues that persons <u>will</u> engage in thought when:

1. A novel situation is encountered for which there is no script.
2. Carrying out the script is effortful.
3. External factors interfere with the completion of the script.
4. The outcomes of the enactment (positive or negative) are discrepant with those that usually follow.
5. Involvement is low.

The brief overview of these various research areas suggests that:

1. Inferences about the intentions of actors from analyses of their talk may be impossible, since actors themselves may be unaware of their intentions.
2. Most everyday social interaction is <u>not</u> characterised by planning, rehearsal, strategy choice, and other alleged precursors of verbal behaviour.
3. Persons will not be able to give extensive self-report information about the motivations for their behaviour when the behaviour is based upon scripts.
4. Individual differences in self-consciousness may strongly influence the degree of relationship between cognition and verbal behaviour.

Implications for the Symposium

There are three major areas in which the previous discussion impacts upon the papers presented in this symposium.   First, the papers by Glendon Drake and Chloris Gormly and colleagues both employ concepts of accommodation (Giles and Smith, 1979)   as a conceptual base.   In particular, the Gormly and colleagues paper presents a rationale for predicting speech adaptations as a function of the relative ages of child interactants.   While the fact that speech accommodation does occur along some speech dimensions and under certain conditions has been demonstrated in many different studies (see Giles and Powesland 1975), there remains the question of the extent to which interactants are <u>conscious</u> of such shifts and the extent to which interactants <u>consciously</u> employ such strategies as convergence in order to become more attractive to the target of their communicative efforts.   Along these lines, Giles and Powesland (1975) suggested that a distinction might be made between <u>overt</u> and <u>covert</u> accommodation. Overt accommodation would include changing from one language to another in a bilingual situation.   Covert accommodation could include changes in accent, speech rate, pauses, etc. which might be <u>outside</u> the conscious awareness of the speaker.   This distinction has yet to receive much empirical attention and within the present context it becomes a crucial issue.   For if we are to <u>explain</u> why convergence takes place, it would seem critical to know whether the speech modifications shown by the interactants flow from attributions which are <u>consciously</u> generated and used to guide speech behaviour or whether the speech modifications are caused by some kind of script which is <u>outside the conscious awareness</u> of the interactants. Moreover, if one's interests are practical and are related to the problem of changing speech patterns in order to produce a more "adaptive communication", it

would seem critical to know whether speech patterns manifested by a client are
consciously produced or whether they are script based. Presumably, the former
would be more easily modified than the latter.

A second, closely related point concerns the relationship between the notion of
verbal strategy and self-consciousness. Bradac and colleagues employ the concept
of verbal strategy and examine the impact of two compliance gaining strategies
(ingratiation and expert) on perceptions of persuasive effectiveness.   In the
latter case, ongoing interaction was not the object of study.   However, the
general problem of inferring some kind of conscious planning or forethought from
the study of verbal behaviour is obvious.   The fact that a particular pattern of
verbal behaviour has the appearance of being "strategic" does not ipso facto mean
that it is the product of conscious selection from among available response alternatives and is aimed at achieving some goal.   Voice intonations may be deliberately manipulated to produce the perception of insult in the auditor, but voice intonations may achieve the same effect in an auditor without conscious intent on the
part of the source.   While this problem might be dismissed by arguing that it is
the perception of the auditor that counts regardless of the intent of the source,
the viability of this argument depends upon what one is interested in explaining.
If one wishes to explain the "strategy selection" of the source, then the preceding argument is considerably weakened and the question of the "generative
mechanisms" underlying the source's speech as well as the issue of awareness become
central concerns.

Finally, two of the studies in the symposium rely either directly or indirectly on
self-reports of communication behaviour.   In the Wiemann and Krueger study, persons
were asked to describe their relationships, and Bradac and colleagues based their
manipulation of compliance gaining strategies on the results of a multidimensional
scaling study of respondent generated social influence strategies (Falbo 1977).
Here the self-awareness issue relates to a concern about the ability of persons to
provide meaningful verbal accounts for their behaviour.   Along these lines,
Nisbett and Wilson (1977) have demonstrated that persons have extremely limited
verbal access to the mental processes which subserve the making of judgments and
the initiation of social behaviour.   Persons frequently show lack of awareness
of the critical stimulus which caused their behaviour, lack of awareness of a
critical response, persons may not see the connection between the two.   Persons
may be aware of the products of complex mental processes, but they do not seem to
be able to access verbally the processes themselves.   The Langer (1978) position
cited earlier is, in a sense, even more extreme in that she apparently argues for
a lack of awareness of both product and process in scripted situations.   In any
case, both of these lines of research suggest that self-reports about communication behaviour are likely to contain an admixture of fact and fiction which might
be impossible for the analyst to disentangle.

Conclusion

The intent (I think) of the preceding discussion is not to suggest that the
studies of the symposium are fatally flawed because they fail to address the
issue of self-consciousness and interpersonal interaction.   Rather, the notion
advanced here is that the role of self-consciousness in conversation and interpersonal interaction has tended to be ignored by those who study interaction through
direct observation as well as those who rely upon less direct methods.   There
seems to be a pervasive tendency to assume that persons are continually scanning
their environments for relevant cues from others and planning their next strategic
moves.   If such a model were to underlie much of everyday interaction, I suspect
that little conversation would ever take place!   Moreover, after a few hours of

"scanning and planning" most persons would be in a state of physical collapse. Much of the time persons appear to operate on a kind of conversational automatic pilot. It is important that we begin to understand how interpersonal interaction is affected when the automatic pilot is both on and off.

REFERENCES

Abelson, R. P. Script processing in attitude formation and decision-making. In J. S. Carroll and J. W. Payne (Eds.) Cognition and social behavior. Hillsdale, New Jersey: Lawrence Erlbaum Associates, 1976

Cooley, C. H. Human nature and the social order (revised edition). New York: Charles Scribner's Sons, 1922

Davis, D. and Brock, T. C. Use of first person pronouns as a function of increased objective self-awareness and prior feedback. Journal of Experimental Social Psychology, 1975, 11, 381-388

Duval, S. and Wicklund, R. A theory of objective self awareness. New York: Academic Press, 1972

Falbo, T. Multidimensional scaling of power strategies. Journal of Personality and Social Psychology, 1977, 35, 537-547

Fenigstein, A., Scheier, M. F. and Buss, A. H. Public and private self-consciousness: assessment and theory. Journal of Consulting and Clinical Psychology, 1975, 43. 522-527

Giles, H. and Powesland, P. F. Speech style and social evaluation. London: Academic Press, 1975

Giles, H. and Smith, P. Accommodation theory: optimal levels of convergence, in H. Giles & R. St. Clair (Eds.) Language and social psychology. Oxford: Basil Blackwell, 1979

Ickes, W. and Barnes, R. D. The role of sex and self-monitoring in unstructured dyadic interactions. Journal of Personality and Social Psychology, 1977, 35, 315-330

Insko, C. A., Worchel, S., Songer, E. and Arnold, S. Effort, objective self-awareness, choice and dissonance. Journal of Personality and Social Psychology, 1973, 28, 262-269

Langer, E. J. Rethinking the role of thought in social interaction, in J. H. Harvey, W. Ickes, & R. F. Kidd (Eds.) New directions in attribution research. Hillsdale, New Jersey: Lawrence Erlbaum Associates, 1978

Mead, G. H. Mind, self and society. Chicago: University of Chicago Press, 1934

Nisbett, R. E. and Wilson, T. D. Telling more than we can know: verbal reports on mental processes. Psychological Review, 1977, 84, 231-259

Schank, R. C. and Abelson, R. P. Scripts, plans, goals and understanding. Hillsdale, New Jersey: Lawrence Erlbaum Associates, 1977

Snyder, M. Self-monitoring of expressive behavior. Journal of Personality and Social Psychology, 1974, 30, 526-537

Turk, J. L. Power as the achievement of ends: a problematic approach in family and small group research. Family Process, 1974, 13, 39-52

Wicklund, R. A. Objective self-awareness, in L. Berkowitz (Ed.) Advances in experimental social psychology (Vol. 9). New York: Academic Press, 1975

The Language of Relationships: I. Description[1]

J. M. Wiemann and D. L. Krueger

*Department of Speech, University of California, Santa Barbara,
California 93106, U.S.A.*

ABSTRACT

This paper examines the way in which people describe their own relationships, and
compares those descriptions to the universally acknowledged relational dimensions,
<u>control</u> and <u>affiliation</u>.   Subjects wrote descriptions of one of three types of
relationships: best liked opposite sex friend, best liked same sex friend, or
described in terms of Affect, Approach–Avoidance and Structure.   In addition,
subjects characterised their positive relationships in terms of Support and their
negative relationships in terms of Incongruity.   Importantly, control appeared
as a sub–set of Structure: one of many constraints, limits and obligations
which define relationships.   Affect appears to be broader than previously
considered, in that several types of cognitive and behavioural representations are
perceived as defining a relationship along this dimension.   Support is a caregiving or caretaking dimension.   Approach–Avoidance is an indication of the
inclusiveness or "tightness" of the relational system.   The dimension identified
as Incongruity in negative relationships encompasses the insincerity or phoniness
enacted by people who are forced into a relationship and try to "put a good face
on it".

<u>Key words</u>

Relationships; communication; affiliation; control; support; approach-
avoidance; phenomenological research; language

INTRODUCTION

The purpose of this report is to explore the manner in which people describe
their own relationships and to see how those descriptions compare with traditional
social science conceptualisations about human relationships.   This concern is
intertwined with, but conceptually separate from, the more usual interest in how
relationships may be "objectively" described by an observer.

---

1. This research was supported, in part, by a grant from the Academic Senate of
   the University of California, Santa Barbara.   An expanded version of this
   paper is available from the authors.

A brief overview of past thinking about characteristics of relationships is presented, followed by an alternative procedure for assessing relational definitions.

CHARACTERISTICS OF INTERPERSONAL RELATIONSHIPS

While a variety of characteristics of interpersonal relationships have been identified, scholars studying relational phenomena are in agreement that there are two universal components of human interaction: control and affiliation (see reviews by Brown, 1965; Carson, 1969; Kemper, 1973). This consensus has emerged from such diverse fields as sociolinguistics (e.g. Ervin-Tripp, 1972), social communication (Foa & Foa, 1972), and task group interaction (Borgatta, 1964).

Despite this consensus we believe that previous research may have distorted or obscured the dimensionality of interpersonal relationships in three important ways: (1) the context of research constrained subject responses so that they were well outside normal relational communication patterns - for example, it is unlikely that behaviour patterns enacted in contrived task groups generalize well to social situations, especially intimate ones; (2) most of this research is monadic in orientation (i.e. individuals, not relationships, are studied); and (3) previous measurement attempts have not fully represented the universe of relational characteristics; scales selected a priori may reflect investigator bias rather than subjects' experience.

A RELATIONAL ANALYSIS SYSTEM

To overcome these difficulties with previous research, a theoretical framework which is phenomenological, interactional (Bateson, 1972; Watzlawick et al., 1967) and which is minimally constraining to respondents is necessary. This framework also holds control and affiliation to be central characteristics of relationships; however, its emphasis is on behaviour patterns in relationships, and not on individuals. By phenomenological we mean not just non-experimental research, but research that focuses on subjects' unconstrained behaviour. Harré and Secord (1972) argue that social behaviour can only be adequately explained from the participants' perspective. This approach is consistent with the notion of the language/reality relationship, articulated by Sapir (1921) and Whorf (1941) and elaborated by symbolic interactionists (cf. Blumer, 1969; Berger & Luckmann, 1966). Consequently, the best indications of the characteristics (or dimensions) of relationships are respondents' descriptions of their own relationships.

Our final consideration, before presenting our data, is the importance of considering negative relationships in a comprehensive study of the characteristics of relationships in general. There are no data to indicate that negative relationships are merely the flip side of positive relationships, although this seems to be implicitly accepted by many researchers. We will offer data to the contrary. First, however, we will proceed to a discussion of how the data were generated.

METHOD

Subjects

Subjects were 216 undergraduates in communication courses at the University of California. Approximately half were males.

Procedures

Subjects responded to a questionnaire designed to elicit descriptionsof a long-standing interpersonal relationship under one of three relational conditions: best liked, same sex friend (BLSS; n = 90); best liked, opposite sex friend (BLOS: n = 60); and least liked other (LL; n = 66).

Analysis

Subjects' descriptions were abbreviated by two coders into single words or short phrases. For example, "He is my boyfriend, and we're very close", was reduced to "boyfriend", and "close". Identical codes from different Ss were tallied, and very similar codes were collapsed; for example, "date frequently" and "date often" were combined into a single descriptor, "date frequently", which thus received two tallies. BLSS yielded 231 descriptors; BLOS, 139; and LL, 98. Using a type of sort analysis, parallel descriptors were grouped; emphasis was placed upon maintaining intragroup similarity and between-group difference, and the fewest possible groups were created.

Next the most reasonable explanation of each group was determined. For example, the group containing the words, "dominating", "rival", "competitive" and "intimidation" was labelled control struggle. Groups were then combined into related clusters, e.g. "positive affect", "intimacy" and the "behavioural manifestations of positive affect" were combined into a cluster interpreted as Affect.

RESULTS

Best liked, opposite sex friend   The clusters and their component groups which organize the Ss' relational descriptors are reported here for each relational condition. A summary of the clusters, their groups, and examples of descriptors which comprise the groups is reported in Table 1.

For BLOS we identified four clusters: Affect, Support, Approach and Structure. Affect consists of positive and negative poles of intimacy, positive affection, and behavioural manifestations of positive affection. Support appears to be a bridge between Affect and Approach, and incorporates the idea of interdependence. Approach contains only behavioural manifestations of approach. The fourth cluster, Structure, embodies organization through constraint, incorporating shared control, and the impact of temporal and spatial limitations on the relationship. Structure consists of spatial constraint, time and shared control.

Best liked, same sex friend   The relational condition BLSS yielded Affect, Support, Approach and Structure, which are similar to those clusters described for BLOS. Affect consists of intimacy, positive evaluation, and neutral description. Support is a single group cluster. Approach is more accurately Approach-Avoidance, consisting of movement both toward (e.g. manifestations of positive affect) and away from (e.g. differentiation) relationships. Structure again consists of spatial constraint, time and control.

Least liked other   In LL four clusters emerged: Affect, Avoidance, Structure and Incongruity. The first three are similar to those in the other relational conditions, but are more negative descriptions. Incongruity appears for the first time and represents a discrepancy between the way S thinks his/her partner feels or behaves, and the way the partner says he/she feels or behaves. Affect consists of neutral, negative evaluation, negative response and manifestations of negative response. Avoidance contains neutral descriptors and behavioural manifestations of avoidance. Structure here parallels the other relational conditions, with the exception that control is control struggle; a fourth group, demand, appears; and time is primarily past history.

J. M. Wiemann and D. L. Krueger

TABLE 1: Dimensions of Relational Communication

BEST LIKED[a] OPPOSITE SEX	BEST LIKED SAME SEX	LEAST LIKED
Affect[b]	Affect	Affect
positive intimacy[c] (lover)[d]	intimacy (love, intimate)	neutral (tolerance, casual)
negative intimacy (not intimate)	positive evaluation (happy, cheerful)	negative evaluation (inconsiderate)
positive affection (affectionate)	neutral description (alike, compatible)	negative response (dislike)
manifestations (fun)		manifestations (fight, insult)
Support	Support	
support (comfort, dependable)	support (care, sympathy)	
Approach	Approach-Avoidance	Avoidance
manifestations (discuss relationship)	manifestations of pos. (confidant)	neutral (no closeness)
	manifestations of neutral (feedback, contact)	manifestations (ignore, never talk)
	manifestations of neg. (no metacommunication)	
	differentiation (try to separate)	
Structure	Structure	Structure
spatial constraint (live near)	spatial constraint (roommate, schoolmate)	spatial constraint (chance proximity)
time (goals for future)	time (long term)	time (divorced, were serious)
shared control (equal)	control (gives advice, influences decisions)	control struggle (competitive, rival)
		demand (pest, demands help)
		Incongruity
		incongruity (insincere, acts like friend)

[a]Relational condition
[b]Cluster or dimension
[c]Groups comprising cluster
[d]Example of descriptor generated by S.

CONCLUSIONS AND IMPLICATIONS

Affect, Approach-Avoidance and Structure emerged as characteristics of all three types, while Support was identified as part of positive relationships and Incongruity as part of negative ones.

Structure   Subjects described controlling aspects of their relationships in
terms of how the relationships are structured, especially by time and space.
Their relationships are defined by the time they spend with the other and by the
spatial contexts they share.   For example, "roommates" is an adequate description for many relationships.   Importantly, these types of constraints are
offered as reasons for liking best-liked others, but as excuses for knowing
least-liked others.   The importance of time and space are especially evident
for LL.   These constraints not only excuse the relationship but, in all likelihood, justify the continuation of the relationship.   Temporal and spatial
relational definitions are also partially dependent on obligations to a third
party.   If A likes B, and B likes X, then A is forced to deal with X.   A
"second hand" interdependence is established and people find themselves unwilling
participants in relationships not of their own making.

Behaviours which social scientists have typically identified as controlling were
used as relational descriptors.   Positive relationships, in particular, were
described in this way, but with some qualification.   Relationships with BLOS
are experienced as mutually controlling or symmetrical;   decision-making is
shared, and influence, bi-lateral.   Complementary control patterns were more
frequently reported in BLSS, with the subject indicating that he/she was in the
"one up" position about as frequently as the reverse.

Negative relationships, on the other hand, engender a competitive orientation.
Several people report that their LL other is a "friend" of the same sex, whom
they know well and in some cases have lived with for a long period of time, but
with whom they frequently compete in sports and school.   Negative relationships
are also characterized by demands.   Subjects described their partners as being
"pests" and, interestingly, as doing favours for them, which they apparently saw
as a demand for a similar response.   Unwanted proximity and behaviour which
obligates one person to another forces an interdependence that is not mutually
desirable.

Affect   A second characteristic of relationships is affect, replicating previous
research.   In contrast to previous research, important distinctions in the modes
of expression of affect were uncovered.   Affect embodies evaluation, description,
cognitive response, and perhaps most importantly, behavioural manifestations of
affect.

This more precise explication of Affect gives greater explanatory power to the
concept.   It is important to know, for example, if a person is evaluating a
relationship highly because of active, behavioural events or because of more
passive, abstract evaluation.

Support   This dimension only appeared in descriptors of best liked others;
non-support was not reported as a relevant description of negative relationships.
Support is superficially related to Affect, but is conceptually different, indicating caretaking and caregiving, rather than liking or disliking.   Items
representative of Support were excluded from previous studies or collapsed with
Affect items, but we feel its conceptual difference from Affect and its identification by our subjects warrants its presentation as a separate relational
characteristic.

Approach-Avoidance   The Approach-Avoidance dimension does not appear in most
studies, but has received considerable support from Schutz (1966) and appears
frequently in the marriage and family literature (see Bochner, 1976).

The descriptors of Approach-Avoidance are primarily behavioural and encompass
movement toward the other, a kind of motionless state and movement away from

the other.   This dimension also appears to have been excluded from past research
or collapsed with Affect; but Approach-Avoidance is generally communicative and
independent of Affect.   In the relational condition BLSS, for example, approach,
neutrality and avoidance were apparent in such affectively neutral descriptors as
"confidant", "feedback" and "try to separate", respectively.

Incongruity   While it emerged as a dimension in LL relationships, incongruity
was mentioned too infrequently to be easily interpretable.

SUMMARY

While Affect emerged as a primary characteristic of the relationships explored in
this study, Control was interpreted as a sub-set of the dimension Structure.
In addition, our subjects also described their relationships in terms of Approach-
Avoidance and Support, characteristics of relationships which have either been
ignored in past research, or collapsed with other dimensions.

The most important outcome of this study is an expanded understanding of control
as a relational concept.   We use Structure to indicate how control can be
construed relationally.   Specifically, Structure encompasses the constraints,
limits and obligations of a given relationship.   Structure is the set of
expectations which relational participants share and upon which they base judgments of appropriateness of behaviour.   Contrast this to more monadic conceptualizations, where one person exercises control upon another.   These approaches to
control treat it as a communicative style in a relational context, rather than
as a feature of the relationship itself.   Structure, on the other hand, does not
beg the question of which strategy - one-up or one-down - is really controlling.
In all but the most unilateral of relationships (e.g. mother-infant) structure
is mutually defined.

Affect was experienced by our subjects in much the way previous research predicts.
But it is more broadly defined by relational participants than was previously
thought.   Evaluation, description, cognitive response and behavioural manifestations all make up the experience of affect.

Support, Incongruity and Approach-Avoidance are also seen by our subjects as
relevant relational characteristics.   The extent to which these are generalizable
to other populations and other social relationships is still an empirical question.

Finally, we must point out that the descriptive, phenomenological perspective
employed in this study permitted us a degree of insight that more mechanical
means of data reduction would not have.   These findings seem to justify the
value of the method.

REFERENCES

Bateson, G. Steps to an ecology of mind. San Francisco: Chandler, 1972
Berger, P. L. and Luckmann, T. The social construction of reality.   Garden City,
    New York: Doubleday, 1966
Blumer, H. Symbolic interactionism: perspective and method.   Englewood Cliffs,
    New Jersey: Prentice Hall, 1969
Bochner, A. P. Conceptual frontiers in the study of communication in families.
    Human Communication Research, 1976, 2, 381-397
Borgatta, E. F. The structure of personality characteristics.   Behavioral Science,
    1964, 2, 8-17
Brown, R. Social psychology. New York: Free Press, 1965
Carson, R. C. Interaction concepts of personality. Chicago: Aldine, 1969

Ervin-Tripp, S.   On sociolinguistic rules: alternation and co-occurrence.
     In J. J. Gumperz & D. Hymes (Eds.), _Directions in sociolinguistics_.   New
     York: Holt, Rinehart & Winston, 1972
Foa, U. G. and Foa, E. B. Resource exchange: toward a structural theory of
     interpersonal communication.   In A. W. Siegman & B. Pope (Eds.), _Studies
     in dyadic communication_.   New York: Pergamon Press, 1972
Harré, R. and Secord, P. _The explanation of social behaviour_.   Totowa, New
     Jersey: Littlefield, Adams, 1972
Kemper, T. D. The fundamental dimensions of social relationship: a theoretical
     statement. _Acta Sociologica_, 1973, _16_, 41-57
Sapir, E. _Language_. New York: Harcourt, Brace, 1921
Schutz, W. C. _The interpersonal underworld_.   Palo Alto, California: Science
     and Behavior Books, 1966
Watzlawick, P., Beavin, J. and Jackson, D. D. _Pragmatics of human communication_.
     New York: Norton, 1967
Whorf, B. L. The relationship of habitual thought and behavior to language.
     In L. Spier (Ed.), _Language, culture and personality: Essays in memory of
     Edward Sapir_.   Menasha, Wisconsin: Sapir Memorial Publication Fund, 1941.

The Social Role of Slang

G. F. Drake*

Linguistics Department, San Diego State University, San Diego, California, U.S.A.

ABSTRACT

Slang is a common linguistic behaviour. Despite this it has been collected rather than defined and studied by linguistics. Dumas and Lighter have attempted to establish criteria for defining the concept, but commit the mistake of neglecting slang as a social psychological phenomenon.

To place slang in a societal frame a variation of Giles' accommodation theory is used. The use of slang is offered as a major index and signal of alienation and solidarity, remarkable in that the same locution can signal both in the same situation.

The development of studies of slang will contribute substantively as a significant component of linguistic and social behaviour and methodologically as a basis for integrating the study of language and society into a unified theoretical framework.

Key words

Slang; intergroup relations; jargon; social status; functions of speech

Labov has called attention to that "... outer, extra linguistic darkness where we cast speculation on the origin of language and articles about slang" (Labov 1972). While this hardly encourages one to write articles about slang, it does capture the aridity of linguistic discussions of slang.

Nevertheless, slang is much discussed; scads of examples of every sort are collected in dictionaries and in such journals as American Speech and in sundry other sources by folklorists, linguists, historians, antiquarians, teachers and others. As a linguist I am called upon by radio, television and newspaper reporters to talk about nothing so much as I am to pontificate on slang. Yet as one recent researcher reports: "... the term 'slang' has rarely been defined in a way that is use-

---

* Now Dean of Arts and Sciences, University of Michigan-Flint, Michigan, U.S.A.

ful to linguists.   Annoyance and frustration await anyone who searches the professional literature for a definition or even a conception of slang that can stand
up to scrutiny.   Instead one finds impressionism, much of it of a dismaying kind."
(Dumas and Lighter, 1978, p.5).   Historically, most rhetoric and grammar books
have warned students away from slang as being imprecise (which it usually is
certainly not) or vulgar (which it often is).   Most students of slang have simply
collected it and arranged it in appropriate taxonomies much in the way amateur
butterfly collectors place specimens on pins according to colour and markings
rather than studying the specimens as an entomologist would.

But the fact that slang is a socially important phenomenon keeps asserting itself
in a persistent but muddled way.   Two contemporary students of slang, Bethany K.
Dumas and Jonathan Lighter, in a recent, interesting article entitled, 'Is Slang
a Word for Linguistics?', have detected that persistent assertion and refined and
extended it in a useful direction, though, I will argue here, to a still inchoate
point due to the lack of an integrative approach which uses social psychological
as well as sociolinguistic theory.

The purpose of this present paper is to demonstrate and make explicit the theoretical value of social psychology to linguistics.   A number of social psychological
theories can be productively applied to the problem of slang.   Due to the constraints of time I will refer here to only some notions of Henri Tajfel and Howard
Giles and their co-workers.

Dumas and Lighter cite a dictionary discussion of slang which raises the social
point:

> The label Slang indicates a style of language rather than a level,
> formality or cultivation.   The distinguishing feature of slang
> as understood in the dictionary is the intention - however often
> unsuccessful - to produce rhetorical effect, such as incongruity,
> irreverence, or exaggeration ...   A word that is strictly denotative ...
> is not slang.   Slang always has strong connotations in addition to
> its denotation ...   Its connotation is intentionally, often
> aggressively informal.
>
> (American Heritage Dictionary 1969, XLVI)

The point that Dumas and Lighter seize on is the speaker's social intention.
Dumas and Lighter also focus on James Sledd's 1965 statement about slang as one
of the few statements that places slang rightfully in a sociolinguistic context.
In his characteristically angry but perceptive manner Sledd wrote:

> When a teacher warns his students against slang, he reaffirms his
> allegiance to the social order that created him.   Typically,
> slang is a para-code, a system of substitutes for statusful ex-
> pressions which are used by people who lack conventional status and
> do not conduct the important affairs of established communities.
> Slang flourishes in the semantic areas of sex, drinking, narcotics,
> racing, athletics, popular music and other crimes - a "liberal"
> language of things done as ends in themselves by gentlemen who are
> not gentlemen and dislike gentility.   Genteel pedagogues must
> naturally oppose it, precisely because slang serves the outs as a
> weapon against the ins.   To use slang is to deny allegiance to the
> existing order, either jokingly or in earnest by refusing even the
> words which represent convention and signal status; and those who
> are paid to preserve the status quo are prompted to repress slang
> as they are prompted to repress any other symbol of potential re-
> volution.
>
> (Sledd 1965, p.699)

Here Sledd has found a handle.   Slang is by implication a <u>group</u> phenomenon and connected with group identity.   However, Sledd captured only part of the picture and so, unfortunately do Dumas and Lighter.   They take as the crucial point of Sledd's remarks not the group implication, but that slang "is used deliberately ... to flout a conventional social or semantic norm" (Dumas and Lighter 1978, p.12).   Indeed, this feature is important, but to focus on it gets one leaning in only one direction in terms of the analysis of slang - in the sociological direction, while ignoring psychological aspects.   To Dumas and Lighter slang is used only to create social distance (cf Peng, 1974).   I will argue later (when I examine the light to be shed on this question by social psychological theories) that slang may be used for solidarity as well as alienation.

However, according to their lights, Dumas and Lighter devise and attempt to delineate a clear set of features with which to define slang.   Dumas and Lighter clearly intend the formulation to be preliminary and they invite criticism in which spirit I proceed.   They claim that a word is "probably" slang if it meets at least two of the following four criteria: 1) The present of a given lexeme "will markedly lower, at least for the moment, the dignity of formal or serious speech or writing."   2) The word used "implies the user's special familiarity either with the referent or with that less statusful or less responsible class of people who have such familiarity and use the term." 3) The word is a "tabooed term in ordinary discourse of persons of higher social status or greater responsibility."   4) The word is "used in place of the well-known, especially in order (a) to protect the user from the discomfort caused by the conventional term or (b) to protect the user from the discomfort or annoyance of further elaboration."   All of these criteria, Dumas and Ligher note, "reflect some aspect of ... rebellion or deliberate lack of dignity."

This focus on lack of dignity leads Dumas and Lighter, as others have been led (e.g. Joos 1961), to urge a distinction between slang and jargon.   The reason for this is that although jargon, i.e. professional terminology, is linguistically rather like slang, jargon is used by high status groups and does not convey a sense of rebellion or lack of dignity.   I submit that when social psychological factors are taken into account, slang and jargon can be seen as the same behaviour fundamentally - that is, as divergence or convergence of individuals from one group to another.   I argue further that the status difference may arrange slang and jargon as different sub-classes of the same behaviour but that for theoretical purposes, the similar cognitive motivations of the two codes take precedence over their status differences.   Both jargon and slang arise from the need for differ-entiation, for the establishment of psychological distinctions between groups. Here it should be clear that social psychological factors enter the analysis; in this case the theory is that of Henri Tajfel, who concluded in a 1974 article that: "... acting in terms of a group rather than in terms of self cannot be expected to play a predominant part in an individual's behaviour unless there is present a clear, cognitive structure of "us" and "them" and unless this structure is not perceived as capable of being easily shifted in a variety of social and psychological conditions."   Both low status users of slang and high status users of jargon are primarily interested in the delineation of "us" and "them"; the use of affront in doing so in the case of slang is relative and secondary.

Linguists refer to sounds as "phones", physicians to injuries as "traumata" and lawyers to hurts as "torts" for essentially the same reason that other individuals may speak of being "stoned", "wasted" or "flying".   A reading of the social psychological literature makes it clear that a group never stops working at the preservation of its distinctiveness.   This is true, of course, of sub-groups also, as for example in an academic discipline.   We academics depend upon more than the programme at a conference to know who is who; the different technical jargon distributes the participants very nicely.   Each of us in the course of

becoming respectable members of our academic school learns very well the jargon of
that school.   Moreover, if we become really accomplished, we may create a special
terminology which identifies our own work specifically.   One measure of our
success may be the extent to which that terminology is taken up by others to become one valued marker of distinctiveness.   There is no need, I think, given this
context to   cite examples.   Both slang and jargon are instruments which at the
same time and often in the same situation may signal both alienation and solidarity, to use older and harsher terms than are usually applied.   It should be of
interest to socio-linguists that this social psychological analysis of the relationship of slang and jargon supports Kenyon's 1948 classic treatment of the same
subject over Joos' classic treatment of 1961.

It seems clear to me that a more integrative approach so far as disciplines are
concerned clarifies such linguistic behaviour as we are discussing here.   One
agrees with Bourhis (1978, p.4) who wrote:

> Social psychological factors help explain why individual speakers
> use speech strategies they do in terms other than just social norms
> and rules.   These factors may consist of speakers' moods, motives,
> feelings, beliefs, and loyalities ..., as well as their perception
> of the inter-group relation situation and their awareness of exist-
> ing socio-linguistic norms.

The point is that sociolinguistic analysis alone may lead one to misapprehend the
nature of slang by over-emphasizing the status function at the expense of the
group function.   Dumas and Lighter are thus led to create for the purpose of
identifying slang, criteria which account for the status lowering function of
slang.   This is an important function, even necessary, but not sufficient to
explain slang.   Nor is slang the only linguistic behaviour that calls attention
to or even boldly announces low status.   Labov (1970) has exposed covert norms
which operate to support and nourish stigmatized grammatical forms in non-standard
speech varieties.   Ellen Bouchard Ryan (1979) has investigated this same
phenomenon, the persistence of low prestige language varieties, from a social
psychological point of view and found that the value of a variety for solidarity
and for identification with a group can often outweigh considerations of status,
prestige or social advancement in maintaining the use of low prestige locutions.
So it is, I suggest, with slang.

Tajfel's theory would suggest that in-group speakers who
value their group membership highly would have a strong drive to make themselves
distinctive on a valued dimension. (cf. Bourhis, 1978, p.14).   Slang, I suggest,
is an instrument for in-group distinction.   What is valued about slang?   The
answer is circular in a sense: Slang is valued because it is a marker of group
distinctiveness.   In this it is no different from many other linguistic behaviours: ethnic, minority languages, for example, or regional dialects, both of
which slang may feed off of as sources for its creation.

In fact slang often becomes confused with dialect. The case of black English is
illustrative.   Among sub-groups of blacks, teenagers, musicians, street hustlers,
and others, slang is an important instrument of in-group solidarity and distinctiveness.   Naive listeners often hear unfamiliar black English and black slang
together and consider them one and the same.   This I take to be one reason that
many speakers of prestige dialects claim that black English is unintelligible,
even though linguistically it clearly is mutually intelligible with prestige
varieties of American English.   To the out-group the slang may _not_ be
intelligible; it is designed to be intelligible _only_ to the in-group.

It is on this point that the ephemeral nature of slang becomes relevant. Often slang is defined by its transient nature (Gleason, 1961, p.6). Closer investigation reveals, however, that the ephemeral character of slang is relative. Some slang is very short-lived; some persists over several generations (Dumas and Lighter, 1978, p.7). Often, too, the temporal factor is used to differentiate slang and jargon, slang being said to be ephemeral and jargon persistent (Joos, 1961). In fact, as any academic knows, much technical jargon is transient indeed. I cannot talk with understanding to linguistic students in the jargon of the 50s, nor in the jargon of the 60s, and I am beginning to experience trouble with that of the 70s.

Often, however, some slang is ephemeral in the extreme, as when the boundaries of groups are soft or when - to use a bit of jargon from Howard Giles - accommodation is practised with some success. In a complex society an individual confronts a complex network of groups and relationships into which he must place himself and he moves about both horizontally and vertically, both synchronically and diachronically. It is a basic tenet of social psychology that identity is in a great measure determined by how an individual finds, creates and defines his place in these networks. As Tajfel says, "It is reasonable to assume that both (an individual's) in-group and out-group attitudes and behaviours must be determined, to some extent at least, by (the) continuing process of self-definition." Insofar as slang and jargon are a means to group definition and distinctiveness and a way of telling the in's from the out's, the locks will be changed now and then in order to see whose keys fit. When some instrumental reason combines with the integrative motivation for slang, such as in the case of needing to differentiate between a drug customer and an undercover narcotics policeman, the locks must be changed constantly. Thus, slang of the drug culture is ephemeral in the extreme.

Howard Giles has provided evidence and arguments in a number of places recently (Giles and Smith 1979; Bourhis, Giles, Leyens and Tajfel 1979; Giles and Powesland 1975; Giles 1977a; Giles, Bourhis and Taylor 1977; Giles 1977b) for an explanation of linguistic behaviour that he terms the accommodation model. The accommodation theory holds that a speaker will under certain conditions, such as an attempt to gain or convey social approval, attempt to alter his persona in order to make it more acceptable to the person addressed.
In terms of speech behaviour one may alter style, variety, accent, pitch, rate or a number of other behaviours to which I would add most specifically slang and jargon. Thus Giles can develop models of convergence and divergence for speakers, according to the social and psychological factors obtaining at the time. I consider these strategies to be related to the solidarity and alienation I perceive in slang, and the model could be used, I think, to explain slang, as it has been used to explain code switching (Bourhis 1978) and accent shift (Giles and Powesland 1975) for two examples.

However, here I should like to extend the notion a bit not only to explain the transient nature of slang, but also to suggest the reason for the rather puzzling and selective appropriation of some slang by the mainstream American culture.

As regards the role of accommodation in the ephemeral nature of slang: because slang is an out-group language and a means to positive social identity for the in-group, successful accommodation (i.e. taking up slang expressions) on the part of out-group individuals has the effect of admitting new members into the in-group, provided the prospective members meet other criteria as well, such as ethnicity or skin colour. In the many cases where the other qualifications are not met the accommodation to slang or jargon on the part of out-group members may blunt the distinctiveness of the in-group and threaten positive social identity. Accordingly, the group must continually create new slang or jargon terms in order to keep the out's out and to be able to identify the in's.

Moreover, the accommodation model may explain the curious social phenomenon of
late generations in the United States by which great amounts of black street slang
has been taken up in the speech of so-called mainstream Americans.   In the late
1950s mainstream "cats" became "cool" and could really "dig".   In the 1960s
mainstreamers "rapped" a lot to get to the "nitty-gritty" and were either "right
on" or "up tight".   By 1970 we became "hip" (Burling 1973, pp.87-88).   (Of
course, many terms were never picked up and the ones that were were quickly
replaced by other terms in black culture.)

What is curious about this is that most aspects of black English have been consistently and widely despised by whites, who have taken a totally different
attitude about vocabulary items in the form of slang.   Only in ridicule would
whites imitate other aspects of black speech (Burling, 1973, p.87).   Yet many
Americans, especially young middle-class Americans, have had an insatiable
appetite for black slang, as they have had for black music, dress and certain
other aspects of black culture.

In this phenomenon can be seen the processes discussed in this paper.   The use
of black slang among blacks demonstrates the notion of slang emphasized by Dumas
and Lighter.   Blacks from lower-class background have been urged by their
schools and by the need for employment to take on the middle-class language as a
symbol and an instrument of the mainstream world they wish to enter.   Toward
standard English, these blacks develop an ambivalent attitude; they want to
learn it but at the same time it stands for what is white and oppressive.
Resultant rebellion of the lower-class blacks against middle-class values involves
many things but language is always there as a symbol (Burling 1973, p.107).   As
Burling has written:

> Consciously or unconsciously, language is used to demonstrate one's
> hope and aspirations, to indicate where one stands, to show the groups
> to which one belongs.   Today, when blacks assert a new pride in their
> heritage and insist that black is beautiful after all, they may feel the
> need for linguistic symbols for their new separatism.   ... if Swahili
> has limited relevance, and if the grammar and pronunciation of non-
> standard English are too bitterly despised to be openly asserted as
> symbols, there is at least black slang.   Because slang is so much less
> stigmatized than the other aspects of black speech, a few blacks have
> come to focus upon it as a valuable black contribution to a common
> language.   Slang, unlike nonstandard grammar, can be used with pride.
> Black slang becomes a symbol of separatism and rejection of middle
> class demands.

Here Burling captures the rebellious intent, as suggested by Dumas, Lighter and
Sledd, and something of the identifactory, solidarity function as suggested by
Tajfel.

In addition, Burling goes on to suggest the rebellion motive of slang in the
cooptation of black slang by whites when he remarks that: "It is understandable
why white youths who want to rebel against many of these same demands eagerly
appropriate the same symbol" (Burling 1973, p.107).   Perhaps here we can productively suggest the accommodation model as having some force as well.   Surely,
part of the motive of some whites involved in the appropriation of black slang
includes the desire to be identified with the rebellion of blacks against middle
class whites; this desire was especially strong in the U.S. during the 1960s.
This in itself fits the accommodation model in that young whites wish to adjust
their persona to take on the speech characteristics and other behaviours of blacks.
However, the appropriation of black slang permeates many other domains of U.S.
society and may very well reflect the general societal accommodation of blacks

that has very clearly occurred in the U.S.A. in the decades since World War II
(Sowell 1978).   This general societal accommodation could be most productively
studied, at least linguistically, using the social psychological models of Tajfel,
Giles and others (cf Giles 1979).

In this paper I have attempted to show how in the area of one small linguistic
subject such an approach may rescue the subject from the outer, extra-linguistic
darkness.

REFERENCES

Bourhis, R. Y. and Giles, H.   The language of intergroup distinctiveness, in
    H. Giles (Ed.) Language, ethnicity and intergroup relations.   New York:
    Academic Press, 1977
Bourhis, R. Y.   Language in ethnic interaction: a social psychological approach
    Paper delivered at Ninth World Congress of Sociology, Uppsala, Sweden,
    August 14-19, 1978
Bourhis, R. Y., Giles, H., Leyens, J. P. and Tajfel, H.   Psycholinguistic
    distinctiveness: language divergence in Belgium in H. Giles and R. St. Clair
    (Eds.) Language and social psychology.   Baltimore: University Park Press,
    1979
Burling, R. English in black and white.   New York: Holt, Rinehart and Winston,
    1973
Doise, W.   Groups and individuals: explanations and social psychology.
    Translated by D. Graham.   Cambridge: Cambridge University Press, 1978
Dumas, Bethany K. and Lighter, J.   Is slang a word for linguists?   American
    Speech, 1978, 53, 1: 5-17
Giles, H. and Powesland, P. F., Speech style and social evaluation.   London:
    Academic Press, 1975
Giles, H.   Social psychology and applied linguistics: towards an integrative
    approach.   I.T.L.: Review of Applied Linguistics, 1977, 33, 27-42 (a)
Giles, H., Bourhis, R. and Taylor, D.   Towards a theory of language in ethnic
    group relations, in H. Giles (Ed.) Language, ethnicity and intergroup
    relations.   New York: Academic Press, 1977 (b)
Giles, H. (Ed.) Language, ethnicity and intergroup relations.   New York:
    Academic Press, 1977
Giles, H. and St. Clair, R. (Eds.) Language and social psychology.   Baltimore:
    University Park Press, 1979
Giles, H. Sociolinguistics and social psychology, in H. Giles and R. St. Clair
    (Eds.) Language and social psychology.   Baltimore: University Park Press,
    1979
Giles, H. and Smith, P. M.   Accommodation theory: optimal levels of convergence,
    in H. Giles and R. St. Clair (Eds.) Language and social psychology.
    Baltimore: University Park Press, 1979
Gleason, H. A. Jr. An introduction to descriptive linguistics.   New York:
    Holt, Rinehart and Winston, 1961
Joos, M. The five clocks.   New York: Harcourt, Brace and World, 1961
Kenyon, J. S.   Cultural levels and functional varieties of English.   College
    English, 1948, 10, 31-36
Labov, W. The study of language in its social context.   Studium Generale, 1970,
    23, 66-84
Labov, W.   Some principles of linguistic methodology.   Language in Society, 1972,
    1, 97-120
Milhauser, M.   The case against slang.   English Journal, 1952, 41, 306-309
Peng, F.   Social distance.   Sciences, 1974, 31, 32-35
Ryan, E. B.   Why do low prestige language varieties persist?   in H. Giles and
    R. St. Clair (Eds.) Language and social psychology.   Baltimore: University
    Park Press, 1979

Sledd, J. On not teaching English usage. <u>English Journal</u>, 1965, <u>54</u>, 698-703

Sowell, T. Ethnicity in a changing America. <u>Daedalus</u>, 1978, <u>107</u>, 213-238

Tajfel, H. Social identity and intergroup behavior. <u>Social Science Information</u>, 1974, <u>13</u>, 65-93

Consequences of Language Intensity and Compliance-Gaining Strategies in an Initial Heterosexual Encounter

J. J. Bradac*, M. J. Schneider**, M. R. Hemphill* and C. H. Tardy*

*Communication Studies, University of Iowa, Iowa, U.S.A.
**Northern Illinois University, DeKalb, Illinois, U.S.A.

ABSTRACT

The effects of high and low language intensity and "expert" and "ingratiating" compliance-gaining strategies, sex of communicator and sex of subjects on judgments of communicator effectiveness and style were investigated. Each subject read one of eight versions of a hypothetical initial encounter between a male and female and subsequently judged the effectiveness of strategies and intensity level along a number of dimensions. Results indicated that the ingratiating strategy was judged as relatively likely to produce compliance; this strategy was also directly associated with perceptions of communicator friendliness. The expert strategy was associated directly with judgments of contentiousness and when employed by a male using high-intensity language it produced a judgment of relatively low competence in the case of female subjects. Male-female judgmental differences and similarities are discussed, and the superiority of the ingratiating strategy in compliance-gaining is discussed in light of previous research on ingratiation.

Key words

Compliance-gaining strategies; sex role; language intensity; communicative competence; language attitudes; conversation; interaction; communication effectiveness

INTRODUCTION AND RATIONALE

Members of every cultural group acquire knowledge of appropriate and inappropriate forms of communicative behaviour, i.e., "communicative competence". Generally, inappropriate messages will be ineffective in achieving the communicator's goal. The research reported here examines an aspect of competence-strategies for gaining compliance in an initial encounter. It seems likely that strategies will vary in terms of their appropriateness and effectiveness in a given context. Our research also examines the consequences for strategists of using high- or low-intensity language. Compliance-gaining strategies are typically encoded verbally, and knowledge of appropriate linguistic forms or styles also comprises an aspect of competence. Competent communicators may know that particular strategies require particular linguistic styles when employed in particular contexts.

What sorts of strategies are used to obtain compliance?   The list is a long one
but recently Falbo (1977) subjected many strategies for getting one's way to a
multidimensional scaling analysis and obtained a simple two-dimensional solution,
the poles being "direct-indirect" and "rational-emotional".   A direct-rational
strategy employed references to one's superior knowledge or skill, whereas an
indirect-emotional strategy employed attempts to alter feelings of the target.
We will label these strategies "expert" and "ingratiating", respectively.
Some research indicates that females are more likely to use ingratiating strategies, whereas males are more likely to use expert strategies (Johnson & Goodchilds,
1976).   This suggests that a male using the expert strategy will be judged more
competent and more likely to gain compliance than will a male using the ingratiating strategy.   Conversely, a female will be judged more competent and more
likely to gain compliance when she uses an ingratiating strategy than when she
uses an expert strategy.   This hypothesis assumes that violations of role expectations constitute inappropriate behaviour which will be judged as ineffective
and indicative of incompetence.

Some evidence also suggests a relationship between communicator sex and intensity
of language used to encode strategies.   For example, Burgoon, Jones and Stewart
(1975) found that a female communicator obtained less attitude change when she
used high-intensity language, whereas a male was relatively ineffective when his
language was low in intensity.   Thus, a male communicator should be judged more
likely to gain compliance and more competent if he uses high-intensity language,
whereas a female using such language should be judged as relatively incompetent
and unlikely to gain compliance.   A converse outcome should occur for low intensity.   We are fully aware that the relationships among communicator sex,
strategies, and intensity we have hypothesized almost certainly reflect stereotypes rooted in a transitory set of social circumstances.   It may be more
interestingly true, however, that relationships among social power, compliance-
gaining strategies, and intensity are relatively stable regardless of the particular determinants of such power.   There may be a pervasive and enduring tendency to expect powerful persons to employ expert strategies which exhibit intense language.

We also examined relationships among our independent variables and several other
dependent variables.   This provided more information about how communicators
employing expert or ingratiating strategies etc. are perceived on a number of
dimensions by male and female subjects.

METHOD

Subjects

Subjects were 96 male and 87 female undergraduates at Texas Tech University,
randomly assigned to conditions.

Strategies, Sex, and Intensity

Eight written versions of a hypothetical initial encounter between "John" and
"Susan" were created.   In one case, "John" was the "initiator" and "Susan" the
"respondent"; in the other case, roles were reversed.   The initiator's
message comprised nine utterances, each about 50 to 75 words in length.   The
respondent's remarks following each initiator utterance were paraphrased and
indicated neutrality.   The topics of initiator utterances were drawn from those
described by Berger, Gardner, Clatterbuck, and Schulman (1976).   They represented a movement from biographical to attitudinal matters.   Subjects were told
that the interactants were previously unacquainted but that the initiator now
desired to "get to know" the respondent.   The final initiator utterance was an

inter-personal request related to this desire.

Each initiator utterance exhibited either the expert or the ingratiating strategy. The expert strategist offered topic-relevant opinions based upon personal experience and reading, whereas the ingratiating strategist employed flattery. Each initiator utterance also exhibited either high- or low-intensity language. High intensity utterances were produced by substituting "strong" words or phrases for neutral ones and low-intensity utterances were formed by substituting "weak" forms. (Generally, manipulation checks indicated that subjects perceived intensity levels and strategies as expected.)

Measures

Nine-point scales were used to assess subjects' judgments of the initiator. These assessed perceptions of communicator (initiator) competence, predictability, the extent to which subjects felt they "knew" the initiator, future initiator and respondent communication intimacy assuming continuance of the conversation, and likelihood of respondent compliance to the initiator's request "Do you want to see a film?" We also selected items representing seven of Norton's (1978) "communicator style" dimensions: "dominant", "dramatic", "contentious", "impression leaving", "relaxed", "open", and "friendly". Normally, Norton's instrument measures self-perceptions of style. We converted it to an instrument measuring perceptions of the initiator's style by changing the form of the items. Two items were selected from each dimension and a single summed score was obtained for each, except for "open", where only one item was used.

Design and Analysis

The design was a 2 x 2 x 2 x 2 factorial. All variables were between-subjects variables. Four-factor analyses of variance were run for each measure, and where interactive effects were obtained these were decomposed into lower order effects.

RESULTS

Tests of Hypotheses

A four-way interaction was obtained for judgments of initiator competence ($p < .03$). Additional tests indicated that female subjects judged the male initiator employing the expert strategy as less competent than the male initiator employing the ingratiating strategy when high-intensity language was used ($p < .04$). A main effect only was obtained for the likelihood of respondent compliance ($p < .01$). The ingratiating strategy was judged more likely to gain compliance than was the expert strategy.

Other Tests

The initiator employing the ingratiating strategy was seen as more likely to escalate conversational intimacy than was the initiator employing the expert strategy ($p < .001$). A three-way interaction was also obtained for this measure ($p < .01$) which indicated that male subjects predicted greater intimacy in the case of the male initiator using high-intensity language than in the case of the female initiator using this intensity level ($p < .04$). Subjects' judgments of the predicted intimacy of the respondent did not differ across conditions. A four-way interaction was obtained for knowledge of the initiator ($p < .04$). Female subjects felt they better knew the female initiator using low intensity when she employed the expert as opposed to the ingratiating strategy ($p < .05$). A two-way interaction was obtained for predictability ($p < .05$). Subjects judged the female initiator using low intensity as more predictable than the male initiator using this intensity level (p <.05).

Main effects for "communicator style" were obtained for "contentious" and
"friendly" (p <.01, < .03).   The initiator employing the expert strategy was
seen as less friendly than the one using low intensity (p <.03).   Three-way
interactions were obtained for "dominant" (p< .02) and "impression leaving"
(p <.01).   Male subjects judged the initiator as more dominant when using high
intensity (p <.01); at low intensity, female subjects attributed higher
dominance to the expert strategy than to the ingratiating strategy (p <.001).
Male subjects judged the male initiator employing the expert strategy as more
likely to leave an impression, whereas they saw the female initiator as more
likely to leave an impression when she employed the ingratiating strategy (p <.01).
Four-way interactions were obtained for "open", "relaxed", and "dramatic" (all
p's < .03).   Female subjects judged the male initiator using low-intensity
language as more open when he employed the expert as opposed to the ingratiating
strategy (p< .06).   Male subjects judged the female initiator using high intensity as more relaxed when she employed the ingratiating as opposed to the expert
strategy (p< .08).   The male initiator using high intensity was judged more
dramatic by both male and female subjects (p <.01 in both cases).   The female
initiator using high intensity was judged more dramatic by female subjects only
(p <.01), and females also judged the female initiator more dramatic when she
used the expert as opposed to the ingratiating strategy (p <.05).

DISCUSSION

Our male and female subjects agreed that the ingratiating strategy was more likely
to gain compliance than was the expert strategy.   A complex interactive effect
was interpreted as indicating that female subjects judged the male initiator as
relatively incompetent when he encoded his expert strategy in high-intensity
language.   Thus, our two hypotheses were not supported.   In fact, the result for
judgments of competence is opposite to what we expected.   It appears that our
female subjects rejected a stereotypic conception of male competence.   This seems
to be a case of relatively favourable attributions resulting from a violation of
role expectations.

Apart from our hypotheses, male and female subjects agreed that the ingratiating
strategy would be associated with increased initiator intimacy and that this strategy indicated high friendliness and low contentiousness.   Further, our subjects
agreed that high intensity indicated friendliness and, when used by a male initiator, a dramatic style.

On the other hand, male and female subjects differed in several respects.   For
example, males judged initiators as dominant if they used high intensity, whereas
females judged initiators employing the expert strategy as dominant even when intensity was low.   Female subjects saw the female initiator as relatively dramatic
when she employed the expert strategy.   Male subjects felt the female initiator
would leave more of an impression when she used the ingratiating strategy.

Generally, the implications for communicators are clear: in an initial hetero-
sexual encounter use an ingratiating strategy if you wish to gain compliance and
to produce an impression of friendliness.   Use an expert strategy if you wish to
be perceived as unfriendly and contentious.   If you are a female and wish to
leave a lasting impression, use an ingratiating strategy; couple this with high
intensity if you wish to appear friendly and relaxed.   If you are a male and wish
to appear friendly, dramatic, and predictable, use high intensity; couple this
with an expert strategy if you wish to appear incompetent.   These perhaps flip-
pant prescriptions are offered tentatively, of course, in light of questions of
external validity involving replicability in real-life situations.

Finally, the clear superiority of the ingratiating strategy for eliciting judgments of the likelihood of compliance merits discussion. This outcome appears
consistent with results of research reported by Jones (1964) which indicate that
persons react favourably to ingratiation attempts, at least when the ingratiator
is of a status equal to that of the target of ingratiation. Our result seems inconsistent with one obtained by Berger and colleagues (1976), however. These researchers found that a high level of flattery (eight compliments) in an initial
encounter produced judgments of low flatterer attractiveness compared to a low
level of flattery (two compliments). Each of our nine initiator utterances comprising the ingratiating strategy contained at least one compliment, so the level
of flattery seems comparable to Berger, et al.'s high level. Perhaps an ingratiating strategy using _fewer_ compliments would have been _more_ effective in obtaining
compliance. Or, perhaps our compliments (or other features of our utterances)
differed from those used by Berger and colleagues in unspecifiable ways. Scrutiny of the Berger and colleagues research materials and further research may
help to explain this apparent disparity.

REFERENCES

Berger, C. R., Gardner, R. R., Clatterbuck, G. W. and Schulman, L. S. Perceptions
    of information sequencing in relationship development. _Human Communication
    Research_, 1976, _3_, 29-46
Berger, C. R., Gardner, R. R., Parks, M. R., Schulman, L. and Miller, G. R.
    Interpersonal epistemology and interpersonal communication. In G. R. Miller
    (Ed.), _Explorations in interpersonal communication._ Beverly Hills: Sage
    Publications, 1976
Burgoon, M., Jones, S. B. and Steward, D. Toward a message-centered theory of
    persuasion: three empirical investigations of language intensity. _Human
    Communication Research_, 1975, _1_, 240-256.
Falbo, T. Multidimensional scaling of power strategies. _Journal of Personality
    and Social Psychology_, 1977, _35_, 537-547.
Johnson, P. and Goodchilds, J. D. How women get their way. _Psychology Today_.
    October 1976, pp. 69-70.
Jones, E. E. _Ingratiation: a social psychological analysis_. New York:
    Appleton-Century-Crofts, 1964.
Norton, R. W. Foundation of a communicator style construct. _Human Communication
    Research_, 1978, _4_, 99-112.

Accommodation in Children's Mixed-Age Social Interactions

C. M. R. Gormly, A. J. Chapman, H. C. Foot and C. A. Sweeney

Department of Applied Psychology, Univeristy of Wales,
Institute of Science and Technology, Cardiff, Wales

ABSTRACT

This paper reviews research on children's mixed-age interactions and overviews the first year of a project in which verbal and nonverbal accommodation is examined. The extent to which five- to nine-year-old children accommodate to younger and older companions and to adults is to be investigated in a series of naturalistic experiments. The experiments will be run in a children's mobile-laboratory on location in schools: the larger of two compartments in the laboratory is a children's play-room and has concealed video-cameras and microphones; the smaller compartment houses the researchers and the recording equipment. After familiarization visits to the laboratory, children will be video-tape-recorded in play activities. Social responsiveness and patterns of interaction are to be derived from subsequent analyses of tapes. In this paper emphasis is given to outlining the range of language measures available. The main trends from several unpublished studies are presented.

Key Words

Behavioural analyses, children, content analyses, mixed-age interactions, nonverbal accommodation, sex differences, verbal accommodation

INTRODUCTION

Not until recent years have researchers shown interest in encounters between children of different ages. Earlier research on child-child encounters had centred almost exclusively on same-age children. However, anthropological and historical evidence indicates that childhood socialization has traditionally taken place within communities where children have interacted regularly with individuals of all ages, especially with other children and within extended families. It has been claimed that even in modern times more than half of child-child interactions, excluding contact between siblings, are between children whose ages differ by more than one year (e.g. Barker and Wright, 1955).

Part of the awakening interest in mixed-age interactions is concerned with the contribution that such interactions make towards general social development. It is assumed that the social skills involved are not identical to those necessary for most same-age interactions: for example, to communicate effectively, a child presumably needs to modify his/her characteristic verbal and nonverbal behaviours

77

to a greater extent when interacting with a child older or younger than him/her-
self.

"Accommodation" in mixed-age social interactions refers to modifications of behaviour in ways which enhance communicative effectiveness.   Following Hartup
(1977) we take accommodation to refer to behavioural changes in directions which
promote closer matching with the behaviours of fellow interactants.   Our studies
are of children in their early school years and our long-term objectives are
threefold: (1) to describe the nature of accommodation in social interaction;
(2) to plot the development of accommodative abilities;   and (3) to relate those
abilities to factors such as birth order, sex of child, number of siblings, age
of siblings, and age of fellow interactants.

RESEARCH ON CHILDREN'S MIXED-AGE INTERACTIONS

Evidently children are capable of accommodating to their companions from an early
age.   Lieberman (1967), for example, reported that the babbling of one-year-olds
is at lower frequencies in the presence of the father than in the presence of the
mother.   Working with older children Shatz and Gelman (1973) found that the
utterances of four-year-olds were shorter and included less complex constructions
and more attention-getting devices when the four-year-olds were placed with two-
year-olds rather than with peers or adults.   It was the youngest two-year-old
companions who elicited the greatest speech adjustments on the part of the four-
year-olds.   However, no differences were found between speech to peers and
speech to adults, and this raises a fundamental distinction regarding children's
verbal and nonverbal behaviours.   As far as nonverbal behaviours are concerned
(e.g. smiling and gaze) accommodation may occur both upwards to an older compan-
ion and downwards to a younger one, but it seems probable that accommodation in
speech rarely occurs in an upward direction: children do not possess the requi-
site linguistic expertise to accommodate upwards to any appreciable extent.   The
products of downward speech accommodation have been termed "motherese" by
Bohannon and Marquis (1977) who discussed the ways mothers speak to their
children.   Clearly, accommodation does not imply exact matching.   Indeed, if
motherese were equivalent to the child's speech, language acquisition and other
learning would be retarded.

To what the child is responding when he/she accommodates is a question addressed
by Lougee, Grueneich and Hartup (1977).   They compared interactions of preschool
children in same-age and mixed-age dyads and found that communications were
generally least frequent in the younger same-age dyads;   they were most frequent
in the older same-age dyads;   and they were intermediate in mixed-age dyads.
According to Lougee and colleagues this may be attributable to the older children
being aware of age-related differences and/or to their being predisposed to react
to the responsiveness of the interactant.   Following Shatz and Gelman (1973),
Masur (1978) found that four-year-olds addressing two-year-olds produced longer
and more complex utterances with those whose speech was more responsive.   The two-
year-olds had been divided into those with high verbal output and those with low
verbal output, and the four-year-olds were thereby shown to be sensitive to the
speech base rates of their younger companions.

It has also been shown that young children make speech modifications in circumstances which exclude feedback.   James (1978) analyzed the speech of children
aged between four-and-a-half and five-and-a-half talking to three different age-
status dolls ("listeners"):   they were of different sizes, representing an adult,
a peer and a younger child.   The subjects used another doll (which they selected
as being most like themselves) through which to address the listeners in command
and request contexts.   Directives were analyzed and, as expected, the most polite
directives under the command conditions were addressed to the "adult", followed by

"peer" and then "younger" doll.   In request conditions the children were more polite to all three dolls, and the only significant difference corresponding to size of doll was between "adult" and "younger" doll.   Results for both contexts were interpreted in terms of status relationships.

There is a consensual, intuitive view that during childhood progressive improvements occur in ability to accommodate.   Appropriate studies have yet to be conducted, and consequently there is a paucity of objective data to substantiate that view.   However examples do exist: a study by Gleason (1973), for instance, found that children over six were better at emulating babies' syntax than were six-year-olds.   Changes in children's concepts of others obviously have important consequences for verbal behaviour, and Flavell (1977) has noted that there are developmental changes in the types of cue to which an interactant responds. Initially it is mainly the interactant's external characteristics (e.g. physical size) which govern responses, but gradually the child learns to respond more to subtle characteristics (e.g. intelligence).   Flavell, Botkin, Fry, Wright, and Jarvis (1968) argue that the ability to communicate effectively depends not just on 'role attribute' discrimination;   it depends also on perceptual and cognitive abilities for encoding information, and of course on verbal skills for clear transmission.

It has been postulated that children are benefited in their ability to accommodate by virtue of having siblings (cf., Foot and colleagues, 1979);   but such benefits have yet to be established empirically.   Also sex differences in inclination or ability to accommodate have been predicted (op.cit.) and here some supportive trends have begun to emerge.   Langlois and colleagues (1978), for example, found that three- and five-year-old girls spoke considerably more in their corresponding mixed-age condition and five-year-old girls spoke an equivalent and appreciable amount in both conditions.   In a study of nonverbal behaviour in seven-, nine- and eleven-year-olds, Chapman (1977) found that boys with younger companions smiled and laughed less and engaged in less eye-contact than they did with same-age companions: no such trends were observed for girls.

It is not the case, of course, that all research on mixed-age interactions has been concerned with, or has given rise to, accommodative responses (cf. Langlois and colleagues, 1978;   Sweeney, Foot and Chapman, 1978).   In our own research, for example, six- and eight-year-olds have emitted more "social speech" and longer "utterance units" in same-age conditions (cf. Sweeney, 1978).   On the other hand, some studies have failed in their stated objective to demonstrate accommodation effects, and a few studies have yielded effects on some measures but not others (e.g. Lougee and colleagues, 1977).   No doubt many factors contribute to conflicts which are beginning to appear in the literature, and one suspects that many of these may relate to the social psychology of the testing environment.   However, we now turn our attention to another major source of misgivings - indices of mixed-age accommodation.

MEASURES   OF   LANGUAGE   ACCOMMODATION

It is our contention that the language measures so far deployed may not be sufficiently sensitive to demonstrate the extent of accommodation in children's mixed-age groups.   From the range of available measures, it is not simply the case that those adopted for particular studies have been drawn from a narrow band.   The problem is more acute: most researchers in this area, by restricting their range of dependent measures, show signs of ignoring that a conversation between two individuals is a two-way dynamic process.   But everyday experiences tell us that during conversation vocalizations rarely occur in unison and that uncomfortable pauses are uncommon.   Instead the flow of conversation is usually smooth as interactants accept regular switching of roles between speaker and

listener.   Of course many turn-taking cues have important nonverbal components,
and some are entirely nonverbal.

It is probable that the young school-child's relative lack of flexibility in conversation arises in no small part from his/her inadequacy in encoding and decoding
cues in combination (cf Mayo and La France, 1978).   The present style of analysis
in our own research is based upon the view that accommodation will be best revealed through various measures of synchrony between interactants.   Hence we are
videotaping child dyads in naturalistic settings, and sequences of interaction
are subsequently analysed in great detail.   For some measures, particularly task
measures, members of dyads are treated as though they were independent units, but
for other measures, particularly those to do with synchronising the interaction,
the dyad members are recognised as being engaged in a dynamic interplay.

We especially advocate fine-grain behavioural analyses, but we are also beginning
to attend to the prosodic characteristics of speech (loudness, timing, tempo,
intonation and pitch variations), and we analyse content of speech in various
ways.   Following the sociolinguistic and psycholinguistic work of others (e.g.
Ervin-Tripp, 1977; Flavell and colleagues, 1968; Garvey and Hogan, 1973; Rondal,
1978; Mischler, 1978; Sachs and Devin, 1976), our battery of measures currently
relate to length and number of utterances, vocabulary, questions posed, imperatives, repetitions, and social consequences of speech.   In this part of the research we are endeavouring to describe how, in mixed-age groups, the older children sometimes use speech corresponding to a developmental level below that which
they exhibit in same-age groups.   At the same time we are examining attempts at
language modification in the younger children, and nonverbal changes in both
younger and older children.

REFERENCES

Barker, R. G. and Wright, H. F. Midwest and its children.   New York: Harper and
    Row, 1955
Bohannon, J. N. III and Marquis, A. L.   Children's control of adult speech.
    Child Development, 1977, 48, 1002-1008
Chapman, A. J. Children's social interactions in same-age and mixed-age dyads.
    Paper presented to the Developmental Section at the London Conference of the
    British Psychological Society, 1977
Ervin-Tripp, S.   Wait for me, roller skate! in S. Ervin-Tripp and C. Mitchell-
    Kernan (Eds.) Child discourse.   New York: Academic Press, 1977
Flavell, J. H., Botkin, P., Fry, C., Wright, J. and Jarvis, P. E.   The development
    of role-taking and communication skills in children.   New York: Wiley, 1968
Flavell, J. H. Cognitive development.   Englewood-Cliffs, New Jersey: Prentice-
    Hall, 1977
Foot, H. C., Chapman, A. J., Sweeney, C. A. and Cormly, C. M. R. Mixed age
    effects in children's social encounters.   Paper presented at the Annual
    Conference of the British Psychological Society, Nottingham, 1979
Garvey, C. and Hogan, R. Social speech and social interaction: egocentrism
    revisited.   Child Development, 1973, 44, 562-568
Gleason, J. B. Code-switching in children's language, in T. E. Moore (Ed.)
    Cognitive development and the acquisition of language.   New York: Academic
    Press, 1973
Hartup, W. W. Peer relations: developmental implications and interaction in
    same- and mixed-age situations. Young Children, 1977, 32, 4-13
James, S. L. Effect of listener age and situation on the politeness of chil-
    dren's directives.   Journal of Psycholinguistic Research, 1978, 7, 307-317
Langlois, J. H., Gottfried, N. W., Barnes, B. H. and Hendricks, D. E. The effect
    of peer age on the social behavior of preschool children.   Journal of
    Genetic Psychology, 1978, 132, 11-19

Lieberman, P. _Intonation, perception and language_. Cambridge, Massachusetts: M.I.T. Press, 1967.

Lougée, M. D., Grueneich, R. and Hartup, W. W. Social interaction in same- and mixed-age dyads of preschool children. _Child Development_, 1977, _48_, 1353-1361.

Masur, E. F. Preschool boys' speech modification: the effect of listeners' linguistic levels and conversational responsiveness. _Child Development_, 1978, _49_, 924-927.

Mayo, C. and La France, M. On the acquisition of nonverbal communication: a review. _Merrill-Palmer Quarterly_, 1978, _24_, 213-228

Mischler, E. G. Studies in dialogue and discourse. III. Utterance structure and utterance function in interrogative sequences. _Journal of Psycholinguistic Research_, 1978, _7_, 279-305.

Rondal, J. A. Patterns of correlations for various language measures in mother-child interactions for normal and Down's syndrome children. _Language and Speech_, 1978, _21_, 242-252.

Sachs, J. and Devin, J. Young children's use of age-appropriate speech styles in social interaction and role-playing. _Journal of Child Language_, 1976, _3_, 81-98.

Shatz, M. and Gelman, R. The development of communication skills: modifications in the speech of young children as a function of listener. _Monographs of the Society for Research in Child Development_, 1973, _38_, (Serial No. 152).

Sweeney, C. A. Children's mixed-age social interactions. Unpublished Masters Thesis, University of Wales, 1978.

Sweeney, C. A., Foot, H. C. and Chapman, A. J. Children's cross-age relationships. Paper presented in the symposium "Studying Friendship" at the Annual Conference of the Social Psychology Section of the British Psychological Society, Cardiff, 1978.

Perceptions and Politics in Language and Sex Research

C. Kramarae

Department of Speech Communication, University of Illinois at Urbana-Champaign, Urbana, Illinois 61801, U.S.A.

ABSTRACT

Many of the feminists researching the relationship of language and sex feel that their experiences have led them to research assumptions and approaches seldom represented in the assumptions, approaches, and accounts in most academic publications. The argument in this essay is not that everyone should hold the same views about language and social structure, but that the perceptions and interpretations offered by women should be acknowledged as legitimate.

Key words

Language and sex; feminist research; sexism in language; language research and politics; perceptions of reality

The study of language and sex[1] has become a field of research and a topic of discussion in books and journals only in the late 1960s and the 1970s. The words used to describe women and men and their behaviour, and women's and men's verbal interaction, have received attention as problematic language structures and activities only since the beginning of the contemporary women's liberation movement.[2]

Of course many academic disciplines are undergoing intensive re-evaluation by people involved in the women's movement. But language and sex is a field which has been created by the movement. In fact, in some respects it is considered central to the re-evaluative work in many disciplines. Dorothy Smith (1978) summarises the argument made increasingly by feminists studying the methods by which women's experiences have been ignored or denied by those who validate "reality":

> ... women have been largely excluded from the work of producing the
> forms of thought and the images and symbols in which thought is

---

1. I prefer the label of language and gender, to stress the social nature of the categories <u>female</u> and <u>male</u> (Kessler and McKenna 1978). But I use <u>sex</u> here to make the terminology consistent with the other papers in this section.
2. Before the 1970s a few anthropologists and linguists wrote comments or essays on the subject but in no sense could the remarks be said to constitute an area of research. See Thorne and Henley (1975) for a review of the relationship of past and contemporary work.

> expressed and ordered.   There is a circle effect.   Men attend to
> and treat as significant only what men say.   (As far back as we have
> records) what men were doing was relevant to men, was written by men
> about men for men. (p.281)

While the serious study of language and sex has been introduced primarily through
the efforts of people involved in the movement, the research process has also been
greatly influenced by the advocates of what Liz Stanley and Sue Wise (in press)
call "hygienic research", i.e. research which is said to be "described" rather
than "experienced", removed from public policy, unemotional, and unaffected by
what the researchers feel about their relationship with the participants of the
study.   Many of the feminists researching the relationship between language and
sex feel that their experiences have led them to research assumptions and approaches which are seldom represented in the research assumptions, approaches and
accounts in most academic journals.   The point is not that everyone should hold
the same views about language and social structure, but that the preceptions and
interpretations offered by women should be acknowledged as legitimate.[3]   What
men consider general interests and experiences are often androcentric.   Women's
experiences are often called invalid.   Below I very briefly discuss the manner in
which women's perspectives have been overlooked or dismissed and the implications
of this for language and sex research.

In his study of the tactics used by people who opposed women's suffrage in Great
Britain, Brian Harrison (1978) found that the suffragists were accused of behaving
irrationally - like women; of behaving like men - and thus unnaturally; of being
deficient in intelligence and self-restraint, and of being physically ugly.
Jennifer Williams and Howard Giles (1978) suggest that similar techniques are used
today by critics who oppose the efforts of those who attempt to redefine and change
the relationships between women and men.   Working with an intergroup theoretical
framework developed by Henri Tajfel (1974), Williams and Giles write that our knowledge of membership in social groups provides each of us with personal and group identity.   For most of us, identity as either female or male is one of our most central sources of personal identity, although we may individually have different
evaluations of the groups, male and female.   Action on the part of members of the
socially inferior group - women - to change the relationship between the two groups
will be met with strong action from members of the dominant group, who will attempt
to maintain their distinctiveness, superiority, and control.

Elsewhere (Kramarae,in press) I have used this theoretical framework to study the
arguments and solutions set forth by those who advocate eliminating usage of masculine terms as "generics" and other linguistic usage which is seen as contributing to inequality, and the arguments set forth by the opponents.   Emphasis by the
opponents has been on why the recommendations made by feminists should be resisted
and on explaining why the usage many people say they perceive as sexist is not
really sexist, rather than on the study of the social nature of language and the
differing views people have of its structure and function.   In this section,
David MacKay, who does give serious consideration to people's differing perceptions
about "generics", has contributed to the growing body of research which indicates

---

3. Stanley and Wise criticise research literature which assumes that the researches
   can be approached as if they contain information which can be transferred - via
   questionnaires, interviews, experiments - to the researcher and that the researcher is an uninvolved receiver of the information.   While most social scientists probably agree in the abstract that all research assumptions and interpretations are products of the researchers' experiences, feminists' discussions of
   their assumptions and interpretations - of their reality - are not often accepted as being as real or valid as the reality of others.

that "generics" influence our thinking, and that women and men sometimes understand the same words to mean different things.

Certainly women and men do share many experiences and interpretations.   However, I think it is important to call attention to what happens when they do not.   An illustration may help.   Recently I was asked to give a conference talk on feminists' critiques of language studies.   The critiques are varied of course but I chose to talk about several concepts, generally accepted by language scholars but questioned or rejected by many feminists.   Included were the following concepts which I called "Truisms in Trouble".

First T in T: Linguistics is an apolitical study, objective and value-free.   The literature which offers counter arguments to this "truism" is increasing.   Julia Penelope Stanley and Susan Wolfe-Robbins (in press) have illustrated, for example, the "patriarchal perspective" through which language scholars select and discard linguistic data to fit the particular biases of the scholars.   Pat Parker (correspondence) has documented the androcentrism which pervades linguistic analysis and argument, including the pedagogical sample sentences which perpetuate traditional, often misogynist, attitudes.

Second T in T: English, like every language, arises from and serves the needs of its speakers in their particular environment.   In actuality, women, excluded from many occupations, have also been excluded from the process by which language is created - or at least printed etymologies do not recognise the involvement of women in determining the language structure and usage called the English language. The volumes edited by Nilsen, Bosmajian, Gershuny and Stanley (1977), Thorne and Henley (1975), Ardener (1975, 1978) and the book written by Miller and Swift (1976) illustrate some of the ways that English is not perceived by women to reflect and transmit experiences equally well for men and for women.

Third T in T: The relationship between language and sex can be defined and explained by simply adding the variable of sex - to go along with those of income, education, age and race - to quantitative sociolinguistic studies.   While many language and sex researchers in the early 1970s utilised the empirical methodology developed by sociolinguistics, now many researchers (see the essays in this section) discuss other approaches which include evaluation of stereotypical "feminine" and "masculine" speech and approaches which, in Fishman's words, consider the way that "socially-structured power relations are reproduced and actively maintained in our everyday interactions".   Their work shows an awareness of the ideas and issues of the women's movement and an awareness of discussions about the types of difficulties women in particular have in asserting authority.

I showed drafts of my convention paper to several of the feminists whose works I referenced, people who indicated my account was accurate.   Then I showed the paper to two people involved in language study who were not familiar with the feminist literature, both of whom said the paper would not do.   One of the men said, "This is not language study.   Ask any linguist and he'll tell you this is not language study". When he said "Ask any linguist", he certainly did not mean the feminist linguists who were quoted in my paper.   He meant any real linguist.

Because universities have a hierarchy of positions with the tenured and administrative positions primarily in the hands of men, women do not have as much authority over what is called knowledge.   Women are greatly under-represented in universities; men determine who is hired and fired, who is admitted to the higher ranks, and what is suitable research.   Further, control of the scholarly journals is almost entirely male.   Men have the authority to continually grade women's work. Many of the features of the grading of student work, set forth by Ian Hextall (1976), apply equally well, I believe, to the grading of women's research in the universities.

1) The evaluation helps establish a social division of labour and reflects and helps form the political-economic context of our lives.

2) The evaluation accords "knowledge" a reality independent of the knowers.

3) The evaluation aids in maintaining the legitimacy of the status quo.

Hextall points out, evaluation is "intensely political" (73).   The analogy between the grading system of schools and the evaluation of women on university faculties is useful in studying how the hierarchical structuring of our universities is maintained and how women are evaluated as if there is some universal, unproblematic interpretation of the world.   Academic evaluation is, as Hextall writes, about who has the right to know.

One of women's recurring experiences is hearing men tell us that we have not, or should not have seen, heard, or felt what we say we have seen, heard, and felt. We say that the "accepted" language structure and usage is inadequate to describe our experiences, and we are told that such a claim is stupid or trivial, that "authorities" do not think it inadequate or sexist, that the current usage has historical precedent, or that the changes proposed are messy, confusing, difficult and unnecessary.   (Maija Blaubergs (in press) and Don MacKay (this volume) have analysed the arguments made by the academic authorities when women indicate that their perceptions of language structure differ from those of men.)   Women are not to transform or create language.

We say that interaction between women and men is often much more framed by the pervasive directives and evaluations of men than by those of women.   Because men hold most of the legitimated positions of authority, rights in conversation seem, to many women, to be unequal.   Women believe that they are restricted in conversations with men in ways that men are not in conversations with women.

The perceptions that women researchers have of the relationship between language and sex merit consideration in their own right.   Further, study of the perceptions of women's and men's speech can aid us in the study of the relationship between language and societal structure.

The academic world in general seems reluctant to regard as scholarly or legitimate the work on the meaning of the categories female/male for men and women, and the work on the degree to which the perceptions of these categories contribute to rank and power differentials, and help to shape interaction.   The following papers in this section all stress the importance, complexity and present fluidity of language and sex research; the researchers' questions, methods and interpretations continue to be guided by the issues and the theorising of the women's movement.

All the authors are concerned with interaction, perceptions and evaluations rather than with static measures of the linguistic units of women's and men's speech. In her study of the self-ratings and judges' ratings of speakers in dyads in which not everyone had equal information for discussion of a problem, Leet-Pellegrini concludes that the interactions and the ratings be best explained by considering both the expertise and the sex of the speakers.   Women and men reacted differently when they were the "experts"; the "expert" men talked more and they were perceived as more dominant and controlling than the women "experts".   She writes of the importance of considering the specific situational factors of female/male interaction.

In a carefully controlled study (in which partners who assumed they were working with the same materials actually had slightly different maps as one partner gave directions to the other), Pedersen found that men and women behaved differently in the roles of "explainer" and "follower".   She agrees with Leet-Pellegrini that sex-linked verbal patterns are complex, and vary depending upon the roles, sex of speakers and situations.

Jose, Crosby and Wong-McCarthy are also concerned with the importance of situation, suggesting that we need to know more about the particular situations in which a speaker's sex and gender identity are particularly salient.   The essays by Smith and by Jose and colleagues recognise that in addition to having membership in a two-division membership category system - male/female - we also have individual identities and intentions.   Their work focuses on others' perceptions of speakers' identity and, in Jose and colleagues, on the dynamics of situation and individual gender orientation.

In her naturalistic study of the conversations of three couples in their homes, Fishman concentrates on the function of specific responses of the women and men. She argues that the linguistic devices which women use to keep conversation going are likely the same as those used by men in conversations with their "superiors". That is, interpretation of conversation needs to include consideration of the relative social status of the individuals in the specific situation - as it is perceived and negotiated by the speakers.

All this work points to the importance of acknowledging and making as explicit as possible the perceptions of all the participants in the research process, including the perceptions of the researcher.   Acceptance of the validity of women's perceptions as well as men's will give all of us a better indication of the reality of language structure and language use for women and men.

REFERENCES

Ardener, S. (Ed.) Perceiving women.   London: Malaby Press, 1975

Ardener, S. (Ed.) Defining females: the nature of women in society.   London: Croom Helm, 1978

Blaubergs, M. An analysis of classic arguments against changing sexist language. Women's studies International Quarterly, in press

Harrison, B. Separate spheres: the opposition to women's suffrage in Britain. London: Croom Helm, 1978

Hextall, I. Marking work, in G. Whitty and M. Young (Eds.) Explorations in the politics of school knowledge.   Driffield: Nafferton Books, 1976

Kessler, S. and McKenna, W. Gender: an ethnomethodological approach.   New York: John Wiley & Sons, 1978

Kramarae, C. Women and men speaking: frameworks for analysis.   Rowley, Mass.: Newbury House, in press

Miller, C. and Swift, K. Words and women.   Garden City, New York: Anchor Press, 1976

Nilsen, A. P., Bosmajian, H., Gershuny, H. L. and Stanley, J. P. Sexism and language. Urbana, Ill.: National Council of Teachers of English, 1977

Smith, D. E. A peculiar eclipsing: women's exclusion from man's culture. Women's Studies International Quarterly, 1978, 1, 281-295

Stanley, J. P. and Wolfe-Robbins, S. Linguistic problems with patriarchal reconstructions of Indo-European culture: a little more than kin, a little less that kind. Women's Studies International Quarterly, in press

Stanley, L. and Wise, S. Feminist research, feminist consciousness and experiences of sexism. Women's Studies International Quarterly, in press

Thorne, B. and Henley, N. (Eds.) Language and sex: difference and dominance. Rowley, Mass.: Newbury House, 1975

Tajfel, H. Social identity and intergroup behaviour. Social Science Information, 1974, 13, 65-93

Williams, J. and Giles, H. The changing status of women in society: an intergroup
    perspective, in H. Tajfel (Ed.) Differentiation between social groups: studies
    in the social psychology of intergroup relations.   European Monographs in
    Social Psychology, 14.   London: Academic Press, 1978

Language, Thought and Social Attitudes

D. G. MacKay*

Department of Psychology, University of California, Los Angeles 90024, U.S.A.

ABSTRACT

This study examines the effects of prescriptive he on attitudes toward and comprehension of paragraphs. In one experiment, students sympathetic to women's liberation read otherwise identical paragraphs containing either plural they or prescriptive he. Female subjects had lower comprehension and personal relevance scores for the prescriptive he than the plural paragraph, whereas the opposite was true of male subjects. And more females than males judged the prescriptive he paragraph to have a male author. An otherwise identical experiment, using students with less favourable attitudes towards women's liberation, replicated only the judgements concerning the sex of the author. Perceived personal relevance and comprehension scores of females were higher for the prescriptive he than plural paragraph. These and other findings suggested that prescriptive he influences attitudes but that its effect depends on the evaluative framework of the perceiver. Implications of these findings for a general theory of the relation between language and thought were discussed along with several other issues of interest to social psychology.

Key words

Language; sex; male; female; he ; attitudes; descriptive vs evaluative concepts; Whorf-Sapir; feminism

INTRODUCTION

Language can be described as a set of social conventions and it is of considerable interest how these conventions are determined and maintained. The present study examines a convention determined by prescriptive grammarians and maintained for the past 250 years by our schools and publishing establishments. The convention is the use of he to mean 'he or she'.

Prescriptive he carries special interest for social psychologists not just because it involves the regulation of social behaviour but because current attempts to de-

* The author gratefully acknowledges the support of NIMH Grant 19964-08 and thanks Toshi Konishi, Robin Baerwitz, Julie Meister, Alfred Nunez, Arlene Arnold, Beth Helmbold, Craig Watanabe and Rod Miyata for help in carrying out the experiments and analysing the data.

fend or analyse the prescription incorporate important social and psychological
assumptions.   The present study examined two of these assumptions, outlined below.

The triviality assumption

MacKay and Fulkerson (1979), Martyna (1978) and Kidd (1971) found that people systematically misinterpret prescriptive he as referring to a male rather than a
generic person.   But under the triviality assumption, misinterpretation of prescriptive he incurs no serious psychological or social consequences.   For example,
Lakoff (1973) argued that prescriptive he is a trivial problem which is "less in
need of changing" than other aspects of sexist language.   Others consider prescriptive he a loaded term with subtle and powerful effects on general attitudes (see
Miller and Swift 1976 and Geiwitz 1978) as well as specific behaviours such as
applying for jobs (see Bem and Bem 1973) and prescriptive he has too many characteristics in common with highly effective propaganda techniques for this view to
be ignored.   As a device for shaping attitudes, prescriptive he has the advantage
of frequency (over 10^6 occurrences in the course of a lifetime for educated Americans: see MacKay 1979), early age of acquisition (prescriptive he is learned long
before the concept of propaganda itself), covertness (questioning the use of prescriptive he is difficult since it is usually not intended as an open attempt to
maintain or alter attitudes), association with high prestige sources (it is especially prevalent in some of society's most prestigious literature such as university textbooks), and indirectness (prescriptive he presents its message indirectly as if it were a matter of common and well-established knowledge).

The language independence assumption

Under the language independence assumption, language and thought involve autono-
mous and independent processes, so that effects of prescriptive he on our thinking
or view of the world are out of the question.   This language independence assumption contradicts the Sapir-Whorf hypothesis which many feminists have endorsed but
which has never been verified and is meeting with growing scepticism.   For unlike
the triviality assumption, there exists good but fragmentary evidence in favour of
the language independence assumption.   For example, Rosch (1973) found that the
conceptual coding of colours and forms is similar for speakers of English and Dani,
languages that code shapes and colours in dramatically different ways.   Moreover,
MacKay and Fulkerson (1979) found no effect of prescriptive he on the conceptual
representation of the classes prescriptive he refers to since subjects accurately
judged the percentages of males and females falling into classes such as doctor,
even though they miscomprehended prescriptive he as male in sentences such as "A
doctor usually sees his patients in an office".

However, subjective attitudes differ in important respects from objective judgements concerning the nature of colours, forms, and occupational classes.   And if
prescriptive he operates as an attitude shaping device, then both the triviality
and language independence assumptions are incorrect.   The present study therefore
examined whether prescriptive he influences attitudes towards the content and
author of paragraphs.   One of the specific issues was whether women unconsciously
evaluate paragraphs containing prescriptive he as less relevant to their personal
lives than do men.

EXPERIMENT I

METHOD

Materials

Since representativeness is important for prescriptive considerations, the present
study used materials characteristic of those encountered in the everyday experience of university students: a paragraph from a UCLA textbook in current use.
The original paragraph (see Appendix) contained 20 uses of the pronoun they re-

ferring to <u>persons</u> or <u>individuals</u>, categories which 80 subjects in MacKay and Fulkerson (1979) rated 49% male and 51% female on the average.

Three additional paragraphs were formed by altering the pronouns and their antecedents. The 'prescriptive <u>he</u>' paragraph was formed by changing the <u>theys</u> to <u>he</u> and singularising the antecedents. The 'Mike Scott' paragraph resembled the prescriptive <u>he</u> paragraph except for the antecedent <u>Mike Scott</u> in the first sentence (see Appendix). The 'Mary Scott' paragraph resembled the <u>Mike Scott</u> paragraph except that <u>Mary</u> replaced <u>Mike</u> and <u>she</u> replaced <u>he</u>. A two word title (Self fulfilment) captioned each paragraph.

Since the content of all four paragraphs was identical, differences in attitudes toward the paragraph could only be due to the pronouns (<u>they</u> versus perscriptive <u>he</u>) or the nature of the antecedent (specific versus non-specific). The sex-specific paragraphs determined whether readers find specific individuals more personally relevant than non-specific individuals while the plural paragraph was an uncontestably generic version for comparison with prescriptive <u>he</u>.

Subjects and procedures

A male and a female experimenter administered the experiment to 234 UCLA undergraduates (115 males and 129 females; mean age 20) in groups of 15 to 165 with the four paragraphs assigned at random within each group.

The subjects were instructed as follows: "This is a study of the comprehension and personal relevance of paragraphs. You will have 2 minutes to read a paragraph absorbing as much information as you can. Following a signal to turn the page, you will use the IBM card provided to answer questions concerning your comprehension of the paragraph and its relevance to your personal experience. Are there any questions?"

Subjects had 7 minutes to answer 15 multiple-choice questions (see Appendix) concerning the content of the paragraph, its relevance to their personal lives, their opinion of the author, their awareness of the independent variables, their attitude toward sex roles, their self concept, their sex and other personal data.

RESULTS AND DISCUSSION

The main results appear in Table 1. Comprehension was significantly better for males than females reading the <u>Mike Scott</u> and prescriptive <u>he</u> paragraphs ($X^2 = 4.18$, df = 1, p < .05) but not for the <u>Mary Scott</u> paragraph ($X^2 = 0.07$, df = 1, $_2$ p < 0.70) and slightly poorer for males than females reading the plural paragraph ($X^2 = 2.88$, df = 1, p < .10). Females comprehended the prescriptive <u>he</u> paragraph worse than any other, whereas males comprehended the prescriptive <u>he</u> and <u>Mike Scott</u> paragraphs better than any other paragraph. Such findings indicate that comprehension of paragraphs with identical content varies jointly with subject sex, paragraph topic and paragraph pronoun.

Comprehension correlated positively with answers to the personal relevance question (r = .16, p < .05), a reasonable outcome which testifies to the validity of answers to the questionnaire. Judged personal relevance was significantly higher for males than females reading the <u>Mike Scott</u> and prescriptive <u>he</u> paragraphs, ($X^2 = 4.38$, df = 1, p $<_2$.05), about equal for males versus females reading the <u>Mary Scott</u> paragraph ($X^2 = 2.91$, df = 1, p $>_2$.05), and slightly lower for males than females reading the plural paragraph ($X^2 = 1.34$, df = 1, p > .20). Personal relevance was significantly higher for males reading the <u>Mike Scott</u> and prescriptive <u>he</u> paragraphs than for all other paragraphs ($X^2 = 4.44$, df = 1, p < .05).

TABLE 1.   Comprehension errors, Personal Relevance and
Assumed Author Male

		Paragraph Conditions				
	Subject Sex	Mike Scott	Prescriptive he	Mary Scott	Plural	Total
Comprehension errors (%)	Female	16	20	16	16	17
	Male	9	10	14	25	15
Personal relevance (% somewhat and highly)	Female	69	81	81	88	80
	Male	93	95	77	78	86
Author question (% likely/very like male)	Female	71	84	36	61	63
	Male	86	68	46	57	64

Results for the author question were similar for males and females reading all but
the prescriptive he paragraph.   Both males and females judged the author to be
male more often for the Mike Scott than Mary Scott paragraph (X^2 = 3.88, df = 1,
p < .05), with the plural paragraph falling in between.   People apparently associ-
ate paragraphs about a female with a female author, paragraphs about a male with a
male author, and truly generic paragraphs with either a male or a female author.
However, females judged the author of the prescriptive he paragraph to be male
more often than male subjects (X^2 = 5.01, df = 1, p < .05) and more often than any
other paragraph (X^2 = 4.97, df = 1, p < .05).   These findings are all the more
striking since females reading the Mary and Mike Scott paragraphs judged the author
to be male less often than did males (see Table 1).   Females were apparently sensitive to the use of prescriptive he in this experiment and judged such usage as
more characteristic of a male than a female author.

Answers to the self-concept questions were unrelated to any of the independent
variables, corroborating the contention that short-term events such as reading a
paragraph have no effect on self evaluation.   Subjects answering the awareness
question (see Appendix) mentioned the paragraph topic (self-fulfilment) as a
factor which might influence their perceived relevance and comprehension but none
mentioned independent variables such as Mike Scott, Mary Scott or prescriptive he.

In summary, the results of Experiment I indicate that prescriptive he influences
comprehension, personal relevance and supposed author of a paragraph, but its
effects vary with sex: superior comprehension and perceived self relevance for
males than females reading paragraphs containing prescriptive he and greater
attribution of prescriptive he to a male author by females than by males.

These effects are readily explained under the hypothesis that prescriptive he unconsciously shapes our attitudes toward what we read.   Under this hypothesis,
females feel excluded from material containing prescriptive he (see Nilsen, 1977)
paying less attention to its content and thereby comprehending it with greater
difficulty.   Males on the other hand readily attend to and comprehend paragraphs
containing prescriptive he since they can easily identify with or relate to the
material in such paragraphs.   Such effects clearly contradict the triviality
assumption and support the hypothesis that prescriptive he has serious psychological consequences.

However, we were concerned with the generality of these findings since other investigators have reported comprehension differences between males and females in the
opposite direction (see Maccoby and Jacklin 1974).   We therefore attempted to replicate and extend the present findings in Experiment II.

EXPERIMENT II: A REPLICATION AND EXTENSION

Students at UCLA generally express overwhelming sympathy for the women's movement. Of a recent sample of UCLA student (N=92) 63% responded supporting or strongly supporting the movement, 5% opposing or strongly opposing the movement and 32% neutral. We therefore wanted to replicate the results of Experiment I with other populations less supportive toward the movement. The population we chose was Los Angeles high school students who Mitchell (1979) described as part of a "self-centred syndrome", an apathetic group in an age of apathy, a "me generation", trying to get ahead within the system. Consistent with this report, in a sample of 117 high school students 19% responded supporting the women's movement, 15% opposing the movement, and 65% neutral.

METHOD

Materials and procedures resembled those in Experiment I. The experiment was administered to 233 high school students (112 males and 121 females; mean age 16 years) in classrooms of size 30 to 52. More men (74%) than women (64%) felt that men had more opportunity to become self-fulfilled than women in our society but more women (77%) than men (70%) felt they were capable of becoming self-fulfilled. Approximately equal numbers of men (60%) and women (63%) expressed a desire to become self-fulfilled.

RESULTS AND DISCUSSION

None of the subjects answering the awareness question mentioned the independent variables as factors that might influence their comprehension and perceived relevance. The main results appear in Table 2. Comprehension was significantly

TABLE 2: Results for Experiment II (in %)

	Subject Sex	Mike Scott	Prescriptive he	Mary Scott	Plural	Total
			Paragraph Conditions			
Comprehension errors (%)	Female	34	20	33	29	29
	Male	34	35	38	38	36
Personal relevance (% somewhat and highly)	Female	63	70	64	64	65
	Male	62	58	69	60	62
Author question (% likely/very like male)	Female	64	74	51	63	63
	Male	62	65	77	58	65

better for females than males reading the prescriptive he paragraph (x^2 = 7.59, df = 1, p < .01), but not for the remaining paragraphs. This finding contrasts with Experiment I where males comprehended the prescriptive he paragraph better than females. Likewise, females in Experiment II comprehended the prescriptive he paragraph worse than any other paragraph.

Comprehension correlated positively with answers to the personal relevance question (r = .21, p < .05). Judged personal relevance was significantly higher for females than males reading the prescriptive he paragraph (x^2 = 5.79, df = 1, p < .02), and males found the prescriptive he paragraph less relevant than any other paragraph.

Comprehension correlated positively with answers to the personal relevance question ($r = .21$, $p < .05$).   Judged personal relevance was significantly higher for females than males reading the prescriptive he paragraph ($X^2 = 5.79$, df = 1, $p < .02$), and males found the prescriptive he paragraph less relevant than any other paragraph.

Females judged the author to be male more often for the Mike Scott than Mary Scott paragraph, with the plural paragraph falling in between.   And they judged the author of the prescriptive he paragraph to be male more often than any other paragraph.   As in Experiment I, females were apparently sensitive to the use of prescriptive he and judged such usage as more characteristic of a male than a female author.

To summarise, prescriptive he influenced comprehension and attitudes toward the paragraph, but in a manner opposite Experiment I: better comprehension and perceived self relevance for females than males reading paragraphs containing prescriptive he.   The only aspect of Experiment I replicated in Experiment II was the greater attribution by females of prescriptive he to a male author.

GENERAL DISCUSSION

This section attempts to reconcile the conflicting results of Experiments I and II and previous studies of language and thought.   The reconciliations are of necessity ad hoc in nature but carry interesting implications for future research into relations between language, thought and social attitudes.

Previous studies failed to find a relation between language and thought because they examined the wrong type of thought: descriptive rather than evaluative thought.   Descriptive thought involves judgements about observable aspects of the external world.   Judgements of the shape or colour of objects as in Rosch (1973) are prime examples of descriptive thought.   So are judgements concerning the sex ratio of occupational classes as in MacKay and Fulkerson (1979).   People rely on more extensive, more reliable, and more accurate language-independent or perceptually based knowledge for making such judgements concerning the nature of the real world.   For example, through extensive real world experience, people come to know that the category person includes females and males in approximately equal proportions and can ignore the language which prescribes he to refer to a person and thereby suggests that this class excludes women.

Prescriptive he may nevertheless influence descriptive thought in the case of children lacking real world or perceptually based information concerning the nature of rarely encountered categories such as technician.   But in general, language is much more likely to influence evaluative thought: subjective or personal judgements concerning the value of objects and events, for which good, perceptually based data are out of the question.   Indeed, the present data support such a hypothesis since prescriptive he influenced attitudes concerning the personal relevance of the paragraphs.   Future research should therefore concentrate on relations between language and evaluative rather than descriptive thought.   For example, no further experiments are needed to show that descriptive thinking about snow is identical for speakers of English and Eskimo even though Eskimo has many more words for snow than English.   Studies of evaluative effects seem warranted, however.   The many Eskimo words for snow may suggest to members of Eskimo society that fine discriminations among different types of snow are important and personally relevant, for example.

Consider now the conflicting results of Experiments I and II.   Taken together, both experiments suggest that prescriptive he unconsciously influences thought but in different ways depending on pre-existing social attitudes of the reader.

Thought is therefore related to language, but only indirectly in somewhat the same way that research conclusions are related to evidence. As Fodor (1975) and Macnamara (1977) point out, thought and interpretation in general resemble a detective's search for clues, guided by a theory of how such and such a murder could occur.   The same clue can lead to different conclusions depending on the theory of the murder.

Implications drawn from the clue of prescriptive he differ depending on one's theory or evaluation of the processes underlying the clue.   UCLA women were predominantly pro-feminist and undoubtedly resented discrimination against women as well as assignment of peripheral status to women in both the language and society at large.   Such resentment could account for their difficulty in comprehending the prescriptive he paragraph.   A similar explanation accounts for their perception of the Mary Scott paragraph as more personally relevant than the Mike Scott paragraph, since pro-feminist women tend to identify with other women (Bate 1975).

By comparison, the prevailing attitudes of the high school students could be characterised as pro status quo.   For whatever reason, the high school women probably accepted the implication of the language and society at large that women in general are peripheral or unimportant.   But since these women felt capable of becoming self-fulfilled even though society provided less opportunity for their self-fulfilment they must have considered themselves an exception to the general rule, each viewing herself as extraordinary and capable of success in a 'man's world'.

This pattern of attitudes could explain why the high school women found the prescriptive he paragraph more personally relevant than the Mary Scott paragraph. 'Establishment messages' signalled by the use of prescriptive he interested the high school women but not messages about another woman, a class they had little desire to identify with.

These contrasting response patterns fit Bate's (1975) description of the Queen Bee and the feminist approach to resolving the cognitive contradiction between being a "generic man" and an "invisible woman".   However these response patterns are quite general in nature, representing two of the ways that people handle inconsistencies between different sources of information (see McGuire 1967) and might best be labelled the assimilation approach (where an oppressed group such as women or blacks assume the values of the dominant culture) and the egalitarian approach (where males and females, whites and blacks are viewed as different but equal).

A third possibility described by Bate (1975) is the conformist approach.   A woman using this approach can overcome the inconsistency between being a person and being excluded from the category person in paragraphs containing prescriptive he by accepting the connotation that women are inferior and peripheral and by "denying such motives as ambition and adventurousness which fail to fit the category woman". (Bate, p.6).   However, it seems unlikely that the conformist pattern played a major role in the present results.   Women are more visible than ever before in American society and the ongoing, widespread discussion of women's abilities and opportunities makes it difficult for contemporary women to accept or believe in the peripheral or inferior status required by the conformist approach.

In conclusion, language influences thought but the nature of its effect depends on the interpretive strategy or evaluative framework of the thinker.   Since different evaluative frameworks can give completely opposite results, future studies of language and thought must take this factor into consideration and previous studies which overlooked this factor must be re-evaluated.

The present findings also refute the language independence and triviality assumptions on which the defence of prescriptive he has rested for so long.   Prescriptive he unconsciously conveys a social message, even though perceivers can localise the message to the sender or class of senders and react to the message in terms of their own framework of thought.   A complete evaluation of prescriptive he therefore requires an evaluation of the frameworks for handling it.   For example, one must evaluate the desirability of the assimilation or Queen Bee framework which entails a loss of sisterhood among women and condescension towards women in general as well as the conformist approach which entails a diminished self concept for women (see Bate 1975).   Determining the full extent of the psychological effects of prescriptive he presents a major challenge for the social psychology of language.

REFERENCES

Bate, B. A. Generic man, invisible woman: language, thought and social change. Michigan Papers in Women's Studies, 1975, 2, 1-13
Bem, S. and Bem, D. Does sex-biased job advertising "aid and abet" sex discrimination? Journal of Applied Social Psychology, 1974, 24, 142-9
Fodor, J. A. The language of thought. New York: Crowell, 1975
Geiwitz, J. Another plea for E. APA Monitor, 1978, August, 3-10
Kidd, V. A study of the images produced through the use of a male pronoun as the generic. Movements: Contemporary Rhetoric and Communication, 1971, 1, 25-30
Lakoff, R. Language and women's place. Language in Society, 1973, 2, 45-80
Maccoby, E. E. and Jacklin, C. N. The psychology of sex differences. Stanford: Stanford University Press, 1974
MacKay, D. G. and Fulkerson, D. C. On the comprehension and production of pronouns Journal of Verbal Learning and Verbal Behavior, 1979, in press
MacKay, D. G. On the goals, principles and procedures for prescriptive grammar. Submitted for publication, 1979
Macnamara, J. Problems about concepts, in J. Macnamara (Ed.) Language learning and thought. New York: Academic Press, 1977
Martyna, W. What does 'he' mean? Journal of Communication, 1978, 238, 131-38
McGuire, W. J. The current status of cognitive consistency theories, in M. Fishbein (Ed.) Readings in attitude theory and measurement. New York: John Wiley and Sons, 1967
Miller, C. and Swift, K. Words and women: new language in new times. Garden City, New Jersey: Doubleday, 1976
Mitchell, J. L. ABCs of the last class of the '70s - from apathy to Appalachia. Los Angeles Times, West Side, June 10, 1979, Part 10, p.1
Nilsen, A. P. Sexism in children's books and elementary classroom materials, in A. P. Nilsen, H. Bosmajian, H. L. Gershuny and J. P. Stanley (Eds.) Sexism and language. Urbana, Ill.: National Council of Teachers of English, 1977
Rosch, E. Natural categories. Cognitive Psychology, 1973, 4, 328-350

APPENDIX (plural version)

Happy, fulfilled individuals display an uncommon absence of approval-seeking. They can function without approval and applause from others.   They do not seek out honours as most others do.   They are unusually free from the opinion of others almost uncaring about whether someone likes what they have said or done.   They neither attempt to shock others, nor to gain their approval.   They are so internally directed that they are literally unconcerned about others' evaluations of their behaviour.   They are not oblivious to applause, they just don't seem to need it.   They can be almost blunt in their honesty since they don't couch their messages in carefully worded phrases designed to please.   If you want to know what they think, that's exactly what you'll hear.   Conversely, if you criticise them they will filter it through their own values and use it for growth.   They recognise that they will always incur some disapproval.   They are unusual in that they are able to function as they, rather than some external other, dictates.

Conversational Dominance as a Function of Gender and Expertise[1]

H. M. Leet-Pellegrini

Judge Baker Guidance Center, An Affiliate to the Children's Hospital and Harvard Medical School, Boston, Mass. 02115, U.S.A.

ABSTRACT

perceived

The study examines how gender and expertise, as bases of power, influenced the emergence of dominance and control in the conversations of 70 pairs of unacquainted college students who discussed television programming for approximately 10 minutes. Independent variables were sex composition of pairs (male-male, female-female, male-female) and expertise (partners equally uninformed or one specially informed).

Typed transcripts of the openings and closings of conversations were used to obtain the following language measures: relative talkativeness, relative production of intrusions into speech, interruptions and overlaps, relative production of varying assent forms. "Powerful" persons (men and experts) were expected to talk more and intrude more than "powerless" persons (women and non-experts). "Powerless" persons were expected to do relatively more assenting or supportive work in conversation. To examine whether "powerless" language features relate to other indices of power, independent judges used opening and closing transcripts to rate subjects on measures reflecting conversational control. Subjects' own ratings of relative dominance were also taken.

In general the interaction of gender and expertise (and not the single factors of being male or being expert) accounted for the major proportion of findings. There was a correspondence across three classes of measures (language features, objective judges' and participants' perceptual ratings) which suggest how male, but not female, experts realised power in conversation. Results for talkativeness and for assent terms supported the view that male experts pursue a style of interacting based on power, while female experts pursue a style based upon solidarity and support. Complex findings for intrusions into speech highlighted the importance of incorporating situational and contextual elements into an understanding of the relations between linguistic form to social function.

1. This article is based on a doctoral dissertation submitted to the Department of Psychology, Tufts University. The author wishes to thank thesis advisor, Zella Luria, as well as Bruce Fraser, Nancy Henley, Elliot Mishler and Jeffrey Z. Rubin for their contributions.

Key words

Conversation; sex; dominance; control; expertise power

INTRODUCTION

At the beginning of any face-to-face encounter all aspects of the situation are
taken into account.   Whenever one member of a conversational pair possesses some
advantageous attribute or some resource important to the ensuing interaction, that
person stands in a position of power relative to his/her partner.   Sex is an obvious cue, and being female in a male-dominated society carries differential attributions of esteem, respect, etc., which place woman and her work in lower, less
powerful positions relative to man and his work (Pheterson, Kiesler and Goldberg
1971;   Lockheed and Hall 1976).   At the same time there can be differential distributions of a resource more specific to the immediate encounter.   For example,
there are differential expectations for the emergence of dominance and control in
conversation when one member of a pair becomes the expert because s/he was given
information critical to the purpose of their conversation (Meeker and Weitzel-
O'Neill 1977).

In the present study gender and expertise were employed as bases of power in order
to observe whether and how power would be realised in the process of two-party conversation.   Would men compared to women, and experts compared to non-experts, use
features of language associated in past research with the exercise of power?
Specifically, would "powerful" persons be more talkative (Strodtbeck 1951;   Soskin
and John 1963) or would they intrude more into the speech of others by means of
interruptions and overlaps (Zimmerman and West 1975;   West and Zimmerman 1978)?
Would "powerless" persons use more assent terms in conversational interaction
(Hirschman 1975;   Zimmerman and West 1978)?   Furthermore, would "powerful" persons be perceived by participants and by independent judges as more dominant and
controlling?   The present study investigated the main effects of gender and expertise as well as the interaction of these two power resources in order to compare, for example, the emergence of dominance and control for female experts compared to male experts.

METHOD

Procedure and design

Seventy pairs of unacquainted college students discussed the negative effects of
television violence upon children and recommended ways for improving the quality
of television programming.   A two-channel recorder was used to tape their conversations lasting approximately ten minutes.   Participants themselves had to negotiate the exact method and moment of exit from the conversations.   The primary
source of data consisted of typed transcripts of the openings and closing of all
70 conversations.   Openings were defined as the beginning exchanges of each conversation which generated one page of 38 lines of transcript.   Closings were defined as the terminal exchanges which also generated one page, the final word(s)
constituting the 38th line of transcript.

The basic design (Design I) of this study is a 2 x 3 unequal n factorial: expertise (equally uninformed or unequally informed) x sex composition of pairs (male-
male, female-female, male-female).   Equally uninformed pairs discussed the topic
as non-experts, i.e. neither partner was provided with relevant information.   In
unequally informed pairs, one partner became the expert by having been given topi-
cally relevant information to read and to ponder before the conversation began.
Twice as many pairs were run in the male-female, unequally informed condition
to account for pairs in which the male was expert as well as pairs in which the
female was the expert.   (See Figure 1).   Two additional equal n designs were in-

cluded to highlight differences among the three mixed-sex pairings (Design II) and
differences among the four pairings in which expertise was an issue (Design III).

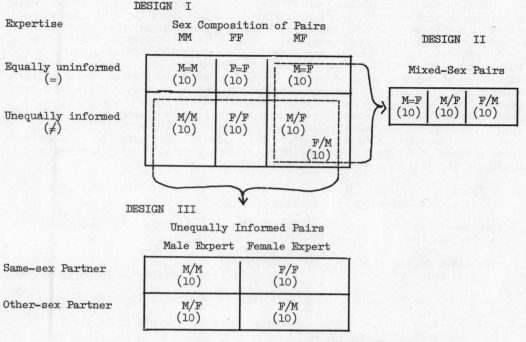

DESIGN I

Expertise   Sex Composition of Pairs
                        MM   FF   MF   DESIGN II

Equally uninformed   M=M   F=F   M=F   Mixed-Sex Pairs
    (=)   (10)   (10)   (10)
                                                                    M=F | M/F | F/M
                                                                    (10)| (10)| (10)
Unequally informed   M/M   F/F   M/F
    (≠)   (10)   (10)   (10)
                                                  F/M
                                                 (10)

DESIGN III

Unequally Informed Pairs

                    Male Expert   Female Expert

Same-sex Partner   M/M   F/F
                       (10)   (10)

Other-sex Partner   M/F   F/M
                       (10)   (10)

Fig. 1.   Source of scores used in analyses for Designs I,
           II and III

For each of these designs a repeated measures factor was added for some independent
variables, when it was possible to look at what happened during openings as well as
closings of conversations.

Difference scores were used in analyses of variance in order to include information about both members of a pair.   The greater the asymmetry (or the larger the
differences between members of a pair), the more participants' jointly constructed
relationship was assumed to be based upon power.   Conversely, the greater the
symmetry (or the smaller the differences), the more the relationship was assumed
to be based upon solidarity.   Absolute difference scores were used in analyses
which included equally uninformed pairs (Designs I and II).   (Wilcoxon matched-
pairs-signed-ranks tests were used in absolute difference scores analyses when it
was necessary to determine which member of a pair accounted for asymmetrical findings.)   Signed differences scores were used when it was possible to hypothesise
that the expert would emerge as relatively more dominant than the non-expert
(Design III).

Dependent measures

The first category of measures included language features hypothetically related
to the differential use of power, which appeared on the one-page transcripts of
openings and closings.   First, a measure was developed to approximate actual talkativeness.   A ratio, consisting of the Number of Lines exceeding one-half of the

page width provided by the most "talkative" partner divided by the Total Number of
Lines of said length, literally measured who filled more of the available space
with the business of talk.   Second, for all 70 pairs asymmetrical distributions
were obtained for interruptions and overlaps which either succeeded (current speaker was halted from completing his/her utterance to at least the next grammatical
boundary) or failed (current speaker continued at least to the next grammatical
boundary irrespective of the intrusion).   Third, the asymmetrical distribution of
assent terms was calculated for all pairs.   These terms consisted of words like
"Yeah", "right", and "uh-huh" as well as quickly interspersed phrases like "Oh,
definitely" or "That's true" which did not interrupt current speaker's conversational flow.   Fourth, the asymmetrical distribution of a special class of supportive utterances was calculated.   Examination of the transcripts uncovered these
special forms which were coded as instances of very active listenership.   Listeners either recycled current speakers' words exactly or they completed current
speakers' apparently intended message.   The following underlined phrases are examples of this as-if-one-voice phenomenon, which almost invariably was not used as
an opportunity to take over a turn.

B: So then, we   several solutions to the
                (A: come up with several solutions)

     (problem   )   One, make other things, things other than T.V. more
     (A: Ha-ha-ha)

     attractive to do, like other activities,
                                      (A: More accessible and attractive)

     make, increase the amount of, uh, education programs on the T.V.

     over (violence   )   uh, educate the parents about the ill
          (A: such as Sesame Street)

     effects of T.V. and the producers   in hopes that ...
                                      (A: Right)

The second category of measures included perceived judgments of dominance and control made by participants as well as by objective judges.   Participants rated
themselves and each other immediately following their conversational interaction on
a 7-point bipolar scale measuring dominance;   self and other ratings were combined
to obtain a single difference score for each pair.   Four independent judges, using
only the typed transcripts, rated participants relative to each other on several
7-point scales reflecting conversational control.   Questions designed to elicit
judges' perceptions of specific control were: a) "Who initially structures the
conversation?" b) "Who initiates the closing?" and c) "Who controls the closing?"
Perceptions of overall control were reflected by the question "Who in general controls the course of conversation?" which judges responded to for openings and then
again for closings.   Judges were uninformed about either the sex of speakers or
their level of expertise, and they rated opening transcripts at separate times and
in a separate order from closing transcripts.   Unbiased estimates of four judges'
reliability (Winer 1971, p.283) ranged between .89 and .98 for the above ratings
of conversational control.   Therefore, the mean of four judges' ratings was used
to obtain a single difference score for each pair.

RESULTS AND DISCUSSION

As expected, manipulation checks indicated that experts were perceived as being the
more informed and more knowledgeable partners by participants ($F(1,64) = 5.56$,
$p < .025$), as well as by independent judges ($F(1,64) = 18.41$, $p < .001$).

Expertise, as a single base of power in the emergence of dominance and control, was limitedly effective in the present study.   There was clear evidence that expertise in general elicited "talkativeness".   Experts literally took control of the conversation by taking up more of the talking space than did their non-expert partners during the entry and exit exchanges of conversations, while no such imbalance occurred in pairs who were equally non-expert, $F(1,64) = 5.86$, $p < 0.25$. Among the perception measures, there was a trend for experts in unequally informed pairs to be perceived as more controlling of the conversation in general than was either member of equally uninformed pairs, $F(1,64) = 3.20$, $p < .085$.

The single base of power, gender, was even less salient as a factor in the development of conversational power.   That is, there were no significant differences among the three equally uninformed pairs;   the hypothesis that other things being equal, male-female interaction is different from female-female or from male-male interaction was not supported.

Clearly, it was the interaction of expertise with gender which produced clear and consistent findings.   Generally, men, but not women, responded differently when they were in positions of power compared to positions of equality.

Analyses of mixed-sex interaction (Design II) indicated power differences such that the male expert was consistently the more dominant partner for openings as well as closings on several measures.   Male experts occupied more "talking space" relative to female partners (M/F, $\bar{X} = .76$) than did female experts relative to male partners (F/M, $\bar{X} = .65$) or males and females relative to each other when both were equally uninformed (M=F, $\bar{X}=.64$), $F(2,27) = 9.09$, $p < .001$.   Also, male experts were perceived by subjects as being relatively more dominant (M/F, $\bar{X} = 2.72$) than were female experts (F/M, $\bar{X} = 1.36$), or either partner of equally uninformed pairs (M=F, $\bar{X} = 1.35$), $F(2,27) = 3.57$, $p < .05$.   Similarly, male experts were perceived by objective judges as relatively more controlling of the conversation in general (M/F, $\bar{X} = 2.80$) than were female experts (F/M, $\bar{X} = 1.72$), or either partner of equally uninformed pairs (M=F, $\bar{X} = 1.87$), $F(2,27) = 6.85$, $p < .01$. Apparently, for men in mixed-sex conversations being male in and of itself was insufficient to activate a show of dominance.   It was the introduction of expertise which created the condition necessary for that display in the context of this study. For female experts, mixed-sex (or even same-sex) interaction elicited no display of dominance.

There was evidence from independent judges' ratings that men differentiate between situations based upon equality and those based upon power in same-sex as well as mixed-sex interaction.   Judges perceived significant differences in initial structuring of the conversation between male pairs with an expert (M/M, $\bar{X} = 4.38$) and those with no expert (M=M, $\bar{X} = 2.33$), $F(2,64) = 4.42$, $p < .05$.   Similarly, judges perceived significant differences for control of the closing between male pairs with an expert (M/M, $\bar{X} = 3.29$) and pairs with no expert (M=M, $\bar{X} = 1.26$), $F(2,64) = 5.82$, $p < .025$.   What is interesting about expert males interacting with other males is that they did not maintain a dominant stance from openings to closings as they did with females.   As Wilcoxon tests showed, it was the expert who structured the conversation initially, but by the end it was not clear which male partner, the expert or the non-expert, was structuring the conversation's exiting moves.   What we may be observing is an instance of conversational jockeying for power, or an attempt by non-expert males to recoup status lost from having been placed in the one-down position.   After all, dominance hierarchies can change. Beta can overturn alpha's advantage.

The major proportion of findings resulted from analyses which compared male and female experts in conversation with same- and other-sex partners (Design III).

Among language measures, significant differences emerged as a function of sex of expert. Male experts tended to take up more space talking than did female experts, $F(1,36) = 3.30$, $p < .085$. However, assenting phenomena most clearly separated the conversational style of male experts from female experts. Women experts ($\bar{X} = 1.23$) used assent terms (yeh, right, uh-huh, etc.:- the whole sample produced 756 instances of these) in conversation with uninformed partners significantly more than did male experts ($\bar{X} = -1.9$), $F(1,36) = 10.46$, $p < .005$. Additionally, the interaction indicated that women experts assented more with male partners (F/M, $\bar{X} = 2.85$) than with female partners (F/F, $\bar{X} = -.40$), $F(1,36) = 4.61$, $p < .05$. Since terms of assent are assumed to be negatively related to dominance and control, negative means supported the hypothesis that uninformed partners would supply the bulk of asymmetrical assenting work in conversation. It is interesting that the direction of the means for assent terms was such that uninformed partners <u>did</u> assent more than experts in all situations but the one in which a female expert conversed with a male non-expert (M/F, $\bar{X} = -2.35$; M/M, $\bar{X} = -1.45$; F/F, $\bar{X} = -.4$; F/M = 2.85). When women who are openly acknowledged as experts interact with men who are openly acknowledged as non-expert, the one-up women support the one-down men. For terms of assent which assist current speaker's ongoing words (repeating words or completing thoughts) the pattern was similar. (The sample produced 84 instances of these special terms of assent.) Female experts ($\bar{X} = 4.0$) assisted partners significantly more than male experts ($\bar{X} = -2.8$), $F(1,36) = 12.94$, $p < .001$). Non-experts supported expert partners only when the male was expert. Again the direction of the means revealed that for female experts the situation was reversed; <u>she</u> accounted for this especially collaborative feature of language more than did her non-expert partners.

Among the perception measures, too, differences were a function of sex of the expert. Subjects' ratings of relative dominance as well as objective judges' ratings on several measures of conversational control provided results consistent with those for language measures. Participants perceived male experts ($\bar{X} = 1.94$) as relatively more dominant than female experts ($\bar{X} = .41$), $F(1,36) = 6.56$, $p <.025$. The Sex of Expert x Same- or Other-sex Partner interaction tended toward significance, $F(1,36) = 3.09$, $p < .07$; the striking difference was in the degree of dominance perceived for male experts with female partners compared to female experts with male partners. The direction of the means illustrates how only in the female expert/male non-expert condition was the expert perceived as overall less dominant than the non-expert (M/M, $\bar{X} = 2.42$; M/M, $\bar{X} = 1.46$, F/F, $\bar{X} = .98$, F/M, $\bar{X} = -.16$).

Judges rated male experts as structuring conversational beginnings significantly more than female experts, $F(1,36)$, $= 14.74$, $p < .001$. The interaction tended toward significance such that male experts with female partners structured more than female experts with male partners, $F(1,36) = 3.66$, $p < 0.75$. The direction of the means for the interaction yields a familiar pattern; for each combination only female experts with male non-experts did overall less structuring than their non-expert partners (M/F, $\bar{X} = 3.12$; M/M, $\bar{X} = 3.32$; F/F, $\bar{X} = 1.46$; F/m, $\bar{X} = -2.44$)

Results for judges' perceptions of conversational control, in general, indicated that male experts ($\bar{X} = 1.60$) were significantly more controlling than female experts ($\bar{X} = .10$) across openings and closings, $F(1,36) = 5.77$, $p < .05$. In this analysis, too, the direction of the means suggests that only when female experts interacted with male non-experts were hypotheses about the exercise of expert power not supported (M/F, $\bar{X} = 2.08$; M/M, $\bar{X} = 1.11$; F/F, $\bar{X} = .44$; F/M, $\bar{X} = -.24$).

Also, judges perceived male experts ($\bar{X} = 1.23$) as tending to control the closings more than female experts ($\bar{X} = -.63$), $F(1,36) = 3.52$, $p < .075$. Again, the direction of the difference shows that hypotheses about the exercise of expert power were supported for male experts and not female experts who generally avoided this particular form of control. There were no significant findings for initiation of the closings, which is perhaps a less powerful determiner of "who's in charge" than is control of the closing.

Given that any interaction is the sum of all the contextual information, (including non-verbal signals, gestures, intonation, cognitive assumptions about situational appropriateness, etc.), it is interesting that subjects who participated in the total context of the conversation and judges, operating from a very limited data base, provided corroborating statements about the emergence of dominance and control. And since results for assenting phenomena clearly correspond to results for perception measures (or extra-conversational aspects of the situation), firm statements can be made about the antithetical function of these assenting linguistic forms to the realization of dominance and control.

Results for interruptions and overlaps, which either succeeded or failed, were provocative. Complex three-way interactions indicated that the production of asymmetrical intrusions shifted from opening to closing exchanges of the conversation in a different way for male experts compared to female experts. Certain findings supported the notion of conversational competitiveness between men, while other findings suggested how shifting contexts can either enhance or depress a female show of dominance. Generally, results for intrusions (to be reported elsewhere) by no means provide the striking asymmetry observed by Zimmerman and West (1975), whereby males routinely interrupted females. Unlike earlier studies, several aspects of situation and context were included in the present study of how intrusions occur systematically in conversational interaction. For example, configuration of dyads interacted with expertise and with change over time. Additionally, asymmetrical findings here could not be attributed to the idiosyncratic style of only a few pairs, since difference scores in the production of these intrusions into speech were used for <u>all</u> 70 pairs in the experiment. Furthermore, interruptions and overlaps were analysed separately on the basis of the success or the failure of the intrusion. Findings suggest that each of the resulting four types of intrusions into speech serves a different social function.

In sum, it is clear that the emergence of power in the present study was not based primarily upon expertise per se, nor upon gender qua gender, but upon a subtle interplay between the two. Correspondence among certain language measures, participants' ratings and objective judges' ratings suggest that in the context of this study it was the use of expert power which definitively separated the sexes. It is no accident that the lexical referent "expert", which appeared 7 times in 140 pages of transcript, occurred only in the female expert/male non-expert condition. In all but one instance it was the male who said something like: "So, you're the expert". Previous work (Raven, Centers and Rodrigues 1975; Johnson 1976) substantiates the hypothesis that expertise is not a legitimate source of power for women. Women with expertise in the present study generally avoided responding in dominant ways. Particularly in the presence of non-expert men, they responded with even more supportive, collaborative work than usual. Perhaps women have to compensate for acquiring this illegitimate source of power. Whereas the name of man's game appears to be "Have I won?" the name of woman's game is "Have I been sufficiently helpful?"

While men may pre-empt forms related to power, women may pre-empt forms related to support or nurturance, a disservice to them both. The intent of the present study has been to bring into awareness conversational practices which serve to keep men and women stuck in their respective games. Awareness is the beginning of making alternatives possible. Linguistic options become available, so that men and women can more freely choose to play a variety of games. Effectiveness in human social interaction is based neither upon relationships of power nor solidarity, but upon having the flexibility to construct whatever kind of relationship is appropriate to the immediate encounter and not to some restricting notion of gender appropriateness.

REFERENCES

Hirschman, L. Female-male differences in conversational interaction.   Paper pre-
    sented at the meeting of the Linguistic Society of America, December 1973.
    Cited in B. Thorne and N. Henley (Eds.) Language and sex: difference and
    dominance.   Rowley, Mass.: Newbury House, 1975
Johnson, P. Women and power. Journal of Social Issues, 1976, 32, 99-110
Lockheed, M. E. and Hall, K. P. Conceptualising sex as a status characteristic:
    applications to leadership training strategies.   Journal of Social Issues,
    1976, 32, 111-124
Meeker, B. F. and Weitzel-O'Neill, P. A. Sex roles and interpersonal behavior in
    task-oriented groups. American Sociological Review, 1977, 42, 91-105
Pheterson, G. I., Kiesler, S. B. and Goldberg, P. A. Evaluation of the perfor-
    mance of women as a function of their sex, achievement and personal history.
    Journal of Personality and Social Psychology, 1971, 19, 114-118
Raven, B. H., Centers, R. and Rodrigues, A.   The bases of conjugal power, in
    R. E. Cromwell and D. H. Olsen (Eds.) Power in families.   New York: Wiley,
    1975
Soskin, W. F. and John, V. P. The study of spontaneous talk, in R. Barker (Ed.)
    The stream of behavior.   New York: Appleton-Century-Crofts, 1963
Strodtbeck, F. L. Husband-wife interaction over revealed differences.   American
    Sociological Review, 1951, 16, 468-473
West, C. and Zimmerman, D. H. Woman's place in everyday talk: reflections on
    parent-child interactions. Social Problems, 1977, 24, 521-9
Winer, B. J. Statistical principles in experimental design (2nd edition) New York:
    McGraw-Hill, 1971
Zimmerman, D. H. and West, C. Sex roles, interruptions and silences in conversa-
    tion, in B. Thorne and N. Henley (Eds.) Language and sex: difference and
    dominance.   Rowley, Mass.: Newbury House, 1975

Sex and Communication: A Brief Presentation of an Experimental Approach[1]

T. B. Pedersen

Institute of Psychology, University of Oslo, Oslo, Norway

ABSTRACT

Criticism is made of earlier studies of sex and language/communication because of their serious theoretical and methodological shortcomings, especially their neglect of communication-situations as <u>social</u> situations.

The present experimental study consists of a 2x2x2x2 design: subjects of two different sexes were given two different roles (Explainer versus Follower) when participating in <u>two</u> different kinds of dyads (same-sex versus opposite-sex) in two different communication situations (simple versus conflict).

The communication was analysed in terms of communication efficiency and relevant qualitative aspects: self-confidence and control. The results clearly show the great importance of situational variation and justify a claim for a broader social-psychological analysis in this kind of research.

Key words

Communication; communication efficiency; conflict; context control; language; self-confidence; sex; social situation.

INTRODUCTION

Recently disciplines other than the traditional philosophical and linguistic ones have defined language and communication as a legitimate area of research, among these psychology and social psychology. Labels such as "psycholinguistics" and "sociolinguistics" reflect these new involvements.

Communication is first and foremost <u>social</u> behaviour (Rommetveit 1974; Rommetveit and Blakar 1979) and as such is complicated and complex behaviour. This important aspect has been neglected in former research to an astonishing degree. By an inte-

---

1. This paper is based on the author's thesis in psychology at the University of Oslo and on an article by Rolv Mikkel Blakar and the present author. The author is in addition indebted to Rolv Mikkel Blakar for valuable comments on this paper and to Olaf Hetland for assistance in problems concerning the use of English.

gration of the theoretical and methodological perspectives of social psychology
into the study of language and communication this field of research could experience a renewed development.   As social scientists we are going to pursue questions, so far seriously neglected, about, for example, the relationship between
characteristics of verbal communication and the social matrix or context in which
it is embedded - and an obvious variable among numerous others in the social matrix is sex.   An interesting question in this connection is: how is sex as a
social category manifested in verbal interaction face to face?   An answer to
this question might increase our understanding of how present use of language and
patterns of communication contribute to maintain and support the present sex
roles.

When we started to search the literature about verbal interaction and sex we were
happy to find many promising and interesting titles, but repeatedly we were dis-
appointed; the titles seldom kept their promises.   Even if ideologically "sound"
and progressive, most of the research was fraught with serious theoretical and
methodological shortcomings (Elert, 1978; Blakar, 1974, 1978b).   For example,
research designed to gain insight into potential subtle sex-bound patterns and
styles of social interaction has to be truly interdisciplinary and capitalise on
sex-role theory, socialization theory, communication theory, etc.   A reasonable
demand to make of studies in sex and communication is that they have an explicit
theoretical foundation in a theory of sex as well as in communication theory.
This modest demand is seldom met.

A topic of study as complex as this has tempted many researchers to make undue
simplification: the aspects studied are often only coarsely operationalised;
there is a general tendency towards using too many, too unsystematised and too
far-reaching variables in one study; in addition the concepts and categories
used for analyses are often too "wide".   These weaknesses probably reflect an
underrating of the complexity of the object being studied.

A very serious part of our critique concerns the fact that very few of the studies
really study the verbal interaction itself.   The results presented are too often
based on some "product" of the interaction (as in the many studies using Prisoner
Dilemma Games) while the underlying verbal interaction has not been examined.

A study of language/communication and sex has to be a study of the relationship
between characteristic features of verbal communication and sex as one important
variable in the social context.   Authors seldom see social context as problematic and do not take into sufficient consideration that a communication situation
is a social situation.   Relevant aspects of social situations are for instance
sex of other persons present, number of persons present and given social roles.
Sex need not be a distinct variable in a social interaction situation.   Different
social attributes (e.g. age, sex, socioeconomic status) will all have different
meanings depending on the context of situation, and sex is just one aspect that
may define interacting persons.   Only through analyses of actual situations is it
possible to determine whether sex represents an important variable in any particular situation and whether sex covaries with other factors.

In addition many of the situations described in the literature are both peculiar
and atypical, and it often is hard to see how they can be seen as real interaction
situations, sufficiently motivating for the subjects.   An over-generalisation of
results is the most probable consequence of these questionable conditions.   To be
able to generalise findings one has at least to study the same verbal behaviour
in two different situations.

This general evaluation of former research in sex and communication may seem to be
harsh.   It is, however, necessary and will serve the future well.   It is our
contention that in our present state of knowledge an appropriate approach to com-

lex processes in verbal interaction is by controlled and standardised situations.

METHOD

Design

The present study involved subjects of two different sexes being given two different roles (Explainer versus Follower) for participating in two different kinds of dyads (same-sex versus opposite-sex) in two different communication situations (simple versus conflict).

Subjects

24 female and 24 male undergraduate students aged 19-21 years all of whom were taking introductory courses ("førebuande prøve") at the University of Oslo, participated as subjects.   The subjects were organised in dyads and given the roles of Explainer or Follower according to the following schedule:

		Follower		
		Woman	Man	Total
Explainer	Woman	6	6	12
	Man	6	6	12
	Total	12	12	24

One important condition for accepting a given dyad was that the individuals had to be unknown to each other.   Knowing nothing about each other except sex and social status (both knew that the partner was also a student), the subjects had to base their attitudes and expectations on stereotypes about sex.   This final selection of subjects chosen "to play against" common hypotheses about sex differences gives a strong base for generalisation.

Materials and procedure: the communication situation

The two persons, A and B, were each given a map of a relatively complicated network of roads and streets in a town-centre.   On A's map two routes were marked with arrows: one short and straightforward (the simple route) and another longer and more complicated one (the conflict route).   On B's map no route was marked.

A's task was to describe the two routes to B, the simple one first.   With the help of A's descriptions, B had to try to find the way through town to the predetermined end-point.   B was allowed to ask questions, to ask A to repeat, or to explain in other ways, etc.

However, the maps held by A and B were not identical (there was one street missing from A's map and hence one street extra on B's).   This was irrelevant to the simple route, but significant for the more complicated one.   Hence A and B were sure to become involved in communication conflicts regardless of the quality of A's description or B's decoding.   While A and B are in two apparently similar cooperative situations, in one a basic prerequisite for communication (a common or shared "here") is satisfied, whereas in the other it is not satisfied.   The theoretical rationale and the development of this particular experimental communication situation has been described by Blakar (1973b).

The two participants were seated at opposite ends of a table with two low screens

preventing them from seeing each other's maps.   The screens were low enough for
the subjects to see each other and to have natural eye-contact (cf Moscovici 1967;
Argyle 1969).   Everything said was tape-recorded, and for certain analyses the
tape was transcribed afterwards.

This experimental method has several important advantages: it is developed within the framework of <u>social-cognitive</u> communication theory (as developed by Rommetveit 1968, 1972a,b, 1974; Blakar 1970, 1973a,b, 1978a; Blakar and Rommetveit
1975; Rommetveit and Blakar 1979).   It is employed in an integrated research
project aiming at a systematic exploration of social background variables in
communication (cf Moberget and Reer 1975; Stokstad, Lagerløv and Blakar 1976;
Øisjøfoss 1976; Dahle 1977; Endresen 1977; Paulsen 1977; Blakar 1978a,b).
Relevant categories for analyses have been developed in the project.

<u>Hypotheses</u>

We based the hypotheses on "common-sense" to find out <u>at what point</u> the results
would force us to go beyond what is taken to be common knowledge.

Elsewhere (Pedersen 1979) I have systematised hypotheses for all possible comparisons of communication efficiency and quality.   Here, however, we concentrate on
the hypotheses about efficiency only:

1) According to general belief about sex roles <u>female</u> subjects should be more
efficient <u>Followers</u>, whereas <u>male</u> subjects should be more efficient <u>Explainers</u>.

2) <u>Sex-bound communication</u> patterns should be particularly highlighted in the
<u>opposite-sex</u> dyads rather than in same sex dyads.   In the Male to Female dyads
both communicators should adhere almost perfectly to their given roles as controlling Explainer and more passive Follower: such dyads should demonstrate
very efficient communication.   In the Female to Male dyads, where the female
was given the information and control vis à vis a male co-actor, we expected <u>both</u>
subjects to have more difficulty in accepting and managing their respective roles.
Consequently, a less efficient communication was expected in this group.

For same-sex dyads, we were in doubt as to what to expect.   According to the
general prejudices within the literature on sex and language/communication, one
might predict that male dyads should be more efficient than females.   On the
other hand, the communication situation - at least for the first task - is a very
simple and straightforward one, and taking the educational level of the subjects
into consideration, one would hesitate to predict any differences in efficiency
between male and female in same-sex dyads because both should make near maximal
scores.

Overall, we expected Female to Male dyads to be less efficient, and Male to Female
dyads to be more efficient than the same-sex dyads.

3) Neither common sense nor the voluminous literature on sex and language seem to
be very helpful in predicting <u>if</u> and <u>how</u> the four categories of role/sex combinations will be influenced by the situational variation.   In the literature the
only "situational" variable systematically considered, concerns content or topic
of discourse.   We therefore refrained from predicting any specific situational
differences.

RESULTS AND DISCUSSION

<u>Simple situation</u>

All 24 dyads managed the simple route without too much trouble ($\overline{X}$ =   4 min.46 sec.)

but the variation in time used (from 32 sec. to 11 min. 14 sec.) indicates that the task was not equally simple for all the dyads. These results correspond to those obtained in earlier experiments with student subjects in the same communication situation (Blakar 1973b; Brisendal 1976).

The data in Table 1 show clearly that male subjects were more efficient Explainers and female subjects were more efficient Followers in this simple communication situation.   Against the background of earlier studies conducted in this standardised communication situation, the clearcut sex-bound differences observed in the simple and straightforward situation are indeed remarkable.

TABLE 1   Time spent on communication tasks by dyads (in minutes and seconds)

		Simple Situation Follower			Conflict Situation Follower		
		Woman	Man	Total	Woman	Man	Mean
Woman		1-17	0-32		0	0	
		2-00	1-30		24-51	29-22	
		2-01	4-15		10-54	18-32	
		4-09	7-36		31-31	0	
		5-47	8-24		24-57	0	
		8-01	11-14		19-13	18-07	
	X̄ =	3-53	5-35	4-44	22-17	22-00	22-10
Explainer							
Man		0-55	1-14		22-40	21-22	
		1-08	2-24		0	10-25	
		1-08	3-08		0	0	
		1-32	4-07		38-34	9-53	
		1-36	4-37		30-03	14-17	
		1-41	9-57		28-29	0	
	X̄ =	1-20	4-15	2-47	29-57	13-59	21-58
Grand X̄ =		2-36	4-50	3-36	25-41	17-25	22-04

0 means problem not solved

In respect of the second hypothesis, female and male same-sex dyads demonstrated almost identical communication efficiency measured in terms of mean and range of time.   Opposite-sex dyads differed from same-sex dyads in the directions predicted from common sense.   Whereas the Female to Male dyads were only moderately slower than the same-sex dyads, the Male to Female dyads were markedly more efficient. Male to Female dyads exhibited only a small variance in the time taken to achieve solution, whereas the variation is large within all the other categories, particularly so in the Female to Male category.   The distribution shown in Table 1 might be thought to imply a rather strong interaction effect (between sex of Explainer and sex of Follower), but an analysis of variance failed to reveal any.[2]

2. The samples are small (only 6 dyads in each category) and there is large within group variation (particularly in the female to male category).   The main effects, however, represent clear tendencies, even though not all of them statistically significant tendencies at the 5% level.   The sex of the follower: $df = 1,20$ (the two values are 1 and 20) $F = 3.781$ $p < .05$ (one-tailed test).   The sex of the explainer: $df = 1,20$ $F = 2.676$ $p > .05$ (one-tailed test).   Two-way interaction: $df = 1,20$ $F = 0.254$ $p > .05$ (two-tailed tests).

Conflict situation

Of the 24 dyads, 16 managed to resolve the induced communication conflict whereas 8 did not.   The latter were shown the discrepancy on the maps after more than 40 minutes had elapsed.

TABLE 2   Distribution of solvers/non-solvers over the four categories of dyads in the conflict situation

		Follower					
		Woman		Man		Total	
		Solvers	Non-solvers	Solvers	Non-solvers	Solvers	Non-solvers
Explainer	Woman	5	1	3	3	8	4
	Man	4	2	4	2	8	4
	Total	9	3	7	5	16	8

Table 1 also shows the time spent by all dyads (non-solvers being marked 0), and yields together with Table 2 a fairly complete picture of communication efficiency.

Whereas the ratio solvers/non-solvers (cf Table 2) did not discriminate between the four categories, amount of time used by the solvers indicated distinctive differences (cf Table 1).   The right hand columns of Table 1 moreover shows a pattern very different from that on the left hand ones.   In order to explore sex-bound patterns of communication more thoroughly, therefore, we had to relate the results obtained in the simple to those observed in the conflict communication situation.

The importance of the situational variation was most clearly revealed in the Male to Female category.   In the simple situation this category of dyads demonstrated the most efficient communication.   In the communication conflict situation, however, this same combination demonstrated the least efficient communication.   In the simple and straightforward communication situation, moreover, same-sex female dyads were slightly more efficient than same-sex male dyads.   In the conflict communication situation, on the other hand, male same-sex solving pairs were markedly faster than female ones.

An analysis of variance of time taken by the 16 solvers revealed two significant effects: in the complex conflict situation, the male subjects were more efficient Followers than the female subjects.[3]   Furthermore a significant interaction effect was revealed in that when the sex of the Follower was held constant, same sex dyads showed a more efficient communication than the opposite-sex dyads.[4] Finally, whereas the Male to Male dyads were the fastest, the Male to Female dyads were the slowest solvers.

In the simple situation the sex-bound communication pattern revealed - with the Male to Female category as the most efficient and the Female to Male as the most inefficient - fits our common sense assumptions.   However, the pattern revealed in the conflict situation is contrary to these assumptions in that here the Male

---

3. df = 1,12, F = 6.114 p < .05 (two-tailed test).   The two values are 1 and 12 in this situation.

4. df = 1,12, F = 5.353 p < .05 (two-tailed test).

to Female dyads demonstrated the least efficient communication.   Our introductory
reservations regarding the general validity of - and basis for - the common sense
(or even the "scientific") knowledge about sex and verbal communication thus seem
to be justified.

Opposite-sex dyads were asked afterwards if they thought that the sex of their
cooperator had influenced their communicative behaviour.   Their answers were
negative.   Reactions to the very question, moreover, varied from astonishment to
vigorous denial.   In only 2 of the 12 dyads was the possibility touched upon that
they could have reacted differently to same-sex partners.   (The same-sex dyads
were not given this question.)   This suggests that patterns of verbal communication can be learned so thoroughly as to have become habitual and generally not
reflected upon.

Analyses of Qualitative Aspects of Communication

A predominant issue in the literature on sex and language/communication has been
that of control: who (men or women) controls the language?   who is defining the
interaction setting?   Mechanisms of control are at the same time of crucial significance in any general theoretical analysis of acts of communication.   Control,
moreover, is the pervading topic in analysis of contractual aspects of discourse
(Blakar 1972, 1978b;   Moberget and Reer 1975;   Glennsjø 1977).   Women's presumed
low self-confidence, moreover, has often been referred to in attempts at explaining sex-bound differences (Brabender and Boardman 1977).   Self confidence is
particularly challenged at critical moments of conflict or lack of mutual understanding during the process of communication (cf Teigre 1976;   Hultberg, Alve and
Blakar 1978).   The willingness to accept control may also depend on one's self-
confidence.

The psychologically intriguing differences between the apparently similar communication situations in the present study may be conceptualised in terms of an interplay of control and self confidence: the roles of Explainer/Follower and speaker/
listener are logically independent in that the Explainer and the Follower take
turns to speak and listen.   But whereas there is a shift of roles in exerting the
speaker's control, the Explainer is continuously in control of the here-and-now in
the sense that only he/she knows the correct route.   This inbuilt asymmetry with
respect to information is the same in the two situations.

The two apparently similar communication situations do, however, make fundamentally
different demands upon the participants.   The change in demands from the simple to
the conflict situation appears to be particularly strongly felt by the Follower.
To ensure successful communication the Explainer has in both situations to give as
adequate and accurate explanations and directives as possible.   The role of the
Follower is, however, markedly different.   In the simple situation successful and
efficient communication can be accomplished by a Follower passively following the
directives/explanations of the Explainer.   However, in the more complicated situation the communication conflict created by the missing street puts a pressure on
the Follower to take a stand to and respond actively to the explanations offered
by the Explainer.   If in this conflict situation the Follower passively and simply
tries to follow the directives given by the Explainer, the dyad will never be able
to unravel the real source of the induced communication conflict.   But the extent
to which the Follower - contrary to the inbuilt asymmetry with respect to information - will assume partial control of the communication process, will depend on
her/his self-confidence.

The above analysis is by no means complete.   Obviously not only the Follower's
(Explainer's) self-confidence, but also the Explainer's (Follower's) confidence in
the Follower (Explainer), and the Follower's (Explainer's) experience of the

other's degree of (lack of) confidence in her/his capability may determine whether or not he/she dares to assume responsibility and control.

It follows from the previous analysis that control and self-confidence are relevant aspects worth examining in verbal interaction between same and different sexes.

The following detailed and time-consuming analyses were carried out: 1) Control patterns in the different categories of dyads as reflected in terms of (a) speaking time by each individual participant; (b) how the contracts monitoring the communication process were endorsed (who proposes the contracts, whose proposals are accepted, etc.). 2) Control strategies in the different constellations as reflected in the form of the contract proposals (the form may be direct or indirect). 3) Patterns of attribution when communication difficulties turned up (the attributions may be to self, to partner, to the maps, etc.)[5]. Whereas the first two analyses were intended to reveal differences in control patterns dependent on role (Explainer/Follower) x sex x situation, the last was to give clues about the level of self-confidence of female or male participants in different roles (Explainer/Follower) in the two different communication (simple/conflict) situations.

The original motivation for these analyses was to try to understand and explain the gross and unexpected differences revealed in communication efficiency. The analyses, together with the theoretical understanding of the demands of the two situations already described, to a certain extent succeeded in throwing some light upon these findings. Of greater interest, however, in this context, may be a presentation and illustration of some of the more general conclusions based on these qualitative analyses.

The main conclusion had to be twofold: on the one hand we found several unequivocal differences between men and women in their communicative behaviour, expected differences as well as surprising ones. On the other hand, however, the sex-linked patterns were extremely complex and complicated, and they varied across situations, roles and sex of partner. A most illuminating sex-difference that we might expect from sex-role theory was revealed by the analysis of who in the dyad uttered the first explicit doubt concerning the identity of the maps. In the 9 opposite-sex dyads in which the identity of the maps was explicitly questioned at least once, this crucial utterance came from the male participant 8 times. Further, regardless of constellation and position, women far more often posed their doubts in the form of a question; the men most often just stated the fact. On the other hand, a maybe surprising discovery was that no more women than men were likely to attribute the communication difficulty to themselves. There was thus no reason to claim that women showed less self-confidence than men. Neither can we assert that men showed more control than women. This study shows how untenable and invalid this kind of generalisation is.

Assertions about self-confidence, about control or any other aspect of interaction have to be specified as to several conditions. This is clearly illustrated by the following findings: given a situation with great communication problems (conflict situation) and given the woman holds a position where it is easy for her to conclude that it is she who has failed (Follower) and given that the partner is a man, then the women do, and to a dramatic degree, attribute the problems to themselves. Under no other conditions did the women deviate from men in this respect.

---

5. For the contractual analysis, see Blakar 1972, Moberget and Reer 1975, Glennsjø 1977; for the analysis of attribution of communication difficulties, see Alve and Hultberg 1974, Haarstad 1976, Hultberg, Alve and Blakar 1978.

Likewise, in the simple situation men did indeed generally take control to a greater degree than women, but the men took control to an exceptional degree when they were Explainers for female Followers. In the conflict situation, however, male Explainers to female Followers exhibited no more control than female Explainers to female Followers. This situational variation is also seen in regard to sex-specific codes of communication. In the simple situation there were indications of such codes in the same sex constellations, but we found no such tendencies in the other complicated situation. In conclusion, in respect of the qualitative aspects of communication, the analyses showed a prevailing tendency for sex-specific behaviour demonstrated in one situation, not to show up, or at least not to the same extent in the other.

The analysis of efficiency in the two situations clearly showed the weakness of common sense; the hypotheses perfectly predicted the outcome of the simple situation while they failed completely in the conflict situation. This was also what happened to the hypotheses about qualitative aspects: they were usually confirmed in the simple situation and had no predictive value in the other.

CONCLUSION

The findings reported from this experimental approach may serve as an impetus to systematic re-thinking of general and often dogmatic claims concerning sex and verbal communication.

Even with the apparently very limited situational variation of the present study, it becomes quite clear that nothing definite can be said about communication efficiency of men versus women without explicit reference to communication situation (cf Stokstad, Lagerløv and Blakar 1976). The present study indicates, moreover, that no simple answer can be given regarding the old issue of whether sex-bound communication patterns are most clearly exposed in same sex or opposite sex combinations. The answer must be a qualified one.

At our present stage of knowledge, until a far broader selection of social situations has been systematically mapped, we must refrain from any general conclusions about the relationship between language/communication and sex. Through these future tasks a social-psychological perspective will be a necessary guide.

REFERENCES

Alve, S. and Hultberg, M. Kommunikasjonssvikt hos foreldre til borderline pasienter. Unpublished thesis, University of Oslo, 1974

Argyle, M. Social interaction. London: Methuen 1969

Blakar, R. M. Konteksteffektar i sprakleg kommunikasjon. Unpublished thesis, University of Oslo, 1970

Blakar, R. M. Ein eksperimentell situasjon til studiet av kommunikasjon: bakgrunn, utvikling og nokre problemstillingar. Stencilled report, Institute of Psychology, University of Oslo, 1972

Blakar, R. M. Sprak er makt. Oslo: Pax, 1973(a)

Blakar, R. M. An experimental method for inquiring into communication. European Journal of Social Psychology, 1973, 3, 415-425(b)

Blakar, R. M. Sprak og kvinneundertrykking - eit mangesidig problem. Ventil, 1974, 4, 3-10

Blakar, R. M. Kontakt og konflikt. Oslo: Pax, 1978(a)

Blakar, R. M. Sprak som makt og kvinneundertrykking: spraksosiologi som motefag. In J. Kleiven (Ed.) Artikkelsamling om norsk spraksosiologi. Oslo: Pax, 1978(b)

Blakar, R. M. and Rommetveit, R. Utterances in vacuo and in contexts: an experimental and theoretical exploration of some interrelationships between what is seen or imagined.   International Journal of Psycholinguistics, 1975,153, 5-32.

Blakar, R. M. and Pedersen, T. B. Control and self-confidence as reflected in sex-
     bound patterns in communication.   An experimental approach.   I Informasjons-
     bulletin fra "Psykopatologi og kommunikasjonsprosjektet", 1978, 7, 3-35

Brabender, V. and Boardman, S. K. Sex differences in self-confidence as a function
     of feedback and social cues. Psychological Reports, 1977, 41, 1007-1010

Brisendal, C-G. Om a misforsta: en kommunikasjonsorientert analyse.   Unpublished
     thesis, University of Oslo, 1976

Dahle, M. Sosial bakgrunn og spraklig kommunikasjon.   Unpublished thesis, Univer-
     sity of Oslo, 1977

Elert, C-C. Rapporter inom planeringsarbetet för forskningsprosjektet "Könsroller
     i sprak".   I Könsroller i sprak 2. Uppsala: Uppsala University, 1978

Endresen, A. Modell för lösning av kommunikasjonskonflikt.   Unpublished thesis,
     University of Oslo, 1977

Glennsjø, K. B. Marital schism og marital skew - en kommunikasjonsteoretisk til-
     nærming.   Unpublished thesis, University of Oslo, 1977

Haarstad, B. E. Anoreksia nervosa.   En eksperimentall studie av familiens Kom-
     munikasjon.   Unpublished thesis, University of Oslo, 1976

Hultberg, M., Alve, S. and Blakar, R. M. Patterns of attribution of communicative
     difficulties in couples having a "schizophrenic", a "borderline" or a "normal"
     offspring.   Informasjonsbulletin fra "Psykopatologi og kommunikasjonspros-
     jektet, 1978, 6.

Moberget, O. and Reer, Ø. Kommunikasjon og psykopatologi: En empirisk-teoretisk
     analyse med vekt pa begrepsmessig og metodologisk avklaring.   Unpublished
     thesis, University of Oslo, 1975

Moscovici, S. Communication processing and the properties of language, in L.
     Berkowitz (Ed.) Advances in experimental social psychology. Vol. III, New
     York: Academic Press, 1967

Paulsen, O. G. Schizofreni og kommunikasjon: en replikasjonsstudie.   Unpublished
     thesis, University of Oslo, 1977

Pedersen, T. B. Kjønn og kommunikasjon: en eksperimentall tilnærming.   Unpub-
     lished thesis, University of Oslo, 1979

Rommetveit, R. Words, meanings and messages. New York: Academic Press, and
     Oslo: Universitetsforlaget, 1968

Rommetveit, R. Sprak, tanke og kommunikasjon.   Oslo: Universitetsforlaget 1972(a)

Rommetveit, R. Deep structure of sentences versus message structure: some criti-
     cal remarks to current paradigms, and suggestions for an alternative approach.
     Norwegian Journal of Linguistics, 1972, 26, 3-22 (b)

Rommetveit, R. On message structure.   London: Wiley, 1974

Rommetveit, R. and Blakar, R. M. (Eds.) Studies of language, thought and verbal
     communication. London: Academic Press, 1979

Stokstad, S. J., Lagerløv, T. and Blakar, R. M. Anxiety, rigidity and communica-
     tion: an experimental approach. Informasjonsbulletin fra "Psykopatologi
     og kommunikasjonsprosjektet", 1976, 3.   (To appear in Rommetveit, R. and
     Blakar, R. M. (Eds.) Studies of language, thought and verbal communication.
     London: Academic Press, 1979

Teigre, H. Ø. Tillit som forutsetning for kommunikasjon.   Unpublished thesis,
     University of Oslo, 1976

Øisjøfoss, Ø.   Makt og kontroll i ekteskapet.   Unpublished thesis, University of
     Oslo, 1976

Androgyny, Dyadic Compatibility and Conversational Behaviour[1]

P. E. Jose, F. Crosby and W. J. Wong-McCarthy

Department of Psychology, Yale University, Box 11A Yale Station, New Haven, Connecticut 06520, U.S.A.

ABSTRACT

This study investigated the relationship between conversational behaviour and sex-role self concept as measured by the Bem Sex Role Inventory (BSRI) and the Personal Attributes Questionnaire (PAQ). More seconds of silence were found in incompatible dyads (as determined by sex-role orientation) than in compatible dyads, but generally sex-role self concept did not predict behaviour very well. We also found that the PAQ femininity scale correlates with self-reported self-esteem and assertiveness whereas the BSRI F-scale does not.

Key words

Conversation; dyads; androgyny; incompatibility; feminity; self-esteem; assertiveness.

Since Constantinople's (1973) criticism of the bipolar, unidimensional scales used to measure sex-role self concept, a number of alternative questionnaires have been proposed (Kelley and Worell 1977). Principal among these new measurement techniques are the Bem Sex Role Inventory (BSRI; Bem 1974) and the Personal Attributes Questionnaire (PAQ: Spence, Helmreich and Stapp 1974). The PAQ and BSRI differ somewhat in their construction. The BSRI is composed of positively-valued personality characteristics which have been rated as more desirable either for males or females. The PAQ items are rated as "ideal" for both sexes but differentiated on the basis of whether the item is more "typical" for males or females. Although technically different, the PAQ and BSRI are logically similar: both use two supposedly independent scales or dimensions, one masculine (M) and one feminine (F). With both, individuals are categorised into one of four sex-role types; masculine (high M, low F), feminine (low M, high F), androgynous (high M, high F) or undifferentiated (low M, low F).

Current sex-role researchers are most interested in the person who reports high levels of masculine and feminine self-descriptions. Bem's predictions are that this androgynous person will be adaptive, flexible and unusually skilful in social situations. Although they are few and are flawed, experiments (Bem 1975; Bem and Lenney 1976; Bem, Martyna and Watson 1976; Jones, Chernovetz and Hansson 1978) have tended to validate behaviourally Bem's sex-role questionnaire and her predictions.

---

1. We are indebted to Lindsay Evans, the students of Psychology 268b and Doug Bunnell for their valuable help with the study. The first author was supported by a National Science Fellowship and the research was supported by Biomedical Research Grant 5-S07-RR07015 to the second author.

Ickes and Barnes (1978) were the first to investigate the effects of sex-roles on verbal and nonverbal interaction strategies in conversations.   Specifically, Ickes and Barnes hypothesised that androgynous persons were more socially skilled than other types and that stereotyped dyads (a masculine male and a feminine female) would exhibit dysfunctional interpersonal behaviours.   It was found that the stereotyped dyads tended to display significantly shorter verbalizations, shorter directed gaze, fewer expressive gestures, less positive affect and less liking than the three other kinds of dyads all of which contained at least one androgynous person.   Ickes and Barnes conclude that sex-role stereotyped dyads are more incompatible than is usually assumed.

The present study extends the work of Ickes and Barnes in several ways.   First, a design difference was introduced that provided a between-subjects factor of type of situation.   Half of the subjects role-played a class-room situation where assertive behaviour is appropriate, and half role-played a party situation where non-assertive behaviour is appropriate.   Second, we emphasised paralinguistic measures (e.g. interruptions) whereas they emphasised other nonverbal behaviours (e.g. body orientation).   Finally, we studied non-extreme scorers in a structured situation, whereas they studied extreme scorers in a non-structured situation.

METHOD

Subjects

Ninety-six Yale College undergraduates (48 males and 48 females) participated in the study.   Due to a small subject sample and an inability to pretest we were unable to construct dyads so as to vary systematically sex-role classification. Therefore the matching of sex-role orientations within dyads was random and somewhat irregular.

Procedure and materials

The experiment consisted of (1) filling out some questionnaires, and (2) participating in a ten-minute discussion of an ethical dilemma.   The dilemma involved saving some lives at the expense of other lives.   Order was counterbalanced. Another between-subjects factor was the instruction set given to dyads.   They were instructed to role-play the discussion very assertively in a classroom situation (instrumental condition), or with primary emphasis upon understanding the other person's choices in a party situation (expressive condition).   Pretesting showed that the classroom instruction adequately operationalised an instrumental situation and that the party instruction adequately operationalised an expressive situation.

Each subject completed four questionnaires: the PAQ, the BSRI, a measure of self-esteem (Texas Social Behavior Inventory; Helmreich, Stapp and Ervin 1974) and a short measure of assertiveness (College Self Expression Scale; Galassi, Delo, Galassi and Bastien 1974).

Treatment of results

Analyses were of two kinds: of individual subjects and of dyads.   The first involved 2 x 2 x 4 ANOVAs (sex of subject x instruction set x sex-role category) on four dependent variables: (1) number of words produced; (2) number of back-channels (e.g. "I see", "okay"); (3) number of interruptions; and (4) number of cuts (being interrupted).   Speaker A was coded as interrupting speaker B if A started talking at least 500 msec before B finished talking.   Every time an interruption was scored for A, a cut was scored for B.   For dyadic analyses, dyads were classified into three types: compatible, neutral and incompatible.   One-way

ANOVAs were performed on the variables: (1) number of turns; (2) seconds of silence; (3) seconds of simultaneous speech; and (4) number of interruptions. All measures were derived from the centre six minutes of the conversation.

The individual subject variables were chosen for the purpose of revealing the relative assertiveness or acquiescence of a person's interaction style.   Interruptions and number of words were thought to be indicative of a more aggressive strategy, whereas cuts and back-channels seem to be descriptive of a more submissive person.

The dyadic measures were chosen to indicate the presence or absence of stress. It was predicted that more seconds of silence, more seconds of simultaneous speech, more interruptions and fewer turns would all characterise interactions in the incompatible dyads.   Incompatible dyads included dyads with two masculine individuals (where both might attempt to control) and dyads with two feminine or two undifferentiated individuals (where both might attempt to yield).   Compatible dyads included at least one androgynous individual or the match masculine-feminine. All other dyads were classified as neutral.

RESULTS

Preliminary analyses

Comparisons of this sample's masculinity and feminity scores show that they are very similar to others: means of 5.01 (M) and 4.85 (F) for the BSRI are within a half of a standard deviation of the original testing norms described by Bem (1974). The median PAQ scores of 21.25 (M) and 21.83 (F) resemble the medians reported by Spence and Helmreich (1978).

Further evidence of comparability is provided by M- and F-scale correlations with each other and with the two questionnaires (TSBI and CSES).   As expected, Bem's M- and F-scales do not correlate with each other; neither do Spence and Helmreich's.

TABLE 1.   Correlations of questionnaire scales

	BSRI F	PAQ M	PAQ F	TSBI	CSES
BSRI M	.00	.78***	.00	.62***	.45***
BSRI F		-.08	.64***	.15	.10
PAQ M			.06	.57***	.33***
PAQ F				.23*	.28**
TSBI					.60***

* p < .05, df = 94; ** p < .01; *** p < .001

The two M-scales and the two F-scales correlate highly as has been found elsewhere (Spence and Helmreich 1978) showing that there is substantial overlap between the two instruments.   Also, as Bem (1977) and Spence and Helmreich (1978) have reported before there is a positive relationship between masculinity and self-esteem. In addition there is a small correlation between PAQ femininity and self-esteem. This same pattern is repeated for the assertiveness scale, due no doubt to a similarity between the two scales (r = .60, p < .001).

Individual analyses

Individual subject ANOVAs revealed no significant differences from the planned

analyses.   To improve the reliability of sex-role classifications, we then repeated our analyses but restricted the sample to the 52 subjects assigned the same
sex-role classification by the two questionnaires.   No results emerged for back-
channels.   The only significant finding for number of words and number of interruptions was that more of each occurred in the classroom situation indicating that
the instruction set affected behaviour.   A sex by instruction set interaction was
found for cuts which showed that females in the party situation were interrupted
twice as often as any of the three other combinations.

Dyadic analyses

Dyadic analyses were performed as described earlier and with dyads similarly
classified by the BSRI and the PAQ (n=28 dyads).   No significant differences can
be reported for number of turns, seconds of simultaneous speech or number of interruptions.   However, ANOVAs on the full sample of 48 dyads for seconds of silence
showed a significant main effect for dyad type on the PAQ ($F=4$, df = 2/45, p <.025)
and a borderline finding for the BSRI (p = .06).   As expected, the less stressed
dyads (compatible) evidenced fewer seconds of silence than the noncompatible dyads.
The same result, but stronger, was found for the dyads similarly classified by the
BSRI and the PAQ (n=28 dyads).

DISCUSSION

Of eight dependent variables studied only one was affected by sex-role classification.   Despite this population's similarity on sex-role scores with other populations, the questionnaires did not predict conversational behaviour very well.
There are a number of reasons why this may be the case.   (1) Perhaps sex-role
questionnaires do not predict language behaviour in general.   Other results of
our research programme (Wong-McCarthy, Jose and Crosby, 1979) do not support
this argument.   (2) Perhaps sex-role questionnaires do not predict these particular language behaviours.   It might be, for example, that sex-role self concept
affects the flow of conversation but not the more static measures used here.   But
because some of our variables are similar to some used by Ickes and Barnes, this
argument is not wholly tenable.   (3) Perhaps we undermined the power of the sex-
role questionnaires by using middle scorers.   Unlike Ickes and Barnes who used
subjects selected from a pretested population of 507 persons, we did not pretest
extreme scorers.   It is possible that in structured situations like ours, and
with our relatively homogeneous sample, sex-role self concept might affect conversational behaviour only in those individuals unusually sensitive to gender and sex-
role.

It was hoped that certain differences would appear between the PAQ and the BSRI in
this study.   Only one difference was apparent: the PAQ femininity scale correlates somewhat with self-esteem and assertiveness whereas the BSRI F-scale does
not.   The greater positivity of the PAQ F-scale items might account for the finding.

Behavioural validations of the primary sex-role questionnaires have been too few in
number to delineate sufficiently their scope.   This study indicates that the scope
is limited but it is not clear whether the constraining element was (1) dilution of
predictive power because of the presence of "middle" scorers, or (2) the use of a
situation wherein a partner's gender was not salient.   Future research in this
area might attempt to disentangle these confounded factors in order to estimate
more accurately the predictive power of people's sex-role self concept.

REFERENCES

Bem, S. L.   The measurement of psychological androgyny.   Journal of Consulting
   and Clinical Psychology, 1974, 42, 155-162
Bem, S. L. Sex role adaptability: one consequence of psychological androgyny.
   Journal of Personality and Social Psychology, 1975, 31, 634-643
Bem, S. L. On the utility of alternative procedures for assessing psychological
   androgyny.   Journal of Consulting and Clinical Psychology, 1977, 45, 196-205
Bem, S. L. and Lenney, E.   Sex typing and the avoidance of cross-sex behaviour.
   Journal of Personality and Social Psychology, 1976, 33, 48-54
Bem, S. L., Martyna, W. and Watson, C.   Sex typing and androgyny: further ex-
   plorations of the expressive domain.   Journal of Personality and Social
   Psychology, 1976, 34, 1016-1023
Constantinople, A.   Masculinity-femininity: an exception to the famous dictum.
   Psychological Bulletin, 1973, 80, 389-407
Galassi, J. P., Delo, J. S., Galassi, M. D. and Bastien, S. The College Self
   Expression Scale: a measure of assertiveness.   Behavior Therapy, 1974, 5,
   165-171
Helmreich, R., Stapp, J. and Ervin, C.   The Texas Social Behavior Inventory: an
   objective measure of self-esteem or social competence.   JSAS Catalog of
   Selected Documents in Psychology, 1974, 4, 79
Ickes, W. and Barnes, R. D. Boys and girls together - and alienated: on enacting
   stereotyped sex roles in mixed-sex dyads.   Journal of Personality and Social
   Psychology, 1978, 36, 669-683
Jones, W. H., Chernovetz, M. E. O. and Hansson, R. O.   The enigma of androgyny:
   differential implications for males and females?   Journal of Consulting and
   Clinical Psychology, 1978, 46, 298-313
Kelly, J. A. and Worell, J.   New formulations of sex roles and androgyny: a
   critical review.   Journal of Consulting and Clinical Psychology, 1977, 45,
   1101-1115
Spence, J. T. and Helmreich, R. L. Masculinity and femininity.   Austin: Uni-
   versity of Texas Press, 1978
Spence, J. T., Helmreich, R. L. and Stapp, J. The Personal Attributes Questionnaire: a measure of sex role stereotypes and masculinity-feminity.   JSAS
   Catalog of Selected Documents in Psychology, 1974, 4, 43
Wong-McCarthy, W. J., Jose, P. E. and Crosby, F.   Sex-role self concept and the
   female register.   Unpublished manuscript, Yale University, 1979

Judging Masculine and Feminine Social Identities from Content-Controlled Speech

P. M. Smith

*Department of Psychology, University of Bristol, 8-10 Berkeley Square,
Bristol 8, U.K.*

ABSTRACT

Listeners gave their impressions of psychologically androgynous, feminine, masculine and undifferentiated male and female speakers, who were tape-recorded reading a short prose passage. Speakers were judged on items relevant to Femininity (F), Masculinity (M), Social Competence (C) and Social Attractiveness (A). Listeners' attributions of F and M were not only consistent and systematic, but correspond closely to speakers' self-assessed gender identities. Attributions of C and A were also systematically related to the three independent variables. These encouraging results suggest that the attribution of sex stereotypical characteristics to people is not simply determined by their sex, and that speech cues are capable of mediating between the expression and perception of conformity to sex stereotypes.

Key words

Androgyny; femininity; masculinity; speech; sex; sex stereotypes

Research on relations between women and men in society has tended to emphasise the homogeneity of differentiation between the sexes at the expense of its variability. Despite the undeniable importance of a person's sex in determining how they will be thought of and treated by others, people vary in the degree to which they consider themselves, and are seen by others to be typical members of their sex class. These deviations from sex-associated beliefs and expectations, or sex stereotypes, result in important variations on the theme of homogeneous male-female differentiation. For example, Harris (1977) found that ratings of female and male stimulus persons on measures of social competence and attractiveness were determined more by the masculinity-femininity and favourability of the personal descriptions than by the person's sex per se. Similarly, Tilby and Kalin (1977) found that stimulus persons were judged to be significantly more maladjusted and more likely to require psychiatric help when their interests and occupations were counter-stereotypical than when they were stereotype congruent. At a time when the legitimacy of sex-associated standards of demeanour and behaviour are a subject of hot dispute (Reid 1975; Coussins 1976; Williams and Giles 1978), there is an urgent need for approaches which are sensitive to the possibility of change and variation in the uniformity of sex-based social differentiation.

Perhaps as a consequence of the emphasis on the homogeneity of male-female relations, little is known about the variables which underlie the perception of conformity to and deviation from sex stereotypes, i.e. the attribution of femininity
(F) and masculinity (M).   Moreover, the objects of social differentiation, being
people themselves, are not likely to remain the passive recipients of discrimin-
ative behaviour aimed in their direction.   Whether they accept or repudiate the
differentiation, they are potentially among those who influence the lines along
which it occurs, and the ways in which it is manifest.   However, despite the
fact that most theorists posit some form of interplay between individuals' self-
assessed M and F, and that attributed to them by others (e.g. Parsons, Frieze and
Ruble 1976; Goffman 1977; Kessler and McKenna 1978; Smith 1978b), virtually
nothing is known about the vehicles which serve this interaction, or the form that
it takes.

Evidence from several sources demonstrates that speech variables at many levels of
analysis provide a basis for reliable inferences about people's F and M.   Yet,
not one of these studies has examined the extent to which these attributions correspond to speakers' gender identities.   Vocal variables such as laryngeal fundamental frequency and vocal tract resonance are arguably among the most salient indices of M and F in speech.   Listeners make very reliable and accurate judgements
of speakers' sex in experimental settings on the basis of such cues (Sachs 1975;
Coleman 1976; Lass, Hughes, Bowyer, Waters and Bourne 1976).   However, given
that there are normally more salient criteria available for the classification of
someone as male or female, such as physical appearance for example, even the most
sex-stereotypical speech cues probably figure less prominently in the process of
sex classification itself, than in the post-categorical process of inferring conformity to sex stereotypes (Smith 1978b).   Nevertheless, when speech stimuli are
the only available cues as to a person's sex, some of them apparently serve as
satisfactory substitutes for the normal arbiters of maleness and femaleness.

Some intonational and paralinguistic features of speech also carry connotations of
M and F.   Speech cues such as the average gradient of pitch shifts, the use of
specific intonational patterns, pitch variability, vocal flatness and thinness,
speech intensity and speech rate, have been shown to evoke reliable attributions
of female- and male-stereotypical characteristics to speakers (Terrango 1966;
Addington 1968; Aronovitch 1976; McConnell-Ginet 1978a, b).   Phonological variables have received less direct attention in this respect, although several
"matched-guise" experiments in England have compared female and male standard-
accented speech to regional-accented speech on dimensions related to M and F
(Elyan, Smith, Giles and Bourhis 1978; Giles and Marsh, 1979; Ford 1979).
From these studies, it would appear that the relative masculine and feminine connotations of standard speech in Britain depend upon the non-standard variant with
which it is compared.   Grammatical, lexical and stylistic variables also have
masculine and feminine connotations, as studies using both spoken and written
materials have shown (Edelsky 1976a, b; Siegler and Siegler 1976; Maxwell 1978).

The discovery of speech correlates of perceived F and M is a worthwhile pursuit
in itself insofar as it results in the discovery of stimuli which are among the
bases for the differential treatment of individuals and groups.   But an important
factor in assessing the significance of these speech-based inferences, from the
point of view of those about whom they are made, is their validity or accuracy.
The study reported below is part of a larger project explicitly designed as a
first attempt to discover whether speech provides a link between gender identity
and attributions of M and F.   The primary aim of this study is to find out if
attributions of F and M based on speech correspond to speakers' self-assessed
gender identities.   A secondary aim is to discern some of the evaluative concom-
mitants of M and F attributions, in terms of the perceived competence and social
attractiveness of the speakers.

METHOD

Selection of speakers

Four women and four men aged between 19 and 25 years were selected from among a larger population (N = 200) which had participated in an earlier study of sex stereotyping and self-concept, and a subsequent sociolinguistic interview (N = 60). One speaker of each sex was chosen to represent each of the four possible combinations of high or low M and F based on their self-ratings on a masculinity scale (M Scale) and a femininity scale (F Scale), each composed of 10 personality-descriptive adjectives found to be highly sex-stereotypical in an earlier study (Smith 1978a: see Table 1).   This approach to the measurement of gender identity is based on the idea that sex stereotypes, representing complexes of expectations

TABLE 1

M Scale	F Scale
Masculine	Feminine
Coarse	Expressive of emotions
Dominant	Nagging
Arrogant	Neat
Aggressive	Sensitive
Hides emotions	Emotional
Uses harsh language	Appearance-oriented
Willing to take risks	Soft-spoken
Loud	Tender
Reckless	Fussy

and beliefs about what men and women are like, are the standards against which individual M and F should be assessed (Smith 1978a).   Therefore a person who endorses female-stereotypic attributes, but not male-stereotypic, as very characteristic of her/his self-presentation has a feminine gender identity, and someone who endorses masculine but not feminine attributes has a masculine gender identity. Someone who endorses relatively high levels of both masculine and feminine attributes is said to have an androgynous gender identity, while one who eschews self-typification in sex-stereotypical terms altogether has an undifferentiated gender identity.

Speech samples

Speakers, who were isolated to minimise the intrusion of unwanted speech style shifts due to the presence of an interviewer (Giles 1973; Smith 1979), were recorded reading a lively short prose passage which had previously been rated as neutral with respect to the probable sex of its author.   The unedited speech samples, of between two and five minutes duration, were spliced on to separate stimulus tapes, comprising the male voices and the female voices.

Listener-judges

One hundred and twenty-eight linguistically naive students, half of each sex, from several University of Bristol faculties, volunteered as judges (Ss), and participated in groups of between 12 and 40.

Procedure and questionnaires

The stimulus tapes were played through once while Ss rated each speaker on five M Scale and five F Scale items (the first five items from each Scale listed in Table

1).   Then the tapes were played through again while <u>Ss</u> rated speakers on the
eight items comprising the Competence (C) and Attractiveness (A) Scales in Table 2.
These items were found to be non-sex-stereotypical in an earlier study of sex
stereotypes.

TABLE 2

C Scale	A Scale
Intelligent	Friendly
Competent	Interesting
Fluent	Reliable
Clear	Sincere

Data analysis

Listeners' judgements were submitted to analyses of variance, which were performed
on the scale sum scores for each scale separately.   Several features of the experimental design are not discussed in this paper due to shortage of space, and so
F-statistics are not reproduced.   The summary of significance levels in Table 3
is abridged from the more complete tables in Smith (forthcoming).

RESULTS AND DISCUSSION

Table 3 presents a summary of the significance levels for the main and interaction
effects, and the direction of the main effects (in parenthesis), for the four independent variables (Speaker Sex, Speaker M, Speaker F, Listener Sex) and four dependent variables (M, F, C and A Scales) of interest.   It can be seen from the absence of effects due to the sex of the listeners, that men and women did not differ
substantially in their attributions.   Listeners' ratings of M and F were influenced by interactions among the three remaining independent variables, so that:

TABLE 3

Source of Variation	Dependent Variables			
	M Scale	F Scale	C Scale	A Scale
Speaker Sex (A)	$p < .001$ (♂)	$p < .001$ (♀)	$p < .001$ (♀)	$p < .001$ (♀)
Speaker M (b)	$p < .001$ (hi M)	$p < .01$ (lo M)	$p < .001$ (hi M)	ns
Speaker F (C)	$p < .001$ (lo F)	$p < .001$ (hi F)	$p < .01$ (hi F)	$p < .01$ (hi F)
Listener Sex (D)	ns	ns	ns	ns
B x C	ns	ns	ns	$p < .001$
A x B x C	$p < .001$	$p < .01$	$p < .001$	ns

(1) female speakers on average were rated higher on the F Scale, and lower on M,
than the males, with the opposite pattern being obtained for male speakers;   (2)
high M and/or low F speakers were rated higher on the M Scale;   and (3) high F and/
or low M speakers were rated higher on the F Scale.   The precise pattern of M and
F attributions depends on the sex of the speaker, as can be seen by referring to
the average values in Table 4.

Ratings of competence and attractiveness were also influenced by interactions
among speaker sex, speaker M and speaker F.   Women overall were perceived to be
more competent and more socially attractive than men, on the basis of speech.

TABLE 4

Scale	Male Speakers				Female Speakers			
	loF/loM	hiF/loM	loF/hiM	hiF/hiM	loF/loM	hiF/loM	loF/hiM	hiF/hiM
M	16.5	14.7	25.4	18.6	11.8	13.8	21.5	12.2
F	16.3	16.7	13.7	22.6	24.0	23.9	19.5	23.5
C	16.7	9.3	15.7	22.6	17.5	21.4	18.0	19.6
A	16.5	14.6	14.3	17.5	19.3	18.4	16.3	18.8

Androgynous speakers, and the feminine woman, were rated as the most, and the feminine male as the least, competent. The four speakers with sex-typed gender identities (i.e. masculine or feminine) were seen to be less socially attractive than speakers who combined aspects of both masculine and feminine identities (i.e. the androgynous and undifferentiated speakers). These results parallel those for another item on the questionnaire, not discussed above. After Ss had rated each speaker on the C and A Scales, they responded to an item labelled, "my overall impression of this speaker is", which was anchored at the poles of the seven-point scale with the labels, "very favourable" and "very unfavourable". Androgynous and undifferentiated speakers created the most favourable impressions on average.

The results of this study, while requiring replication with different speakers, perhaps in more normal speech situations, are encouraging. They suggest that vocal cues alone elicit reliable stereotypes of speakers' gender identities, which correspond closely to speakers' actual gender identities. That is, these stereotypes are not determined simply by the sex of the speaker, but are sensitive to variations among people of the same sex who differ in the degree to which they share a social identity seen as typical of other members of their sex. Finally, even content-controlled speech readily elicited judgements of social competence and social attractiveness which bore a systematic relationship to masculine and feminine gender identity, and to attributions of masculinity and femininity. Within the limits imposed by the methodology of this study at least, speech has been shown to serve as a link between gender identity and attributions of conformity to sex stereotypes.

REFERENCES

Addington, D. W. The relationship of selected vocal characteristics to personality perception. Speech Monographs, 1968, 35, 492-503

Aronovitch, C. D. The voice of personality: stereotyped judgements and their relation to voice quality and sex of speaker. Journal of Social Psychology, 1976, 99, 207-220

Coleman, R. O. A comparison of the contributions of two voice quality characteristics to the perceptions of maleness and femaleness in the voice. Journal of Speech and Hearing Research, 1976, 19, 168-180

Coussins, J. Equality Report. London: National Council for Civil Liberties, Unit for Women's Rights, 1976

Edelsky, C. Subjective reactions to sex-linked language. Journal of Social Psychology, 1976, 99, 97-104 (a)

Edelsky, C. The acquisition of communicative competence: recognition of linguistic correlates of sex roles. Merrill-Palmer Quarterly, 1976, 22, 47-59 (b)

Elyan, O., Smith, P., Giles, H. and Bourhis, R. Y. RP-accented female speech: the voice of perceived androgyny? in P. Trudgill (Ed.) Sociolinguistic Patterns in British English. London: Arnold, 1978

Ford, B. Accented speech as a basis for stereotyped class and sex trait attributions. Unpublished honours thesis, University of Bristol, 1979

Giles, H. Accent mobility: a model and some data. Anthropological Linguistics, 1973, 15, 87-105

Giles, H. and Marsh, P. Perceived masculinity and accented speech. Language Sciences, 1979, 1, 301-315

Goffman, E. The arrangement between the sexes. Theory and Society, 1977, 4, 301-331

Harris, M. B. The effects of gender, masculinity-femininity and trait favorability on evaluations of students. Contemporary Educational Psychology, 1977, 2, 353-363

Kessler, S. J. and McKenna, W. Gender: an ethnomethodological approach. New York: Wiley, 1978

Lass, N. J., Hughes, K. R., Bowyer, M. D., Waters, L. T. and Bourne, V. T. Speaker sex identification from voiced, whispered and filtered isolated vowels. Journal of the Acoustical Society of America, 1976, 59, 675-678

McConnell-Ginet, S. Intonation in a man's world: signs. Journal of Women in Culture and Society, 1978, 3(3), 541-59 (a)

McConnell-Ginet, S. Intonation in the social context: language and sex. Paper delivered at IXth World Congress of Sociology, Uppsala, Sweden 1978 (b)

Maxwell, E. Reactions to women's language variation. Paper presented at the IXth World Congress of Sociology, Uppsala, Sweden, 1978

Parsons, J. E., Frieze, I. H. and Ruble, D. N. Introduction. Journal of Social Issues, 1976, 32, 1-5

Reid, E. Women at a standstill: the need for radical change, in Women Workers and Society: International Perspectives. Geneva: International Labour Office, 1975

Sachs, J. Clues to the identification of sex in children's speech, in B. Thorne and N. Henley (Eds.) Language and sex: difference and dominance. Rowley, Mass.: Newbury House, 1975

Siegler, D. M. and Siegler, R. S. Stereotypes of males' and females' speech. Psychological Reports, 1976, 39, 167-170

Smith, P. M. Talking about androgyny: getting there is half the fun. Resources in Education, ERIC document 151686, 1978 (a)

Smith, P. M. Speaker sex as a dependent variable in sociolinguistic research. Paper presented at the IXth World Congress of Sociology, Uppsala, Sweden, 1978 (b)

Smith, P. M. Sex markers in speech, in K. Scherer and H. Giles (Eds.) Social markers and speech. Cambridge University Press, 1979

Smith, P. M. Language variables and intergroup relations: the voices of masculinity and femininity. Unpublished Ph.D. dissertation, University of Bristol, forthcoming

Terrango, L. Pitch and duration characteristics of the oral reading of males on a masculinity-femininity dimension. Journal of Speech and Hearing Research, 1966, 9, 590-595

Tilby, P. and Kalin, R. Effects of sex-role deviant life styles in otherwise normal persons on the perception of maladjustment. Canadian Journal of Behavioural Science, 1979, 11, 45-72

Williams, J. A. and Giles, H. The changing status of women in society: an intergroup perspective, in H. Tajfel (Eds.) Differentiation between social groups: studies in the social psychology of intergroup relations. London: Academic Press, 1978

Conversational Insecurity[1]

P. M. Fishman

Department of Sociology, Queen's College, The City University of New York,
Flushing, New York 11367, U.S.A.

ABSTRACT

Concrete ways that women talk are frequently explainedas a result of female "personality" and socialization. This paper offers an alternative social explanation for the depiction of women as "insecure", using data from tape recording of three male-female couples in their homes. Looking at the seemingly insecure behaviour of women in actual conversational settings, their activity can be demonstrated to be embedded in the necessary work involved in producing successful interactions.

Key words

Conversational analysis; male-female conversation; question-asking; women's - insecurity, personality, speech; "you know"; socialization

INTRODUCTION

Discussions of the way women act, including the way they talk, often rely on some notion of a female "personality". Usually, socialization is used to explain this personality. Women are seen as more insecure, dependent and emotional than men because of the way that they are raised. Socialization is seen as the means by which male-female power differences are internalised and translated into behaviour producing properly dominant men and submissive women (Bardwick and Douvan 1977; Lakoff 1975). Lakoff (1979) has probably been the most explicit in offering this personality-socialization explanation for women's speech patterns:

"Linguistic behavior, like other facets of the personality is heavily influenced by training and education. Women speak as they do - and men speak as they do - because they have from childhood been rewarded for doing so, overtly or subtly. Also they speak as they do because their choice of speech style reflects their self-image." (p.141)

I want to propose an altogether different analysis. Instead of viewing the behaviour of adult women as indicative of a gender identity acquired through childhood socialization, I will examine the behaviour in terms of the interactional

---

1. I thank Mark Fishman and Linda Marks for their comments.

situation in which it is produced.   As a methodological strategy, I advocate
that _first_ we examine the situational context for the forces that explain why
people do what they do.   If no such forces can be found in the immediate context,
only then should we rely on prior socialization to explain present behaviour.

In this paper I will consider two examples of women's conversational style:
question-asking and the use of _you know_.   Both are seen as indicative of women's
tendency to be more "insecure" and "hesitant" and are said to arise from a
socialized female personality.   Rather than using these as evidence of personality traits, I shall explore the character of conversational interaction in which
they occur.   By doing so, we will see that these speech patterns are attempted
solutions to the problematics of conversation.

The illustrative data in this paper come from 52 hours of taped natural conversation, $12\frac{1}{2}$ hours of which have been transcribed.   Three male-female couples
agreed to have tape recorders placed in their apartments for periods ranging from
4 to 14 days.   Because the couples operated the recorders manually, uninterrupted
recording lengths ran from 1 to 4 hours.   The apartments were all small one-bed-
room units, and the recorders picked up all kitchen and living room conversation
as well as louder talk from the bedroom and bath.   The six participants were between the ages of 25 and 35, white and professionally oriented.   The three men
were graduate students, as were two of the women.   The third woman was a social
worker.   Two of the women were feminists.   The other woman and all of the men
were sympathetic to the women's movement.   The participants could erase anything
they wished before giving me the tapes, though this was done in only three instances.

ASKING QUESTIONS

Lakoff argues that the asking of questions is a prime example of women's insecurity and hesitancy.   She deals with women's extensive use of two interrogatory
devices: tag questions ("Isn't it?"   "Couldn't we?") (1975) and questions with
declarative functions ("Did you see this in the paper?"   "Should we do a grocery
shopping?") (1979):

> "... women are more apt than men to use a question when there is a
> choice for this reason: a woman has traditionally gained reassurance
> in this culture from presenting herself as concerned about her accept-
> ance as well as unsure of the correctness of what she's saying ... a
> woman, believing that a hesitant style will win her acceptance, will
> adopt it, and phrase her opinions ... deferentially. ... The single
> greatest problem women are going to have in achieving parity is surely
> this pervasive tendency toward hesitancy, linguistic and otherwise.
> (1979, p. 143)

My transcripts support Lakoff's claim that women use tags and declarative questions
much more often than men.   In fact, women ask more questions of any kind.   Out of
a total of 370 questions asked in $12\frac{1}{2}$ hours of conversation, the women asked 263,
two and a half times as many as the men.   About a third of the women's questions
(87) were tags or were ones that could have been phrased as declaratives.   The
women asked three times as many tag or declarative questions as the men (87 to 29)
and twice as many requests for information or clarification (152 to 74).   (There
were 28 questions which I could not categorise, half because of the lack of trans-
cribable words.   Twenty-four were asked by the females, four by the males).   A
substantial number of women's questions theoretically need not have been questions
at all.   Why do women speak this way?   And why do women ask so many more questions generally?

Instead of interpreting question-asking as the expression of an insecure personality, let us consider the question's interactive attributes.   What work does a
question do?   Question-asking attempts to establish one of the prerequisites of
conversation.   In order for two or more people to talk to one another, they must
agree to do so.   They must display that agreement by entering into mutual orientation to one another, and they must speak and respond to one another as one aspect of their mutual orientation.   They must take turns speaking, and they must
display connectedness between what they say to one another.

Sacks, working within this interactional perspective, has noted that questions are
part of a category of conversational sequencing devices; questions form the first
part of a pair of utterances, answers being the second part (Sacks 1972).   Questions and answers are linked together, conversationally and normatively.   Questions are both explicit invitations to the listener to respond and demands that
they do so.   The questioner has rights to complain if there is no response forthcoming.   Questions are stronger forms interactively than declaratives.   A declarative can be more easily ignored.   The listener can claim they did not know the
speaker was finished, or that they thought the speaker was musing aloud.

Evidence for the strength of the question-answer sequence can be seen from an
analysis of who succeeds in getting their topics adopted in conversation.   In
earlier work (Fishman 1978) I found that women, using a variety of utterance
types to introduce topics, succeeded only 36% of the time in getting their topics
to become actual conversations.   In contrast, all but one of the men's topic
attempts succeeded.   However, when we look at the number of topic attempts that
women introduced with a question, their success rate jumps considerably.   Of 18
introductory attempts which were questions, 13 succeeded.   This 72% success rate
is exactly double the women's overall success rate of 36%.   Men used questions
to introduce topics six times out of 29, all of which succeeded.

Women ask questions so often because of the conversational power of questions, not
because of personality weakness.   Women have more trouble starting conversation
and keeping it going when they are talking with men.   Their greater use of questions is an attempt to solve the <u>conversational</u> problem of gaining a response to
their utterances.

"YOU KNOW"

Lakoff discusses hedging as another aspect of women's insecurity.   By hedges, she
is referring to the frequent use of such phrases as "sorta", "like", and "you
know".   I shall deal here with "you know", since it is a device which I have addressed in my own analyses of conversations (1979).   In my transcripts, just as
Lakoff would predict, the women used "you know" five times more often than the
men (87 to 17).   Why is this?

Let us consider where "you know" appears in conversation.   According to Lakoff,
one would expect "you know" to be randomly scattered throughout women's speech,
since its usage is supposed to reflect the general insecurity of the speaker.
If, however, "you know" does some kind of work in conversation, we would expect
its occurrence to cluster at points in conversation where the interactional context seems to call for its usage.   And this is just what I found.   Thirty of the
women's 87 "you know's" occur during six short segments of talk.   These were all
places where the women were unsuccessfully attempting to pursue topics.   The six
segments of talk total 10 minutes.   This means that nearly 35% of the uses occur
in less than 2% of the transcribed hours of conversation.   (The "you know's" were
not counted for 1½ hours of transcript where four people, rather than the couple,
were conversing.   Thus, the total transcript time here is 11 hours (10/660 = 1.5%)
Also during 2 hours of one couple there were no clustered "you know's".   Subtract-
ing those 2 hours, we are left with 10/540 = 1.9%, a ratio well under the 35% of

the total "you know's" which fall in that time.)

"You know" displays conversational trouble, but it is often an attempt to solve
the trouble as well.   "You know" is an attention-getting device, a way to check
with one's interactional partner to see if they are listening, following and attending to one's remarks.   When we consider "you know" interactively, it is not surprising to find that its use is concentrated in long turns at talk where the
speaker is unsuccessfully attempting to carry on a conversation.   If we look
briefly at the two longest segments in which "you know" clusters, we can clarify
how it works in actual conversation.

In the two transcripts which follow, the numbers in parentheses are the time in
seconds of the pauses.   The vertical lines in the second transcript indicate overlapping talk.   The first segment is five minutes long and only parts of it are
reprinted (the full text can be found in Fishman 1979).   Here, the woman is
attempting to engage the man in conversation about an article she has just read.
During the five minutes the man responds only six times, and the woman uses "you
know" 16 times.   Ten of her 16 uses fall in the 2 minutes when there is no response from the man at all:

F   "... he's talking about the differences, that the women (1.3) uhm (0.8)
       that the black women represent to the black men, (o.5) white society (0.8)
       and that uhm (1.5) they stand for all the white values like they're
       dressed much neater than the men.   They're obviously trying much
       harder, y'know, and they're more courteous and polite etcetera, etcetera,
       you know.   (1.5) It seems to me that the women because of our (0.7)
       chauvinism in this society are constantly being put down for things that
       the same set of the same traits in a man would be put up. (1.5)   Like
       this - he uses different words, you know? (1.5) uhmm(1).   For instance
       you know they try more they're more conscientious.   This sort of thing
       the goddamn blighter used to say about a man, 'n'-, and so on.(1)   It's
       just obvious that -(3) uhh(1), he doesn't know what to do with the fact
       that the women, the black women (1) uh you know, for a multitude of
       reasons probably, have come out to be much stronger in many ways than
       black men. (1) Y'know they hold families together, they're also the bread
       earners, (1) they just have to go through a lot more shit than the men
       it seems, and they're stronger for it. (1) and uhm (1.5) he doesn't know
       what to make of the fact that (0.9) they do all these things, (2)y'know,
       and so he just puts them down.   In a blind and chauvinistic way. (2.5)
       In other words black women are white. (2) Y'know it's really a simplistic
       article (0.5) you know he starts off saying - this - (1) y'know, (0.8)
       sort of this gross, indiscriminate, black versus white (1) vision and ..."

Eight out of ten of the "you know's" occur immediately prior to or after pauses in
the woman's speech.   Pauses are places where speaker change might occur, i.e.
where the man might have responded.   Because the man does not respond and the
woman continues talking to keep the conversation going, the pauses become internal
to the woman's speech.   "You know" seems to be an explicit invitation to respond.
At the same time, it displays the man's position as a co-participant when he has
not displayed it himself.

"You know" appears to be used somewhat differently in the second segment.   In this
2-minute piece, the woman uses "you know" five times.   (The "Richard" referred to
in this segment is a mutual friend.   He was born in a foreign country which the
couple were discussing immediately prior to this piece of conversation).

F   "Many of the men I've met have been incredibly uhh provincial (2) in a
       sense (1) Umm and it also you know you've got a-, mind you, I know that
       Richard has had a very good education (2) but he's a very taciturn man

and very bitter (0.6) very bitter about the way he's been treated. He's ve-, you know old family in regards

M   umphhh

F   Well you know some people got caught up in it I mean

M   oh of course (1.1)

F   You know I mean (0.6) yes I'm sure I mean he's very conservative, right? I mean I'm (1) he hates everything (0.7) and I am I am sure he didn't before but (1) whenever you talk to his father about it (0.6) he (1.5) he is very confused. I mean apparently he, he was (0.7) very active (0.6) hated Germany (2) and yet turned around afterwards (1) you know which is sort of

M   Oh the trouble is that he turned against everything, even in the war.

(F then makes another attempt to pursue the topic of Richard's politics, which M responds to with a discussion of cities in the country of Richard's birth).

Two of the five "you know's" here follow internal pauses, as in the first transcript we examined. The other three cluster around the man's two minimal responses. Minimal responses display minimal orientation but not full participation. They fill the necessity of turn-taking but add nothing to the substantive progress of the talk, to the content of the conversation.

The use of "you know" around minimal responses displays and attempts to solve the same problem as its use around pauses. In both cases there is a speaker change problem. The women are either trying to get a response or have gotten an unsatisfactory one. The evidence for women's insecurity is in fact evidence of the work they are doing to try to turn insecure conversations into successful ones.

CONCLUDING REMARKS

I do not mean to imply that women may not find themselves feeling insecure and hesitant in such conversations. The point is that the feelings are not necessarily something women carry around with them as a result of early socialization. Rather, the feelings arise in situations where the women's attempts at conversation are faltering or failing and they are forced to do considerable work for dubious results.

And why do women have more conversational trouble than men do? Because men often do not do the necessary work to keep conversation going. Either they do not respond minimally to conversational attempts by the women. In the few instances where men have trouble in conversations with women they use the same devices to try to solve their problems. I suspect that in conversations with their superiors men use what has been regarded as women's conversational style. The underlying issue here is likely to be hierarchy, not simply gender. Socially-structured power relations are reproduced and actively maintained in our everyday interactions. Women's conversational troubles reflect not their inferior social training but their inferior social position.

REFERENCES

Bardwick, J. M. and Douvan, E. Ambivalence: the socialization of women, in P. J. Stein, J. Richman and N. Hannon (Eds.), <u>The Family: functions, conflicts and symbols</u>. Reading, Mass.: Addison-Wesley, 1977

Fishman, P. M. Interaction: the work women do. <u>Social Problems</u>, 1978, <u>25</u>, 397–
    406
Fishman, P. M. What do couples talk about when they're alone? in D. Butturff
    and E. L. Epstein (Eds.) <u>Women's language and style</u>. Akron: University of
    Akron, 1979
Lakoff, R. T. <u>Language and woman's place</u>. New York: Harper Colophon Books, 1975
Lakoff, R. T. Women's language, in D. Butturff and E. L. Epstein (Eds.) <u>Women's</u>
    <u>language and style</u>. Akron: University of Akron, 1979
Sacks, H. On the analyzability of stories by children, in J. Gumperz and D. Hymes
    (Eds.) <u>Directions in sociolinguistics: the ethnography of communication</u>.
    New York: Holt, Rinehart and Winston, 1972

Ethnicity and Language:
A Social Psychological Perspective

D. M. Taylor[1]

*Department of Psychology, McGill University, P.O. Box 6070, Montreal Station 'A',
Quebec, Canada*

Ethnicity and its relation to language is a persistent and pressing social issue.
Ethnic awareness, which was relatively dormant in the sixties, has evolved into a
world-wide social phenomenon.   And the social consequences have not been, and
will not be, trivial.   A quick cataloguing of the societal implications of the
rise of Black consciousness in the United States, the move toward political independence among Francophone Canadians, similar pressures in Wales and Scotland,
indeed the ethnic movements on all continents make it clear that issues of social
justice in the form of collective rights for minority ethnic groups must be
addressed.

Equally clear is the intimate relationship of language to ethnicity.   Its role is
obvious in cases where ethnicity is largely defined through language (e.g. French
Canadians - Taylor, Bassili and Aboud, 1973; Welshmen - Giles, Taylor and Bourhis,
1977) or where, in the struggle against colonialism, emerging nations work towards
implementing a national language, as in the case of India or the Philippines.
But language also strikes to the core, albeit more subtly, in unilingual nations
such as England, Australia, the United States and many countries in Western Europe.

The challenge for social science is enormous.   For this universal ethnic revival
was not a phenomenon that social scientists anticipated or predicted (see Fishman
1977).   Instead, real people, with real needs, belonging to groups with real
feelings of injustice forced home a reality that governments and society cannot
ignore.   Social scientists, by and large, have responded to this reality only in
a post hoc fashion and if the social sciences are to provide some leadership,
cooperation across disciplines is not only desirable but essential.

The aims of the present volume were articulated in the Introduction.   They are
predicated on the assumption that social psychology may have something to offer
those persistent and fundamental issues in sociolinguistics.   The very thrust of
this volume makes it clear that language and ethnicity has been a neglected issue
in mainstream social psychology.   Therefore it is to some extent understandable
that sociolinguistic research has not as yet capitalised on theory and research in
the field of social psychology.   At this early stage of cross-fertilisation be-

---

1. I would like to thank Marianne Ebertowski for helpful comments on an earlier
   version of this paper.

tween the disciplines then a sophisticated integration is not to be expected.
Rather the aim is to engage in "consciousness raising", alerting ourselves to
critical places in sociolinguistic enquiry where social psychological issues, concepts, processes and theories might be relevant.   A few of the papers in this section, written as they were by social psychologists, discuss and incorporate social
psychological processes directly.   The majority of the papers, which are more
linguistically based, allude to social psychological interpretations only indirectly.   Thus the reader is challenged to bridge the gap between descriptive sociolinguistic phenomena and the potentially rich social psychological literature
which may provide some much needed explanation.

Papers in this section

The first three papers in this section focus on some of the social barriers to
learning the language of another group.   The final four are concerned with relations between ethnolinguistic groups.   The reader is reminded that while some
authors provide detailed accounts of the social psychological processes to which
they refer, others rely more on the background knowledge of the reader.   In these
latter cases it is hoped that the specific terminology and key references provided
are sufficient to enable an evaluation of the heuristic potential of the research
strategies which are outlined.

The paper by Cherry emphasises "status and power as the underpinnings of human
social interaction".   Inequities in status are linked specifically to learning
another group's language.   Certain key references are cited but there remains a
volume of literature left unexplored.   True, the social psychological literature
on status and power is relatively sparse.   Nevertheless, there are a number of
well known formulations which could usefully be applied.   To cite one early example, the various forms of power discussed by French and Raven (1953) may be relevant.   They distinguish five conceptually distinct forms: reward power, coer-
cive power, legitimate power, referent power and expert power.   Space does not
permit a detailed discussion of each but it would seem reasonable to expect that
relations between ethnolinguistic groups which are characterised by different
forms of power may be associated with differential motivation and success in
second language learning.

The paper dealing with second language learning by Clément directly discusses a
number of social psychological constructs.   Specifically the notions of integrative and instrumental motivation, ethnolinguistic vitality, social identity and
personal self-confidence are treated thoroughly and key references are provided.

The third paper in this section on social grammar by Grayshon alludes to status
but concentrates more on the sociolinguistic norms which permit those with such a
shared understanding to communicate effectively.   Grayshon demonstrates clearly
the misunderstandings which arise when facility in a second language is not accompanied by a knowledge of the normative social meaning associated with the formal
linguistic and para-linguistic elements of a language.   The social psychology of
norms is addressed in detail in the paper by McKirnan and Hamayan.   Their paper
not only provides key up-to-date references but also extends the existing literature and applies it to the role of language for ethnicity and intergroup relations.

The paper by Platt refers to six factors potentially involved with language choice
in a multilingual setting.   Two that have particular relevance for social psychology are roles and social identity.   The concept of role and its function has received a good deal of attention (see Sarbin and Allen, 1968) and social identity
has been the subject of an important social psychological theory of intergroup relations (Tajfel, 1978; Tajfel and Turner, 1979).

Hinnenkamp provides us with an insightful social analysis of the language situation of the foreign worker in Germany.   The paper describes in detail the survival oriented context of the worker and demonstrates how language personifies this
totally subordinate social role.   Several key issues which have been addressed
in the social psychological literature could usefully be applied to this context.
The consequences of subordinate status in terms of locus of control (Rotter, 1966)
self-fulfilling prophecy (Rosenthal and Jacobson, 1968) and deindividuation (Zimbardo, 1970) literature might be particularly relevant.

All the papers thus far have been approached from the point of view of what social
psychology might offer to sociolinguistics.   The final paper in this section by
Taylor and Royer illustrates how social psychology can benefit from theoretical
developments in the field of language.   The experiment described in the paper is
based on the argument that social psychological theory and research has paid insufficient attention to group processes.   The group polarisation phenomenon,
from the social psychology of group processes, is applied to Giles's accommodation
theory as an illustration of how social psychology must itself take greater account of group process, and of how sociolinguistic research has been partly responsible for alerting social psychologists to this issue.

Each of the papers in this section addresses important issues for ethnicity and
language, and the brief outline presented here is not intended as a substitute
for the substantial material contained in them.   Rather the aim is to alert
readers to the various areas of social psychological enquiry which have had a
rich tradition of theory and research but which have not as yet been applied to
sociolinguistic issues.

A framework for research on language and ethnicity

There are a number of striking features to the papers in this section, representing as they do a cross-section of current interests in language and society.
First, while a number of potentially important concepts are introduced, in most
cases they are not developed to the stage where they permit the construction of
concrete hypotheses and thereby new insights.   Second, while each paper is concerned with the same general topic, there is little or no overlap among how the
issues are formulated.   This lack of a common conceptual perspective makes it
difficult to pinpoint areas of agreement and disagreement, both necessary for a
systematic understanding of the relationship of language to ethnicity.

One major obstacle to truly cumulative research in this area is the absence of a
theory or framework which is broad enough to address the full range of important
issues, but which is also specific enough to generate empirically testable integrated propositions.   At this early stage in the application of social psychology
to sociolinguistic issues, such an integrated theory could hardly be expected.
As an initial step Taylor and McKirnan (1978) have proposed a theory which attempts to predict the stages involved in the dynamics of relations between groups.
The theory is outlined briefly here because it is one that grows out of two important areas in current social psychological thought: processes of causal attribution (Iteider, 1958; Jones and Davis, 1965; Kelley, 1973), and social comparison
(Suls and Miller, 1977).

The theory builds on important advances in the field of intergroup relations introduced by Tajfel (1978) and Tajfel and Turner (1979).   The present framework posits four stages to relations between groups; stable hierarchically organised intergroup relations, social mobility,   consciousness raising, competitive intergroup relations.   In a more detailed discussion of the theory 'paternalistic'
(Van der Berghe, 1967) intergroup relations such as feudal, caste and slave social
structures are discussed.   However, for the present purpose discussion is limited

to group relations typified by social class and those of ethnolinguistic minority groups which are the focus of recent attention in current sociolinguistics.

Stage 1: Stable hierarchically organised intergroup relations
This arbitrary starting point represents the traditional social stratification that is associated with ethnolinguistic diversity.   As was pointed out by several of the papers in this section, group status is fundamental to understanding relations between ethnolinguistic groups.   The important theoretical issue to be confronted at Stage 1 is the mechanism by which members of the disadvantaged group come to tolerate, if not accept totally, their disadvantaged position.

One of the keys to this acceptance lies in the fact that disadvantaged group members attribute their status internally;   that is, they take individual responsibility by attributing their position to their own efforts and abilities, or lack of them.   Of course advantaged group members propagate an ideology that reinforces a pattern of attribution and social comparison designed to maintain the existing status hierarchy.   With respect to attribution this entails an ideology which emphasises individual social mobility based on effort and ability.   The same individualism is contained in the social comparison feature of the ideology.   Individuals are encouraged to make comparisons between their own status and that of other individuals.   Viewed as illegitimate are intergroup comparisons which may imply that an individual's status is determined by group membership rather than individual achievement.

At this stage then disadvantaged group members are continuously reinforced for maintaining their status, and accepting responsibility for it.   Such people may learn the language or code of the advantaged group, but not with any belief that this will be accompanied by a change in status.   Rather they will learn the language because it is required in order to survive in the economic, political and social milieu.   As such the motivation will be to acquire a functional use of the advantaged group's language.   So the fact that the acquired speech is non-native like and clearly marked will not be crucial, indeed it serves to reinforce the person's status in the intergroup context.   This leads to the proposition not addressed directly in the papers in this section; namely, that disadvantaged group members in a Stage 1 relationship will not expect nor be motivated to learn the language or code of the advantaged group with native-like capacity.

Stage 2: Social mobility
At this stage individual members of the disadvantaged group, in search of a more positive social identity, attempt to pass into the advantaged one.   However, only a selected few members of the disadvantaged group attempt a passing strategy. Attempts at individual social mobility are only made by those few members of the disadvantaged group who have a relatively high status within the disadvantaged group, and who have sufficient contact with the advantaged group to make, on an individual basis, realistic social comparisons with members of the advantaged group.

Such individuals are highly motivated to earn acceptance by the advantaged group. Cherry, in her paper notes that status is a barrier to learning another group's language.   The present analysis leads to the opposite prediction when the intergroup situation is at Stage 2.   The prediction here is that disadvantaged group members, but only a select sample of them, because they make internal attributions for their status, will be highly motivated to learn the language of the advantaged group with the expectation of a rise in social status.   Indeed, unlike at Stage 1, the aim will be to acquire the language with native-like proficiency.   As well, Clément refers to the present Stage 2 formulations as one of two major opposing forces which motivate the individual to become an accepted member of the other group.

Stage 3: Consciousness raising

Attempts at social mobility by certain key disadvantaged group members are not always successful.   Members of the advantaged groups have vested interests in the passing process.   Promoting a limited amount of passing serves two functions. First, it usurps human resources from the disadvantaged group with the hope that this will be put to use in strengthening the advantaged group's position.   Second, a limited amount of passing provides others with visible evidence that the ideology based on internal attribution and individualistic social comparison has some reality.   Those few disadvantaged group members who do pass, assimilate to the advantaged group in the extreme.   Linguistically this would be manifested in terms of total speech convergence (Giles, 1978; Giles and Powesland, 1975) as when members of one ethnolinguistic group adopt the language of another and attempt to erase all evidence that might link the person to the former group.

Those disadvantaged individuals who fail to pass, or are not permitted access to the advantaged group, experience dramatically altered perceptions of social stratification.   They no longer attribute their disadvantaged status internally; rather they attribute their status to external causes, more specifically they attribute responsibility to the injustice of the system controlled by members of the advantaged group, not their own ability and effort.

Unsuccessful attempts at passing make it clear that a rise in status cannot be accomplished individually but must arise from an increase in the status of the disadvantaged group as a whole.   As a first step then these key individuals attempt to persuade all members of the disadvantaged group that (a) their status is collectively defined; (b) that from intergroup comparisons their group's status is illegitimate; and (c) that collective action is required.

Consciousness raising involves a shift in perception from a belief in a system of stratification which is individually based to one where members of a particular ethnolinguistic group perceive that they share a common fate, a common set of objectives and share an externally based attribution for the group's status in comparison with other groups.   This transformation of individuals into a collectivity will be largely mediated through language.

A number of examples can be found in the papers in this section.   The refusal of foreign workers to learn the host society's language may well be motivated by the desire to solidify their own collective identity in response to perceived injustice toward the group (Hinnenkamp).   Clément proposes that members of a language community will be influenced by two opposing forces.   The present framework proposes that these opposing forces will be evidenced at different stages.   The first, a desire to become an accepted member of the other group, has already been discussed as operating at Stage 2.   The opposing force, fear of assimilation, is a group process whereby there is active avoidance of learning or using the language of a dominant group.   As such it is a Stage 3 process where group solidarity is generated as response to the frustrations of not being granted access to the dominant group.

Finally, McKirnan and Hamayan describe a number of structural changes to a community's language norms which may be the outgrowth of intergroup relations at Stage 3.   Specifically from their formulations it might be inferred that as the consciousness raising process progresses it will be reflected in language norms which have a narrow range, high distinctiveness and extreme evaluation.

Stage 4: Competitive intergroup relations

Group solidarity growing out of the consciousness raising process is now manifested in terms of collective action in competition with the advantaged group.   At this stage of course, the social comparisons are intergroup in nature.   The consciousness raising process also has a profound effect on attributions.   Whereas

disadvantaged group members attribute their past and present status <u>externally</u>
they now view their future <u>internally</u>.   That is, the forward looking belief is a
collective one that "it is up to us to determine our own status compared to the
other group".

A number of collective strategies may be used to actualise this new group status,
but all are motivated by a sense of comparative injustice in terms of material and
social rewards (see Tajfel, 1978; Tajfel and Turner, 1979 for the most thorough
review of these strategies).   Collective action may be direct as when members of
a disadvantaged group actively compete with advantaged group members on already
established social values.   These may include certain agreed upon abilities,
training and values for the achievement of status.

The competition may be indirect, as when disadvantaged group members reinterpret
the value of their own characteristics.   This re-evaluation is mediated by the
changes in attribution for the outcomes of intergroup comparison.   The disadvantaged group attributes the low value placed on their physical features, social
values and language to the advantaged group.   As such the evaluation is now
viewed as illegitimate and is therefore replaced with a renewed pride in the
group's own characteristics.

Numerous examples of this process were discussed in the papers in this section.
Platt describes choice of a language in Singapore as at times motivated by the
desire to assert social identity or a renewed pride in one's language.   Clément
notes that certain groups may refuse to learn the other group's language while
taking a new pride in speaking their own for precisely the same reasons.   This
same motivation may explain the language strategy of the foreign workers described
by Hinnenkamp.   However the severe legal restrictions may make it difficult for
these workers to compete effectively with their hosts.

The important assumptions about the relationships among the stages proposed by
Taylor and McKirnan (1978) have been summarised elsewhere by Taylor and Giles
(1979):

> "First the stages are hypothesised to be sequential such that they
> operate in order for any given intergroup context, although the time
> spent at any one stage will vary depending upon a number of situational
> variables.   It is possible, then, for an entire generation to be born
> into an intergroup situation which has developed to Stage 3 and the shift to
> the next stage may vary in time from months to generations.   At no time
> is it possible to skip a stage despite great variations in the time spent
> at the various stages.   Secondly, once Stage 4 has been reached a new
> balance will be achieved between the groups in question.   The balance
> will never be total equality but as long as one group is not totally
> dominant and the other inevitably disadvantaged, "healthy" competition
> will ensue.   If one group becomes continually disadvantaged, the stages
> become cyclical such that there will be a return to Stage 1 and the process
> will begin anew".

(Taylor and Giles, 1979, p.238)

The potential value of the present framework is twofold.   First, the stages cover
a wide range of conditions involving ethnicity and language.   As such it may
serve to organise conceptually the diversity of empirical findings which characterise the field at this early phase.   The papers in this section describe a number
of processes but there is little basis for predicting when any particular process
will be operative.   The present framework makes concrete hypotheses about when
these language strategies become functional.   Attention must now be directed at
putting these hypotheses to the empirical test.

The second value to the framework for the present context is its reliance on the important social psychological processes of attribution and social comparison. The focus on these processes alters the emphasis from a descriptive to an explanatory approach to the study of ethnicity and language. It also paves the way for these and other social psychological concepts both to contribute to and benefit from sociolinguistic enquiry.

REFERENCES

Fishman, J. A. Language and ethnicity, in H. Giles (Ed.) Language ethnicity and intergroup relations. London: Academic Press, 1977

French, J. R. P. and Raven, B. The bases of social power, in D. Cartwright and A. Zander (Eds.) Group dynamics: research and theory. New York: Harper and Row, 1953

Giles, H. Linguistic differentiation between social groups, in H. Tajfel (Ed.) Differentiation between social groups: studies in the social psychology of intergroup relations. London: Academic Press, 1978

Giles, H. and Powesland, P. F. Speech style and social evaluation. London: Academic Press, 1975

Giles, H., Taylor, D. M. and Bourhis, R. Y. Dimensions of Welsh identity. European Journal of Social Psychology, 1977, 7, 165-174

Iteider, F. The psychology of interpersonal relations. New York: John Wiley, 1958

Jones, E. E. and Davis, K. E. From acts to dispositions: the attribution process in person perception, in L. Berkowitz (Ed.) Advances in experimental social psychology (Vol. 2) New York: Academic Press, 1965

Kelley, H. H. The process of causal attribution. American Psychologist, 1973, 28, 107-128

Rosenthal, R. and Jacobson, L. Pygmalion in the classroom: teacher expectation and pupils' intellectual development. New York: Holt, Rinehart and Winston, 1968

Rotter, J. B. Generalised expectancies for internal versus external control of reinforcement. Psychological Monographs, 1966, 80 (1, whole no. 609)

Suls, J. M. and Miller, R. L. Social comparison processes. New York: John Wiley & Sons, 1977

Sarbin, T. R. and Allen, V. L. Role theory, in G. Lindzey and E. Aronson (Eds.) Handbook of social psychology (Vol. 1). Reading, Mass.: Addison-Wesley, 1968

Tajfel, H. Differentiation between social groups: studies in the social psychology of intergroup relations. London: Academic Press, 1978

Tajfel, H. and Turner, J. C. An integrative theory of intergroup conflict, in W. G. Austin and H. Worchel (Eds.) The social psychology of intergroup relations. Monterey: Brooks-Cole, 1979

Taylor, D. M., Bassili, J. and Aboud, F. E. Dimensions of ethnic identity: an example from Quebec. Journal of Social Psychology, 1973, 89, 185-192

Taylor, D. M. and Giles, H. At the crossroads of research into language and ethnic relations, in H. Giles and B. St. Jacques (Eds.) Language and ethnic relations. Oxford: Pergamon, 1979

Taylor, D. M. and McKirnan, D. J. Four stages in the dynamics of intergroup relations. Unpublished manuscript, McGill University, 1978

Van der Berghe, P. C. Race and racism. New York: Wiley, 1967

Zimbardo, P. G. The human choice: individuation, reason and order versus deindividuation, impulse and chaos, in W. J. Arnold and D. Levine (Eds.) Nebraska symposium on motivation. Lincoln: University of Nebraska Press, 1970

Ethnicity and Language as Indicants of Social-Psychological Status

F. Cherry

Department of Psychology, Carleton University, Ottawa, Canada

ABSTRACT

The analysis of social behaviour abounds with examples of the joint impact of personality and situational variables (Cherry and Byrne, 1977). This theme is reit-
erated in broader terms by developmental psychologists who espouse the importance
of both a cognitive-developmental and a social learning approach to the acquisition
of social behaviour. However, it is less often that one sees social psychologists
apply an interactional framework to the acquisition and communication of language.
My intent in the conference presentation is to explore a framework for discussing
language communication which isolates some of the relevant person variables (e.g.
gender, ethnicity, ESL/non-ESL, motivation) and some of the relevant situational
variables (e.g. explicitness of learning environment, teacher behaviour, minority/
majority ratio).

I am particularly interested in applying this analysis to the problems encountered
by non-English speaking children in pre-school environments where no official language instruction is available. Many children in Canada, of pre-school age, will
experience day-time care in either group home or institutional facilities where
attention could be paid in a formal way to language instruction. It is becoming
clearer that English cannot be learned adequately by the informal social contacts
available in these group settings and a study was conducted to explore the extent
of the problem. An extensive observational analysis of 3 and 4 year olds' social
contacts, play preferences and speech behaviour was undertaken in a local pre-
school setting. ESL children (represented by a variety of different ethnic groups)
approached peers less frequently and were contacted less frequently than English-
speaking children. ESL children grouped together creating a similarity effect not
unlike that found by Lucas (1975). They spent more time in solitary play and
watching others. Language communication was, for the most part, inappropriate.
The number of months's attendance at pre-school was positively correlated with appropriate speech behaviour. By 11 months, ESL children were engaging in more appropriate speech behaviour. However, it was still not at the level of their
English-speaking peers. Despite the absence of explicit language learning goals
in the pre-school, some environmental restructuring might well increase the contacts between groups such that formal language instruction would not become necessary. Further research is required to determine whether instruction is necessary
or advisable. Some researchers have focused on the subtractive aspects of second-
language learning for Canada's minority children. It seems possible that as early
as 3 or 4 inroads can be made which foster both bilingualism and biculturalism.

However, this will likely take some joint understanding of the social and cognitive aspects of the language learning and communicating environment.

Key words

Second language learning; ethnicity; status; power; contact hypothesis; osmosis principle

My area of interest in social psychology is neither ethnicity nor language per se. Rather, I am interested in how both of these factors urge us in the direction of examining status and power as the underpinning of human social interaction.   It is now almost commonplace to assert that social psychologists have neglected the study of status and power in human relations.   Less well articulated is how one might approach the study of status and power at the individual psychological level.   It is my intention to use ethnicity and language as two of the aspects of persons which seem to me important in beginning to analyse social-psychological functioning at a sociopolitical level.

In social psychology, variables such as race, ethnicity, language designation, class and gender have been treated as separate classificatory systems.   In studies of a wide range of social behaviours, these classifications place empirical limits on universal laws of social interaction.   They are the background noise in the analysis of variance which interacts with the major variable of concern, namely, some systematic manipulation of the situation.   Even in personality psychology, where one might expect to find a more thoroughgoing treatment of these variables, the 'person' in the person X situation interaction is not some intermixture of these classificatory labels but rather a personality type.   Indeed, it is diffi-cult to find social psychological theory or research which looks at aspects of the person, conceptualised as race, ethnicity, language, gender or class, in more than a demographic or classificatory way.   More and more, I am led to the conclusion that to examine these factors as static characteristics and in isolation from one another is to miss the point of their importance in psychological and social change.

There are, I find, striking similarities in the social psychological research on racial/ethnic, sex and class differences.   Whether one is looking at the body of research on cultural deprivation of North American racial and ethnic minorities, the underachievement of women or the linguistic impoverishment of the lower class, there is a sameness in the assumptions made and conclusions drawn.   Each area re-flects a bipolarity, with one pole as the standard and the other pole as a contrast of inferior functioning.   The bipolar classification may conceal an important con-tinuum of psychological identity.   Differences between the nominal groups are accounted for by arguments of biology and/or socialization with little regard for the broader economic and political importance of these differences.   Each area has provided empirical documentation of group inferiority on which compensatory pro-grammes have been based to move individuals towards the higher status pole of the classification.   Despite these limitations, I feel reasonably confident that re-search is possible which links together classificatory variables not as summary la-bels for biological givens or family socialization practices but as keys to the in-dividual's psychological and social status in daily social interaction.   The task for the social scientist becomes less the separation of distinct problem areas - race relations, sex-role development - but rather the unification of these areas into an understanding of an individual's treatment of and by others in society, using status hierarchy as the principal variable.

As an exercise in this endeavour, I would like to turn to ethnicity and language in more specific terms.   I will limit my comments to second-language acquisition where an understanding of power and status dimensions of social behaviour are par-ticularly important.   I choose this particular context because I have discerned an interesting parallel in the literature on prejudice in social psychology and the literature on second-language acquisition. These two parallel notions are termed the contact hypothesis and the osmosis principle.

THE CONTACT HYPOTHESIS

In the literature on prejudice, Allport (1954) provided an early statement of the notion that intergroup hostility could be modified through intergroup contact.   To be effective in creating positive change, however, the contact should be between groups of equal status.   Furthermore, to prevent contact from intensifying inter-group hostility, group members must cooperate in their pursuit of a shared goal.

In the real world of social interaction in the neighbourhood, the school or the workplace, the results of contact have not always facilitated a reduction in inter-group hostility between diverse racial and/or ethnic groups.   This is perhaps be-cause equal status contact is not just difficult to attain but is rather part of the definition and substance of ethnic minority/majority relations.

A review of the research on the contact hypothesis by Amir (1969) suggests that its utility in a multi-ethnic society has to incorporate a thorough analysis of the contact situation itself.   Amir includes such factors as "the degree of proximity between races", the norms of interracial association, relative status, and so on. What is interesting about this list, and indeed Allport's original list of vari-ables affecting the outcome of contact, is its similarity to factors which are con-sidered important in the successful acquisition of a second-language (Schumann 1978). Schumann suggests that factors of social dominance, integration norms or strategies affect the extent and quality of contact between language groups and hence language acquisition itself.   It seems that whether one is examining ethnic groups or lang-uage groups, the relative status of the group is a key to understanding the psycho-logical functioning of the individual, be this the expression of prejudice or the acquisition of another language.

THE OSMOSIS PRINCIPLE

Although not as formally stated as the contact hypothesis, there is the notion in second-language acquisition that young children exposed to a speech environment will absorb the new language from contact with their peers.   In fact, in many countries formal second-language instruction does not begin until age seven and in-formal contact provides the basic learning mechanism.   Inherent in the osmosis principle is the assumption that young children will have easy access to an envir-onment in which the target second language is spoken.   Once again, we have to assume, as in the case of reducing prejudice, that equal status contact with peers is possible and that factors of ethnicity and/or inability to communicate in the target language do not impede the essential contact upon which we rely for acqui-sition.

What has become apparent in my reading of the bilingualism literature is that chil-dren learning a second language who are not members of an official language group (e.g. French or English in the Canadian context) are at an immediate disadvantage. Whether through voluntary immigration, expulsion, colonization, conquest or indus-trialisation, the lower status of a variety of ethnic groups has come to define the social-psychological context for the individual who shares that ethnic background. Just as inequities in status affect the quality of contact underlying attitude change, these same inequities appear also to impede language acquisition.

While we see the success of early immersion programmes in Canada of a French-Eng-lish nature, these results have not always generalised to lower status unofficial language groups, e.g. Spanish-English programmes for Chicano children.   On this point Haugen and Bloomfield (1976) write:

"We need to think in terms of dominant and nondominant but these are terms
we don't like to talk about because they are ultimately political. ...
Children are sensitive to the pressure of society through their parents
and their peers.   I think the opposition of dominant and nondominant is
so important that I wonder if Lambert's good results may not be accounted
for by the fact that he is teaching the members of a dominant group a
nondominant language which has potentialities of dominance, while in Texas
or New Mexico we are teaching a dominant language to a nondominant group."

The suggestion here is that relative status is a major input to second-language acquisition.   Ethnicity is the classification variable which provides us with one
way in which persons share in the status and power of the society in which they
live.   Chicano children in the United States, as members of a nondominant language
and cultural grouping, fall behind in both their home language and in their second
language.   Non-dominant ethnic minorities run the risk, through second-language
acquisition, of weakening their ties to their first language and first culture.

It would appear that contact between members of dominant and non-dominant groups is
not a sufficient condition for second-language acquisition, particularly among very
young children.   Recently, two studies (Hoffman, 1978; Lucas, 1972) suggest that
the osmosis principle has severe limitations.   Both of these studies found that
preschool children learning English as a second-language interacted significantly
more often with language-similar peers.   Furthermore, Hoffman and I found that
ESL children engaged more frequently in solitary play than children speaking English as a first language.   Experience with the pre-school environment did correlate positively with measures of contact.   However, even after 11 months of pre-
school experience children who were attempting to acquire English did not match
the levels of contact observed among English-speaking preschoolers.

At this early an age (3 to 5 years), it may be that the inability to communicate
in the target language is sufficient to disrupt patterns of contact.   However, at
least by five years of age, I would assume that the child has linked his or her
ethnicity and culture to an understanding of the status implications of that group.
Ethnicity becomes a barrier to contact with the target language group, in this case
English, largely because it summarizes or stands for inferior status.   In Sweden,
for example, where provisions are being made for home language training, one would
assume that the typical lower psychological status of immigrant groups would be
minimised, particularly for the young child.

SUMMARY

I began by stating that my specific interest was neither ethnicity nor language,
but rather how these factors reflect the status of individuals as they attempt to
interrelate in society.   I took as a particular problem area how status (classified as membership in a particular ethnic group) affects the acquisition of a second-language by modifying the quality of contact between groups, and by presenting
individuals with conflicting value systems.   Social psychologists have stressed
the importance of equal status contact in bringing about changes in attitudes and
behaviour between conflicting groups.   A parallel formulation in the area of second-language acquisition, namely, the principle of osmosis, would appear to require
some of the same qualifications as the earlier statement of the contact hypothesis.

With respect to language acquisition, I have intended my comments to show how a
particular classification variable can shed light on the nature of the contact
situation itself.   I have found the taxonomies of Amir, Allport and Schumann helpful in arriving at dimensions of the situation which tell us something about the
quality of contact which can be expected.   Furthermore, these taxonomies alert us
to the psychological dimensions of the classificatory variable.   While terms such
as assimilation, accommodation, separation and/or preservation are often taken to

refer to ethnic/language group strategies for group survival, I think it also possible that these terms will be useful in understanding aspects of the person which
affect social interaction and social communication.   My comments are not intended
to rule out individual cognitive or personality factors as important in second-
language acquisition but only to stress that person factors which carry with them
status implications for social interaction should not be overlooked in the person
X situation analysis.   Finally, my comments are intended to shed some light on
what Giles and Powesland (1975) have already noted as the complex interrelation-
ship between language and ethnic identity.

REFERENCES

Allport, G. W. The nature of prejudice. Reading, Mass.: Addison-Wesley, 1954
Amir, Y. Contact hypothesis in ethnic relations. Psychological Bulletin, 1969,
    11, 319-342
Giles, H. and Powesland, P. F. Speech style and social evaluation.   London:
    Academic Press, 1975
Haugen, E. and Bloomfield, M. (Eds.) Language as a human problem. New York: W.
    W. Norton, 1976.
Hoffman, M. S. A comparison of the social interaction patterns of preschoolers
    who speak English as a first or second language.   Unpublished Honours
    thesis, Carleton University, 1978
Lucas, E. Language in the infant's playground. Multiracial School, 1972, Vol. 1
    no. 3, 18-22; Vol. 2 no. 1, 20-23
Schumann, J. H. Social and psychological factors in second language acquisition,
    in J. Richards, (Ed.) Understanding second and foreign language learning.
    Rowley, Mass.: Newbury House, 1978
Cherry, F. and Byrne, D. Authoritarianism, in T. Blass (Ed.) Personality
    variables in social behavior. New Jersey: Erlbaum Associates, 1977

Ethnicity, Contact and Communicative Competence in a Second Language[1]

R. Clément

School of Psychology, University of Ottawa, Ottawa, Ontario K1N 6N5, Canada

ABSTRACT

A theoretical framework is presented which traces and relates the individual's acquisition, practice and maintenance of communicative competence in a second language to the social/structural characteristics of a community. These characteristics are mediated by a two-stage motivation process hypothesised to impact on fluency in a second language. Such competence will in turn, depending on structural aspects of the milieu, bring about integration or assimilation as social consequences. The implications of this formulation for future research are discussed and specific hypotheses outlined.

Key words

Motivation; communicative competence; integrativeness; fear of assimilation; ethnolinguistic vitality; self-confidence; assimilation; integration; inter-ethnic contact

INTRODUCTION

In the past, inter-ethnic communication has attracted the attention of many researchers, resulting in a variety of theoretical concepts, relations between these concepts and theoretical formulations. The evident relationships existing between phenomena, all pertaining to inter-ethnic communication, are not matched, however, with comparable efforts to integrate the different conceptualisations in one theoretical framework.

Researchers have addressed the issue of individual factors related to second language acquisition and shown the importance of language aptitude and attitudinally based motivation (e.g. Clément 1978; Gardner and Lambert 1959; Gardner and Smythe 1975). Even though these researchers have repeatedly acknowledged the importance of the influence of the milieu on individual processes (e.g. Gardner 1979) this approach has not been extended to include concepts and relationships formally describing the acknowledged linkage. Furthermore, research on second language acquisition has, in the past, considered only individual outcomes such

---

1. The author is grateful to Dr. R. C. Gardner for his comments on a draft of this paper.

as linguistic competence.   It seems likely, however, that members of one community, sharing the same social milieu, might develop comparable levels of fluency in a second language.   The shared outcome might therefore result in collective consequences such as assimilation or cultural isolation of a community, thus influencing the structure of the milieu and through it, individual processes.

Conversely, in research on the influence of the social milieu and the collective consequences of fluency in a second language, little attention is given to individual mediational processes.   Giles, Bourhis and Taylor (1977) have suggested that the influence of social factors on cross-ethnic communication can be described in terms of 'ethnolinguistic vitality'.   Ethnolinguistic vitality is defined by three structural variables: the status of a language in a community, the absolute and relative number of its locutors (demographic characteristics) and the institutional support (e.g. governmental services, schools, mass media) for the language.   Giles and colleagues (1977) have linked ethnolinguistic vitality to Tajfel's (1974) theory of intergroup relations and Giles' (1977) theory of speech accommodation.   No attempt has been made, however, to describe the individual mediational processes linking structural characteristics and linguistic outcome.   The same comment can be made about research on the collective outcome of bilingualism.   Authors such as Comeau (1969) or Lamy (1977, 1978, 1979) have related assimilation, the disappearance of a language in a community, to structural characteristics of a population such as the demographic density of the assimilated group.   Again, little attention is given to the individual processes linking structural characteristics to individual outcomes.   Yet, it seems important in order to evolve from a taxonomy of factors to dynamic processes, to identify and describe the individual mechanisms mediating the influence of the milieu on the individual and collective consequences of inter-ethnic communication.

In the following, I will therefore describe the bases of a framework designed to encompass the theoretical formulations related to social/structural, individual and collective aspects of inter-ethnic communication.   It is necessary beforehand, however, to state an assumption of the model in order to reconcile the scope of the three original formulations.   The bulk of the research on individual processes is aimed at explaining variations in linguistic competence.   In contrast, the other two approaches are much more similar in that they address the broader issue of inter-ethnic communication and relations, thus encompassing a variety of non-linguistic behaviours.   It is therefore assumed here that linguistic competence is but one aspect of inter-ethnic communication which includes, as well, the acquisition of norms, values and patterns of behaviour which are characteristic of the second language culture.   Further, it is assumed that the same processes underlie the acquisition, maintenance and practice of linguistic and paralinguistic skills, now subsumed under the term 'communicative competence'. These assumptions are consistent with Gardner's (1979) recent extension of his framework to include 'paralinguistic' skills as well as recent findings linking individual processes to aspects other than linguistic competence (see Gardner, Smythe, Clément and Gliksman 1976).

TOWARD AN INTEGRATED FRAMEWORK

Research and theory stemming both from sociological and psychological traditions (e.g. Fishman 1977; Giles, Taylor and Bourhis 1977; Taylor, Bassili and Aboud 1973) acknowledge that language is one of the most important dimensions of individual identity.   If this is the case, the status and prestige afforded to a language in a community should have an impact on the individual's inter-ethnic behaviour.   Such status and prestige could be described in terms of Giles (1977) concept of ethnolinguistic vitality.

As described before, ethnolinguistic vitality refers to structural characteris-

tics such as status, demographic representation and institutional support pertaining to a language and its locutors in a given community.   In a multi-ethnic setting it would be expected that it is the language of the group showing the strongest ethnolinguistic vitality which is likely to predominate.   Thus, members of
non-dominant groups would be expected to devalue their belonging to their mother-
tongue group in favour of the dominant group's language and culture.   There should
therefore, be a direct relationship between the ethnolinguistic vitality of a culture and its attractiveness to members of out-groups.

The process might, however, be more complex.   Cummins (1978, 1979) has suggested
that, at the linguistic level, adequate knowledge of a first language might facilitate the acquisition of a second language.   Cummins (1979) further traces the
deficit observed among many second language students to societal conditions which
are adverse to the 'potency' of their first language.   At the social level, this
'interdependence hypothesis' implies that the acquisition and practice of the
skills necessary to interact with the second-language speaking group might require,
a priori, a thorough identification with the first language group.   This latter
condition would be fulfilled only if the first language group itself is characterised by a reasonable measure of ethnolinguistic vitality.   To this point, only
tangential evidence exists in support of the social corollary of the 'interdependence' hypothesis.   Berry, Kalin and Taylor (1977) report a positive relationship
between confidence in one's own group and attitude toward bilingualism and out-
groups.   Clément, Gardner and Smythe (1977a) report factor analytic evidence
suggesting that Francophone students' attitudes toward the self and French Canadians are positively related to attitude toward Anglophones.   Although not conclu-
sive, these results suggest the existence of a dynamic process, still to be explored, linking ethnic identity to ethnolinguistic vitality.

In the proposed framework, ethnolinguistic vitality does not have a direct impact
on individual and collective outcomes.   Rather, it initiates an individual motivational process which mediates the influence of the milieu on communicative competence.   This motivational process is depicted in Figure 1.

The conditions prevailing in the milieu (i.e. the relative ethnolinguistic vitality of the groups present) will influence what has been labelled here 'Primary Motivational Process'.   This process consists in the operation of two antagonistic
forces: the desire to become an accepted member of the other culture ('integrativeness') and the fear that such belonging might result in the loss of the first
language and culture (fear of assimilation).   Under different names, 'integrativeness' has been the foundation stone of much theorising in the area of second
language acquisition.   From the early Gardner and Lambert (1959) study to the
most recent formulations (e.g. Gardner, Gliksman and Smythe 1978; Gardner 1979;
Clément 1978) the links between the individual's affective predispositions toward
the second language group, his motivation to learn the language and his linguistic
and paralinguistic skills have been empirically documented.   'Integrativeness'
represents the individual's affective predispositions toward the second language
group and constitutes here the positive basis of the Primary Motivational Process:
the willingness to become like valued members of an attractive community.

'Fear of assimilation' is a relatively new concept.   It represents the negative
affective basis of the primary motivational process and corresponds to the fear
that loss of the first culture and language might result from learning the second
language.   Taylor and Simard (1975) first suggested that such fear might be an
impediment to cross-ethnic communication.   At the empirical level, Taylor, Meynard and Rheault (1977) found a negative relationship between fear of assimilation
and self-ratings of fluency in a second-language.   Clément (1978) reports factor
analytic evidence suggesting the existence of a negative relationship between fear
of assimilation and affectively-based motivation.   These results suggest the ex-

istence of a force which would moderate the influence of the well documented integrative motive on competence in a second language.

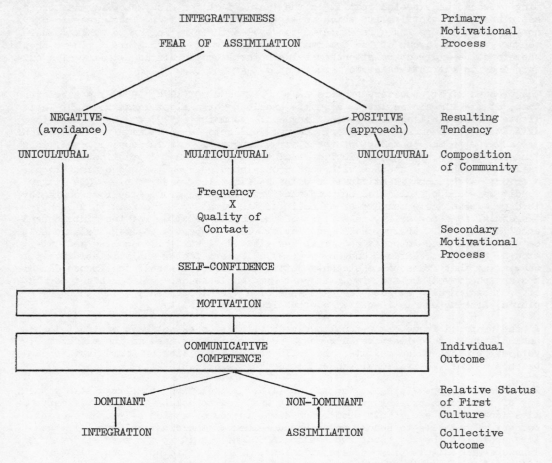

INTEGRATIVENESS	Primary Motivational
FEAR OF ASSIMILATION	Process
NEGATIVE (avoidance) · · · POSITIVE (approach)	Resulting Tendency
UNICULTURAL · MULTICULTURAL · UNICULTURAL	Composition of Community
Frequency X Quality of Contact	Secondary Motivational Process
SELF-CONFIDENCE	
MOTIVATION	
COMMUNICATIVE COMPETENCE	Individual Outcome
DOMINANT · NON-DOMINANT	Relative Status of First Culture
INTEGRATION · ASSIMILATION	Collective Outcome

Fig. 1   Schematic representation of individual mediational
         processes

As mentioned earlier, important determinants of these two forces are the relative ethnolinguistic vitality of the first and second cultural groups.   Hypothetically 'integrativeness' might be related to the attractiveness or ethnolinguistic vitality of the second culture.   Fear of assimilation, on the other hand, might be a negative function of the vitality of the first culture.   Whether the resulting tendency is positive or negative would be determined by a delicate balance, here expressed as a subtractive relationship, of the respective statuses of the first and second culture in a given community.   This would be consistent with the 'interdependence hypothesis' described earlier.

In unicultural settings, the tendency resulting from the Primary Motivational Process would be directly associated with the individual's motivation to acquire competence in the second language.   It would be expected that those for whom fear of assimilation predominates would be less motivated to acquire and eventually less competent in communicating with the second language group than those who manifest a relatively high level of 'integrativeness'.

The importance of this affectively-based process (here the Primary Motivational Process) has been repeatedly demonstrated in settings where there is a clear predominance of one culture (e.g. Gardner and Lambert 1972; Gardner and Smythe 1975).

In multicultural settings, recent evidence suggests that another process, here the secondary motivational process, might be operative. Gardner (1979) reports that, in bilingual settings in Canada, the anxiety experienced by the student when using a second language, is a better predictor of competence than attitudes or motivation. Clément and colleagues (1977a) found that among Francophone students in Montreal, a factor analytic cluster reflecting the individual's self-confidence in his ability to communicate in English evidenced a stronger association with indices of English achievement than the factor reflecting his attitudinal predispositions toward the second-language group. The results of Gardner (1979) and Clément and colleagues (1977a) therefore support the existence of an additional motivational process related to the self-confidence experienced by the individual when communicating in a second language. Such self-confidence appears, furthermore, to result from frequent contacts with members of the other ethnic group.

Frequency of contact should not, however, be the only aspect influencing self-confidence. It seems evident that the quality or pleasantness of such contact is a relevant dimension. Indeed, authors have repeatedly stressed the importance of this aspect for the outcome of inter-ethnic contact programmes (e.g. Amir 1969; Cook 1970; Wrightsman 1972). Whether the qualitative aspects of contact are directly related to aspects of the situation such as competition or intimacy or the result of a more complex mechanism involving prior expectations remains to be investigated. In any case, it seems reasonable, within the context of the present framework, to hypothesise that quality of contact would be directly related to self-confidence. Furthermore, on a logical basis, it would be expected that self-confidence would be an interactive function of the frequency and quality of contact: a high frequency of pleasant contacts will have a more positive outcome than a low frequency. Conversely, much unpleasant contact will have a more negative effect than a little contact.

Aspects of inter-ethnic contact in multicultural settings would, therefore, be crucial to the development of self-confidence and, ultimately, communicative competence. This does not detract, however, from the importance given to the Primary Motivational Process. In fact, if the development of self-confidence hinges on aspects of the contact situation, the individual's willingness to enter such contact might be dependent upon the resultant tendency from the Primary Motivational Process. Clément, Gardner and Smythe (1977b) and Desrochers and Gardner (1978) report a positive relationship between the individual's attitudes toward the second language group and the frequency with which he will make contact with its members in the context of a bi-cultural excursion. Thus, in multicultural settings, an individual's motivation would be determined by both the Primary and Secondary Motivational Processes operating in sequence.

In summary, the motivation to acquire communicative competence in a second language would, therefore, be a function of self-confidence and/or of the tendency resulting from the Primary Motivational Process, depending on the context. Communicative competence per se is, in turn, a direct function of motivation which mediates the primary and secondary processes. As mentioned earlier, the importance given to motivation as a central concept has already been documented in relation to numerous linguistic and paralinguistic outcomes, in a variety of settings. The mediational function of motivation has also been demonstrated for Canadian Anglophones living in unicultural and bicultural settings (Gardner 1979) and Canadian Francophones living in a bicultural milieu (Gardner and Smythe 1976).

The motivational process, taken as a whole, is heavily influenced by characteristics of the setting in which the individual lives. As such, the predispositions and competencies of locutors sharing a common milieu should evidence some resemblance and thus, influence the collective outcome of communicative competence.

Numerous authors have addressed the issue of the cognitive consequences of bilingualism (e.g. Cummins 1978, 1979; Lambert 1978; Peal and Lambert 1962). Few, however, have considered the social consequences. Two social outcomes of competence in a second language seem possible: either members of a community will participate in two cultures (integrate) or lose their first language and culture and join exclusively the other group (assimilate). Previous research suggests that the occurrence of either outcome is dependent upon structural characteristics of the community.

Studying the relationship between bilingualism and ethnic identity, Lamy (1977, 1978, 1979) reports Canadian data which suggest that this relationship is indeed tenuous. Rather, he argues, it is contact with members of the other group expressed in terms of the demographic characteristics of a community which effects a change in ethnolinguistic identification. In line with Lamy's findings, integration would result when members of a dominant group acquire communicative competence in a second language. The same skills acquired by members of a non-dominant group would, however, result in their assimilation into the dominant group's language and culture. That is, communicative competence should be directly related to integration or assimilation, depending on the relative ethnolinguistic vitality of the first and second language cultures.

This last step concludes the description of my proposed framework and, at the same time, brings us back to the start: the influence of the milieu on the Primary Motivational Process. Communities characterised by different levels of integration or assimilation should influence differentially their members' integrativeness and fear of assimilation.

CONCLUSION

The elaboration of a framework characterised by greater generality and precision makes blatant the definitional imprecisions of the original formulations and increases markedly the number of undocumented hypotheses. From the point of view of theoretical advancement, this hopefully encourages integration and conceptual clarity in future formulations. At this point, it seems that the unanswered questions could be classified into one of two categories. The first category includes questions about the boundaries of the framework, as formulated. Most of the relationships between the processes and outcomes are hypothetical. I have tried to state these hypotheses as clearly as possible when they were appropriate.

The second category of questions concerns the scope of the present framework. Evan though it attempts an integration of much of the research related to social and affective aspects of inter-ethnic communication, it would seem that two other fields of research could be meaningfully integrated with the present theorising. The first of these consists in the study of the cognitive mechanisms involved in second language acquisition. From the elaboration of the concept of language aptitude by Carroll (1962), hypothesised cognitive constructs have grown both in terms of their number and the complexity of their inter-relationships (see, for example, Bialystok and Fröhlich 1977; Cummins 1976; Krashen 1977). This field of research has evolved in a parallel manner to that of social factors. It seems obvious that a thorough understanding of inter-ethnic communication would require a unified framework.

A second line of research which could enrich our understanding of inter-ethnic communication is related to its developmental aspects. In this case, although psychologists have been interested in cognitive-developmental aspects, no one, to my knowledge, has addressed the issue of social-developmental aspects as they relate to second language acquisition.   Yet, it seems obvious that careful observation of the evolution of the processes depicted here would provide us with valuable data on their specific dynamics.   Furthermore, assuming common processes, this type of study could also tell us about the socio-affective bases of first language acquisition, a topic which remains virtually unexplored.

We might find, after answering these questions and unifying the field, that little is left of the original framework.   Although possible through experimental disconfirmation, such an outcome is even more likely if we first address, as we should, the fundamental epistemological issue of the language in which we cast our theoretical formulations.   Do the concepts of attitude and motivation as they now stand, with their specific historical and cultural origins allow us to describe fully and precisely the phenomena we observe?   Are causal sequences subtle enough to account fully for the intricate processes we postulate?   As suggested by the articles included in a recent issue of the Journal of Personality and Social Psychology (1978, 36, (3)), these meta-theoretical questions are coming to the forefront and proper answers seem to be essential to the development of the field.

REFERENCES

Amir, Y. Contact hypothesis in ethnic relations. Psychological Bulletin, 1969, 71, 319-342

Berry, J. W., Kalin, R. and Taylor, D. M. Attitudes à l'égard du multiculturalisme et des groupes ethniques au Canada. Ministère des approvisionnements et services du Canada, 1977

Bialystok, H. and Fröhlich, M.   Aspects of second language learning in classroom settings. Working Papers on Bilingualism, 1977, 13, 1-26

Carroll, J. B. The prediction of success in intensive language training, in R. Glaser (Ed.) Training research and education. Pittsburgh: University of Pittsburgh Press, 1962

Clément, R. Motivational characteristics of Francophones learning English. Québec City: International Center for Research on Bilingualism, Laval University, 1978

Clément, R, Gardner, R. C. and Smythe, P. C. Inter-ethnic contact: attitudinal consequences. Canadian Journal of Behavioural Sciences, 1977, 9, 205-215 (b)

Clément, R., Gardner, R. C. and Smythe, P. C. Motivational variables in second language acquisition: a study of Francophones learning English. Canadian Journal of Behavioural Sciences, 1977, 9, 123-133 (a)

Comeau, P. A. Acculturation ou assimilation: technique d'analyse et tentative de mesure chez les Franco-ontariens. Canadian Journal of Political Science 1969, 2, 158-172

Cook, S. W. Motives in a conceptual analysis of attitude-related behavior, in W. J. Arnold and D. Levine (Eds.) Nebraska Symposium on Motivation. Lincoln, Nebraska: University of Nebraska Press, 1970

Cummins, J. The influence of bilingualism on cognitive growth: a synthesis of research findings and exploratory hypotheses. Working Papers on Bilingualism, 1976, 9, 1-43

Cummins, J. Educational implications of mother tongue maintenance in minority language groups. The Canadian Modern Language Review, 1978, 34, 395-416

Cummins, J. Bilingualism and educational development in Anglophone and minority Francophone groups in Canada. Interchange, 1979, 9, 40-51

Desrochers, A. and Gardner, R. C. Cross-cultural contact: correlates and consequences. Research Bulletin No. 455, Department of Psychology, University of Western Ontario, London, Canada, 1978

Fishman, J. A. Language and ethnicity, in H. Giles (Ed.) Language, ethnicity and intergroup relations. London: Academic Press, 1977

Gardner, R. C. Social psychological aspects of second language acquisition, in
        H. Giles and R. St. Clair (Eds.) Language and social psychology,
        Oxford: Basil Blackwell, 1979

Gardner, R. C., Gliksman, L. and Smythe, P. C. Attitudes and behaviour in second
        language acquisition: a social psychological interpretation. Canadian
        Psychological Review, 1978, 19, 173-186

Gardner, R. C. and Lambert, W. E. Motivational variables in second-language acqui-
        sition. Canadian Journal of Psychology, 1959, 13, 266-272

Gardner, R. C. and Lambert, W. E. Attitudes and motivation in second language
        learning. Rowley: Newbury House, 1972

Gardner, R. C. and Smythe, P. C. Second language acquisition: a social psycholo-
        gical approach. Research Bulletin no. 332, Department of Psychology,
        University of Western Ontario, 1975

Gardner, R. C. and Smythe, P. C. The role of attitudes in acquiring the language
        of another ethnic group. Language Research Group Research Bulletin no.
        7, Department of Psychology, University of Western Ontario, London,
        Ontario, Canada, 1976

Gardner, R. C., Smythe, P. C., Clément, R. and Gliksman, L. Second-language
        learning: a social psychological perspective. The Canadian Modern
        Language Review, 1976, 32, 198-213

Giles, H. Social psychology and applied linguistics: towards an integrative
        approach. ITL: Review of Applied Linguistics, 1977, 33, 27-42

Giles, H., Bourhis, R. Y. and Taylor, D. M. Towards a theory of language in eth-
        nic group relations, in H. Giles (Ed.) Language, ethnicity and inter-
        group relations. London: Academic Press, 1977

Giles, H., Taylor, D. M. and Bourhis, R. Y. Dimensions of Welsh identity. Euro-
        pean–Journal of Social Psychology, 1977, 7, 165-174

Krashen, S. Adult second language acquisition and learning: a review of theory
        and applications. Unpublished manuscript, University of Southern
        California 1977

Lambert, W. E. Cognitive and socio-cultural consequences of bilingualism. The
        Canadian Modern Language Review, 1978, 34, 537-547

Lamy, P. Education and "survivance" French language education and linguistic
        assimilation. Paper presented at the annual meeting of the Western
        Association of Sociology and Anthropology, Calgary, Alberta, 1977

Lamy, P. Bilingualism and identity, in I. Haas and W. Shaffir (Eds.) Shaping
        identity in Canadian society. Canada: Prentice Hall, 1978

Lamy, P. Language and ethnolinguistic identity: the bilingualism question.
        International Journal of Sociology of Language, 1979, 20, 23-36

Peal, E. and Lambert, W. E. The relation of bilingualism to intelligence.
        Psychological Monographs, 1962, 76, 546

Tajfel, H. Social identity and intergroup behaviour. Social Science Informa-
        tion, 1974, 13, 65-93

Taylor, D. M., Bassili, J. N. and Aboud, F. E. Dimensions of ethnic identity:
        an example from Québec. Journal of Social Psychology, 1973, 89, 185-
        192

Taylor, D. M., Meynard, R. and Rheault, E. Threat to ethnic identity and second-
        language learning, in H. Giles (Ed.) Language, ethnicity and inter-
        group relations. London: Academic Press, 1977

Taylor, D. M. and Simard, L. M. Social interaction in a bilingual setting.
        Psychologie Canadienne, 1975, 16, 240-254

Wrightsman, L. S. Social psychology in the seventies, First edition.
        Belmont, California: Wadsworth Publishing Company, 1972

Social Grammar, Social Psychology and Linguistics

M. C. Grayshon

University of Nottingham School of Education, University Park,
Nottingham NG7 2RD, U.K.

ABSTRACT

Social Grammar of language is concerned with the total communication process which
it sees as human behaviour; a social activity modified and moderated by individuals' activity. How are the various signal levels used by individuals to maintain
themselves in society? We look for universals in the functioning of society and
not in the forms of language as forms are the product of functions. The various
signal levels move from word and word order, via items usually referred to as
paralinguistic, through to body movements received as visual signals. Different
language groups use different levels for the same purpose and the same level for
different purposes. The social problems caused by this difference in use is
illustrated by examples across Nigerian languages and the English language, and
also in sub-groups of the English language.

Key words

Grammar; social psychology; linguistics; social grammar; body language

INTRODUCTION

The fundamental view of language that is the basis of SOCIAL GRAMMAR is that
human communication is both a social activity modified by individual behaviour and
an individual activity modified by social activity. It is a behaviour pattern
based upon physiological activities which both allows a range of choice of signals
and at the same time limits this choice of signals. As language is a human behaviour pattern the manipulation of forms is only a small, but essential, part of
the process.

The reasons for signalling are fundamental to an individual's life and living.
The purpose behind signalling is to inform people, constrain people, persuade
people, order people, refuse people, etc. and this is, of course, an interactive
process. As I attempt to influence you, so you are trying to influence me. The
society in which I live, and also the sub-society in which I live limits the
choice of signals which is open to me and also limits the choice of actions which
I have. I may know what I want to do with my language behaviour, I may have all
the personal language resources to do it but my position in society precludes many
of my choices. This is tied in to status: the higher my status the more options,
the lower the status the less the options.

The communication process has produced a great many forms, traditionally linguistics has been concerned with the defining and analysing the forms and the relations of forms to each other.   Even more limiting has been the concentration on words and word order.   This has produced descriptions of languages but these descriptions are only comparable across languages if languages use the same signalling systems for carrying similar messages.   If the information to be passed moves from the signalling system of one language to another signalling system in another language then language descriptions according to form are useless.   If, as well, different messages are sent using the same signalling system, there is more room for confusion.   Even more, if the messages are sent by a system below the awareness of the sender and receiver and interpreted at this sub-awareness level, then there is danger of misinterpretation of the message sent; and consequential unfavourable deductions being made about the social behaviour of the other person.

Traditionally linguistics ('is' linguistics) has been concerned with the describing of forms and is very necessary.   But then there comes the stage of asking how these forms are used, in what situations, in what way and by what people ('does' linguistics).   This, I suggest, covers both sociolinguistics and psycholinguistics and is wider than both.   The <u>social grammar of language</u> is an attempt at a macro theory and in such a short paper any description is impossible.   However, a brief attempt to list one or two salient points is made.

LEVELS OF COMMUNICATION

First of all we need a very wide definition of 'language' to limit it to words and word order is cutting out far too many information sources.   I suggest that we send messages by using the whole of the human body and we can make an initial breakdown as follows:

For the moment these codes can be shown as follows:

> LANGUAGE (T)   The total communication system
> LANGUAGE (U)   Utterances: which subdivide into:
>
>   Language (l) - lexis (words)
>   Language (s) - syntax (word order)
>   Language (p) - phonetics
>   Language (i.s.) - paralinguistic features
>   i - tone (voice movement up and down)
>   ii - pitch (tone contrast)
>   iii - loudness and softness
>   iv - emphasis (loud and soft contrast)
>   v - rhythm
>   vi - timbre (open/closed throat)
>   vii - pause
>   viii - permutations and combinations of these.
> LANGUAGE (F)   Facial expressions and head movements
> LANGUAGE (B)   Body movement and posture
>   i - body posture
>   ii - arm positions
>   iii - leg positions
>   iv - body space utilisation.

(Writing is a sub-category with its own rules and problems depending upon whether it is phonetic/alphabetic or ideographic).

This range of signals is based upon a limited number of physiological dyads that are linked in a very simplex way in the human nervous system:

	Initiator of Signal	Receiver of Signal
1.	Sound/silence	Hearing (ears)
2.	Movement/non-movement	Sight (eyes)
3.	Body contact	Body contact (all over)
4.	Smell (all over)	Olfactory (nose)
5.	Taste	Taste (mouth)

Two things to notice here are <u>first</u> that the complex messages from the initiator are received (except for 3.) by one single apparatus, so that, for example, all the visual signals coming from all over the initiator's body (plus the environment) are taken in and decoded by the eye and what lies behind it; <u>second</u> that the child learns to communicate with 3., 4., and 5. initially and then probably with 2. and almost simultaneously with (i.s.) from 1.   Before it starts refining communication by using the codes of word and word order it is performing many of the communication processes and operating many of the relationships in the society to which it belongs.

We see then, that we have a whole range of signals to choose from to pass a message. These signals can be used alone or in a variety of combinations.   There is an order of priority in English: normally we use levels (1) + (s) + (i.s.) + (F) + (B).   However, when there is contradiction between the signalling levels then the reverse order gives the priority of correctness, i.e. if there is contradiction between (1) and (s) on the one hand and (i.s.) on the other, then the (i.s.) signal gives the correct information.   If there is contradiction between (s) and (1) on the one hand and (F) + (B) on the other, then (F) and (B) give the correct information.   These levels have a great deal to do with indicating status and emotion and are learnt by the child before the (1) and (s) levels.

At the present state of my research I suggest that these priorities are true of all languages.   This would be logical because children are first reassured by tactile information levels (i.e. being cuddled, fed on the breast - or its substitute, made comfortable at the other end) from birth and for the first months of life.

However, one of the major findings is that all languages do not use the same signalling levels in the same way to carry similar messages.   That where some languages use lexis and syntax (words and word order) others use the (i.s.) levels and others use the Language B and F levels.

There would seem to be some physiological imperatives present which determine basic patterns.   The most that can be said here is that there are at least two major groups of languages at each end of a continuum.   One group has short vowels, equal accentuation and the change of pitch over a VCV cluster gives a change of meaning; this change of pitch is then added to a terraced falling tone over a sentence and the return to the basic frequency of the individual voice.   This is called a <u>Lexical semantic tonal language</u>.   The other group has long and short vowels with the associated strong and weak stress.   It uses varieties of change of pitch over a sentence, or phrase, to change meaning, and it uses the plagual and perfect cadences at the end of the utterance to indicate the end of the speaker's utterance unit.   This is called a <u>Syntactic semantic tonal language</u>.   There are three things to note about these two groups:

i. the information carried in (i.s.) in the second group moves up to (1) and (s) in the first group, and/or down to (F) and (B).
ii. that it is very difficult indeed for people in one group to gain a fluent mastery of languages in the other group.
iii. the basic make-up of these languages, the operating at the levels other than (1) and (s) seems to be laid down in early childhood.

How far these differences are widely spread amongst Nigerian and other African
languages has yet to be discovered.   Whether they are at either end of a continuum of languages or in strict opposition remains to be discovered.   (As there is
one language which seems to have redundant lexical tone the former seems possible).

CONSEQUENCES

The consequences of these discoveries and the theory derived from them and other
works has a number of applications.   In this paper there is reference only to
some discoveries which lead to grave disquiet for the social consequence of social
interaction for people whose languages belong to the two different groups.

The original work (Grayshon, 1977) gave evidence for the conclusions above.   In a
further project in Nigeria in 1975/76 funded by the Nigerian Government the writer
carried out other experiments.   Amongst these was one where a recording of a message in English was made twice.   Each time the word and word order remained exactly the same but the (i.s.) was changed.   In the first recording the speaker
was clearly rebuffing the listener, giving her the brush off;   in the second recording the speaker was very apologetic and wished to placate the hearer.   The
message was played to 251 students in secondary school and teacher colleges in
Nigeria where the medium of instruction was English.   The results were very disturbing: 92 (36.65%) heard no difference between the two recordings;   a further
152 (60.55%) heard a difference but gained no meaning.   Only 7 understood the
difference.   Thirty-nine languages were involved and four institutions used.   The
Igbo language is known, by 'is' linguistics, as a terraced tone language, i.e.
over a sentence the voice comes down the scale starting high and finishing low.
Meaning is carried by change of tone inside a word so a VCV cluster can have nine
meanings according to whether the Vs are said high, low or in the middle.   However in English one form of the falling tone is used to give orders;   orders can
be given only to low status people.   If a low status person gives an order to a
high status person, then social judgements are made that the speaker is 'rude',
'impertinent' etc.   When a low status person is giving instruction to a high status person in English at the request of the high status person, the order form
must not be used.   In Igbo it is permissible for a low status person to use an
instructional form when asked for instructions by an inferior.   So when I was
given a young person as a messenger to take me in the car, she used the straightforward English instructional form, "Turn left", "Turn right", etc.   This was
said with mother tongue interference at the (i.s.) level where here terracing
came in, and to the English ear she was using the order form of (i.s.) so we have
a junior giving orders in an abrupt form to a senior ...   "How rude!"   Multiply
this over the whole range of communication and you have a large contribution to a
racial stereotype of a bumptious, rude, impertinent people.   (The full description of these two experiments is being prepared for publication).

In Grayshon (1973) it was shown that the Merkwen have a word 'nga' which appears
as 'No' in dictionaries.   However, Merkwens use the single word 'nga' in many
situations in English where 'No' is unlikely to be used and where a whole series
of politeness words and phrases are used.   Merkwen moves this politeness signal
down to (B).   Our Merkwen student had a number of very unhappy incidents in his
first weeks in the U.K.

Confusion at the (i.s.) level easily occurs inside English because we assume that
sub-cultural groups use (i.s.) patterns for similar messages.   The child from the
home where mother uses the falling tone (used for orders only in other sub-groups)
on most occasions together with the order words (i.e. no politeness words).   However the child is loved and cherished and takes this tone to be the norm for conversations.   The first day at school the infant teacher, wishing to reassure and
comfort, uses the rising inflection and also includes politeness words such as

'Please' and forms from (s) level. Our child has rarely, if ever, met this way of behaving and wanders around somewhat lost. At the end of the day the teacher says to a colleage, "... That little Kevan is backward, he lacks language experience". He does not: he lacks <u>her</u> language experience.

There is another area of possible confusion that is shown up by Social Grammar analysis. The Jukun is a highly authoritative tribe and when the Chief says do this or that, the person spoken to has the choice of doing, or going away and not doing and hoping that the Chief will forget. In the adjacent Yala tribe there is a much more democratic situation: it is possible to refuse the superior by offering a valid reason, "... I cannot hoe your yam patch because my father expects me to hoe his". This is taken as reasonable – the refusal is not directed at the order-giver, but at the action. What happens when the Jukun and Yala children are in the tribally mixed school with a Jukun/yala teacher? The jukun teacher judges the Yala child to be wilful, disobedient, etc. The Yala child judges the Jukun teacher to be oppressive etc. The Jukun child may be over-passive in a child-centred learning situation; the Yala teacher thought to be a softy and indecisive by the Jukun child. As teaching is currently conducted in English which allows for all possible forms of social relationship, there is possibility of even more confusion.

In this research twelve languages were looked at in an introductory survey. They fell in to the two groups, but it soon became obvious that inside the groups there are many differences of uses of signalling levels. It is possible that languages will group themselves together according to how they function, how they <u>use</u> the various codes to carry information. This then becomes of direct relevance to social psychologists and to sociolinguists because it suggests that many current descriptions of language use are culture bound, and that if we wish to compare across cultures we need a set of universals which are available across all cultures and sub-cultures. It is the hope of the author that Social Grammar has laid down the broad outlines of these.

REFERENCES

Grayshon, M. C. On saying no. <u>Nottingham Linguistic Circular Vol.iii</u>, No.1, November 1973

Grayshon, M. C. Towards a social grammar of language, in <u>Contributions to Sociolinguistic Series</u>. No.18. The Hague: Mouton, 1977

Language Norms and Perceptions of Ethno-Linguistic Group Diversity

D. J. McKirnan* and E. V. Hamayan**

**Department of Psychology, University of Illinois at Chicago Circle, Box 4348,
Chicago, Illinois 60680, U.S.A.
**Bilingual Education Service Center, North West Educational Cooperative,
500 S, Dwyer, Arlington Heights, Illinois 60005, U.S.A.*

ABSTRACT

This paper outlines a general research and conceptual framework for studying perceptions of and reactions to ethno-linguistic diversity. In particular, a psychologically based model of social norms is presented, and discussed vis-à-vis its heuristic value for the study of speech norms and inter-group perceptions. This model,
which attempts to integrate both social psychological and larger group processes,
views norms as consisting of an overall cognitive structure, and a socially situated "focus". The specific components of this model are discussed in light of existing data on normatively regulated language behaviour.

Key words

Ethnicity; attitudes; social norms; conflict

INTRODUCTION

An increasingly important issue in social psychology concerns the stable conceptions or "rules" we use cognitively to organise and generate expectancies toward
our complex, stratified social environments. An integral feature of this is perceptions of social groups; the basis for differentiating among and assigning characteristics to the members of groups, and the personal and social significance of
such distinctions, are fundamental to individual and collective social behaviour
(Tajfel 1974). Language is central to these distinctions in that it has the social and personal importance, visibility and flexibility to underlie a range of social categorizations (Giles, Bourhis and Taylor 1977). However, both the general
social significance of language and its effects on intergroup relations are often
discussed in isolation from basic social psychological principles (see, however,
Giles and Powesland 1975; Taylor 1977). The present paper thus outlines a general social psychological model of the identification of social diversity, wherein
language is viewed as one of many domains of behaviour underlying perceptions of
group differences. The individual's need for a stable conceptual organisation of
the environment is seen as underlying the different components of the model.

The social psychological study of groups has been hampered by several factors.
First is a conceptual malintegration between the microscopic study of individuals
vis-à-vis psychological processes, and more macroscopic studies of larger social
groups (Tajfel 1974; Taylor and Brown 1979). Thus, there is a need for a unit of
analysis that represents a basic psychological process, yet addresses the shared,

social basis of behaviour.   The present paper then posits shared social norms as
an interface between the individual psychological need for cognitive organisation
and the demands of group membership within a complex, stratified social environment.   A second difficulty in this area is a lack of larger conceptual and research frameworks linking together psychological principles, group processes and
speech.   While normatively regulated language behaviour represents a logical
focus for such links, integrated conceptual frameworks have been conspicuous in
their absence (see, however, Smith and Giles 1978;   Taylor 1977).   This is despite a plethora of studies indicating systematic variation in speech style across
social groups and contexts, and evidence that perceivers make clear distinctions
in their evaluations and expectancies of such speech varieties (Giles and Powesland 1975;   Labov 1966;   Lambert 1967;   Shuy 1969).   The general conceptual and
research framework outlined here is then hoped to have heuristic value for the
study of these processes.   The first major component of this model is elaborated
in the present discussion.

The overall research framework hypothesises that in areas of potential conflict
such as the differentiation of psychologically normal from deviant individuals,
or the distinction of ideological ingroup from outgroup members - there are three
stages to the identification of deviance or social diversity.   First, conflict
or "problem" recognition represents the perception that the other conforms to or
deviates from the perceiver's norms, with these norms forming the basis for the
recognition of the other as "deviant" or an outgroup member.   Second, the rami-
fications of such recognition will be a product of the denotative and connotative
"definition" of the individual's behaviour.   Third is the "problem resolution
strategy", wherein behaviour toward the outgroup member will be determined by the
larger socio-political context of the interaction, and the judgements made in the
"definition" stage.

THE RECOGNITION OF SOCIAL DIVERSITY

The social psychological process underlying the recognition of social diversity
is that of social norms.   A social norm is defined as a stable, shared conception
of the behaviour appropriate or inappropriate to a given context, that dictates
expectancies of others' behaviour, and provides "rules" for one's own behaviour.
Norms are central to the establishment of "cognitive control" over the environment (Zimbardo 1969), in that these beliefs and expectancies function to organise
our experience (Sherif and Sherif 1969;   Triandis 1971) and to make predictions
about the consequences of (and thus to guide) our behaviour (Kelly 1955).   The
need for a consistent, organised perception of ourselves and the environment is
basic both to cognitive theories (Kelly 1955;   Piaget 1971) and to a range of
social psychological constructs, including cognitive consistency theory (Heider
1958), stereotypes (Taylor and Aboud 1973), attribution theory (Kelley 1972),
attitude theory (Triandis 1971) and theories of inter-group relations (Tajfel
1974).

The application of a normative model to perceptions of ethno-linguistic groups is
based on the general hypothesis that larger social groups are a fundamental feature of the social environment, and that group membership has associated with it
a network of shared beliefs and norms that both underlies group members' social
identity and serves as a natural line of fracture between members and non-members
(Kelley 1952;   Tajfel 1974).   Thus the need for cognitive control may motivate
us to hold stable norms concerning the behaviours that clearly differentiate the
members of different groups.   Given its ubiquity, sensitivity and flexibility,
speech is a likely candidate for the focus of such norms (Giles, Bourhis and
Taylor 1977;   Taylor 1977).   Further, there is evidence that stable norms or
"cognitive organisations" both strongly affect perceptions of, and are affected
by, social stress, threat or conflict (see Averill 1973;   Erdelyi 1974;   Taylor
1977).   Thus speech norms may represent a logical unit of analysis for under-

standing individuals' cognitive organisation of the social environment, and for examining changes in cognitive organisation in response to social threat or conflict.   However, the concept of "social norm" has been used in varying and often conflicting ways in sociology and psychology.   This discussion will then present a psychologically oriented model of norms, wherein they are viewed as being comprised of two major constituents: the structure of beliefs and expectancies – consisting of normative "content", "range" and "distinctiveness" – and the focus of a norm, representing the social context it applies to and its level of analysis or "communality".

THE OVERALL STRUCTURE OF SOCIAL NORMS

The content of a norm is a stable belief regarding the optimal level (quantity or frequency) of a target behaviour, shared by the members of a social group, that serves as a "benchmark" for one's own and for expectancies of others' behaviour. This is similar to what is described in cognitive psychology as a "core concept" (Nelson 1974), "scheme" (Furth 1969), "prototype" (Rosch 1975) or "ideal" (Bregman 1977), in that it is a relatively abstract concept underlying situated behaviour, generally denoted by a verbal label.   Of particular interest here is that subset of norms that differentiates between members and non-members of a given group (or "social category").   Hence in applying the concept of normative "content" to speech, two basic questions arise: are there consciously held "best ways" of speaking, and do these clearly vary across different groups?

The answer to the first of these questions is clearly "yes": a plethora of ethno-methodological data show language use, despite its apparent diversity, to be exquisitely rule governed (Hymes 1972), although not necessarily by formal linguistic properties (see Garfinkel 1972).   As to the second, and more important question, regarding group differences, there is abundant evidence that speakers recognise "prototypes" of the speech appropriate to specific social groups.   Examples here would include Labov's (1966) classic work with Black youth gangs, or Shuy's (1969) finding of powerful socio-economic and racial differences in phenomena such as deletion of final consonants ("mine" for mind, "tess" for test ...) or the use of "in" for "ing".   A further important feature of Shuy's (1969) now common finding was that listeners' socio-economic, racial and age status was virtually irrelevant to their ability to classify speakers on the basis of these linguistic features, indicating the existence of a widely shared, stable normative "content". Other linguistic features, while differentiating social groups, were far less powerful, indicating that a major aspect of the "group differences" question concerns the specific language features constituting these norms.   Labov (1972a), Ervin-Tripp (1972) and others have noted that phonological, syntactic and lexical differences often co-occur, hence some of these norms may have generality beyond a specific language feature.   However, these features will clearly interact in complex ways, raising a major empirical question concerning the particular contexts where these language features do or do not co-vary.   In other terms, this question concerns the particular dimensions of speech that constitute "linguistic variables" (Labov 1972b; Ervin-Tripp 1972) or socially evaluated aspects of speech for a given socio-historical context.

The range component of norms.   The second structural component of social norms consists of the range of normative variation around the content or optimal target behaviour.   This is an integral feature of traditional discussions of norms. Sherif and Sherif (1969) describe norms as "latitudes" of acceptable behaviour, rather than fixed standards, while Jackson (1969) views the normative range as bounded by the points where behaviour meets shared disapproval.   Further, viewing norms in terms of both an optimum and a range of behaviour is consistent with current perspectives in cognitive psychology.   Given that overt behaviour (or a given behavioural rule) represents the transformation of a prototype into a socially situated instance or expectancy, there may be more or less "fit" between the "ideal" and the "real". This is a familiar theme in Piagetian thought, where a schema, as manifested in behaviour, represents a contextually "corrected" schema (see Furth, 1969), thus allowing for a range of approximations to the prototype. Further, concept identification is generally seen as the judgement of the "goodness of fit" of an exemplar to a prototype (Bregman 1977). This pertains to an important element of the range component of norms, in that the range is seen as governing the clarity with which the norm is articulated. A norm with a wide range of acceptable behaviour would be more inclusive of progressively "less optimal" behaviour than would be a norm with a narrower range, thus making the "cut-off" for inclusion or exclusion more equivocal.

This range component clearly applies to speech norms, on several levels. Shuy (1969) argues that speakers are socially categorised via the frequency of a specific speech characteristic. Thus, a norm may be bounded by conceptions of acceptable frequencies of, for example, dropped final consonants rather than the simple presence of a given form. On a second level, Labov (1972b) has argues that socially stratified phonological varieties may be quantifiable along a continuum of "stigmatised form" to "hypercorrection", with movement in either direction being recognised as some degree of deviation from a standard form. Thus norms may contain a range of approximations to a phonological optimum. Finally, general judgements of "grammaticality" or linguistic "goodness" have been found to be continuous rather than categorical (Quick 1966, cited in Labov 1972a). Thus, from a normative perspective, a "linguistic variable" may be clearly or unclearly articulated, depending upon the range of acceptable behaviour it encompasses. This may control both the specific behaviours relevant to judgements of social diversity, as well as the certainty with which such judgements are made.

The distinctiveness of norms.   Distinctiveness, which is generally not included in traditional models of norms, is based on the assumption that norms represent expectancies both of ingroup members' behaviour, and that of prototypic outgroup members.   Given that these expectancies represent ranges of permissible behaviour, they may overlap to a greater or lesser extent.   Distinctiveness refers to the lack of such overlap, in that a linguistic variable specific only to one group will allow for less equivocal social categorizations than variables with larger degrees of overlap.   This component of norms is suggested by the general "cognitive control" orientation promulgated above; maintaining a clear and distinctive cognitive organisation of the environment requires the maintenance of such "contrastive ideals", particularly in domains of potential social conflict.   Further, this is important to the "interactive" quality of norms.   The ability to "take the role of the other" (Mead 1934) and anticipate reactions to one's behaviour (e.g. as in speech accommodation) is based on one's sense of the other's norms, and the their distinctiveness vis-à-vis one's own.

The distinctiveness component of norms is also suggested by ethnographic studies. The language forms that Shuy (1969) finds to be potent predictors of social category are those that the present model would describe as highly distinctive. Similarly, Labov (1972b) argues that a specific linguistic variable may acquire different statuses, e.g. as an "indicator", "marker" or "stereotype", reflecting different degrees to which the linguistic variable is used only by a specific group, or only in a particularly extreme form by that group.   In present terms, these different statuses correspond to progressively more distinctive norms.

There is evidence that this normative structure is directly manifested in behaviour, whereby members of different groups maintain "behavioural distinctiveness". Thus a number of writers have described ethno-linguistic groups' use of speech style to maintain or articulate group identity and distinctiveness (Labov 1966; Giles, Bourhis and Taylor 1977).   Similarly, while middle class (MC) and lower class (LC) speech styles have much in common, in a given social context LC individuals often use a less formal register than MC individuals (Labov 1966; Taylor

and Clément 1974), thus unintentionally maintaining behavioural distinctiveness.
Further, Taylor and Simard (1977) point out that there may be both positive and
negative consequences of the norms governing a linguistic variable becoming distinctive enough for mutually held stereotypes to develop.   The negative consequences would consist of the conflict or social stratification resulting from the
designation of one group's characteristic speech style as "stigmatised" or as a
"lower" variety, as in a stable diglossic context (see Fishman 1972a; Lambert 1967)
In contrast, a subordinate group may effect social change by developing normatively distinctive, socially valued areas of behaviour, wherein groups share mutually
distinctive norms, and positively evaluate both their own and the other group's
characteristics.

Conceptualising norms according to their distinctiveness has two heuristically
useful implications.   First, it alerts us that members of a speech community
(Hymes 1972) learn not only "appropriate" language forms, but (receptively) learn
deviant forms that are contrastively used for social categorization.   It is hypothesised that both the presence and distinctiveness of these forms are a product
of the degree of contact and, more importantly, the potential social conflict between the groups in question.   Second, this conceptualization indicates that, as
with the range component, normative distinctiveness is a quantitative feature of
a linguistic variable.

Normative structure and evaluative reactions.   The structure of a social norm
represents the "content" or prototype of the target behaviour of oneself or one's
own group, as well as of an outgroup or "deviant" individual.   Operationally,
these norms represent ranges of appropriate variations, with range size governing
the clarity of the norm.   The overlap of the ingroup and outgroup ranges further
governs the distinctiveness of a norm.   This overall structure is itself related
to the evaluation of behaviour, in that clear and distinctive norms have associated with them stronger positive evaluations for normative behaviour and stronger
negative evaluations for non-normative behaviour than do less clear or distinctive
norms (Jackson 1969; McKirnan 1977).   These evaluative reactions will be strongly related to behaviour toward individuals perceived as conforming to or violating
norms, or, in the present context, as being an ingroup or outgroup member.

Viewing the structural and evaluative aspects of social norms as being in a dynamic relationship may have some heuristic value for the study of social change.
For example, the maintenance of a stable bilingual or bidialectal context, particularly with diglossia, will necessitate clear and distinctive norms.   Violation
of language norms in such a context - whether through linguistic incompetence or
intentional divergence - will generate stronger evaluative reactions than in a
less clearly structured or non-diglossic context.   Further, as the norms become
more structured, either through social evolution or direct legislation, the
strength of evaluative reactions will increase.

This model of norms can also be viewed from the other direction, whereby the
mechanism of social change comes from changes in the strength of evaluative reactions rather than from changes in normative structure.   In a bilingual or bidialectal context where intergroup relations become more conflictual (or "evaluative-
ly intense") over time, one would expect normative structure to become clearer
and more distinctive.   This is similar to Taylor's (1977) argument that "ego protection" and the accurate perception of the environment are in a dynamic balance,
such that under conditions of threat, ego protection is accomplished via increasingly simple, self-serving and inaccurate conceptualisations of the social environment.   The present model extends the generality of this conception by positing
changes in general normative structure as a response to threat.   Hence, a threatened group's norms are expected to yield clearer and more distinctive expectancies, some of which will be accurate and some of which will not.

THE FOCUS OF A NORM

The second major constituent of a norm, which has been the major concern of ethnographic studies of speech, is its focus.   This consists of the social context it
applies to and the level of analysis, i.e., the nature of the social group within
which the norm is shared.

The social context of language norms. This component is crucial, in that all
social norms operate within a specific social context: normative behaviour is
situation-specific (Moos 1973).   Further, there may be overriding context effects
that apply to virtually any social norm.   For example, middle class individuals
appear to make clearer distinctions between the contexts of behaviour than do
lower class individuals, whether the behaviour in question concerns language (see
Labov 1966) or perceptions of psychological deviance (McKirnan 1977).   Similarly,
it would appear that one dimension of a social context that affects virtually all
normatively regulated behaviour is its degree of formality or explicit social constraint (Ervin-Tripp 1972; Labov 1966; McKirnan 1977; Shuy 1969).   Thus, there
may be "universals" in normatively regulated behaviour, that allow us to approach
speech norms from a broader perspective.

A major empirical question that has emerged in the ethnographic
study of language has been the precise nature or "level" of social context.   For
the present discussion, it would appear that a reasonable unit of analysis – and
one that corresponds to other studies of norms – is the "social situation" (similar
to Fishman's (1972b) "domain") such as "work", "leisure" or "social gathering", in
that this level has a widely shared social and behavioural meaning vis-à-vis the
goals, history and social significance of such contexts.   Many studies can thus be
thought of as more microscopic analyses of social situations, focusing on issues
such as the role relations of participants, specific locales, or personal goals
being maximised in a specific speech event (Hymes, 1972).   Similarly, a major area
of study consists of the more "macroscopic" socio-historical underpinnings of such
contexts, particularly vis-à-vis larger socio-economic, sex or ethno-linguistic
group relations.   Thus it is expected that in a social system characterised by
stable inter-group conflict, some social contexts will become particularly salient
to the groups in question, either as loci of frequent inter-group contact (e.g.
governmental or educational contexts) or as symbolising a history of inter-group
conflict (e.g. the work situation).   The increased evaluative intensity of such
domains may lead to particularly clear and distinctive norms, thus facilitating
perceptions of social diversity.   These factors may then operate in addition to
more general elements such as formality or social class effects.

A second major question concerns the specific characteristics of speech that are
modulated by the social context.   Much of the ethnographic literature has been
devoted to this question, ranging from address rituals (Ervin-Tripp 1972) to code
switching (Gumperz 1972).   However, one difficulty with this literature is that
both speech 'rules' and social contexts have been studied in a somewhat fragmentary fashion; the different levels and qualities of social settings have often
been examined separately, as have the specific language features affected by them.
Thus a significant heuristic advantage of including social context in a larger conception of norms is that the overall structure of norms is expected to vary across
contexts in systematic ways, possibly leading to more comprehensive and integrated
study of these factors.

The level of analysis of a norm.   The second component of the focus of a norm
concerns the level at which it is analysed, ranging from a dialect shared by a
larger social group (Fishman 1972b) to an idiolect, i.e. the idiosyncratic conventions pertaining to particular interlocutors in a specific speech event (Hymes
1972).   The major empirical question here then concerns how broadly based the focus
must be in examining language and social groups, or, in other terms: "what is a

speech community".

The salience of shared norms to the definition of a speech community has been clearly established, to the extent that both Labov (1966) and Hymes (1972) explicitly define a speech community as a set of speakers sharing the same norms concerning speech use, rather than vis-à-vis common language, locale or other demographic characteristics.   This definition of speech community is important in orienting us toward the salience of norms, and in indicating that some "ways of speaking" may be normative only within specific groups.   An excellent example of this is Labov's (1966) analysis of "sounding", an elaborate, normatively regulated system of ritual insults used by black American adolescents to establish group identity and ingroup status.   Similar examples can be found in studies of psychologically deviant behaviour, such as Agar's (1973) study of heroin addicts' speech norms or Room's (1975) studies of alcoholics.   However, there are two difficulties with this general approach.   First, social norms governing virtually all domains of behaviour contain both shared and idiosyncratic features (McKirnan 1977). Hence, in a multilingual context, "English speakers" may represent the most logical level of analysis, while in a monolingual context other, more specific, demarcations may be most salient.   Second, viewing a speech community as wholly coincident with a set of norms is partially circular, in that the community must be posited as both the result and the cause of the norms.   Larger factors such as the political and economic "vitality" (Giles, Bourhis and Taylor 1977) of a group may then bear examination.

The level of analysis of a norm may then be seen as somewhat arbitrary, in that it must be determined by the empirical question.   Hence, in examining groups such as youth gangs, the concept of speech community as normative consensus within a small, clearly demarcated group may be most appropriate.   Alternatively, the study of larger intergroup processes, for example subordinate groups' use of language to facilitate group solidarity, distinctiveness and positive social identity (Giles, Bourhis and Taylor 1977), may require the study of the wider social and political status of the language (or dialect) across an entire society.

The focus of a norm thus addresses the "socially situated" character of behaviour. As regards speech, this has been most directly addressed in ethnographic studies, where a rich descriptive vocabulary of speech contexts is rapidly developing (Gumperz 1972; Hymes 1972).   The heuristic value of the present approach is in integrating these considerations into a larger framework, where "social context" represents socially structured, historically common situations that carry both individual and pan-cultural meaning, while the level of analysis represents an empirical question concerning the appropriate integration of phenomenological and demographic parameters of "speech community".   The present model of norms may expedite the study of both of these areas, by providing a larger perspective and by positing measurable changes in normative structure as a reasonable operational definition of an "effective" characterisation of social context, or an "appropriate" level of analysis.

CONCLUSION

In conclusion, the present discussion attempts to provide an integrated social and psychological model of speech norms.   Norms are seen as consisting of two major constituents.   The first pertains to their cognitive structure and is analysable in terms of basic psychological principles.   The second pertains to the focus or "socially situated" character of normative regulation.   Insofar as language represents the actual focus of intergroup distinctions and conflicts, or serves as a marker for them, these norms will underlie the recognition of the speaker as a member of a particular social group or category.   This represents the first stage of the overall conceptual framework outlined above.   It is hoped that this model

will have heuristic value in stimulating more integrated and theoretically oriented studies of speech norms and inter-group behaviour.   The significance of the
recognition of diversity will, however, be strongly affected by the second stage
of the overall framework, that of the social and personal meaning or "definition"
of the interaction.   Finally, both the short and long term outcome of the situation will be a product of the different processes underlying the development of
problem resolution strategies.   By approaching these issues within an integrated
research and conceptual framework, it is hoped that systematic, theory based studies of these processes will be expedited.

REFERENCES

Agar, M. Ripping and running: a formal ethnography of urban heroin addicts.   New
        York: Seminar Press, 1973
Averill, J. R.   Personal control over aversive stimuli and its relationship to
        stress.   Psychological Bulletin, 1973, 80, 286-303
Bregman, A.   Perception and behaviour as compositions of ideals.   Cognitive
        Psychology, 1977, 9, 250-292
Erdelyi, M. H.   A new look at the new look: perceptual defense and vigilance.
        Psychological Review, 1974, 81, 1-25
Ervin-Tripp, S.   On sociolinguistic rules: alternation and co-occurrence, in
        J. J. Gumperz and D. Hymes (Eds.) Directions in sociolinguistics.   New York:
        Holt, Rinehart and Winston, 1972.
Fishman, J. A.   The sociology of language: an interdisciplinary social science
        approach to language in society.   Rowley, Mass.: Newbury House, 1972 (a)
Fishman, J. A.   Domains and the relationship between micro- and macrosociolinguis-
        tics, in J. J. Gumperz and D. Hymes (Eds.) Directions in sociolinguistics
        New York: Holt, Rinehart and Winston, 1972 (b)
Furth, H. Piaget and knowledge.   Englewood Cliffs, New Jersey: Prentice Hall
        1969
Garfinkel, H.   Remarks on ethnomethodology, in J. J. Gumperz and D. Hymes (Eds.)
        Directions in sociolinguistics. New York: Holt, Rinehart and Winston, 1972
Giles, H. and Powesland, P. F.   Speech style and social evaluation.   London and
        New York: Academic Press, 1975
Giles, H., Bourhis, R. Y. and Taylor, D. M.   Towards a theory of language in eth-
        nic group relations, in H. Giles (Ed.) Language, ethnicity and intergroup
        relations.   London and New York: Academic Press, 1977
Gumperz, J. J.   Linguistic and social interaction in two communities.   American
        Anthropologist, 1972, 66, 137-153
Heider, F. The psychology of interpersonal relations.   New York: Wiley, 1958
Hymes, D.   Models of the interaction of language and social life, in J. J. Gum-
        perz and D. Hymes (Eds.) Directions in sociolinguistics.   New York: Holt,
        Rinehart and Winston, 1972
Jackson, J.   Structural characteristics of norms, in I. D. Steiner and M. Fish-
        bein (Eds.) Current studies in social psychology.   New York: Holt, Rine-
        hart and Winston, 1969
Kelley, H. H.   Two functions of reference groups, in G. E. Swanson, T. M. Newcomb
        and E. L. Hartley (Eds.) Readings in social psychology.   New York: Holt,
        1952
Kelley, H. H.   Causal schemata and the attribution process.   New York: General
        Learning Press, 1972
Kelly, G. A. The psychology of personal constructs.   New York: Norton, 1955
Labov, W.   Language in the inner city: studies in black English vernacular.
        Philadelphia: University of Pennsylvania Press, 1966
Labov, W.   The study of language in its social context, in J. B. Pride and J.
        Holmes (Eds.) Sociolinguistics.   London: Penguin, 1972(a)
Labov, W.   On the mechanism of linguistic change, in J. J. Gumperz and D. Hymes
        (Eds.) Directions in sociolinguistics.   New York: Holt, Rinehart and
        Winston, 1972 (b)

Lambert, W. E. A social psychology of bilingualism. _Journal of Social Issues_, 1967, _23_, 109

McKirnan, D. J. A community approach to the recognition of alcohol abuse: the drinking norms of three Montreal communities. _Canadian Journal of Behavioural Science_, 1977, 9, 108-122

Moos, R. H. Conceptualizations of human environments. _American Psychologist_, 1973, _28_, 652-665

Nelson, K. Concept, word and sentence: interrelations in acquisition and development. _Psychological Review_, 1974, _81_, 267-285

Piaget, J. _Biology and knowledge_. Chicago: The University of Chicago Press, 1971

Room, R. Normative perspective on alcohol use and problems. _Journal of Drug Issues_, 1975, _5_, 358-368

Rosch, E. Cognitive representations of semantic categories. _Journal of Experimental Psychology_: Human Perception and Performance, 1975, _104_, 192-233

Sherif, M. and Sherif, C. W. _Social psychology._ New York: Harper and Row, 1969

Shuy, R. W. Subjective judgments in sociolinguistic analysis, in J. E. Alatis (Ed.) _Monograph Series on Languages and Linguistics_, 20th Annual Round Table Washington, D.C.: Georgetown University Press, 1969

Smith, P. M. and Giles, H. _Sociolinguistics: a social psychological perspective_. Paper presented at IXth World Congress of Sociology, Uppsala, Sweden, August 1978

Tajfel, H. Social identity and intergroup behavior. _Social Science Information_ 1974, _13_, 65-93

Taylor, D. M. _Towards a preliminary theory of the functions of speech markers_. Paper presented at a Conference of Social Markers in Speech, Paris, October 1977

Taylor, D. M. and Aboud, F. E. Ethnic stereotypes: is the concept necessary? _The Canadian Psychologist_, 1973, _14_, 330-338

Taylor, D. M. and Clément, R. Normative reactions to styles of Quebec French. _Anthropological Linguistics_, 1974, _May_, 202-217

Taylor, D. M. and Brown, R. Toward a more social social psychology? _British Journal of Social and Clinical Psychology_, 1979, _18_, 173-180

Taylor, D. M. and Simard, L. M. _Ethnic identity and intergroup relations_. Paper presented at the Canadian Ethnic Studies Association National Conference on Emerging Ethnic Boundaries, Quebec, 1977

Triandis, H. C. _Attitude and attitude change_. New York: John Wiley and Sons, 1971

Zimbardo, P. G. _The cognitive control of motivation_. Glenview, Ill.: Scott, Foresman, 1969

Mead, G. H. _Mind, self and society_. Chicago: University of Chicago Press, 1934

The Lingue Franche of Singapore:
An Investigation into Strategies of
Inter-Ethnic Communication

J. Platt

Department of Linguistics, Monash University, Clayton, Victoria 3168, Australia

ABSTRACT

It is suggested that six main factors are involved to a greater or lesser extent
in LF selection in a multilingual setting where more than one LF is in use:

(a) the set of features relating to the background of the addressee, (b) the situation identification in relation to a particular domain or sub-domain, (c) the set
of features relating to the background of the speaker, conditioning his social
identity and his verbal repertoire, (d) the speaker's personal preference of LF
based on his social identity, (e) the speaker's wish to accommodate or otherwise,
based essentially on his personality and his role relationship to the addressee(s),
and (f) the functional configuration of the LFs themselves.

In an LF selection, (a) and (b) would be processed by the speaker in the light of
(c), (d) and (e) and then matched against (f).

The LF selection outlined above is discussed with reference to the four main
lingue franche of Singapore: Bazaar Malay, Hokkien, Mandarin and Singapore English.

Key words

Accommodation (to addressee); domain; functional configuration (of lingua franca);
lingua franca (LF) selection; polyglossic network; selection device (personal
preference); social identity; sub-domain; verbal repertoire

Much has been said about the structure and development of certain types of lingue
franche such as pidgins (e.g. Hymes, 1971) and of the possible social and political significance of a lingua franca (e.g. Fishman, 1968). This paper will centre
on the problem of what happens in multilingual societies where more than one lingua
franca (LF) exists in the polyglossic network of the community and where each LF
may have different as well as similar functions. Why do speakers in these regions
select a particular lingua franca for particular situations? Can certain features

The research in Singapore was supported by Australian Research Grants Committee
grants A68/16801 and A77/15355. My thanks go to H. Weber for assistance with the
Singapore research project.

be established which determine to some extent the probability of a particular LF
being selected in a particular situation? In other words, is it possible to establish something like a 'functional configuration' for each LF and ascertain what
role it plays in LF selection and whether or not other factors are involved as
well?

Characteristics which should be considered in such a 'functional' set for any
type of lingua franca are: its ontogenetic background, its status within the
polyglossic network of the region, its ethnicity link, its education link, its
link to certain demographic factors, e.g. number of users, age, and possibly sex
of users and lastly its acceptability as a code in the major spheres of everyday
activity in the region.

When discussing some general principles of code selection in a multilingual-polyglossic society (Platt, 1977b), I stated that in addition to the appropriateness
of the code and the verbal repertoire of speaker and addressee, other features
needed to be considered, e.g. the ethnicity, education, sex, age and socio-economic background of both speaker and addressee. Naturally, these factors would
also apply to LF selection.

If the speaker is cognisant of the various characteristics of his addressee, then
a selection would be relatively easy, but in many cases, e.g. in transactions
with strangers, no prior information would be available to the speaker and he
would have to rely firstly on his direct perception of the addressee, judging the
addressee's ethnic background and approximate age by physical appearance, and his
educational level, socio-economic background and possibly even type of education
by the addressee's dress and general bearing. Secondly, the speaker would be
aided in his judgement of the addressee's characteristics by the domain and sub-
domain to which the particular situation belonged. For instance, if the speaker
was seeking an interview with the manager of a large bank he would expect his
addressee to have certain characteristics possibly demanding the choice of a different LF than if he was addressing a porter in a hotel lobby.

We have then to consider three different sets of characteristics or features
which all play a part in LF selection:

(1) the features which form the functional configurations of the LFs,
(2) the characteristics of the speaker,
(3) the characteristics of the addressee, which are: (a) known to the speaker, or
    (b) perceived by the speaker directly via the addressee and indirectly via the
    situation, that is assuming that it is a congruent situation where the man
    behind the bank manager's desk is indeed the bank manager and not the cleaner
    in disguise.

In addition, as stated in Platt (1977b), there is also the recognition by the
speaker of the domain and sub-domain to which a particular speech situation belongs and the codes considered appropriate for use in this sub-domain according
to the norms of the polyglossic network of his society.

Figure 1 shows the suggested process of LF selection and the various factors involved, where I1 signifies the perceived information concerning the addressee's
background, I2 the deduced information about the addressee's background on
account of situation recognition and I3 the perceived information concerning the
situation and its belonging to a particular domain or sub-domain.

An additional factor before final LF selection takes place would be not only the
speaker's own background but also a selecting device based on the speaker's social
identity, i.e. a type of filter which selects the speaker's own preference, if
circumstances permit. That this device may be of considerable importance in

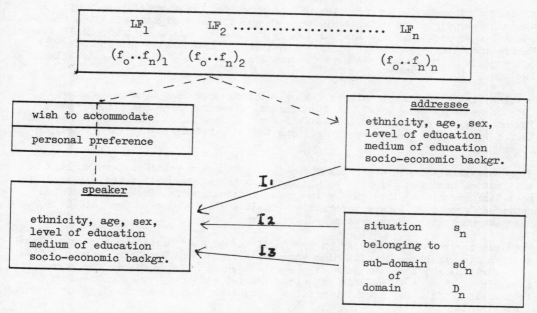

Fig. 1   LF selection procedure

shaping selection will be shown later.   To what extent it is allowed to operate
would depend on the degree of accommodation the speaker is prepared to give to
the addressee, in other words, to what extent he allows his own preference to decide the choice rather than the perceived information regarding the addressee.
The degree of accommodation would depend on the speaker's personality as well as
his role relationship to the addressee.

The model suggested in Figure 1 will be applied to LF selection in a particular
multilingual setting, namely Singapore, with its four main lingue franche:
Bazaar Malay, Hokkien, English and Mandarin.   Table 1 shows some of the main
features which constitute the functional configurations for these particular LFs.

TABLE 1   Functional configurations of the four main LFs of
Singapore: English (E) Mandarin (M) Hokkien (H)
and Bazaar Malay (BM)

LF	Ontogenetic background	Status	Education link	Ethnicity link	Demographic features		
					used by %	speakers are	age of users
E	creoloid – stand.lang.	$M - H_1$	+	–	> 50	increasing	$O < Y$
M	creoloid – stand.lang.	$M - H_2$	+	+	> 50	increasing	$O + Y$
H	reduced language	$L^+ - M$	–	+	> 50	decreasing	$O > Y$
BM	pidgin	L^-	–	–	> 50	decreasing	$O > Y$

As far as ontogenetic characteristics are concerned, Bazaar Malay is a pidgin,
which developed in contact situations between Chinese immigrants and the indigenous Malay population.   It was adopted by immigrant Indians in communication with
Malays and Chinese and later on by the British.   Essentially its structure is a
convergence of Malay and Southern Chinese dialects with a predominantly Malay
lexicon.

Hokkien, the predominant Chinese dialect of Singapore is a Reduced Language.
Once connected more strongly to its original standard, Amoy Hokkien, spoken in
Fukien province of mainland China, it has now become functionally restricted and
therefore, linguistically speaking, 'stunted' - particularly as far as lexicon is
concerned.

Singapore English took over from the original Standard South-eastern English of
the British administration.   It was acquired through education and was used by
most learners almost immediately in everyday situations.   It is at present a
continuum from what I have referred to (Platt 1975, 1978) as a Creoloid to a Standard Language with an increasingly local norm.

Mandarin is spoken natively by only 0.1% of the population.   The number of Chinese schools in the region teaching through the medium of Mandarin increased stead-
ily, particularly from the time of the establishment of the Kuomintang regime in
mainland China.   Now Mandarin is, after English, the next important medium of
instruction, with the other two official languages, Malay and Tamil, playing only
a minor role.

In multilingual societies where more than one LF is in use, one of them is usually
the language acquired through the medium of education and therefore has more prestige than an LF which may have developed from a pidgin or has still remained a contact pidgin.   Of the four LFs of Singapore, only two: Singapore English and Mandarin have the feature: + education.

In Platt (1977a) I suggested, on the analogy of Ferguson's concept of diglossia
(1959), that in many multilingual communities a state of polyglossia exists with
speech varieties ranging from H(igh) status via M(edium) to L(ow) status varieties.
The status features of the four Singapore LF's vary considerably, with Singapore
English occupying the range M-H$_1$, Mandarin M-H$_2$, Hokkien L$^+$-M and Bazaar Malay
classed as L$^-$.

Giles, Bourhis and Taylor (1977) comment on the fact that "ingroup speech can
serve as a symbol of ethnic identity and cultural solidarity".   An ethnicity link
or the lack thereof may have considerable significance in LF selection.   Although
an LF may be the 'native' language of only a small minority in a particular region,
it may nevertheless have strong and wider connotations, such as the concept of
'Chineseness' associated with Mandarin in Singapore.   Singapore English itself
has virtually no ethnicity link but is gradually gaining wider significance as an
all-embracing nationality symbol, i.e. it contributes to the identity of 'being a
Singaporean'.

Demographic characteristics of LFs are not so easy to establish.   The Singapore
population distribution according to ethnic background is approximately 76% Chinese,
15% Malay, 7% Indians and 2% small minority groups.   43% of the Chinese are
Hokkien.   According to the SRM Media Survey 1972, approximately 73% of Singaporeans claim to understand Hokkien, 55% Mandarin, 47% English and 57% Malay.   This,
of course, includes Standard as well as Bazaar Malay.   Since then, with increased
enrolment in English-medium streams at school, the figure for English has been
rising whilst the figure for Bazaar Malay has been declining.

TABLE 2   Domain acceptability for the four main LFs of
            Singapore

LF	Friend-ship	Trans-action	Emp.	Ed.	Media	Govern-ment	Law	Religion	Cult. Act.
E	A	A	A	A	A	A	A	A	A
M	A	A	A	A	A	RA	RA	A	A
H	A	A	A	NA	RA	NA	RA	A	RA
BM	A	A	A	NA	NA	NA	RA	NA	NA

Table 2 gives an acceptability matrix for the four LFs as far as the major domains are concerned, with A signifying 'acceptable', RA - 'Acceptable under certain conditions' and NA - 'not acceptable'.

In structured interviews with 100 Singaporeans on code selection and attitudes to
codes we obtained some interesting data concerning LF selection.

Where the particular domain and sub-domain to which a situation belongs are more
clearly defined, identification of the situation and with it deduction of the
addressee's background play a very strong part in the selection procedure (I2 and
I3 in Fig. 1).   English was the first choice as LF for shopping at larger department stores and in fashionable boutiques.   The interviewees stated that they
were aware that many of the sales staff in these establishments, particularly
younger ones, were English-medium educated and therefore would converse fluently
in English.   Most interviewees also felt that the setting demanded English, recognised as a language of education and status.   Thus the main features in the
LF which attracted selection were: +education, +younger generation, +status (at
least Medium status).   The ethnicity link feature played a relatively small
part, only 9% of the interviewees claiming that they selected Mandarin first, 8%
that they would use Hokkien and 2% that they would first use Bazaar Malay.

The ethnicity link feature plays an important part in situations related to other
sub-domains of the Transactions Domain, e.g. shopping at markets, hawker stalls
and in small provision stores.   Here, the situation again assists in deducing
addressee's background (I2).   It is generally assumed that vendors at these establishments are not very highly educated, most likely not English-medium educated, and the ethnicity link feature can often be ascertained either by shop signs,
type of shop or location of the market (I2) as well as, of course, from the vendor's external appearance (Il).   The first LF choice was either Bazaar Malay
(-education, -ethnicity), if the vendor was not a Chinese, or otherwise Hokkien
(-education, +ethnicity).

I have mentioned previously the need for a personal preference device, based to
a large extent on the speaker's social identity.   Naturally, depending on the
degree of accommodation, the device would either be deliberately suppressed if a
high degree of accommodation was desirable, e.g. a Mandarin-educated loan seeker
using English to the bank manager although his LF preference would have been Mandarin, or it could be allowed to over-ride accommodation needs.   An example of
this will be given later.

When we questioned our interviewees about their first LF choice a number of
typical first preferences emerged.   These can be seen in Table 3.

Up to now I have limited myself to the dyad speaker - addressee.   In a group situation, an even more complex selection procedure would take place, depending in

TABLE 3   Relation of speaker's social identity to LF
           preferences

Social identity	LF preference

Singaporean
   (-ethnicity, +nationality, +education
    +younger age group)
	Singapore English

Singaporean and ethnically Chinese (+ethnicity, +education, +younger age group)	Mandarin
Ethnic Chinese (+ethnicity, -education, +older age group)	Hokkien
Ethnic Malay or Indian (-education, +older age group)	(Bazaar) Malay

addition to the factors already mentioned on the number of users of each LF and
often on the personality of the official (or unofficial) group leader(s).

A pattern of LF use in three small Singapore workshops will demonstrate this (cf.
Table 4, adapted from Platt and Weber, in press).   In this sub-domain of the
Employment Domain either Colloquial Singapore English, Hokkien or Bazaar Malay
would be acceptable.

TABLE 4   LF use in three Singapore workshops

	Workshop A	Workshop B	Workshop C
Number of employees:	12	10	14
Mechanic in charge:	Hokkien (Eng.- med. educated)	Cantonese (Eng.-med. educated)	Arab (Eng.-med. educated)
Ethnicity of rest of employees:	Hokkien 6 Teochew 1 Cantonese 3 Hakka 1	Hokkien 2 Cantonese 2 Malay 4 Tamil 1	Arab 2 Chinese 3 Malay 8 (2 with Eng.-med.ed.)
Predominant LF used:	Hokkien	(Cantonese) English	Bazaar Malay

In Workshop A, the choice of Hokkien was the logical one.   The Teochew dialect
is closely related to Hokkien and the non-Hokkien workers were all able to speak
Hokkien.

In Workshop B, the mechanic in charge was forceful and rather arrogant.   He used
Cantonese if at all possible, although more than half of his staff were not very
familiar with it.   His second choice was English, although two of the Malay workmen were not English-medium educated and at a considerable disadvantge.   He was
of a younger age group and his Bazaar Malay was shaky.   By using his native dialect and an LF with which he was familiar, he managed to maintain a superior role
relationship, even if his code selection bordered on strong non-accommodation to
one section of his staff.   Needless to say, this verbal behaviour created an unpleasant atmosphere in the workshop.

In Workshop C, the most frequently used LF was Bazaar Malay, although the mechanic in charge, a Singaporean Arab, admitted that his own LF preference was English. He was a generous thoughtful man and realised the need for accommodation to all his co-workers.   In his own words, "with such a mixed bunch, it is necessary to choose a language everyone can understand".

REFERENCES

Ferguson, C. A. Diglossia. Word 1959, 15, 325-340

Fishman, J. A. Some contrasts between linguistically homogeneous and linguistically heterogeneous polities, in J. A. Fishman, C. A. Ferguson and J. Das Gupta (Eds.) Language problems of developing nations. New York: John Wiley & Sons, 1968

Giles, H., Bourhis, R. Y. and Taylor, D. M. Towards a theory of language in ethnic group relations, in H. Giles (Ed.) Language, ethnicity and intergroup relations. London: Academic Press, 1977

Hymes, D. Pidginization and creolization of languages. London: Cambridge University Press, 1971

Platt, J. T. The Singapore English speech continuum. Anthropological Linguistics. 1975, 17, 363-374

Platt, J. T. A model for polyglossia and multilingualism (with special reference to Singapore and Malaysia). Language in Society. 1977a, 6/3, 361-178

Platt, J. T.   Code selection in a multilingual-polyglossic society. Talanya. 1977b, 4, 64-75

Platt, J. T. The concept of a 'creoloid'. Exemplification: basilectal Singapore English. Papers in Pidgin and Creole Linguistics I. Pacific Linguistics A54, 1978, 53-65

Platt, J. T. and Weber, H. English in Singapore and Malaysia: status - features - - functions. Kuala Lumpur: Oxford University Press, in press.

The Refusal of Second Language Learning in Interethnic Context

V. Hinnenkamp

*Universität Bielefeld, Fakultät für Literaturwissenschaft und Linguistik,
48 Bielefeld, Postfach 8640, Federal Republic of Germany*

ABSTRACT

The language situation of foreign workers ('gastarbeiter') in West Germany is to a great extent characterised by an official policy that has failed to integrate the bilingual needs of the immigrant worker and his family. Especially in the realm of encounters with authority, where communication is embedded in the survival-orientated context of a bureaucracy controlling their very existence, the 'gastarbeiter' feels powerless in face of what he perceives as a kind of 'total' institution. These communications are constantly experienced as irresoluble 'double-binds'. Refusing to accept the 'host society's' means of communication reflects one resort of the second language learner's reaction to these situations.

Key words

Second language learning; ethnicity; assimilation; integration; double-bind; gastarbeiter; sociological forces; perceived helplessness.

Immigrants can have many reasons for refusing to accept the 'host society's' language. I want to differentiate in this context between intrinsic and extrinsic factors. The former is intended to refer to features such as ethnicity, cultural and linguistic particularities. Here I wish to concentrate upon extrinsic factors which are dependent on various societal and interactional constraints.

INTRODUCTION

From an assertion like that of Bickerton who wrote that "the difference between arriving at a pidgin and arriving at a reasonably accurate version of a standard language lies mainly in the availability of target models and the amount of interaction with speakers of the target language" (1977, p.55), we could draw the conclusion that the availability of the different colloquial varieties of Standard German was the crucial problem in respect of the natural acquisition of German for the gastarbeiter in West Germany. At the same time it would be hard to explain why the gastarbeiter-German has developed or is developing into a pidgin, which appears to be what is happening. Views like that quoted above omit important social factors. Communication does not take place in formal and value free interaction between individuals and between groups but it is a concrete phenomenon of the social relations between groups and between classes within concrete social and power structures. This means that individuals and groups do not encounter each

other indifferently or as individuals only but as personifications of economic and
social relations.   These actual economic and social conditions including the antecedents reflecting forced emigration and experiences following immigration, allow
Germans and gastarbeiter in general, and gastarbeiter and specific groups of Germans in particular, to interact asymmetrically.   This necessitates a definition
of those variables which could explain why the "interlanguage" of most gastarbeiter
fossilises on a level rightly termed pidgin in its social and social-psychological
markedness.[1.]

The quantity of availability of target varieties is granted by many contacts of
varying degrees at work, out shopping, in leisure time, in contacts with neighbours,
intercourse with the authorities and with officials, and gradually also in intra-
family contexts because many children of the gastarbeiter develop bilingual patterns and even converse in German at home.   In addition, further availability - at
least passively - is provided by television, radio and the like.   If Bickerton's
hypothesis is correct a quantitative increase in the incidence of these events and
encounters should then bring about an approximation to or acquisition of the model
language instead of further pidginization.

However, in addition to cognitive and purely psychological restrictions it is particularly barriers of social power that, objectively as well as subjectively, lead
to a lingo-integrative negation in interethnic interaction.   These variables are
of qualitative nature, qualitative in the sense of their restrictive effect despite
a relatively high apparent "availability of target models".

ALTERNATIVE HYPOTHESIS

My hypothesis is that pidginization of 'gastarbeiter'-German is among other things
the result of a subjective strategy of refusal by the second language learner,
originating in a permanently experienced frustration, that to communicate with
Germans, who are primarily socially above them or function as superiors or officials, means communicating against themselves - at least in its social dimensions.
This experience is especially strong at work, but even stronger and more sanction-
ising in the intercourse with the many authorities with which the gastarbeiter is
forced to interact, because of his legal and social status.

RATIONALE FOR ALTERNATIVE HYPOTHESIS

If we examine in this context the structural model of Giles, Taylor and Bourhis
(1977, p.306ff) on ethnolinguistic vitality it is noticeable that it does not
explicitly include components like the special legal status of ethnic minority
groups either within its three main variables (status, demography, institutional
support) or within its more detailed list of subvariables.

In fact, economic, social as well as interior and exterior language status in West
Germany, are to a high degree defined by laws such as the Immigrants Act (Ausländer-
gesetze), the Regulations for Duration of Stay (aufenthaltsrechtliche Bestimmungen),
the Work Promotion and Demarcation Act (Arbeitsförderungsgesetz), and the Legis-
for Provision of a Place of Work (Arbeitsplatzerlaubnisverordnung), - to mention
only a few.

These laws and regulations have at least the following character and consequences:

---

1. The notion of pidgin and/or pidginization of 'gastarbeiter' German is a debat-
   able one.   In our context we refer to Schumann (1978:viii) "Pidginization
   occurs when a language is restricted to the communication of denotative referential information and is not used for integrative and expressive functions".

i) While West Germany may be a target country for immigrants, no citizenship is available for the gastarbeiter for at least eight years;

ii) there has been a prohibition on immigration since 1973 for most categories of foreigners;

iii) normal civil rights like the freedom of assembly or the freedom of political activities are not guaranteed for such persons;

iv) gastarbeiter are almost without exception deportable;

v) there are three 'classes' of gastarbeiter: from EEC countries; from associated EEC countries; from non-EEC countries.

This differentiation covaries with prejudicing in job-finding, etc. in the predictable direction:

vi) a later immigration of the family members (Familiennachzug) granting of a work permit for a spouse, etc. are subjected to further restrictions.

In addition to these discriminations there are further regulations rationing or preventing gastarbeiter from moving into certain areas and town districts (Zuzugssperre), special differentiation against the gastarbeiter's children in school,[2.] and of course a generally non-institutionalised prejudice in public and daily life. The quantity and quality of laws and decrees but briefly outlined here result in a permanent state of insecurity for the gastarbeiter, for example:

vii) a permanent supervision by and intercourse with the authorities; and

viii) an economic, social, psychological and, in the final analysis, a total dependence on the decisions of authorities and officials.

Language competence assumes a double character in this totality for gastarbeiter:

i) On the one hand it is an indispensable prerequisite for integration in the sense of an alliance with Germans, especially with German workers, and for the ability to verbalise their needs and difficulties, formulating their criticisms, obtaining appropriate information, etc.;

ii) on the other hand its mastery can frustrate (with an increasing approximation to the target model and an accompanying increase in perceptive abilities of communicative strategies) expected social-integrative (affirmation of social identity) and expressive roles (verbalising psychological needs) of the second language.

This enables us to formulate a second hypothesis:

Interethnic communication, embedded in the specific context of being 'trapped' between two cultures and of being deprived of basic rights of citizens, which the gastarbeiter experiences in particular at work and in encounters with the authorities, evolves as a pervasive 'double-bind' situation with specific consequences for the second language learner.

For our purposes we have to view the particular character of the authorities the gastarbeiter has to deal with as total institutions, and secondly to illustrate and explain the double-bind in the interaction in this realm.

The rules of interactional conduct in institutions are governed by the institutions themselves. The participants are submitted to specific institutionally ordered constraints of interaction in terms of:

---

2. Gastarbeiter children enter so-called Promotion Classes and after two years should transfer to ordinary classes. However instruction and provision in Promotion Classes is poor and less than 40% of foreign children achieve an ordinary Hauptschule.

> who is allowed to participate
> where and when communication has to take place
> which competence the participants have to have at their disposal
> which performances are permissible and desirable
> how these performances have to be realised.

A more or less properly organised institutional conduct has to provide that the institution-specific conventions are presupposed (known) by its participants. Any deviation from the institutionally sanctioned organisation, especially deviations by those expecting something from the institution, requires explicit justification; tolerance of variation is limited by the immutable functional character of the institution. Of course every person dealing with the authorities is submitted to these conditions. The 'totality' for the gastarbeiter as opposed to the character of the authority for the average citizen, is reflected in the qualitatively much farther reaching entanglement with the institutions of bureaucracy.

According to Goffman (1961) one of the central features of total institutions is that the boundaries which normally separate the spheres of sleep, leisure-time, and work are suspended. This suspension is in the type of institution Goffman describes - an asylum - an objective fact. The notion can be extended in our context in that formally and locally separated spheres of daily life are perceived as a totality because of its subjectively experienced unity. This totality is arrived at by "bureaucratic organisations of whole blocks of people" (ibid.p.6), which penetrate all interactional conduct:

i) The institution itself defines the social status and the social status again legitimates the institution to wield control and act restrictively.

ii) The above mentioned laws and special decrees symbolise the restriction of social intercourse with the Germans. The laws do not exist to protect minority rights but to 'protect' the native society from the gastarbeiter.

iii) All crucial matters of life, such as the existentially necessary presuppositions for normal reproduction, are decided upon by the authorities: duration and kind of work, duration of work permits, family life etc., which are "imposed from above by a system of explicit formal rulings and a body of officers." (ibid. p.6)

iv) With the entry into the new society and its accompanying procedures of reception the gastarbeiter has to put up with the mutilation or loss of his psychological and cultural identity: he is not identified by his pre-arrival occupation, the status he held in the 'old' society, his family and village, but his whole personality and biography is being subsumed under an undifferentiating category gastarbeiter, and he can even be deprived of his proper name. At the same time he is submitted to a hitherto unknown file, which renders all the important information about the gastarbeiter at any time.

In sum, the average gastarbeiter is, as a result of his dependence on authorities and institutions, surrendered to them in a total way.

EXPLICATION OF THE DOUBLE BIND

The double-bind effect in this context arises because two incompatible features of interaction are realised simultaneously:

i) an assumption of simple but elementary relevance, namely expected acceptance of the participants as humans through communication. This means that effective communication always presupposes a reciprocity of acceptance of the communicating partners founded on an assumption of a mutual wish to establish a rapport.

ii) However, communications for gastarbeiter, in particular in their encounters with authority and at work <u>deny</u> their acceptance as social agents because their communication with authority is <u>coercive communication</u>.

This is further reinforced by (a) the immutable character of the authorities with whom gastarbeiter have to deal; (b) the assymetrical bilingual situation, due to the fact that actually none of the institutions provides interpreters, not even for the major gastarbeiter nationalities; (c) the actual and institutionally ascribed communicative competence of the official. The gastarbeiter communicates in an even more unequal situation: his competence is the reflection of his social role and in this role his "naturally" acquired second language. The official on the other hand has at his disposal a whole set of "talking down" and "foreigner talk" registers, which he is able to apply according to the actual "moves" in the interaction - either successively or concurrently.

This set comprises: 'foreigner talk' with its various verbal and non-verbal characteristics; patronising speech; sympathetic friendliness; kind rejection; admonishing or warning appeal; openly threatening attitudes; switching from 'Sie' (polite address) to 'Du' (informal address); reference to not being understood or not being able to understand 'broken German'.

On the content level: reference to incompetence or superior instance; reference to the gastarbeiter's file; reference to existing laws, regulations etc.

The negation of the gastarbeiter as a person and the coercion through encounters with authorities   in pursuit of the maintenance of his material existence, leaves the gastarbeiter "in an intense relationship that has a high degree of physical and/or psychological survival value" (Watzlawick, Beavin and Jackson 1967, p.212). This <u>intense relationship</u> and consequent dependencies are not only experienced in dyadic interaction like that of mother/child or teacher/pupil, but also in societal apparata of various natures. In our case it is the extensively discussed dependence of the gastarbeiter on federal German authorities and their application of relevant legislation. Appreciating this kind of relationship is one important prerequisite for comprehending the <u>double-bind</u> effect. Another one is, that the <u>victim</u> of the <u>double-bind</u> is repeatedly or permanently entangled in this <u>intense relationship</u>.

The offered communicative/interactive alternatives mutually exclude both being achieved. This last point is indexed in particular because:

i) The gastarbeiter becomes aware within the interethnic communication that his affirmation as a social being presupposes the accomplishment of the expected conventions of the actual communicative conduct. Communicative competence thus putatively becomes the carrier of social acceptance and hence the accomplishment of the anticipated societal roles and wishes.

This view of the <u>victim</u> is supported by the illusion that the encounter with authority is not conducted with an anonymous apparatus, but is mediated by another human being: the official, whose own non-tolerance within and dependence on this apparatus is not perceived by the gastarbeiter. Hence the first "non-alternative" to lessen the physical dependence is experienced only as a fallacy by the second "non-alternative".

ii) That is, accomplishing a relative high communicative competence - at least according to his own judgment. In the actual communication, however, it becomes clear that the various communicative strategies of the official (see previous page) - even supposing these strategies could be counteracted - are not the decisive barriers of communicative and social affirmation. The actual communication reveals that acceptance by the official through adequate communicative intercourse cannot disantagonise the psychological and physical character of the <u>victim's</u> dependence.

It is this irresoluble contradiction which the gastarbeiter finds himself constantly involved in, while at the same time, however, not being adequately perceived by
him.   These are the two channels, the two paradoxical injunctions, which do not
allow either positive alternative.   This is reflected, for example on the conversational level, by analysing the verbal strategies of the official and the successful counterstrategies of the gastarbeiter.   (Space limitations preclude the inclusion of examples which are available from the author).

The double-bind phenomenon has, of course, effects of grave consequences for the
natural second language acquisition process.   Under 'normal' circumstances there
are at least two possible reactions to solve or to handle this contradiction.   The
first one would be to verbalize the experience.   A second possibility is simply to
escape these situations.   Both, of course, are not possible for the gastarbeiter;
particularly as this would presuppose to have consciously perceived the character
of the double-bind.   "The third possible reaction would be to withdraw from human
involvement", or, where this is not possible, at least "by blocking input channels
of communication" (Watzlawick and colleagues 1967, p.218).   This 'blocking' is exactly what we mean by the 'refusal of second language learning'.   Whether this
blocking reaches pathological dimensions such as the catatonic has to be found out.
The symptoms at least are obvious.   This is further supported by the fact that in
double-bind-free contexts, i.e. primarily intragroup communication, these symptoms
do not occur.

POSSIBLE RESOLUTIONS OF THE DOUBLE-BIND

How are these situations to be countered?   Primarily of course by the abolition of
the segregating legislation and special obligations for the gastarbeiter.   Secondly
all institutions gastarbeiter have to deal with should be obliged to provide interpreters.   Furthermore, some positive attempts are being made from inside the gastarbeiter communities, through self-help organisation, to meet with authorities
collectively;   this is often supported by members of their own group, who are more
effectively competent in dealing with German officials.   The issues discussed
above are certainly in contention.   Our discussion has to be regarded as an attempt
at finding some evidence in social psychologically-related matters to find an explanation for interethnic communication breakdown, which already has disastrous consequences for the necessary integration into West German society of gastarbeiter.

To return to the starting point: while it would certainly not be legitimate to describe pidginization as a pathological process, however, this pidginization comprises countless varieties of very rudimentary and sometimes of actually non-identifi-
able qualities, despite the speaker sometimes having worked more than a decade in
West Germany.

REFERENCES

Bickerton, D.   Pidginization and creolization: language acquisition and language
        universals,   in A. Valdman (Ed.) Pidgin and creole linguistics.   Indiana:
        Indiana University Press, 1977
Giles, H., Taylor, D. M. and Bourhis, R. Y.   Toward a theory of language in ethnic
        group relations,   in H. Giles (Ed.) Language, ethnicity and intergroup re-
        lations.   London: Academic Press, 1977
Goffman, E.   Asylums.   Chicago, Ill.: Aldine Publishers Co., 1961
Schumann, J. H.   The pidginization process.   A model for second language acquisi-
        tion.   Rowley, Massachusetts: Newbury House, 1978
Watzlawick, P., Beavin, J. H. and Jackson, D. G.   Pragmatics of human communication
        New York: Norton, 1967

Group Processes Affecting Anticipated Language Choice in Intergroup Relations

D. M. Taylor and L. Royer

*Department of Psychology, McGill University, Stewart Biological Sciences Building,
1205 McGregor Avenue, Montreal, P.Q. Canada H3A 1B1*

ABSTRACT

The experiment was designed to illustrate the importance of placing greater emphasis on group processes in the study of language and ethnic relations.   The "group
polarization" phenomenon was applied to accommodation theory which proposes that
individuals adjust their speech in order to be more similar to, or different from,
another, depending upon whether the motivation is for social approval or disapproval.   It was hypothesised that group discussion would enhance the speech adjustments usually made in a dyadic context.   The hypotheses received confirmation,
and there was evidence that the assertion of ethnic identity was an important motivation for choosing a linguistic strategy.

Key words

Speech accommodation; convergence; divergence; group polarization; language
choice; ethnic identity

INTRODUCTION

The social psychology of language and ethnicity necessarily involves group processes and yet these have not received the attention they deserve.   The experiment
reported in this paper illustrates the heuristic potential of more careful attention to group processes.   Specifically, the risky-shift, or more generally the
group polarization phenomenon will be examined in the light of a current theory of
speech accommodation.

Giles's theory of speech accommodation is one of the more influential in the social
psychology of language generally, and in relating language and ethnicity specifically (Giles, 1978; Giles and Powesland 1975).   The theory attempts to explain
the dynamics of speech adjustment in the process of interaction.   The underlying
assumption is that individuals subtly and indirectly communicate approval or disapproval of one another by altering their speech so as to be more similar to or
different from the other.   Speech accommodation can take two forms; convergence
and divergence.   Convergence involves shifting one's speech toward that of the
interlocutor, the motivation being to express or receive social approval.   A shift
away from the other's speech style in order to communicate disapproval constitutes
speech divergence.

The process of speech convergence has been empirically demonstrated by means of several linguistic indicators including pronunciation (Giles 1973), speech rate (Webb 1970), pause and utterance lengths (Jaffé and Feldstein 1970; Matarazzo 1973), vocal intensity (Natalé 1975), and language choice (Giles, Taylor and Bourhis 1973).   More recently attention has focused on speech divergence where it would appear that such a process has particular relevance for asserting ethnic id- entity in the context of intergroup relations.   For example, it has been found in both Wales (Bourhis and Giles 1977) and Belgium (Bourhis, Giles, Leyens and Tajfel 1979) that a member of one ethnolinguistic group will accentuate the unique as- pects of his/her own group's speech style when speaking to an outgroup member who makes derogatory remarks about their linguistic and cultural heritage.

Accommodation theory has received strong empirical support when studied in the context of the dynamics of individual speech strategies in social interaction. An important extension to the theory would be a systematic consideration of group processes.   A growing number of social psychologists (e.g. Billig 1976; Moscovici 1972; Sampson 1977; Steiner 1974; Tajfel 1972; Taylor and Brown 1979) have criticised current theory and research generally for its individualis- tic bias, and Taylor and Giles (1979) have raised this issue specifically in the context of language and ethnic relations.   The need to emphasise group processes is especially relevant to accommodation theory.   Although the theory is rooted in individually based social psychological concepts (similarity-attraction, social ex- change, causal attribution) it refers to group identity directly in explaining mo- tivations for speech divergence.

For example, in a study by Giles, Taylor and Bourhis (1973) English speaking sub- jects responded to a tape-recorded message from a French speaker.   In two of the conditions the speaker chose to communicate in French or English.   The speaker's choice of language had the predictable effects on both the attitudes of the sub- ject toward the speaker and the degree of convergence and divergence the subject displayed in a return communication to the speaker.   Thus when the speaker used French the subject responded in English, whereas the response was in French when the speaker chose to communicate in English.

Although group identity played a role in the subject's interpretation of the speaker's choice of language, the experiment was clearly individualistic in its emphasis.   Individual subjects were by themselves when they expressed their at- titudes toward the speaker and prepared their own return message.   Behaviour was not assessed in a public forum; that is, at no time did the subject make judg- ments in the presence of, or discuss his or her own judgments with, members of his or her own group.

What would be the effect of studying accommodation in a group context?   Evidence in the social psychology of group decision making suggests that extrapolation from the individual to the group context would be inappropriate.   What was labelled initially as the "risky-shift" phenomenon (Kogan and Wallach 1964) has been stated more generally as the "group polarization" hypothesis (Myers and Lamm 1976).   The proposition is that following group discussion, individuals will make more extreme decisions than the average of their individual decisions prior to group discussion. The direction of the polarization will be the same as the pre-group decisions.

When applying the "group polarization" phenomenon to accommodation theory directly two specific hypotheses emerge:

1. Anticipation of interaction with a cooperative outgroup member will result in more convergence when speech strategies are formulated in a group as opposed to individual context.

2. Anticipation of interaction with a non-cooperative outgroup member will result
in more divergence when speech strategies are formulated in a group as opposed to
individual context.

Current intergroup relations in Quebec provide an ideal context for addressing
these hypotheses. Anglophones have long enjoyed the status of an elite minority
in Quebec, but the rise of Francophone nationalism has altered the situation considerably. New language laws protecting and enhancing the French language and
culture at all levels of society are concrete evidence of the changing relations
between the two groups. Language choice among Francophones when interacting with
Anglophones then provide an excellent context for testing the group polarization
effects on accommodation.

METHOD

Subjects   Eighty Francophone male and female students from a French speaking
junior college participated in this experiment. The students ranged in age from
sixteen to nineteen.

Procedure   The experiment was conducted in three phases and required that four
subjects be tested at a time.

Phase 1

The experiment began by having each of the four subjects seated in a separate
cubicle to receive the instructions. Subjects were led to believe that they
would be meeting with an Anglophone student in order to discuss the appropriate
language of education for Quebec; an extremely sensitive issue where Francophones
in the large majority are in favour of, and Anglophones somewhat anxious about,
the increased role of the French language. If the subjects for a particular
session were one of ten, four person groups randomly assigned to the cooperative
condition, they were told that the Anglophone they would meet shared their opinion
that French should be the appropriate dominant language in education. The ten
groups of four subjects assigned to the non-cooperative condition were told that
the prospective Anglophone was in total disagreement with increasing the use of
French in education.

At this point each of the four subjects was asked to indicate, in the privacy of
their cubicle, the linguistic orientation they planned to adopt when interacting
with the Anglophone student. Specifically there were two questions. For the
first question the subject was to assume that he or she was fluently bilingual,
whereas for the second question subjects took into account their actual fluency
in English. For both questions subjects responded by indicating which of eleven
alternative speech strategies they would adopt; the options ranged from 100%
French to 50% French - 50% English to 100% English.

Phase 2

All four subjects were brought together in the same room. Their task was to discuss the issue of an appropriate language orientation toward the Anglophone they
anticipated meeting and to come to a concensus as to their preferred orientation.
In order to eliminate fluency as a confounding variable, subjects were to assume
that they were functionally bilingual. The group indicated their chosen orientation using the standard eleven point scale ranging from 100% French to 100%
English.

Phase 3

The subjects were again returned to their individual cubicles where they were
asked for a final decision about the linguistic orientation they proposed to use.
In addition subjects were asked a series of questions about their own reasons for
the linguistic strategies they chose and the approach they anticipated their
Anglophone counterpart would take.   These questions were designed to assess the
motivational bases for subjects' decisions about language choice and were asked
at the end of the experiment so they would not contaminate subjects' actual choice
of a linguistic strategy.

In terms of their own motivation, subjects were asked the extent to which their
own linguistic strategy was influenced by such factors as the linguistic orientation they expected from the Anglophone student, their own desire to assert
French identity, the desire to maximise communicational efficiency or because the
meeting would be held at their own French college.   In every case responses were
made on an eleven point scale defined at one end by "not at all important" and at
the other by "extremely important".

Finally, subjects indicated on the standard eleven point scale what linguistic
strategy they expected from their Anglophone counterpart.   As well, they were
asked about the Anglophone's motivations for the linguistic strategy they expected.
These motivational questions for the Anglophone paralleled the questions they were
asked about their own motivations.

RESULTS AND DISCUSSION

The results are presented in two sections.   The first deals directly with the
hypotheses relating group polarization to accommodation, and the second focuses
on the motivational bases for subjects' linguistic orientation.

Group polarization and accommodation

Accommodation was assessed by means of a 2 X 3 analysis of variance where the independent variables were the anticipated spirit of the interaction (cooperative
versus non-cooperative) and the repeated measure of response context (alone versus
group versus post group).   For the first analysis the dependent variable was the
percentage of French chosen, where subjects took into account their fluency in
English.   Although 80 subjects participated in the study, the actual N for the
analysis was reduced to 20 since in the group condition four subjects generated
only a single response.   Thus in the alone and post group conditions the average
of the four responses served as the raw data for the analysis.

The analysis yielded a significant interaction ($F(2,36) = 3.84$, $p < .05$) providing
confirmation of the hypotheses.   The results are presented in Figure 1 where the
operation of the group polarization phenomenon is clear.   Subjects anticipating
interaction with a cooperative Anglophone accommodate more by planning to speak
less French and more English in the group condition then in either of the alone
conditions.   By contrast, in the non-cooperative condition the effect of the
group is to elicit plans for even greater use of French.

From Figure 1 it is also clear that the basic formulations of accommodation theory
are supported.   In all three response conditions more divergence, or planned use
of French, is evidenced in the non-cooperative as opposed to cooperative condition.
The fact that the main effect did not reach acceptable levels of significance was
due no doubt to the reduced N arising from having to average individual responses.

A second 2 X 3 analysis of variance was performed where subjects in the alone con-

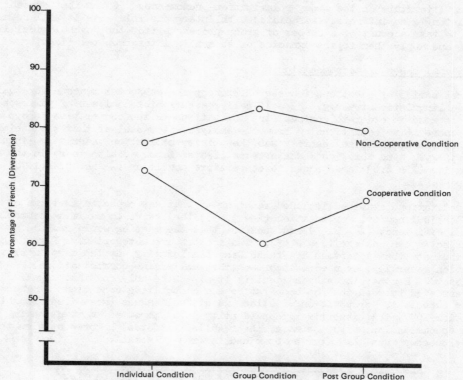

Fig. 1   Significant interaction involving the effects of
          anticipated spirit of interaction and response
          context on accommodation

dition imagined they were functionally bilingual.   In this case only the two main
effects were statistically significant.   The main effect for spirit of interaction was only marginally significant ($F(1,18) = 3.27$, $p < .07$), however it is
clear that in the cooperative condition subjects planned to use less French
($\overline{X} = 66.67\%$) than they did in the non-cooperative condition ($\overline{X} = 78.92\%$).   This
again confirms, albeit modestly, the postulates of accommodation theory.

The main effect for response condition ($F(2,36) = 8.31$, $p < .01$) only partially
confirms the group polarization effect.   In the group condition more French was
planned ($\overline{X} = 71.50\%$) than in the alone condition ($\overline{X} = 59.13\%$), and the shift to
increased use of French in the group condition was maintained in the post group
decisions ($\overline{X} = 73.63\%$).   The group condition clearly influences accommodation
but not precisely in the manner predicted by the hypotheses.   Given the complete
confirmation obtained in the earlier analysis it would seem that in the present
case asking individuals to assume they were bilingual for their first judgment
provided subjects with a set to use a great deal of English.   Thus in the group
condition that followed, the shift was likely to be toward an increased use of
French, not only in the non-cooperative condition, but in the cooperative condition as well.

In summary, the analyses provide good evidence that group processes do influence
accommodation generally, and there is some evidence that the effect is consistent

with the literature on the group polarization phenomenon.   Given that speech accommodation is so intimately associated with intergroup relations it will be necessary to take account of a number of group processes from the psychological literature and apply them to the dynamics of speech in intergroup relations.

Motivational bases of accommodation

The first series of questions focused on Francophone subjects' reasons for their
proposed linguistic strategy.   Specifically, a series of analyses of variance
were performed in order to contrast the motivations in the cooperative as opposed
to non-cooperative conditions.   From the analyses it was clear that the desire
to assert French Canadian identity was the primary motivation underlying linguistic strategy.   And this issue was of even greater importance to those in the non-
cooperative ($\overline{X} = 6.83$) as opposed to cooperative condition ($\overline{X} = 4.48$, $F(1,78) =$
8.32, $p < .01$).

Other motivations examined included reacting to what was expected in terms of the
Anglophone's linguistic orientation ($\overline{X} = 3.99$), the desire to maximise communicational efficiency ($\overline{X} = 4.65$), and the fact that the meeting would be held at
the subject's own college ($\overline{X} = 2.85$).   Two factors are noteworthy.   First, the
means indicate that assertion of French Canadian identity was the most important
motivation generally, even more important than maximising communicational
efficiency.   Second, the ethnic identity item was the only one that significantly
differentiated between the non-cooperative and cooperative conditions.   These
results support the proposition of Giles and his colleagues (see Giles, Bourhis
and Taylor 1977) that asserting group identity is an important motivation in
speech accommodation.   Furthermore, the results reinforce the present view that
group processes must heretofore be examined in greater detail.

TABLE 1   Subjects' explanations of the linguistic orien-
            tation of Anglophones and the motivations for
            this evaluation

	Cooperative condition	Non-cooperative condition	F
Percentage of French anticipated from Anglophone	69.25%	24.25%	74.06**
Desire to assert English Canadian identity	2.90	8.23	46.28**
Desire to maximise communicational efficiency	7.80	4.75	26.68**
The fact that meeting would be held at French college	7.58	4.55	27.68**

** means $p < .01$

Subjects were not only sensitive to their own linguistic strategies but expected
Anglophones to respond in reciprocal fashion.   This pattern is clear from the results which are summarised in Table 1.   Thus, in the cooperative condition Francophone subjects expected significantly more French to be spoken to them than they
did in the non-cooperative condition.   Beyond this they judged that non-cooperative Anglophones would be motivated to assert English Canadian identity more than
Anglophones in the cooperative condition.   Finally, cooperative Anglophones were
seen as especially sensitive to communicational efficiency and to the fact that
the meeting would be at a French speaking college.

CONCLUSIONS

From the results of the present study three conclusions seem warranted. First, consistent with the findings of accommodation theory, Francophones propose converging and diverging speech strategies in the context of intergroup communication. Second, subjects appear to be aware of their own motivations for speech accommodation, and expect members of the other group to behave reciprocally. Specifically there is an awareness of the importance of speech divergence for asserting ethnic identity. Third, and most central to the present context, group processes would appear to be a necessary extension to accommodation theory. Specifically, hypotheses derived from the social psychology of group decision making received confirmation when applied to accommodation theory. The logical extension to the present study would be one that actually involved interaction between two ethnolinguistic groups. The linguistic strategies adopted in both realistic, individualistic and group contexts, would provide unequivocal evidence for the social significance of group processes.

Finally, there is a need to examine a wide range of group processes which social psychologists have studied extensively. Conformity, norms, group cohesion, social identity, are only a few of the processes which have been addressed by social psychologists and which will be usefully applied to issues in the field of language and ethnicity.

REFERENCES

Billig, M. The social psychology of intergroup relations. London: Academic Press, 1976

Bourhis, R. Y. and Giles, H.   The language of intergroup distinctiveness, in H. Giles (Ed.) Language, ethnicity and intergroup relations. London: Academic Press, 1977

Bourhis, R. Y., Giles, H., Leyens, J. P. and Tajfel, H. Psycholinguistic distinctiveness: language difference in Belgium, in H. Giles and R. St. Clair (Eds.) Language and social psychology. Oxford: Blackwell, 1979

Giles, H. Accent mobility: model and some data. Anthropological Linguistics, 1973, 15, 87-105

Giles, H. Linguistic differentiation between ethnic groups, in H. Tajfel (Ed.) Differentiation between social groups: studies in the social psychology of intergroup relations. European Monographs in Social Psychology. London: Academic Press, 1978

Giles, H. and Powesland, P. F. Speech style and social evaluation. London: Academic Press, 1975

Giles, H. Bourhis, R. Y. and Taylor, D. M. Towards a theory of language and ethnic relations, in H. Giles (Ed.), Language, ethnicity and intergroup relations. London: Academic Press, 1977

Giles, H., Taylor, D. M. and Bourhis, R. Y. Towards a theory of interpersonal accommodation through speech: some Canadian data. Language in Society, 1973, 2, 177-192

Jaffe, J. and Feldstein, S. Rhythms of dialogue. New York and London: Academic Press, 1970

Kogan, N. and Wallach, M. A. Risk taking: study in cognition and personality. New York: Holt, Rinehart and Winston, 1964

Matarazzo, J. D. A speech interaction system, in D. J. Kiesler (Ed.), The process of psychotherapy. Chicago: Aldine, 1973

Myers, D. J. and Lamm, H. The group polarization phenomenon. Psychological Bulletin, 1976, 83, 602-627

Moscovici, S. Society and theory in social psychology, in J. Israel and H. Tajfel (Eds.), The context of social psychology. London: Academic Press, 1972

Natalé, M. Convergence of mean vocal intensity in dyadic communication as a
    function of social desirability. Journal of Personality and Social Psycho-
    logy, 1975, 40, 827-830

Sampson, E. E., Psychology and the American Ideal. Journal of Personality and
    Social Psychology, 1977, 35, 767-782

Steiner, I. D. Whatever happened to the group in social psychology? Journal of
    Experimental Social Psychology, 1974, 10, 94-108

Tajfel, H. Experiments in a vacuum, in J. Israel and H. Tajfel (Eds.) The con-
    text of social psychology. London: Academic Press, 1972

Taylor, D. M. and Brown, R. J. Towards a more social social psychology? British
    Journal of Social and Clinical Psychology, 1979, 18, 173-180

Taylor, D. M. and Giles, H. At the crossroads of research into language and eth-
    nic relations, in H. Giles and B. St. Jacques (Eds.) Language and ethnic
    relations. Oxford: Pergamon Press, 1979

Webb, J. T. Interview synchrony: an investigation of two speed rate measures in
    an automated standardised interview, in A. W. Siegman and B. Pope (Eds.)
    Studies in dyadic communication. Oxford: Pergamon, 1970

Language Attitudes: Social Meanings of Contrasting Speech Styles

E. B. Ryan

Department of Psychology, University of Notre-Dame, Notre-Dame,
Indiana 46556, U.S.A.

The term Language Attitudes refers to a broad collection of empirical studies concerned with the distinctive social meanings of contrasting language varieties. The particular contrasts that have been investigated include different languages; ethnic, social class, and regional dialects; and specific linguistically defined variations in pronunciation, lexical choice and grammar.

Although a comprehensive theory of language attitudes is not yet available, the concepts of class-related and context-related standards (Giles and Powesland, 1975) seem to be relevant to both between and within languages in numerous settings across the world. A class-related standard is the style of speech which is viewed as the most prestigious language or language variant in a given culture and which is characteristic of the social group with the highest socioeconomic status. A context-related standard, on the other hand, is a style of speech regarded as the most appropriate for particular socially defined situations. Considerable agreement exists in most societies, even across subgroups, concerning the standard style appropriate to public and formal contexts, while views of appropriateness for informal and private contexts are much more variable. Although the class-related standard usually coincides with the context-related standards for the highest social groups, the standards typically conflict for members of the lower status groups. Most investigations in this area have addressed issues related to class standards.

In terms of assessment of language attitudes, two basic approaches have been employed: direct and indirect measurement. Direct measurement involves questionnaires with items concerning the value of language variety X versus language variety Y for particular purposes or in particular settings (cf. Fishman, Cooper and Conrad 1977; Gardner and Lambert. 1972). Indirect measurement, typically the social evaluation of speakers with contrasting speech styles, has been employed because of its greater relevance to interpersonal situations and because of the greater likelihood of tapping a respondent's private reactions (Lambert 1967). A key advantage of the direct measurement method is the relative ease of examining the effects of differing contexts on language preference.

The studies reported here are all concerned with reactions toward English, one (Roberts and Williams) with Welsh versus English, and the others with contrasting variations within English. Four papers have utilised the indirect method based on social evaluations of communicators, two reports (Wober; Roberts and Williams) have employed the direct questionnaire method. While most of the papers focus upon class-related standards, Smith and Bailey have addressed the effects of context.

In the first paper, Kalin, Rayko and Love consider how English-speaking Canadians perceive and evaluate fluent speakers of English with four foreign accents. Playing the role of personnel consultants for a firm, listeners evidenced discrimination among the speakers in their job suitability ratings. The favouritism hierarchy (British, German, South Asian and West Indian) obtained in this speaker evaluation study matched the evaluative hierarchy of ethnic groups in Canada previously established through direct measures. Although the ethnicity of the accents was not always correctly identified, confusions in identification tended to be with ethnic groups of similar evaluative status. Thus, this employment-analogue experiment simulated real-life decision making and yielded support for a class-related continuum of foreign accents among English Canadian listeners.

In the second paper, Sebastian, Ryan, Keogh and Schmidt suggest that negative stereotypes held for individuals of particular ethnic backgrounds may not be the only determinants of negative reactions to speakers of nonstandard ethnic variants of English. In particular, they consider the relevance of the reinforcement-affect model of interpersonal attraction to Anglo-American evaluations of speakers of Spanish-accented English. When a standard English speaker was heard in a noise condition which interfered substantially with the listeners' performance on a communication task, he was downgraded in a manner very similar to that typical for Spanish-accented speakers. The negative social judgments occurred even though responsibility for task difficulty was overtly attributed to the tape and not to the speaker. These data support the hypothesis that negative affect aroused by accented speech may contribute to unfavourable reactions toward the speakers. Although the reduced level of noise in the second experiment was not sufficient to interact with accentedness or to yield similar downgrading of standard speakers for personality and social evaluations, the noise did affect willingness to participate with the speakers in a future communication experiment. The results, as a whole, suggest that serious attention be given to the negative affect mechanism in the social evaluation of nonstandard speech styles. Of some importance, also, is the fact that the previous within-group findings regarding the downgrading of Spanish-accented speakers were replicated here with a between-group design.

In the third paper, Smith and Bailey explored both context-related and class-related standards for various regional and ethnic dialects of American English. Two groups of Southern American subjects evaluated the same ten speakers on two occasions. The first group rated the speakers on two different activities, reading a prose passage and engaging in free conversation, while the second group rated the speakers on two instances of the same activity, two different samples of free conversation. Evaluations for many speakers varied not only on different activities but also on different instances of the same activity. The authors concluded that it might be possible to talk about fixed attitudes toward American English varieties only for speech styles which are either prestigious or socially stigmatised. For all other varieties, attitude measurement seems dependent upon a speaker's specific activity. More generally, this paper raises the question of reliability in speaker evaluations.

In the fourth paper, Bradac, Courtright and Bowers are also concerned with the social evaluation of a communicator, but evaluations were based on a written message rather than a taped speech sample. Previous research by communication scientists has established that evaluative judgments of a communicator are affected by three lexical variables: language intensity, verbal immediacy and lexical diversity. Subjects read one of eight versions of a belief-discrepant message, each version representing one of the orthogonal combinations of two

levels (high versus low) of the three language variables. Ratings of the communicator and the message partially confirmed the authors' complex set of predictions concerning the relations between the language variables and the dependent
measures. The finding that diversity, in particular, was a relatively powerful
characteristic contributes to the linguistic specification of a class-related
standard since previous research has indicated that a high level of diversity is
associated with high social status.

The fifth paper, by Wober, illustrates the direct measurement approach to language attitudes by examining British attitudes toward a limited set of lexical
items. The same arguments leading to universal adoption of English as the international language have been used against preservation of the English system of
measurement. Thus, the British people are experiencing various pressures to
adopt the metric system (the superposed variant) as opposed to the Imperial System (the vernacular). Wober found that a majority of the respondents preferred
their traditional system and that the social categories of age, sex and social
class did not predict attitudes well. Specific experiences, such as possessing
a metric appliance and frequent exposure to the use of a metric unit (e.g. the
Celsius degree), were related to more receptive attitudes. Seeking a solution
to the resistance to official 'language' policy, Wober resorted to the notion of
a context-related standard in suggesting that a more successful policy might insist on metric jargon only for formal scientific business and government contexts,
not for everyday speech.

The final paper, by Roberts and Williams, views language erosion and maintenance
as aspects of intergroup relationships, with erosion indicating accommodation by
the minority group toward the dominant group and maintenance indicating rejection
of accommodation. Their study of Welsh-speaking adolescents in two Welsh communities differing in language density supported both of their predictions.
First, attitudes toward the minority language (Welsh) were comparatively low
where institutional support for Welsh was low and where social networks consisted
of a mixture of bilingual and monolingual English speakers. Second, involvement
with voluntary ethnic associations influenced language attitudes comparatively
less in the area with more heterogeneous language use than in the community with
more cohesive Welsh language social networks. The influence of social institutions, both formal and informal, and of language density on the formation of
language attitudes is an issue highly relevant to the development of language
attitudes within individuals as they grow up in a given community and also to the
prediction of language maintenance trends for the community as a whole.

In conclusion, these papers provide a good sampling of current language attitude
research. Several important, but often ignored, empirical and methodological
aspects of the overall picture are given serious attention by at least one of
these reports: careful linguistic specification of contrasting variants (Bradac
and colleagues); between-group design (Bradac and colleagues, Sebastian and colleagues); context variation (Smith and Bailey); individual differences among respondents (Roberts and Williams; Wober); role of social institutions (Roberts and
Williams); search for explanatory mechanisms (Sebastian and colleagues): and concern with social issues (Kalin and colleagues; Wober). In terms of future research, one critical issue which requires more direct analysis by researchers in
this area concerns the relationship between attitudes towards language varieties
and attitudes towards speakers of those varieties. A personal preference not to
use metric or Spanish does not necessarily imply a corresponding dislike and downgrading of an individual who has switched to metric or one who speaks Spanish.
Furthermore, dislike and downgrading of speakers of a given variety would not
necessarily preclude a desire to learn that variety for instrumental reasons. A
complete understanding of language attitudes in any cultural context will be best
achieved through combined use of direct and indirect assessments.

REFERENCES

Fishman, J. A., Cooper, R. L. and Conrad, A. W. The spread of English. Rowley,
    Mass: Newbury House, 1977
Gardner, R. C. and Lambert, W. E. Attitudes and motivation in second language
    learning. Rowley, Mass: Newbury House, 1972
Giles, H. and Powesland, P. F. The social evaluation of speech styles. London:
    Academic Press, 1975
Lambert, W. E. The social psychology of bilingualism. Journal of Social Issues,
    1967, 23, 91-109

The Perception and Evaluation of Job Candidates with Four Different Ethnic Accents

R. Kalin, D. S. Rayko and N. Love

Department of Psychology, Queen's University, Kingston, Ontario, Canada

ABSTRACT

This paper describes two experiments. In the first, 50 subjects listened to 16 speakers with four accents (English, German, West Indian and South Asian), rated them for comprehensibility and tried to identify them. Correct identifications ranged from 20% to 94%, but were all better than chance. English speakers were rated more comprehensible than all others; German accented speakers were found to be more comprehensible than South Asians and West Indians. In the second experiment, 64 subjects acted as personnel consultants who were to rate the suitability of the 16 speakers for four jobs varying in status. Analysis revealed a strong Ethnicity x Job Status interaction. For the highest status job (Foreman) English accented candidates were rated most suitable followed by German, South Asian and West Indian. For the lowest status job (Industrial Plant Cleaner) the order was reversed. Results were explained in terms of prejudice toward the ethnic groups represented by the speakers.

Key Words

Ethnicity; accents; judgments of occupation; accent identification; attitudes.

INTRODUCTION

Dialect or accent is a non-content speech quality previously shown to be an important cue in the social evaluation of speakers (Giles and Powesland, 1975). Lambert (1967) has argued that responses to speech cues associated with ethnicity are more likely to reveal listeners' private reactions to ethnic groups than direct attitude questionnaires. There may be discrimination against individual speakers to the extent that there is prejudice against the groups represented by the speakers. Such discrimination becomes particularly serious for ethnic minorities with discernible accents.

Several recent studies have investigated the role of speech in the evaluation of occupational suitability. Hopper and Williams (1973) investigated the relationship between the ethnicity of speakers, as revealed in accents, and judgments of job suitability. They found that intelligence-competence perceived in speech samples was strongly involved in predicting employment decisions while judged ethnicity was but minimally implicated.

In a Canadian context, however, Kalin and Rayko (1978) found that ethnicity, as revealed in accents, did exert an important effect on judgments of job suitability. Speakers with English-Canadian as compared with foreign accents were rated more suitable for higher status jobs, and less suitable for lower status jobs.   Among the foreign accents represented no significant difference was found.   This failure to find differences is surprising in the light of earlier studies which have found a consistent hierarchy of Canadians' evaluations of various ethnic groups (Berry, Kalin and Taylor, 1977).   There are several features in the study by Kalin and Rayko which may have obscured real differential preferences for ethnic groups: the limited status range of the ethnic groups involved in the study, a contrast effect between Canadian and foreign speakers and inability to identify speakers' accents.

The present study sought to eliminate these possible obscuring factors.   The basic procedure was an elaboration of that reported by Kalin and Rayko.   To guarantee a wider range of perceived status, accents were selected from different levels of the evaluative hierarchy of ethnic groups in Canada (Berry, Kalin and Taylor, 1977). The highest rated group (English), the lowest rated group (South Asian), one slightly above average group (German), and one below average group (West Indian) were chosen.   To remove the possible contrast effects, English Canadians were not included.   Finally, a preliminary study was conducted to ascertain whether correct ethnic labels would be assigned to the speech samples presented.

EXPERIMENT   1

METHOD

Subjects

Fifty Canadian undergraduate students at Queen's University (19 male and 31 female) were individually recruited to volunteer for a study in speech perception.

Materials

Audiotape recordings of the voices of 16 male students and professors at Queen's University were used.   Four had English accents (i.e. from England), four had German, four had West Indian and four had South Asian accents.   All spoke English fluently.

The 16 passages heard by subjects were spoken in an informal, conversational mode. They dealt with current concerns (such as the weather, or a neighbour's dog) and were not related to jobs.   To eliminate systematic variance due to speech content, four versions of the tape were prepared such that each of the 16 passages appeared exactly once in each version of the tape, and each passage was associated with each accent category exactly once across the four tape versions.   Order of speakers was randomised and different in each of the four tape versions.

Procedure

Subjects heard 30 second samples of each of 16 foreign accented male voices, and rated each for comprehensibility and attempted to identify the type of accent. For the identification, eight alternatives were provided (English, Italian, German, Polish, West Indian, Chinese, East Indian and "Other").

RESULTS

Correct identifications ranged from 20% to 94%.   Tests for differences in proportions revealed that all speakers were correctly identified at better than chance level (p < .05), with chance level being defined as one eighth, or 12.5%.   English accented speakers, as a group, were correctly identified more frequently than the other voices (X^2(df = 1) = 106.47, p < .001, corrected for continuity).

With respect to comprehensibility ratings, a Newman-Keuls test indicated that the English accented voices were significantly more comprehensible than each of the three other accents while the German accented voices were, in turn, significantly more comprehensible than the West Indian and South Asian voices (p < .05).

EXPERIMENT 2

METHOD

Subjects

Sixty four Canadian undergraduates from Queen's University (21 male and 43 female) served as subjects.

Procedure

Participants were asked to put themselves in the place of a personnel consultant working for a large manufacturing enterprise.   The firm was hiring individuals as foremen, industrial mechanics, production assemblers and industrial plant cleaners.   Extensive job descriptions were provided.   The task was to rate the suitability of each of 16 candidates for each of the four jobs by using 9-point scales.   Information on candidates was provided through biographical dossiers (randomly assigned to speakers) and raters heard 30 second audio recordings of each candidate speaking, purportedly an excerpt from a job interview.   The same audiotapes were used as in Experiment 1.

Design

Three independent variables were manipulated.   Sixteen different job candidates were presented (Speaker).   Four candidates spoke with one of each of four types of ethnic accent (Ethnicity of Accent).   Each candidates was rated on four jobs of different socioeconomic status (Job Status).   Thus, four levels of Speaker were nested within each of four levels of Ethnicity, which were factorially crossed with four levels of Job Status.

RESULTS

An analysis of variance was conducted on the suitability ratings for the design Speaker within Ethnicity x Job Status.   Speaker was treated as a random effects variable.   Quasi-F ratios were computed and appropriate df determined following Meyers (1972).   No significant main effects for either Ethnicity or Speaker were obtained, but a significant main effect for Job Status (F = 28.88, p < .001) and significant interactions for Job Status x Ethnicity (F = 10.10, p < .001) and for Job Status x Speaker (F = 1.81, p < .01) emerged.

The meaning of these findings may be better understood by reference to Figure 1, in which mean job suitability ratings are plotted for the four accent categories across levels of Job Status.   There were general increases in suitability ratings as job status decreased across the first three levels, then a fall in suitability ratings for the lowest status level.

The Job Status x Ethnicity interaction is clearly displayed.   For the highest status job (foreman) English accented candidates were rated the most suitable, then German, South Asian and finally West Indian accented candidates.   But for the

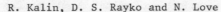

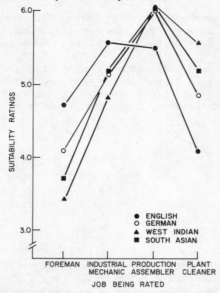

Fig. 1. Mean suitability ratings for English, German, West Indian and
South Asian accented speakers for four jobs.

job of least status (industrial plant cleaner) the order of the mean suitability
scores was exactly reversed.

The Job Status x Speaker interaction followed a similar pattern.   Within each
level of Ethnicity of Accent the individual who received the highest suitability
ratings on the highest status job also received the lowest suitability ratings on
the lowest status job, and vice versa.

Orthogonal comparisons computed at each job status level revealed that English
accented candidates received significantly different suitability ratings from the
others at all job status levels.   German accented candidates were rated more suitable for the highest status job and less suitable for the lowest status job than
the South Asians and West Indians.   South Asians were rated more suitable for the
two highest status jobs and less suitable for the lowest status job when compared
with the West Indians.   Raters clearly made discriminations on the basis of ethnicity at each job status level.

DISCUSSION

The present study demonstrated stable discrimination among the speakers with
various ethnic accents.   This discrimination took the form of favouritism and
denigration.   Favouritism was indicated by judgments of a group of speakers as
suitable for high status jobs and unsuitable for low status jobs.   Denigration
was indicated by the reverse pattern of judgments.   A clear favouritism hierarchy
in the order: English, German, South Asian and West Indian was evident in the
judgments.   The discrimination was triggered by the ethnicity of speakers because
other possibly relevant factors (background information and speech content) were
controlled.

Several explanations can be considered for the major finding.   Comprehensibility
differences may seem like a reasonable explanation since English accented candidates were most comprehensible and were rated most suitable for the highest status

job.   However, comprehensibility is an inadequate explanation for at least two reasons.   First, high comprehensibility can only be an asset, not a hindrance, thus the most comprehensible group ought not to receive the lowest job suitability ratings, as it did for plant cleaner and industrial assembler.   Second, despite the fact that no statistically significant difference was found between the comprehensibility ratings of West Indians and South Asians, raters discriminated between the two groups in job suitability judgments for three of the four job status levels.

Nor is familiarity with English, and therefore ability to comprehend, an adequate explanation.   The two groups receiving highest and lowest ratings at all job status levels were English and West Indian accented speakers.   Yet these are the two speech groups that share English as a mother tongue.

Identification of speakers' ethnicity is a more complex factor.   While it is true that the ethnicity of each speaker was correctly identified at better than chance level, percentages of correct identifications varied considerably, from 20% to 94%, with the English accented voices being well identified and the others considerably less so.   Despite a general lack of correct identification for the non-English accented speakers, there was considerable agreement in the evaluation of speakers.   Or to put it differently, within ethnicity of accent group, homogeneity of evaluation accompanied heterogeneity of ethnic identification.   To find the basis for this result, misidentifications of each accent group were examined. These misidentifications tended to be with the ethnic groups adjacent in the evaluative hierarchy of ethnic groups in Canada discovered by Berry et al., 1977. English speakers were sometimes misidentified as Scottish or Irish, Germans as Polish and South Asians and West Indians were frequently confused with each other. Expressed in different terms, misidentifications in Study 1 were generally consistent with suitability ratings in Study 2.

The most likely reason for the discrimination shown is prejudice against the ethnic groups represented by the speakers.   It is possible that this discrimination is not so much the result of prejudice in the emotional sense, but reflects a consensual perception of social reality.   The existence in Canada of an ethnic hierarchy in terms of socio-economic status has been well documented by Porter (1965). According to this hypothesis, South Asians have higher status than West Indians. South Asian speakers are therefore rated to be more suitable for higher status jobs.   This explanation can be extended to judgments regarding English and German speakers if we assume that in the perceived social status hierarchy the groups appear in the order: English, German, South Asian, West Indian.   In the process of making occupational judgments about stimulus persons, subjects make reference to a consensual social status hierarchy and place individual speakers at the level of the group with which they are identified.   While judgments made on this basis do not necessarily reflect prejudice in the purely emotive sense, they still reflect prejudice.   By suggesting that ethnic groups are best suited for occupations fitting their perceived social status, respondents advocate the perpetuation of the status quo where social status is based on criteria (e.g. ethnicity) which are irrelevant to merit.

REFERENCES

Berry, J. W., Kalin, R. and Taylor, D. M.   Multiculturalism and ethnic attitudes
    in Canada.   Ottawa: Minister of Supply and Services Canada, 1977
Giles, H. and Powesland, P. F. Speech style and social evaluation.   London:
    Academic Press, 1975
Hopper, R. and Williams, F. Speech characteristics and employability.   Speech
    Monographs, 1973, 40, 296-302
Kalin, R. and Rayko, D. S. Discrimination in evaluative judgments against foreign
    accented job candidates. Psychological Reports, 1978, 43, 1203-1209

Lambert, W. E. The social psychology of bilingualism. <u>Journal of Social Issues</u>, 1967, <u>23</u>, 91-109

Meyers, J. L. <u>Fundamentals of experimental design</u>. 2nd ed. Boston: Allyn and Bacon, 1972

Porter, J. <u>The vertical mosaic.</u> Toronto: University of Toronto Press, 1965

The Effects of Negative Affect Arousal on Reactions to Speakers[1]

R. J. Sebastian, Ellen Bouchard Ryan, T. F. Keogh and A. C. Schmidt

*Department of Psychology, University of Notre-Dame, Notre-Dame,
Indiana 46556, U.S.A.*

ABSTRACT

Two studies were conducted to test the hypothesis that speakers associated with
negative affect and/or frustration will be negatively evaluated. As part of a
colour recognition study, the participants in the first experiment listened to
tape-recorded colour descriptions by a male speaker of standard English. The
tape was either free from noise or punctuated by bursts of white noise. The subjects in the noisy tape condition performed significantly worse on the colour recognition task, and consistent with the hypothesis, judged the speaker less favourably. Participants in the second study listened to the colour descriptions of
either a standard or Spanish-accented speaker of English which were presented on
tapes with no noise, continuous white noise or bursts of white noise. Colour
recognition accuracy was significantly influenced by both noise and accent alone
as well as in combination. Accented speakers were responded to more negatively
than standard speakers on most measures, including several social evaluation
scales. Noise significantly affected other measures, including the ratings of
speaker's communication effectiveness, tape responsibility for task difficulty,
and ease of understanding. The results, as a whole, suggest that serious attention be given to the negative affect mechanism in the social evaluation of nonstandard speech styles.

Key Words

Ethnicity; judgments of accents; accents, social evaluation, communicative
effectiveness.

INTRODUCTION

In comparison to speakers of the standard variety of a language, individuals who
speak nonstandard or low prestige varieties are generally evaluated more negatively on a number of dimensions, including status and personality (Giles and Powesland
1975). Spanish-accented speakers of English, for example, have been viewed by
Anglo-American listeners as lower in status and social class, less similar in atti-

1. Reprints may be requested from Richard J. Sebastian, Department of Psychology,
   University of Notre-Dame, Notre-Dame, Indiana 46556. The authors gratefully
   acknowledge the Zahm Travel Fund for providing travel support.

tudes, less desirable as "partners" in a range of social interactions, and sometimes less friendly than speakers of standard English (Ryan and Carranza, 1975;
Ryan and Sebastian, in press; Sebastian, Ryan and Corso, submitted). The explanations of such findings frequently involve assumptions about the negative stereotypes held for individuals of Spanish ethnicity and/or the lower class, and evidence for these stereotype explanations exists (Ryan and Sebastian, in press; Sebastian and colleagues).It is plausible, however, that other mechanisms may also contribute to the frequently observed downgrading of Spanish-accented speakers and
other individuals or groups who speak nonstandard varieties of a language.

One such mechanism essentially involves the arousal of negative affect in individuals listening to accented English and the later devaluation of those speakers
who are associated with the negative affect (cf Clore and Byrne, 1974). Subjects in our previous studies have reported that listening to Spanish-accented
speakers made them feel more uncomfortable and caused them greater difficulty in
understanding than listening to speakers of standard English. In the research of
Sebastian and colleagues these ratings were significantly correlated with all
other evaluative reactions, suggesting that the negative affect experienced by the
listeners may have contributed to their other responses.

This negative affect mechanism may be especially likely to operate in interpersonal
communication situations where the individuals involved are at least minimally motivated to understand one another. An Anglo-American's difficulty in understanding Spanish-accented speech in these settings may be at least mildly frustrating.
Further frustration may be experienced by the Anglo-American if his difficulty in
understanding the Spanish-accented speech diminishes his ability to carry on a
conversation or to execute other interaction demands successfully. Under these
circumstances, derogation of the Spanish-accented speaker would be expected from
theories of interpersonal attraction which predict that persons associated with
frustration or negative affect will be disliked (Clore and Byrne, 1974; Lott and
Lott, 1972).

A fairly direct test of the negative affect mechanism can be made by experimentally
varying the affective circumstances under which subjects are exposed to the same
speaker. White noise, especially intermittent and unpredictable white noise, is
known to be subjectively annoying (Glass and Singer, 1972). A person associated
with this kind of noise should be less attractive than the same individual who is
not associated with this aversive stimulation, especially if the persons evaluated
are not physically present (Kenrick and Johnson, 1979). In addition to its intrinsic effects, the noise may interfere with a communicated message, thereby also
impairing performance of a task based upon the communicated information. These
additional frustrations should lead to even further devaluation of an individual
associated with them.

STUDY 1

On the basis of the above reasoning, college students in the first study listened
to the tape-recorded descriptions of difficult -to-describe colours given by a
male speaker of standard English as part of a colour recognition experiment. The
tapes were either noise free (normal) or punctuated by bursts of noise (noisy).
It was predicted that the speaker would be evaluated more negatively in the noisy
than normal tape condition.

METHOD

Thirty volunteer undergraduate students were assigned randomly to two conditions.
Participants were tested in a language laboratory which had individual cubicles.
They were told that the study concerned the ability to recognize hard-to-describe

colours on the basis of another person's description of them.   Also, they were
told that mechanical difficulty during preparation of the tapes had caused some of
the tapes to have some static or noise on them.   After listening to each of six
taped colour descriptions (approximately 25-words each in length), subjects chose
the colour being described from a set of five stimulus colours.   For the normal
condition, the colour descriptions of a male speaker of standard English were
recorded.   The taped descriptions for the noise condition were prepared by superimposing bursts of white noise upon the original tape.

After the colour recognition task, the participants were asked to complete a questionnaire about the speaker.   The questionnaire included seven-point Likert-like
scales on personality characteristics (successful, unfriendly, trustworthy, unin-
telligent), judged attitude/belief similarity, willingness to participate with the
speaker in a future communication experiment, effectiveness of colour descriptions,
responsibility of the speaker for any difficulties experienced with the task, and
responsibility of the tape recording for any task difficulties.   An item for estimating social class was also included.   In addition, three speech items were
included: accentedness, discomfort associated with listening to the speaker, and
ease of understanding the speaker.

RESULTS

Scores on the questionnaire items (except the two on responsibility) were trans-
posed so that high numbers represent favourable responses to the speaker.   As in
our previous research two dimensions of personality ratings were analysed: status
(successful and intelligent) and solidarity (trustworthy and friendly).

TABLE 1   Mean colour recognition accuracy and speaker evaluations
under normal and noisy conditions

	Normal condition	Noisy condition
Colour Accuracy	3.73	1.67***
Status	4.97	3.90**
Solidarity	4.90	4.33*
Social Class	4.73	3.80**
Perceived Belief/Attitude Similarity	4.07	3.47
Willingness for Future Experiment Together	5.53	2.40***
Speaker Responsibility	2.87	3.07
Tape Responsibility	4.53	6.47**
Effective	5.13	2.53***
Accented	5.00	5.00
Comfortable	6.20	3.27***
Ease of Understanding	4.00	1.07***

*p < .05   **p < .01   ***p < .001

The group means for the standard and noisy tapes are presented in Table 1.   As can
be seen in the table, colour identification was substantially worse in the noise
condition.   Consistent with the fact, the speaker in the noise condition was
viewed as less effective.   The noisy speech was evaluated as uncomfortable and
extremely difficult to understand, but the mean accent rating was predictably
identical under both conditions. ·Although the tape (but not the speaker) was
seen to be more responsible for task difficulties under noise, indirect measures of

speaker responsibility revealed evidence of the generalisation of discomfort and frustration to evaluations of the speaker.   In particular, although the speech was in fact standard the typical pattern of derogation for speakers with nonstandard English was assigned: lower status, solidarity, and social class, and greater "social distance".

STUDY 2

The second study extended the first by examining listeners' evaluation of Spanish-accented speakers as well as speakers of standard English.   The study also compared continuous noise with bursts of noise and no noise tapes.   In an effort to equate the performance on the colour recognition task, two additional changes were made.   For the bursts condition, the noise was introduced on the tape in such a way that no critical colour information was masked.   Secondly, two of the colour sets were modified to raise the average level of recognition accuracy.   It was predicted that speakers associated with noise and accented speakers would be evaluated more negatively than speakers who communicated over noise-free tapes and standard speakers.

METHOD

Ninety undergraduate students participated in this study, which was conducted in a manner similar to Study 1.   Tape recordings of the same colour descriptions were prepared for three male speakers of standard English and for three male speakers of Spanish-accented English.   From each speaker's recording, two noisy versions were prepared.   The Continuous-Noise tapes were created by superimposing bursts of white noise.   Five listeners were assigned to each of the 18 recordings.   A nine-point Likert-like mood questionnaire was administered in this study after completion of the colour recognition task and before evaluation of the speaker.

RESULTS

The results were analysed by a 3 x 2 x 3 analysis of variance with two between factors (noise and accent) and one nested factor (speakers).   The subjects' colour recognition accuracy was significantly influenced by noise, accent and the interaction of these factors.   As seen in Table 2, performance on the task was especially depressed in the continuous noise, accented speaker condition.   Analysis of participants' estimates of their performance on the colour recognition task closely parallel those of the performance data.

In support of one of the major hypotheses of the study, accented speakers were evaluated more negatively than standard speakers on several of the personality and social dimensions: status, social class and attitude/belief similarity.

Although noise did not significantly affect the subjects' responses on the major personality and social evaluations, main and interaction effects for noise were obtained on other response measures.   The subjects' reported willingness to participate in a future communication experiment with the speaker was marginally ($p < .10$) affected by the noise, with the least willingness expressed by individuals in the continuous noise condition.   The perceived effectiveness of the communications was also significantly influenced by the noise and marginally ($p < .10$) affected by accent.   For speaker responsibility, a marginal main effect for noise indicated that subjects held the speaker least responsible in the bursts condition. A marginally significant interaction and subsequent simple effect test indicated that this was true <u>only</u> for the standard speaker.   Subjects saw the tape as more responsible for their difficulties in both noise conditions, especially when the speaker was <u>accented</u>.

TABLE 2 Mean colour recognition accuracy and evaluations for speakers of standard and accented English (A) under normal and noisy conditions (N)

| | Normal | | Continuous Noise | | Burst Noise | | Significant |
	Standard	Accented	Standard	Accented	Standard	Accented	Effects
Colour Accuracy	4.27	4.87	4.73	2.73	4.20	4.13	N,A,NA
Guessed Colour Accuracy	3.73	4.07	4.07	2.67	4.13	3.60	N+,A,NA
Status	5.13	4.10	4.80	3.97	4.47	4.23	A
Solidarity	5.13	4.93	5.00	4.67	4.87	4.90	
Social Class	4.67	3.07	4.40	3.47	4.67	3.53	A
Perceived Belief/ Attitude Similarity	3.40	2.73	3.67	3.07	3.53	3.27	A
Willingness for Future Experiment Together	4.73	4.67	4.07	3.67	4.47	3.93	N+
Speaker Responsibility	4.00	3.40	3.13	3.80	2.27	3.47	N+,NA+
Tape Responsibility	2.33	2.00	4.40	6.27	5.40	6.60	N,A,NA
Effective	4.87	4.53	4.67	3.60	5.07	5.00	N,A+
Accented	5.33	2.20	5.67	3.33	5.53	2.20	N+,A
Comfortable	6.00	5.13	6.07	4.80	5.87	5.27	A
Ease of Understanding	6.27	4.73	3.87	2.13	4.27	3.87	N,A
Mood	7.20	7.00	6.60	5.60	7.40	7.13	N,A+

All effects reported are significant beyond the .05 level unless marked by a + in which case they are marginal ($p < .10$).

The measures directly concerned with speech were also influenced by the independent variables. Main effects for accent were obtained on all speech measures: accentedness, comfort, and difficulty in understanding. A main effect for noise on the difficulty in understanding measure, reflected particular difficulty for the continuous noise condition.

The analysis of the mood scale indicated that subjects in the continuous noise condition experienced the most negative affect while subjects who listened to accented speakers tended to feel more negative affect.

DISCUSSION

Several features of the reported research are especially noteworthy. Striking support of the negative affect mechanism is provided by the first study in which the noise was quite clearly disruptive of the subjects' ability to perform the task. The fact that the speaker of standard English who was associated with the noise and resulting frustrations was severely derogated cannot be explained in terms of stereotypes.

Since the noise manipulations in the second study did not yield different levels of colour recognition for standard speakers, this study served as a more rigorous test of the effects of noise per se on evaluative judgments. Even though little evidence was obtained for the influence of noise on the evaluative reactions toward speakers associated with it, further research with more aversive noises (louder, unpredictable) and with more direct measures of affect should be conducted.

An additional significant feature of the second study centres on the pronounced devaluation of the Spanish-accented speakers.   Given the controversy about the validity of results obtained with within-subjects designs (cf. Giles and Bourhis, 1973; Lee, 1971), this replication of earlier findings with a between-subjects design further justifies the use of the more efficient design in which listeners judge several speakers.

In summary, although the results of the present research do not unequivocally support the negative affect mechanism, there is sufficient evidence for it in our data as well as the extant literature to justify its serious consideration as a source of negative evaluations of speakers of nonstandard language varieties.

REFERENCES

Clore, G. L. and Byrne, D.   A reinforcement-affect model of attraction, in T. L. Huston (Ed.), Foundations of interpersonal attraction.   New York: Academic Press, 1974

Giles, H. and Bourhis, R. Y.   Dialect perception revisited.   Quarterly Journal of Speech, 1973, 59, 337-342

Giles, H. and Powesland, P. F.   Speech style and social evaluation.   New York: Academic Press, 1972

Glass, D. C. and Singer, J. E.   Urban stress: experiments on noise and social stressors.   New York: Academic Press, 1972

Kenrick, D. T. and Johnson, G. A.   Interpersonal attraction in aversive environments: a problem for the classical conditioning paradigm?   Journal of Personality and Social Psychology, 1979, 37, 572-579

Lee, R. R. Dialect perception: a critical review and re-evaluation.   Quarterly Journal of Speech, 1971, 57, 410-417

Lott, A. J. and Lott, B. E.   The power of liking: consequences of interpersonal attitudes derived from a liberalized view of secondary reinforcement, in L. Berkowitz (Ed.) Advances in experimental social psychology (Vol. 6).   New York: Academic Press, 1972

Ryan, E. B. and Carranza, M. A.   Evaluative reactions toward speakers of standard English and Mexican American accented English.   Journal of Personality and Social Psychology, 1975, 31, 855-863

Ryan, E. B. and Sebastian, R. J.   The effects of speech style and social class background on social judgments of speakers.   British Journal of Social and Clinical Psychology, in press

Sebastian, R. J., Ryan, E. B. and Corso, L.   Social judgments of speakers with differing degrees of accentedness.   Manuscript submitted for publication, 1979

Attitude and Activity:
Contextual Constraints on Subjective Judgments

M. K. Smith* and G. H. Bailey**

**Department of Psychology, University of Tennessee, Knoxville,
Tennessee 37916, U.S.A.*
***Linguistic Atlas of the Gulf States, Emory University, Atlanta,
Georgia 30322, U.S.A.*

ABSTRACT

The purpose of the present paper is to explore the effects that differing activities might have on subjects' evaluation of speakers of regional dialects within
the United States.   In order to do this two experiments were run.   In Experiment
1, a group of Southern American subjects rated the same 10 speakers on two different activities: reading a prose passage and engaging in free conversation.   In
Experiment 2, another group of subjects rated these same speakers on two instances
of the same activity, i.e. on two different free conversation passages.   Results
of these experiments indicate that evaluations for many speakers varied not only
on different activities but also on different instances of the same activity.
Only the ratings of two groups of speakers were constant: North Midland speakers
and Southern blacks.   Thus, within American English, it might be possible to talk
about fixed attitudes toward language only when talking about speech which is
either prestigious or socially stigmatized.   For all other speakers, an attitude
measurement will have to take into account a speaker's specific activity.

Key Words

Dialect; social evaluation; situational variation; speaker evaluation;
attitudes to dialects.

INTRODUCTION

During the last twenty years a number of researchers have investigated attitudes
toward regional varieties of English which are spoken within a single country.
In most cases the researchers have discovered stereotyped reactions to those
regional varieties.   For example, in Britain, Giles (1970) used a matched-guise
technique to study reactions to thirteen English accents.   He concluded that
English accents can be ranked along a continuum of prestige, with Received Pronunciation at the top and Birmingham speech at the bottom.   Tucker and Lambert (1969)
in a study of the attitudes of three groups of college students toward six American dialects, found that the variety rated most favourably by all groups was "Network English", the variety used most often on national radio and television.
Underwood (1974), on the other hand, in a study of the attitudes of Arkansawyers
toward different varieties of American English, found no evidence for a consensus
prestige variety: Arkansawyers gave the highest rating to speech most like their
own.   Houck and Bowers (1969), however, found that Northerners' rating of the

speech of Southern Americans was variable: Southerners were rated more favourably
when they were talking about issues relevant to the South.

The discrepancy among the findings of Lambert and Tucker, Underwood and Houck and
Bowers is puzzling.   In fact, it makes one wonder whether or not there are fixed
attitudes toward different varieties of a language.   The idea that people have
fixed attitudes toward different varieties of their language becomes even more
tenuous when one realises that most earlier studies, as Giles and Powesland (1975)
note, rely exclusively on stimulus voices reading emotionally neutral prose passages.   These studies, then, ignore the possible effects of a speaker's activity -
whether he is reading a standard passage, talking about a neutral issue, talking
about personal experiences and so forth.   The study by Houck and Bowers is a
notable exception.   They find that varying the content of the stimulus passage
causes a change in the evaluation of certain speakers.   The purpose of this study
is to explore in more detail the relationship between what a speaker is doing -
his activity - and how he is perceived.   If the evaluations of speakers do not
change with changes in activity, then we can talk about fixed attitudes toward
dialects with some certainty.   If, however, evaluations of speakers do change
with changes in activity, then we can only talk about attitudes toward dialects
in specific contexts.

In order to determine the relationship between activity and evaluation, two experiments were designed.   In the first experiment, we had subjects rate the same
group of speakers on two different activities: reading and free conversation.
In the second experiment we had subjects rate those speakers on two instances of
the same activity, that is, on two samples of free conversation.

EXPERIMENT 1

METHOD

Subjects

Our subjects were 35 students enrolled in two spring-quarter freshman English
classes (one an early morning class, the other an early afternoon class) at The
University of Tennessee at Knoxville.   Nineteen of the students were enrolled in
the afternoon class, sixteen in the morning class.   Of the students 54% were male,
89% were white, and 91% were native Tennesseans.   The mean age was 18.8 years.

Materials

Our materials consisted of a semantic differential scale which made use of 12
pairs of adjectives and two tape recordings of 10 speakers from different parts of
the United States.   The format of the semantic differential was that used by
Underwood (1974): the adjectives were divided into two groups, one of which consisted of adjectives designed for evaluation of a speaker's speech, the other of
which were adjectives designed for evaluation of the speaker as a person.   The
pairs of adjectives designed for the rating of speech were good-bad, careful-
sloppy, pretty-ugly, smooth-harsh, graceful-clumsy, and relaxed-tense.   The adjectives designed for the rating of the person were smart-dumb, rich-poor,
friendly-unfriendly, city-country, energetic-lazy and polite-rude.   A seven point
scale was used.

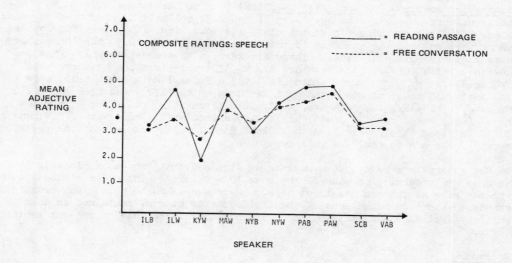

Fig. 1. Composite Speech Scores for 10 speakers on two activities (Reading and Free Conversation).

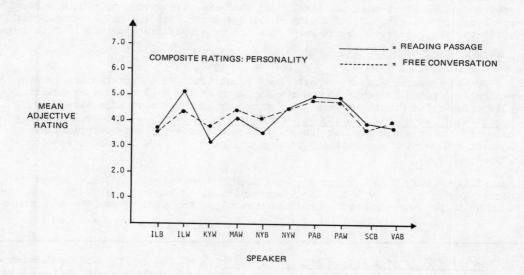

Fig. 2. Composite Personality Scores for 10 speakers on two activities (Reading and Free Conversation).

The two tape recordings were made from the collection of tapes used by the Dictionary of American Regional English (DARE)[1]. The DARE tapes used in this experiment were chosen by the custodian of the DARE collection, who tried to match black and white speakers for social class and education within specific locales which were selected as examples of various American dialects. The 10 speakers were from five dialect areas. Three speakers, a Massachusetts white (MAW), a New York white (NYW), and a New York black (NYB) were from the Northern area. Two speakers, a Pennsylvania white (PAW) and a Pennsylvania black (PAB) were from the North Midland, and one speaker, a Kentucky white (KYW), was from the South Midland. Finally, two speakers, a Virginia black (VAB) and a South Carolina black (SCB) were from the South, and two speakers, an Illinois white (ILW) and an Illinois black (ILB), were from the Inland North. It took each of the speakers about 45 seconds to read the passage.

On the second tape we dubbed a passage of free conversation (approximately 45 seconds per speaker) for each of the same 10 speakers. The order of the speakers was the same as that on the first tape. Care was taken to choose conversational passages which contained none of the fieldworker's speech, contained no long periods of silence and contained no overt non-linguistic cues to race or social class.

Procedure

Both tapes were played for the subjects, but the second one, the one consisting of passages of free conversation, was played a month after the first, the one with the reading passage. In both cases the procedure was the same: the teacher explained the use of the semantic differential at the beginning of class and then asked the students to evaluate each speaker on tape using that tool. The tape was played for the entire class at once (i.e. all students in each class evaluated the speakers at the same time), and students were given one minute between speakers for evaluation. The purpose of the experiment was not discussed with students, and students did not know that the same speakers appeared on both tapes.

RESULTS[2].

A repeated measure, within subject ANOVA (Condition /Free Conversation versus Reading/ x Speaker x Subject) was run for each of the twelve adjective pairs. Main effects for Condition were found for four of the twelve adjective pairs (pretty-ugly, good-bad, smooth-harsh and careful-sloppy). However, the Speaker main effects were significant for all twelve adjectives; more importantly, Speaker x Condition interactions were significant ($p < .01$ in each case) for all the adjectives.

Correlations were also performed over all adjective pairs. All six adjectives pertaining to speech were highly intercorrelated, as were the six adjectives pertaining to personal traits. From these results, the authors decided to compute

---

1. The Dictionary of American Regional English is edited by Frederic G. Cassidy of The University of Wisconsin, and is supported by a grant from the National Endowment for the Humanities. We would like to thank Professor Cassidy for allowing us to use DARE tapes in conducting our research.

2. We would also like to thank Jeffrey L. Smith for his assistance in the processing of the data.

both a mean speech score (i.e. an average of the six adjectives) and a mean personality score. Graphs of the mean values can be found in Figure 1 (for speech) and Figure 2 (for personality). ANOVA's were also run on these mean scores; all effects were significant except for the main effect for Condition on the personality variable.

From Figure 1 it is clear that subjects' evaluations of reading were higher than their evaluations of free conversation, with differences the greatest for the three speakers: ILW, MAW and PAB. Two speakers, KYW and NYB, show large differences in the opposite direction: they were rated higher on free conversation. The two task ratings were very close for two speakers, NYW and PAW, and for four of the five black speakers. From Figure 2 it can be seen that the pattern of results for the evaluation of personality is almost identical to the pattern for the evaluation of speech, with these exceptions: MAW and VAB were rated somewhat higher when engaging in free conversation and the two scores for MAW and PAB are very close.

EXPERIMENT 2

METHOD

Subjects

The subjects were twenty students (ten male, ten female) enrolled in introductory psychology classes at The University of Tennessee. All students were white, native Tennesseans with a mean age of 19.1 years. Each student received extra credit for participation in the experiment.

Materials

For this experiment a second passage of free conversation for each speaker was selected from DARE records and put on a second tape. The order of the speakers was randomised. Otherwise, all materials were identical to those used in Experiment 1.

Procedure

The subjects came in groups of five to a psychology laboratory at The University of Tennessee. As part of their extra credit requirement, the subjects were asked to return one month later, ostensibly for a different experiment. In all other respects the rating procedure was identical to that used in Experiment 1. During the first session, subjects were asked to rate the speakers on Free Conversation Tape 1, that is, on the Free Conversation tape used in Experiment 1. During the second session, subjects rated the speakers on Free Conversation Tape 2. All subjects participated in both sessions.

RESULTS

ANOVA's similar to those used in Experiment 1 were run, with the two components for Conditions this time being Free Conversation I versus Free Conversation II. No significant main effects for Condition were found; all Speaker main effects were significant except for the friendly-unfriendly pair. Only four interactions were significant: pretty, good, smooth and smart.

Mean speech and personality scores were once again computed because of the high intercorrelations among variables. Graphs of these means can be found in Figure 3 (for speech) and Figure 4 (for personality). ANOVA's on these two variables were also run; the only variables which were significant were both Speaker main effects and the interaction effect for speech.

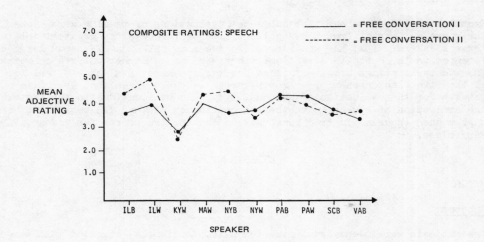

Fig. 3. Composite Speech Scores for 10 speakers on two instances
of the same activity (Free Conversation).

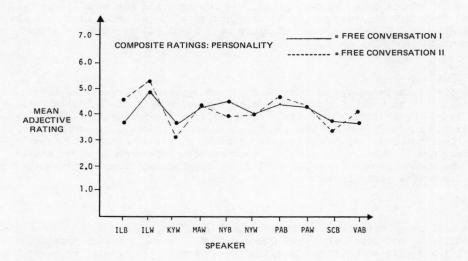

Fig. 4. Composite Personality Scores for 10 speakers on two
instances of the same activity (Free Conversation).

An examination of Figure 3 shows that the interaction effect was significant because of differences between the evaluations of four speakers: ILB, ILW, NYB and MAW. The other speakers' ratings were almost identical across the two tasks. On Figure 4, small discrepancies can be seen for three speakers: ILB, KYW and NYB. None of the differences, however, are significant.

DISCUSSION

Are there fixed attitudes toward regional varieties of American English? The results of the present experiments suggest a tentative yes and no. The findings of Experiment 1 indicate that a change in activity often produces a significant change in the way a speaker is evaluated. Evaluations of both speech and personality may be altered. It should be noted, however, that a change in activity does not affect the rating of all speakers. The results of Experiment 2 indicate that even on two instances of the same activity there may be significant differences in the evaluation of the speech, though not of the personality of the speakers.

In general, the speakers for whom evaluations were most constant were those from the North Midland area – speakers whose speech is probably closest to Network English – and Southern blacks – speakers whose speech is usually considered to be socially stigmatised. The fact that the North Midland speakers were ranked highest in several, though not all of the conditions perhaps lends support to Tucker and Lambert's notion of a prestige variety of American English. However, there is no evidence for the existence of a prestige continuum of American dialects such as Giles found in England. In fact, the rank ordering of speakers changes with a change in activity.

The findings of the present study suggest that we can only tentatively talk about attitudes toward different varieties of the same language. There seem to be fixed attitudes toward the most prestigious and most stigmatised dialects, at least in the contexts under investigation here, but attitudes toward other varieties may be influenced by the speaker's activity and, as Houck and Bowers demonstrate, even by a speaker's topic. Thus, before we talk about stereotyped attitudes toward different dialects of the same language, attitudes must be investigated in a variety of activities, and with speakers discussing a variety of topics.

REFERENCES

Giles, H. Evaluative reactions to accents. Educational Review, 1970, 22, 211-227
Giles, H. and Powesland, P. F. Speech style and social evaluation. London: Academic Press, 1975
Houck, C. L. and Bowers, J. T. Dialect and identification in persuasive messages. Language and Speech, 1969, 22, 180-186
Tucker, G. R. and Lambert, W. E. White and Negro listeners' reactions to various American-English dialects. Social Forces, 1969, 47, 463-468
Underwood, G. N. How you sound to an Arkansawyer. American Speech, 1974, 49, 208-215

Effects of Intensity, Immediacy and Diversity Upon Receiver Attitudes Toward a Belief-Discrepant Message and Its Source

J. J. Bradac*, J. A. Courtright** and J. W. Bowers*

*Department of Communication Studies, University of Iowa, Iowa 52242, U.S.A.
**Cleveland State University, Cleveland, Ohio 44115, U.S.A.

ABSTRACT

During the last fifteen years, over fifty studies have been done on the attitudinal consequences of three language variables: language intensity, verbal immediacy and lexical diversity. We recently constructed a comprehensive theory integrating previous research on these variables which comprises 26 axioms, 66 novel theorems and a causal model. The research reported here is an initial test of a part of the causal model and selected theorems; 183 persons participated. Each read one of eight versions of a message pretested for belief discrepancy. The versions represented orthogonal combinations of two levels (high versus low) of each of the three language variables. Subjects responded to 24 seven-interval scales which measured their judgments of the communicator and her message. Results indicate that diversity is directly related to judgments of competence, trustworthiness, predictability, similarity and receiver favourableness toward the belief-discrepant message. Immediacy is inversely related to judgments of competence at low diversity and of trustworthiness at high diversity. Immediacy is inversely related to liking when intensity is high. Intensity is directly related to predictability when immediacy is low. The results partially confirm our predictions. They indicate also that diversity is a more powerful determinant of receiver judgments and attitudes than are immediacy or intensity.

Key Words

Language intensity; verbal immediacy; lexical diversity; language attitudes; impression formation; speech style; theory testing; message variables.

INTRODUCTION

Abundant evidence indicates that receivers' judgments of communicator attributes and abilities are influenced by the type of language he or she uses (cf Giles and Powesland, 1975). Dialectal variations especially have been subjected to experimentation which supports this claim. Communicative consequences of other variations in language have also been studied. For example, three language variables have recently received much attention from communication scientists: language intensity, verbal immediacy and lexical diversity. Briefly, intensity refers to linguistic cues indicating the communicator's departure from affective neutrality; immediacy refers to cues which indicate association with or dissociation from the topics or referents of the message; and diversity refers to the degree of

217

lexical redundancy (conversely, vocabulary richness) exhibited by the communicator.

We recently constructed a comprehensive theory integrating previous research on these variables (Bradac, Bowers and Courtright, 1980).   The theory comprises 26 axioms, 66 novel theorems and a causal model.   The research reported here is an initial test of a part of the causal model and some of the theorems.   We examine the individual and combined effects of the three variables on receiver attitudes when the communicator's message is belief-discrepant from the stand-point of her receivers.

Our model predicts that:

1) Language intensity (of a non-obscene type) in belief-discrepant messages is inversely related to post-communication ratings of source competence.
2) Language intensity in belief-discrepant messages is inversely related to message effectiveness (attitude change).
3) Language intensity in belief-discrepant messages is inversely related to receiver attributions of source similarity.
4) Verbal immediacy is directly related to receiver judgments of source competence and character (trustworthiness).   (This prediction is based on a single study by Conville (1975); we speculate that it will not be supported in the case of a belief-discrepant message.)
5) Verbal immediacy in belief-discrepant messages is inversely related to receiver attributions of source similarity.
6) Lexical diversity is directly related to receiver judgments of source competence.
7) Lexical diversity is directly related to message effectiveness (attitude change).
8) Lexical diversity is directly related to receiver attributions of source similarity.

Our theorems indicate that:

1) Lexical diversity is directly related to receiver judgments of source predictability (i.e. inversely related to uncertainty).
2) Lexical diversity is directly related to receiver liking for source.
3) For a belief-discrepant message, intensity and immediacy are inversely related to receiver judgments of source predictability (i.e. directly related to uncertainty).
4) For a belief-discrepant message, intensity and immediacy are inversely related to receiver liking for source.

The research reported below tests these predictions.

METHOD

Subjects

Subjects were 183 undergraduates at Cleveland State University, randomly assigned to conditions.

Belief-Discrepant Message

We constructed a message arguing in support of a tuition fee increase at Cleveland State University.   The fact that an increase had occurred at this institution just prior to the study suggested to us that this would be a salient, belief-discrepant proposition.   As expected, a pretest indicated that persons from the target population were opposed to a fee increase ($\overline{X}$ = 2.24 on a seven-point scale with 1.0 as the value indicating maximal opposition).   Message length was approximately 450 words.   The source of the message was described as a female assistant professor of economics at Cleveland State University.

Lexical Manipulations

From the "kernel" belief-discrepant message, we generated high- and low-diversity versions.   High diversity was operationalised as a mean segmental type-token ratio for 25-word segments of approximately .88;   the ratio for low-diversity versions was approximately .76.   This means that on the average six words were repeated per segment in the low diversity messages, whereas three words were repeated for high diversity messages, a difference of three repetitions.   Accordingly, for each 25-word segment we included three words which were high or low in intensity, immediacy and diversity.   Levels of immediacy were produced by varying adjectives (the versus that), verb tense (present versus past), order of occurrence of references (earlier versus later), implied voluntarism (want versus must), mutuality (Dave and I do x versus I do x with Dave), and probability (Bob and I will versus Bob and I may). (cf Mehrabian, 1968).   Intensity levels were produced by including words and phrases rated maximally different in terms of intensity in a pretest given to persons from the target population (e.g. "extremely costly" versus "somewhat costly"). (cf Bowers, 1963).   Thus, eight message versions were created: high versus low intensity x high versus low immediacy x high versus low diversity.

Measures

Subjects read one of the eight message versions and subsequently responded to 24 seven-interval scales which measured their judgments of communicator competence, trustworthiness, predictability, likeability and similarity and their attitudes toward the message's proposition (the tuition increase).   With an eigenvalue criterion of 1.0, factor analyses confirmed the six hypothetical dimensions underlying the scales.   Generally, the appropriate items were loaded above .60, with split loadings below .40.

Design and analysis

The design is a 2 x 2 x 2 factorial with three between-subjects variables. Accordingly, three-factor analyses of variance were run on scores representing each of the six factors.   These scores were obtained in each case by summing across the scales loading on the factor.   Where interactive effects were obtained, simple effects tests were conducted subsequently.

RESULTS

1. A main effect was obtained for competence ($F = 23.85$; $p < .0001$).   High diversity produced higher ratings than did low.   An immediacy x diversity interaction was also obtained ($F = 3.82$; $p < .05$).   Simple effects tests indicated that when diversity was high, immediacy levels did not differ;   when diversity was low, higher competence was attributed to the source of the message exhibiting low immediacy ($p < .08$).   Effects of diversity differed at both high and low immediacy ($p < .05$, $< .01$, respectively).

2. A main effect was obtained for trustworthiness ($F = 6.50$; $p < .01$).   High diversity produced higher ratings than did low.   An immediacy x diversity interaction was also obtained ($F = 4.98$; $p < .03$).   Simple effects tests indicated that high immediacy produced lower ratings of trustworthiness when diversity was high ($p < .08$);   at low diversity, immediacy levels did not differ.   When immediacy was low, the two levels of diversity differed ($p < .01$);   when immediacy was high, they did not.

3. A marginal main effect was obtained for liking ($F = 2.85$; $p < .09$).   Low immediacy produced greater liking than did high.   A marginal intensity x immediacy interaction was obtained also ($F = 2.91$; $p < .09$).   Simple effects tests indica-

cated that when intensity was high, low immediacy produced greater liking than did high ($p < .05$); immediacy levels did not differ at low intensity. High and low intensity did not differ at either level of immediacy. There was no evidence of a relationship between diversity and liking.

4. A main effect was obtained for predictability ($F = 3.91$; $p < .05$). High diversity produced a judgment of greater predictability than did low. An immediacy x intensity interaction was also obtained ($F = 3.96$; $p < .05$). At low immediacy, high intensity produced a judgment of greater predictability than did low ($p < .07$); at high immediacy, intensity levels did not differ. High and low intensity did not differ at either level of immediacy.

5. A main effect was obtained for similarity ($F = 7.99$; $p < .01$). High diversity produced a judgment of greater similarity than did low.

6. A main effect was obtained for attitude toward the tuition increase ($F = 4.27$; $p < .05$). High diversity produced a more favourable attitude than did low.

DISCUSSION

The outcomes for diversity support four of the five predictions: diversity was directly associated with message effectiveness and judgments of source competence, predictability and similarity. The prediction indicating a direct relationship between diversity and liking for the source was not supported; we found no evidence of a relationship between these variables. This is surprising given the evidence supporting a direct relationship between perceptions of similarity and interpersonal attraction (Byrne, 1971).

Generally, the predictions for intensity and immediacy were not supported. On similarity and attitude toward the tuition increase, these variables had no significant effect. Some evidence indicates that low immediacy produced higher likeability ratings than did high immediacy when intensity was high, which is partially supportive of our prediction. Our results point to an inverse relationship between immediacy and source credibility (competence and trustworthiness), which does not support our prediction but which does support our speculation that the direct relationship predicted would not occur in the case of a belief-discrepant message. For competence, the inverse relationship held at low intensity only; for trustworthiness it held only at high intensity. One result is opposite to what we predicted: high intensity produced a judgment of relatively high source predictability when immediacy was low.

Our predictions assume that intensity, immediacy and diversity will produce main effects only, that they are related orthogonally (additively), and that the variables will have an equal impact upon receiver judgments and attitudes. Our results indicate that these assumptions are to some extent incorrect. Interactive effects were obtained for competence, trustworthiness, liking and predictability. The main effect assumption seems correct only in the case of diversity's relationship to similarity, predictability and attitude toward the message's proposal. Also, diversity accounted for more of the variance in judgments than did the other variables. For example, the R^2 for the diversity main effect on competence was .12, whereas the R^2 for the immediacy x diversity interaction was .01. It should be noted that this type of information about relationships among language variables can be obtained only when such variables are manipulated conjointly in a single factorial design. Very few studies of the effects of language variation have employed a design of this sort, perhaps because of the great difficulty involved in devising stimulus messages by initially varying one aspect of language while holding other aspects constant, then varying the other aspects, etc.

Finally, in this study and in others (Bradac, Davies, Courtright, Desmond and Murdock, 1977; Bradac, Desmond and Murdock, 1977), diversity has been shown to be a relatively powerful variable. Why should a communicator's level of diversity play a more important role in impression formation than does his or her level of intensity or immediacy, for example? We can only speculate at this point, but there is reason to believe that intensity and immediacy together reveal the communicator's degree of liking for the topics or referents of his message, whereas diversity reveals nothing about this.   On the other hand, diversity may indicate the extent to which the communicator is in control of his or her behaviour.   A low level of diversity is associated with judgments of low socioeconomic status and high anxiety (Bradac, Davies, Courtright, Desmond and Murdock, 1977), and both sorts of judgments seem likely to produce perceptions of low behavioural control.   Perhaps for many receivers, a communicator's degree of behavioural control is more important, more fundamental, than the extent to which he or she likes or dislikes something. In an extreme case, low diversity may produce a judgment of severe abnormality or pathology, whereas for most topics even extremely intense and immediate language probably would not do so.   We will investigate this "behavioural control" hypothesis in the near future.

REFERENCES

Bowers, J. W. Language intensity, social introversion and attitude change.
    Speech Monographs, 1963, 30, 345-352
Bradac, J. J., Bowers, J. W. and Courtright, J. A.   Variations in intensity,
    immediacy and diversity: an axiomatic theory and causal model, In
    R. St. Clair and H. Giles (Eds.), The social and psychological contexts of
    language.   Hillsdale, New Jersey: Lawrence Erlbaum (1980)
Bradac, J. J., Davies, R. A., Courtright, J. A., Desmond, R. J. and Murdock, J. I.
    Richness of vocabulary: an attributional analysis. Psychological Reports,
    1977, 41, 1131-1134.
Bradac, J. J., Desmond, R. J. and Murdock, J. I.   Diversity and density: lexical-
    ly determined evaluative and informational consequences of linguistic complex-
    ity. Communication Monographs, 1977, 44, 273-283
Byrne, D. The attraction paradigm. New York: Academic Press, 1971
Conville, R.   Linguistic nonimmediacy and self-presentation. Journal of Psycho-
    logy, 1975, 90, 219-227
Giles, H. and Powesland, P. F.   Speech style and social evaluation. London:
    Academic Press, 1975
Wiener, M. and Mehrabian, A. Language within language: immediacy, a channel in
    verbal communication. New York: Appleton-Century-Crofts, 1968

Attitudes Towards Metric and Imperial Systems of Measurement

M. Wober

The Independent Broadcasting Authority, Research Division,
70 Brompton Road, London SW3 1EY, U.K.

ABSTRACT

The Independent Broadcasting Authority is required by Parliament to provide Broadcasting services "for disseminating information, education and entertainment". It does this through a structure which is essentially regional emphasising local news and weather reports, and other items intended to reflect the cultural life of each region.

Cutting across this cultural pluralism is found a doctrine of universalism of expression, one of those manifestations is the support by a Metrication Board for the International System of Units. These affect broadcasters particularly since the hertz (Hz) has replaced the metre in defining channel position; and since the degree Celsius ($^{\circ}$C) is intended to replace the degree Fahrenheit.

A survey among Londoners discloses net opposition to the introduction of each of six Units explored, from kilometres (most strongly) to Centigrade (least strongly opposed). Recent school education seems unlikely to have been primarily responsible for accepting attitudes towards new jargon; rather, experience (exemplified by the use of a radio marked in Hz) was the independent variable best related to support for new jargon.

The results are discussed briefly with an aim to finding a compromise in the extent to which metrication might totally replace jargon which is an evocative part of local and national culture.

Key Words

Attitudes; metrication; cultural values; social change.

INTRODUCTION

If a language is seen as a complete system for communication about life, while jargons label limited ranges of objects or functions within a particular culture, we should consider the Metric and the Imperial measurement systems as jargons. Measurement systems, nevertheless, are highly pervasive within any culture, describing how its material world is divided up and experienced. Such systems may be idiosyncratic within a culture or they may be shared across cultures. The design and choice of a measurement system may therefore express, and implement a universalism on the one hand (as is the intention with the spread of the Metric system) or individuality and identity on the other.

A relevant case to contemplate is that of Iran, where atavistic pressures oppose 'western' or internationalist innovations which are felt as threatening local cultural integrity.   Thus in the 1960s the Encyclopaedia Britannica could say that "the metric system of weights has been officially adopted but in the country districts old standards still prevail".   The old standards ill serve the ways of science and industry, but do link directly with the roots of that culture's social experience;   thus the farsakh is about 4 miles, the distance a laden horse can travel in an hour, and the kharvar is about 650 lbs, a full donkey load unit of weight.   It must be extremely doubtful that the Khomeini regime would officially establish such antique measures;   yet to accept the metric system would symbolise in one way at least how some codes for the expression of cultural individuality are forsaken even by such a passionately radical movement as that in Iran.

In the United Kingdom the doctrine of a universalist jargon of measurement was promoted by a series of paragovernmental committees and study groups.   Thus in 1965 the Federation of British Industry told Government that a majority of its members (industrialists) favoured metrication.   A Metrication Board was set up in 1969 as a promotional organisation.   This Board conducts surveys and in its 1976 Report (London, HMSO) referred (para. 3.19) to "an improvement in overall awareness of, and attitudes to, metrication".   No figures were given in the Report to indicate the extent of approval, if any.   However, in September 1978 a survey carried out by National Opinion Polls for the Board* found that those not in favour of metrication were 11% more than those in favour of it.   As distinct from approval, 74% believed that "It is still Government policy to go metric totally", while 19% accepted the statment that "The Government has stopped the metrication programme"; 81% agreed that metrication "is bound to happen so we might as well learn to use it" and 80% that "I'm sure I can cope with metric when I have to".

THE   PRESENT   STUDY

The Independent Broadcasting Authority is set up by an Act of Parliament which requires the Authority to provide broadcasting services "for disseminating information, education and entertainment".   The definition of 'education' is not made explicit, certainly not in the fashion of some countries where broadcasting is seen as a tool for 'nation building', social engineering or implementing cultural change.   However, it is widely believed both among one school of media researchers and by lay observers that broadcasting may have pervasive effects at psychological, social and cultural levels.   One field of effects may relate to the fact that broadcasting brings new units of measurement to the public in two ways.   One is that radio station location is now based on the Hertz unit of frequency rather than the metre;   the other is that weather forecasting is done with the Centigrade scale overlapping the use of Fahrenheit.   No conversion scales are overtly publicised, nor are other forms of metric measurement conspicuously taught or supported in programming.

To explore attitudes to new terms of location for radio stations, and to relate these attitudes to those on metrication more generally, a questionnaire was posted in February 1978 to 1130 adults recruited as a panel for assessing television programme appreciation in the London area.   Among 603 programme appreciation diaries returned, were 402 attitude questionnaires.   These were weighted by known quotas of adults by sex, age and social class to represent the population of the region.

* Information by courtesy of the Metrication Board

RESULTS

The first table examines simple approval and disapproval for separate sub-fields of jargon change.

TABLE 1   Attitudes to six new metrics being brought into use in Britain, among a representative sample of London adults

	I approve (%)	I disapprove (%)	% NET DISAPPROVAL
For each of the following new ways of measuring things:-			
Distance between places in kilometres rather than miles	18	71	53
Liquids in litres rather than pints and gallons	23	64	41
Weights in kilograms rather than pounds and ounces	24	58	34
Lengths and height in metres rather than feet and yards	26	60	34
Radio stations in KiloHertz and MegaHertz rather than metres	20	48	28
Temperature in Centigrade rather than Fahrenheit	35	46	11
Average (first four items)	23	63	41
N: Weighted London sample	400	400	400

The average covers the first four items, which pose contrasts between metric and imperial jargons, while the final two items can be said to be contrasts between different approaches to metrication.

The second table examines relationships between variables.

Clearly, where a person favours one new type of measure, he or she tends also to approve the others.   Sex and social class (assessed by the five-fold system common to the market research industry) bear little relation to acceptance of new metrics, but age shows a more consistent though small link: younger people accept innovation more readily.

DISCUSSION

It is sometimes suggested that school teaching, now using metric jargon, would promote more favourable attitudes towards metrication.   The present evidence in which the lowest correlation with age concerns the use of kilometres and the greatest involves the use of Hertz does not fit in with this hypothesis.   It is more clearly the possession of a radio set marked in KiloHertz (though not of one capable of VHF reception) that relates to favourable attitudes to new metrics.   This suggests that there may be an interaction between explicit educational and other experiences such as possessing a new piece of apparatus, or hearing a frequently used unit such as the Centigrade degree that relates to more receptive attitudes.

On balance, it remains clear from the present figures, as also with those from the Metrication Board, that there is net disapproval for the arrival of new measurement

TABLE 2   Correlations (r) between personal attributes, radio ownership and attitudes to metric innovation

	Personal:			Most used Radio has:		Attitude to:					
	Sex	Age	Class	VHF	KHZ	Kgr.	Metres	Cgr.	Km.	Litr.	KHz
Sex	1.0	.02	.08	.01	.03	.10	.08	.15	.05	.07	.07
Age		1.0	.18	-.02	-.03	.14	.16	.18	.07	.10	.18
Class			1.0	.10	.06	.05	.07	.12	.03	.02	.04
VHF				1.0	.43	.00	.02	.08	.04	.02	.09
KHz					1.0	.15	.17	.14	.21	.15	.27
Kgr.						1.0	.88	.70	.79	.85	.69
Metres							1.0	.72	.84	.85	.71
Cgr.								1.0	.70	.67	.66
Km.									1.0	.83	.73
Litres										1.0	.69
KHz											1.0

jargons.   Disapproval is greatest for items that have not yet been transformed, like miles instead of kilometres.   This supports subjective statements that the approval noted quantifiably was rendered 'faute de mieux', as with the agreement measured for the Metrication Board reported above.

Metrication is a field of change where two of the three analytically separable aspects of inter-European integration are mixed.   These aspects are the cultural, economic and political facets of integration.   The electorate may have approved integration (by referendum) basically on political and to some extent economic imperatives.   However, language and jargon are cultural (in the limited sense of the word) constructs and it seems likely that the London public (who are more cosmopolitan than the wider British public) wish to retain cultural identity even if they have agreed to other dimensions of integration.   These analytic distinctions should be (or should have been) more thoroughly explored so as to support decisions on the means, or extent to which metrication may eventually be implemented as an integrated British experience.   Other projects of deliberate economic and cultural change, not least in 'third world' countries but also in the first two 'worlds' suggest that populations try to separate economic from cultural innovations, accept the former and reject the latter.   Schisms may thus be promoted within a society either between groups, some of whom live and express themselves in more traditional ways while others are more modern, or within individuals, parts of whose lives function within one cultural environment which is at odds with another climate that regulates other facets of behaviour and expression.   In the case of metrication, it is already the case that the more formally controllable sectors of industry and commerce are moving towards international metric systems, while demotic spheres of exchange such as common speech and street markets cling to more traditional units of expression.   In order not to emphasise strains then, it may be possible to be administratively selective about metrication, establishing metric jargons where international economic and scientific considerations may be paramount.   However, other systems could live on where their place in the language of the people is linked to common experience and if the nature of the jargon is arbitrary and convenient (as with sizes of shoes, or temperature scales for describing climate) rather than inseparable from a demotic engagement with a common culture of science.

Attitudes and Ideological Bases of Support for Welsh as a Minority Language

C. Roberts and G. Williams

Department of Social Theory and Institutions, University College of North Wales, Bangor, N. Wales

ABSTRACT

In a study of the relationship between attitudes towards the Welsh language among fourteen year old school children and their involvement in institutions which offer support for the Welsh language, a positive relationship was found between attitudes to the Welsh language and involvement in religious institutions, other voluntary associations which offer support for the Welsh language, the extent of family support for the language and exposure to Welsh language media. Where the Welsh language is not the community language the influence of voluntary institutions is less. The relationship of these findings to ideology is discussed.

Key Words

Attitudes; ethnic institutions; minority-majority languages; ideology.

1. Theory and hypotheses

The study of attitudes rarely relates to such contentious concepts as legitimisation, power, inequality and control. Yet the way in which we see the world is clearly the result of the impact of ideological forces which attempt to construct and control our social and cultural perceptions. Both the Marxist and neo-Marxist orientations to social science make this perfectly clear in the manner in which the relationships between infrastructure, superstructure and ideology are discussed. It is perhaps most explicit in the work of Gramsci (1971), whose major contribution involved his explication of what he referred to as ideological hegemony. However, he never saw the exercise of hegemony and consciousness as total or static nor as something which was the exclusive prerogative of the ruling class. On the contrary, he saw hegemony as a matter of the degree of equilibrium that pertains between the state and civil society. Let us conceive of civil society in a bi-ethnic context as consisting of independent institutional structures which pertain to both ethnic groups. Those institutions relating to the dominant group may well have an all-pervasive ideological influence upon the entire population. On the other hand the institutions of the minority ethnic group and their ideological potential will be limited to the members of that group. This does not mean that the counter ideological potential of the minority institutions will exist within the minority cultural context which in itself can serve to colour the world view of the constituent members. This approach involved a tension between the established order which is capable of manipulating attitudes

227

through media, education, language, culture etc., and a conflicting order which might question the legitimacy of the established order and may draw upon its own social and authority relations, cultural patterns and life-styles as the basis for its reaction.   This counter hegemoney is capable of generating and supporting its own attitudinal basis. Given the importance of the ideological structure for the legitimisation of the process of social and cultural reproduction, this conflict deserves far more attention than it has received.   Perhaps it should not be surprising that psychology has failed to incorporate such ideas into its wide spectrum of interests since it does itself serve as part of the established ideological order.   By reducing all problems to the level of the individual, it conspicuously fails to accommodate the inevitable conflict which derives from the structural level.   Thus any inadequacy tends to be discussed in terms of individual weakness, lack of accommodation, socialisation failures etc. rather than in terms of social position.

Yet there is no reason why the implicit conflict between dominant and subordinate language groups cannot be discussed in terms of a social psychology which focuses attention upon attitudes as a measure of the relationship between conflicting ideological systems.   Such a perspective would hold that language erosion and language maintenance are aspects of the relationship between the two interest groups, with erosion indicating a tendency towards accommodation on the part of the minority language group, and maintenance a rejection of such accommodation, at least in part.   An intervening variable is the ideological order which serves to structure attitudes towards the respective languages, thereby conditioning the process of erosion and maintenance.   However if we follow Gramsci's dictum, we would recognise two conflicting ideological orders encompassed in different institutional settings, each with different perspectives towards the minority language.

Surprisingly this rather self-evident viewpoint has been ignored by those studying attitudes towards the Welsh language, the data almost exclusively having been divorced from any reference to the institutional and ideological structure.[1]   Thus the most extensive study of the attitudes of school children towards the Welsh and English languages (Sharp, Thomas, Price, Francis and Davies, 1973) operated at the methodological level of the school and made little or no reference to the wider community.   This study, not surprisingly, found that attitudes towards the Welsh language declined substantially between the ages of eleven and fifteen.   Yet we would maintain that if the data were disaggregated, substantial differences would appear in these figures according to the degree of exposure to the different ideological systems incorporated in the institutional structures.   Thus we hypothesise that where the institutional support for the minority language is low and where social networks consist of a mixture of bilingual and monoglot dominant language speakers, attitudes towards the minority language will be low.   This assumes that ideological transfer occurs both via the institutional structure and through peer group norm enforcement which itself derives in part from the ideological order.   Conversely where institutional support for the minority language is strong and where social networks are homogeneous in terms of minority language ability the attitudinal change will be much less.   Since attitudinal change is most evident during the early teens, at a time when children come under the ideological influences of both the institutional order and the commercial order while the ideological role of the family declines in importance, a study of secondary schoolchildren appears to be perfectly relevant.

---

1. This omission may in itself constitute part of the dominant ideological order, with the focusing on attitudes leading to the obscuring of more 'political' issues.

2. Methods and procedures

Two schools located in research areas designated below as Ll and A were chosen as the focus of the research.   School Ll is located in a small market town which serves a rural hinterland of small farming communities.   School A on the other hand is located in another small town which serves a more varied economic function including small scale manufacturing, tourism, retirement and services.   We would like to underline that our analysis in no way relies upon a rural-urban dichotomy. What does emerge in the difference between the two areas is the proportion of the population which is bilingual.   Sixty per cent of the children attending school Ll and fifteen per cent of those attending school A were bilingual.   This is partly a reflection of the different occupational structures, and in particular the relationship of the minority language to the ownership of the means of production.   Area Ll has a substantial portion of its population employed on and owning agricultural enterprises with Welsh being the language of the relations of production in this sector.   The means of production of the economic enterprises located in area A on the other hand are owned largely outside of Wales and this has a profound influence on the prestige of the Welsh language and on the language employed in the relations of production (Williams, 1979a; Williams, Roberts and Isaac, 1978).[2]

As Giles, Bourhis and Taylor (1977) have suggested, where language density is low, institutions which use the minority language are limited in number and scope. Furthermore the peer group will consist of a substantial number of actors who do not speak the minority language, at least in those domains which lie outside of the minority institutional structure.   Thus the language of the peer group will inevitably be the dominant language, regardless of individual attitudes.   The institutional support afforded the Welsh language has been outlined elsewhere (Stephens, 1973).   Briefly it consists of the non-conformist chapels which organise and support both religious and secular activities, young people's institutions such as the Urdd (Welsh League of Youth), and the Young Farmers' Clubs, among other voluntary associations.   Institutions which do not use the Welsh language include some religious institutions and 'British' institutions such as the Guides and Scouts as well as sports clubs which cater for activities such as badminton and horse riding.

The respondents consisted of all fourteen year old students of both sexes who were fluent in Welsh.   This gave 34 respondents in school Ll and 47 respondents in school A.   For comparative advantage the attitude test administered was the Thurstone test used by Sharp, Thomas, Price, Francis and Davies (1973) in their study of school children's attitudes towards Welsh and English.   In addition information concerning language behaviour, membership and involvement in voluntary associations, attitudes towards Welsh youth culture and sociometrics was gathered by structured interview.   Limited space precludes the inclusion of all of the relevant data in this paper and we will focus attention upon attitudes to Welsh and institutional support for Welsh.

3. Results

It has been suggested that social networks as they relate to the language ability of the constituent members is a far more meaningful basis for understanding language behaviour than the concept of domain (Committee on Irish Language, 1975). Thus it was necessary to establish the nature of the social networks of the respondents as they related to language ability and use.   Cubbitt (1973) has suggested that only one or two high density cliques or clusters are required to form

---

2. See Williams (1979b) for an elaboration of the infrastructural differences.

a norm-enforcing group, and that this structure is more influential than the whole
extended network for norm-enforcement.   Thus a high density network which uses the
Welsh language is influential in the maintenance of that language.   In a highly
cohesive network we would expect the language to be the same, that is all Welsh or
all English, since the greater cohesiveness of the group results in a greater degree of norm sharing, including that of language use.   In less dense networks
language use is more likely to be individualised and more context dependent.
The results of the study clearly show this to be the case.   All the dense networks
were made up of respondents who spoke Welsh with one another, while the others consisted of dyads with their own patterns of language use, mainly English in school
A and Welsh in school Ll.   Thus the language use patterns are as expected, mostly
Welsh at school Ll and English at school A.   If language behaviour is closely related to language attitude it is reasonable to assume that if language behaviour
reflects peer group cohesiveness then attitudes towards language can be expected to
be equally cohesive.

As the model offered by Giles, Bourhis and Taylor (1977) suggests, institutional
support assumes both a formal and informal context.   We define institutional support as the support given in the form of language use in the activities conducted
within the institutions both within the community and the wider society.   Formal
institutional support is related to areas such as education and government services.
It relates to the function of language in power domains.   Informal means of support can be expressed through the mass media and popular culture including literature.   It is also expressed through other channels such as clubs and societies,
religion and work, which may carry both a formal and informal element.   The motivational basis for involvement in institutional activities may be diverse and need not
concern us here.

The chapel is held to be a major source of support for various aspects of culture
associated with the Welsh language.   Of the respondents from area A 40% attended
chapels using the Welsh language, 30% attended religious institutions which use
English and 30% did not attend any religious establishment.   The comparable figure
for those respondents from area Ll were 76.4%, 8% and 15.6%.   However, the difference between the two groups of respondents was greater when frequency of attendance
was taken into account with a much greater involvement being found among the respondents from area Ll, and a greater tendency for these respondents to attend from
choice rather than as a result of parental pressure.   There was also a significant
empirical relationship between the frequency of attendance and the amount of Welsh
spoken with peers and siblings with 62.5% of those who attended chapel at least
once a week speaking Welsh with peers and siblings, compared with only 10.5% of
those attending with less frequency.

The same contrast between the two groups emerges when we consider involvement in
secular institutions which use the Welsh language.   The respondents from area Ll
were involved almost exclusively in clubs where the dominant language of activity
was Welsh.   However this did not mean that the respondents from area A were not
involved in secular institutional activities but that those activities which were
undertaken within the institutions with which they were involved were invariably
conducted through the medium of English.

Another facet of institutional support and one which has a very strong and explicit
ideological ingredient is that which is generally referred to as popular culture.
The respondents from area Ll tended to read more literature in Welsh, to listen to
more Welsh language pop music and to watch more Welsh language television than their
counterparts in area A.   Thus thirty-eight per cent of respondents in area Ll were
exposed to all three aspects of media compared with only fourteen per cent in area
A.

The family can also be viewed as an important source of informal institutional support. Not only are the voluntary associations run by parents, but children are often encouraged to speak Welsh by their parents. This is evident from the relationship between language spoken with kin and attitude towards Welsh.

The relationships between institutional support and attitudes towards Welsh is presented in Table 1. Since all of the respondents were themselves Welsh speakers it is perhaps not surprising that the number of unfavourable scores were few. Yet

TABLE 1.   Correlations between Attitudes to Welsh and Institutional Support

	School Ll (n = 34)				School A (n = 47)				Total Sample (n = 81)			
	VA	FS	R	M	VA	FS	R	M	VA	FS	R	M
Attitudes to Welsh	.75	.87	.79	.79	.41	.81	.58	.79[+]	.56	.83	.66	.79
Voluntary Associations		.45	.74	.63		.50	.60	.40[+]		.57	.69	.57
Family Support			.56	.66			.66	.47			.66	.59
Religion				.57				.57				.60
Media												

[+] p <.003, all other r's p <.001

the range of the scores is significant. The measure of institutional support was established by allocating equal weight to the use of the Welsh language in the family, religious institutions, voluntary associations and media exposure of the respondents. The data would appear to support our hypotheses. However it is interesting to note that the relationship between institutional support and attitudes is weaker among those respondents from area A. Table 1 gives a clearer indication of the relationship between the different areas, the different aspects of institutional support and attitudes. It is evident that while all the product moment correlations are significant beyond the 0.001 level involvement in voluntary associations appears to have less of an influence on attitudes in area A. The variations between the other correlation coefficients is far less.

As the partial coefficients indicate (Table 2) the key variables are 'family' and 'religion' although the other variables should not be ignored. The role of the family becomes even more important in area A. This we would expect in that where the voluntary associations which use the minority language are wek or absent it is to be expected that peer groups will cluster less around such institutions and their language leaving the family as virtually the only supporting agency for the minority language.

The difference between the two areas might be explained by the fact that Welsh is the dominant community language in area Ll. In contrast in area A Welsh is restricted to what might be termed 'ethnic institutions'. Thus the status of Welsh in the two areas is expected to differ and this is reflected in the attitude scores. Nonetheless we should not ignore the positive relationship between institutional support and attitudes to Welsh which does exist among the respondents from area A.

4. Discussion

The preceding data support our hypothesis concerning the relationship between institutional support for a language and attitudes towards that language. This would appear to point towards far reaching theoretical and practical implications. Firstly it would allow us to make heuristic statements concerning language and cultural reproduction. The institutions in which the minority language functions often consist of what Weber (Gerth and Mills, 1948, p.174) has referred to as status groups. As such they tend to draw their membership across class position and being the main agencies of minority cultural transmission it means that unlike the wider

TABLE 2.   Partial Correlations between Attitudes to Welsh and Institutional Support

Attitudes to Welsh	School Ll (n = 34)				School A (n = 47)				Total Sample (n = 81)			
	VA	FS	R	M	VA	FS	R	M	VA	FS	R	M
Partialling out VA		-.42	.29	.41		-.54	.40	.24		-.47	.33	.32
Partialling out F	.19		-.25	.30	.13		-.10	.04	.07		-.16	.18
Partialling out R	.06	.36		-.38	.10	.40		-.07	.06	.39		-.24
Partialling out M	.07	.26	.23	-	.07	.49	.33	-	.15	.42	.29	-
	if r = 33, p = .05				if r = 29, p = .05				if r = 22, p = .05			

order (Bourdieu 1973) minority cultural reproduction bears no direct relationship to social reproduction as it pertains to class distinctions.   Secondly, the minority institutions, insofar as they are the exclusive domains of the minority language have a potentially powerful ideological basis which constitutes a threat to the dominant ideological order.   Thus the dominant language group will seek either to eliminate or to expropriate the minority language, that is it will seek to control the ideology expressed through the institutions which support the minority language. It is our belief that social psychology and studies of attitudes must move to encompass issues such as these rather than remain rooted in issues of individual reductionism.

REFERENCES

Bourdieu, P.   Cultural reproduction and social reproduction,   in R. Brown (Ed.) Knowledge, education and cultural change. London: Tavistock Press, 1973
Committee on Irish language – Report on attitudes towards the Irish language. Dublin, 1975
Cubitt, T.   Network density among urban families,   in J. Boissevain and J. C. Mitchell (Eds.) Network analysis studies in human interaction.   The Hague: Mouton, 1973
Gerth, H. and Mills, C. W. (Eds.) From Max Weber: essays in sociology.   London: Routledge and Kegan Paul, 1948
Giles, H., Bourhis, R. and Taylor, D. M.   Towards a theory of language in ethnic group relations,   in H. Giles (Ed.) Language ethnicity and intergroup relations.   London: Academic Press, 1977
Gramsci, A.   Selections from the prison notebooks.   New York: International Publishers, 1971
Sharp, D., Thomas, B., Price, E., Francis, G. and Davies, I.   Attitudes to Welsh and English in the schools of Wales.   London and Cardiff: Macmillan/University of Wales Press, 1973
Stephens, M. (Ed.) The Welsh language today.   Llandysul: Gwasg Gomer, 1973
Williams, G.   Language group allegiance and ethnic interaction,   in H. Giles and B. Saint-Jacques (Eds.) Language and ethnicity.   London: Pergamon Press, 1979a
Williams, G.   Economic marginalization, social structure and contemporary nationalism in Wales.   Paper presented at the First Annual Conference of Europeanists, Washington D.C., April 1979b
Williams, G., Roberts, E. and Isaac, R.   Language and aspirations for upward social mobility,   in G. Williams (Ed.) Social and cultural change in contemporary Wales.   London: Routledge and Kegan Paul, 1978.

Personality, Emotion, Psychopathology and Speech

K. R. Scherer

*Department of Psychology, Justus-Liebig University, Otto Behaghel Str. 10,
6300 Giessen, Federal Republic of Germany*

Science always deals with abstractions.   In many cases, the complexity of the
real world is not amenable to study and scientists have to take recourse to a somewhat idealised version of reality in order to advance theory and research.   However, such idealised versions of reality concentrating on a few salient aspects of
a problem and neglecting other factors and interactions become dangerous if they
are idolised to the point where the importance of the neglected factors is out-
rightly disputed.   Students of language have not been too successful in avoiding
this danger and have succumbed to the temptation of keeping things tidy.   One
convenient strategy has been to construct models of the speaker/hearer which emphasise rule systems or structural/situational norms abstracting from the messy
day-to-day or person-to-person variations by relegating these to the status of
peripheral error variance.

One such model which has been with us for quite some time could be termed "homo
linguisticus" or "homo psycholinguisticus" (discovered, of course, by Chomsky) an
idealised speaker/hearer who functions like a speech synthesis/recognition computer with a complex set of rules (most of them hardware logic).   More recently,
we have seen the phenomenal rise of a somewhat different model which could be
called "homo sociolinguisticus" or "homo ethnolinguisticus", a speaker/hearer whose
speech processing is determined by social categories, cultural context and situational variation.   Homo psycholinguisticus, in its extreme version, speaks a
universal language (probably assembler), whereas for homo sociolinguisticus there
is quite some variety of speech styles depending on category, culture and situation.   However, even this more realistic model of speaking man seems to assume,
for example, that all adolescent female Hottentots show the same speech behaviour
at marriage ceremonies (if there are no bilinguals around to induce code-switching).

We all know that these models are not realistic.   They disregard, among other
things, individual differences between speakers in terms of types or traits and
psychological states such as emotions or moods.   We know for a fact that traits
and states of this sort affect speech behaviour quite strongly and we also know
that listeners use speech markers of traits and states to infer or attribute a
wide variety of speaker characteristics (cf. Scherer, 1979a, 1979b).   However,
we know very little about the details of trait/state effects on speech and the
nature of the inferences made on the basis of these.   Whereas animal communication researchers have long since realised that individual differences among
animals and their emotional state have a strong impact on the nature of signalling
and have started to study these effects systematically, students of speech and

233

language have been remarkably reticent in this respect.   This is true even for
psychology, the discipline that is presumably in charge of phenomena such as personality and emotion.   Interestingly enough, it seems to have been an anthropologist, Edward Sapir, who first suggested the importance of studying personality and
speech (Sapir, 1927).   While there were some early flurries of excitement in
psychology in the thirties and forties (Pear, 1931; Allport and Cantril, 1934;
Sanford, 1942), the enthusiasm died very rapidly and, as systematic reviews of the
literature for both personality and emotion show, we can find little more than
some isolated, and often rather weak pieces of research in this field (cf
Scherer, 1979a, 1979b).   It is not difficult to think of the reasons why psychologists have ceased to study the effects of personality and emotion on speech.
As many of the early studies show, the methodological difficulties were quite
overwhelming both in terms of measuring personality and emotion as well as in
obtaining appropriate speech samples and extracting the relevant variables.
Furthermore, both the behaviouristic and the cognitive preoccupation which have
succeeded each other in dominating psychology in the past decades, seem to have a
rather extreme distrust of all things emotional.   One of the consequences is
that the psychology of emotion is one of the most underdeveloped subareas within
scientific psychology.   Finally, the enormous numbers of personality psychologists have not much advanced research on personality and speech as they have generally contented themselves with checkmarks on questionnaires and the interrelationships between these.

Consequently, since psychology has not done its part, it could hardly be expected
from linguists, sociologists, anthropologists or even social psychologists to
fill the gap, particularly as all these groups seem strongly to doubt the existence of personality and emotion anyway.   Surprisingly, there has been a fair
amount of work on the relationships between psychopathology and speech behaviour
(cf. Scherer, 1979a; Vetter, 1969).   Much of this work, however, has been done
by psychiatrists who have been mainly interested in the diagnostic use of speech
patterns in assessing the underlying psychopathological syndromes.   It is regret-
able that few researchers primarily interested in language have looked at the
effects of psychopathological syndromes on speech.   In many disciplines, the
study of deviations, abnormality and experimental destruction provides an important tool to discover the normal functions of the structures and processes under
investigation.   Since psychopathology often consists of mood and/or personality
disorders, such research would have thrown light on the role of personality and
emotion in speaking behaviour.

In order to get beyond the stage of isolated studies by isolated researchers, a
situation patently detrimental to a serious accumulation of research findings and
theoretical insights, the study of the effects of personality, emotion and psychopathology has to take its proper place in the study of language and speech.
Since these factors interact with both cognitive processes and the effects of
social structure and situation, this proper place seems to be within a broadly conceived social psychology of language.   The papers in this section show some
possible approaches to combining interest in personality, emotion or psychopathology with the kinds of questions that are usually asked within the social psychology of language.   Bruce Brown discusses the methodological problems involved in
detecting emotion in vocal qualities and points to some possible methodological
advances which could render research on speech and voice correlates of emotion
more meaningful.

At the conference, a number of papers in this symposium were concerned with communication patterns in disturbed or handicapped populations. Judith Duchan reported on communication patterns in interactions with an autistic child, and Ivan Leudar reported results from a study on the verbal and nonverbal communication between normals and persons suffering from Down's syndrome.

The paper by Rainer Krause presents an intriguing theory of affect repression in stuttering. His data from a large scale study on stutterers interacting with fluent speakers confirm this theory and provide important information on the relationship between verbal and nonverbal communication and the nature of the production processes. Heiner Ellgring and his associates deal with depression and anxiety and the impact of changes in the state of depression on speech and looking behaviour. They also provide a discussion on the coordination between speech and gaze behaviour. The paper by Harald Wallbott and Klaus Scherer introduces the speculative notion that psychiatrists may be strongly influenced by speech patterns in assessing improvement of psychiatric patients, based on a notion of normality of speech behaviour in terms of social norms. Data from a study with nine schizophrenics support this notion and provide information on the nature of speech changes over therapy.

Finally, the paper by Ursula Scherer, Hede Helfrich and Klaus Scherer addresses the question of whether paralinguistic behaviour is determined by "internal push" factors (such as personality or emotional arousal) or "external pull" factors (such as situational demands or social norms). In many ways, this aspect is central for the study of personality, emotion and psychopathology within the social psychology of language, since it focusses directly on the interaction between individual and social variables in determining speech behaviour. As the evidence presented in this symposium suggests, "homo sociopsycholinguisticus" will have to be studied in terms of both <u>external</u> pull and <u>internal</u> push.

REFERENCES

Allport, G. W. and Cantril, H. Judging personality from the voice. <u>Journal of Social Psychology</u>, 1934, <u>5</u>, 37-55

Pear, T. H. <u>Voice and personality</u>. London: Chapman & Hall, 1931

Sanford, F. H. Speech and personality. <u>Psychological Bulletin</u>, 1942, <u>39</u>, 811-845

Sapir, E. Speech as a personality trait. <u>American Journal of Sociology</u>, 1927, <u>32</u>, 892-905

Scherer, K. R. Nonlinguistic indicators of emotion and psychopathology, in C. E. Izard (Ed.) <u>Emotions in personality and psychopathology</u>. New York: Plenum Press, 1979 (1979a)

Scherer, K. R. Personality markers in speech, in K. R. Scherer and H. Giles (Eds.) <u>Social markers in speech</u>. Cambridge: Cambridge University Press, 1979 (1979b)

Vetter, H. <u>Language behaviour and psychopathology</u>. Chicago: Rand McNally, 1969

The Detection of Emotion in Vocal Qualities

B. L. Brown

Department of Psychology, Brigham Young University, Provo, Utah 84601, U.S.A.

ABSTRACT

Previous studies of the vocal expression of emotion can be considered in two categories: (1) subjective reaction studies that deal with the ability of human
judges to recognise accurately emotion from vocal qualities and (2) objective
voice measurement studies that seek to establish the acoustic properties of vocal
reflections of emotion. There have been a number of studies of the first kind,
but very few of the second.

The subjective reaction studies are faced with the problem of holding speech content constant to ensure that the accuracy in judgments is due to vocal reflections
of emotion, and many techniques have been devised to do this. Both kinds of
studies are plagued with the problem of obtaining replicated samples of speech
with natural rather than portrayed emotion, and the even bigger problem of establishing presence of an emotion and the necessity of the particular label given to
it.

Preliminary results are given of some studies designed to compare the level of
accuracy of identification of more natural emotion with the accuracy found in
earlier studies using portrayed emotion. Projected studies are discussed which
use speech synthesis methods to test precisely hypotheses concerning the emotional
meaning of various acoustic dimensions of vocal para-language.

Key Words

Emotion; vocal quality; identification of emotions; acoustics of emotion;
natural emotions

There have been numerous studies of the vocal indicators of emotion, but as
Scherer (1979) demonstrates in his review, there is much yet to be done. A few
fairly strong findings emerge. Increased pitch has been found in numerous
studies to accompany nonspecific arousal or stress. Streeter, Krauss, Geller,
Olson and Apple (1977) and Apple, Streeter and Krauss (1979) have demonstrated the
pitch increase effect in relation to the stress accompanying deception, both with
an analysis of vocal properties while "lying" (under experimental instruction to
do so), and with truthfulness judgments of computer synthesised speech experimentally raised in pitch. Anger has been found to be characterised by "high pitch,
wide pitch range, loud voice and fast tempo", and grief/sadness by the opposite

237

ends of each of these vocal dimensions.

This paper will deal with two issues: (1) an assessment of the ability of judges
to detect accurately spontaneous natural emotion as compared to emotion portrayals
and (2) the use of speech synthesis techniques to test hypotheses that come from
the findings of these "natural emotion" studies and the previous "portrayed
emotion" studies.   Very few studies have examined natural emotion in spontaneous
speech, and those few are very disappointing.   In the words of Scherer, "If the
speech samples used in simulation studies are not natural enough, the samples
consisting of spontaneous speech are not emotional enough ...: in each of these
studies, both the intensity and the specificity of the emotional states of the
speakers probably fall far below the levels attained in real life or in simulation studies." One notable exception is one of the studies reported in the
Williams and Stevens (1972) paper.   They acoustically analysed the recorded
commentary of the radio announcer who witnessed and described the Hindenburg
disaster as it happened.   It is difficult to imagine a more realistic natural
emotion and one more extreme.   Comparisons between the actual recording and a
portrayal by an actor who had not heard the recording but only read the transcript
showed similar emotion/non-emotion differences, suggesting that, at least for
this one kind of very extreme emotion, portrayals are not so bad.   What is missing in these data are replications to determine whether such emotion cues are consistent across persons.   An experimental study with a number of emotion-producing
situations and a number of speakers would allow statistical inference and tests of
consistency as to the relationships between emotive states and vocal properties.

In addition to the study just discussed, Williams and Stevens (1972) also reported
a study that utilised the recorded voices of professional actors reading the dialogue of short scenarios written to portray anger, fear, sorrow and a neutral
situation.   Qualitative and quantitative analyses were made of the three actors'
voices, showing among other things a lowered pitch and slower rate for sorrow and
a raised pitch and increased pitch variance for anger.   They did not examine the
accuracy of judges in the identification of emotions from these portrayals, but
such data have been gathered for the expression of emotion by actors in two other
studies, the classic Davitz and Davitz (1959) study of the vocal communication of
feelings, and Kramer's (1964) study of the effect of eliminating verbal cues in
judging emotion from voice.

Davitz and Davitz (1959) had subjects express each of ten emotions by reciting the
alphabet "using the letters as if they were words", after reading a brief description of a situation which might generate the feeling in question.   Judges were
then faced with the task of deciding which feeling situation was being expressed.
They found the highest percent of correct identifications for anger (65%) followed
by nervousness (54.2%), sadness (49.2%), happiness (43.5%), sympathy (38.8%),
satisfaction (30.8%), fear and also love (25%), jealousy (24.6%) and pride (20.8%).
(Davitz and Davitz do not report percent correct statistics but they do give, in
their Table 1, the number of correct identifications for each emotion portrayed.
These percent figures were obtained by dividing the number correct for each emotion by the total number of portrayals, which was 240 in each case.)

Kramer (1964) used only five emotions but their acted portrayals used actual
speech rather than letters of the alphabet, and the results were displayed more
completely in confusion matrix form (thus allowing more careful comparison with
the other studies to be reported in this paper).   In order to hold verbal content
constant so that it would not be a cue in determining the emotion portrayed, they
arranged to have three sentences that were equivalent for each of the scenarios
for the five emotions.   Only those three sentences were presented to judges for
the identification task.   The three sentences of recorded portrayals were
presented to judges in three ways: untouched English portrayals, the same English

portrayals filtered to pass only frequencies below 400 Hz., and untouched portrayals in Japanese.   These conditions were used to test the consistency of the pattern of confusions under each method of disguising content (filtering and using a
language unknown to the judges.)   Table 1 displays the results of the Kramer
study presented in a format that allows maximal comparison with the other studies
of this paper.   Two of the emotion names, anger and love, are the same for the
Kramer study and the Davitz and Davitz study (although it is not easy to determine
whether the scenarios, the real definition of the emotion, are), and grief in the

TABLE 1   Confusion matrices, information theory statistics and percent correct
           statistics for English unfiltered, English filtered and Japanese
           voices portraying five emotions.   (Data from Kramer, 1964, Table 1,
           with information theory and corrected percent correct statistics
           added)

English unfiltered voices

Intended emotion	judged emotion a	c	g	i	l	median percentage of judgments that were correct	median corrected percentage of judgments	percent information transmitted (coefficient of constraint)
anger	74	26	0	0	0	74	67.5	46.4% of the
contempt	3	85	3	9	0	85	81.3	information
grief	2	5	58	4	31	58	47.5	for the five
indifference	1	16	4	76	3	76	70	emotions was
love	2	14	17	11	56	56	45	transmitted

English filtered voices

Intended emotion	judged emotion a	c	g	i	l			
anger	77	23	0	0	0	77	71.3	38.0% of the
contempt	6	48	4	36	6	48	35	information
grief	0	3	71	5	21	71	63	for the five
indifference	6	11	7	63	13	63	53.8	emotions was
love	0	12	20	19	48	48	35	transmitted

Japanese voices

Intended emotion	judged emotion a	c	g	i	l			
anger	67	29	0	3	1	67	58.8	42.5% of the
contempt	0	20	17	52	11	20	0	information
grief	0	0	90	1	10	90	87.5	for the five
indifference	2	21	2	73	2	73	66.3	emotions was
love	1	7	3	52	38	38	22.5	transmitted

Note: These confusion matrix data are in percent form as Kramer reported them
        rather than in the frequency tally form of Table 2.

Kramer study could be thought of as being at least roughly comparable to sadness in the Davitz and Davitz study. Of those three, in both studies anger is most often correctly identified (between 67% and 77% in the three Kramer conditions and 65% correct in Davitz and Davitz), sadness/grief is next (58% to 90% in Kramer and 49.2% for Davitz and Davitz), and love is least correctly identified in both studies (38% to 56% in Kramer and 25% in Davitz and Davitz).

If one wishes to be precise, neither the Kramer nor Davitz and Davitz studies really measured judgment accuracy, since in both cases the experimenters had identified each scenario as an "anger" scenario, a "love" scenario, etc. and gave judges the task of identifying which emotion name best fitted each utterance. The necessity of the connection between any scenario and the emotion name attached to it by the experimenters has not been established, nor could it conceivably be established. In the strictest terms, a true accuracy study would allow judges to read the scenarios and then judge which utterance is the result of portraying which scenario, since the ultimate definition of what emotion each actor is portraying is in the content of the scenario, not in the emotion label applied to it by the experimenter. This is the major problem of all studies of the vocal indices of emotion (and also of vocal indices of personality). One way to approach this problem is the strategy implied by Scherer (1979): to get sufficient knowledge of the physiology of non-specific arousal and discrete emotions and their effects upon the vocal apparatus to begin to build a theory to guide hypothesis testing. Rather than waiting for an adequate definition of emotion, vocal indicators research could help to build such a definition. Vocal indices can be measured very precisely, but what is to be the independent criterion for an emotion (or a personality trait)? (It seems strange that a matrix of the pooled judgments of a number of judges would have less information transmitted than any of the individual judges but that is in the nature of information theory mathematics. They take into account not only the proportion of correct judgments but also the number of incorrect ones that are consistent, but the incorrect consistencies wash out when judges matrices are pooled.) This is an even bigger problem for studies of natural emotion than for studies of portrayed emotion unless we can find ways to get natural emotion in which the definition of the emotion can be the situation that led to it.

Even if we could be fortunate enough to be in the right places at the right times with our tape recorders (and enough right places and right times to get a variety of emotions with replications for some group of subjects), and assuming all of the problems of ethics and consent could be solved, we would still have the difficulty of defining the emotions. Even a situational definition would be limited by the adequacy of our perception and description of the situation. So, we do the best we can with a world that is imperfect for the needs of ideal science.

In order to move one step closer to natural emotion in spontaneous speech, we designed an experiment to obtain speech samples of five male undergraduates in reaction to six films quite diverse in emotional impact. It is not easy to define the emotion generated by each film, but having the judges also view the film provides a situational definition That is, judges are faced with the question "Which film led to this utterance?" to which there is one indisputably correct answer and five indisputably incorrect ones. The emotion involved is probably somewhere between real emotion and portrayed: the vicarious emotion of the spectator. Even though it could be argued that this is one step further removed from real emotion than portrayals are in that it is an observation of a portrayal, one crucial element makes it more comparable to real emotion: the emotion is subsidiary to the task the viewer is carrying out rather than being the focus of his attention as in portrayals. (Subsidiary and focal are being used here in the sense Polanyi (1958, chapter 4) employs them.) The great weakness of studies like those of Kramer (1964) and Davitz and Davitz (1959) lies in the problem that it is one thing to ask whether the feelings and emotions a person experiences in natural situations are detectable in vocal qualities and quite a different thing to ask whether a person can produce vocal portrayals of emotions or feelings that are recognisable. The former are likely to be much more subtle. The latter run the risk of being nothing more than a stylised caricature.

The six films were chosen for high impact and diversity from one another. Two were intended to be light and humourous:

"Litterbug" - A Walt Disney Donald Duck colour cartoon.
"Dream of a Rarebit Friend"- A black and white slapstick comedy, vintage
                1920's.

Two were intended to be very serious with elements of sadness but overall positive in tone:

"Leo Beuerman" - A biographical sketch of the courage of a badly deformed
                man and how he meets the difficulties of his life.
"Peege" - A family visits a failing, elderly grandmother in a rest home
        who seems nearly catatonic as they talk past her, until they
        leave and one son returns and reminisces over their happy times
        together and she responds.

Two others were chosen to be very serious, but this time with a decidedly negative tone, with strong elements of injustice and senseless brutality:

"Love to Kill" - An excerpt from the motion picture "Bless the Beasts and
                the Children" where some boys try to save some buffalos
                from being slaughtered by blood-thirsty hunters and one
                boy is accidently killed.

"Lottery" - A portrayal of a devastating short story showing the yearly
                ritual of a fictional New England town where lots are drawn
                and the loser is stoned to death.

In order to mask content so that the ability of judges to assess accurately which film led to each utterance on the basis of vocal qualities alone, the five speaker subjects were fluent Spanish bilinguals who have English as their first language and cultural orientation. None of the judges knew Spanish. In the Kramer (1964) study the confusion patterns for emotion identification for the English and Japanese portrayals were reasonably comparable, even though their Japanese speakers were culturally Japanese with that as their first language. Our speakers would be expected to have even more consistency with an English comparison group, since their cultural background is English and Spanish is probably more similar to English in terms of paralinguistic display rules than Japanese.

Each speaker was instructed to describe each movie after viewing it so as to convey clearly to another the content of the movie. Two kinds of judgments were made of the voice recordings. A group of eighteen male and female undergraduates who had not viewed the films were instructed to listen to each voice sample and rate it on the 13 emotion categories shown in Figure 1. That figure summarises the results of a factor analysis of these subjective ratings. All of the average factor score positions for voices in reaction to the films fit what would be expected ("Love to Kill" high on disgust, anger, hatred; "Peege" high on love, reverence; "Litterbug" high on humour, happiness, etc.) with the exception of one movie - "Lottery". It is an overwhelmingly negative experience to view "Lottery", the effect lasting for a day or so. We noticed a lot of nervous laughter among speakers when they viewed the film, but it is very curious that their voice when describing the film would be judged to have some humour in it as well as some contempt.

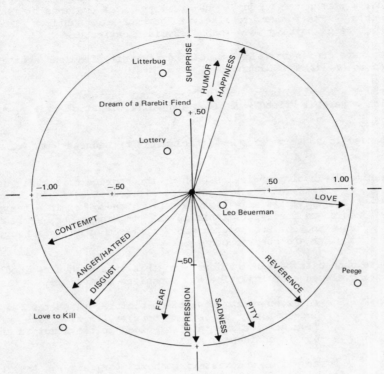

Note: The circle represents unit length for the emotion vectors which was
        arbitrarily made to coincide with one standard deviation unit (1σ) on the
        factor score plotting space for the plotting of the average factor score
        for each film.

        Fig. 1. Film-judging study - plotting of the thirteen emotion
                vectors in the two factor space, with a plotting of
                the mean factor scores for the received ratings of the
                six films superimposed.

The second test of these voice samples, the judgments of which film led to each
voice sample (as judged by four male undergraduates who had viewed all six films
but did not know Spanish) is shown in Table 2.   In comparing these results to
those of Kramer and of Davitz and Davitz, one would expect the most information
to come from the movie that generates anger ("Love to Kill").   It is high, but
even higher is "Leo Beuerman" (62.5% correct) which in Figure 1 does not seem to
be very extreme on any dimension.

The most comparable thing across the three studies is probably the amount of
information transmitted statistics (the coefficients of constraint).   The information theory statistics in Table 2 indicate that the percent of information (concerning film identity) received by individual judges ranges from 29.8% to 51.7%,
and the percent transmitted by individual speakers ranges from 47.2% to 58.8%.

TABLE 2. Film-judging study – confusion matrix, information theory statistics, and percent-correct statistics for the pooled judgments of all judges, and information theory statistics for individual speakers and judges.

Actual Film	judged film						percentage of judgments that were correct	corrected percentage of judgments*
	Litterbug	Dream	Leo Beuerman	Peege	Love to Kill	Lottery		
Litterbug	6	3	1	4	2	4	30	16
Dream	6	6	1	3	4	0	30	16
Leo Beuerman	1	2	10	1	0	2	62.5	55
Peege	1	2	5	6	1	1	37.5	25
Love to Kill	1	3	1	0	8	3	50	40
Lottery	2	0	5	5	3	5	25	10

Information theory statistics for the pooled judgments

percent information transmitted (coefficient of constraint) for individual judges and speakers

median % correct: 33.75   20.5

*note: the percent of guesses that would be correct by chance is 16.67% for six alternatives. The percent correct, corrected for guessing (Pc) is computed by the formula:

$$P_c = \frac{P - .1667}{.8333}$$

uncertainty in sender: 2.58 bits

transmission: .461 bits

percent of information transmitted: 17.9% (coeff. of constraint)

judges	speakers
29.8%	40.6%
36.0%	47.2%
46.9%	51.8%
51.7%	58.0%
	58.8%

Unfortunately comparable figures are not available from Kramer and cannot be computed from his tables, but the percent of information transmitted in the pooled matrix of all judges and all speakers was computed from his tables and is presented in Table 1 of this paper. For his English, filtered, and Japanese conditions 46.4%, 38.0% and 42.5% information was transmitted, respectively. The comparable figure for this film identification study for pooled judgments is 17.9%. Kramer's Japanese condition is most comparable to our results, and even in that condition he accounts for more than twice as much information being transmitted. It is obvious that tacit, evoked emotion is much more subtle than intentionally portrayed emotion.

Information theory statistics cannot be computed for Davitz and Davitz data, but the three studies can be compared on percent correct statistics corrected for guessing. For the Davitz and Davitz study, the corrected percents range from 12% to 61% with a median of 27.6 (corresponding uncorrected valued are 20.87%, 65% and 34.8%). From Table 2 it can be seen that these figures are only slightly higher than the corresponding ones for the judgment of films study, but the values of Table 1 show that judges in that study were about twice as accurate as judges in the other two studies. Although they use portrayed rather than evoked emotion, presumably the Davitz and Davitz judges do relatively badly because of speakers using alphabet recitation rather than more natural speech.

TABLE 3 Birth study: confusion matrices, information theory statistics and percent correct statistics for the pooled judgments of four male judges and the pooled judgments of four female judges.

Male Judges

actual situation	judged situation				median percentage of judgments that were correct	median corrected percentage of judgments	percent information transmitted (coefficient of constraint)
	doc's office	labour room	deliv- ery	post- delivery			
doctor's office	68	8	0	44	56.7	42.3	27.3% of the information for the five emotions was transmitted
labour- room	48.5	24.5	12.5	34.5	20.4	less than chance	
delivery	0	29	91	0	75.8	67.7	
post- delivery	47.5	18.5	7.5	46.5	38.8	18.4	

Female Judges

actual situation	judged situation						
	doc's office	labour room	deliv- ery	post- delivery			
doctor's office	32	52	23	13	26.7	2.3	22.6% of the information for the five emotions was transmitted
labour- room	51	5	5	59	4.2	less than chance	
delivery	2	22	94	2	78.3	71.1	
post- delivery	20	21	37	42	35.0	13.3	

Note: when each judge heard each speech sample, rather than just indicating which time frame he thought it came from, each was given ten tallies that could be allocated according to his relative feelings of the likelihood of each alternative. One of the male judges opted to cast half tallies for some alternatives, giving rise to the non-integral values in the confusion matrix for male judges.

Other studies are now being conducted to extend assessments of accuracy of emotion identification to more natural emotion. Preliminary results of one such study are shown in Table 3. Recordings were made of the voices of a young couple upon the occasion of the birth of their first child.* In studies of life span evaluations, we have found that many people indicate that as one of the happiest events in their lives. However there are also some moments of real tension. Approximately 20 second segments were taken (and played backwards to mask content) from four segments of the tape: doctor's office visit, in the labour room at

* In return for their participation, couples were given a copy of the tape recordings of the occasion. We were very careful to preserve anonymity and use the voices for testing only in the content masked form.

delivery, and after delivery.   Four male and four female judges were asked to judge from the voice, which time frame it came from.   It is surprising that these male judges were more accurate than the females (Table 2) and that males seldom judged the "office" voice to be the "labour room" voice, but females often did: 22.6% of the information was received by male judges, and 27.3% by female judges, which, interestingly, is not as high as comparable figures for individual speakers in the film study which ranged from 40.6% to 58.8% (Table 2).   There is little doubt about the emotion in this study being real and fairly intense, but playing voices backwards may obscure more of the necessary vocal information for identification than speaking in an unknown tongue.

Other studies of natural emotion are also being conducted using: (1) the voices of athletes before and after winning and losing, (2) recordings of reminiscences of happy, sad, difficult, etc. life experiences, etc. and acoustic speech synthesis is being used to test the emotional significance of changes in acoustic parameters.

REFERENCES

Apple, W., Streeter, L. A. and Krauss, R. M.   Effects of pitch and speech rate on personal attributions.   Journal of Personality and Social Psychology, 1979, 5, 715-727

Davitz, J. R. and Davitz, L. J.   The communication of feelings by content-free speech.   Journal of Communication, 1959, 9, 6-13

Kramer, E.   Elimination of verbal cues in judgments of emotion of voice. Journal of Abnormal and Social Psychology, 1964, 68, 390-396

Polanyi, M. Personal knowledge.   New York: Harper, 1958

Scherer, K. R.   Nonlinguistic vocal indicators of emotion and psychopathology, in C. E. Izard (Ed.) Emotions in personality and psychopathology.   New York: Plenum Press, 1979, 495-529

Streeter, L. A., Krauss, R. M., Geller, V., Olson, C. and Apple, W.   Pitch changes during attempted deception.   Journal of Personality and Social Psychology, 1977, 35, 5, 345-350

Williams, C. E. and Stevens, K. N.   Emotions and speech: some acoustical correlates.   Journal of Acoustical Society of America, 1972, 52, 1238-1250

Some Aspects of Communication in Down's Syndrome*

I. Leudar

Psychological Laboratory, The University, St. Andrews, Scotland

ABSTRACT

Communication with retarded people is often a problem because of their inadequate
command of language.   However, studies of their linguistic competence have to be
supplemented by research on how different aspects of their linguistic deficiency
affect their communication and by research on how they overcome their problems with
language.   Results of two experiments are reported.   In the first, it was found
that clarity of their speech did not affect the frequency with which they used
speech.   In the second experiment, it was shown that mongols are socially sensitive
but that they express this in NVC rather than by changing the pattern of their
verbal communication.

Key Words

Acquaintance; articulation; communication; Down's Syndrome; language; posture.

INTRODUCTION

Communication between any two people may be a problem.   With a retarded person it
is a problem most of the time.   This is due to their inadequate command of language.
It is not certain if impairment of linguistic competence necessarily implies communicative incompetence.   Perhaps not, since communicative competence may have
extralinguistic origins (Bruner, 1976).   The work, which will be reported below,
suggests that even severely linguistically retarded Down's syndrome subjects have
the social skills needed for communication.

By calling communication a problem, I do not mean to focus attention on its deviations from more fluent conversations.   I mean that when a normal person communicates with a retarded person, he has to <u>act</u> differently from when he interacts with
another fluent language user.   He can rely less on conventional means of expression
since these need not be present or may be unclear.   He must pay attention to extra-
linguistic cues on which he would not usually <u>focus</u>, since they may be useful in
solving a problem: "What did he mean?"   The retarded speaker also has to monitor

---

* The research was supported by a grant from the Scottish Home and Health Department.   I express my gratitude to Dr. W. I. Fraser and to Professor M. A. Jeeves
  for their help.

behaviour of his audience in order to engage in "repair work" when he feels he was
misunderstood.   The process of communication under these circumstances requires
creativity and ingenuity from both participants.

Shortcomings of Mongols' linguistic competence have been studied in the past.
The development of their syntax is delayed, but follows the same course as in nonretarded population (Blanchard, 1964; Lennenberg, Nichols and Rosenberger, 1964).
It has been claimed, however, that mongols' grammatical errors are less consistent
than those in other comparable groups.   Acoustic properties of mongols' voices
make judgements of their age and sex difficult (Michel and Carney, 1964; Hollien
and Copeland, 1965; Montague, Brown, and Hollien, 1974).   The most striking aspect of their language is the lack of clear articulation, which is also inconsistent (Dodd, 1976).   Finally, mongols' language production is more delayed than
is their comprehension (Dodd, 1975).

It has been frequently pointed out that insights into language can be gained by
study of its disfluencies (e.g. slips of a tongue, aphasia, etc.).   Our problem
here is communication in mental retardation.   The limitation of research on
linguistic competence is that it does not specify the contribution of particular
deficits (semantic, syntactic or phonological) to communication failure.   One has
to ask the following questions: Which of the deficits will hinder communication
most?   The answer may be important for effective planning of remedial teaching.
A second question which is perhaps more interesting is how, despite more than one
constraint on their linguistic competence, mongols make themselves understood at
all?

Price-Willams and Sabsay (1979) have shown that even severely linguistically retarded mongols are not necessarily communicatively retarded.   The men they observed were capable of securing the attention of their audiences and used complex
strategies to establish shared reference.   The mongols monitored understanding
by their audiences and would repeat their utterances, rephrase them and gesture in
order to correct misunderstandings.   They were capable of initiating speech acts
(e.g. greetings, questions, instructions) and reacted to speech acts of their
partners appropriately.   They answered questions and made assertions relevant to
topics introduced by their partners.   In other words, communication was a problem
but mongols both followed conventions and were able to deal with misunderstandings.

What we need to know is how fluent speakers react to mongols' language disfluencies
as well as how mongols react to such reactions.   Which means of expression, other
than language, do mongols use and for what purposes?   How does the social relation
of interactors affect the process of communication?   What kinds of content are
mongols able to express using the limited means they have available?

                                EXPERIMENT 1

The first of the present studies I will refer to was concerned with the relation
between the degree of articulatory disfluency of an individual and the frequency
with which he uses language.   The subjects were all trainees at Dalgairn Adult
Training Centre, Cupar.   They were 25 years old on average.   Their average
mental age was 4 years 11 months.   Their vocabulary corresponded to that of an
average 5 year old.

To assess each subject's articulatory disfluency, he was asked to imitate a set of
words (spoken by a local man) containing all the phonemes of English.   The
clarity of their imitation was assessed in two ways.   Firstly, by counting the
number of mispronounced vowels and consonants, omitted phonemes, reduced consonant
clusters, etc.   Secondly, by presenting a recording of the mongol's imitations
to naive judges, whose task was to identify the imitated words.   The two measures

gave similar results ($r = 0.89$, $N = 12$, $p < .001$).   The less clear an individual's speech, the more likely he is to be misunderstood.   This is likely to lead to communicative distress and so to decreased language use in future.   On the other hand, if language is an inefficient means of communication, another means might be expected to be used (e.g. gesture).   It was expected that the clearer speakers would use language more frequently, whereas the less articulate speakers would use gesture more frequently.   Each of the mongols was observed in the training centre for ten minutes.   The number of acts of communication realised in speech only, in speech accompanied by gesture, and in gesture only, was noted.   The results were against expectations.   There was no correlation between speech clarity and the frequency of realisation of communication in speech ($r = 0.17$, $N = 12$).   But individuals who spoke more also gestured more ($r = 0.72$, $N = 12$, $p < .01$).

Obviously, these results have to be treated with care.   Perhaps the range of articulatory abilities was too small for the expected effects to appear. Perhaps imitation is not the best test of clarity of spontaneous speech.

However, the fact remains that some individuals communicated more both in gesture and in speech.   Why should this be so?   One of the factors may be an individual's social relation with his partners.

EXPERIMENT 2

This experiment deals with mongols' interactions with nonmongol strangers or acquaintances.   Each mongol was asked to construct a jigsaw, once with a stranger (a nonretarded adult from outside the centre, who had no previous experience of interacting with a retarded person), and once with an acquaintance (member of Dalgairn staff).   Strangers and acquaintances were matched in age and sex. Mongols and nonmongols were matched in sex, but not in age.

The members of each interacting dyad sat across a corner of a rectangular table, alone in the room, but their interaction was filmed.   The first 500 seconds was used for subsequent analysis.   In posture analysis, the 500 seconds of film was sampled at 5 sec. intervals.   The first 25 sample points were called the first period, the last 25 sample points the fourth period.

Posture Analysis

Posture classification is shown in Figure 1 below.

The categories of posture (tilt, orientation, distance) were discussed by Dittman (1978).   He suggested, that even though physically they may vary continuously, their extremes (e.g. near, far) may be treated as discrete categories by perceivers.   The position of arms reflects openness/closeness of a posture (e.g. arm held on one's chest closes one's posture).   Not only actual postures, but also their mobility was investigated.   Mobility was defined as the ratio of observed over possible posture changes.   Each posture change consisted of alteration of one or more scoring features.   Average number of features altered per posture change was calculated and called the 'extent of change'.   Both posture mobility and the extent of change were calculated separately for each body part and each period.

Two questions can be asked about these postures:

i) Was the choice of a certain parameter dependent on the kind of audience a participant faced (e.g. did mongols sit far from strangers and near to their acquaintances)?

(a) BODY			(b) HEAD		(c) ARMS	
Tilt	Orientation	Distance	Tilt	Orientation	Near Arm (X°)	Distant Arm (X°)
Forward	Towards	near neutral far	Forward	towards neutral away	135	135,90,45,0
	Neutral	near neutral far	Straight	towards neutral away	90	135,90,45,0
	Away	near neutral far			45	135,90,45,0
Straight	Towards	near neutral far			00	135,90,45,0
	Neutral	near neutral far				
	Away	near neutral far				

Fig. 1 Body posture: scoring categories

ii) Were the <u>relationships</u> between features of a posture dependent on social
relations of partners interacting together (e.g. did a mongol keep near a
stranger only if oriented neutrally and far if oriented towards him, and with
an acquaintance, were orientation and distance independent)?   In other words,
was the syntax of Posture a reflection of social relations between the participants?

In the present paper I deal only with the first question.

Analysis of verbal interactions

Each speech act was classified according to (a) its spontaneity, (b) the demands
made on its recipient, and finally (c) according to whether it referred to another
speech act or to previously unverbalised actions of the two participants (see
Figure 2).

It was expected that mongols would communicate less spontaneously with strangers
and that they would make fewer demands on them because of their lack of familiarity
with them.   It was expected that this effect would disappear as interactions progressed.   The last factor, (c), was chosen to capture the level at which cohesion
of conversations was achieved.   If speakers refer to actions and experiences, but
not to each other's speech acts, then their conversation is made cohesive only by
their shared experience of interaction.   In other words it would be hard to understand verbal transcripts of such conversations.   On the other hand, speakers can
cross-refer their speech acts explicitly, through linguistic devices such as, for
example, anaphora and ellipsis.   Such conversations are easier to understand in
the absence of information about the speakers' physical actions.

Dimensions of a speech act			Examples	
Initiative	Requirements on addressee	Speech act refers to	Addressee's antecedent action	Addressor's speech act
spontaneous	understand (?)	NV action	Joins two pieces	"Well done"
		Speech act	"I like jigsaws"	"So do I"
	reply	NV action	breaks jigsaw	"Why did you do that?"
		Speech act	"I like jigsaws"	"Why?"
	act	NV action	Whistles	"Do it again"
		Speech act	"These go together"	"Well do it"
reaction	understand (?)	NV action	Points at a piece	"Yes, that's the one"
		Speech act	"What about this?"	"Yes, that's the one"
	reply	NV action	Touches addressor	"What do you want?"
		Speech act	"What is the time?"	"Where is your watch?"
	act	NV action	Points at a piece	"You try"
		Speech act	"Do these go together?"	"You try"

Fig. 2.   Analysis of verbal communication

Posture analysis results

Mongols kept their heads and bodies oriented <u>towards</u> nonmongols less frequently. They kept far from their partners more frequently.

Mongols distinguished strangers and acquaintances in terms of head orientation, body distance, body orientation, position of their arms and also in their mobility: they kept their head oriented towards strangers and neutrally relative to acquaintances. They kept far from strangers during the first period, far from acquaintances during the fourth period. With strangers they kept their near arm on their chest (closed posture) more frequently, even though this meant that they had to use their nonpreferred hand for manipulation. With strangers during the first period, they changed their posture rarely, though their mobility increased during the fourth period. The extent of posture changes was greater with acquaintances than with strangers.

On the other hand, there were only two differences between the postures of strangers and acquaintances.   A stranger would keep his body straight more often and
kept his near arm on his chest less often (i.e. his posture was more open).
(Each of the above described differences was significant at least p = 0.05).

Verbal interaction results

Mongols spoke fewer acts (SA) per period than nonmongols did (21.8 SA per period).
Their spontaneity of language use was less (56% of their speech acts) than that
of their nonmongol partners (94%).   This might have been so because mongols were
of lower status and lower ability than nonmongols.   As expected, mongols talked
less to strangers than to acquaintances (10.0 and 17.8 SAs per period respectively).
Surprisingly, mongols used language relatively more spontaneously with strangers
(64%) than with acquaintances (38%).   This was due to the behaviour of their
partners.   Acquaintances asked more questions (13.6 per period) than strangers
did (3.4 questions per period).   Since mongols answered questions readily, the
relative spontaneity of their speech decreased.   But in fact, they spoke as
spontaneously with strangers as with acquaintances (7.1 and 7.6 spontaneous SAs
per period respectively).   Finally, mongols asked few questions of either
acquaintances or of strangers (1.0 and 1.5 questions per period respectively).
Unfortunately, the analysis of conversation cohesion was impossible, since too
many of mongols' utterances were unclear: it was impossible to decide what they
referred to.

DISCUSSION

How one interacts with a stranger and an acquaintance can be a response to their
distinct behaviours.   But even if a stranger and an acquaintance behave identically, their actions may be interpreted differently.   Using language, mongols
reacted to demands of their audiences.   The initiative of their own language and
the demands they made on their partners were the same with strangers and with
acquaintances.   It is interesting to note that asking them many questions did not
make them speak more nor ask more questions in return.

There were several aspects that differentiated mongols' posture (and its change)
with strangers and acquaintances.   But there were only two which distinguished
the posture of strangers and acquaintances.   Mongols could have adopted
different postures spontaneously.   This could be tested by observing their behaviour with strangers and acquaintances who would posture and speak identically.
On the other hand, their posture could have been elicited by (a) the differences
in acquaintance-stranger posture that were observed or alternatively (b) the
different verbal communicative styles of their respective audiences.

In the first case, the conclusion would be that mongols were more interactive in
a nonverbal than in a verbal medium: it will be remembered mongols' spontaneous
speech was unaffected by the behaviour of their audiences.   In the second case,
the situation would be as follows: while the difference in behaviour of strangers
and acquaintances was mainly in their speech, mongols reacted to it in a nonverbal
medium.

So it seems that mongols' social relations were expressed mainly in NVC.   They
either spontaneously distinguished strangers from acquaintances by their posture
or they reacted to their audiences distinct communicative styles by adopting
different postures.

SUMMARY

The results of the first experiment were surprising.   The competence of mongols' articulation did not affect the frequency with which they used language.   The second experiment has shown that how often they used language spontaneously did not depend on the type of audience they faced, though they were sensitive to whether they interacted with a stranger or an acquaintance, but they expressed it in their posture rather than in their speech.

REFERENCES

Blanchard, I.   Speech pattern and etiology in mental retardation.   *American Journal of Mental Deficiency*, 1964, 68, 612-617

Bruner, J. S.   The ontogenesis of speech acts.   *Journal of Child Language*, 1975, 2, 1-19

Dittman, A. T.   The role of body movements in communication, in A. W. Siegman and S. Feldstein (Eds.) *Nonverbal behaviour and communication*, Lawrence Erlbaum Associates, 1978, pp 69-95

Dodd, B.   Recognition and reproduction of words by Down's syndrome and non-Down's syndrome retarded children.   *American Journal of Mental Deficiency*, 1975, 80, 306-311

Dodd, B.   A comparison of the phonological systems of mental age matched normal, severely subnormal and Down's syndrome children.   *British Journal of Disorders of Communication*, 1976, 11, 27-42

Hollien, H. and Copeland, R.   Speaking fundamental frequency (SFF) characteristics of mongoloid girls.   *Journal of Speech and Hearing Deficiency*, 1965, 30, 344-349

Lennenberg, E., Nichols, I. and Rosenberger, E.   Primitive stages of language development in Down's syndrome.   *Disorders of Communication XLII*, 1964, 119-137.   Research Publications.   Association for Research in Nervous and Mental Disease.

Michel, J. F. and Carney, R. J.   Pitch characteristics of mongoloid boys.   *Journal of Speech and Hearing Deficiency*, 1964, 29, 121-125

Montague, J. C., Brown, W. S. and Hollien, H.   Vocal fundamental frequency characteristics of institutionalised children.   *American Journal of Mental Deficiency*, 1974, 78

Price-Williams, D. and Sabsay, S.   Communicative competence among severely retarded persons.   *Semiotica*, 1979, 26, 35-63

Interactions With an Autistic Child

J. Duchan

Department of Communicative Disorders and Sciences, State University of New York/Buffalo, Buffalo, New York 14226, U.S.A.

ABSTRACT

This study examines and compares the interactions of a severely autistic child with four people: his teacher, mother, brother and a stranger to him. Analyses are made of interaction routines, features of verbal turn-taking, types of breakdowns in interaction sequences, and kinds of repair work following the breakdowns. All four interactants constructed activities and verbal action routines which they used to keep the interaction going. The amount of work needed to keep the interaction going was considerable, thereby accounting for why autistic children are deemed socially withdrawn and noninteractive.

Key words

Autism; interaction; social withdrawal; initiation; response; routines

INTRODUCTION

There are a number of checklists for determining whether or not a child has autistic characteristics. One of the qualifying characteristics of autism on all these lists is the child's lack of social interaction (Creak 1961; Kanner 1943; Wing 1976). This study attempts to examine how normal adults come to feel that autistic children are non-interactive. Further, it asks what approaches people develop for interacting with this "non-interactive" child and how the child responds to their different attempts.

The interactions are between a nine-year-old autistic child, Robbie, and another interactant. There are four different interactants: his mother, his classroom teacher, his brother, and a stranger, namely a speech pathologist whom he has just met and who is unfamiliar with autistic children. Each of the four were video-taped as they worked with Robbie; and in each case the purpose of the interaction was to get Robbie to show what he knows. Thus the event was skewed in the direction of the interactant doing what Pam Fishman (1978) has called the interactional work, where the work is to set up an interaction sequence and to keep it going.

The tapes were made within one month of each other. The length of the video-session was 30 minutes each for interaction with his mother, teacher and the stranger, and 10 minutes for his brother. The sessions were divided into sequences which were labelled by some of the interactants as "activities". These

units, recently called speech events by Ervin-Tripp and Mitchell-Kernan (1977),
were sometimes given a more specific title by the interactants such as "learning
dressing skills", "playing ball", or "naming objects".   The activities contained
sequences of verbal-action routines which were prescribed in that the person who
initiated them regarded their success as dependent on the correct execution of a
well defined sequence of actions and verbal exchanges.   These routines also had
beginnings and endings and, when they were aborted, the interactant made varied
attempts to repair them and thereby achieve their completion.   Between these activities and sometimes within them (but between the verbal-action routines) were
transition periods where the direct attempts to carry out the activity or its
routines were suspended, and Robbie was talked to or allowed to do what he would
while the interactant focussed on something else.

The results of the analysis of the four interactions are presented in terms of the
work which each of the interactants do to set up these activities and verbal-
action routines.   Particular attention is given to whether the verbal-action routines are carried out, why and when they break down, and how the breakdowns are
repaired.

ACTIVITIES

The mother tape comprised four activities defined in several ways by Robbie's
mother.   The first activity she called "dressing skills", and labelled it as such
at the beginning of the tape when she announced to an imagined viewer of the tape
that: "The first thing that we usually do in the morning is start out with dressing skills".   The activity entailed having Robbie work with buttoning buttons,
snapping snaps, zippering zippers and tying knots and bows.   It began when she
introduced a cloth book with pages containing buttons and button holes, zippers,
etc., and ended when she finished all the tasks she had planned beforehand.

The second activity was "body parts" and involved making a replica of a person out
of clay while naming the parts of the body.   The third activity involved commands
to find objects around the room.   There was a follow-up variation where Robbie
was asked yes-no questions such as "Is this a hat?" and was required to tell if the
noun was the correct term for the object in hand.

The mother concluded the session with a musical instrument activity where Robbie
was asked to name the musical instrument, to find those which one could blow,
hit, shake, and to differentiate which of the blows and hits were loud and which
were soft.

There were three separate activity structures in the teacher's session with Robbie.
The first was to have Robbie identify objects in terms of their name, function or
attribute.   For the second, Robbie played ball with the teacher following her
specific instructions to throw, roll, and catch the ball.   The third was to identify the missing object.

The third interactant was Robbie's six-year-old brother, Eric.   His activity
structuring was not as clearly defined as that of Robbie's mother and teacher, and
seemed to evolve as the session progressed depending upon what Eric found available
to use and upon the mother's suggestion for what Eric might try with Robbie.   In
some cases the activity seemed to evaporate in that it failed to end and instead
Eric or Robbie became involved in doing something not in the original activity
structure.   Eric's activities were having Robbie understand the name and function
of objects, to name pictures and to play ball.

The last interaction was that between a student speech pathologist and Robbie.
There were six discernible activities in this session.   The first and last were

activities where Robbie was instructed to either give a designated object to someone or to put it somewhere.   The second was a picture task where Robbie was asked
to name and answer questions about the pictured object.   A third was ball playing
where Robbie was asked to throw and catch the ball.   For a fourth, Robbie was
asked to identify parts of his body by name.   A fifth was a sentence imitation
task, which was a clinical procedure used to evaluate Robbie's syntactic skills.

ROUTINES

Most of the activities were comprised of one or more verbal-action routines.   The
routines were in some cases so tightly linked to the activity that the activity
was indeed defined by them.   For example, the yes-no question and answer routine
was the main means for carrying out the activity.

Other routines were more loosely related to the activity structure.   The object-
naming routine was interspersed into a number of activities and could in some
cases be seen as the primary component of the activity.   In other cases it could
be regarded as a precursor to the main event which defined the activity.   For an
example of the precursor routine, Robbie was first asked to identify objects and
then to determine which was missing, or he was asked to name the shoelace before
being instructed in how to tie it.

Most routines were single exchanges repeated through an activity where Robbie was
given a highly familiar command or question and he responded with his half of the
prescription either verbally or nonverbally.   Samples of these exchanges can be
divided into five types - all related to objects.   Object-naming routines were
begun with initiation phrases such as: "What is this?"   "Is this an X?"
Object-placement routines were started by commands such as: "Bring me X".
"Give Y the X".   Object-function routines were initiated by utterances such as:
"What do you do with an X?"   "Do you Y it?"   Object-attribute routines were
typically started by questions such as: "What colour is X?"   "Is it X colour?"
"How many are there?"   Object-possession routines were: "Do you have an X?"
and "Whose X is this?"

In some cases routines were associated with particular activity structures as was
the case for the "What's missing?" and "Yes-no question" routines.   Other routines occurred in many activities.   For example, the object-naming routine was
used in any activity involving objects or pictures.   Some routines were tied to
particular objects.   Object-possession routines, for example, were regularly
used with clothing, object-location routines with furniture toys, object-attribute routines with blocks and heads, and object-function routines with household
tools..

These exchanges qualify as routines on several counts.   First, they were very
frequent, comprising 27% of all of the interactants' verbal utterances to Robbie
in all four sessions.   Secondly, Robbie's verbal segments were highly stereotyped in intonation and syntax as in, "This is an X".   They were also often only
partially completed or wrongly answered as when he said "This is a _" and paused,
omitting the answer; or when he answered with the wrong colour or the wrong yes-
no answer in order to complete his turn.   Thirdly, an uncompleted routine was
more likely to be repaired by the initiator than the other verbal exchanges in
the sessions and seemed to require a single correct answer.   These factors give
the routine a feel of being a unitary event, a gestalt which requires closure.

The four interactants differed in their use of verbal routines.   Eric, Robbie's
six-year-old brother, initiated only one routine and used it in 49% of his utterances to Robbie.   That was the object-naming routine.

Robbie's teacher used routine structuring for 59% of her talk to Robbie.   Her
interaction with Robbie consisted of a number of unvarying routines.   Robbie's
mother relied on the object-naming routine and object-function routines, but seldom used others.   Robbie's mother's routines comprised only 21% of her talk to
Robbie.

The clinician used the widest variety of routines.   In some cases she began with
polite forms and used complex sentences.   When these and their paraphrases failed
to elicit Robbie's turn, she resorted to the more direct routines, and incidentally was more successful then in eliciting a turn from Robbie.   She used routines
in 37% of her utterances directed to Robbie.

Robbie in no case initiated routines.   He often completed them and, as was mentioned, sometimes tried to complete them even when he did not know the "answer".

BREAKDOWNS AND REPAIRS

The activities and verbal-action exchanges continued until they achieved a natural
conclusion, such as when the picture book was completed or the hidden objects were
all found;   or until they were aborted for some reason.

Most of the breakdowns were due to Robbie's lack of participation or to his wrong
or unintelligible answers, or to his not taking his turn and instead engaging in
self stimulatory behaviour or whining or leaving the scene.   Another source of
the breakdowns came from the interactant not carrying out the structure.   This
was characteristic of the Eric-Robbie interchange where Eric got involved in his
self-directed pursuits.   A third source of breakdown and one most common in the
teacher-Robbie and clinician-Robbie exchanges was that the interactant did not
perceive that Robbie had indeed taken his turn and in some cases had even answered
correctly. At these times, Robbie typically had answered very quickly and his
answers were internally directed.   That is, there was no mutual gaze, they were
under-articulated and of low volume.

In these cases of breakdown, the initiator tended not to move to something else,
but attempted to repair the breakdown instead.   The repairs were of the following
four types: First was a <u>verbatim repetition</u> or <u>revision</u> of the initiation utterance.   The revisions took different forms.   In some cases the utterance was
changed in degree of politeness (becoming either more or less polite), in others
the pronoun was changed.   There were also lexical, paralinguistic and intonational alterations.   A second type of repair was to provide Robbie with <u>hints</u> to the
answer or give him the whole answer.   These hints could be gestural where interactants showed Robbie what to do, or verbal where they gave him the response or
the first sound or syllable of the response.

The first two repair types did not alter Robbie's half of the prescription.   A
third repair type was to change to <u>another routine</u> which required a different answer from Robbie.   A commonly occurring example was to shift from a "What's this?"
initiator to a "yes-no question" initiator as did the clinician in the following
exchange: C: "What are these?"; R: "These are bagel"; C: (Not understanding
Robbie) "Are these rings?"

Finally, a considerable amount of repair work was done outside the verbal-action
routine structure.   This involved <u>attention getting devices</u> such as calling,
touching, restraining, pointing to the object, or disciplining Robbie.

SUMMARY

This was a study of what people do when in a face-to-face interaction with an autistic child.   The fact that they did all the work in planning, setting up, and initiating interactions, and repairing them when they failed, leads us to understand how people can easily come to feel that autistic children, such as Robbie, are non-interactive, at least in situations which are designed by the interactants. (We have done other studies of interactions with Robbie from his point of view and have found evidence that he is highly interactive in non-obvious ways.   See Duchan 1979; Prizant 1979).   What is now needed is a study which structurally analyses Robbie's sense of the different activity structures and routines and from there we hope to determine the value of using different activities and routines in his acquisition of knowledge, social competence, and language.

REFERENCES

Creak, E. M. Schizophrenic syndrome in childhood: progress report of a working
    party. Cerebral Palsy Bulletin, 1961, 3, 501
Duchan, J. Temporal aspects of self stimulating behaviors, in M. Davis (Ed.)
    Interaction rhythms. New York: Human Sciences Press (in press)
Ervin-Tripp, S. and Mitchell-Kernan, C. Child discourse. New York: Academic
    Press, 1977
Fishman, P. Interaction: the work women do. Social Problems, 1978, 25, 397-406
Kanner, L. Autistic disturbances of affective contact. Nervous Child, 1943, 2,
    217
Prizant, B. An analysis of the functions of immediate echolalia in autistic
    children. Buffalo, New York: State University of New York at Buffalo,
    Unpublished doctoral dissertation, 1979
Wing, L. Early childhood autism. New York: Pergamon Press, 1976

Stuttering and Nonverbal Communication: Investigations about Affect Inhibition and Stuttering

R. Krause

Institute of Psychology, University of Zurich, Switzerland

ABSTRACT

Stutterers who were openly stuttering and stutterers who were using hiding techniques were filmed talking to fluent speakers in greeting situations and during political discussions. The non-verbal behaviour of all participants, especially the expression of affect in the face, was compared to dyads of fluent speakers in similar situations using FACS (Facial Affect Coding System) and other coding techniques for the body and the hands. Stutterers do, disregarding the hearability of the speech disturbance, induce different non-verbal behaviour in their partners. Their own non-verbal behaviour pattern differs from that of the fluent speakers in the speaking position as well as during listening. The results are discussed in the framework of a new conception of the disturbance. Possible consequences for treatment are highlighted.

Key words

Affect; affect inhibition; automatic vocal transaction analyser; display rules of affect; facial action coding system; illustrators; listener response; regulators; speech disturbance; stuttering.

INTRODUCTION

Research treatment in the area of stuttering is in a deplorable state. There are approximately ten partially contradictory models of the stuttering response, its development and maintenance as well as the stutterer personality, although a lot of researchers doubt whether the latter exists.

An adult stutterer looking for treatment has a 30% chance of being healed and there is a lot of controversy about the definition of healing in the context of stuttering.   It is surely not the disappearance of the symptom alone.   Short-lived success in getting rid of the speech disturbance is relatively easy to ob-tain, by a multitude of techniques and tricks.

Despite this rather chaotic situation of research and treatment the following re-sults can be considered as relatively stable:

1. In the industrialised countries the disturbance is present in about 1% of the population, with a sex distribution of approximately 3.5 to 1 disfavouring the male.
2. Despite the expenditure of a tremendous amount of time and money the quest for somatic causes of the disturbance has been unsuccessful to date.
3. No stutterer stutters all the time - under certain social as well as emotional conditions the stuttering is reduced or disappears completely.
4. Negative affects and emotional states like anxiety, anger, shame, etc. seem to foster the speech disturbance.
5. Many stutterers report that the intensity of the negative affects influences the stuttering response.   Mild degrees of subjectively felt anger augments stuttering dramatically, whereas the very rare fits of rage are accompanied by completely fluent speech.

Based on these results as well as on the observation of stutterers in group therapies for quite a long time, I suspected that stutterers are trying to keep their arousal level, especially in relation to negative affects, on an extremely low level.   Most of the treatment approaches which are used nowadays favour this kind of affective monitoring also, since they recommend and teach the stutterer relaxation and internal peace, correctly assuming that speech is more fluent in these kinds of states.   Alas, most really important talks are not held in such a state.   These ideas were published in a theoretical paper in 1976 (Krause, 1976).

Based on these facts and speculations, I was expecting that stutterers do not only stutter but that they are using a communicative style which follows a display rule of general but incomplete affect inhibition.   I was especially expecting a reduc-tion of the variability and intensity of the affect expression in the face as well as a suppression of illustrators and regulators as the behavioural events which have a particularly close connection between affect expression and speech.   Illus-trators are movements of the extremities, the trunk or the upper face which are in a very close connection with the content and the temporal organisation of speech. Regulators are patterns of movement of the face as well as other parts of the body, especially the hands, as well as variations in pitch which monitor the change between speaker and listener (Ekman, 1977; Duncan, 1975).   The investigations I am now discussing, were conducted at the Psychologisches Institut der Universität Zurich, the Human Interaction Laboratory of the University of California, and the Speech Laboratory of the University of Maryland, Baltimore County.

The subjects were 28 male stutterers with different intensities of the speech dis-turbance.   The control group consisted of 50 male speakers who had no speech pro-blems.   They were matched so that every stutterer had a speaking partner who was roughly equivalent in age and occupational status.   Of the fluent speakers, 11 had other fluent speakers as partners, they were the control group.   The speaking partners, who did not know one another in advance, sat in a comfortable group therapy room, equipped with three remote control video cameras.   The experimenter left the room with the remark that he would be busy adjusting the cameras for about four minutes, so people should get acquainted with one another.   In fact, this part of the interaction was already being filmed.   After four minutes he came back and explained to the subjects that we were doing research on problem-solving behaviour; especially we were curious about how people solve political problems. The task to be solved by the subjects was to come to an agreement within twenty minutes on the three most important political and social problems needing to be solved within the next year in Switzerland. It was not mentioned that it was an observation study in the realm of stuttering and many of the subjects never realised this. Instructions and observation methods for the control group were identical. In Figure 1 the form of data observation and storage can be seen.

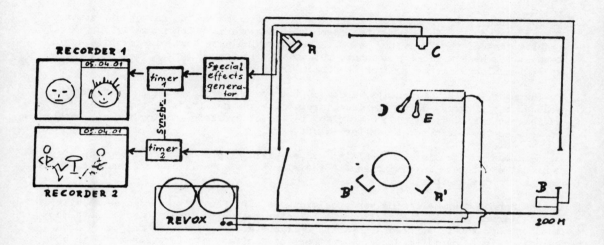

Fig. 1. Set-up of data recording within the experiment

(Cameras A and B are equipped with remote-control zoom lenses. Person's A' and B' faces are filmed for 5 minutes using these cameras. Then a 5 minute torso film follows, then the face again etc. The recordings of the two interactants are fed into recorder 1, using a special effects generator together with a digital clock with 1/100 sec precision. Camera C with a wide angle lens, records both interactants in full size on recorder 2. A second timer synchronized with the other one is fed into this recording. Sound is recorded separately on a 4 track Revox recorder using the two gun microphones D and E fixed to the ceiling.)

Later, two independent raters decided on the basis of listening to the audiotapes whether stuttering was audible or not. Reliability of these judgments was 0.95 (Phi-coefficient). Of the 26 stutterers, 16 stuttered audibly with different degrees of intensity; 10 used either hiding techniques or really did not stutter in this social situation.

For the analysis of the mimical expression we used the Facial Action Coding System (FACS by Ekman and Friesen, 1978), a coding system allowing an exhaustive description of all occurring muscular phenomena in the face.   The Automatic Vocal Transaction Analyzer (AVTA), an automatic computerized system for the statistical analysis of sound-silence-segments or on-off patterns of two speakers, developed by Feldstein and others at the University of Maryland (Feldstein and Welkowitz, 1978), was used for the analysis of the audible part of the discussion.   For body movements and positions we used an extensive coding system developed at the University of Berne (Frey and Pool, 1976).

RESULTS

1. The variability of mimical expression of stutterers who do not openly stutter is very reduced.   Especially the forehead and eye area which normally show lively innervations of the frontalis as well as the orbicularis oculi is immobile.   In respect to these mimical phenomena, but usually in the context of a stutterer spell in which it is of greater temporal duration.

2. The number of headmovements, accompanying speech production is significantly reduced in the group of stutterers disregarding whether there is stuttering audible or not.   This is in comparison to fluent speakers talking to one another as well as the partners of manifest stutterers.

3. Headnods in the listener position are significantly reduced in the group of manifest stutterers in comparison to their partners as well as to fluent speakers talking to one another.

4. The range of angle of the head positions is significantly reduced especially in stutterers who keep control over their disturbance.   Turning of the head to the partner as well as head downwards positions are in regard to frequency and duration significantly reduced.   Partners of manifest stutterers react with a prominent intensification of headmovements toward the stutterer.

5. The speaking partners of manifest stutterers smile during 22 per cent of their speaking and listening time compared to only 4 per cent of the speaking partners of stutterers who keep control of the disturbance.   The differences are highly significant.

In dyads where stutterers are involved one finds a frozen smiling, whereas smiling in a control group of fluent speakers talking to one another is relatively balanced. The group of fluent speakers talking to one another has significantly more synchronizing of smiling and brow raising.   The accuracy of the synchronizing of smiling and brow raising is worse in both groups in which stutterers are involved for the beginning of the mimic activities as well as for their completion.

6. Stutterers who openly stutter held their eyes partly or totally closed during 22 per cent of their listener times compared to 11 or 13 per cent of the time for the group of fluent speakers talking to one another.

7. Manifest stutterers show a significant augmentation of mouth movements during listening, be it that the mouth is opened or closed and lips are heavily pressed together.

8. Mimic activities which may allow inferences on states of negative affective arousal are significantly reduced in stutterers who keep control of the disturbance compared to fluent speakers talking to one another as well as the manifest stutterers.

9. The following significant differences in body behaviour between stutterers and
fluent speakers are found: stutterers turn their trunks more to their speaking
partners but, at the same time, head positions are turned away. The average
openness of hands and arms is defined as the average position of hands and arms
away from the trunk. Stutterers are less open in this respect. Symmetric positions of the legs are rare in stutterers. Complexity of movement behaviour is
defined as the number of all body parts simultaneously involved in one movement.
Stutterer's movements are significantly less complex, nominal differentiation of
movements was defined as the relation of the empirically found number of different
positions and the maximal possible number of different positions. This nominal
differentiation is significantly reduced in stutterers.

DISCUSSION

I consider our hypotheses as generally confirmed, especially for the group of
stutterers who keep control over their disturbance. They are characterised by
a great behavioural rigidity, be it in the face or in the body. Their speaking
partners, however, develop a similar pattern of behaviour, so the dyad seems to be
inhibited. Stutterers who stutter openly do not have - at least in the speaking
position - a severe reduction of mimic activities. However, many of the visible
mimic co-activities seem to be part of the stutterer response. It can hardly be
said whether this is pseudo-affective behaviour. Both groups of stutterers
react with a significant reduction of listener behaviour such as headnods, eye
contact and turning in of the head. They seem to be pretty bad listeners. It
might be that it is this behavioural strategy which leads to the fact that the
stutterers occupy significantly more speaking time during the political discussion
than their partners. Again this holds true too for the group of nonmanifest
stutterers. Partners of manifest stutterers react with an intensification of
listener responses such as augmentation of smiling, over-exaggerated forms of
heavy headnods and turning in of the head. Partners of non-manifest stutterers
react with the reduction of these behaviour patterns.

In dyads of fluent speakers congruence of speech parameters like average vocalisation, duration of pause length, etc. can be observed. This congruence process
is disturbed in dyads where a stutterer is involved in the sense that fluent
speakers adapt their behaviour to the stutterer and never the other way round.
(See Krause, 1978, 1979). The phenomenon of congruence of nonverbal behaviour,
especially of these speech characteristics, was considered by some authors as a
possible behavioural correlate of empathetic processes. People who are forced
to control their own affects all the time should do the same thing with the
affects of their interaction partners, because the behaviour of the other person
might function as a trigger as powerful and potent as their own internal arousal
processes. In that sense the communicative style, at least of the non-manifest
stutterers, is functionally successful in inhibiting spontaneous affective and
expressive behaviour in the speaking partner as well as their own behaviour.
For the treatment I propose that we should re-evaluate the following problems in
stutterer therapy and prevention:

1. With the first appearance of speech disfluence in children under affective
arousal it is probably unwise to react with relaxation and speech control techniques, as happens today.   It would be more adequate to observe the
interactive patterns of children and parents in relation to affect expression and
speech production and they should be changed in the direction of speech under
arousal and not, as is the case presently, to speech without arousal.

2. Adult stutterers should not be treated with affect control techniques like systematic desensitization, hypnoses, self-suggestion techniques, autogenic training,
etc. It seems that they are useless anyhow, but they are permanently applied

nevertheless.   In my opinion they might be a methodologically refined augmentation of the fatal control techniques the stutterer is using for himself anyhow.
Instead of these techniques, sensitisation techniques to affective states and
arousal should be learned.

3. Observation of their own behaviour must play a central role in stutterers'
treatment.   This happens best in groups of stutterers.   The secondary gain of
the disturbance disappears when they talk to other stutterers.

4. Techniques heavily relying on speech are probably not very adequate, because,
in my opinion, there is nothing to be learned about speech.   Group techniques
relying on nonverbal processes and exercises seem to me more adequate.   I am
thinking of certain strategies of Gestalt, body work and psychodrama.

REFERENCES

Duncan, S.   Interaction units during speaking turns in dyadic face-to-face
       conversations, in A. Kendon, R. M. Harris and M. R. Kay (Eds.) Organization
       of behaviour in face-to-face interaction. Paris: Mouton, 1975
Ekman, P.   Biological and cultural contributions to body and facial movements,
       in D. Blacking (Ed.) Anthropology of the Body. San Francisco: Academic
       Press, 1977
Ekman, P. and Friesen, W. V. Manual for the facial action code.   Palo Alto:
       Consulting Psychologists Press, 1978
Feldstein, S. and Welkowitz, J. A chronography of conversation: in defense of
       an objective approach, in A. Siegman and S. Feldstein (Eds.) Nonverbal
       behavior and communication. Hillsdale: Lawrence Erlbaum, 1978
Frey, S. and Pool, J. A new approach to the analysis of visible behavior.
       Forschungsbericht aus dem Psychologischen Institut der Universität Bern.
       Bern, 1976
Krause, R.   Probleme der psychologischen Stottererforschung und Behandlung.
       Zeitschrift für Klinische Psychologie und Psychotherapie, 1976, 24, 20-37
Krause, R.   Nonverbales interaktives Verhalten von Stotterern und ihren
       Gesprächspartnern.   Schweizerische Zeitschrift für Psychologie und ihre
       Anwendungen, 1978, 3, 16-31
Krause, R.   Stottern und nonverbale Kommunikation.   Eine neue Theorie der
       Störung und ihrer Behandlung, in Sonderpädogogik, 1979, Sonderheft,
       Sprachstörungen.

Psychopathological States and Their Effects on Speech and Gaze Behaviour*

H. Ellgring, H. Wagner and A. H. Clarke

*Max Planck Institute for Psychiatry, Kraepelinstrasse 10, D-8000 Munchen 40,
Federal Republic of Germany*

ABSTRACT

Internal characteristics such as depressed mood, anxiety and general negative
emotions are accompanied, particularly during depressive illness, by changes in
observable behaviour.   Accordingly, the following questions may be examined:
are intra-individual changes in speech and gaze behaviour related to changes in
the internal psychopathological state?   Further, do these changes occur synchronously to changes in the state of subjective well-being?

A longitudinal study was made on depressed patients.   Their behaviour was observed
during standardised interviews and diagnostic-therapeutic discussions held at regular intervals.

Various speech and gaze parameters were examined with respect to their coordination
and their relationship to the subjective state of well-being.

Considerable variation was found in the temporal relationship amongst these variables.   The results are discussed with respect to the relevance of speech parameters and the coordination of verbal and nonverbal behaviour as indicators of
the psychopathological condition.

Key Words

Social interaction; depression; verbal and nonverbal behaviour; speech; looking
behaviour; dyadic interaction; single case study; longitudinal study; communication and psychopathology; social psychology.

INTRODUCTION

When investigating the relationship between psychopathology and communicative behaviour it is generally assumed that specific changes in the internal state of the
individual are associated with changes in communicative behaviour.

---

* The work reported in this paper was carried out in connection with an interdisciplinary research project on endogenous depression.   The support of the
  Deutsche Forschungsgemeinschaft Angrag Nr.El 67/1 is also gratefully acknowledged.

The following questions are examined in this contribution: are intra-individual changes in speech and gaze behaviour related to changes in the internal psychic state? Further, do these changes occur synchronously with changes in subjective well-being?

Assuming that speech activity yields some indication of the "social energy output" during depression, it may be analogously said of the gaze behaviour, that it should yield some indication of the capacity of the individual to be receptive towards visible social information, i.e. as an indicator of "input capacity".

According to the hypothesis of general reduction in performance capacity during depression, it is to be expected that such states of higher demand should occur less, or be avoided more.

DEPRESSION AND MEASURES OF SPEECH

To date there exist few, and to some degree inconsistent reports on the relationship between depression and temporal measures of speech. Aronson and Weintraub (1967) and Hinchliffe, Lancashire and Roberts (1971a) found that depressive patients exhibited a lower rate of speech than control persons. In an early article Rutter and Stephenson (1971) reported significantly reduced speech activity during an interview situation in both schizophrenic and depressive groups as compared to a normal control group. However, in a recent publication Rutter (1977) found that during natural conversation, such patients exhibited no significantly different behaviour. Thus, it seems doubtful that consistent group differences are to be observed. The question may be posed, however, as to whether the individual exhibits notable differences in his behaviour for varying internal states.

Starkweather (1974) compared the speaking rate intraindividually over three interviews for 4 depressive patients during both depressive and improved phases. For three of the patients the speaking rate increased from 14-18% to 45-62%. With the fourth patient, diagnosed as agitated depressive, the relatively high initial values of about 60% had not changed notably after improvement. In a longitudinal study with four depressive patients, based on series of 10 or more interviews, Ellgring (1977) found a negative correlation between speech activity and depressive state. A similar, but less close relationship was found for the amount of gaze at partner.

DEPRESSION AND GAZE BEHAVIOUR

The few investigations of the relationship between gaze behaviour and depression appear no more consistent than those regarding the speech activity. The reduced amount of gaze at partner during depression reported by Waxer (1974) supports the hypothesis of reduced reception of social nonverbal information. Hinchliffe, Lancashire and Roberts (1971b) measured 23% gaze at partner in a group of depressive patients compared to 51% gaze at partner in a group of improved patients.

However, less clear results were obtained by Rutter and Stephenson (1972a) and Rutter (1977). According to Rutter (1977) both schizophrenics and controls exhibited a relative duration of ca. 55% gaze at partner, and depressives 45%, whereas patients with neurotic or personality disorders exhibited only 35%. Not surprisingly, a corresponding inconsistency is to be found in the reports concerning simultaneous looking and speaking (Hinchliffe et al. 1971b; Rutter and Stephenson 1972b; Rutter 1977). The general inconsistency of the results concerning the temporal aspects of speech and gaze may be due to the influence of various topics of conversation, as Rutter (1977) supposed or to the heterogeneity of the groups as Rutter (1973) suggested in a review article.

The question remains as to whether the reduced verbalisation and gaze found in some depressive patients is associated with a tendency towards social withdrawal; or, on the other hand, whether the influence of the situational context on some individuals is so strong that the internal psychic state is not observable at the behavioural level.

The work reported in this paper involves an approach, by means of longitudinal single case studies, to assess under which conditions and to what degree the internal state becomes manifest in the observable behaviour. In this way the application of parameters derived from such communicative behaviour for the inference of depressive state can be evaluated in more detail.

METHOD

Single case, longitudinal studies were carried out with patients who had been diagnosed for endogenous depression (ICD 296). For the present analysis only those patients were selected who had shown a notable change in their state of well-being during clinical stay. These included 5 female and 4 male patients, aged between 33 and 57 years.

The patients were videorecorded twice weekly during the course of their clinical stay. Each recording consisted of a standardised interview, followed by a period of free conversation. The patients were recorded in a dyadic situation with a psychiatrist and on alternate days, with a clinical psychologist.

The first five minutes of each standardised interview and free conversation were analysed. The number of interviews recorded for each patient ranged from 11 to 39, corresponding to one to four months clinical stay. Details of the interview and the recording procedure have been reported elsewhere (Ellgring and Clarke, 1978).

The subjective well-being of the patients was assessed by means of a self rating scale which ranged from a feeling of extreme comfort (= 0) to extreme discomfort (= 112). This assessment was administered directly before each recording.

The on-off patterns of speech and gaze of the patient and the interviewer were registered continuously by four independent observers. The reliability, as measured continuously for point-to-point agreement, was found to be 96% for speech registration and 94% for registration of gaze at the partner. The agreement between human observer and acoustic detector for speech was found to be 94%. This observation procedure yields four binary channels of information corresponding to the presence and absence of speech and gaze at partner.

A review of the relationship between subjective well-being and the speech and gaze behaviour of the patient will be dealt with in the following. First of all, these variables will be presented in detail for one patient who was found to exhibit a particularly illustrative course of depression. The remainder of the results involve a somewhat condensed description of the longitudinal data for the 9 selected patients. This is presented in a compatible form to that of Starkweather (1967.), whereby the first and final interviews are compared.

RESULTS

A single case, longitudinal study of depression

The following results illustrate the different temporal courses of the subjective and behavioural variables recorded from a 57 year old female patient.

As can be seen in Figure 1, the patient's initial subjective well-being was good,
indeed showing a tendency to improve until the 25th day.   At this point a sudden
lapse into a deep depression occurred.   The subjective well-being appeared to improve until the 80th day.   A slight relapse occurred between the 100th and 120th
day.   The patient was treated from the 29th day with Amitriptylin.   The observed

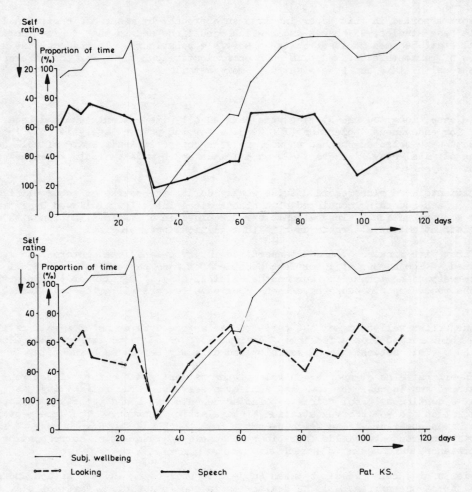

Fig. 1.   Course of depression in a 57 year old female patient.
           (ICD 296.3)

behaviour was found in this case to correspond generally to the subjective well-
being.   As shown in Figure 1, the proportion of speaking was found to decrease
during the depressive phase (ca. 70% to 18%).   A similar reduction in the proportion of gaze at partner was found (ca. 60% to 9%).   The proportion of speaking
averaged over interviews 1-3 and 4-6 remained constant (mean values 70%), whereas
the proportion of gaze was found to drop from 63% to 51%.

Thereafter, the proportion of gaze appears to have increased more rapidly.
Between the 60th and 90th day, however, a decrease to an average value of 52% was
measured.   This precedes the observed relapse in the subjective well-being.

Over the final three interviews, an average level of 63% gaze at partner was measured.

There are various points of interest in this single case study.   Firstly, there appeared a systematic relationship between the fluctuations of the subjective well-being of the patient and the observed behaviour.   Secondly, the speech behaviour was found to fluctuate between more stable levels and with larger shifts of level than the gaze behaviour, and finally, the changes in gaze behaviour were found to occur in advance of the changes in the subjective well-being.

Intraindividual comparisons

It can be seen from Figure 2 that the relationships between subjective well-being and observed behaviour hypothesised in the introduction are not to be found in all cases.

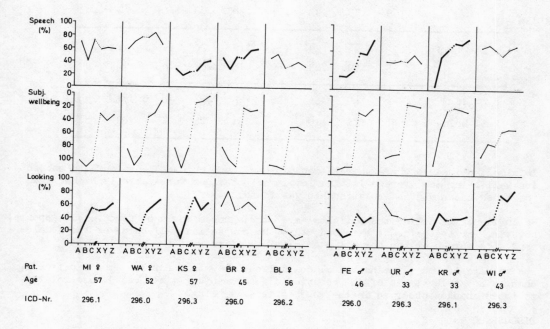

Fig. 2.   Results from the longitudinal study of nine depressive patients.
For each plot, values were taken for the first (A B C) and final (X Y Z) three interviews recorded during clinical stay.
Heavy line sections emphasise relationship between subjective well-being and the respective behaviours.
For patient KS, A B C represent interviews 7 to 9.

The proportion of speech was found to increase with clinical improvement in four of the patients, the proportion of gaze in six.   In only three of the patients were both variables found to increase simultaneously.

The results listed in Table 1 indicate, for those patients who did in fact exhibit the expected changes, an average increase in speech activity between 10 and 40%, and in gaze between 22 and 41%.   The patient KR attained a stable level of gaze activity as early as the second interview, and the patient MI after the third interview.

TABLE 1   Mean proportion of speech and looking at partner
during initial (a) and final (b) three interviews
and corresponding subjective well-being.

		Patient								
---	---	MI	WA	KS	BR	BL	FE	UR	KR	WI
p(Speech)	a	.60	.69	.27	.42	.45	.23	.44	.40	.66
	b	.59	.75	.37	.55	.38	.63	.47	.74	.63
p(Looking)	a	.33	.28	.29	.65	.32	.20	.55	.41	.39
	b	.55	.59	.63	.60	.15	.45	.43	.46	.80
Subject	a	106	97	93	97	110	109	91	75	79
Well-being	b	36	26	10	24	51	25	15	20	51

In almost all cases where no relationship was found between behaviour and subject-ive well-being the average initial levels in behaviour were markedly higher than for those cases where a relationship was found.

No influence regarding the patients' age or diagnoses could be found.   It appears, however, for the patients examined, that the subjective well-being of the females tended to worsen at the beginning of clinical stay.

The results of the intraindividual comparisons show that for 7 of the 9 patients, changes in at least one of the behavioural components (mainly gaze) were related to those changes observed in the subjective well-being.

DISCUSSION

The proportion of speech and looking at partner does not appear in all cases to be related to the internal state, or subjective well-being, of the patient.   A pre-condition appears to be an initially low level of the behavioural activity during depression.   It can therefore be expected that those patients who exhibit a low level of such behaviour during a depressive phase should also exhibit an increase parallel to clinical improvement.   This agrees with the results of the single case studies carried out by Starkweather (1967) with respect to speech.

There also seems to be some evidence for the argument that behavioural changes may precede changes in subjective well-being.

It may be concluded that neither the "optimistic" view expressed by Hinchliffe, Lancashire and Roberts (1971b), "... that eye contact is recording the affective changes in the patient adequately", nor the more sceptical opinion of Rutter (1977)

regarding the indicative value of speaking and looking at partner, can be fully
supported.   Both variables can be shown, for particular cases, to change systematically and to some extent with a temporal shift to the patient's self-rated internal state.

The fact that such changes occurred more often in gaze may suggest that this behaviour is more independent of the situational demands than speech, i.e. possibly
a certain compensation may be made in the energy output whereas the limited input
capacity, as expressed by the proportion of gaze, remains uncompensated.   The
higher proportion of speech in those cases where no relationship exists to the
subjective well-being can perhaps be explained as a coping strategy on the part of
the patient to match the demand characteristic of the interview situation.   There
is some evidence that parameters such as utterance length may yield further information on this.   The observed temporal shifts amongst the behavioural and subjective variables might further be explained as resulting from the presence of separate
temporal systems governing the associated psychological levels.

REFERENCES

Aronson, H. and Weintraub, W. Verbal productivity as a measure of change in
    affective status. Psychological Reports, 1967, 20, 483-487
Ellgring, J. H. Kommunikatives verhalten im verlauf depressiver erkrankungen,
    in W. H. Tack (Ed.), Bericht über den 30. Kongress der Deutschen Gesellschaft
    für Psychologie in Regensburg 1976, Bd. 2. Göttingen: Hogrefe, 1977, S.
    190-192
Ellgring, J. H. and Clarke, A. H. Verlaufsbeobachtungen anhand standardisierter
    videoaufzeichnugen bei depressiven patienten, in H. Helmchen and E.
    Renfordt (Eds.) Fernsehen in der psychiatrie. Stuttgart: Thieme, 1978, S.
    68-77
Hinchliffe, M. K., Lancashire, M. and Roberts, F. J. Depression: defence
    mechanisms in speech. British Journal of Psychiatry, 1971(a), 118, 471-472
Pope, B., Blass, T., Siegman, A. W. and Raher, J. Anxiety and depression in speech
    Journal of Consulting and Clinical Psychology, 1970, 35. 128-133
Rutter, D. R. Visual interaction in psychiatric patients: a review. The British
    Journal of Psychiatry, 1973, 123, 193-202
Rutter, D. R. Visual interaction in recently admitted and chronic long-stay
    schizophrenic patients. The British Journal of Social and Clinical Psych-
    ology, 1977, 16, 47-56
Rutter, D. R. and Stephenson, G. M. Visual interaction in a group of schizophrenic
    and depressive patients. British Journal of Social and Clinical Psychology,
    1972(a), 11, 57-65
Rutter, D. R. and Stephenson, G. M. Visual interaction in a group of schizophrenic
    and depressive patients: a follow-up study. British Journal of Social and
    Clinical Psychology, 1972(b), 11, 410-411
Starkweather, J. A. Vocal behaviour as an information channel of speaker status,
    in K. Salzinger and S. Salzinger (Eds.) Research in verbal behaviour and some
    neurophysiological implications. New York: Academic Press, 1967, pp.253-265
Waxer, P. Nonverbal cues for depression. Journal of Abnormal Psychology, 1974,
    53, 319-322

Normal Speech - Normal People? Speculations on Paralinguistic Features, Arousal and Social Competence Attribution

H. G. Wallbott and K. R. Scherer

Department of Psychology, Justus-Liebig University, Otto Behaghel Str. 10,
6300 Giessen, Federal Republic of Germany

ABSTRACT

It is suggested that various aspects of nonverbal vocal behaviour, especially para- and extralinguistic features play an important role for social skills and inter- actional competence, and that some variants of these features may lead to the attribution of "abnormality". Results from our studies with schizophrenic pat- ients indicate that differential improvement can be predicted from paralinguistic data from an interview before therapy, i.e. patients judged as more improved after therapy show more speech "abnormalities" before therapy (e.g. long hesitation pauses, slow speech rate, high fundamental frequency)! Results are interpreted as indicating either improved social competence of the patients or reduced psych- ological arousal and tension after successful therapy.

Key Words

Abnormality; arousal; attribution; paralinguistics; schizophrenia; depression; social competence; social skills; speech behaviour.

"Normality" or "abnormality" of a person's behaviour is an essential concept in both folk psychology and clinical psychology. Behaviour is more likely to be considered "normal" the more it corresponds to the modal behaviour or certain norm- ative standards in a social group. Consequently, institutions like psychiatric hospitals, prisons, etc. are expected to change the behaviour of their "abnormal" clients and bring it back into line with these norms and standards.

However, the concept of normality as used in psychiatry and much of psychology is coming increasingly under attack. Many "anti-psychiatrists" claim that schizo- phrenics and depressives are not abnormal or mentally ill, but rather that they behave differently from the majority of the people in a society (cf Laing, 1961; Szasz, 1961; Goffman, 1967). According to this view labelling a certain beha- viour as "abnormal" is the result of attribution processes and therefore not a use- ful diagnostic category in terms of a medical model of mental illness.

Recently, a third view of mental illness has been proposed, which takes these at- tribution processes into account. It is maintained that lack of interactive competence or social skills (cf Argyle, 1969; Trower, Bryant and Argyle, 1978) can give rise to attributions of "abnormality". Once this lack of social skills

is alleviated by appropriate training procedures, mental patients are seen as
"improved" or "normal".   However, the various components of social skills and the
part they play in facilitating attributions of "normality" or "abnormality" has as
yet only been tentatively identified.   Thus the effect of nonverbal, especially
paralinguistic aspects of behaviour has remained rather unclear.

It seems possible that deviant paralinguistic speech behaviour reflecting absence
of essential social skills is as likely to lead to a perceived need for some kind
of "therapy" as are bizarre behaviour patterns or affect disturbances.   Consequently, changes of speech patterns in the direction of cultural expectation may
contribute significantly to the impression of "improvement" after therapy.   Thus,
we propose to test the hypothesis that deviations from social norms concerning
paralinguistic aspects of speech behaviour contribute to the attribution of abnormality or social incompetence.   Psychiatrists and clinical psychologists may judge
the improvement of patients who have shown unusual speech behaviour at the beginning of therapy by the degree to which they have returned to the modal type of
speech behaviour, particularly with respect to paralinguistic aspects (cf Wallbott,
1975).

We will describe some results from a pilot study conducted in our Giessen laboratory, which are pertinent to these hypotheses.   In this study we used materials
originally collected by Ekman and Friesen (cf. 1975).   Semi-standardised interviews with hospitalised psychiatric patients (American females) were video- and
audiotaped immediately after admission to the hospital (admission interview) and
shortly before discharge following clinical improvement (discharge interview).
The audiotapes were analysed with respect to different elements of speech behaviour
(results are reported in detail elsewhere: Tolkmitt, Scherer, Helfrich, Standke
and Wallbott, in prep.).   We will focus here mainly on the relationships between
perceived improvement and paralinguistic aspects of speech for nine schizophrenic
patients (for further details see Wallbott, 1975).   The following variables were
measured in our laboratory for the first four minutes of each interview: number
of words, speech rate, number of silent pauses, silence-quotient, speech disturbances, proportion of self-reference, interaction rate and type-token-ratio (cf.
Wallbott, 1975).   In addition fundamental frequency of the voice (pitch) was ex-
tracted from the speech signal using digital computer analysis (autocorrelation
procedures, cf. Tolkmitt and colleagues, in prep.).   Trained judges rated the
patients' improvement on the basis of their records (nurses' comments and ratings,
psychiatrists' judgments: cf Kiritz, 1973).   The results seem to support our
hypotheses.

Table 1 shows the major results on the speech patterns for the nine patients whi3h
had been discharged at the time of the final interview.   These patients were categorised into two groups, "much improved" and "little improved" on the basis of a
fixed cut-off point in the improvement scale used by the expert raters (+ 1.0 on a
+ 5.0 to - 5.0 scale).   The data show clearly that the groups differ quite strongly in terms of the variables measured at the time of the admission interview, but
not at discharge (the former differences are significant in randomisation-tests,
cf. Siegel, 1956, although the small size of the sample suggests some caution in
the interpretation of the differences found).   This implies a (significant) change
over therapy for the "much improved" group - larger number of words, faster speech
rate, fewer and shorter silent pauses, lower interaction rate (all of which are
highly intercorrelated) and lower fundamental frequency - and little change for the
"little improved" group.

These results could be interpreted as showing that the rather dramatic change in
paralinguistic speech behaviour of the much improved group from admission to discharge - presumably in the direction of modal speech behaviour in American society -
is directly responsible for the degree of perceived improvement.   This would es-

TABLE 1   Differences between patient groups and interviews

Patient Groups	Speech variables (for the first 4 minutes of each interview)	Admission interview		Discharge interview	
		$\overline{X}$	S	$\overline{X}$	S
Patients rated as much improved after therapy N = 5	Fundamental frequency (F_0 in Hz)	243.8	26.0	220.2	17.6
	Number of words	160.4	39.8	431.0	140.1
	Speech rate (# words / speaking time)	103.2	27.3	224.2	68.2
	Silent pauses (# silent pauses / # words)	14.7	3.9	10.1	4.6
	Silence quotient (duration of silent pauses / speaking time)	52.3	9.3	27.9	7.7
	Interaction rate (number of speaking turns)	24.2	2.9	15.0	7.4
Patients rated as little improved after therapy N = 4	Fundamental frequency (F_0 in Hz)	207.6	29.7	199.4	28.8
	Number of words	477.5	195.1	422.8	165.9
	Speech rate (# words / speaking time)	234.3	82.1	241.5	71.8
	Silent pauses (# silent pauses / # words)	9.3	2.7	8.5	.8
	Silence quotient (duration of silent pauses / speaking time)	31.7	11.7	31.4	11.2
	Interaction rate (number of speaking turns)	12.5	5.1	16.5	4.7

(Between admission and discharge, much improved group: $p < .05$)

(Between the two patient groups, admission interview: $p < .05$ [1] ; discharge interview: n.s. [2])

(Between admission and discharge, little improved group: n.s.)

[1] except: "F_0" $p < .20$

[2] except: "number of words" $p < .05$

tablish a link between the conformity of paralinguistic speech patterns to cultural norms and attributions of normality or social competence.   Proponents of the "lack of social competence" view of psychopathology might even hold that the much improved patients have learned (or relearned) cultural expectations concerning paralinguistic behaviour patterns and have acquired the appropriate speaking skills.

However, the marked decrease in fundamental frequency of the voice in the much improved group suggests an alternative explanation in terms of changes in the underlying psychopathological symptoms.   It has been shown that fundamental frequency is a major indicator of psychological arousal (Scherer, 1979).   This allows us to interpret the decrease in fundamental frequency after therapy as a pronounced reduction of arousal or tension and a sign of relaxation in the much improved group. These patients may have had much more severe symptoms and higher tension levels and the reduction of these is consequently seen as greater improvement than changes in patients who were less aroused to begin with.

It is not possible to decide on the basis of the data available from the study whether the changes in paralinguistic behaviour were primarily due to changes in psychological state, particularly to the reduction of abnormally high tension, or to an increase in social competence which could be due either to an increase in concern with social norms concerning paralinguistic speech patterns and/or the acquisition (or re-acquisition) of the appropriate speaking skills in terms of paralinguistic behaviour, or possibly to all of these determinants.   Similarly, on the level of attribution, it remains unclear whether these speech cues serve mainly as inferences of psychological states or as assessments of "normality".

Further studies on the role of paralinguistic behaviour in psychopathology and clinical change brought about by therapy could provide insights for both the nature of psychopathology and the role of paralinguistic behaviour in social interaction

REFERENCES

Argyle, M. Social interaction. London: Methuen, 1969
Ekman, P. and Friesen, W. V.   Nonverbal behavior in psychopathology, in R. J. Friedman and M. M. Katz (Eds.) The psychology of depression. Contemporary theory and research.   New York: Winston, 1975, pp. 179-216
Goffman, E. Interaction ritual.   Garden City: Double Day, 1967
Kiritz, S. A. Hand movement and clinical ratings.   Unpublished dissertation. San Francisco, 1973
Laing, R. D. The self and the others.   London: Tavistock, 1961
Scherer, K. R. Nonlinguistic indicators of emotion and psychopathology, in C. E. Izard (Ed.) Emotions in personality and psychopathology.   New York: Plenum Press, 1979, pp. 495-529
Siegel, S. Nonparametric statistics for the behavioral sciences.   New York: McGraw-Hill, 1956
Szasz, T. S. The myth of mental illness.   London: Secker & Warburg, 1961
Tolkmitt, F., Scherer, K. R., Helfrich, H., Standke, R. and Wallbott, H. G. Therapy effects on voice and speech in schizophrenic and depressive patients. In prep.
Trower, P., Bryant, B. and Argyle, M. Social skills and mental health. London: Methuen, 1978
Wallbott, H. G. Paralinguistische Aspekte der Sprache Schizophrener. Unpublished diploma thesis, 1975

Paralinguistic Behaviour:
Internal Push or External Pull?

U. Scherer, H. Helfrich and K. R. Scherer

*Department of Psychology, Justus-Liebig University, Otto Behaghel Str. 10,
6300 Giessen, Federal Republic of Germany*

ABSTRACT

Data from two studies are reported which illustrate that various paralinguistic
aspects of speech, particularly fundamental frequency of the voice, can be explained by internal determinants such as personality traits or affective states or
external determinants such as conformity to social expectations and/or self-presentation.   Various explanations are shown to be feasible to account for the inverse relationship between voice pitch and life satisfaction in elderly women
found in the first study reported and the pitch of public officials' voices in
interacting with different types of clients observed in the second study.

Key Words

Paralinguistics; pitch of voice; interactive speech; personality traits,
affective states; self presentation; speech norms; interactive competence.

Are paralinguistic features such as tempo and rhythm of speech and pitch and
quality of voice determined by an internal, intrapersonal "push" exerted by personality traits and dispositions as well as affective states, or by the external
"pull" of social norms and expectations concerning the appropriateness of particular speech patterns and the need for adequate self-presentation?

For example, a number of studies on silent pauses raises the question whether
speakers' hesitation patterns are based on personality traits and/or affective
states or whether they are the result of an attempt to meet social expectations
with regard to paralinguistic speech patterns. Siegman (1978) explained findings
of negative relationships between extraversion and both number and duration of
silent pauses in terms of a biophysical factor of impulsivity. However, in one
of our studies (Scherer, 1979b), while we found a similar negative relationship
for American speakers, we found a positive relationship (extraverts pausing more)
for German speakers. One can argue that Americans attribute introversion (which
seems to be negatively evaluated in their culture) to speakers who show many
hesitation pauses, and that American extraverts may therefore attempt to avoid
hesitation pauses to demonstrate their extraversion (cf Scherer, 1979b).
Similarly, fundamental frequency of the voice (F$\emptyset$) could be affected by both internal push and external pull. On the basis of studies conducted in a number of
different laboratories, it is safe to assume that the fundamental frequency of the

human voice is one of the most important vocal indicators of psychological arousal
or stress, an essential internal push, possibly due to the effect of general muscle
tension (for a review, see Scherer, 1979a).

At the same time, vocal pitch (perceived F∅) may well be subject to external pull
in terms of social expectations and preferences.   For example, Laver (1975) has
pointed out that there may be a cultural stereotype favouring low fundamental frequency in the American culture, and in one of our own studies (Scherer, 1979b) we
were able to show that American males had significantly lower pitched voices than
German males in jury simulation studies using highly similar subject pools.

Moreover, pitch seems to play a major role in the attribution of personality traits
and psychological states from speech.   Both male and female speakers with higher
pitch are perceived as being less benevolent and competent (Brown, Strong and
Rencher, 1975), more immature (Aronovitch, 1976), more nervous and less truthful
(Apple, Streeter and Krauss, 1977), less emotionally stable (Scherer, in prep.),
and more withdrawn, tense and agitated (Ekman, Friesen and Scherer, 1976; cf
Scherer, 1979b, pp.44-54).   These results can explain why habitually low fundamental frequency of voice may be an important component of interactive competence
or may be used instrumentally for self-presentation purposes.

In this paper we report data relevant to the question of whether it is affective
arousal or social competence in terms of orientation towards cultural norms which
accounts more adequately for differences in paralinguistic behaviour, particularly
F∅, between different groups.   Heinl-Hutchinson (1975) and Sedlak (1975), working
in our laboratory, studied the speech paterns of 12 elderly women living in a home
for the aged.   These women were selected on the basis of questionnaire data on
life satisfaction and number of social contacts.   A number of paralinguistic
variables, including F∅, were assessed on the basis of speech samples which consisted of free descriptions of the subjects' saddest and nicest life experiences
as well as of their daily routines in the home.   Out of the many speech variables
studied (tongue slips, filled pauses, mannerisms, self references, speech rate,
TTR, verb-adjective quotient and F∅) only F∅ showed a consistent relationship to
the social adjustment measures across all three speech situations.   F∅ correlated
$r = -.65$ ($p < .05$) with life satisfaction and $r = -.56$ ($p < .06$) with number of
social contacts.

There are several possible explanations for these results.   On the one hand one
might argue that higher pitch of voice is an indicator of the emotional tension
associated with lack of social contacts and dissatisfaction with one's life.   On
the other hand, assuming that pitch is an important component of interactive competence which provides important cues for the attribution of traits and states,
two further hypotheses can be formulated to account for the variation in pitch of
voice among these elderly women.   First, persons who speak in a lower voice may
attract more social contacts and consequently may be more satisfied with their
lives (these two variables were correlated with $r = .89$ in the sample).   Second,
persons who often interact with others may attempt to elicit favourable attributions by lowering their voices.   This vocal setting may then be adopted habitually.   The latter hypothesis presumes that individuals can in fact control their
larynxes in such a way that long term changes in fundamental frequency are produced.
The existence of cultural preferences, i.e. lower pitch range in American males as
adaptation to cultural stereotypes (cf. Scherer, 1979b), suggests that this may be
the case.

The issue of affect or arousal versus interactive competence and/or self presentation as determinants of pitch of voice surfaces again in another study conducted
by our group.   In a large-scale series of experimental simulations of bureaucratic
encounters (Scherer and Scherer, 1979) 39 public officials from welfare agencies had

to interact in two typical cases with high status or low status clients behaving
either aggressively or submissively (ANOVA design using two lay actors with
different appearances and behaviour instructions).   While the analyses so far
have focussed on nonverbal behaviour some paralinguistic variables, including Fø
have been assessed.

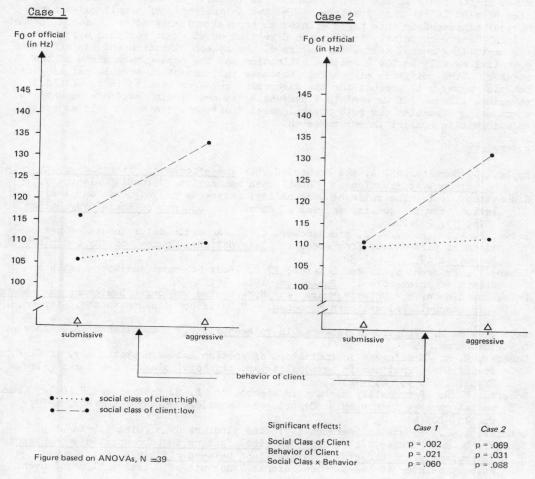

Figure based on ANOVAs, N =39

Significant effects:	Case 1	Case 2
Social Class of Client	p = .002	p = .069
Behavior of Client	p = .021	p = .031
Social Class x Behavior	p = .060	p = .088

Fig. 1.   Voice pitch of officials as indicator of arousal
in interactions with clients

As Figure 1 shows, there is evidence for Fø as an indicator of psychological
arousal in that officials spoke in a significantly higher voice in interactions
with aggressive clients, a more stressful situation compared to interactions with
submissive clients.   At the same time, some of the results seem to show the
effects of attempts at self-presentation in paralinguistic behaviour.   Regardless
of the behaviour of the clients, the officials' voices were lower when interacting
with middle class clients than with lower class clients (cf Fig. 1).   Possibly

the officials attempted to impress the clients (manager and teacher) favourably (in fact officials with lower voices were judged in more positive terms by raters).

Which of the two assumed hypothetical relationships is correct, cannot be determined on the basis of the present data.   It is quite possible that both tendencies coexist in the same speakers.   The two determinants of paralinguistic behaviour discussed in this paper - internal arousal and adaptation to social expectations - may work jointly in the same direction or at cross purposes depending on the prevailing social norms, the nature of the speech situation and its affective potential as well as the cognitive evaluation and the coping mechanisms of the speaker.   The multitude of possible outcomes in terms of observable paralinguistic behaviours may well account for the discrepant research results in the field of paralinguistics.   If we want to disentangle the conflicting evidence we have to start using variables for both psychological traits and states as well as social and linguistic context in our research.

REFERENCES

Apple, W., Streeter, L. A. and Krauss, R. M. The effects of pitch and speech rate on personal attributions. Unpublished manuscript, Columbia University, 1977

Aronovitch, C. D. The voice of personality: stereotyped judgments and their relation to voice quality and sex of speaker. Journal of Social Psychology, 1976, 99, 207-220

Brown, B. L., Strong, W. J. and Rencher, A. C. Acoustic determinants of perceptions of personality from speech. International Journal of the Sociology of Language, 1975, 6, 11-32

Ekman, P., Friesen, W. V. and Scherer, K. R. Body movement and voice pitch in deceptive interaction. Semiotica, 1976, 16, 23-27

Heinl-Hutchinson, M. Untersuchungen zur Sprechweise und deren Beziehung zur Lebenszufriedenheit bei aelteren Menschen. Unpublished diploma thesis, Giessen, 1975

Laver, J. D. M. Individual features in voice quality. Unpublished Ph.D. thesis, Edinburgh, 1975

Scherer, K. R. Nonlinguistic indicators of emotion and psychopathology, in C. E. Izard (Ed.), Emotions in personality and psychopathology. New York: Plenum Press, 1979, pp. 495-529(a)

Scherer, K. R. Personality markers in speech, in K. R. Scherer and H. Giles (Eds.) Social markers in speech. Cambridge: Cambridge University Press, 1979, pp. 147-209(b)

Scherer, K. R. Speech and personality: the juror study. Giessen, in prep.

Scherer, U. and Scherer, K. R. Psychological factors in bureaucratic encounters: determinants and effects of interactions between officials and clients. Paper presented at the NATO conference "Analysis of Social Skills", Leuven, Belgium, June 1979

Sedlak, L. Gerontologische Studie zur Psycholinguistik - Soziale und emotionale Aspekte. Unpublished diploma thesis, Giessen, 1975

Siegman, A. W. The tell-tale voice: nonverbal messages of verbal communication, in A. W. Siegman and S. Feldstein (Eds.) Nonverbal behaviour and communications. Hillsdale, New Jersey: Erlbaum, 1978, pp. 183-243

Temporal Aspects of Speech: Prologue

S. Feldstein

*Department of Psychology, University of Maryland, 5401 Wilkens Avenue,
Baltimore, Maryland 21228, U.S.A.*

As an area of study, interaction chronography must still be considered relatively
new.   Although it might be said to have begun officially with the publications
of Chapple (1939) and of Norwin and Murphy (1938), it was only by the mid to late
sixties that more than just a few investigators began to show any serious interest
in pursuing the initial findings.   The papers presented in this section demonstrate that not only has interest in the area expanded considerably, but also that
the interest has been accompanied by increasingly sophisticated inquiries.

My intention in this prologue is simply to provide at least a minimal structure
that might help to integrate the seemingly diverse set of papers that comprise
this section.   I comment upon, and raise questions about, the papers in the epilogue that follows them.

The name, <u>interaction chronography</u>, was first used by Chapple (e.g. 1949) to refer
to the timing of all the vocal behaviours and muscle movements involved in conversational interactions between two persons.   Since Chapple, the area of interaction
chronography has taken a number of directions.   One extreme, for example, is
represented by the work of Duncan and Fiske (1977) who examine a broad spectrum of
the behaviours that occur in an interaction.   The other extreme is represented by
the research of Jaffé and Feldstein (1970) who time only the vocal sounds and silences of an interaction.   Less radical positions examine the time patterns of
speech and gazing behaviours in interactions. Although two of the papers that
follow involve the timing of gazes, all of them are primarily concerned with the
temporal aspects of speech.   For that reason, let me very graphically illustrate
the temporal parameters of a dyadic verbal interaction in Figure 1.   Note that
there are five main parameters: <u>speaking turns</u>, <u>vocalizations</u>, <u>pauses</u>, <u>switching
pauses</u> and <u>simultaneous speech</u>.   Notice also that a switching pause <u>precedes</u>
rather than follows a change in which speaker has the floor.   Finally, notice that
simultaneous speech is divided into <u>interruptive</u> and <u>noninterruptive simultaneous
speech</u>.   Interruptive simultaneous speech involves a change of which speaker has
the floor while noninterruptive simultaneous speech does not.   These are essentially the parameters that are used by all the symposium participants except Siegman
and Crown.   The latter investigators used <u>latencies</u> instead of switching pauses,
the difference having to do with the point at which the floor changes hands (or
mouths).   In other words, although a switching pause and latency are the very same
interval of silence, the speaker switch occurs at the <u>end</u> of a switching pause but
at the <u>beginning</u> of a latency.   The fact that the experimental interactions used by
Siegman and Crown were interviews rather than unconstrained conversations justifies

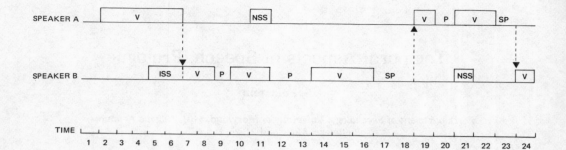

Fig. 1   A diagrammatic representation of the sound-silence sequence of a conversational excerpt.   The letter V stands for <u>vocalization</u>, P for <u>pause</u>,
and the letters SP for <u>switching pause</u> (the silence that often occurs
immediately prior to a change in the <u>speaking turn</u>, i.e. in which
speaker has the turn, or floor).   The arrows that point downward denote
the end of <u>A</u>'s turns;   the arrow that points up denotes the end of <u>B</u>'s
turn.   ISS and NSS refer to <u>interruptive</u> and <u>noninterruptive simultaneous speech</u>, respectively.   The numbered line at the bottom represents
300 msec. - units of time.

the use of latencies rather than switching pauses.

Clarke and his associates use a four-state probability model to describe dialogic
patterns, and the parameters depicted in the figure can be derived directly from
their model (Jaffé and Feldstein, 1970).   Brown uses speech rate, a close
estimate of which can be computed from the proportionality constants of pauses and
vocalizations (Feldstein, 1976).   In addition to using latencies, Siegman and
Crown use pauses and vocalizations.   Finally, Cappella and Dabbs use exactly those
parameters described in Figure 1.

Perhaps the most useful framework for organizing the presentations is that provided
by the expectations of almost all those who investigate the time patterns of dyadic
interactions.   There are three basic general expectations.   One is that <u>the tem-</u>
<u>poral patterns of a verbal interaction affect the meaning conveyed by the lexemes</u>
used in the interaction.   It is an expectation that few studies have tried to address.   A somewhat indirect approach was taken by Alberti (1974), who related
speaking turn frequencies to verb tense with the hypothesis that present tense
verbs are associated with more frequent turn-taking.   The paper by Dabbs is, in
part, concerned with the temporal patterning of social and intellectual conversations, and that concern can probably be viewed as pertinent to this first expectation.

Another expectation is that <u>the temporal patterns carry information about each of</u>
<u>the individuals involved in an interaction.</u>   Research concerned with this expecta-
tion has primarily addressed itself to the study of relations between the temporal
parameters and personality characteristics, between the parameters and impression
formation (Crown, in press;   Feldstein, in press;   Feldstein, Alberti and Ben Debba
1979;   Feldstein and Welkowitz, 1978;   Hayes and Bouma, 1977), and between the parameters and various psychopathological conditions (Chapple, 1942;   Glaister, Feldstein and Pollack, 1979).   The expectation is addressed by three of the present
papers.   Brown discusses the relation of personality attributions and competency
evaluations to rates of speech that have been experimentally manipulated.   Siegman

and Crown are concerned with the effects of the ways in which interviewers behave upon the temporal behaviour of interviewees, and how that temporal behaviour relates to the interviewees' perceptions of the interviewers and attraction to the interviewers.

Dabbs, who is interested in the temporal patterning of both speech and gaze behaviours, reports the ways in which they are affected by the degrees of self-monitoring in which the participants in an interaction engage. Self-monitoring behaviour is presumed to reflect a personality characteristic.

Dabbs is also interested in the effects upon speech and gazing behaviour of pairing individuals who are similar and different in the extent to which they engage in self-monitoring. Thus, his studies are also pertinent to the third expectation, namely, that the temporal patterns of an interaction are sensitive to the relationship between the participants in the interaction. This relevance of his work to the third expectation is reflected in his exploration of the relation between the self-monitoring behaviours of the two participants and the degree to which they influence, or accommodate to, each other's temporal patterns.

Also relevant to the third expectation is Cappella's paper. In it, he proposes techniques for estimating the extent to which the temporal patterns of two participants in an interaction become similar, a phenomenon I have elsewhere called "temporal congruence" (Feldstein, 1972) but which may, more profitably perhaps, be considered an aspect of interpersonal accommodation. Essentially, then, Cappella attempts to provide the means with which the third expectation may be tested more effectively.

The report by Clarke, Ellgring and Wagner is also methodological. It offers a probabilistic grammar to account for the observed patterns and underlying structure of the time and gaze patterns of dyadic interactions. The fact that the authors have taken the trouble to construct a model of these patterns suggests that they view at least one of the basic expectations as viable. Presumably, their efforts are directed towards facilitating the testing of any of the expectations.

Another type of framework is possible and probably useful. It classifies studies into three categories. One category comprises those investigations that are methodological in the sense that they model the temporal patterns or provide techniques for their analysis. The papers by Cappella and by Clarke and his associates fit into this category. A second category consists of those papers that relate the temporal patterns to other variables of interest. The contributions by Brown, Dabbs and by Siegman and Crown represent this category. The third category is comprised of those studies that explore the temporal patterning not only of verbal behaviour but also of other behaviours that are involved in dyadic interactions. The presentations of Dabbs and of Clarke and his associates can be considered appropriate to this category as well as to the second and first category, respectively.

The framework not withstanding, the papers that follow are concerned with issues central to the area of dyadic temporal behaviour. Moreover, they provoke interesting questions about the direction of further work, some of which I shall discuss in the epilogue.

REFERENCES

Alberti, L. Some lexical correlates of speaker switching frequency in conversation. Paper read at the Eighteenth International Congress of Applied Psychology, Montreal, July 1974

Chapple, E.D. Quantitative analysis of the interaction of individuals. Proceedings of the National Academy of Sciences, 1939, 25, 58-67

Chapple, E. D. The interaction chronograph: its evolution and present application
    Personnel, 1949, 25, 295-307
Chapple, E. D. and Lindermann, E.   Clinical implications of measurements of inter-
    action rates in psychiatric interviews.   Applied Anthropology, 1942, 1-11
Crown, C. L. Impression formation and the chronography of dyadic interactions,
    in M. Davis (Ed.) Interaction rhythms.   New York: Human Sciences, in press
Duncan, S. Jr. and Fiske, D. W. Face-to-face interaction: research, methods and
    theory.   Hillsdale, New Jersey: Erlbaum Associates, 1977
Feldstein, S.   Temporal patterns of dialogue: basic research and reconsiderations
    in A. W. Siegman and B. Pope (Eds.) Studies in dyadic communication.   New
    York: Pergamon, 1972
Feldstein, S.   Rate estimates of sound-silence sequences in speech.   Paper read
    at the Acoustical Society of America, San Diego, November 1976
Feldstein, S., Alberti, L. and Ben Debba, M. Self-attributed personality charac-
    teristics and the pacing of conversational interaction, in A. W. Siegman
    and S. Feldstein (Eds.) Of speech and time: temporal speech patterns in inter-
    personal contexts.   Hillsdale, New Jersey: Erlbaum Associates, 1979
Feldstein, S. and Welkowitz, J. Adronology of conversation: in defense of an
    objective approach, in A. W. Siegman and S. Feldstein (Eds.) Nonverbal
    behavior and communication.   Hillsdale, New Jersey: Erlbaum, 1978
Glaister, J., Feldstein, S. and Pollack, H. Chronographic speech patterns of
    acutely psychotic patients.   Paper read at the Clinical Research Society of
    Toronto, Toronto, Canada, March 1979
Hayes, D. P. and Bouma, G. D. Patterns of vocalisation and impression formation.
    Semiotica, 1977, 13(2), 113-129
Jaffé, J. and Feldstein, S. Rhythms of dialogue.   New York: Academic Press, 1970.
Norwine, A. C. and Murphy, O. J. Characteristic time intervals in telephonic con-
    versation.   Bell System Technical Journal, 1938, 17, 281-291

Situational Effects on the Syntax of Speech and Gaze Behaviour in Dyads[1]

A. H. Clarke, H. Ellgring and H. Wagner

*Max-Planck-Institute for Psychiatry, 8 München 40, Kraepelinstr. 10,
Federal Republic of Germany*

ABSTRACT

A substantial literature exists on the coordination of speaking and looking behaviour and their significance as indicators for the production and reception of social information. Within this framework, the temporal organisation of such behaviour has been shown to reflect both the coordination within the individual and between participants in a situation.

In this paper, it is proposed that observed behavioural sequences may be formally described by rules of syntax, thus implying the likelihood of structural organisation as opposed to, for example, linear time dependence between behavioural states. This being the case, differing sets of rules and grammars respectively can be expected for various social situations.

Clinical interviews and discussions between couples on a topic of marital conflict were analysed, the on-off patterns of speech and gaze being taken as data.

The resulting behavioural repertoire was regarded, in the sense of a formal grammar, as the terminal vocabulary. A set of rewriting rules was determined and their associated probabilities inferred.

The situational conditions were found to be reflected in the syntactic features of the grammatical model – the terminal vocabulary, the production rules and the production probabilities.

Key Words

Social interaction; verbal and nonverbal communication; mathematical linguistics; grammar; rules of syntax; behavioural analysis; pattern recognition; social psychology.

INTRODUCTION

It is well known that the behaviour observed during social interaction is influenced by such factors as the internal states and mental capacities of the partici-

---

1. The work reported in this paper was supported by the Deutsche Forschungsgemeinschaft, Antrag El 67/1

pants, the dominance relationships between participants and the situational demands. This has been variously reported for both verbal and nonverbal behaviour (Cicourel, 1973; Scheflen, 1967). In this context, the significance of the temporal coordination of speech and gaze behaviour has been recognised (Jaffé and Feldstein, 1970; Argyle and Cook, 1976). It is proposed here that examination of behavioural sequences involving verbal and nonverbal behaviour - in the present case, speech and gaze - should yield results which conform to a structural or syntactic model. That is, as Duncan (1969) has suggested "an underlying system or set of rules somewhat analogous to those for languages" may be sought. A similar approach has been recently described by D. D. Clarke (1979) for the verbal aspects of conversation and Slama-Cazacu (1976) has suggested a "mixed syntax" for the verbal and nonverbal components of interaction.

Various possibilities for the formalisation of such a model have been developed in mathematical linguistics and pattern recognition (Fu, 1976). The methods discussed here attempt to exploit both the structural and the external variable approaches for the formal analysis of speaking and related looking behaviour.

This approach therefore involves implications about the regularity of behavioural sequences and their rules of syntax. That is to say, beyond a taxonomy of behavioural units yielding statistical descriptors of frequency, duration, etc. whether rules of syntax can be formulated for the observed behavioural sequences. It is maintained here that the observed behaviour during social interaction should reflect, on the one hand, factors such as the situational conditions and the participants' understanding of their roles, and on the other, internal states of the participants such as arousal level and mental capacity. The influence of these factors may be likened to a form of rule-governing, and the internal states may be seen as contributing to the manner in which the rules are followed. How these aspects are compounded remains to be clarified. An example of such a rule for speech and gaze behaviour could be that during a clinical interview, only the physician may pose questions. At a micro level in the behavioural hierarchy the effect of the participants' internal states could, for example, be thus described: when the mental load associated with speech preparation or production is too high, in terms of cognitive or emotional capacity, eye contact with social partner must be reduced. According to the concept of rule governed behaviour, it can be argued that during dyadic interaction each participant will assume a role, and behave according to his understanding of the rules which govern that role. Also, this rule dependence should become evident in those aspects of verbal and nonverbal behaviour which are understood by the participant as belonging to his role. Thus, what may be likened to an underlying, or deep structure of the interaction is reflected in the observed behaviour.

Observed material and data

The material being analysed involves videorecordings of clinical-psychiatric interviews with depressive patients which have been made for a number of single case, longitudinal studies (see Ellgring, Wagner and Clarke, this volume). Further material includes extracts of conversations between couples attending marital therapy. In principle, the data transcription involves the scoring of the presence, respectively absence, of the speech and gaze of the two participants. This yields four binary channels of data, corresponding to a possible behavioural repertoire of sixteen combinatorial states (Clarke, Wagner, Rinck and Ellgring, 1979) The sixteen possible states in the behavioural repertoire can be ordered into four subgroups corresponding to the four possible speech activity conditions, namely: a) mutual silence, (b) participant A speaking, (c) participant B speaking, and (d) simultaneous speaking. Each of these subgroups contains each of the four possible gaze combinations, namely: (a) no one looking, (b) participant A looking at B, (c) participant B looking at A, and (d) mutual gaze.

This coding scheme gives a complete description of the sequence of behaviour at the level of observation. The states defined are mutually exclusive and represent the behavioural elements in the subsequent analysis (see Appendix 1).

Structural model

As a formal model, a probabilistic grammar, based on a Chomsky Type 2 grammar has been explored (see Appendix 2). Thus, for each analysed episode the interaction is described by means of: a repertoire, or terminal vocabulary of behavioural elements, a structural description in the form of a set of rewrite rules, to which a set of probabilities is allocated.

A probabilistic grammar was selected as a model following the assumption that the observed strings of behavioural elements represent 'noisy images' of ordered structures. Accordingly, the behavioural strings are generated on a grammatical level, and to some extent deformed on the probabilistic level (Grenander, 1969).

The grammars are constructed in practice as follows:

1) The behavioural repertoire is defined by the 16 possible combinations of the binary coded channels. These behavioural states are taken as terminal syntactic elements.
2) It is assumed that the observed strings of syntactic elements can be structurally described by the rewrite rules of a corresponding grammar. The observed strings thus represent the units of analysis (in contrast to the unit of analysis with grammars of natural language, which is the sentence, it is generally the case here that the unit of analysis corresponds to an exchange between participants).
3) Each of the rewrite rules of the grammar may be allocated a probability estimated for each analysed episode according to the frequencies of occurrence of the observed strings.

For each observed episode a sequence of approximately 300 - 400 behavioural elements is recorded. This sequence is examined for recurring behavioural strings. Examples are shown in Figures 1a and 1b. The strings which are found may be described by a derivation of the type shown in Figure 1. This is equivalent to the structural description in terms of rewrite rules. The set of rewrite rules required for the complete episode yields a qualitative description of the structure of the observed sample.

Thus, for Figure 1a, a dialogue exchange (nonterminal element: D) can be "rewritten as consisting of the floortime or turn of participant A (nonterminal element A) and the turn of participant B (nonterminal element B)". Similarly the turns of each participant can be rewritten as required, as consisting of those states during which the participant actually speaks (A_S, B_S) and in pauses (Pa).

These states can then be rewritten as terminal elements (10, 2, 6).

In turn, the frequences of occurrence of the behavioural strings yield the frequencies of application of each of the rewrite rules for the generation of the observed sample. This takes into consideration the probabilistic aspect or noisiness, of the behaviour, and represents a quantitative description of the structural relationships between behavioural elements.

Two grammars, constructed from the data from (a) a clinical interview and (b) a conversation between a marital couple, are listed in Table 1. As can be seen the grammars (G) are defined as quintuples (V_N, V_T, P, S, p), differing from phrase structure grammars in that a set of probabilities (p) is included. To

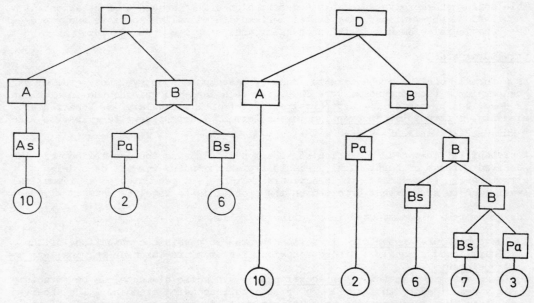

Fig. 1   Examples of possible structural derivations of
strings involving three and five behavioural states.

each rewrite rule in the set (P) a probability is allocated.   In the nonterminal
vocabulary (V_N) the element (Ch) refers to interpersonal speech pauses, whilst the
element (Pa) refers to intrapersonal pauses.

In each grammar rule 1 defines the exchange between participants – floortime A (A),
speaker switch (Ch), floortime B (B).

In the case of the interview (where part. A is the interviewer, part. B the
patient), it can be seen that the terminal vocabulary (V_T) consists of a repertoire reduced to only 5 of the possible 16 behavioural states.   This can largely
be attributed to the depressive state of the patient at the time of the interview.
This is further reflected by the number of pause states (0,2,3) and the number of
rewrites involving pausing (rules 6, 8–11).

The probability values indicate that the interviewer spends most of his floortime
speaking (rules 2, 3) with little pausing, and further that while speaking his
gaze is directed at the patient (rule 4).   On the other hand, the patient spends
less of his floortime speaking (e.g. rule 6), and when speaking, his gaze is always directed away from the interviewer (rule 7).   The probabilities relating to
the pause behaviour indicate that all interpersonal pauses (rule 12) involve state
2 – the interviewer looking at the patient and the patient not looking at the interviewer.   The majority of the intrapersonal pauses also involve this state
(rules 8–11).

In connection with the single case, longitudinal studies mentioned earlier, a matrix can be constructed which contains the rewrite probabilities for each of the
series of interviews.   This enables measurement of intraindividual changes in
behavioural repertoire, coordination, structural complexity, etc.

The second grammar describes a conversation between a marital couple.   In this
example, the nonterminal vocabulary (V_T) includes 11 of the 16 possible states.

TABLE 1   Probabilistic grammars for a) a clinical interview, and b) a conversation between a marital couple.

a) Interview: Fe1m03

G = (V_N, V_T, P, S, p)

V_N = (D, A, B, Ch, Pa, As, Bs)

V_T = (O, 2, 3, 6, 10)

1) D $\longrightarrow$ A Ch B

2) | A $\xrightarrow{.85}$ As

3) | A $\xrightarrow{.15}$ Pa As

4) | As $\xrightarrow{1.0}$ 10

8) | Pa $\xrightarrow{.22}$ 2 B

9) | Pa $\xrightarrow{.62}$ 2

10) | Pa $\xrightarrow{.07}$ 2 3

11) | Pa $\xrightarrow{.09}$ 2 O

12) | Ch $\xrightarrow{1.0}$ 2

5) B $\xrightarrow{.46}$ Bs

6) B $\xrightarrow{.54}$ Bs Pa

7) Bs $\xrightarrow{1.0}$ 6

b) Dialogue: 5455

G = (V_N, V_T, P, S, p)

V_N = (D, A, B, Ch, As, Bs)

V_T = (1, 4, 5, 6, 7, 8, 9, 10, 11, 13, 14)

1) D $\longrightarrow$ A Ch B

2) | A $\xrightarrow{.44}$ As

3) | A $\xrightarrow{.56}$ As A

4) | As $\xrightarrow{.12}$ 8

5) | As $\xrightarrow{.44}$ 9

6) | As $\xrightarrow{.20}$ 10

7) | As $\xrightarrow{.24}$ 11

8) B $\xrightarrow{.49}$ Bs

9) B $\xrightarrow{.51}$ Bs B

10) Bs $\xrightarrow{.29}$ 4

11) Bs $\xrightarrow{.19}$ 6

12) Bs $\xrightarrow{.40}$ 5

13) Bs $\xrightarrow{.12}$ 7

14) Ch $\xrightarrow{.41}$ 13

15) Ch $\xrightarrow{.20}$ 1

16) Ch $\xrightarrow{.39}$ 14

Also, more rewrite rules are required than for the interview, and the more symmetrical structure of the situation is reflected. The terminal vocabulary includes only one pause state (1), and this always occurs as an interpersonal pause (rule 15). From the estimated probabilities for rules 14-16 it can be seen that speaker switching occurs mostly via states 13 and 14 - states involving mutual speaking and one participant with directed gaze. The symmetry of the situation is indicated by the closely matched rules 2-7 (part A) and 8-13 (part B). For the rules 2, 3 and 8, 9 the probabilities are comparable. It is possible to calculate a measure of symmetry with respect to asymmetry from the rewrite probabilities of the complementary rules within a grammar. Without going into detail, the measures of asymmetry found for the examples described were, for the conversation 0.05, and for the interview 0.36. This measure of asymmetry is of particular interest in the study concerning marital couples. For the interview situations it seems more useful to calculate a difference measure from interview to interview as mentioned earlier.

CONCLUSION

The present study has been concerned with the application of such concepts as rule governed behaviour and the hierarchical organisation of behaviour to the description of the process of dyadic interaction. The use of a grammatical, or linguistic model has been explored. However, this should be distinguished from the linguistic analogy of Birdwhistell; the present approach is to be understood within the framework of generative grammar, as opposed to the earlier structuralist grammar to which the so-called linguistic analogy subscribed. This distinction applies, above all, to the emphasis on the importance of the syntactic rules and the description of the underlying structural relationships. The model of a probabilistic grammar furthermore provides a quantitative measure of these relationships.

This corresponds to the research strategy recently proposed by Duncan and Fiske (1978), in which both structural and statistical aspects of the interaction process ought to be taken into consideration. However, whether the model can be further developed to include reference to the semantic aspect of the behavioural elements remains to be shown.

The features of the probabilistic grammar, namely the behavioural repertoire, the structural description and the probability measure enable the determination of structural changes in the interaction process, both for situational and for role dependencies.   On the basis of these features, such measures can be obtained as comparison of situation - determined by the quantitative changes in the rule pro- babilities between situations; or, symmetry of interaction - calculated from the probabilities of the complementary rules within a grammar.

Generally, the approach has explored and to some extent demonstrated the practica- bility of the grammatical model for behavioural sequence analysis.   Although the examples described involve a particular type of observational data, it seems quite feasible that the method be implemented for most types, given that some sequential order is to be expected.

REFERENCES

Argyle, M. and Cook, M. Gaze and mutual gaze. London: Cambridge University
    Press, 1976
Clarke, A. H., Wagner, H., Rinck, P. and Ellgring, J. H. A system for computer
    aided observation and recording of social behaviour. (in press)
Clarke, D. D. The linguistic analogy or when is a speech act like a morpheme? in G.
    P. Ginsburg (Ed.) Emerging strategies in social psychology. New York: Wiley, 1979
Cicourel, A. V. Cognitive sociology. London: Cox and Wyman, 1973
Duncan, S. and Fiske, D. W. Face-to-face interaction. New York: Wiley, 1977
Ellgring, H., Wagner, H. and Clarke, A. H. Psychopathological states and their
    effects on speech and gaze behaviour. (See this volume)
Fu, R. S. Foundations of pattern analysis. Quarterly of Applied Mathematics
    XXVII, No. 1, 1969
Jaffé, J. and Feldstein, S. Rhythms of dialogue. New York: Academic Press, 1970
Scheflen, A. E. On the structuring of human communication. American Behavioral
    Scientist, April, 1967
Slama-Cazacu, T.   Nonverbal components in message sequence: "mixed syntax".
    Language and Man, World Anthropology Series, Mouton, 1976

Appendix 1.   Repertoire of behavioural states   (0 = on, 1 = off)

Speech A B	Gaze A B	State	Speech A B	Gaze A B	State	Speech A B	Gaze A B	State
0 0	0 0	0	0 1	0 1	5	1 0	1 0	10
0 0	0 1	1	0 1	1 0	6	1 0	1 1	11
0 0	1 0	2	0 1	1 1	7	1 1	0 0	12
0 0	1 1	3	1 0	0 0	8	1 1	0 1	13
0 1	0 0	4	1 0	0 1	9	1 1	1 0	14
						1 1	1 1	15

Appendix 2.

A probabilistic grammar G is defined as a quintuple: $G = (V_N, V_T, P, S, p)$ where V_N is a finite, non-empty set of non-terminal elements; V_T is a finite, non-empty set of terminal elements; P is a set of rewrite rules; S is the start symbol. $V_N \cap V_T = \emptyset$ $V_N \cup V_T = V$ P, the set of rewrite rules is composed of three elements (α_i, β_j, p_i), where p_{ij} is a real number indicating the probability that a given element α_i will be rewritten as β_j. p_{ij} is termed the production probability.

Effects of Speech Rate on Personality Attributions and Competency Evaluations

B. L. Brown

Department of Psychology, Brigham Young University, Provo, Utah 84601, U.S.A.

ABSTRACT

With the development of Fourier analysis and related speech synthesis techniques, it is possible to isolate experimentally the effects of one vocal paralinguistic feature at a time. So far, speech rate is the single dimension that has been found to have the most reliable and clear cut effects. The early studies found a monotonically increasing relationship between rate and evaluations of the speaker on competence-related adjectives (with higher competence being attributed to higher speaking rates) and an inverted U relationship between rate and evaluations of the speaker on benevolence-related adjectives (with middle ranges of rate receiving the highest ratings). There have been substantial methodological improvements in later studies with the development of experimental paradigms to assess the effects of rate manipulations on natural spontaneous speech, but the early findings remain essentially unchanged. New work is beginning using more sophisticated methods of analysing and synthesising temporal patterns rather than just increasing and decreasing rate.

Key Words

Attributions; evaluations of competence; benevolence; speech rate

INTRODUCTION

The studies reported here had their beginning in the work of Lambert's social psychology of language research in Montreal in the 1960s. In particular they grew out of an extension of the matched guise studies (see Lambert, 1967 and Brown, Strong and Rencher, 1973 for reviews) to an assessment of the reactions of French Canadians to other French Canadians differing in social class level (see Brown, 1969 and Brown and Lambert, 1976). When Lambert and I used correlational methods to assess the correspondence of linguistic dimensions to personality ratings, it became obvious that an experimental approach was needed. A year later, as I began teaching at Brigham Young University, I met an acoustic physicist, William J. Strong, with the necessary skills, and we began using speech synthesis to assess experimentally the effects of acoustic manipulations on personality judgments from voice.

The first studies were concerned with experimentally assessing the effects of speech rate manipulations and intonation manipulations (variance of FØ) on personality ad-

jective ratings and with assessing the realism of these experimentally altered
voices (Brown, Strong and Rencher, 1973).   Rate manipulations were accomplished
in two ways: by a computer-based fast Fourier transform method of analysis/syn-
thesis, and by a mechanical tape recorder device (the Eltro Automation Rate
Changer) which can alter either pitch or speaking rate while the other is held
constant.   The latter device is useful only for rate manipulations (in that it
raises or lowers all formant frequencies by the same proportion that the fundamental frequency is increased or decreased), and even for rate manipulations the computer method is potentially superior in that the rate changer speeds or slows all
segments of the utterance the same;   whereas in actual speech, speeding is
primarily accomplished in the vowels with the consonant durations remaining constant.[1]

The fundamental finding with respect to rate manipulations, which has little surprise value, is that decreases of rate caused the voices to be evaluated as less
competent (adjectives such as intelligent, confident, ambitious, etc.) and increases of rate caused them to be evaluated as less benevolent (adjectives such as
kind, sincere, polite, etc.).   Somewhat more surprising is the finding that when
compared to manipulations of intonation (variance of fundamental frequency), rate
manipulations have much larger and much more consistent effects upon adjective
ratings of the voices.   Whereas the general trend is for increases of intonation
to make the voices sound both more competent and more benevolent and decreases to
make them sound less competent and less benevolent (this trend accounts for 61%[2]
of the variance in ratings), when one looks at individual speakers, there is not
much consistency of pattern.   Rate manipulations, on the other hand, were found
to affect every voice tested in the same way (increased rate equals decreased
benevolence and decreased rate equals decreased competence).   The rate manipulation accounted for about 95% of the variance in speaker ratings in the two factor space.

The next study (Brown, Strong and Rencher, 1974; also see Brown, Strong, Rencher
and Smith, 1975 for a simple summary) was a factorial one in which the interactions among rate, pitch, and intonation could be assessed as well as the relative
magnitude of the simple effects of each.   Two voices, each speaking a very brief
sentence, "We were away a year ago", were each synthesised in 27 forms (all possible combinations of three levels of each of rate, pitch and intonation).   In

---

1. This is a very important point, in that all of the studies of the effects of
rate manipulations (including all of the studies from our research group as well
as the Apple, Streeter and Krauss, 1979 study reviewed in this paper) are crude in
this regard.   That is, whereas it is very possible to use the computer synthesis
scheme to produce voices that are increased or decreased in rate the same way
natural variations occur, with a differential amount of change in vowels and consonants, or at clause boundaries or phrase boundaries, etc., this would require
gathering considerable data first to determine the properties of such natural
changes in rate and it also requires the incorporating of such data into the synthesis process.   Although we are now beginning some work in that direction, all
of the studies of rate manipulations up to now could just as well have used the
mechanical rate-changer device, in that the computer synthesis method that was employed changed all segments of the utterance uniformly.

2. This was determined by taking one minus the Wilks' lambda value (1-lamda) from
the multivariate analysis of variance.   See Cooley and Lohnes (1971, pp 223-242)
for the rationale of this percent of variance statistic.

each case the levels of manipulation were selected to be at the extreme limits one could expect in actual speech in order to maximise the chances of getting an effect on intonation and to make the relative effects for the three (rate, pitch, and intonation) as comparable as possible. Again, rate was found to have effects that were by far the greatest in magnitude and the most consistent. The only interaction found to be significant was the rate by intonation interaction. The estimates of "variance accounted for" in competence ratings were 86%, 4%, 3% and 1% for rate, pitch, intonation, and rate by intonation interaction respectively. For benevolence ratings, the percents accounted for were 48%, 1%, 6% and 1% for rate, pitch, intonation and rate by intonation interaction respectively.

Bruce L. Smith noticed in the interaction between rate and intonation an interesting thing: whenever the normal rate voice has a competence value near the mean or lower, increasing the speaking rate gives rise to an increased competence rating. In other words, the interaction seemed to be accounted for by a kind of "ceiling effect". When a voice was fairly high in its received competence rating in the normal speaking rate form, increasing the speaking rate would not cause an increase in competence rating but only a decrease in the rating on benevolence adjectives. On the other hand, if a voice in its normal speaking rate form is medium or low in its competence rating, increasing the speaking rate would cause an increase in both competence adjective ratings and benevolence adjective ratings. He further argued that the earlier studies would have found a monotonically increasing relationship between speaking rate and competence, if the original unmanipulated voices had been more representative. (All of the voices used up to this time had been the most accessible ones, university students or professors).

Smith set out to test these notions in his master's thesis (reported in Smith, Brown, Strong and Rencher, 1975). He improved upon the earlier studies not only by getting a more representative sample of voices, but also by having four levels of rate increase and four levels of decrease as compared with only one of each in Brown and colleagues' (1974) study and two of each in their 1973 study. Ratings of the voices of 28 adult males of diverse socioeconomic and educational background were obtained on the same adjectives as the earlier studies and six of the voices representative of the possible positions in the competence/benevolence space were selected for analysis/synthesis. Each of the six was synthesised in the nine rate levels (including normal rate) shown in the key to Figure 1. As Smith had predicted, ratings on competence-related adjectives were found to be a monotonically increasing function of speech rate, with the normal rate receiving the highest benevolence ratings. These two relationships are very robust ones. Not only are they consistent with the results of the earlier studies, but they have also been confirmed in two more recent studies which vary markedly in design from the Smith and colleagues study.

A recent study by Apple, Streeter and Krauss (1979) employs some important methodological improvements over these earlier studies. Rather than using recitations of standard sentences, they used natural speech: the spontaneous answers of subjects to two questions (what he would do if he suddenly won or inherited a large sume of money, and his opinion of college admissions quotas designed to favour minority groups). 27 speakers were selected from 40 to have their answers to the two questions presented to judges in one of the nine combinations of increased, normal, and decreased rate and increased, normal and decreased pitch (three subjects were assigned to each manipulation combination). The analysis/synthesis and manipulations were performed by a computer based method similar to the ones employed in the Brown, Strong and Rencher series of studies. Judges listened to all 54 answers (two answers each for the 27 speakers), so, of course, any one speaker could not be presented in more than one of the nine manipulation combinations, otherwise judges would hear the same answer twice and recognise that they were hearing the same speaker again. Therefore, although this study has the advantage

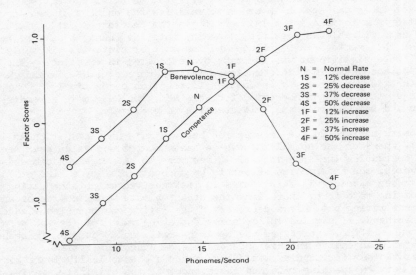

Fig. 1.   Means over speakers of factor scores
          for the competence factor and the
          benevolence factor. (From Smith et al., 1975)

over the earlier ones in utilising natural speech with content free to vary, it
has the disadvantage of not using each speaker as his own control.[3]

Three studies using this tape are reported.   The first involved "truthfulness"
evaluations of the voices, the second impressions of the speaker's personal characteristics, and the third ratings of speaker affect.   Only the second is relevant
to the concerns of this paper.   Unfortunately only nine bipolar adjective scales
were used for the ratings of speakers' personal characteristics, and also unfortunately, they were semantic differential adjectives.   It is not easy to see how
"thin-thick", "sweet-sour" would correspond to the personality rating adjectives
used in the earlier studies.   As has been argued elsewhere (Hart and Brown, 1974;
Brown, Strong and Rencher, 1973, p.33) Osgoodian semantic differential adjectives
do not correspond well to the more natural dimensions people use in describing
other people, as determined by multidimensional scaling (Smith, Pedersen and Lewis,
1966).   The results of Apple et al. also show this: in their factor analysis
they found "strong-weak" (the lead pair for the potency factor) crossing over into
the activity factor and "slow-fast" (an activity pair) highly related to the other
two potency adjectives.   (When we have included semantic differential adjectives
in our adjective set we find both "active-passive" and "strong-weak" correlating

---

3. Speakers were randomly assigned to treatment combinations and an analysis of
variance was computed on pre-manipulation pitches and rates, and it was found that
a preponderance of slow speakers were, unfortunately, assigned to the slow rate
condition.   Apparently the study had already been completed when this check was
run, since, rather than altering the speaker assignments for a more careful experimental control, analysis of covariance was used to statistically accommodate the
problem.   Covariance, of course, assumes a linear relation.   Smith's finding of
a curvilinear relation between benevolence adjectives and speaking rate suggests
that the covariance analysis may not have solved all of the problems.

highly with one another and with other competence related adjectives.) They found a significant rate effect on the activity factor, but only for the slow manipulation (which was rated less active), not for the fast one. They also found a rate by question interaction. Surprisingly, on their evaluative factor (which corresponds somewhat to our benevolence factor) they found no significant effects for rate. On their quasi-potency factor ("thick" and "large" but not "strong") they found a monotonic effect for rate: the faster, the less "potent". It is hard to relate this to our earlier results. If their activity factor is like our competence factor, it is hard to see why increased rate did not increase activity ratings. It could be a problem with the adjectives used, or it could be a design/analysis problem as discussed in Footnote 3, or it could be that their study has revealed that the earlier findings are not applicable to natural speech of the kind they studied.

This past spring we conducted a study to test more adequately the extension of our earlier research to spontaneous natural speech and in addition to compare the effects of conscious alterations in rate to the effects of computer manipulations of rate, and to test the effects of rate change on judgments of the quality of a person's expressed opinion. The design of the experiment was in some ways similar to that of the Apple et al. study but with a smaller number of speakers, since each speaker was to be his own control. That is, every speaker's voice received all of the manipulations. Seven male college students were recorded as they responded to three questions, one on their opinions about the encouraging of childhood myths and two that would stimulate more emotional involvement, their opinions of racial quotas in college admissions (the same question used by Apple et al.) and their opinions concerning Proposition 13 (tax repeal). Seven manipulations were constructed for each of these 21 answers: (1) the person's normal answer, (2) the same answer "acted" back by the person (word for word) at a normal rate, (3) the answer acted back at the fastest manageable[4] rate, (4) acted back at the slowest manageable rate, (5) computer synthesised normal rate, (6) synthesised fast (143% normal rate), and synthesised slow (77% normal rate).

Before the personality ratings were assessed, six judges were asked to estimate the phonemes per second (pps) rate (using a 100 cm. scale with anchor voices) of each of the 49 samples (7 manipulations x 7 speakers) for the "quotas" question only, in order to determine the correspondence of perceived rate to actual.[5] There is a general tendency to overestimate rate for all seven manipulations (see Figure 2), but it is least pronounced for the "acted back" voices. Acted back medium rate voices are 2.36 phonemes per second faster on the average than normal voices, but are only perceived to be .82 pps faster. This non-spontaneous programmed speech sounds slower relatively than normal or computer-manipulated normal. (Perhaps a plotting of perceived pps by actual could be a way of separating spontaneous from non-spontaneous speech. Can a listener recognise it?)

Seven testing tapes were made for the ratings of voice manipulations on personality adjectives, with each tape having all seven answers to the "myths" question first,

---

4. The experimenter worked with each speaker in repeated tries to reach the maximum and minimum rates that still sounded like real speech.

5. These data were gathered and analysed by Brett E. Murri as a project for an experimental psychology class, and the data for the other ratings of these voices and the gathering and synthesis of the voices are from a similar project by Mark A. Stewart and Stephen Stewart. A more detailed analysis is forthcoming in a jointly authored paper.

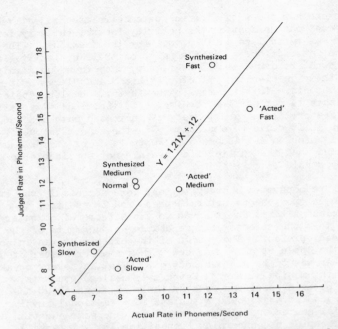

Fig. 2.   Bivariate scatter plot and regression line for the
relationship between actual and perceived speaking
rates for average or normal voices and averages of
six manipulations.

the "quotas" question second and the "Proposition 13" question last.   Each speaker only appeared once for each of his three questions on each of the tapes in a
Latin-Square-like constrained random order.   This design has the advantage of
having each speaker as his own control, while any judge only hears each speaker
once on each of his questions.   Figures 3, 4 and 5 present for each question
respectively the averaged-over-speakers factor scores for the seven manipulations.
These are superimposed upon the factor pattern, which is the adjective vectors in
their relative positions.   The rotation problem does not exist with this kind of
presentation, since one need not even name factors.   The whole picture is nothing
more than a two dimensional simultaneous presentation of the average ratings on
all 15 adjectives where one gives up 20%, 22% and 18%[6] of the information in original adjective ratings (for Figures 3, 4 and 5 respectively) for the sake of simplicity and clarity.   If one were to drop mental perpendiculars from the average
factor score plots to any one adjective, the resulting relative positions would on
the whole account for 80%, 78% and 82% of the variance in the actual ratings.

The results with this more natural speech, spontaneous answers to opinion questions,
are amazingly consistent with the findings from the earlier, more artificial
studies: decreases in rate bring about lower ratings in both competence and benevolence adjectives, and increases in rate bring about lower ratings in benevolence
adjectives and higher ratings in competence ratings.   There are interactions
with question, a number of slight variations on the general pattern (such as,
little if any increase in competence ratings on the "quota" question with increased rate).   It is interesting to note the high correspondence of conscious

6. These figures are taken from the eigen values for the three factor analyses for
the data of the "myths", "quotas" and "Proposition 13" questions respectively.

manipulation results to computer manipulation, with the main difference being the
uniformly higher benevolence adjective ratings of conscious manipulations.   (Perhaps some of the rate manipulation studies could have been done more cheaply).
On the two more emotionally involved questions ("quotas" and "Proposition 13"),
no voice sounds more competent (confident, intelligent, etc.) than the normal one,
but on the "childhood myths" question, both fast voices do.   Before making the

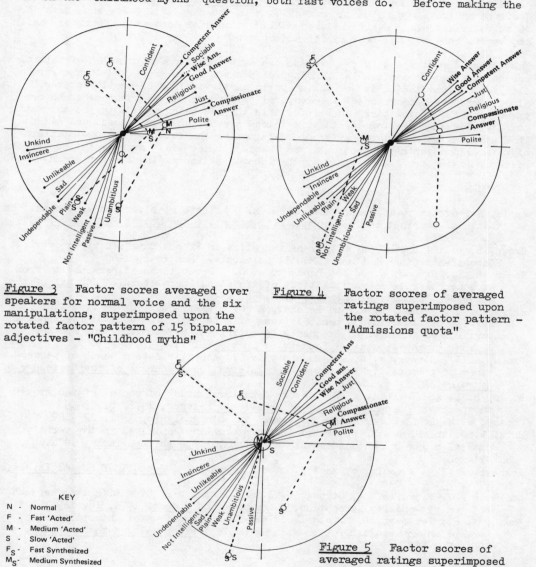

Figure 3   Factor scores averaged over
speakers for normal voice and the six
manipulations, superimposed upon the
rotated factor pattern of 15 bipolar
adjectives - "Childhood myths"

Figure 4   Factor scores of averaged
ratings superimposed upon
the rotated factor pattern -
"Admissions quota"

KEY

N   -   Normal
F   -   Fast 'Acted'
M   -   Medium 'Acted'
S   -   Slow 'Acted'
F_S -   Fast Synthesized
M_S -   Medium Synthesized
S_S -   Slow Synthesized

Figure 5   Factor scores of
averaged ratings superimposed
upon the rotated factor pattern -
"Proposition 13"

Note: For clarity only the right poles of the bipolar adjectives on the personality
rating sheet are shown in these three figures. The opposite pole is obvious for most,
but for 'plain' the paired opposite is 'good-looking'. The vectors for the four ratings
of the adequacy of the content of each answer are labelled in all bold letters.

adjective ratings the judges had listened to the tapes twice, once to rate the
overall quality of each spoken answer and once to rate the quality of the answer
on the three dimensions of competent, just and wise.   The location of the vectors
for these three variables in Figures 3-5 shows that the ratings of the <u>content</u> of
the answers on "competent", "wise" and overall adequacy of the answer are highly
correlated with ratings of the speakers' <u>personalities</u> on competence related adjectives and rate manipulations affect both in the same way.   The same high cor-
relative relationship exists between ratings of answer content on "compassionate"
and benevolence related personality adjectives.

Further studies are now in progress to use this acoustic manipulation of natural
speech paradigm to confirm the findings of other studies (reported in the Personality symposium) indicative of the acoustic manifestations of emotive states.
Also, a precise comparison of the temporal patterning of the spontaneous as compared with the "acted back" answers of this tudy is being made using an automatic
computer-based scheme for identifying voiced speech, unvoiced speech and silence.
This same analysis will be applied to determining the relative temporal patterns
of natural and portrayed emotions, and future studies will investigate the effects
of manipulating temporal patterns rather than just increasing and decreasing rate.

REFERENCES

Apple, W., Streeter, L. A. and Krauss, R. M.   Effects of pitch and speech rate on
     personal attributions.   <u>Journal of Personality and Social Psychology</u>, 1979,
     <u>5</u>, 715-727
Brown, B. L.   A social psychology of variation in French Canadian speech style.
     Unpublished dissertation.   McGill University, Montreal, 1969
Brown, B. L., Strong, W. J. and Rencher, A. C.   Perceptions of personality from
     speech: effects of manipulations of acoustical parameters.   <u>Journal of the
     Acoustical Society of America,</u> 1973, <u>54</u>, 29-35
Brown, B. L., Strong, W. J. and Rencher, A. C.   Fifty-four voices from two: the
     effects of simultaneous manipulations of rate, mean fundamental frequency and
     variance of fundamental frequency on ratings of personality from speech.
     <u>Journal of the Acoustical Society of America</u>, 1974, <u>55</u>, 313-318
Brown, B. L., Strong, W. J. and Rencher, A. C.   Acoustic determinants of percep-
     tions of personality from speech.   <u>International Journal of the Sociology of
     Language</u>, 1972, <u>6</u>, 11-32
Brown, B. L. and Lambert, W. E.   A cross-cultural study of social status markers
     in speech.   <u>Canadian Journal of Behavioral Science</u>, 1976, <u>8</u>, 39-55
Cooley, W. W. and Lohnes, P. R.   <u>Multivariate Data Analysis,</u> 1971, 223-242
Hart, R. J. and Brown, B. L.   Personality information contained in the verbal
     qualities and in content aspects of speech.   <u>Speech Monographs</u>, 1974, <u>41</u>,
     371-380
Lambert, W. E.   A social psychology of bilingualism.   <u>Journal of Social Issues</u>,
     1967, <u>23</u>, 91-109
Smith, B. L., Brown, B. L., Strong, W. J. and Rencher, A. C.   Effects of speech
     rate on personality perception.   <u>Language and Speech</u>, 1975, <u>18</u>, 145-152
Smith, K. H., Pedersen, D. M. and Lewis, R. E.   Dimensions of interpersonal
     perception in a meaningful on-going group.   <u>Perceptual and Motor Skills</u>,
     1966, <u>22</u>, 867

Turn-by-Turn Matching and Compensation in Talk and Silence: New Methods and New Explanations

J. N. Cappella

Center for Communication Research, Department of Communication Arts,
University of Wisconsin, Madison, Wisconsin 53706, U.S.A.

ABSTRACT

Research into the temporal structure of communicative interchanges in informal conversations has observed that partners influence one another's expressive behaviours in pause duration, latency duration, loudness, vocalisation duration, nonverbal immediacy behaviours, verbal aggression, verbal intimacy, verbal intensity and lexical diversity.

A number of different explanations have been put forward to explain processes of mutual influence, and a number of different methodologies have been employed to establish the existence of mutual influence. The present paper focuses exclusively on the objectively defined talk and silence variables, vocalisation, pause and switching pause duration. Mutual influence between conversational partners on each of these variables has been observed typically in the mean and typically as positive, so that partners match one another. These mean similarities have not been satisfactorily explained.

Using time-series procedures commonly employed in econometrics and in engineering, turn-by-turn mutual influence is studied on a dyad-by-dyad basis. If the data series are stationary, one can employ time-series procedures to establish for each person in each dyad the size and direction of the person's influence on the other. Turn-by-turn influence, if present, can account for similarity in the mean response level and can detect compensatory as well as matching processes.

Explanations of mutual influence in talk and silence variables must be offered which have the possibility of explaining matching, and compensation not only in talk and silence variables but also for other expressive behaviours. Competing explanations of mutual influence processes are described and evaluated relative to the criteria (1) that the explanation be capable of accounting for both matching and compensation processes and (2) that the explanation be capable of accounting for mutual influence in expressive behaviours other than talk and silence.

Key Words

Conversation; dyad; talk; silence; time; compensation; matching; arousal.

Research on the temporal structure of communicative interactions in informal conversations has shown that partners influence each other's expressive behaviours.
Such influence has been observed for pause duration (Jaffé and Feldstein, 1970),
vocalisation duration (Feldstein 1968), nonverbal immediacy (Argyle and Dean, 1965;
Coutts and Schneider, 1976), vocal intensity (Natale, 1975), intensity of verbal
intimacy (Bradac, Hosman and Tardy, 1978), as well as other verbal and nonverbal
behaviours.   The observation of similar processes between very young children and
their primary caretakers (Stern, 1974) suggests the centrality of these control
phenomena in human interactive behaviour.

In the limited space available I wish to raise three questions about mutual influence in expressive behaviours: (1) What statistical procedures are appropriate to
the study of the temporal process (turn-by-turn) of mutual influence?   (2) Can
these procedures contribute substantially to extant research on mutual influence in
talk and silence behaviours?   (3) What can data on the temporally evolving process
of mutual influence tell us about explanations of this process?

Statistical procedures for mutual influence

In unravelling the effects of person A on B and B on A over the course of a conversation, the researcher typically acquires a string of data for A and for B over
time.   These data may be categorical or continuous and observed in event time or
clock (real) time (Gottman and Bakeman, 1979).   Regardless of the type of data, it
may always be re-expressed in continuous form (given sufficient observations).
Given continuous data defined in real or event time, a conversation may be abstract-
ed as a strong of two time series of observations representing the expressive
behaviours of A and B across time.   Questions of mutual influence become questions
of the influence of the time series for A on that of B and vice versa.

The two most well known techniques for studying continuous level time series data
are (in the time domain) the Box-Jenkins techniques (Box and Jenkins, 1976), made
available to the behavioural sciences by Glass, Willson and Gottman (1975), and
(in the frequency domain) spectral techniques (Jenkins and Watts, 1968), applied
by Gottman (1979) to dominance patterns in marriage.   I wish to suggest that
neither of these techniques is suited to the study of mutual influence processes.
My argument against them hinges on two presumptions about mutual influence processes: (1) Influence may occur from A to B, B to A, or both simultaneously.   (2)
A's subsequent behaviour may depend upon A's own prior behaviour at various lags;
similarly for B.   While either or both of these assumptions may be false in any
particular case, it would be an error to begin our study of mutual influence by
blithely assuming away simultaneity and indirect feedback through methodological
narrow-mindedness.

Box-Jenkins techniques permit indirect feedback but not simultaneity while spectral
techniques permit indirect feedback with results which are difficult to interpret
when there is simultaneity (Meyer and Arney, 1974).   If it is appropriate to
assume no feedback or if one can identify one series as the input series, then
either or both of the above techniques become viable approaches for unravelling
mutual influences.   When such powerful assumptions are inappropriate, time series
regression (TSR) procedures commonly used in econometrics may be profitably employed (Hibbs, 1974).   The most general (linear) description of a two-person
mutual influence process is

$$(1) \quad A(t) = \sum_{i=1}^{m} b_i A(t-i) \; + \; \sum_{k=0}^{n} g_k B(t-k) \; + \; \text{error term}$$

$$(2) \quad B(t) = \sum_{i=1}^{m} b_i' B(t-i) \; + \; \sum_{k=0}^{n} g_k' A(t-k) \; + \; \text{error term}$$

where $A(t)$ and $B(t)$ are measures of A's and B's expressive behaviour at various times, the b_i and b_i' are feedback coefficients at lag i, and g_k and g_k' are the cross (or influence) coefficients at lag k.

With few time series points but many cross sections (i.e. dyads), data must be pooled and mutual influence processes can only be studied in the aggregate (Hannan and Young, 1977; Simonton, 1977). If the number of time series points is large (typically 50 to 100 or at least 4 to 5 times the order of the process), then mutual influence in individual dyads can be studied using regression-type procedures (Hibbs, 1974; Cappella, in press).

With a large base of time series points fewer ad hoc assumptions about systems like Equations (1) and (2) need to be made than with a small base. In either case some assumptions must be made about the order of the process (the size of n and m in the equations above) which indicates how far back influence and feedback operates and in the case of few time series points some assumption about correlation between adjacent errors must be made. Typically in the small data base situation one assumes that m = 1 and n = 0 (that is, mutual influence is first order) with errors correlated through some equally simple first-order process (Hannan and Young, 1977).

Mutual influence in talk-silence sequences

While previous research has shown that individuals in conversation become more similar in mean duration of pauses and switching pauses, research has not studied the process through which this similarity is generated, nor has it observed increasing dissimilarity of response levels (see however Harper, Wiens and Matarazzo, 1978, p.49; Jaffé and Feldstein, 1970, p.47 note 7). In an experiment reported in Cappella (1978) modelled after Jaffé and Feldstein's study 2 (1970, p.30), data on 12 informal dyadic conversations were obtained to test for turn-by-turn mutual influence. Audio transcripts were analysed by a computer hardware and software system, FIASSCO by name, comparable to Jaffe and Feldstein's AVTA (Cappella and Streibel, in press). FIASSCO generates continuous data from audio recordings on floor time, vocalizations, pauses, and switching pauses for each turn of each person. A twenty minute conversation generates between 150 and 300 such turn summaries.

Because of the large number of data points each conversation can be analysed separately. Bivariate time series using TSR techniques were undertaken to explain the following peculiar observations: in correlating the mean duration of floor time, vocalisation, pause and switching pause between partners across all conversations, it was observed that mean switching pauses correlated at .750, mean pause durations did not correlate (.007), and both floor time and vocalisation exhibited negative correlations between partners (-.283 and -.565 respectively). The first correlation is consistent with previously reported data while the latter three are not. Can these correlations in the mean be accounted for by some turn-by-turn process? Does the absence in correlation in means imply no mutual influence within dyads?

Since the nemesis of time series data is correlation among residuals, a preliminary analysis was undertaken to determine the extent of autocorrelation in residuals. Following techniques discussed by Hibbs (1974) autocorrelations and partial autocorrelations among consistently estimated residuals to order 10 were generated. No strong patterns of autocorrelation emerged (usually less than .3 even when significant) making the task of estimation much simpler because in this case ordinary regression procedures can be employed.

The large number of data points permitted us to expand the number of feedback terms and cross influence terms from 1 to 6 in steps of 1 without appreciable loss of power.   The following rather ad hoc but (I think) reasonable procedure was used to establish the order of the mutual influence process and the size and direction of the influence for each variable and for each dyad.   The order of the process was determined by the longest lagged term which met an alpha-criterion of 0.20.   Thus, if B's lag-4 switching pause predicted A's switching pause significantly (at least at alpha less than 0.20) and B's lag-5 and lag-6 failed to do so, then the process was fourth order in switching pauses for person A in that dyad.   Next, since other lags less than 4 may have been significant but of the same or possibly a different sign and since we wish to characterise the overall influence of B on A, a sum of B's four values was taken as the independent predictor of A's switching pause. This sum had the effect of summarising in a single regression coefficient the effect of B on A due to B's lag-1, lag-2, lag-3 and lag-4 switching pause.   A careful inspection of the summary coefficient and its separate counterparts revealed that when the separate coefficients were of different sign the summary coefficient either tended toward zero or weighed toward the larger independent effect.   This is the desired result.

Based upon the sign and the magnitude of these summary coefficients[1], we were able to determine the number of diverging, converging, and unrelated dyads for floor time, vocalisations, pauses and switching pauses (see Table 1).

TABLE I.   Number of dyads increasing in similarity, difference, or neither on each of four continuous conversational variables.

	Conversational Variables			
	Floor Time	Vocalisations	Pauses	Switching Pauses
No. Converging	4	2	5	9
No. Diverging	7	6	4	1
No. Unrelated	1	1	1	1
No. Indeterminate	0	3	2	1

As the frequencies show, the number of diverging dyads is greatest for floor time and vocalisations which showed the moderate to strong negative correlations in mean durations between partners.   On pauses, 5 pairs were converging while 4 were diverging which explains why the overall mean correlation on pauses was not significantly different from zero.   The overwhelming majority of dyads converged on switching pauses paralleling the strong positive correlation in the mean duration between partners.

Overall these data and procedures show that similarity or dissimilarity in mean response is a result of an underlying turn-by-turn process which can be observed in

1. If both influence coefficients are positive, or one positive the other zero, or one positive the other negative but less in absolute value, then the dyad is converging;   if both are negative, or one negative the other zero, or one negative the other positive but less in absolute value, then the dyad is diverging;   if both are zero, there is no mutual influence.

individual dyads. Second, they show that the absence of similarity or difference
in mean response does not necessarily imply the absence of turn-by-turn mutual
influence as the pause data above illustrates. Clearly the correlation between
mean values across persons can be a misleading indicator of mutual influence.
Furthermore that correlation gives no indication of who is influencing whom; the
TSR procedures above clearly separate covariation from Causal influence.

Implications for explanation

Having established that persons in conversations can influence one another's
expressive behaviour (positively or negatively) through turn-by-turn effects does
not explain the process. Whatever explanation is finally offered, we now know that
it must be capable of explaining not only increasing similarity but increasing
difference as well, when individual's "opt out" of conversations. Consequently,
explanations which can only handle increasing similarity such as explanations from
imitation (Bandura, 1965) or from Natale's communication model (1975) will simply
not do. Rather the explanations must be able to account for increasing similarity
under certain conditins and difference under others. I believe that an arousal
based explanation, not unlike that offered by Patterson (1976) to account for
compensation and matching in verbal and nonverbal immediacy behaviours, has
potential payoff in explaining talk and silence mutual influence processes.

Whiel an arousal explanation may seem far-fetched at first glance, it has several
characteristics which recommend it:

1. There is some evidence that physiological arousal tracks external ambient
stimuli (Fiske and Mddi, 1961).
2. Various types of arousal in the form of anxiety and stress have been shown to
affect different output measures of talk and silence (Siegman, 1978).
3. Absolute stimulus value need not be the predictor of arousal or response since
most theories hold that the arousal value of the stimulus is relative to some
expected baseline (Berlyne, 1960; Mandler, 1975).
4. Given the low level of conscious awareness at which mutual influence processes
there is little "cognitive weighing" in mutual influence, explanations must
minimise the mental periphrenalia in responding with increased similarity or
difference.[2]
5. Arousal explanations of talk-silence mutual influence can link up with arousal
explanations of other simple expressive behaviours (Patterson, 1973, 1976) yielding
the rudiments of a unitary theory of mutual influence in expressive behaviours.

REFERENCES

Argyle, M. and Dean, J. Eye contact, distance and affiliation. Sociometry, 1965,
      28, 289-304
Bandura, A. Behavioral modification through modeling procedures, in L. Krasner and
      L. P. Ullman (Eds.) Research in Behavior Modification. New York: Holt,
      Rinehart and Winston, 1965
Berlyne, D. E. Conflict, arousal and curiosity. New York: McGraw-Hill, 1960
Bradac, J. J., Hosman, L. A. and Tardy, C. H. Reciprocal disclosures and language
      intensity: attributional consequences. Communication Monographs, 1978, 45,
      1-17

---

2. Meltzer, Morris and Hayes (1971) make a similar argument concerning interruptions. The mechanism through which interruptions are won or lost must be
   very simplistic (that is, noncognitive and noncontent) because interruption
   decisions are made with great rapidity.

Box, G. E. P. and Jenkins, G. M.   Time series analysis.   Second edition.   San
    Francisco: Josey-Bass, 1976

Cappella, J. N.   Structural equation modeling: an introduction, in P. R. Monge and
    J. N. Cappella (Eds.), Multivariate techniques in communication research.
    New York: Academic Press, in press

Cappella, J. N.   A within- and between-situation analysis of talk-silence sequences
    in informal two-person conversations.   Paper presented at the International
    Communication Association meetings, Philadelphia, P.A., 1978

Cappella, J. N. and Streibel, M.   Computer analysis of talk-silence sequences: the
    FIASSCO system.   Behavioral Research Methods and Instrumentation, in press.

Coutts, L. M. and Schneider, F. W.   Affiliative conflict theory: an investigation
    of the intimacy equilibrium and compensation hypothesis.   Journal of Person-
    ality and Social Psychology, 1976, 34, 1135-42

Feldstein, S.   Interspeaker influence in conversational interaction.   Psychologi-
    cal Reports, 1968, 22, 826-828

Fiske, D. W. and Maddi, S.   A conceptual framework, in D. W. Fiske and S. Maddi
    (Eds.), Functions of varied experience.   Homewood, Ill.: Dorsey, 1961

Glass, G. V., Willson, V. L. and Gottman, J. M.   Design and analysis of time series
    experiments.   Boulder, Co.: Colorado Associated University Press, 1975

Gottman, J. M.   Time series analysis of continuous data in dyads, in M. E. Lamb,
    S. J. Suomi and G. R. Stephenson (Eds.), Social interaction analysis.
    Madison, Wi.: University of Wisconsin Press, 1979

Gottman, J. M. and Bakeman, R.   The sequential analysis of observational data, in
    M. E. Lamb, S. J. Suomi and G. R. Stephenson (Eds.), Social interaction ana-
    lysis.   Madison, Wi.: University of Wisconsin, 1979

Hannan, M. T. and Young, A. A.   Estimation in panel models: results on pooling
    cross-sections and time series, in D. R. Heise (Ed.), Sociological
    methodology 1977.   San Francisco: Jossey-Bass, 1977

Harper, R. G., Wiens, A. N. and Matarazzo, J. D.   Nonverbal communication.   New
    York: Wiley, 1978

Hibbs, D. A.   Problems in statistical estimation and causal inference in time
    series regression models, in H. L. Costner (Ed.), Sociological methodology
    1973-74.   San Francisco: Jossey-Bass, 1974

Hibbs, D. A.   On analyzing the effects of policy interventions, in D. R. Heise
    (Ed.), Sociological methodology 1977.   San Francisco: Jossey-Bass, 1977

Jaffe, J. and Feldstein, S.   Rhythms of dialogue.   New York: Academic Press,
    1970

Jenkins, G. M. and Watts, D. G.   Spectral analysis and its applications.   San
    Francisco: Holden-Day, 1968

Mandler, G.   Mind and emotion.   New York: Wiley, 1975

Meltzer, L., Morris, W. and Hayes, D.   Interruption outcomes and vocal amplitude:
    explorations in social psychophysics.   Journal of Personality and Social
    Psychology, 1971, 18, 392-402

Meyer, T. F. and Arney, W. R.   Spectral analysis and the study of social change,
    in H. L. Costner (Ed.), Sociological Methodology 1973-74.   San Francisco:
    Jossey-Bass, 1974

Natale, M.   Convergence of mean vocal intensity in dyadic communication as a func-
    tion of social desirability.   Journal of Personality and Social Psychology,
    1975, 32, 790-804

Patterson, M. L.   Compensation in nonverbal immediacy behaviors: a review.
    Sociometry, 1973, 36, 237-252

Patterson, M. L.   An arousal model of interpersonal intimacy.   Psychological
    Review, 1976, 83, 235-245

Siegman, A. W.   The telltale voice: nonverbal messages of verbal communication,
    in A. W. Siegman and S. Feldstein (Eds.), Nonverbal behavior and communi-
    cation.   Hillsdale, New Jersey: Lawrence Erlbaum, 1978

Simonton, D. K.   Cross-sectional time-series experiments: some suggested statisti-
    cal analyses.   Psychological Bulletin, 1977, 84, 489-502

Stern, D. N.   Mother and infant at play, in M. L. Lewis and L. Rosenblum (Eds.)
    The origins of behavior, Volume I.   New York: Wiley, 1974

Temporal Patterning of Speech and Gaze in Social and Intellectual Conversations

J. M. Dabbs, Jr.

Department of Psychology, Georgia State University, Atlanta, Georgia 30303, U.S.A.

ABSTRACT

The function of a conversation may be revealed in its underlying temporal form. Fifty 10-minute conversations were obtained from subjects who were high or low in social skill or who received instructions producing a social or an intellectual set. Computer techniques were used to examine second by second changes in speech and gaze and compute amount and mean duration of speech and gaze episodes, conditional probabilities linking speech with gaze, and congruence between subjects in speech parameters. The notion that people converse for social or intellectual reasons, with their attention focused respectively upon their partners or upon lexical meaning and abstract ideas, provides a scheme for understanding a number of aspects of nonverbal patterning.

Key Words

Conversation; nonverbal; gaze; temporal; patterning; social; intellectual; computer.

I am a representative of the Southern United States, where we have long doubted the rationality of human behaviour, where words are so often so clearly an excuse for talking, where politicians and preachers have been models in showing that what one says counts for far less than how it is said.

I would like to consider why people talk and how their reasons for talking may be revealed in patterns of speech and gaze. One function of conversation appears to be purely social. People use their voices to fill silences, establish social bonds, entertain one another, and communicate affection, dominance and nurturance. Conversations can be entered or left at any point without loss. The words make sense, but one gets the feeling that the exchange of symbolic information is not really important. A second function is more intellectual. The meaning of the words is important, and people explain, inquire, instruct and deal with practical matters and abstract ideas. Their words summarize knowledge about the nature of the world. Conversation can thus be either social, serving the relationship between participants, or intellectual, dealing with ideas that transcend the participants' attitudes toward one another.

Social and intellectual functions often occur together, but they are to some extent mutually incompatible. Social conversation requires attending to one's partner,

307

which produces more eye contact, which interferes with thinking.   Intellectual
conversation requires the pursuit of ideas, which flow unpredictably and can disrupt a smooth and superficial exchange.   I suggest that the underlying non-verbal
form of a conversation, including its temporal patterning, will vary depending
upon whether the conversation is more social or intellectual.   Specifically, the
function of a conversation may be revealed in part in its temporal patterning of
speech and gaze.

Study 1, examined conversations among subjects high or low in self monitoring, on
the presumption that high self monitors would talk in a more "social" manner.
High self monitors are actors on the social stage, more concerned with playing a
part than with presenting a true picture of the self.   Low self monitors cannot
or will not bend to the situation, displaying behaviour that more truly represents
the self across all situations (Snyder, 1974).   High self monitors appear to
have more social skill than lows.   We expected highs to be more responsive toward
their partners, looking at them more, matching their vocal patterns, interjecting
more vocalizations while the partner spoke, and in general displaying a conversational style that is smoother and faster paced.

In Study 1, 48 subjects were recruited from the extreme fifths of a pool of undergraduates who completed Snyder's self monitoring scale (1974).   Subjects were run
in pairs, matched with partners similar to themselves in sex and self monitoring.
Subjects reporting to the laboratory were seated on opposite sides of a table and
left for 10 minutes to talk with one another.   On the table between them was a
2 by 2 foot wooden box with an opening through the centre, through which subjects
could see each other.   In the opening were two lightly silvered mirrors, which
looked like clear glass to the subjects but which diverted images of their faces
into a TV camera inside the box.   The camera output was recorded on $\frac{3}{4}$ inch videotape.   Subjects wore lapel microphones, and the output of the two microphones was
recorded on two audio channels on the videotape.   The single videotape thus preserved a synchronized record of both faces and both voices for subsequent scoring.

Speech was scored electronically.   An integrated circuit device decoded the voices
from the two microphones and converted them to binary on-off signals, attributing
each to the proper subject.   Gaze was scored by two judges, each watching one subject's face on the videotape and pressing a button when that subject looked directly forward.   A subject appearing to look directly forward out of the videotape
monitor would have been looking directly toward the partner's face in the original
session.

A microcomputer sampled the voice channels and gaze switches four times per second
and transmitted these data to a computer centre.   A programme in the computer
centre expanded the on-off speech codes from each subject into six more detailed
codes, as defined by Feldstein and Welkowitz (1978):

    Turn: time during which one subject has the floor, beginning when the subject
             speaks alone and ending when the partner speaks alone;
    Vocalization: speech or sound uttered by the subject who has the floor;
    Pause: silence between vocalizations within a subject's turn;
    Switching Pause: silence ending a turn and lasting until the partner speaks;
    Simultaneous Speech: sound interjected by one partner while the other is
             already talking.   Simultaneous speech is "Interruptive" if it leads
             to a change of turn and "Noninterruptive" if it does not.

The computer preserved for each dyad a continuous record of the on-off state of
four basic talk and gaze codes, plus the six expanded speech codes for each subject, a total of 16 codes.   Other programmes summarized this stream of information, computing the amount of time each code occurred, the number of episodes of

each code, and the mean duration of the episodes of each code. These programmes also computed the conditional probability of gaze given each of the speech codes. Scores generated by these programmes could be analysed using conventional analysis of variance.

In Study 1, with subjects conversing with partners similar to themselves in sex and self monitoring, females looked more than males, with less frequent but longer glances. High self monitors had shorter turns and emitted more interruptive simultaneous speech than low self monitors.

Congruence in vocal patterns was also observed, where congruence is a greater than chance agreement between paired subjects in their mean values of a parameter. Correlations between subjects across the 24 pairs were r = .72 for pause length and r = .69 for switching pause length. We found congruence in interruptive simultaneous speech but not in noninterruptive simultaneous speech. Perhaps interruptive is more likely than noninterruptive simultaneous speech to catch the partner's attention, making possible a congruent response. There was no congruence in turn or switching pause length, and high and low self monitors did not differ in congruence.

To examine the relationship between speech and gaze, each subject's conditional probability of gaze was computed given each of 10 vocal states (vocalization, pause, switching pause, interruptive and noninterruptive simultaneous speech of subject and of partner). Gaze dropped when a subject spoke, dropped even further during pauses, rose when the partner interjected simultaneous speech, and rose to its highest levels when the subject listened and the partner spoke or paused. This pattern was the same for both sexes and for subjects high or low in self monitoring. Mutual gaze - the state of A and B looking together - was examined as a separate code. Across the whole experiment the probability of a subject's gaze was .74 and the probability of mutual gaze was .56, placing mutual gaze about where it would fall as the chance coincidence of the independent gazes of the two partners. Further, within each of the different vocal states, mutual gaze was within one per cent of the chance value predicted by the probability of A's gaze times the probability of B's gaze. Mutual gaze thus apparently occurred largely as the outcome of the two randomly coupled gazing machines, neither of whose looking was affected by whether or not the other was looking.

Study 2 involved bringing 36 of the subjects back for another conversation, with each subject meeting with a new partner similar in sex but opposite in self monitoring. Congruence of vocal parameters, gaze in different conversational states, and mutual gaze apparently resulting from the random matching of individual gaze were approximately the same as in Study 1. To see more precisely how subjects might have reacted differently to having a similar or an opposite partner, data from the two studies for these 36 subjects were examined in a repeated measures format. Differences in self-monitoring were greater in Study 2 than in Study 1. Highs now had longer turns than lows, and lows gazed more than highs (perhaps because one gazes more when one's partner talks more). Lows also increased their interruptive simultaneous speech. Even though they talked less than highs in Study 2, lows were equally as likely to initiate turns with interruptive simultaneous speech; apparently the style of the highs was "catching".

The patterns of speech and gaze in these two studies fitted reasonably with Snyder's description of high and low self monitors, but the differences between highs and lows were not as great as expected. We had expected high self monitors to converse in a somewhat much more "social" manner than lows. Perhaps our measures did not adequately capture the differences that were there, or perhaps differences were attenuated by giving all subjects the same highly social task of making small talk.

In Study 3 we examined conversations generated by an intellectual instructional set. Subjects reporting to the laboratory were told we had been studying social conversations and now wished to study more serious discussions. They were introduced to each other and given sheets containing questions on the fuel crisis. They were taken to separate rooms to gather their thoughts for 10 minutes, then taken to the experimental room for a 10 minute discussion.

Data from only the first eight pairs have been analyzed. Patterns of speech and gaze seem to show more cognitive and less social involvement in this third study. The conversations contained longer turns, fewer but longer vocalizations, shorter gazes, and markedly less gaze during the pauses within a subject's turn and the switching pauses preceding the turn. Noninterruptive simultaneous speech was higher than in the earlier social conversations, perhaps because longer turns somehow "demanded" more interjections from the listener. Overall gaze and vocalization were about the same as before, as was the variation in conditional probability of gaze across the different vocal states. (While a shift toward intellectual activity may interfere with congruence between subjects in vocal parameters because congruence requires attending to the partner, eight pairs of subjects were too few to provide a stable estimate of congruence.)

These studies were motivated by a desire to understand why people talk. The content of a conversation often does not tell us much, because people can use virtually any content for any purpose. They laugh and joke and have fun talking about the most serious issues in the world, and they pursue abstract and intellectual understandings of the most intimate social relationships. Perhaps the form of a conversation, including its temporal patterning, provides a better clue as to the real function of the conversation.

Some kind of theoretical framework that considers the function of a conversation is imperative, because the data are otherwise overwhelming. Our analysis dealt with 40,000 bits of information in each 10 minute conversation, without even considering such things as facial expressions, gestures, smiles, tone of voice or other non-verbal signals. The intricacy of this information could be tracked out forever, in the process becoming a projective test for the investigator. I have suggested that a contrast between social and intellectual, an old distinction in social psychology, might be useful in organising the data. The relative salience of social or intellectual functions at a given moment may affect a variety of features, with the shift from one function to the other being the occasion for the turning on or off of whole classes of nonverbal signals.

Social implies a focus of attention toward one's partner; intellectual implies a cognitive load. Attending to a partner makes it difficult to pursue ideas. Attending to an idea makes it difficult to be responsive to one's partner. Intellectual conversation should be marked by less attention to the partner, including lower gaze, especially at moments such as pauses where more cognitive activity takes place. Intellectual conversation should also be less predictable in its temporal patterning, because the natural flow of ideas leads to vocalizations and pauses of erratic length. It remains to be seen how often conversation can be neatly segmented into social and intellectual, and whether temporal parameters of speech and gaze will bear usefully upon a social-intellectual distinction.

Our approach is in part a study of style, which in turn is a blending of content and form, including temporal form. People can say outrageous things, if they say them gracefully. Style can be a way of couching words and making them palatable. Or it can become the primary feature of an exchange, with the words, for all their apparent importance, being simply a medium through which style is conveyed.

REFERENCES

Feldstein, S. and Welkowitz, J.   A chronology of conversation: in defense of an objective approach, in A. W. Siegman and S. Feldstein (Eds.) Nonverbal behavior and communication. Hillsdale, New Jersey: Erlbaum, 1978
Snyder, M. The self-monitoring of expressive behavior. Journal of Personality and Social Psychology, 1974, 30, 526-537

Interpersonal Attraction and the Temporal Patterning of Speech in the Initial Interview: A Replication and Clarification[1]

A. W. Siegman and C. Crown

Department of Psychology, University of Maryland, 5401 Wilkens Avenue, Baltimore, Maryland 21228, U.S.A.

ABSTRACT

Using an interview paradigm, it was found on the basis of between–subjects and within–subjects comparisons that interviewees responded with longer reaction–times and with more frequent within–response pauses to reserved and neutral interviewers than to friendly ones.   Since interviewees were significantly less attracted to the reserved interviewers than to the friendly ones, we may infer an inverse relationship between interpersonal attraction and silent–pausing in speech.   It is proposed that these pauses – their specific location and duration varying as a function of task and relationship variables – involve both self–monitoring and the monitoring of one's partner.

Key words: pauses; pause latency; interpersonal attraction; self–monitoring

INTRODUCTION

The results of several studies conducted recently in our laboratory indicate that interviewees' responses to warm and friendly interviewers are associated with shorter within–response silent pauses and faster speech–rates than their replies to reserved and neutral interviewers (Siegman, in press b, c; Siegman and Reynolds in press).   Since interviewees are also more attracted to the warm and friendly interviewers than to the reserved and neutral ones (this effect is a very strong one, frequently without overlap between conditions), it can be inferred that there is a general inverse relationship between interpersonal attraction and silent pauses in speech.   If these findings hold up under replication, their implications are indeed significant.   Firstly, they broaden the range of nonverbal cues that are used to encode the giving or withholding of affection to others.   It is not unreasonable to assume that the more nonverbal channels are involved in the expression of affection and positive regard for others, the more likely it is that such behaviour can be decoded in a reliable and valid manner.   Secondly, it has been shown that the temporal patterning of speech, especially the duration of nongrammatical silent pauses, is a potent source of personality attributions.   Specifically, we tend to attribute negative personality traits to individuals who speak slowly with long silent pauses, unless these pauses can be attributed to the inti-

---

(1) The authors wish to express their profound gratitude to Dr. Marilyn Wang without whose statistical assistance this research would not have been possible.

mate nature of the topic under discussion or to another such external circumstance
(Siegman and Reynolds in press).   Thirdly, as discussed elsewhere in some detail
(Siegman in press b, and c), the availability of speech indices such as pause
duration and speech-rate as measures of interpersonal attraction has many methodological advantages.   Unlike the paper-and-pencil measures of interpersonal
attraction currently being used by social psychologists, which are subject to a
host of response biases, temporal measures provide us with readily quantifiable
and yet at the same time subtle and unobtrusive indices with which to assess not
only overall attraction level but also to track changes in interpersonal attraction
over time.

All our previous studies followed a specific experimental paradigm.   In order to
control for interviewees' expectations regarding the interviewer's warmth, the
interviewees were always forewarned about the interviewer's style (warm and
friendly or reserved and neutral), although in some studies the interviewers sometimes deliberately behaved in a manner which was inconsistent with the interviewees' expectations.   In naturalistic settings, however, interviewees have to decide for themselves whether the interviewer is warm and friendly or reserved or
perhaps even cold, although they may very well do so within the first few minutes
of the interview.   Also, in naturalistic settings interviewers may fluctuate between the giving and withholding of social reinforcers, rather than behave in a
consistently warm or reserved manner, as they did in our experiments.   Finally,
in our previous studies the interviewers always followed a prepared script, which
inevitably gives the interview an air of stiffness and artificiality.   The purpose of the study to be summarised in this paper was to test the generality and
ecological validity of our previous findings by using an experimental paradigm
which approximates naturalistic interviews more closely than was the case with our
earlier studies.

METHOD

Interviewers, interviewees and the interview

Five especially trained female graduate students interviewed 63 female undergraduates.   All interviews started with the introductory questions: "Tell me something
about your family", with the remaining questions being either all intimate or non-
intimate.   (Interviewee responses were not included in the analyses).   Each interview consisted of four ambiguously phrased, pre-programmed core questions, each of
which was followed by two spontaneously selected specific questions (e.g. How did
you feel about that?   Could you explain that?).   The order of the four core
questions in both the intimate and non-intimate interviews was partially counterbalanced: A, B, C and D versus C, D, A and B.

Experimental conditions

There were four experimental manipulations of interviewer warmth-reserve.   The
interviewers behaved either in a consistently warm and friendly manner (W-W), or in
a consistently neutral and reserved manner (R-R), or changed their demeanour at
mid-point from warm to reserved (W-R) or vice versa.   The specific interviewer
behaviours defining warmth and reserve are detailed elsewhere (Siegman in press b
and c).

The design of the study made it possible to assess the effects of interviewer
warmth on the temporal patterning of interviewees' speech both on the basis of
between-subjects comparisons (W-W versus R-R) and on the basis of within-subjects
comparisons (W-R versus R-W).   The order of the four interviewer warmth conditions,
the two types of interview (intimate and non-intimate) and the two question sequences were counterbalanced across interviewees.

Dependent variables

The major dependent variables were response latency or reaction time (RT), pause frequency (PF) and average pause duration (APD), with the latter two being measures of within-response pausing. RT was defined as the period between the last word of an interviewer's question and the first word in an interviewee's response. PF is the number of pauses 300 msec. and over per core unit. PF is typically adjusted for productivity by dividing the total number of pauses by vocalisation time. However, this method is subject to a variety of methodological objections (Marsden, Kalter and Ericson 1974). We have therefore used interviewees' unadjusted PF scores, with their vocalisation times as a covariate. APD is self-explanatory. Additionally, we analysed interviewees' Productivity scores, with Productivity defined as the summed duration of interviewees' vocalisations per core unit. The temporal components of the various indices which were used in this study, i.e. vocalisations and pauses, were measured automatically by AVTA (Jaffé and Feldstein 1970), which samples the interviewee's response every 300 msec. for both vocalisations and pauses.

Interviewees' RT, APD and Productivity scores were subjected to analyses of variance for repeated measurements, and their PF scores to an analysis of covariance for repeated measurements. The between-subjects variables were warmth condition with three degrees of freedom and intimacy with one degree of freedom. Table 1 lists the number of subjects in each condition. The within-subjects variables were: sessions (first half versus second half of each interview) and questions nested within sessions (core unit 1 versus 2 and core unit 3 versus 4). The main effect of interviewer warmth, with three degrees of freedom, was broken down into the following three separate contrasts: R-R + W-W versus R-W + W-R, R-R versus W-W and R-W versus W-R, with the latter two as our primary focus of interest. Each of these contrasts and their interactions with intimacy and the within-variables were tested in each possible order, so that we could assess their independent as well as their unique contributions to the total variance.

TABLE 1   Number of subjects in the various interview
conditions

Interviewer Warmth	Question Type	Interviewees n	Interviewer Warmth	Question Type	Interviewees n
W-W	Intimate	7	W-W	Nonintimate	8
R-R	Intimate	8	R-R	Nonintimate	9
W-R	Intimate	10	W-R	Nonintimate	8
R-W	Intimate	7	R-W	Nonintimate	6

Post-interview ratings

At the completion of the interview, and prior to the debriefing, the interviewees rated their interviewer's warmth. These ratings, together with the evaluations of the interviewer's warmth by "blind" judges from behind a one-way mirror, served as manipulation checks. Interviewees also rated their own anxiety level, the interviewer's competence and their own level of attraction to the interviewer.

RESULTS

Ratings

The interviewers who behaved in a consistently warm manner obtained significantly higher warmth ratings from their interviewees than interviewers who behaved in consistently reserved manner ($F(1,26) = 7.97$, $p < .02$). Moreover, the judges

achieved 100 per cent accuracy in their identifications of the interviewer's experimental condition. The interviewees were also significantly more attracted
to the consistently warm than to the consistently reserved interviewers $(F(1,25) =$
6.11, p < .05). However, the interviewer warmth manipulations had no significant
effect on interviewees' anxiety and competency ratings.

Temporal indices

The interviewer warmth manipulations were a significant source of variance on
interviewees' RT scores $(F(3,55) = 2.77, p = .05)$. Interviewees responded with
significantly longer latencies to interviewers who behaved in a consistently
reserved manner than to interviewers who behaved in a consistently warm and
friendly manner. With the contributions of the other contrasts partialled out
$(F(1,55) = 4.97, p = .03)$. However, the interaction of the W-W versus R-R contrast by sessions was of borderline significance $(F(1,55) = 2.74)$, p = .10).
This interaction reflects the fact that the effect of interviewer warmth on interviewees' latencies increased from the first half to the second half of the interview $(F(1,30) = 1.02$ and 5.11 respectively). The interaction of the W-R versus
the R-W contrast by session was also of borderline significance $(F(1,30) = 2.46$,
p = .10). This interaction reflects the fact that interviewer reserve was
associated with longer latencies in the W-R condition $(F(1,16) = 6.17, p < .05)$
but not in the R-W condition (p < .1).

The analysis of covariance of interviewees' PF scores yielded a significant main
effect, W-W versus R-R $(F(1,54) = 5.06, p < .03)$ and a significant interaction
effect: the W-R versus R-W contrast by session $(F(1,54) = 6.39, p < .02)$.
Interviewers responded with more frequent pauses to the reserved than to the
friendly interviewers on the basis of both between subjects and within subjects
comparisons.   The experimental manipulations had no significant effect on interviewees' APD scores.

Finally, in relation to interviewees' productivity or summed duration of vocalisation scores, there was one significant interaction: the W-W versus R-R contrast by sessions $(F(1,55) = 5.08, p < .03)$. When the interviewers behaved in
a consistently warm manner the interviewees' productivity levels increased with
time, with precisely the reverse pattern characterising interviewees' behaviour
when the interviewers behaved in a consistently reserved manner. Moreover, if
we combine all first half sessions in the four conditions, we find that the
interviewees were significantly more productive in the reserved than in the warm
conditions, provided the interviewers asked intimate questions $(F(1,30) = 5.32$,
p < .05).

DISCUSSION

Basically, the results of the present study with its improved design, which includes an adequate sampling of interviewers, the use of an experimental paradigm
which approximates naturalistic interviewee-interviewer interactions more
closely than that of earlier studies, and the reliance on both between-subjects
and within-subjects comparisons, confirm our previous finding of an inverse relationship between interpersonal attraction and pausing. While in previous
studies this pausing took the form of longer within-response silent pauses, in
the present study it took the form of longer response latencies and more frequent within-response short silent pauses. Perhaps the many specific questions
which were used in the present study, in contrast to the more general questions
that were used in our previous studies, prevented the interviewees from "fili-
bustering" and forced them to do their screening prior to starting their response.
Elsewhere (Siegman 1978b; in press a) we have argued for the "functional equiva-
lence" of hesitation phenomena. Evidence is presented that the specific hesi-

tation phenomena associated with cognitive decision making - and these hesitation
phenomena include silent pauses as well as "ah's" and even phenomena usually subsumed under "speech disturbances" (Mahl, 1956) - are a function of the social context, type of decision-making (i.e. syntactic versus semantic) and response condition (i.e. pressure to respond promptly or to continue talking). The results
of the present study suggest that the type of question is yet another source of
variance, as far as the location of relatively long pauses is concerned.

It remains to be explained, however, why the interviewees' relatively long latencies had to be supplemented by frequent within-response short silent pauses.   In
our previous discussions of the meaning of the silent pauses that occur when talking to a partner whom one does not like, it was suggested that such pauses involve
self-monitoring, i.e. decisions about <u>what</u> to disclose and <u>how</u> to disclose it.
The possibility was left open, however, that such pauses may also be devoted to the
monitoring of one's partner. According to Goldman-Eisler (1968), the response
latency period is devoted to thematic planning. Even if we concede that such
pauses also involve syntactic planning they can hardly serve the purpose of providing the interviewee with feedback from the interviewer since the interviewer
has yet to begin his remarks. This type of other-monitoring may take place during
the short within-response pauses.

An assessment of the effect of interviewer warmth on interviewees' latency scores,
by comparing the conditions in which the interviewers switched from a warm and
friendly manner to a reserved and neutral one and vice versa yielded ambiguous
findings. While the change from a warm and friendly interviewer demeanour to a
neutral and reserved one was associated with a corresponding significant increase
in interviewees' latencies, the change from a neutral and reserved manner to a
warm and friendly one produced no such significant effect. This is not particularly surprising since even a consistently warm and reserved interviewer manner
does not significantly affect interviewees' response latencies until the interview
is well on its way. This is not to be interpreted as an indication that the latency measure is not very sensitive to changes in the interviewer's warmth and
friendliness, since a change from a warm and friendly demeanour to a cold and reserved one fairly promptly produces an increase in interviewees' latencies.   Instead, our data suggest that interviewees tend to reserve judgment of an interviewer's reserved and neutral manner and that they do not immediately respond with
a defensive speech style, unless the interviewer's reserve follows a previous period of warmth and friendliness. Of course, a relentlessly neutral and reserved
interviewer manner will eventually produce a sharp increase in interviewees' latencies. Elsewhere (Siegman, in press b) we have pointed out that many of our social
psychological theories assume a symmetry in people's response to positive and negative experiences, which in fact may not exist. One such lack of symmetry in how
people respond to positive versus negative events in their lives, i.e. a kind of
positivity bias, is suggested by the above finding.

In three consecutive studies we were unable to replicate an early finding (Pope
and Siegman 1972) that interviewees tend to be more productive in response to warm
and friendly interviewers than to reserved and neutral ones. However, since the
early study was based on within-subjects comparisons and the later ones on between-
subjects comparisons we were reluctant to dismiss the earlier finding, despite the
repeated replication failures. In the light of the results obtained in the present
study, in which we used both between-subjects and within-subjects comparisons, it
should be clear that interviewer warmth has no advantage as far as interviewee productivity is concerned. Although the interviewees were significantly more attracted to the warm and friendly interviewers (in the W-W condition) than to the reserved and neutral ones (in the R-R condition), this did not significantly increase
interviewees' productivity levels. In fact, there is evidence that at least initially interviewer reserve tends to increase interviewee productivity. This ini-

tial positive association between interviewer reserve and interviewee productivity can be explained in terms of the mediating role of anxiety-arousal, which has been shown to increase interviewee productivity (Siegman 1978; Siegman and Pope 1972). However, interviewees are likely to adapt to an interviewer's reserved manner, and hence the transitory nature of the facilitating effect of interviewer reserve on interviewee productivity level.

In conclusion it should be pointed out that we need more research on the effects of different patterns of silent pausing in speech on listeners' attribution of positive or negative personality traits to the speaker, and hence on their attraction to the speaker. Previous findings (Siegman and Reynolds, in press) indicate that long silent pauses in interviewees' speech, whether they precede their responses or whether they occur within their responses, detract from the interviewers' attraction to the interviewees, provided that these pauses cannot be justified in terms of the nature of the material (e.g. highly intimate) or some other external circumstance. Results of regression analyses performed on the data of the present study confirm the earlier findings in relation to within-response pausing but not latencies. The increase in R^2 contributed by interviewees' within-response pauses to the interviewers' attraction scores was 6 per cent ($F(1,51) = 3.79$, $p < .06$). In the present study, however, the duration of interviewees' latencies did not contribute significantly to the interviewers' attraction ratings. Perhaps this was the case, because in the present study long latencies could be justified in terms of the specific nature of the interviewer's questions. As pointed out earlier, such questions force interviewees to plan their responses before they start responding, and tend to produce relatively longer latencies. There is some suggestive evidence, then, that personality attributions that are made on the basis of nonverbal cues involve fairly subtle, and one should add, reasonable discriminations on the part of the listener. Perhaps it is possible, after all, to pause and do one's information processing without creating a bad impression.

REFERENCES

Goldman-Eisler, F. Psycholinguistics: experiments in spontaneous speech. New York: Academic Press, 1968
Jaffé, J. and Feldstein, S. Rhythms of dialogue. New York: Academic Press, 1970
Mahl, G. F. Disturbances and silences in the patient's speech in psychotherapy. Journal of Abnormal and Social Psychology, 1956, 53, 1-15
Marsden, G., Kalter, N. and Ericson, W. A. Response productivity: a methodological problem in content analysis studies in psychotherapy. Journal of Consulting and Clinical Psychology, 1974, 42, 224-230
Pope, B. and Siegman, A. W. Relationship and verbal behavior in the initial interview, in A. W. Siegman and B. Pope (Eds.) Studies in dyadic communication. New York: Pergamon Press, 1972
Siegman, A. W. The telltale voice: nonverbal messages of verbal communication, in A. W. Siegman and S. Feldstein (Eds.) Nonverbal behavior and communication Hillsdale, New Jersey: Lawrence Erlbaum Associates, 1978
Siegman, A. W. Cognition and hesitation in speech, in A. W. Siegman and S. Feldstein (Eds.) Of speech and time: temporal speech patterns in interpersonal contexts. Hillsdale, New Jersey: Lawrence Erlbaum Associates, in press a.
Siegman, A. W. Interpersonal attraction and verbal behavior in the initial interview, in R. St. Clair and H. Giles (Eds.) The social and psychological contexts of language. Hillsdale, New Jersey: Lawrence Erlbaum Associates, in press b.
Siegman, A. W. and Pope, B. The effect of ambiguity and anxiety on interviewee verbal behavior, in A. W. Siegman and B. Pope (Eds.) Studies in dyadic communication. New York: Pergamon Press, 1972
Siegman, A. W. and Reynolds, M. Interviewer-interviewee nonverbal communications: an interactional approach, in C. Arensberg and M. Davies (Eds.) Interaction rhythms. New York: Human Services Press, in press

Temporal Aspects of Speech: Epilogue

S. Feldstein

Department of Psychology, University of Maryland, Baltimore County,
5401 Wilkens Avenue, Baltimore, Maryland 21228, U.S.A.

COMMENTS AND QUESTIONS

In its own way, each of the papers in this section represents an advance beyond previous research. Perhaps the clearest example of such an advance is Cappella's paper. Those who have explored the phenomenon of temporal congruence, or temporal accommodation, have tended to use relatively simple correlational techniques to estimate its occurrence and degree (e.g., Marcus, Welkowitz, Feldstein and Jaffé, 1970; Natale, 1975). They are techniques that permit conclusions about groups of dyads but not about a single dyad. Cappella, however, appears to have more successfully used time series regression procedures to characterise individual dyads in terms of whether, for each of the temporal parameters, the values of the two participants converge, diverge, or show no relationship. Granted that the procedures need further exploration and refinement, the consequences of the advance they represent are exceedingly important for future research, and possibly in none more so than in clinical research. For example, a colleague and I have been investigating the relation between marital "harmony" and temporal congruence. A number of other colleagues and I (Glaister, Feldstein and Pollack, 1979) are examining the chronographic patterns of interviews with acute psychotic patients as a function of treatment and length of hospital stay. Inasmuch as there are marked differences among married couples in terms of type and degree of discord, and among psychiatric patients (even among those with the same diagnosis), it becomes almost imperative to treat the investigations as series of single-case studies and compute within-interview rather than across-interview estimates of temporal congruence. It is only now, however, that such estimates may be obtained.

A large part of Dabbs' paper describes the temporal speech patterns of high and low self-monitors and the degrees to which they accommodate their patterns to each other in conversational interactions. It also describes the time patterns of the gazing behaviour of high and low self-monitors and their relation to speech patterns. Parenthetically, one fascinating bit of information was the finding that the likelihood that a speaker would gaze at his or her partner was not affected by the direction of the partner's gaze. In other words, the extent to which the participants in a conversation engaged in mutual gazing appeared to be a function of chance. Although it may well be confirmed by subsequent research, the finding seems counterintuitive. People tend to believe that they most often engage in mutual gazes for particular reasons or as a function of some emotion, such as love and/or hate. It is likely, however, that the belief can be experimentally tested. In any case, it seems to me that the part of Dabbs' work that represents an advance

is his concern distinguishing between the time patterns of social and intellectual conversations.   This effort to delineate the patterns of conversations that
have different goals represents an important if indirect thrust into the level of
conversational semantics.   It is an effort somewhat related to an hypothesis I
suggested some years ago, namely, "... that dialogic time patterns are related to
semantic content such that there are some patterns and content that frequently co-
occur and others that rarely co-occur". (Feldstein, 1972, p.110).

Dr. Clarke and his associates have proposed a 16-state probability model that describes the combined surface structure of speech and gazing behaviours.   It is,
indeed, quite similar to the 16-state matrix of transitional probabilities suggested a number of years ago by Dabbs and his colleague Bakeman (Bakeman and
Dabbs, 1976) to account for the same behaviours.   You will have noted that Dabbs
made clear, in his paper, that he still uses the 16 states or "codes" that are,
in fact, the 16 possible observable states of speech and gaze behaviours.   However, Clarke and colleagues have pushed beyond the 16-state model to further propose what they call a "probalistic grammar" that presumably describes the underlying structure of speech and gaze patterns.   The structure is represented by a
set of rewrite rules, and the probabilities are those with which the rules occur.

Since modeling is intended to accomplish much more than the accumulation of
data, it is not surprising that it is a risky procedure and that the results are
more vulnerable.   For example, Clarke asserts that the grammar he and his colleagues have proposed is based upon induction and experience.   Is it not possible,
therefore, that another investigator may devise a different grammar and thus a
different structure for speech and gaze patterns?   It seems to me possible although, given the set of behaviours and the intention to devise a generative
grammar, it also seems unlikely that the resulting rewrite rules would be strik-
ingly different from those presented by Clarke.   Of much more importance is the
question of whether the probabilistic grammar is, in this instance at least, more
useful than the 16-state probability model.   Is it capable of generating predictions?   Does it provide any more useful distinction between interviews and unconstrained conversations than the probability matrix?   Finally, does it imply
assumptions about the users (i.e. the speakers and gazers) that are tenable?

One issue raised by both the report by Dabbs and that by Clarke and his colleagues
has to do with the linkages between or among the various types or dimensions of
nonverbal behaviour, for example, visual or gazing behaviour, facial behaviour,
gestural behaviour, etc.   Investigators who study a single dimension operate upon the implicit or explicit assumption that each dimension may be considered –
if only for the purposes of research – independent of the other dimensions even
if it functions, as each usually does, in coordination with the other dimensions.
One implication of this position is that the components of that dimension are defined independently of other dimensions.   The end of a hand movement, for instance, is not defined in terms of whether the person making the movement initiated or terminated eye contact with his or her partner in the interaction.   Nor,
as another instance, is the beginning of one person's speaking turn defined in
terms of the other person's gestural behaviour or facial behaviour.   Clearly,
however, the position is not one that is unanimously accepted; there are investigators who define the parameters of one dimension in terms of the parameters of
other dimensions (e.g., Duncan, 1972).   The issue is important because the type
of information obtained is based upon the approach taken to the phenomena being
examined.

The series of studies that Brown and his colleagues have previously conducted and
those he has reported have yielded results that, as he states, are "amazingly consistent" across computer-synthesised and more natural speech.   This consistency
suggests that the results must be taken quite seriously.   But there is another

reason for taking them seriously. They seem to explain, at least in part, the findings of a number of other studies by other investigators. Specifically, Brown found that as his speakers increased their rates of speech, they were perceived to be more competent but less benevolent. The other studies to which I refer (e.g. Miller, Maruynama, Beaber and Valone, 1976) found that individuals who spoke faster were perceived to be more persuasive than those who spoke at a relatively normal rate but also somewhat less trustworthy. Given both sets of results, it seems not unreasonable that persons who are seen as <u>more</u> competent but <u>less</u> benevolent might be considered more persuasive but less trustworthy than those who appear to be <u>less</u> competent but <u>more</u> benevolent. I do not think that the various dimensions have all been included in one study but, clearly, they ought to be.

One other issue is worth mentioning. It concerns the notions of self-monitoring used as a personality construct by Dabbs and simply as a cognitive activity by Siegman and Crown. The two notions may perhaps be distinguished by considering that the latter is deliberate while the former is not. My understanding, however, is that both serve the purpose of conveying a particular impression. It seems likely, therefore, that the two ostensibly different notions ought to bear some relation to each other. Otherwise, perhaps their names ought to be different.

Apart from these issues, the Siegman and Crown study not only replicates the findings of a considerable number of previous experiments conducted by Siegman (e.g. 1979), but demonstrates their viability within the context of a much more naturalistic and complex interview format.

In short, the papers presented in this section characterise the methodological sophistication and healthy variety of interests that investigators are bringing to the study of interaction chronography.

REFERENCES

Bakeman, R. and Dabbs, J. M., Jr. Social interaction observed: some approaches to the analysis of behavior streams. <u>Personality and Social Psychology Bulletin</u>, 1976, <u>2</u>, 335-345

Duncan, S., Jr. Some signals and rules for taking speaking turns in conversations. <u>Journal of Personality and Social Psychology</u>, 1972, <u>23</u>, 283-292

Feldstein, S. Temporal patterns of dialogue: basic research and reconsiderations, in A. W. Siegman and B. Pope (Eds.) <u>Studies in dyadic communication</u>. New York: Pergamon Press, 1972

Glaister, J., Feldstein, S. and Pollack, H. <u>Chronographic speech patterns of acutely psychotic patients</u>. Paper read at the Clinical Research Society of Toronto, Toronto, Canada, March, 1979

Marcus, E. S., Welkowitz, J., Feldstein, S. and Jaffe, J. Psychological differentiation and the congruence of temporal speech patterns. Paper presented at the meeting of the Eastern Psychological Association, Atlantic City, April 1970

Miller, N., Maruynama, G., Beaber, R. J. and Valone, K. Speed of speech and persuasion. <u>Journal of Personality and Social Psychology</u>, 1976, <u>34</u>, 615-624

Natale, M. Social desirability as related to convergence of temporal speech patterns. <u>Perceptual and Motor Skills</u>, 1975, <u>40</u>, 827-830

Siegman, A. W. The voice of attraction: vocal correlates of interpersonal attraction in the interview, in A. W. Siegman and S. Feldstein (Eds.) <u>Of speech and time: temporal speech patterns in interpersonal contexts</u>. Hillsdale, New Jersey: Erlbaum Associates, 1979

What is Planned During Speech Pauses?

R. Hänni

Institute of Psychology, University of Bern, Gesellschaftsstr. 47-49,
3012 Bern, Switzerland

ABSTRACT

Since speech pauses have become a matter of psychological concern, several authors have tried to strengthen the hypothesis that speech pauses are an exterior phenomenon of interior, i.e. cognitive processes. This means that one accepts that speech is interrupted either because there is nothing ready to be uttered (speaking has been faster than thinking, hence a pause) or there is a need for certain acts of planning to be executed mainly during non-speech periods. If the latter is true, it follows that speaking is interfering with planning.

To test this interference hypothesis, the following experiment has been carried out:

Two groups of subjects either had to comment on a short film shown on a TV screen (group A) or to reproduce orally its contents immediately after its termination (group B). While speaking, their speech pauses were automatically filled with speech fed to the subjects' earphones from a pre-recorded tape. Speech behaviour was tested against two control groups, one each for the two conditions (groups CA and CB), which groups did not receive experimental treatment.

The rationale for investigating the two different situations lies in the assumption that they differ in the type of possible cognitive planning activities requires (need for content retrieval, idiosyncratic structuring and interpretation of the shown story, etc.)

Results show no differences in the frequency distributions of pause length, mean length of pauses, percentage of pause time of the total speaking time, mean number of uttered words, mean number of errors of articulation per word, or mean number of subordinate clause introductions within A and AC and B and BC respectively. Mean number of uttered words is higher in A than in B, mean number of errors of articulation per word is lower in A than in B. These last two variables are the only ones that lead to a difference between A and B on a quantitative level of analysis and, together with some differences produced by a more qualitative, i.e. Transcript analysis, justify the investigation of the two situations.

Note: This paper on temporal factors was presented in addition to those in the symposium.

Interpretation of the results regarding the lack of differences between A and AC
and B and BC leads to two possible conclusions: (1) that planning does not occur
during pauses; and (2) if it does occur, it cannot easily be disturbed.

The question remains - why should we need pauses in order to plan our spoken output?   But pauses do occur and they have been looked at on a less cognitive level
and perhaps with more success.

Key words

Speech pauses; interference; planning; questions; latency of speech.

For about twenty years speech pauses have been a matter of psychological interest.
Maclay and Osgood (1959) and especially Goldman-Eisler in the sixties viewed them
as one of the indicators of speech planning and drew conclusions on the basis of
their location within the syntactic and semantic structure of speech.   Although
Goldman-Eisler (1968) carried out some of her experiments in interview situations
she was not particularly concerned with possible interactive functions of pausing.
This contrasts with investigations made by Martin and Strange (1968) and later by
Jaffé and Feldstein (1970) and others.   Whereas Martin and Strange do not concede
that pauses may have interactive functions because they are, in many cases, not
consciously perceived by the listeners, Jaffe and Feldstein have shown that pausing varies according to personality characteristics of the dialogue partners for
instance.   The first study[1] presented here was concerned with cognitive aspects
of pausing.   The second study investigated some interactive phenomena of pausing.

As mentioned above, speech pauses in spontaneous speech have been viewed as
exterior symptoms of interior processes, i.e. cognitive planning of forthcoming
speech.   Pauses would occur because there is no more speech ready to be uttered
(speaking has been faster than thinking).   If one looks at pauses in this way,
the question arises as to why there should be a need for certain acts of speech
planning to be executed during non-speech periods.[2]   One possible answer would
be that speaking is in some ways interfering with planning.   As it is difficult
to have people speaking while they are pausing in order to interfere with their
planning, I chose another means to test this interference hypothesis.

Subjects in Group A had to comment on a short film shown on a TV screen.   Subjects in Group B had to reproduce its contents orally immediately after the film
had finished.   All subjects were led to believe that somebody was listening in
the next room and that it was the aim of the investigation to find out how
accurately this listener could retail the story afterwards without having seen the
film.   In reality no one was listening.   While speaking, subjects' speech pauses
were automatically 'filled' with speech fed to the subjects' earphones from a pre-
recorded tape by means of a sound key.

Speech production of each of the two experimental groups was compared with that of
two control groups (Groups AC and BC) who had the same task as their experimental
counterparts but did not have their pauses filled with speech.

---

1. Method and results presented here are based on an earlier study (Hänni, 1973
   and 1974) but the interpretation of data is different in certain respects.

2. About 80% of the speech pauses were shorter than one second and only about 5%
   or less were longer than three seconds (Goldman-Eisler, 1968; Hänni, 1974).
   Planning must therefore refer to processes different from those we are consciously aware of during long pauses.

Subjects in Group A had to process incoming visual information (there was of course no sound in either situation) into verbal output concurrently with planning and producing their utterances, finding words for pictures, forming sentences and articulating them.   Possible planning deficiencies should therefore show themselves in difficulties of word retrieval, unusual grammatical constructions, and/ or changes in pausing behaviour.

Subjects in Group B in preparing to recall the story, had to give it a sense, to choose from important and less important details and so on.   This leads one to expect that in this situation planning consists, in addition to what has been mentioned for Group A, in structuring the whole story of the film, requiring planning activities on a higher cognitive level.   If this is the case and pauses are needed for planning there should be differences in mean pause length and/or pause length frequency distribution at least.

RESULTS

As can be seen in Table 1, comparisons between Groups A and AC and between B and BC show no statistic differences at all.   What has happened?

TABLE 1   Characteristics of speech as a function of pause telling

Variable	Treatment of Group Means*			
	A	AC	B	BC
- pause length (secs)	2.24	1.56	.91	.87
- pause time in percentage of total speaking time	52	47.5	38.5	32.5
- number of uttered words	723	752	391	269
- errors of articulation per word	.02	.02	.03	.04
- number of subordinate clause introductions	14.7	13.0	11.4	9.4

*No differences between A and AC or B and BC are statistically significant

At the beginning I set out to find good evidence for the strengthening of the interference hypothesis.   Now I am almost sure that this hypothesis is wrong and further that we do not necessarily need speech pauses in order to speak correctly. Why should we?   We are capable of knitting, watching, speaking and listening to music at the same time without manifesting such coarse, that is temporally measurable, external symptoms of planning as is the case with speech pauses.   It is of course possible that the experimental treatment of the S's did not affect their planning while pausing.   The present data do not allow a decision in this direction.   While they were performing, most of the S's showed signs of heavy stress: they blushed, clenched their fingers and showed all the signs of being very nervous, a fact confirmed by them in a subsequent brief interview.   Despite this they produced normal everyday speech with no difference on the more qualitative variables such as type of lexical constructions, subordination index, and adequacy of the contents of the story.   Nevertheless, the phenomenon of pausing is real, speech pauses do occur and I am still interested to find out more about them.

In a second study which is not yet completed I looked at them on a quite different level, i.e. their possible function in verbal interaction.   The study aimed to

find out whether S's could identify signals of forthcoming turnchanges while listening to a dialogue and if they were able to do so, of what nature these signals
would be.   For this purpose I took one of my previously collected tape recorded
dialogues and cut it up into single utterances.   These utterances were then recorded on magnetic tape in their chronological order with an artificial pause of
about seven seconds between each of them.   S's were instructed to press a button
if, and as soon as they expected a turnchange.   They had an opportunity to press
this button from the beginning of the utterance until the end of the immediately
following artificial pause.   If they felt that no change of speakers would occur
they were not to press the button.   Preliminary results show that none of the
twenty S's pressed the button before an utterance ended, which clearly indicates
the limitations of such an experiment in that if they had pressed before the end
of an utterance this action would have corresponded to interrupting one's partner.

It is, nevertheless, interesting to look at further results, e.g. mean time of
latency (the time elapsed from the end of an utterance until the button had been
pressed was computed for each utterance).   Analysis of those items that have
caused shorter latencies than minus one standard deviation shows that with one
exception they are all questions.   This means that there should be shorter pauses
after questions than after any other type of statement.   This is actually true
for the particular dialogue used.   For the time being it is not possible to tell
whether this holds for pauses after questions in general or not because analysis
of more dialogues is still in progress, and no data are yet to hand.   Nevertheless I have started to interpret these initial results and they are, of course,
open for discussion.

Looking at speech pauses in interactive situations, in a dialogue in this case, includes assigning possible interactive functions to them.   In this sense short
pauses after questions could occur for the following reasons.   Because the intonation and/or syntax of questions are readily noticeable signals for the listening
partner that the speaker wants him to speak now, he does not need additional signals such as pauses in order to appreciate the intention of turn change.   A long
pause after a question would tell him nothing more, whereas such a pause after almost any other statement is possibly one of the few indicators of an intended turn
change, apart from visual signals, of course.   There is additional evidence for
this interpretation.   There were altogether nine questions in the dialogue.
Nineteen of the twenty S's pressed the button after every question, anticipating
a turn change.   One S did not press the button after two questions.   This leads
to a mean anticipation rate of turn change after questions of 96%, as compared
with the percentage for the remaining utterances of 48.

Furthermore, the dialogue included two questions put in alternative form of the
type: 'Are you the experimenter or are you the subject?'   (Translated from Swiss-
German into English for the purpose of this paper by the author).   Since both
utterances of this turn are clearly put in an interrogative way one would expect
after what has been said above that in the button pressing experiment the S's
would be misled to anticipate a turn change i.e. an answer immediately after the
first utterance, where as in the original dialogue the speaker of this question
should try to minimise pausing between the two parts of the turn, this in order
not to risk being interrupted after the first part of such particular turns.   The
question concerning the misleading of the S's is already answered: they have actually been misled.   As for the suppression of the pause in the original dialogue
I can only note that there was no measurable pause in either instance but it would
be daring indeed to generalise from two cases.   We are now investigating similar
types of turns and hope to answer this question later.   If what has been said
here is true, one would expect that interruptions in dialogues should be more frequent if the rule of making no or very short pauses after such questions is vio-
lated.   This is the reason why we are now looking at such interruptions in order

to get more and stronger evidence.

Before the conclusions are summarised, one more detail is possibly worth mention. A preliminary analysis of contents and linguistic form of the utterances which caused longer latencies than one standard deviation shows that this happens in the case of the utterances or turns being very short, i.e. one or two words only. The interpretation for this would be that listeners in general are surprised to get back the floor so soon and/or because many of the short utterances are in some ways incomplete and listeners expect completion. A long pause is in this case an indicator for a turn change where other signals, verbal or nonverbal, are absent. This is in line with what has been mentioned above, and involves no contradiction, but it is also well known from research in nonverbal communication that speakers not willing to lose their turn communicate this by giving signs like turning away their heads.

It is also well known that people rarely answer questions raised in the titles of their papers. I am no exception. I still do not know what is planned during speech pause, if there is any planning. While it is clear that theories cannot be falisfied by such findings as presented in this paper they may add to a reconsideration of speculations widely taken for granted. In terms of the arguments proposed in this paper one would have to explain why pausing characteristics change in the course of dialogues (e.g. Feldstein, Alberti and Ben Debba, 1979) and why temporal patterns very similar to those of adult speech occur between mothers and their babbling infants (Aebi-Hungerbühler and Alberti, 1979). It is certainly hard to explain the latter in terms of semantic and/or syntactic characteristics of speech. And why should the placement of speech pauses as a structuring element not have been learned simply together with language acquisition?

I am convinced that speech pauses are significant for maintaining a normal interactive exchange. Just as we continue to give visual signals when speaking on the telephone, the S's in the first experiment, despite the situation being a monologue may have kept their normal dialogue pausing habits. The functions certain pauses have for turn changing may not be their only role, but I think it is an important one. They do not depend on speaking partner characteristics only, but also upon linguistic form and contents, and so their investigation may allow us to learn more about language and language use.

REFERENCES

Aebi-Hungerbühler, E. and Alberti, L. Entwicklung des "Sprecherwechsels" in der Mutter-Kleinkindinteraktion, in L. Alberti and R. Hänni (chair), Dialoganalyse. Symposium presented at the 21.Tagung experimentellarbeitender Psychologen, Heidelberg, 1979

Feldstein, S., Alberti, L. and Ben Debba, M., Self-attributed personality characteristics and the pacing of conversational interaction, in A. W. Siegman and S. Feldstein (Eds.) Of speech and time: temporal speech patterns in interpersonal contexts. Hillsdale, New Jersey: Lawrence Erlbaum Associated 1979

Goldman-Eisler, F. Psycholinguistics. New York: Academic Press, 1968

Jaffe, J. and Feldstein, S. Rhythms of dialogue. New York: Academic Press, 1970

Hänni, R. Sprechpausen unde die planung des sprechens. Unpublished doctoral dissertation, Berne (Switzerland), 1973

Hänni, R. Auswirkungen der störung von sprechpausen, in L. H. Eckensberger and U. S. Eckensberger (Eds.) Bericht über den 28.Kongress der Deutschen Gesellschaft für Psychologie in Saarbrücken 1972. Volume 1. Göttingen (Germany): Hogrefe, 1974

Maclay, H. and Osgood, C. E. Hesitation phenomena and spontaneous English speech. Word, 1959, 15, 19-44

Martin, J. G. and Strange, W. Determinants of hesitations in spontaneous speech. Journal of Experimental Psychology, 1968, 76, 474-479

Bilingualism, Multilingualism, Code-Switching

C. M. Scotton

Department of Linguistics, University of Michigan, Ann Arbor, Michigan, 48109, U.S.A.

INTRODUCTION

The papers presented at this symposium represent an important step in the development of a theory to explain code selection. This is so for two reasons. First, all of them go beyond the taxonomic approach which has characterised many sociolinguistic studies. That is, these papers attempt to explain code selection rather than simply describe the conditions associated with different selections. Second, in general these papers discuss personal motivation factors, a set of variables well known to social psychologists but largely ignored by sociolinguists.

The first sociolinguistic studies generally saw code choice as a function of the formal features of both speakers and the settings in which the speech event takes place. Many of these studies were purely taxonomic with no explanatory power. Lists of demographic features of speakers and of the possible variations in time, setting, topic, and participants which could occur in the speech situation were simply assembled. Rarely was any attempt made even to rank these factors in relative importance as independent variables associated with code choice, although studies which are notable exceptions do exist. In all cases, however, the premise of these studies was the same - that is, that the far majority of code choices could be correlated with the social characteristics of speakers and situations. This correlation became the implicit explanation of choice.

A more recent approach developed as a protest against the view that code choice correlates consistently with such "static" factors. Sociolinguists following this alternative approach are either members of, or influenced by, the school of ethnomethodology. They argue that linguistic choices can only be understood within the specific interactional context in which they occur; therefore, methodologically they rule out large-scale surveys and self-reports. These interactionist sociolinguists take cognizance of the macro-societal factors which the correlationist sociolinguists emphasise. But the interactionists view choices as more of product of speakers influenced by a specific discourse context than by their group identities. Implicit in this approach is that no general explanation of code selection is possible since each interaction must be explained on its own. In this sense, this approach is also taxonomic since lists of speech event characteristics, even though they deal with single interactions, are its main product.

The papers presented at this symposium take account of both sets of factors emphasised in the previous approaches. That is, they recognise the constraints of societal norms on behaviour for specific identities in specific situations as factors which influence code choice.   They also recognise the effect of the dynamics of the interaction itself on subsequent code choices as the interaction unfolds. However, both of these sets of factors deal with the 'how' of code choice since they deal with the mechanics of selection.

All the papers presented deal to a greater or lesser extent with a third set of factors which is more closely related with the 'why' of code choice.   They emphasise the motivation behind code choice.   Implicit in the approach these papers take is the view that speakers use code choice for their own ends, to signal perceptions they have regarding their own status and the type of role relationship they want, or consider appropriate, between themselves and others.   In this sense code selection is seen as a personally-motivated statement of social identity.

Radical Grammars: Interplays of Form and Function

M. B. Kendall

Department of Anthropology, Indiana University, Rawles Hall, Bloomington, Indiana 47405, U.S.A.

ABSTRACT

Standard Chomskian grammatical theory not only treats language as a bounded system of rules, but considers it a property of "mind" as well, putting it squarely in the domain of individual psychology. Although he does not discuss the issue of multi-lingual competence, it seems to follow from Chomsky's main arguments that different languages must be stored separately as non-overlapping systems in the minds of multi-lingual individuals. In this essay we will try to develop a more adequate formal model of multilingual competence, and suggest how such a model might articulate with a model of language use. What is abundantly clear from empirical evidence is that multilinguals present special problems for the "individual psychological" view of grammatical competence.

Six months of observations on the spontaneous daily social interactions of eleven multi-lingual friends and co-workers serve as the data base for this study. Depending on the particular constellation of individuals present at any given time, recorded conversations revealed the whole spectrum of multi-lingual speech possibilities, from isolated borrowings, to multi-lingual code-switches, to true pidginization. On the other hand, observation of this group also showed that multi-lingual speech obeyed many structural or grammatical constraints, and was in no sense a case of "anything goes" - just as multilingual speech is not a case of unconstrained functional variation.

We have numerous examples of social interactions that led to restructuring of individual's formal linguistic competence, suggesting a dynamic and processual model of language - one which is socio-psychological rather than individual.

Our observations bear on the question of the permeability of codes and the kinds of social and structural factors affecting it. We offer the notion of "radical grammars", extensions of, restructurings of, or stabs at the "normal" grammatical rules of an official code.

Key words

Code switching; conversation; radical grammar; pragmatics; semantics; grammatical competence; negotiation.

Code-switching studies focus on the complex and processual interplay of etiquette, impression management, expectation, social solidarity or distance, and inequalities of power in multi-lingual situations.   The best of these studies (Parkin, 1974, a, b, c; Scotton and Ury, 1975) address questions of the relationship between individual choices and the social impact these choices have.   They focus on the meanings that an individual's behaviour have for persons with whom the individual interacts.   This methodological stance, making reference as it does to shared expectations and evaluations, denies in effect that meanings are strictly situational.   Rather, it assumes that norms guide or shape, but do not entirely determine, the forms that interactions can take.

Code-switchers must not only have a range of linguistic alternatives available to them in order to communicate functional meanings effectively; they must also be able to project correctly the interpretation that their choice of code will receive.   Thus, if a person's intent in switching from code A to code B is to demonstrate superior education or refinement, then he or she must assume that members of the reference group define code B as the idiom of the cultivated.   If the speaker projects this on the basis of idiosyncratic or mistaken beliefs - and members of the reference group actually define code B as the idiom of social climbers and pretenders - then a switch from code A to code B could have negative consequences.   Conceptualising code-switching in this way highlights the fact that language choice can be manipulated to establish the tenor and direction of particular interactions; it also recognises that the communicative effect of language choice is constrained by social convention.

This model is very similar to those the philosophers Grice (1957, 1968, 1969) and Searle (1969, 1979) propose to characterise linguistic meanings.   For both Grice and Searle linguistic forms are subject to two kinds of interpretation: one produces conventional readings - the so-called "semantic meanings" that forms have in neutral or abstract contexts; the other produces "situational" or "pragmatic" interpretations - the idiosyncratic interpretations linguistic forms have when contextualised.   We follow Searle in arguing that conventional meanings limit or constrain the situational interpretation of linguistic forms just as we follow Scotton in proposing that social conventions inform and delimit the production and interpretation of other social behaviours.

As is the case with other social norms, the rules generating linguistic behaviours are neither inviolable nor static.   They are created in the process of social exchange, and hence change in response to actual experiences with different reference groups.   And, interestingly enough, violating linguistic rules leads to many of the same kinds of judgements as does transgressing other norms, i.e. norm-breakers may be deemed creative, original, playful, forgetful, drunk, incompetent, etc. depending on how the audience construes the situation.

We want to discuss interplays of social and linguistic norms in code-switching behaviour, basing our views on six-months' participant observation in a small multilingual speech community of friends and co-workers.   We will try to make the case that a code-switcher's assessment of the formal grammatical competence of his or her audience bears on the switcher's choice of codes and on his or her subsequent interpretations of the interlocutor's response.   We will argue that code-switching itself can restructure the developing competence of incipient bilinguals and consequently affect other speakers' assessments of these individuals' progress. Reassessments of competence in turn generate new expectations about how much an incipient bilingual can produce and understand, resulting in new linguistic and social responses to them.

Our study revealed that, depending on the particular constellation of individuals present at a given time, members of our speech community produced the whole spectrum of multi-lingual speech possibilities, from isolated borrowings, to code-mixes and code-switches, to true pidginizations. On the other hand, observation of this group also showed that our friends' multilingual speech obeyed structural or grammatical principles and was in no sense a case of "anything goes" on a formal level.

We would like to clarify what we mean by competence, a term responsible for much debate and misunderstanding in the social and behavioural sciences. Competence, as we see it, is an abstraction from performance (Miller 1975). It is a set of principles organising and accounting for behaviour, this set derived on the basis of social interaction. Linguistic competence guides speech but, at the same time, is structured and restructured by it. Linguistic competence can be relatively stable and well-established or relatively unstable and partial, depending on the quality and frequency of a person's social exchange with speakers of a particular code. Competence is what allows a speaker of a language, no matter how fluent or inarticulate that person may be, to produce a potentially infinite number of utterances in that language. It allows native speakers to recognise "normal" word order and violations thereof, as well as synonymy, constituency and ambiguity; and it allows the partially fluent to produce more or less successful approximations of what the fluent speaker produces.

In our speech community, individual competence in particular languages was distributed very unevenly. Every member spoke some French and some English, the degrees of fluency ranging from that of beginner to that of native speaker. In addition to English and French, Bambara, Wolof, Spanish, Arabic and Tamachaq were recorded – again with varying levels of fluency represented.

In examining the ways that particular individuals employed particular codes, we found that every speaker at some time produced utterances in a language in which he or she had no competence – that is, in a language he or she could not be said to know. These zero-competence exchanges were inevitably examples of "supportive rituals", or "phatic communications". They were, in descending order of frequency: greetings and leave-takings, indications of assent or disagreement, blessings and curses, responses to one's name, exclamations of surprise, delight or distress, and, finally, condolences. Such interchanges were pure tokens of social solidarity.

Assessments of group members' fluency within the group were remarkably uniform. Group members' judgements of each other's capacities to speak and understand specific languages agreed, and these group assessments agreed with self-assessments as well. Significantly, these judgements did not seem to depend strictly on a group member's ability to produce a particular language; rather, evidence that he or she could comprehend a code was commonly taken into account. We recorded a number of conversations where French speakers spoke French to English speakers and received English replies, which only makes sense if the French speakers can assume that the English speakers comprehend French and vice versa. Everybody involved in these kinds of conversations reported feeling very comfortable with them, i.e. they enjoyed being able to speak a language in which they were fluent, without requiring anyone else to operate in a language in which he or she would have less facility. Such conversations, then, seemed to be viewed as additional indices of group solidarity, cooperation and mutual respect. Furthermore, they demonstrated that, whether or not our group members could articulate a distinction between production and comprehension, all of them tacitly recognised one.

It is difficult to assess the effect such conversations have on people's abilities to produce alien languages, but they do seem to contribute to people's abilities to understand them. On the other hand, speaking a language in which one has little fluency can lead to dramatic reorganisations of skills.   Two members (L and B) of the group were paradigm cases of the effect of performance on competence. Neither L nor B initially had very firm grasps on the structural principles allowing production of each other's languages, although B had passive competence in L's second language, French.   The two characteristically spoke French at first, their only common language, although this meant a considerable sacrifice in expressive power for B.   Since L was attempting to learn B's language, English, they agreed to speak to each other only in the language in which each was most incompetent so that each could practise that code.   The result of this pact was pidgin conversations, in which each participant had to infer from extremely degenerate data what the other was trying to say, then had to formulate what he or she hoped was an appropriate response in an imperfectly controlled idiom.   Since both of them were projecting and inferring grammatical structures, each relied on lexical items to carry their meaning and each produced sentences bearing more structural resemblance to languages they controlled than to the languages they were trying to produce, e.g. "Yesterday I am gone to marché with Sagiko".   The logic of these conversations is exactly that logic underlying the production of pidgins (Bickerton, 1973, 1978).

Part of L and B's pact was an agreement to help the other learn to generate normal or correct forms in his or her target language.   We thus have numerous examples of social interactions that led to restructurings of individual's formal linguistic competence, including simple, but not uninteresting cases of speaker's aiding each other in vocabulary retrieval (e.g. B: "J'ai un photo de Mamadou avec un ... uh ... comment dit-on 'knife'?"   L: "couteau"), as well as more intricate corrections of irregular verb forms, prepositions, auxiliaries and other function words.   What was significant about these error corrections was how often they were effective in altering faulty production.

More interesting socially, however, is the fact that not just L and B, but all audiences corrected faulty sentences productions in the direction of more standard forms only when the speaker was by consensus defined as a language learner.   The group developed a strong etiquette dictating that one should not correct the errors of individuals who present themselves as fluent or semi-fluent speakers.

This meant that all the real incompetents improved their skills in particular codes over time, and this in turn meant that the kind of pidgin exchanges appearing early in the study eventually disappeared.   As the incipient bilinguals assimilated the norms for producing expected and appropriate linguistic behaviour, they progressed into phases where they generated mixed-code utterances that showed some appreciation of grammatical structure.

The notion that structure constrains production is crucial here.   When speakers had little competence in particular languages, i.e. when they were merely guessing at the form of the grammatical rule they were trying to obey, they could, and did, do great violence to grammar.   Auxiliary verbs, tense and aspect markers, verb plus particle constructions, and prepositions and post-positions were particular vulnerable structural points.

Speakers competent in both French and Bambara were not able to switch codes at certain structural points, but incipient bilinguals were.   Particular structural categories seemed to entail commitments to continuing in one code until the governing category in question was structurally complete.   For example, in Bambara, an SOV language where auxiliaries separate subjects from objects, fluent bilingual speakers rejected the possibility of switches after choosing Bambara auxiliaries. On the other hand, an incipient bilingual actually did produce such sentences, much to the consternation of all Bambara speakers who heard it.

Since Bambara is a language with postpositions rather than prepositions, a speaker must either switch out of Bambara to produce a prepositional phrase or, having selected a Bambara noun first, stay in Bambara, i.e. the speaker cannot attach Bambara postpositions to unassimilated French noun phrases, or attach French prepositions to Bambara nouns, at least not without doing violence to both languages. Thus fluent speakers would accept the first of the following examples, but reject the second and third as impossible combinations. Yet it is just this kind of sentence incipient speakers of Bambara are capable of making up.

> "Il est tombé (sesi nin kan)"$_{Bambara}$
> he has fallen (chair this onto)
> <u>He fell on the chair</u>

> "Il est tombé sur (sesi)"$_{Bambara}$
> <u>He fell on the chair</u>

> "A binna (cette chaise)$_{French}$ (kan)"$_{Bambara}$
> <u>He fell on the chair</u>

Learning a language is nothing if it is not learning how words fit together, which includes learning the syntactic entailments of function words like articles, demonstratives, prepositions, auxiliaries and complementizers. Since function words are generally the last grammatical categories a speaker acquires in gaining linguistic competence, incipient bilinguals perform code-switching manoeuvres at points where fluent speakers do not, and feel they <u>can</u> not. The more fluent one is, the more salient and the less permeable grammatical structure becomes. This is not a paradoxical statement: one can only observe boundaries if one knows where to look for them.

We would like to offer here the notion of <u>radical grammars</u>, extensions of restructurings of, or approximations of what most competent speakers would consider the normal or "official grammatical rules" (i.e. ways of saying things) in their language. Radical grammars, whether they are intentional or unintentional creations, are products of social-linguistic exchanges in particular kinds of speech communities, or in particular kinds of social situations. Diverse motivations produce such grammars: they can represent speaker's attempts to follow linguistic principles which they believe people around them are following (Collett, 1977), leading to pidgins, creole continua, code-switches; they can represent fluent speakers' attempts to involve semi-fluent or inarticulate interactants in social exchange, producing the kind of speech used to foreigners, people in shock, babies and small children, and animals; they can represent deliberate attempts to produce abnormal linguistic structures so that a particular category of interactors is excluded from the interaction, as is the case with secret language, code-switching, glossolalia and related phenomena. In all these instances speakers seem to be acknowledging - either by observance or violation - what Grice (1975) calls "the cooperative principle", the assumption that, other things being equal, social actors with whom one is involved collaborate to carry out the requirements of the interaction at hand.

SUMMARY AND CONCLUSIONS

In the interests of brevity, we list our conclusions in summary form:

1) The whole range of multi-lingual speech phenomena from borrowings, through pidginization and code-mixing, all the way to sophisticated metaphorical code-switching can be scaled according to the competence of the speakers in the various languages in contact. Grammatical competence is a set of norms that

allows speakers to produce and interpret formal linguistic objects.   Like
other kinds of hypotheses about how things ought to be done or what things
mean, grammars are individual projects or constructions of social realities.

2) Social competence, linguistic and otherwise, grows out of social interaction
   and, at the same time, structures it.   Another way of saying this is to state
   that competence is an abstraction from performance, or that pattern (structure)
   stands in relation to behaviour as both its potential cause and unintended
   consequence (Giddens, 1976;   Moore, 1975).

3) Studying small group multi-lingualism diachronically, especially where speakers
   have unequal competences, can contribute greatly to our understanding of
   language use, including language learning situations, as both social and individual phenomena.

4) Viewing linguistic competence as a particular kind of social norm accounts
   effectively for both linguistic structure and for variation, since this model
   automatically incorporates indeterminacies at crucial points.   Speakers impute inferential structures to their audiences and audiences impute intentions
   to speakers – but in no case do these imputations actually determine behaviour.
   Individual behavioural variations are to be expected as social actors assess
   and weigh their options for action within and across reference groups.

What we are talking about here, in sum, are linguistic and non-linguistic evaluations informing socio-linguistic decisions.   We have discussed them as components
of a model which is only roughly predictive, but which nevertheless accounts for
regularity and change in both language and social behaviour in adequate and
interesting ways.

REFERENCES

Bickerton, D. The nature of a creole continuum. Language, 1973, 49.3, 640-669
Bickerton, D. Pidginization and creolization: language acquisition and language
     universals, in A. Valdman (Ed.) Pidgin and creole linguistics. Bloomington,
     Indiana: Indiana University Press, 1977
Collett, P. The rules of conduct, in P. Collett (Ed.) Social rules and social
     behavior. Totowa, New Jersey: Rowman and Littlefield, 1977
Giddens, A. New rules of sociological method. London: Hutchison and Co.Ltd.,1976
Grice, H. P. Meaning. Philosophical Review, 1957, 66, 377-388
Grice, H. P. Utterer's meaning, sentence meaning and word-meaning. Foundations
     of Language, 1969, 4, 225-242
Grice, H. P. Logic and conversation, in P. Cole and J. L. Morgan (Eds.) Syntax
     and semantics III: speech acts. New York: Academic Press, 1975
Miller, G. A. Some comments on competence and performance, in D. Aaronson and R.
     W. Reiber (Eds.) Developmental psycholinguistics and communication disorders.
     New York: Annals of the New York Academy of Sciences, 1975, 263, 201-204
Moore, S. F. Uncertainties in situations, indeterminacies in culture, in S. F.
     Moore and B. G. Myerhoff (Eds.) Symbol and politics in communal ideology.
     Ithaca: Cornell, 1975
Parkin, D. (a) Nairobi: problems and methods
           (b) Language shift and ethnicity of Nairobi: the speech community of
               Kaloleni
           (c) Language switching in Nairobi
     in W. H. Whiteley (Ed.) Language in Kenya. Nairobi: Oxford University Press,
     1974
Scotton, C. M. and Ury, W. Bilingual strategies: the social functions of code-
     switching. International Journal of the Sociology of Language, 1975, 13,5-20
Searle, J. Speech acts. Cambridge: Cambridge University Press, 1969
Searle, J. Ten lectures on the theory of speech acts. Indiana University, 1979

Evaluative Reactions to Code Switching
Strategies in Montreal[1]

R. Y. Bourhis*[2] and F. Genesee**[3]

*Department of Psychology, McMaster University, 1280 Main Street, West, Hamilton,
Ontario, Canada
**Department of Psychology, McGill University, 1205 Ave.
Dr. Penfield, Montreal, Quebec, Canada

ABSTRACT

This study is one of a series designed to explore the language switching strategies French Canadians (FCs) and English Canadians (ECs) most commonly use in various types of cross-cultural encounters in Montreal. In the current study FCs, ECs and EC French immersion students gave their reactions to a simulated dialogue between a French speaking salesman and an English speaking customer. The language used by each speaker (French or English) was varied in different experimental conditions. It was predicted that evaluative reactions towards these various language switching strategies could reflect combinations of the following (1) the willingness of FCs and ECs to accommodate each other's linguistic needs; (2) the influence of situational norms which suggest that 'the client is always right' and should be served in the language of his choice; and (3) emerging socio-cultural norms which favour French as the only language of communication in Quebec including client/clerk encounters. Results indicated that use of English by the salesman and the customer was accepted and perceived favourably by both anglophone and francophone listeners. Use of French by the salesman was not viewed favourably by either anglophone or francophone listeners. Thus language usage patterns in this setting were evaluated by the listeners mainly in terms of situational norms favouring the use of English despite emerging socio-cultural norms which favour French language usage in Quebec. Moreover, EC immersion students appeared less tolerant towards the use of French in this setting than even the unilingual EC students. The results are discussed in terms of interpersonal speech accommodation and the salience of situational and socio-cultural norms in determining appropriate language behaviour in the Quebec intergroup context.

---

1. This research was supported in part by a McGill University Graduate Faculty Research Grant and by a research grant to the Instructional Services Department of the Protestant School Board of Greater Montreal from le Ministère de l'Education, Gouvernement du Québec.

2. The first author is conducting a research project on Code Switching in Montreal which includes a sociolinguistic survey and a series of field studies conducted in various settings in the Montreal Metropolitan area.

3. Reprints may be obtained from the authors.

Key Words

Convergence;   divergence;   speech maintenance;   speech strategies;   speech accommodation;   situational norms;   emerging socio-cultural norms.

In multilingual communities language switching often occurs in conversations between members of different ethnolinguistic groups.   The social and motivational bases of code switching strategies have been discussed in recent papers by Bourhis (1979), Giles, Bourhis and Taylor (1977) and Scotton and Ury (1977).   These authors have pointed out that not all language switches can be explained simply in terms of social norms dictating appropriate language behaviour in particular situations.   For instance, Giles, Taylor and Bourhis (1973) developed a model of speech accommodation which seeks to explain the motivations underlying changes in people's speech styles during interpersonal verbal communication.   According to this approach, speakers can enhance mutual liking by making their speech style (accent, speech rate, etc.) similar to that of their interlocutor: a strategy known as speech convergence (Giles and Powesland 1975).   The social psychological significance of this speech strategy has been illustrated in cross cultural encounters in Québec by Giles, Taylor and Bourhis (1973).   In this study it was found that bilingual English Canadian (EC) students perceived French Canadian (FC) bilinguals more favourably when the latter communicated in English than when they used French.   Moreover, the EC students were more likely to communicate in French with their FC interlocutor if the latter had previously converged to English than if he had maintained his communication only in French.

However not all encounters favour language convergence.   A speaker may choose to dissociate himself from his interlocutor by deliberately maintaining or using a speech style that differs from that of his interlocutor.   These linguistic strategies are known as speech maintenance and speech divergence and may be used by speakers because they personally dislike their interlocutor or because they wish to assert their group identity (Bourhis and Giles, 1977).   A study in Belgium by Bourhis, Giles, Leyens and Tajfel (1979) has shown that language divergence can be used to assert group identity in threatening encounters with outgroup interlocutors. In this study trilingual Flemish students in response to the perception of ethnic threat from an outgroup French speaking Bruxellois, diverged by switching from English, a previously agreed upon neutral language, to their native language, Flemish.

So far, the social psychological significance of using different speech strategies has been examined mainly in settings which lacked clear situational and socio-cultural norms which could interact with the process of speech accommodation (e.g. Bourhis, Giles and Lambert, 1975).   In addition, few studies have investigated interpersonal speech accommodation during verbal exchanges of more than two speech acts.   The purpose of the current study was to extend research in bilingual communication by examining listeners' reactions to different patterns of language usage during extended verbal exchanges as a function of the following: (1) the process of speech accommodation, (2) the social roles of the interlocutors portrayed in a specific situation and (3) the socio-cultural status of the two languages used by the interlocutors.   In order to examine the relationship between these variables, listeners were presented with a simulated dialogue between a FC salesman and an EC customer, each using various combinations of French and English in a Montreal store.

In Montreal, client/clerk encounters may be particularly salient since they constitute one of the few settings where there is frequent cross-cultural contact between English and French speaking Quebecans.   In addition to frequently being the actors in such settings, FCs and ECs may often be witnesses of client/clerk encounters as bystanders in Montreal stores.

Traditionally, in the Montreal context, the English language has dominated the French language in prestige value and as the language of economic activity (Joy, 1972). In a client/clerk situation such as that depicted in the present study the above historical trends would favour the use of English rather than French (Taylor, Simard and Papineau, 1978). In addition, existing situational norms which imply that the 'customer is always right' suggest that the FC salesman in the scenario would be perceived more favourably if he converged by using English with the customer than if he maintained French. Conversely, emerging socio-cultural norms, as reflected in the passage of Bill 101 which favours the use of French as the only official language of communication in Québec, suggests that the EC customer should accommodate to the FC salesman and use French: to not do so could result in relatively unfavourable impressions of the customer. Arguably enough, Bill 101 may be perceived as a manifestation of an emerging socio-cultural norm since numerous 'Québecois' FCs elected the 'Parti Québécois' with the mandate of enshrining French as the only official language of Québec. Indeed Bill 1 later amended as Bill 101 was the first legislation adopted by the 'Parti Québécois' government after its election in 1976.

The perceived salience of the above situational and socio-cultural norms may also vary depending on the ethnicity and linguistic skills of the listener subjects. Three groups served as subjects in this study: unilingual francophones, unilingual anglophones and bilingual anglophones who learned French in immersion classes. Most simply, for reasons of loyalty to one's ingroup language, francophones were expected to favour the use of French in the scenarios, while unilingual anglophones were expected to favour the use of English. On the basis of previous research with immersion students (Genesee, 1979), the linguistic preferences of anglophone bilinguals were expected to fall midway between those of francophone and anglophone unilinguals.

METHOD

Subjects

Three groups of 17 year old students matched for middle class status and sex were recruited, all were in their final year of secondary school in Québec.[4] (A) The French Canadian (FC) group was made up of 144 francophone students attending French-language high school who had studied English as a second language since grade 5. (B) The English Canadian (EC) group was made up of 85 anglophone students attending English-language high school who had received instruction in French as a second language since primary school. (C) The EC Immersion (Imm) group was comprised of 94 anglophones attending English language high school. However, these students had been in a one year French immersion programme during grade 7 and had subsequently taken a number of special French courses in grades 8 to 11 (for a description of this immersion programme see Genesee, Polich and Stanley, 1977).

Information collected in response to a questionnaire shows that the FC sample was quite homogeneous and 'pure' with respect to their cultural and linguistic background, whereas the EC and Imm samples were more heterogeneous from a linguistic and cultural point of view. In addition, whereas 91% of the anglophone students identified themselves as either Canadian or English Canadian, only 41% of the francophone students identified themselves as Canadians or French Canadians. The majority of the FC students (59%) preferred to identify themselves using the label 'Québécois'.

---

4. We would like to express our thanks to all the teachers and students who made this research possible.

Procedure

The subjects were tested in groups during their regular class hours and were told they would hear a pre-recorded 'conversation' between a French speaking salesman and an English-speaking customer in a small toy store in Montreal.   A bilingual FC played the role of the salesman and a bilingual EC played the role of the customer.[5]   The dialogue consisted of three speech acts in the order FC salesman – EC customer – FC salesman.   Four different content controlled dialogues were recorded varying in terms of the language of response of the customer (English or French) and of the salesman (French or English).   The salesman was always recognisable as a French-speaking Canadian since his initial speech act was always in French and since he had a noticeable French accent when he spoke in English. The customer was always recognisable as an English-speaking Canadian because of his noticeable English accent when speaking French.

The students heard each speech act twice, the first time they simply listened and the second time they answered questions pertinent to that section of the tape. Each student heard one stimulus condition only.   Subjects indicated their reactions to each speaker and each speech act using 9-centimetre straight line rating scales.   They indicated their impressions of the salesman after his first speech act on 7 evaluative scales including friendly, kind, competent, nationalistic, intelligent, considerate and honest.   Subjects also rated how anxious the salesman was to make a sale, how likely they themselves would be to buy something from the salesman and how much they would like to be served by him.

In addition to rating their impressions of the customer on the same evaluative scales as those used for the salesman, subjects also indicated how tense, comfortable and confident they thought the customer felt in the situation and how much they thought the customer liked and respected the salesman.

After hearing Speech Act 3, subjects rated the salesman using the same scales as before.   Finally Ss rated how pleased, insulted, comfortable and annoyed they thought the customer was after the salesman's French or English response.

RESULTS AND DISCUSSION

Ratings on each scale were analysed separately using analysis of variance procedures.   The main variables were subjects' language GROUP (FC, EC, Imm), language used by the CUSTOMER (English, French), and language used by the SALESMAN during Act 3 (English, French).   As well, TIME (Act 1, Act 3) was included as a variable in the analyses of Act 3.   Newman-Keuls Tests of Multiple Comparisons were performed to isolate significant main effects and interactions revealed by the analysis of variance.   Only major findings will be discussed in this paper.

As can be seen in Table 1 statistically significant findings for ratings of the salesman after Act 1 emerged as GROUP main effects on 4 of the 10 rating scales; these were friendly, considerate, honest and would like to be served by this salesman.   In all cases except 'considerate', the Imm students rated the FC salesman significantly lower than did the FC students.   These results show that the FC students tended to view the French speaking salesman somewhat more favourably than did the Imm and EC students.

---

5. We also thank Marc Berval and Brian Doan for their excellent voice recordings.

TABLE 1   Scales with mean ratings showing group effects in
evaluating the FC salesman after Speech Act 1.

| TRAITS | GROUPS | | | F-ratio | df |
	FC	EC	IMM.		
Kind	7.03	6.58	6.17	10.49***	2,309
Considerate	6.77	6.12	5.89	11.35***	2,309
Honest	5.91	5.80	5.36	4.45**	2,309
Like to be served by	4.76	4.82	4.24	4.53**	2,309

**p < .01;   ***p < .001

Statistically significant findings for the students' ratings of the EC customer
emerged on most traits.   Significant GROUP main effects appear in Table 2 and
show that EC and Imm students rated the EC customer to be more considerate,
friendly, competent and honest than did the FC students.   Imm.students also rated
the EC customer to be more nationalistic than did the FC students, while EC students rated the customer to be kinder than did the FC students.   Interestingly
enough the FC students felt that the EC customer liked and respected the FC salesman significantly more than did the EC and Imm.students.

These results show that whereas the FC salesman tended to be preferred by the FC
students, the EC customer was favoured by the anglophone students.   Thus, both
linguistic groups displayed patterns of ingroup favouritism when evaluating representative speakers of their own group.   These results contrast with previous findings using the matched guise technique which showed that FCs denigrated members of
their own group relative to outgroup EC speakers (Lambert, 1970).

Essentially, for the three subject groups, the EC customer was seen to be as
friendly, considerate, kind, honest, competent and intelligent whether he used
English or French with the FC salesman.   Thus the EC customer was not viewed more
favourably when he converged to French than when he maintained English.   Indeed
the three subject groups rated the EC customer to be more nationalistic, confident,
comfortable and tense when he maintained English than when he converged to French.
These results suggest that despite recent changes in language policies in favour of
French in Québec, use of English may still be viewed as acceptable, especially for
speakers occupying the role of customers in commercial establishments.

Two questions arise as a consequence of the salesman's reply in Speech Act 3.
1) How will the salesman be perceived depending on whether he maintains his use of
French or converges to English to accommodate the EC customer?   2) Will the perceptions of the salesman's use of French or English depend on the customer's previous language choice?   Students' ratings of the salesman as a function of whether
he maintained French from Act 1 to Act 3 or converged to English in Act 3 are represented graphically in Figure 1.   Five of the eight interactions were statistically
significant.   Newman-Keuls analyses of these results indicate that the EC and Imm
students rated the FC salesman less considerate, less friendly, less kind, less

TABLE 2   Scales with mean ratings showing group effects in
          evaluating the EC customer after Speech Act 2.

TRAITS	GROUPS			F-ratio	df
	FC	EC	IMM.		
Considerate	5.99	7.13	7.00	13.55***	2,309
Friendly	7.02	7.34	7.12	14.09***	2,309
Competent	4.72	6.25	5.62	15.07***	2,309
Nationalistic	4.53	4.96	5.31	5.53**	2,309
Kind	6.56	7.06	6.95	3.04*	2,309
Honest	6.32	7.31	7.37	10.39***	2,309
Tense	4.44	3.76	4.01	4.06**	2,309
Comfortable	4.50	3.89	4.13	3.67*	2,309
Customer likes Salesman	5.62	4.70	4.60	12.56***	2,309
Customer respects Salesman	6.60	5.02	5.39	7.15***	2,309

**p < .05;   **p < .01;   ***p < .001

competent, and less intelligent when he maintained French in Act 3 than after initially hearing him in French during Act 1.   Even the FC students rated the FC
salesman less considerate, kind and competent when he maintained French with the
EC customer.

All three groups of students agreed that the salesman appeared more nationalistic
but less honest and less anxious to make a sale when he maintained French than
when he switched to English.   Thus, the salesman's decision to maintain French
seems to have cost him significantly in terms of other's impressions of him;   this
was particularly true in the case of the Imm. students, to a lesser extent in the
case of the EC students and to a much less extent in the case of the FC students.

At the same time, the salesman who switched to English was rated pretty much the
same by all three groups after making the switch in Act 3 as he was when he spoke
French in Act 1, although he was seen to be more considerate and intelligent by
the EC and Imm. students when he used English.   In general then, the salesman
gained relatively little by switching to English.   Thus, it seems that the salesman's use of English was interpreted as compliance with the situational norm and

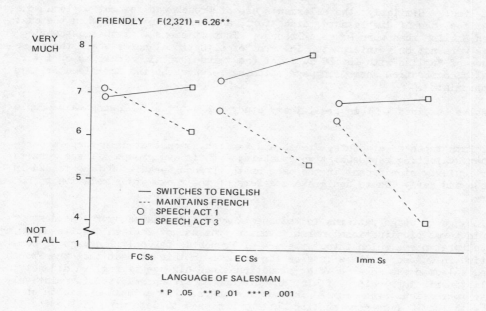

Fig. 1   Students' impressions of the FC salesman after Act 1
          and after Act 3.   Similar patterns of results emerged
          for the following traits: Kind: F = 4.64**;
          competent: F = 5.30**; intelligent: F = 13.19***;
          and considerate: F = 16.03***.

was not appreciated as language accommodation towards the EC customer.

With respect to the second question, it appears that the students' reactions to the
salesman's use of English or French in Act 3 did not depend upon whether the customer himself had previously used French or English.   This result provides additional evidence that the students were responding to the interaction in terms of situational norms rather in terms of speech accommodation.   According to speech
accommodation, one may have expected more favourable impressions of the FC salesman in those conditions when the language he used matched that used by the customer, but this pattern of results did not emerge.

Significant interaction effects emerged on student ratings of how the customer felt
in reaction to the salesman's response after Act 3 on four traits including how
pleased (F = 5.97; df= 1,314; p < .05), comfortable (F = 8.56; p < .01), insulted (F = 28.93; p < .001) and annoyed (F = 12.14, p < .001) the customer felt.

Newman–Keuls analyses of these interactions revealed the following results.   For
the 3 subject groups the salesman's use of English was thought to result in generally positive feelings in the customer regardless of which language he had previously used; conversely, the use of French by the salesman was thought to arouse less
positive feelings in the customer.   In addition, the students thought that the customer who had previously used French would be just as pleased and comfortable as
the customer who had used English if the salesman responded in English.   Nevertheless, the salesman's use of English was thought to lead to stronger feelings of
annoyance and insult when the customer had previously used French than when he had

used English.   Similarly, the salesman's use of French was thought to lead to stronger feelings of displeasure, discomfort, annoyance and insult when the customer used English than when he used French.   Thus it seems that the customer's feelings were not only interpreted in terms of situational norms where the salesman's use of English with the EC customer was valued but also in terms of interpersonal accommodation where language matching between the two interlocutors was also appreciated.

The results obtained in this preliminary study suggest the following main conclusions.

   1. Both types of students, French and English demonstrated ingroup favouritism when evaluating representative speakers of their own group.   These results are particularly significant in the case of the French Canadian Ss who tended in the 1960s and early 70s to denigrate speakers of their own group relative to EC speakers.

   2. Language usage patterns in this setting were evaluated by the students mainly in terms of situational norms favouring the use of English despite emerging socio-cultural norms which favour the use of French as the only language of communication in Québec.   It is interesting to note in this respect that the French speaking salesman was in a NO-WIN situation since his use of English did not improve listener's impressions of him, and his use of French resulted in relatively negative impressions even from FC ingroup listeners.   Nevertheless results obtained with the FC listeners must be further analysed to determine if FCs identifying as "Québécois" could be more favourably disposed towards French language usage in this setting than FCs identifying as "Canadians" or "French Canadians".

   3. There were important differences in the value that the three groups of students attached to the speakers' language switching strategies.   For example, results obtained with the Imm. students suggest that competence in French as a second language does not necessarily precipitate the adoption of favourable attitudes towards French language usage in Québec or even towards members of the French language group.   Instead, Imm. students appeared less tolerant towards the use of French in this setting than even the unilingual EC students.   An ongoing study in which the clerk is an EC and the customer is a FC will determine if Imm. and EC students still favour English in a situation where French language usage is the prerogative of the FC client.

   4. Finally, this experimental paradigm provides a useful and sensitive technique for studying the role played by situational, cultural and social psychological variables in the dynamics of interpersonal and cross-cultural communication. In addition, this technique appears quite useful as a subtle tool for studying the psychological and sociolinguistic impact of controversial language planning programmes in various intergroup contexts.

REFERENCES

Bourhis, R. Y. Language in ethnic interaction: s social psychological approach, in H. Giles and B. Saint-Jacques (Eds.) Language and Ethnic Relations Oxford: Pergamon Press, 1979
Bourhis, R. Y. and Giles, H.   The language of intergroup distinctiveness,   in H. Giles (Ed.) Language, ethnicity and intergroup relations.   London: Academic Press, 1977
Bourhis, R. Y., Giles, H. and Lambert, W. E.   Social consequences of accommodating one's style of speech: a cross-national investigation. International Journal of the Sociology of Language, 1975, 6, 53-71
Bourhis, R. Y., Giles, H., Leyens, J. P. and Tajfel, H.   Psycholinguistic distinctiveness: language divergence in Belgium, in H. Giles and R. St. Clair (Eds.)

Language and social psychology. Oxford: Blackwell, 1979

Genesee, F. Les programmes d'immersion en français du bureau des Ecoles Protestantes du Grand Montréal. Etudes et documents, (S.R.E.P.). Ministère de l'Education, Gouvernement du Québec, Québec, 1979

Genesee, F., Polich, E. and Stanley, M.H. An experimental French immersion program at the secondary school level: 1969-1974. The Canadian Modern Language Review, 1977, 33, 318-332

Giles, H. and Powesland, P. F. Speech style and social evaluation. London: Academic Press, 1975

Giles, H., Bourhis, R. Y. and Taylor, D. M. Towards a theory of language in ethnic group relations, in H. Giles (Ed.) Language, ethnicity and intergroup relations. London: Academic Press, 1977

Giles, H., Taylor, D. M. and Bourhis, R. Y. Towards a theory of interpersonal accommodation through language: some Canadian data. Language in Society, 1973, 2, 177-192

Joy, R. J. Languages in conflict. Toronto: McClelland and Stewart, 1972

Lambert, W. E. What are they like, these Canadians? A social psychological analysis. The Canadian Psychologist, 1970, 11, 303-333

Scotton, C. M. and Ury, W. Bilingual strategies: the social function of code-switching. International Journal of the Sociology of Language, 1977, 13, 5-20

Taylor, D. M., Simard, L. M. and Papineau, D. Perceptions of cultural differences and language use: a field study in a bilingual environment. Canadian Journal of Behavioural Science, 1978, 10, 181-191

The Relation Between Accommodation and Code Switching in a Multilingual Society: Singapore[1]

J. Platt

Department of Linguistics, Monash University, Clayton, Victoria 3168, Australia

ABSTRACT

It appears that in multilingual societies, code switching in the two most private domains, the family domain and the friendship domain, is quite strongly linked to accommodation, particularly in transitional situations where either one or more participants leave the conversation or join it.   The relationship of accommodation to pure topic related code switching can be assessed to some degree numerically by self-report of those using more than one code in any one of the domains or their sub-domains.

In mixed domains, e.g. family <u>and</u> friends, particularly where there is a considerable difference in the verbal repertoires of the participants, strategies are at times employed to resolve the conflict arising from differing needs for accommodation.   These strategies are often signalled by code switching, either spontaneous or requested.   The type of strategy may differ according to the situation and its success may often depend on achieving, at least temporarily, a state approaching a quasi-similarity condition in verbal repertoires.

<u>Key words</u>

Accommodation-related code switching;   conflicting accommodation needs;   family domain;   friendship domain;   multilingual verbal repertoires;   topic-related code switching;   transitional situations.

In multilingual-polyglossic societies complex systems of code selection operate (Platt 1977a, 1977b) based not only on the speaker's own verbal repertoire but also on the addressee's known or expected verbal repertoire.   Another important factor is the degree of accommodation which the speaker is willing to make.   Giles and Powesland (1975) suggest that "accommodation through speech can be regarded as an attempt on the part of the speaker to modify or disguise his persona in order to make it more acceptable to the person addressed" and that "in addition, speech

---

1. The research in Singapore was supported by Australian Research Grants Committee grants A68/16801 and A77/15355.

accommodation may be a device by the speaker to make himself better understood".
I feel that, in cultural settings such as can be found in parts of Asia, accommodation is also a gesture of courtesy towards the other interlocutor(s) (Platt
1977c).

There have been a number of discussions of and explanations for code switching,
e.g. Blom and Gumperz (1972), Clyne (1972), Ervin-Tripp (1971), Fishman (1972),
Scotton and Ury (1977).   Often investigations have centred around more public
domains, e.g. shopping, public transport.   The questions to be raised in this
paper are: what types of code switching occur in the more private domains, e.g.
family, friendship and what are the characteristics of code switching when several
codes are accepted as appropriate for any one domain, depending on the multilingual repertoires of the participants?

My hypothesis is that in such situations code switching can be: (a) topic related,
(b) accommodation related, or (c) a mixture of the two.

Code switching of Type (a) occurs if one of the participants cannot adequately
discuss a topic in Code X and he switches to Code Y in which he possesses a more
suitable lexical range.   Type (b) occurs if accommodation (convergent or divergent) is involved.   This may be accommodation either to some active participant(s)
or silent participant(s).   Type (c) occurs if a speaker switches from Code X to
Code Y because, although he himself can discuss Topic 2 in Code X, he knows that
his addressee cannot, or not as well as in Code Y.

Besides distinguishing between these three main reasons for code switching, it is
also necessary to distinguish between two types of situation:

(1) Static situations, in which the participants remain constant.
(2) Transitional situations, in which others join or drop out or when a silent par-
    ticipant becomes an active participant.

It may be argued that "silent participants" are not participants at all.   I would
disagree.   Firstly, as far as language ability is concerned, a person may be able
to decode a speech variety to some extent but be unable to encode it and secondly,
probably a more important consideration, the silent participant may considerably
affect the behaviour of the active participants in a speech situation.

In order to facilitate a better understanding of the empirical data to be presented in support of my hypothesis, it is necessary to give a very brief sketch of
the multilingual-polyglossic network of Singapore. The 1976 population figure
for Singapore was 2,249,000, consisting of 76.1% Chinese, 15.1% Malays, 6.9% Indians and 1.9% small minority groups including Eurasians.   However, the ethnic make
up is considerably more complicated than this.   Among the Chinese, there are
three major 'dialect' groups: the Hokkien (approximately 42%), the Teochew
(approximately 22%) and the Cantonese (approximately 17%) and minor groups, e.g.
the Hainanese and Hakka.   Among the Indians, about 67% are Tamil, 12% Malayali
and 8% Punjabis.

Four languages have official status: English, Mandarin, Malay and Tamil.   Over
the last twenty years, primary and secondary education has, in principle, been
available through the medium of any of these four.   When English is not the medium of instruction it is the compulsory second language.   Typical verbal repertoires of Singaporeans are given in Table 1 (adapted from Platt and Weber, in
press).

In structured interviews with 100 Singaporeans of different ethnic, educational
and socio-economic backgrounds, information was elicited as to code selection and

TABLE 1   Typical verbal repertoires of Singaporeans

Ethnic Group	usually includes	may include
Chinese	Native Chinese dialect or Baba Malay* (spoken by Peranakan Chinese) Dominant Chinese dialect: Hokkien (if native dialect not Hokkien) Bazaar Malay*	English + Mandarin + Other Chinese dialect(s)
Malay	Colloquial Singapore Malay 'Standard' Malay	English +
Indian	Native Indian language Some Tamil if a Dravidian and own language not Tamil Bazaar Malay*	English +

(adapted from Platt and Weber, in press); * decreasingly so among younger people; + increasingly so among younger people.

code switching in the Family and Friendship domains.   Admittedly, the method of self-report has its obvious disadvantages, but no investigator could, strictly speaking, investigate speech variety use and code switching in any family but his own.   If he entered any other family situations as an investigator or even as a friend, his mere presence could modify the results as this would not be a pure family situation any more and therefore there could be conflicting needs of accommodation, as will be shown later.   Of the 100 interviewees, 71 claimed to use two or more codes in the Family domain and also stated that they practised code switching.

To the question: why would you switch from Code X to Code Y? we were given various reasons, with quite a number of the interviewees giving more than one reason. The overall results of the response analysis for this domain can be seen in Table 2.

TABLE 2   Number of interviewees giving various reasons for code switching in the Family domain

(Total number of speakers: 71)

a	b1	b2	c1	c2	Type of
Topic	Accom. to participant	Accom. to silent participant	Topic + Accom. to participant	Topic + Accom. to silent participant	Situation
58	12	1	32	1	Static
9	62	8	11	2	Transitional

As far as static situations are concerned, the most common reasons for code switching given was a change of topic, e.g.

"I tal(k) Cantonese to my sister when we tal(k) abou(t) clo(the)s a. Then we tal(k) school, maybe éssáy, maybe ma(th)s - then switch to English.

Don('t) know all the word(s) in Cantonese."

But quite often topic was coupled with accommodation to the other participant(s), particularly if they were less fluent in one code than the speaker, e.g.

"Sometime, you know, I converse with my mother in English. She understand(s) English, can speak a little, you know. But if topic too difficul(t) for her to follow in Englihs, I switch to Hokkien."

This strategy is also quite common with siblings. It has been a practice in some Chinese families to give some children a Chinese (Mandarin)-medium education and some an English-medium education. Thus reasons were given such as:

"Sometime I tal(k) English to my brother(s) (Chinese-medium educated). They wan(t) to practise English. But if matters too difficul(t) for thém, you know, politic or some things, I switch to Hokkien."

When asked: "Why don't you speak Mandarin to them?" the answer was:

"Ah canno(t). Sometime they joke. I talk English to thém, they use Chinese to make me mad. My Chinese no(t) very goo(d), y'see."

Here the reason for switching is a deliberate non-accommodation as a joke.

Accommodation was one of the main reasons given for code switching in the wider family domain (i.e. a mixture of several sub-domains), particularly in transitional situations, e.g.

"I tal(k) English to my sister(s) bu(t) when my mother come into the room, we use Hainanese. You see, my mother speak little English, no schooling."

When asked: "Would you switch to Hainanese in the middle of a conversation" the answer was:

"Ya, I think so - usuallý."

As was to be expected, reasons connected with accommodation to a silent participant were not very frequent, but several interviewees were aware of this problem. One stated that sometimes, when talking to his wife, he switched from Hokkien to Mandarin as he had suddenly become aware of the children's presence and he did not want them to hear what was being discussed. His pre-school children knew only Hokkien and some colloquial English.

Of the 100 interviewees 69 claimed to use more than one code in the Friendship domain and of these 55 (i.e. 80%) admitted to using more than one code to any one friend or group of friends. The rest would constantly use one code to one group, e.g. Hokkien to their Chinese friends, another code to another group, e.g. Bazaar Malay to Malays and Indians.

The code combinations are dependent to a large extent on the speaker's own verbal repertoire and on his circle of friends and their repertoires. The combination usually consists of one of the local native Chinese dialects or a local language in its colloquial form and either colloquial Mandarin or colloquial Singapore English.

The reasons given for code switching in the Friendship domain were very similar to those for the Family domain - and so was their distribution. See Table 3.

TABLE 3 Number of interviewees giving various reasons for
code switching in the Friendship domain

(Total number of speakers: 55)

a	b1	b2	c1	c2	Type of Situation
Topic	Accom. to participant	Accom. to silent participant	Topic + Accom. to participant	Topic + Accom. to silent participant	
51	6	-	9	-	Static
2	49	4	3	-	Transitional

The most common reason by far was accommodation to a new participant in the conversation, e.g. when a Chinese-medium educated Chinese joined into a conversation
conducted by English-medium educated Chinese, or if an Indian or Malay joined a
conversation conducted by Chinese-medium educated Chinese.

The reason: Topic + Accommodation was less frequently given than in the Family
domain. This was not surprising. Usually friends share to some extent a common
background and may all be able to discuss Topic A better in Code X and Topic B
better in Code Y. There would be less need for accommodation on account of topic.

It is not possible to discuss here the whole investigation into code switching and
accommodation where there is a fusion of two domains, e.g. friends in the family
circle. I shall concentrate only on one point which appears to me of particular
interest: the conflict in accommodation needs and its relationship to code switching. Within the family domain such conflicts are often resolved by the hierarchy
of fixed role relationships. In a mixed domain such role hierarchies would not
be so easy to establish.

I feel that in such conflicts, attempts are often made to find a solution and that
code switching or the deliberate lack thereof is involved. I also feel that different strategies of resolving the conflict are dependent upon a number of factors:
the number of participants, the role relationships between the participants and to
what extent these relationships would be recognised and acted upon and last but not
least the participants' own multilingual verbal repertoires. I feel that a solution, even if temporary, which would bring varying repertoires into some kind of
"apparent similarity condition" by means of code switching would be a considerable
step towards resolving many conflicts arising out of different accommodation needs
in a multilingual setting.

Structured observations were made in five different Singaporean households in order
to isolate different strategies used for overcoming conflicting accommodation needs.
Details are given in Table 4.

Four different types of strategies were isolated, all related to code switching in
one way or another. Their structure and use can be seen in Table 5.

S1 is an attempt to resolve the conflict by systematic and frequent code switching
with the accommodator functioning as a quasi-interpreter, e.g. in HH1: Host's
mother and sister talk in Punjabi; friend joins; sister (in English) to friend:
we have been speaking about ...; friend (responds to topic in English); sister
(in Punjabi) translates for mother what has been said, etc.

TABLE 4   Five events investigated for code switching

	Event	Particip. Number	Family	Friends*	'Problem' Codes
HH1	dinner	small	Indian (Punjabi) govt.clerk	Eurasian	Punjabi English
HH2	lunch	small	Malay businessman	Chinese	Malay, Teochew English
HH3	afternoon refreshm.	small	Chinese (Hokkien) salesman	Indian	Hokkien, English Mandarin
HH4	21st birthday party	large	Chinese (Hakka) cook	Chinese Eurasian Indian	Hokkien Hakka English
HH5	buffet dinner	large	Peranakan Chinese primary school teacher	Indian Chinese	Baba Malay English Cantonese

*excluding the two observers

TABLE 5   Structure and observed use of four strategies

Strategy Type	Structure	Observed Use				
		HH1	HH2	HH3	HH4	HH5
S1	$P_1(X \longleftrightarrow X)AP(Y \longleftrightarrow Y)P_2$	4	1	2	1	-
S2	$AP_1 \nearrow^{AP_2(X \longleftrightarrow X)P_3}_{(X \longleftarrow \longrightarrow X)}$	2	2	3	1	1
S3	$AP(X \longleftrightarrow X)P_1$ $P_2(Y)$	1	5	3	6	-
S4	$(A)P_1(X_1 \longleftrightarrow X_1)P_{1'}$ $(A)P_2(X_2 \longleftrightarrow X_2)P_{2'}$ $\cdots$ $(A)P_n(X_n \longleftrightarrow X_n)P_{n'}$	1	1	-	3	5

where some Xs may be identical

P = participant(s)   AP = accommodating participant   X,Y = codes
$\longleftrightarrow$ = reciprocal use of a particular code

S2 is an attempt to resolve the conflict by persuading one (or several) of the participants to switch to a code they are less familiar with, in other words, asking them to accommodate to the other participants, e.g. HH1: Host joins group mentioned above and speaks in Punjabi to his mother; mother giggles and looks somewhat embarrassed; host (in English) to friend: I ask my mother to speak to you in English.   She knows some English; mother speaks to friend slowly in halting

English.

In S3, the fact that a conflict exists is ignored (at least temporarily) and accommodation is made only to one participant (or group of participants), disregarding the needs of the others, e.g. in HH2, the wife spoke fast colloquial Malay to accommodate to her mother although one of the Chinese friends could not follow.

S4 is a break up and reformation into small groups according to verbal repertoires of participants.   This can be done spontaneously by all participants or manipulated by a few, e.g. the host or hostess, e.g. in HH5, some of these groups were

family:	grandmother - hostess (Baba Malay);
family:	siblings (Colloquial Singapore English);
mixed:	grandmother - observers (Baba Malay/Malay);
mixed:	daughter-in-law - Cantonese friends (Colloquial Singapore English)

In conclusion, I can summarise briefly

1) that in more private domains of everyday activity, code switching appears to be quite strongly linked to accommodation, particularly in transitional situations, and
2) that in mixed domains, code switching is closely related to the various strategies employed to resolve the conflict arising from different accommodation needs.

REFERENCES

Blom, J-P. and Gumperz, J. J. Social meaning in linguistic structures: code switching in Norway, in J. J. Gumperz and D. Hymes (Eds.) Directions in sociolinguistics. New York: Holt, Rinehart and Winston, 1972
Clyne, M. Perspectives on language contact. Melbourne: The Hawthorn Press, 1972
Ervin-Tripp, S. M. Sociolinguistics, in J. A. Fishman (Ed.) Advances in the sociology of language I. The Hague: Mouton, 1971
Fishman, J. A. The sociology of language. Rowley: Newbury House, 1972
Giles, H. and Powesland, P. F. Speech style and social evaluation. London: Academic Press, 1975
Platt, J. T. A model for polyglossia and multilingualism (with special reference to Singapore and Malaysia) Language in Society, 1977, 6, 361-378 (a)
Platt, J. T. Code selection in a multilingual-polyglossic society. Talanya, 1977, 4, 64-75 (b)
Platt, J. T. Review of H. Giles and P. F. Powesland Speech style and social evaluation. Lingua, 1977, 43, 98-100   (c)
Platt, J. T. and Weber, H. English in Singapore and Malaysia: status - features - functions. Kuala Lumpur: Oxford University Press, in press
Scotton, C. M. and Ury, W. Bilingual strategies: the social functions of code-switching. International Journal of the Sociology of Language, 1977, 13, 5-20

Social Motives in the Transmission of a Minority Language: A Welsh Study[1]

G. Harrison

Department of Psychology, University College, Cardiff, Wales

ABSTRACT

Four predictions were derived from the integrative/instrumental distinction in language learning theory. They concerned differences between the behaviour, attitudes and expectations of bilingual mothers rearing bilingual children and those rearing monolingual children; the additional language of the bilingual children having to be a minority language. A study of 311 bilingual Welsh/English mothers in Wales provided a test of the predictions which were all confirmed. Compared with the bilingual mothers of monolingual (English) children, the bilingual mothers of bilingual children were more tolerant of baby talk, more frequently selected Welsh in a comparable setting, more often expected their children to settle in Wales, and more often saw Welsh as helpful for work. These confirmations are set against some additional findings, but overall support is adduced for extending to early bilingualism the distinction of integrative from instrumental motives in mastering languages.

Key words

Language transmission; integrative motivation; instrumental motivation; bilingualism; Welsh; child rearing; mothers.

The psychology of language learning distinguishes two principle motives for adults acquiring a second language. These motives are instrumental and integrative. Their separateness is a theme of Gardner and Lambert's book of 1972. Richards (1972) and Christophersen (1973, pp 21-22) accepted the theme. Happily Lambert has more recently shown he sees the distinction as useful. For example, he employs it when considering 'Culture and language and factors in learning and education' (1977).

---

1. Cyngor yr Iaith Gymraeg supported the work reported here; B. Piette and W. Bellin greatly helped it.

This paper applies the distinction of integrative and instrumental motivation to
parents transmitting language to their children.   Instrumentally motivated learners are characterised by particular and often material goals.   Integratively
motivated learners seek social and cultural rewards.   Acquiring English as a
second language often rests on instrumental grounds.   These may include career
advancement, access to the many publications in English, and the increased likelihood of communicating with someone anywhere.   Acquiring languages like Scots,
Gaelic or Lappish could only rarely be undertaken on such grounds.   Learners of
those minority languages almost always want to relate to the community and culture
of native speakers of their target language.   Acceptance within a community and a
shared regard for its traditions will be typical grounds for learning its historic
language.   Briefly their motives will be integrative.

Commonly speakers of minority languages need another language to respond to legis-
lative and administrative demands and to trading patterns which ignore their first
language.   Additionally languages of power help in pursuing goals like career advancement.   Commonly, langauges of power, like English in Britain, India and
America, and like French in France and Gabon are for some speakers languages of
the home.   Exposure to a language of power often occurs in a society where it is
also language of the home.   These coinciding uses may influence bilinguals with a
minority language lacking general leverage in the state.   These bilinguals may
turn from their minority language to concentrate on the one they see both in public and commercial and in social and domestic use.   Lambert (1977) suggested that
maintaining an indigenous language, when acquiring, say, English might require
learners to want to be integrated in two cultures.   Without that orientation the
transmission of the minority language to the next generation could weaken.   Seaman's (1972) study of Modern Greek in the United States agrees with this view
"... for most Greek Americans Modern Greek is a secondary language rapidly dimin-
ishing in linguistic importance, ... practically extinct already in the third generation, and will be totally extinct in the fourth generation unless some new factors occur".

Drawing together the distinction between integrative and instrumental motives with
work on language transmission leads to predictions about bilingual mothers and
whether they will have bilingual children:-

  i) Bilingual mothers of monolingual children will have more specific expectations
about how their children will speak, compared with mothers of bilingual children.
A single language gives a narrower target.   A disinclination to accept occasional
mixes may foster a general intolerance that encompasses 'baby talk'.

  ii) Bilingual mothers of monolingual children will discount their own bilingualism
in advancing in society, more often than will mothers of bilingual children.

(This second prediction needs placing in the context of mothers' ideas about work
and social position. Mother may admit medical treatment, say, can be facilitated
by a relevantly bilingual doctor, but becoming a doctor does not depend on bilingualism.   Accordingly, mothers' views on their children becoming bilingual may be
unaffected.   Again, mothers may not envisage some occupations needing fluency in
a minority language as suitable careers for their children).

Bilingual mothers who maintain their minority language rather than turn from it,
seem likely to value the social and cultural opportunities it affords them.   A
probable result of so valuing their minority language will be its transmission to
their children.   From this view two predictions arise about bilingual mothers who
have bilingual children in a correspondingly bilingual community.   Both predictions compare bilingual mothers with others having monolingual children.

iii) Bilingual mothers with bilingual children will more often select their minority language and use it when talking to others known to share their bilingualism.

iv) They will less often think of their children, when adult, settling away from the area where their minority language is spoken.   This fourth prediction rests on the mothers' concern for being a member of the minority language community and investing that concern in their aspirations for their children.

The four predictions may be tested using data from countries where the historic language has become a minority language generally lacking power compared with some introduced language.   Wales is such a country.   Only since 1967 has Welsh regained any of the legal recognition lost in 1536.   Census data show the number of Welsh speakers has continually declined since 1901.   Monolingual Welsh speakers are very rare.

An opportunity to test the four predictions arose in a study asking: Why do only some bilingual mothers in Wales have bilingual children?   Ten areas across Welsh speaking Wales were studied.   Twelve bilingual field workers each visited from 20 to 40 mothers at home and used a standard questionnaire in each mother's preferred language.   Of 311 bilingual mothers, 118 (38%) had bilingual children and 193 (62%) had monolingual.   Field work could only last five weeks.   Urgency meant using all willing bilingual mothers with at least one child aged between 2 and 7. Subsequent comparisons of mothers grouped by children's language(s) confirmed groups' similarity in family size, age and sex distributions, modal social class, and parental age structures.

Six items in the questionnaire directly related to the hypotheses.   The item about intolerance of baby talk was in English:-

> Sometimes children of three or four use baby talk.   For example, "chuf - chuff", "bow wow".   Is this something you: encourage, take no notice of, discourage?

Table 1 summarises their responses.

TABLE 1   Frequencies of mothers' responses to baby talk

Response:		Encourage	Ignore	Discourage		Totals
Mothers'	Bilingual	2	65	50	=	117
children are	Monolingual	7	65	120	=	192
Totals:		9	130	170	=	309

$$(x^2 = 14.2, \text{ (df, 2)}, \; p < 0.001)$$

Oddly, more mothers of monolingual children encouraged baby talk.   However, their 2/7 split is not statistically significant and relates to just 3% of the mothers. From 170 (55%) of the mothers who reported discouraging baby talk disproportionately more have monolingual children ($p < 0.001$).

Two items sought mothers' views on bilingualism as an asset for work.   These items were:

> In which of the following places in Wales where people work do you think their knowing both English and Welsh is a help?   The National Folk Museum, The Midland Bank, Primary Schools, Hospitals, Newspaper offices,

Police stations.

In Wales it can help in getting work to speak both English and Welsh.
For example, a speech therapist who speaks both languages in Anglesey
would be able to do more to help all the patients she might see.
Would you think being able to speak the two languages would sometimes
be useful in getting work in: Clwyd, Dyfed, Gwent, Mid-Glamorgan,
Gwynnedd, Powys?

The results from these two items revealed little about the validity of the second
prediction. Although in the predicted direction the data about work and bilingualism and counties showed no significant differences between the groups of bilingual mothers. Overall the data on particular work places did confirm the second
prediction. There were, over the six places, 1812 answers about bilingualism
being a help at work; 283 held that bilingualism would be no help. Of the negative replies 198 (70%) came from mothers of monolingual children. That proportion is significantly more than chance expectation, given the total numbers of
answers from the two groups (p < 0.01). For all six work places mothers of monolingual children gave higher proportions of negative answers. Hence while no results contradicted the second prediction, some supported it.

The third prediction was illuminated by responses to two items:-

Are there any people in the area who are bilingual with whom you only
use one of your languages? Yes, No. Who? What language do you
use together? (This latter enquiry was put for up to four people)

Suppose you're out shopping with //naming child nearest to 4// and
you meet five people individually. How many would you expect to
be bilingual: 1, 2, 3, 4, 5? How many would you speak to
in Welsh: 1, 2, 3, 4, 5?

Of the mothers of bilingual children and of those of monolingual children 85.5% of
each said they used only one language with some people. That equality facilitates
the ease of analysis of responses on language use. What emerged clearly was that
bilingual mothers with bilingual children more often preferred using just Welsh,
whereas both sets of mothers preferred Welsh overall. The greater preference for
Welsh among mothers of bilingual children achieved high statistical significance
(p < 0.002).

The item on meeting people shopping also confirmed Prediction iii as Table 2 shows:

TABLE 2   Reported numbers of Welsh speakers met with, and
           spoken to in Welsh by average bilingual mothers
           meeting people while shopping

Welsh speakers:	Met	Spoken to
Mothers of bilingual children	4.51	4.02
Mothers of monolingual children	4.15	3.35

(Entries are Contra-harmonic means)

Table 2 derives from distributions that are significantly different: for Welsh
speakers met (p = 0.03), and for Welsh speakers spoken to (p < 0.001). Briefly,
Prediction iii was supported: the bilingual mothers of bilingual children more
often selected their minority language.

The fourth prediction was tested against responses to the item:-

When your children grow up do you expect them to settle: within 20
miles, in the county, elsewhere in Wales, beyond Wales? (This enquiry
was put for up to four children per family).

This item, like the rest, had been pilot tested in places allowing the implied
transitivity that "in the county" subsumed "within 20 miles".   In the study proper this transitivity sometimes clearly failed.   To escape this problem, the data
in Table 2 pool responses for the two zones.   For brevity only data on eldest
children are given there.

TABLE 3   Bilingual mothers' expectations of where their
          eldest children would settle

	Within 20 miles or in the county	Elsewhere in Wales	Beyond Wales	Total
Bilingual children	36	41	9	86
Monolingual children	46	50	38	134
Totals	82	91	47	220

The distributions of Table 3 significantly differ from chance ($p < 0.05$).   Data
for younger children confirmed the pattern.

Hence the four predictions from the integrative/instrumental distinction were
generally confirmed empirically and no data emerged contrary to them.   Admittedly
we would have hoped that some findings might have been more compelling: the responses about bilingualism being useful for work gave only an overall difference.

The posited integrative/instrumental difference in bilingual mothers' motivation
cannot account for all differences in their children's language acquisition.
Children have two parents.   Bilingual mothers' husbands commonly father their
wives' children, but spouses do not always share bilingualism.   94% of the 311
mothers gave answers clearly indicating their children's father was a family member.   We lack data about how many families had two bilingual parents.   Field
notes from mothers' conversations showed that in 32 families (11%) fathers were
monolingual English and in 21 of those families children were monolingual.

Mothers were not asked about their husbands' languages, but were asked about their
own parents' languages.   We found that bilingual mothers who had two bilingual
parents have bilingual children more often than do bilingual mothers with one, or
no, bilingual parent.   Probably if one can, for 311 mothers, obtain a maternal
grand-parent effect and for 32 families obtain a paternal effect in language transmission, then generally there will be paternal effects among those 261 families
where fathers' languages were unknown to us.   Such paternal effects may often be
separate from mothers' motivations.   Additionally data showed mothers' post-
school education was definitely and significantly related to whether their children were bilingual.   The complexity of influences affecting language transmission
in Wales is apparent.   Doubtless other environments are similarly complex.

No single account predicts whether bilingual mothers will rear their children bi-
lingually.   However the four hypotheses here were confirmed.   Accordingly support accrues for usefully extending the distinction between instrumental and integrative motives in developing bilingualism in individuals.   Specifically, it
appears that, beside drawing together work on adults becoming bilingual, these mo-

tives help to explain why some children, reared by bilingual mothers, are not similarly bilingual, while others, reared by other bilingual mothers, are.   The evidence suggests that instrumental motives predominate in the former group of mothers, and integrative ones in the latter.

REFERENCES

Christophersen, P.   Second language learning.   Harmondsworth: Penguin, 1973
Gardner, R. and Lambert, W.   Attitudes and motivation in second language learning.
    Rowley, Mass.: Newbury House, 1972
Lambert, W. Culture and language as factors in learning and education, in F. R.
    Eckman (Ed.) Current themes in linguistics.   Washington: Hemisphere, 1977
Richards, J. Social factors, interlanguage and language learning.   Language
    Learning, 1972, 22, 159-188
Seaman, P. Modern Greek and American English in contact.   The Hague: Mouton,
    Janua Linguarum, Series Practica, No. 132, 1972.

Explaining Linguistic Choices as Identity Negotiations[1]

C. M. Scotton

Department of Linguistics, Michigan State University, Wells Hall, East Lansing, Michigan 48824, U.S.A.

ABSTRACT

A negotiation model to explain linguistic code choices is presented, taking account of three sets of factors: (1) a person's own personality system, (2) his group identities and group behavioural norms, and (3) the dynamics of each interaction. The model allows for individual variations in choices, with the proviso that their meanings are constrained by reference to a common interpretative component shared by all members of the speech community. Choices are viewed as either unmarked or marked in well-defined role relationships; unmarked choices are negotiations to identify with the terms of the role relationship, and marked choices are negotiations to dis-identify. In weakly-defined role relationships, all choices initially are exploratory, but the speaker's aim is to have his choice accepted as unmarked so that the relationship is identified by his definition. Examples of negotiation maxims which speakers follow and which influence attitudes toward other participants are also presented.

Key words

Linguistic code choice; identity negotiation; multilingualism; code switching; language attitudes

One way of explaining linguistic code selection is to begin by regarding the making of linguistic choices as synonymous with symbolising status. Statuses become meaningful only in interactions, as individuals express their statuses by the roles they take. Making linguistic choices is one of the most "visible" aspects of role-taking.

But where do statuses come from? In a role relationship, how do participants know their relative statuses? This leads to an underlying question: to what ex-

---

1. Field work to develop and test parts of this model was conducted in Kenya in 1977 under a grant from the Joint Committee on African Studies of the American Council of Learned Societies and the Social Science Research Council. This model is part of a longer work by Scotton on identity negotiations now in manuscript.

tent are the meanings of statuses based on the dynamics of each individual interaction, or to what extent do such meanings exist on a supra-interactional, societal level as interpreted by overall norms?   Put another way, does each interaction somehow "create" statuses anew, by making salient only certain aspects of a
persona, or is it that statuses and the norms which identify them pre-exist interactions of the moment and that they are simply realised in interactions, so that
statuses are more of "givens" than identities which can be assumed at will?

These questions raise the major differences between interactionist sociolinguistics, represented by the work of Sacks and Garfinkel, and to an extent, Goffman
and Gumperz, and correlationist sociolinguistics, represented by Fishman and
others who emphasise the normative association of linguistic choices with demographic and situational variables.

I want to present here a model   which reconciles the differences between these
two poles within sociolinguistics and which also takes cognizance of personal
motivation factors, such as those which figure in Giles' accommodation theory
(Giles, Taylor and Bourhis (1973), Giles and Powesland (1975)). I suggest data of
the papers from this symposium be considered in terms of this model. This model
is a reconciliation because it takes account of the potency of both interactional
dynamics and also of social features and overall societal norms in explaining any
linguistic choice.

According to the model, linguistic choices can be explained as individually-moti-
vated negotiations of identity.   But the success of these negotiations depends on
the extent to which they both abide by and exploit the constraints of the commun-
ally-recognised norms on which any linguistic choice relies for its meaning.
This is a negotiation model, then, and what is being negotiated is the speaker's
self-identification of persona - that is, the status he holds in a role relationship.   His identification of the relative personae of others in the relationship
is also part of the negotiation.   Like accommodation theory, this model stresses
personal motivation strategies.   But it situates these strategies within a clearly normative framework, something accommodation theory does not emphasise.

Within this normative framework, all linguistic choices are distinguished as
either unmarked or marked in terms of the expectations of specific role relationships.   The unmarked:marked opposition is crucial in the interpretation of
choices, as will become clear.

In each well-defined role relationship, one code selection is always more unmarked than others.   That is, the unmarked choice is that choice which the norms
of society indicate represents the most expected choice for a particular status-
holder in a particular role relationship in a particular situation.   The unmarked
choice can be identified empirically;   it is the most expected because it is, in
fact, the choice most often made.

No claim is intended that identity negotiations necessarily involve conscious behaviour;   in fact most code choices are probably unconscious in much the same way
as are grammatical choices which a speaker makes, such as word order, subject verb
agreement and the like.

The psychological reality of the societal association of a particular linguistic
code as unmarked with participation in a certain role relationship could be tested
empirically to see if listeners anticipate this code and therefore delay in their
processing of other codes, or even fail to process them as communicative.   Ervin-
Tripp (1976, p.59) comments about selection among various styles of directives in
American English:

"... the social norms reported in this paper suggest that the work of the hearer need not begin with the utterance, but that the set or priming of the hearer can be so great that a nod is a directive.   But if the form is inappropriate to the context, it may not be heard as a directive at all."

Even though the unmarked choice is well recognised, speakers do make marked choices in many well-defined role relationships, at least in some societies.   This is why interactionist sociolinguists protest the one-to-one correlation of code selection with social features in any situation (Gumperz 1976, p.8).   While I agree, of course, that more than one choice is possible in many interactions, marked choices differ in important ways from the unmarked choice in their interpretation so that quite different motivation strategies are involved in the two types of choices.   Further, the range of marked choices is always limited by the normative framework.   As Irvine (1974, p.167) points out, specifically in reference to Wolof greeting strategies:

"Although the greeting allows for personal strategies and manipulation of its structure, these must be in accord with basic ground rules which in fact limit the kinds of personal motivations that may be culturally appropriate."

A third kind of choice, the exploratory choice, exists in those role relationships which are weakly-defined.   When the relative statuses which are salient to an interaction are unknown, a weakly-define role relationship exists.   Such a relationship also holds when the salient statuses of participants may be known, but the unmarked negotiation of a desired role relationship is unclear.   This second situation arises for speakers who are new arrivals in a speech community and unfamiliar with the norms.

Code switching may be any one of the three types of choices.   It is probably most often exploratory or marked, but it can also be unmarked.   For example, for many bilinguals in multilingual societies, the act of code-switching itself seems to be the unmarked strategy to identify a role relationship with another similar bilingual as that of peer-to-peer.

As stated above, the model being presented here characterises all linguistic choices as negotiations of identity within societal constraints.   The major differences among the choices involve the interpretation process which each type of choice evokes and the resulting evaluations of the speaker.   These differences are set forth in these hypotheses:

1) If a role relationship between two or more participants is well-defined, societal norms will identify generally one code as the unmarked choice for each side of the role relationship.   (This may or may not be the same code.).   A speaker's choice of this unmarked code will signal he is negotiating <u>identification</u> with a status implied as his by the role relationship.

Based on this linguistic choice, members of the speech community will form a consensus in defining the speaker's negotiated identity.

2) If a role relationship is well-defined, even though role expectations favour the unmarked choice, the speaker may make a marked choice.   Role expectations will bias the interpretation of the marked choice so that it will be viewed as a <u>dis-identification</u> with the status implied by the role relationship.   Further, by implication, the marked choice will be viewed as identification with another status and role relationship for which the current marked choice would be an unmarked choice within the speech community.

Because it is a dis-identification, a marked choice generally provokes an emotional response from others in the current role relationship.   For example, anger arises if the speaker's dis-identification involves the bid for a different status which changes his position in the power differential for the better.   Humour occurs if the speaker's dis-identification is viewed as patently incongruous, given other social factors.   Feelings of warmth, or insult, may occur because the dis-identification is the negotiation of a new role relationship involving less social distance between the participants than that in the current role relationship.

Based on this linguistic choice, members of the speech community will form a consensus in defining the speaker's negotiated identity.   This identity will be different from that associated with the unmarked choice in the same interaction.

3) If the role relationship is weakly-defined, then no choice is initially marked or unmarked.   Exploratory choices will characterise such a relationship.   An exploratory choice is a negotiation to identify the type of role relationship which is evolving and the speaker's status in it.   If other participants reciprocate with a choice congruent with the exploratory choice (i.e. the same or complementary), acceptance of the role relationship as identified is signalled.   The exploratory choice and the reciprocal choice then become unmarked for the remainder of the interaction.   If other participants do not respond with a choice congruent with the original exploratory choice, then the response choice becomes the candidate for the unmarked choice, which other participants may accept or reject.   Exploratory choices are presented until the negotiation of unmarked choices is accepted.

Based on these linguistic choices, members of the speech community will form a consensus in defining the negotiated identities.

These hypotheses can be tested and their terms defined relative to specific speech communities.   First, a panel of judges from the community can delimit well-defined role relationships from those which are only weakly-defined.   One way of doing this would be to show judges video tapes of community members in an interaction, with cues available, such as the setting and the participants' non-verbal behaviour.   (It is expected that relatively few role relationships in some societies, expecially Western ones, will be characterised as well-defined in any a priori sense.   Well-defined relationships would likely include that of salesperson-customer, religious leader-congregation member, judge-defendant and the like.)   Second, judges can establish by their consensus interpretations of the meanings of both marked and unmarked choices in well-defined relationships and of exploratory choices in weakly-defined relationships.   The same method can be used as that employed in Scotton and Ury (1977), in further field work by Scotton, and somewhat modified by Bourhis and Genesee (1980).   That is, judges can be presented with facsimile tape recordings of interactions and asked to interpret linguistic choices.

A second set of hypotheses regarding the frequency of types of choices and the factors with which they are most closely associated are these:

1) In well-defined role relationships in which a power differential is a factor in status-identification, unmarked choices will dominate.   In such relationships, code selection can best be predicted in terms of salient group identities of the participants and other situational factors.

2) In well-defined role relationships in which a power differential is an incidental factor in status-identification, marked choices may occur depending on the dynamics and content of the interaction.   Marked choices will occur with a higher frequency in these relationships than in those in which a power differential is a

factor.

3) In weakly-defined role relationships, which particular exploratory choices are presented for unmarked status will depend on the nature of the goals participants have for the relationship. For example, whether they have long or short-term goals for the duration of the relationship is a potential independent variable. Individual personality characteristics, including goals, will be better predictors of linguistic choices than are group identities or situational factors.

The model proposed here also provides for a set of negotiation maxims patterned after those proposed by Grice (1975) as conversational implicatures. Grice's maxims dealt with the content of conversations; the maxims proposed here deal with the use of conversations to negotiate social identity. Grice's maxims apparently were intended as universals, but it is unlikely they apply universally. Keenan (1974), for example, has pointed out their inapplicability in Malagasy society. It is just as likely that the following negotiation maxims will not hold universally, although I do not know now of exceptions. The following set of maxims is by no means exhaustive; these maxims are merely suggestive of the type of conditions which a negotiation model implies.

(1) The gains maxim. If any participant expects relatively higher gains than costs in the current interaction, he will suspend his assessment of linguistic choices made by other participants. That is, he will suspend the marked:unmarked distinction in choices. Further, he will accommodate others in regard to his own choices, if necessary also suspending the negotiation of the identity which would be unmarked for him, given the role relationship and societal norms.

Moles (1974, p.456) discusses data which support the existence of this maxim in role relationships between Indians and non-Indians in Peru. In interactions in which either side expects exceptional gain, seemingly deviant pronoun usage is accepted.

(2) The topic change maxim. Changes in topic represent natural boundaries for changes in role relationships among the same participants. This is so because new topics make salient new aspects of the social profile of participants. Speakers who wish to negotiate a role relationship shift will take up the option to change their code when a new topic is introduced. Note this change is only an option. Such a choice will be treated initially as exploratory - as if the role relationship has become weakly-defined. Such a choice is seen as an identification, not as a dis-identification, as a marked choice would be. The choice may or may not be accepted as unmarked for the remainder of the interaction, or until a new topic is introduced; that is, a new role relationship may or may not be accepted with a topic change.

(3) The multiple identities maxim. A participant in any role relationship, but most typically in a weakly-defined role relationship, who hopes to negotiate a favourable status may engage in code switching. He chooses more than one code because he seeks to negotiate for himself something of the favourable statuses and role relationships with which each code is associated as an unmarked choice. In an additive fashion, then, he negotiates a multiple identity.

Scotton (1976) explains the high incidence of code switching among multi-ethnic co-workers in several African cities in this way. Agheyisi (1977) notes what she calls "interlarded speech" in office interactions between members of the same ethnic group, particularly between a boss and secretary. English is the unmarked choice for their role relationship as boss-secretary, while their mother tongue is the unmarked choice to identify their shared ethnicity and a role relationship of less social distance. Schenkein (1978, p.72) also comments on identity adding in

an American English interaction in which the role relationship of salesman-client
already exists.   He says:

> "Each can surely turn the generation of unofficial identities (other than
> salesman and client) by the other (namely the client's involvement with
> other kinds of insurance and the salesman's involvement with military
> obligations) into an occasion for affiliation or disaffiliation, approval
> or disapproval, curiosity or incuriosity, and so on."

(4) The _virtuosity_ maxim.   A listener's interpretation of any code choice as
marked or unmarked depends in part on his assessment of the speaker's formal grammatical competence in codes which would be unmarked for the implied role relationship.   The competence of listeners is taken into account by any speaker in his
code selections.

(5) The _first in_ maxim.   Many new school teachers in North America are given this
advice: 'never smile until Christmas'.   The assumption is that once the new teacher has established a role relationship with students in which he has the status
as a dour authoritarian, he can then relax with the students and make more friendly overtures if he wishes - with the assurance that the students will not take advantage of these friendly messages since the original message of 'no smiles' will
remain foremost in their minds as the symbol of the identity which the teacher can
assume at any time.

Any speaker can follow this negotiation maxim in his linguistic choices, but it is
a maxim favoured especially by persons who have the social identities which normally would allow them to assume the more powerful status in a particular role relationship.   Once having negotiated his identity with the unmarked choice for
this powerful status, the speaker can then make other marked choices which dis-
identify him with this status, especially those which narrow the social distance
in the role relationship.   Therefore, while the role relationship may well change,
the initial status he negotiated leaves its trace.

Let me now suggest very briefly how some of the data in the papers presented at
this symposium might be considered within the negotiation model of this paper.   I
want to emphasise I am making no attempt to do justice to the rich data and
thoughtful analyses which the writers have provided; time and space do not permit
such a discussion.

The evaluation by subjects of the salesman in Bourhis and Genesee (1980) can be
explained in terms of the gains maxim, as well as the hypotheses proposed about
well-defined relationships and unmarked choices.   Once the salesman realises the
customer is an English Canadian, if he wants to increase the likelihood of pleas-
ing the customer and making a sale, the gains maxim exhorts him to speak English.
That is, the salesman ignores the official promotion of French as the unmarked
choice in public situations in Quebec.   According to the gains maxim, norms regarding markedness are suspended.   This is how I would explain the fact that subjects in the study rate the salesman no more favourably once he has switched from
his opening remark in French to English in his second speech than they did when
they heard only his initial statement in French.   Since all the salesman is doing
is following the gains maxim, he receives no special credit for his accommodation
to the customer's mother tongue, English.   Further, by the first in maxim, the
salesman has the satisfaction of knowing he has established some salience of his
identity as a French Canadian before he switches to English.   The gains maxim also explains why the subjects judge the customer satisfied with the salesman's response to him in English, even if the customer himself has spoken French.   That
is, the customer recognises it is an option for people expecting gains to follow
the gains maxim, so he does not discount the salesman for doing so.

The negotiation model is compatible with the results of Harrison's (1980) study. Both groups of mothers, whether they have integrative or instrumental motives regarding their children's acquisition of languages, want their children to learn the unmarked code or codes of the role relationships in which they want them to take part.   The point is they see their children in different role relationships. Since one set of role relationships may be perceived to have a different unmarked choice than another set, it follows that some mothers believe their children need learn only English and others believe they should know both Welsh and English.

It seems possible to interpret much of the code switching in the data from Singapore presented by Platt (1980) in terms of the multiple identities maxim and the topic change maxim.   Both of these depend on shared recognition of unmarked choices for different role relationships.   Assuming multiple identities is, in many ways, the most neutral form of accommodation in a group where several role relationships are operating at once.   But perhaps more importantly, the multiple identities strategy maximises the speaker's changes of having a favourable status since it situates him in more than one role relationship.   If a speaker takes up the option of the topic change maxim to propose a new code as unmarked, the speaker may also negotiate a more favourable status.

Kendall (1980), the ultimate negotiator, proposes that not only may almost all elements of social reality be negotiated, she also suggests that the concept of grammatical competence itself is even partially open to negotiation as 'radical grammars' are created.   She recognises that norm-breakers may be termed odd, but also points out that norm-breakers may be seen as original, creative, playful and the like.   Much of the behaviour discussed can be accommodated in the model according to the virtuosity maxim, which suspends notions of markedness.   Kendall goes beyond this suspension, though, and provides us with a notion of how restructurings of what is marked and unmarked become part of a new system.

REFERENCES

Agheyisi, R. N. Language interlarding in the speech of Nigerians, in P. F. A. Kotey and H. Der-Houssikian (Eds.) Language and linguistic problems in Africa.   Columbia: Hornbeam Press, 1977

Bourhis, R. Y. and Genesee, F.   Evaluative reactions to code switching strategies in Montreal, this volume.

Ervin-Tripp, S. Is Sybil there?   The structure of some American English directives.   Language in Society, 1976, 5, 25-66

Giles, H., Taylor, D. M. and Bourhis, R. Y. Towards a theory of interpersonal accommodation through language: some Canadian data.   Language in Society, 1973, 2, 177-192

Giles, H. and Powesland, P. F.   Speech style and social evaluation.   London: Academic Press, 1975

Grice, H. P. Logic and conversation, in P. Cole and J. L. Morgan (Eds.) Syntax and semantics: speech acts. New York: Academic Press, 1975

Gumperz, J. J. The sociolinguistic significance of conversational code switching in J. J. Gumperz and J. Cook-Gumperz (Eds.) Papers on language and context. Berkeley: University of California Language Behaviour Research Laboratory Working Paper No. 46, 1976, 1-46

Harrison, G.   Social motives in the transmission of a minority language: a Welsh study. (This volume)

Irvine, J. T. Status manipulation in the Wolof greeting, in R. Bauman and J. Scherzer (Eds.) Explorations in the ethnography of speaking.   London: Cambridge University Press, 1974

Keenan, E. Norm-makers, norm-breakers: uses of speech by men and women in a
     Malagasy community, in R. Bauman and J. Scherzer (Eds.) <u>Explorations in the
     ethnography of speaking</u>. London: Cambridge University Press, 1974
Kendall, M. B. Radical grammars: interplays of form and function, this volume.

Moles, J. A. Decisions and variability: the usage of address terms, pronouns and
     languages by Quechua-Spanish bilinguals in Peru. <u>Anthropological Linguis-
     tics</u>, 1974, 16, <u>2</u>, 442-463
Platt, J. The relation between accommodation and code-switching in a multilingual
     society: Singapore, this volume.
Schenkein, J. Identity negotiations in conversation, in J. Schenkein (Ed.)
     <u>Studies in the organization of conversational interaction</u>. New York:
     Academic Press, 1978
Scotton, C. M. Strategies of neutrality: language choice in uncertain situations
     <u>Language</u>, 1976, <u>52</u>, 4, 919-941
Scotton, C. M. and Ury, W. Bilingual strategies: the social functions of code-
     switching. <u>International Journal of the Sociology of Language</u>, 1977, <u>13</u>,
     5-20

Language in the Courtroom*

B. Danet

*The Communications Institute and the Department of Sociology,
The Hebrew University of Jerusalem, Israel*

INTRODUCTION

In the last five years a new interdisciplinary field has emerged, the study of
language as it relates to the law and to the legal process.   Work on language in
the courtroom, the subject of this paper, is, consequently, part of a broader trend.
While lawyers and jurists have, in the past, discussed some language-related issues,
e.g. Bishin and Stone 1972;   Probert 1972;   Mellinkoff 1963;   see Danet 1978a, 1980,
the work now emerging differs in that it is empirical rather than speculative, and
emphasises law talk (Probert, North Carolina Law Review, 1974), the spoken language
of legal professionals, their clients, and various others with whom they come into
daily contact, rather than dealing almost exclusively with the written language of
appellate opinions and statutes.

Two complementary trends account for the consolidation of interest in law and
language.   On the one hand, social scientists interested in the law are beginning
to look to language, and to ideas and methods from sociolinguistics and psycholinguistics, as a way of illuminating the legal process, as it works in practice.
The Law and Social Science Program of the American National Science Foundation
helped to launch this new work in the United States by funding four team projects,
two of which have focussed on courtroom questioning (see for example O'Barr and
Conley 1976;   Erickson, Lind, Johnson and O'Barr 1978;   Danet and Kermish 1978;
Danet, Hoffman, Kermish, Rafn and Staymon 1979;   Danet, in press), the other two
dealing with the comprehensibility of jury instructions (Charrow and Charrow 1976,
1978;   Sales, Elwork and Alfini 1976, in press).   In another development, the Law
and Society Review has commissioned a review article on language in the legal process for a special issue on Contemporary Issues in Law and Social Science (Danet
1980).   Research reports on language in the legal process are beginning to appear
on the programmes of legal and socio-legal conferences, e.g. Loftus 1978;   Danet
1978b;   Danet and Bogoch 1979b.   Even practising lawyers are beginning to take an

* Activities of the author in the area of law and language have been supported by
  the Law and Social Science Program of the National Science Foundation (Grant SOC-
  74-23503);   Israel Foundations Trustees- Ford Foundation; and the Faculty of
  Social Science, Hebrew University.   I am grateful to Bryna Bogoch for help in
  preparing this paper.   For further details on the five papers presented at the
  Symposium on Law and Language, see Parkinson (1979);   Naylor (1979);   Danet and
  Bogoch (1979a);   Phillips (1979);   and Atkinson (1979).

interest in this work; for instance O'Barr has been deluged with requests for information by lawyers hoping to turn findings from his team's research into tips on how to win cases, and Loftus, an expert on language and memory (cf Loftus and Palmer 1974; Loftus 1975; Loftus 1976), frequently appears in court as an expert witness, and gives workshops for trial lawyers.

The second trend accounting for the consolidation of the field of law and language is the increasing tendency for psycholinguists and sociolinguists to choose legal settings for their research. Here, the prime incentive may be the recognition that legal settings offer rich opportunities for linguistic theory and research. However, cooperation between members of the legal profession and social scientists interested in language is fraught with difficulties. Perhaps the most important of these is the fact that the stance of social science is inherently threatening to the legal profession and its institutions. Good social science frequently debunks and de-mystifies what the legal profession may prefer to leave unexamined. Until very recently, the legal profession managed to insulate itself from investigation by outsiders, but growing social criticism is now changing this situation (see, for example, in relation to the United States, Auerbach 1974; Rosenthal 1974; Nader and Green 1976; Illich 1977; Tisher, Bernabei and Green 1977; Lieberman 1978; Abel 1979; Time Magazine 1978; - in relation to Britain, Carlen 1976; Bankowski and Mungham 1976; Baldwin and McConville 1977; McBarnet 1979).

Growing institutional support for sociolinguistic and psycholinguistic work using legal materials is evident from the fact that three language conferences have featured sessions on law and language since 1976. The first conference to do so was the Fifth Annual Colloquium on New Ways of Analysing Variation in English at Georgetown University, Washington, D.C. Second, the Program on Sociolinguistics at the 1978 World Congress of Sociology in Uppsala, Sweden, included an interest group session on language in the legal process. Finally, the fact that the conference on which this book is based also included a symposium on the same topic will undoubtedly strengthen international interest in it.

LANGUAGE AND THE TWO BASIC FUNCTIONS OF LAW

The two basic functions of law in society are, first, to organise things so that society can go about its daily business, and second, to provide a means to resolve disputes when order breaks down, so that society can return to its business. Briefly, we may call these the facilitative-regulative function and the dispute-processing function (for further discussion of the functions of law see, for example, Hoebel 1954; Aubert 1969; Schwartz and Skolnick 1970; Fuller 1971; Friedman 1977).

<u>Language and the facilitative-regulative function of law</u> The facilitative-regulative function of law provides recipes for living, for doing, for creating relationships where none existed before. Thus, the law provides the means to get married (civil marriage), to engage in a contract, to create a corporation, to dispose of property. To take advantage of options available in the law, the public has generally been dependent on services of members of the legal profession. Legal language has long been recognised as difficult and obscure to the lay person, but only recently has there been talk of reform of "legalese" as part of a general attempt to make legal services either unnecessary or, at least, more accessible to the public.

The so-called "Plain English Movement" in the United States is a response to the growing criticism of language in public life - in politics, advertising, bureaucracy, and the professions. President Carter's promise to reform the language of federal bureaucratic regulations is part of this trend. The movement includes reform of the language of insurance policies, credit loan forms, and landlord-tenant agreements.

In 1972, Dwight Bolinger, then President of the Linguistic Society of America, argued that "truth is a linguistic question", meaning that linguists should get involved in fighting misuses of language in public life.   But professional linguists have been slow to get involved.   This work is still mainly being carried out by self-styled experts on "Plain English" with little or no training in linguistics.   We need serious work on the linguistic description of legal language, on the identification of those features which obscure meaning, and above all perhaps, on the limits of reform.

Most of the work conducted so far on the reform of legal language has addressed itself to written documents.   There is much to be done on the language of members of the legal profession in interaction with lay persons.   Does lawyers' language mystify their clients?   Do clients learn to talk "legalese"?   To what extent can communication between professionals and non-professionals be improved?   These questions cannot be separated from the broader sociological question: what are the limits to deprofessionalization (see, for example, Abel 1969)?

<u>Language and dispute processing</u>   The second major theme of work on law and language is that focussing on dispute processing.   There is a well-established tradition of research since the 1960s in the sociology and anthropology of law dealing with this topic (for example, Nader 1969; Nader and Todd 1978; Roberts 1979), though the ethnographic materials typically do not deal with disputes at a level specific enough to examine language issues in detail.   Basically, societies resolve disputes by fighting or by talking, by physical fights or by <u>fighting with words</u>.   Research till now has been concerned, among other things, with the analysis of the conditions under which fists or words predominate, or under which a verbal dispute deteriorates into a physical brawl (for example, Roberts 1979). A sociolinguist would ask, given the choice of words rather than fists, what is it about the words that is important?   In what ways do words matter?   How do features of the social situations of dispute processing constrain choices made by participants?   How do speech patterns relate to justice?   The study of talk in disputes offers a fruitful way to illuminate how actors perceive social rules and how they use them in pursuing their interests.

Most of the sociolinguistically oriented work on the language of disputes has focussed on trials as conducted under the ground rules of the Anglo-American adversary system of justice.   This work examines such variables as "powerful" versus "powerless" speech of witnesses and its effect on judgments of their credibility (O'Barr and Conley 1976; Erickson, Lind, Johnson and O'Barr 1978), semantics and presuppositions in questions (Loftus 1978; Loftus and Palmer 1974; Kasprzyk, Montano and Loftus 1975; Danet, in press), and coerciveness of question form (Danet, Hoffman, Kermish, Rafn and Stayman 1979; Danet and Kermish 1978; Danet and Bogoch 1979a; Phillips 1979).   Atkinson and Drew's (1979) work, heavily influenced by ethnomethodology, follows a rather different course; it is an attempt to describe formal, structural and sequential properties of verbal interaction in courts, and to identify systematic features of sequences like those involving blame allocation during cross-examination.   For lack of space, I shall devote the remainder of this paper to brief summaries of each of the five papers presented in this symposium at Bristol, and to a discussion of their implications.

LANGUAGE IN THE COURTROOM : THE FIVE STUDIES

Of the five papers presented at Bristol in the Symposium on Language and Law, three dealt with criminal trials: Danet and Bogoch, Parkinson, and Naylor; a fourth, by Phillips, dealt with changes of plea, a criminal procedure in which a defendant who formerly pleaded not guilty to a certain charge had decided to

plead guilty instead, and had to go before a judge to make the change official;
the fifth paper by Atkinson dealt with an aspect of civil law and procedure, the
small claims court hearing.

Paper 1.   <u>Michael Parkinson: speech patterns and the outcome of trials</u>

Parkinson reported results of a study in which he chose 19 criminal cases in which
the defendant had been acquitted, and matched them with similar cases in which the
defendant had been convicted.   He then sampled the speech of all attorneys and
witnesses by analysing certain features of the first 40 turns-to-talk in each sequence of interrogation of witnesses, yielding a sample of 300 to 1500 words for
each.   Variables studied included the presence or absence of the features of
"powerless" speech (hedges, intensifiers, hyper-correct grammar, polite forms);
legal jargon (terms appearing in Black's Law Dictionary); verbosity (total words
in the subject's speech sample); duration of question line (for attorneys only;
number of questions referring to a specific topic); and specificity of questioning (number of questions eliciting more detailed information than contained in the
previous response); syntactic features analysed using the Syntactic Language Computer Analysis programme.

Parkinson found that prosecutors who win cases differ significantly in their
speech patterns from those who lose them.   Successful prosecutors were verbally
assertive, speaking longer, asking more questions referring to the witness, and
making more indicative statements than did less successful counterparts.   Second,
successful defence attorneys used speech patterns distinct from those of prosecutors.   For them it was important to use abstract or ambiguous language; successful defence attorneys used more legal jargon and fewer "afferent" words (those
referring to concepts that can be sensed with the five senses).   Finally, defendants who were more polite and spoke in more grammatically complete sentences
tended more often to be acquitted.

Paper 2.   <u>Paz Buenaventura Naylor: linguistic and cultural interference in
                          testimony</u>

Naylor called attention for the need to analyse in depth the sources of linguistic
and cultural interference in the testimony of witnesses whose native language is
not the language of the court.   A native of the Philippines herself, she drew her
ideas from a controversial 1977 case in which two Filipino nurses working at a
Veterans' Administration Hospital in Ann Arbor, Michigan, were convicted on char-
ges of conspiracy and seven counts of poisoning patients.   The prosecution
claimed that the nurses had injected the alleged victims with Pavulon, a drug
which would have fatally affected their breathing.

Because the trail was based on circumstantial evidence only, the credibility of
witnesses was absolutely crucial.   Naylor's main point was that linguistic and
cultural interference in the testimony of the two defendants made them appear to
be lying and trying to mislead the jury.   She identified the following sources
of interference: differences between English and Tagalog with respect to tense
and aspect distinctions; differences in English versus Tagalog verbs along an
axis she calls "punctual" versus "durative"; differences in the sociolinguistically appropriate use of indirection; and, finally, differences in the use of a
mitigating phrase like "I believe".

As an illustration, one of these four sources of interference can be briefly
described.   Asked "How did you feel when you <u>came</u> to the Veterans' Hospital and
found out that the understaffing was worse?" one of the defendants replied, "I
didn't know that until I was in the V.A."   For a speaker of Tagalog the verb
"came" can only mean the actual act of coming, of arriving, and has no duration;

thus, the defendant's reply appears strange and non-responsive, though she is trying to reply to the question.   Naylor presented whole sequences of testimony in which the effect of confusion caused by such sources of interference was cumulative.   Given the critical importance of one's ability to account for one's movements over time in such a case, it is not difficult to understand why the jury believed the nurses to be guilty.

Paper 3.   **Brenda Danet and Bryna Bogoch: lawyers' combativeness in the adversary system of justice**

Danet and Bogoch presented results of an empirical study of lawyers' combativeness in six criminal trials recorded in the Superior Court of Boston, Massachusetts in 1976.   Analysis of all of the testimony on direct and cross-examination of the defendant and of one prosecution witness in each of two murder trials, two rape trials, and two assault and battery trials yielded a sample of approximately 5000 question-response sequences.   Four empirical measures of combativeness pertaining to two speech acts prominent in lawyers' courtroom performance, asking and objecting, were used: (1) the total number of questions asked; (2) the form of the question ("coerciveness of question form" - see Danet, Hoffman, Kermish, Rafn and Stayman 1979; Danet and Kermish 1978); (3) the topic (whether the question was about the defendant or not); and (4) the rate of objecting to the other side's questions or responses.

Three basic prerequisites for a successful adversary system of justice are that the parties should be highly combative, that they should be evenly matched, and that the decision-maker-umpire should be impartial.   Variations in the four measures of combativeness were analysed in relation to three independent variables, side (prosecutor versus defence attorney); type of examination (direct versus cross); and degree of seriousness of the offence.   The findings were as follows: (1) Prosecutors were consistently more combative than defence attorneys, and, unexpectedly, the more serious the offence, the more combative their linguistic strategies became; (2) Defence attorneys were rarely or only weakly influenced by the offence; the judge was generally impartial in his handling of lawyers' objections, with some interesting exceptions.

Paper 4.   **Susan Phillips: syntactic variation in judges' use of language in the courtroom**

Phillips observed and tape-recorded nine judges' handling of the criminal procedure known as change of plea in a court of general jurisdiction in Arizona.   She began her paper by presenting a linguistic analysis of the extent to which the form of questions addressed to defendants supplies the elements of the reply. She pointed out that the extent to which questions constrain the syntactic form of the reply derives not only from the syntactic structure of the question itself but from the authoritative role of the questioner as well.   She then analysed how the legal purposes of the procedure affect it.   One purpose is to make sure that defendants knowingly and voluntarily waive their constitutional rights to a jury trial; the other is to make sure that there is a factual basis for the plea.   Despite considerable ritualisation in the procedure, she found a large amount of syntactic variation in judges' questions.   The most legally significant portions of the proceeding varied the least.   This was because judges wanted the legally critical portions to be acceptable to the higher courts.   Open-ended wh-questions (who, what, where, etc.) appeared rarely, but when they did, it was usually in the establishment of the factual basis of the plea.

Phillips found that whether judges used open-ended questions to allow defendants to provide the facts, or preferred relatively closed questions (declaratives, yes/ no questions) merely to get the defendant's assent, in both cases, the reasons they gave had nothing to do with the search for truth.   Judges who preferred the open-ended style did so because if a defendant actively made admissions, s/he was more likely to stand by his/her plea, and because it increased the likelihood that the defendant knowingly and willingly pleased guilty to the charge, thus strength- ening the judge's own position in case of appeal.   Other judges reported prefer- ring the more ritualised way of eliciting assent through controlled questions be- cause such assent is all that is legally necessary for a voluntary and knowing plea.   Younger judges were less likely to have routinised their procedures; Phillips speculated that they may still be capable of taking an interest in the problematic nature of the fit between "facts" and statutory interpretation.

Paper 5.   J. Maxwell Atkinson: displaying neutrality – the management of an interactional problem in small claims court hearings

Atkinson presented some preliminary results from a study of tape-recorded English small claims court hearings.   The report focussed on a three turn sequence that was found to recur with some regularity, and could be characterised as follows: (1) a 'question' by arbitrator projecting a 'minimal response' (e.g. one word, such as 'yes', 'no', 'here', 'there', etc.) as a sequentially relevant next turn; (2) a 'non-minimal' response (i.e. one which does something more than or different from what was projected by the prior turn) by recipient; (3) a turn by arbitrator preceded by a pause and comprising (a) a receipt marker in turn initial position (e.g. 'yes', 'certainly', 'okay', etc.); (b) a pause (c) a next 'question' that avoids assessment or uptake of the relevances projected by the 'non-minimal' response.   An example of such a sequence is:

   (SC:1B:BS) (Simplified transcription – numbers in brackets represent pause
                lengths to the nearest tenth of a second)

(1) Arbitrator: ... when you talk about a bespoke sandal (0.2), this is
                       one made (0.3) to your (0.3) order

                       (0.5)

(2) Plaintiff: Uh (0.4) when you say to my order ehm I would expect
                       to get a wearable pair of sandals out of it ehm ah –
                       it was done in discussion with Mister Naddas he an I
                       talked about it – eh (1.8) I think it yes it's fair
                       to say that he said that the sandals would be (0.3)
                       acceptable

                       (0.7)

(3) Arbitrator: Certainly (0.6) eh – can we now (0.3) look at the
                       (0.2) uh (0.7) dispute between the two of you about
                       fittings.   (1.0) You say that there was only one

Particular attention was given to the third turn, and evidence from naturally occurring conversation and higher court hearings was introduced in support of the proposal that receipt markers and uptake avoidance seldom occur in such sequential positions in these other environments.   In small claims hearings, however, such utterance constructions are placed there quite regularly by different arbitrators, in different hearings, and in response to utterances by both plaintiffs and de- fendants.

A possible interpretation of this finding is that such utterances may be a device for resolving an interactional problem routinely faced by arbitrators, namely that of how to avoid displaying either affiliation (which tends to be done at similar points in conversation) or disaffiliation (which tends to be done at similar

points in cross-examination) with the person being questioned.   The problem
arises because, in contrast with formal adversarial proceedings where there is a
division of labour between questioners (counsel) and decision-makers (judges),
small claims courts involve arbitrators in doing both.

IMPLICATIONS

These five papers overlap and complement one another in a number of ways.   The
studies by Parkinson and by Danet and Bogoch are each concerned with the verbal
behaviour of lawyers in criminal trials.   Both find that prosecutors are highly
assertive.   Whereas Danet and Bogoch highlighted the effect of situational constraints on the verbal choices of each type of attorney, Parkinson was most interested in the correlation between linguistic strategies and the outcome.

Phillips, like Danet and Bogoch, is interested in coerciveness of question form
and its relation to the response.   Although dealing with different criminal procedures, the two studies lead to similar negative conclusions about the workings
of the American system of justice.   Danet and Bogoch's finding that prosecutors
were more combative when the offence was serious may mean that prosecutors are
doling out a form of symbolic punishment, even before defendants have been convicted.   Second, the finding that defence attorneys apparently did not become
more combative as the offence became more serious suggests indifference to the
challenge of defending their clients.   Similarly, the reasons that Phillips'
judges gave for choosing open or closed question forms had nothing to do with
eliciting the truth.   Like the defence lawyers in the Boston study, they appeared
to respond primarily to organisational and professional constraints, rather than
to the needs of defendants (see Blumberg 1967;   Skolnick 1970;   Casper 1972;
Baldwin and McConville 1977 for further critiques of the adversary system).

Naylor's discussion of the trial of the two Filipinos points to a new kind of work,
which should sensitise members of the legal profession to the special problems of
non-native speakers of the official language of any court.   Her paper will become
part of a growing body of research on multilingualism and its implications for the
legal process.   At the same time, it is a continuation of the type of research
undertaken by O'Barr and his colleagues on speech style of witnesses and judgments
of credibility (O'Barr and Conley 1976;   Erickson, Lind, Johnson and O'Barr 1978).

Like the others, Atkinson too is ultimately concerned with the "doing" of justice.
Probably the most obvious implication of his paper is the suggestion that questioning of witnesses to elicit "facts" as carried out in the continental inquisi-
torial model of justice will be structurally quite different from that carried out
according to the adversary model (see Thibaut and Walker 1975;   Damaska 1975).
We should also note that the use of devices like "Yes" and "I see" to display
neutrality is by no means a guarantee of substantive neutrality in any adjudica-
tive situation.

The conclusions of these five studies must be regarded as tentative.   Danet and
Bogoch's analysis is based on only six trials in the courtroom of one American
judge;   Phillips worked with only nine judges;   Naylor's work focusses on only one
trial and is still in the stages of discovery of important variables;   Parkinson's
claims about his ability to predict the outcome of a trial from small samples of
the speech of participants awaits replication;   Atkinson's work needs to be extended to a larger number of small claims hearings, at the very least.   Still, taken
together, these studies are highly suggestive of the ways in which language in the
courtroom may affect both substantive and procedural justice.

REFERENCES

Abel, R. L.   Delegalization: a critical review of its ideology, manifestations
    and social consequences, in E. Blankenburg, E. Klausa and H. Rottleuthner
    (Eds.) Alternative rechstformen und alternativen zum recht, 6 Jahrbuch für
    Rechtssoziologie und Rechtstheorie. Opladen: Westdeutscher Verlag, 1979
Atkinson, J. M. Displaying neutrality: management of an interactional problem in
    small claims court hearings.   Paper presented at the International Conference
    on Language and Social Psychology, University of Bristol, England, July 16-20,
    1979
Atkinson, J. M. and Drew, P. Order in court: the organisation of verbal inter-
    action in judicial settings.   Oxford Socio-Legal Studies, London: Macmillan
    Press, 1979
Aubert, V. (Ed.) The sociology of law.   Harmondsworth, Middlesex: Penguin, 1969
Auerbach, J. S. Unequal justice: lawyers and social change in modern America.
    New York: Oxford University Press, 1974
Baldwin, J. and McConville, M. J. Negotiated justice.   London: Martin Robertson
    1977
Bankowski, Z. and Mungham, G. Images of law.   London: Routledge and Kegan Paul,
    1976
Bishin, W. R. and Stone, C. P. Law, language and ethics.   Mineola, New York:
    The Foundation Press, 1972
Blumberg, A. S. Criminal justice.   Chicago: Quadrangle Books, 1967
Bolinger, D. Truth is a linguistic question.   Language, 1973, 49, 3, 539-550
Carlen, P. Magistrates' Justice.   London: Martin Robertson, 1976
Casper, J. D. American criminal justice: the defendant's perspective. Englewood
    Cliffs: Prentice Hall, 1972
Charrow, V. and Charrow, R. Lawyers' views of the comprehensibility of legal
    language.   Paper delivered at the Fifth Annual Colloquium on New Ways of
    Analysing Variation in English, Georgetown University, Washington, D.C.,
    October 1976
Charrow, V. and Charrow, R. The comprehension of standard jury instructions.
    Working Paper, Xerox, 1978
Damaska, J. Presentation of evidence and factfinding precision.   University of
    Pennsylvania Law Review, 1975, 123, 1083-1105
Danet, B. Language in the legal process: an overview.   Paper presented at the
    Program in Sociolinguistics, World Congress of Sociology, interest group on
    Language in the Legal Process, Uppsala, Sweden, August 1978 (a)
Danet, B. Communication in the courtroom.   Paper presented at the Mid-winter
    Convention, American Association of Trial Lawyers, Monte Carlo, Monaco,
    February 1978: International Symposium on Communications and Psychology in the
    Courtroom. (b)
Danet, B. Language in the legal process.   Law and Society Review, 1980: special
    issue edited by Richard Abel on Contemporary Issues in Law and Social Science.
Danet, B. and Bogoch, B. Have you stopped beating your wife? A sociolinguistic
    study of courtroom questions as weapons, cues and punishment.   Paper presented
    at the International Conference on Language and Social Psychology, University
    of Bristol, England, July 16-20, 1979 (a)
Danet, B. and Bogoch, B. Fixed fight or free-for-all? An empirical study of
    combativeness in the adversary system of justice.   Paper presented at the
    Conference on the Sociology of Law, the International Sociological Association,
    Cagliari, Sardinia, September 19-22, 1979 (b)
Danet, B., Hoffman, K., Kermish, N., Rafn, H. J. and Stayman, D. G. An ethnogra-
    phy of questioning, in R. Shuy and A. Shnukal, (Eds.) Language use and the
    uses of language: papers from the Fifth Annual Colloquium on New Ways of
    Analysing Variation in English. Washington, D.C.: Georgetown University
    Press, 1979

Danet, B. and Kermish, N. C. Courtroom questioning: a sociolinguistic perspective, in L. N. Massery, (Ed.) Psychology and persuasion in advocacy. Washington, D.C.: Association of Trial Lawyers of America, National College of Advocacy, 1978, 412-441

Danet, B. 'Baby' or 'foetus'? Language and the construction of reality in a manslaughter trial. Semiotica (in press)

Daniels, A. K. How free should professions be? in E. Freidson (Ed.) The professions and their prospects. Beverly Hills, California: Sage Publications 1971

Erickson, B., Lind, E. A., Johnson, B. C. and O'Barr, W. Speech style and impression formation in a court setting: the effects of 'power' and 'powerless' speech. Journal of Experimental and Social Psychology, 1978, 14, 266-279

Friedman, L. M. Law and society. Englewood Cliffs: Prentice Hall, 1977

Fuller, L. I. Human interaction and the law, in R. P. Wolff (Ed.) The rule of law. New York: Simon and Shuster, 1971

Hoebel, E. A. The law of primitive man. New York: Atheneum, 1954

Illich, I. V. Disabling professions. London: Marion Boyars, 1977

Kasprzyk, D., Montano, D. E. and Loftus, E. F. Effects of leading questions on jurors' verdicts. Jurimetrics Journal, 1975, 16, 48-51

Lieberman, J. K. Crisis at the Bar: lawyers' unethical ethics (and what to do about it). New York: Norton, 1978

Llewellyn, K. The normative, the legal, and the law jobs. Yale Law Journal, 1940, 49, 1355

Loftus, E. F. Leading questions and the eyewitness report. Cognitive Psychology, 1975, 7, 560-572

Loftus, E. F. Influence of language on memories and images. Paper delivered at the Fifth Annual Colloquium on New Ways of Analysing Variation in English, Georgetown University, Washington, D.C., October 1976

Loftus, E. F. Semantics and courtroom questioning. Paper presented at the Mid-Winter Convention, American Association of Trial Lawyers, Monte Carlo, Monaco, February, 1978. International Symposium on Communications and Psychology in the courtroom.

Loftus, E. F. and Palmer, J. C. Reconstruction of automobile destruction: an example of the interaction between language and memory. Journal of Verbal Learning and Verbal Behavior, 1974, 11, 5, 585-589

McBarnet, D. J. Conviction: the law, the state and the construction of justice. London: Macmillan, 1979

Mellinkoff, D. The language of the law. Boston: Little, Brown, 1963

Nader, L. (Ed.) Law in culture and society. Chicago: Aldine, 1969

Nader, L. and Todd, H. F. Jr. The disputing process: law in ten societies. New York: Columbia University Press, 1978

Nader, R. and Green, M. (Eds.) Verdicts on lawyers. New York: Thomas Y. Crowell, 1976

Naylor, P. B. Linguistic and cultural interference in legal testimony. Paper presented at the International Conference on Language and Social Psychology, University of Bristol, England, July 16-20, 1979

North Carolina Law Review Developments in law and social sciences research. Assessment Conference sponsored by the National Science Foundation. The North Carolina Law Review, 1974, 52, June 5

O'Barr, W. M. Legal assumptions about language. Paper delivered at the Fifth Annual Colloquium on New Ways of Analysing Variation in English. Georgetown University, Washington, D.C. October, 1976

O'Barr, W. M. The language of the law - vehicle or obstacle? Manuscript, 1976b

O'Barr, W. M. and Conley, J. When a juror watches a lawyer. Barrister, 1976, 3, 3, 8-11

Parkinson, M. Language behavior and courtroom success. Paper presented at the International Conference on Language and Social Psychology, University of Bristol, England, July 16-20, 1979

Phillips, S. U. Syntactic variation in judges' use of language in the courtroom.
    Paper presented at the International Conference on Language and Social Psycho-
    logy, University of Bristol, England, July 16-20, 1979
Probert, W. Law, language and communication. Springfield, Illinois: Charles
    C. Thomas, 1972
Roberts, S. Order and dispute: an introduction to legal anthropology.
    Harmondsworth, Middlesex: Penguin, 1979
Rosenthal, D. E. Lawyer and client: who's in charge? New York: Russell Sage
    Foundation, 1974
Rosenthal, D. E. Evaluating the competence of lawyers. Law and Society Review,
    special issue on Delivery of Legal Services, 1976, 11, 257-286
Sales, B., Elwork, A. and Alfini, J. A psycholinguist's approach to rewriting
    jury instructions. Paper delivered at the Fifth Annual Colloquium on New
    Ways of Analysing Variation in English, Georgetown University, Washington, D.C.
    October, 1976
Sales, B., Elwork, A. and Alfini, J. Improving comprehension for jury instruc-
    tions, in B. Sales (Ed.) Perspectives in law and psychology. Volume 1:
    The criminal justice system. New York: Plenum (in press)
Schwartz, R. and Skolnick, J. H. Society and the legal order: cases and materi-
    als on the sociology of law. New York: Basic Books, 1970
Skolnick, J. Social control in the adversay system, in G. Cole (Ed.) Criminal
    justice: law and politics. North Scituate, Mass.: Duxbury Press, 1976
Time Magazine   Those ≠X!!! Lawyers! Time Cover Story, April 10, 1978
Thibaut, J. and Walker, L. Procedural justice: a psychological analysis.
    Hillsdale, New Jersey: Lawrence Erlbaum Associates, 1975
Tisher, S., Bernabei, L. and Green, M. Bringing the Bar to justice: a compara-
    tive study of six Bar associations. Washington, D.C.: The Public Citizen,
    1977

Dynamic Dimensions of Language Influence:
The Case of American Indian English

W. Wolfram

*Center for Applied Linguistics, 1611 North Kent Street, Arlington,
Virginia 22209, U.S.A.*

Within the tradition of linguistics, there is sufficient precedent for a descriptive concern with languages in contact. From Weinreich's (1964) classic summary
of the types of influences languages in contact may have on each other to the
current interest in pidgin and creole languages (e.g. Hall 1966, Hymes 1971,
DeCamp and Hancock 1974, Bickerton 1975), a continuing interest in this topic has
been evidenced. At the same time this concern was being demonstrated, and, in
some ways, related to it, a strong tradition of interest in non-mainstream
varieties of English developed within sociolinguistics. Given the converging
interests, it is surprising that the English of native American Indian communities
has received such little descriptive attention. Despite the persistent pleas of
Leap (1974, 1975, 1977) these varieties remain the object of selective, and, in
some cases, inappropriate attention. Some of the fundamental questions we might
ask about any variety of English still persist - namely, what are the linguistic
characteristics of those varieties called 'Indian English', how did these
varieties emerge, and what is their relationship to other varieties of English?
There is a sense, then, in which these linguistic facts are basic to the consideration of the phenomenological world of speakers and hearers in the context of
society - those legitimate concerns of the social psychology of language.

The presentation that follows is dedicated to the prospect of showing how the
development of English in American Indian communities, particularly those set off
on reservations, has taken place in some rather intricate and fascinating ways.
These descriptive details are a prelude to considering some of the attitudes,
motivations, intentions and expectations that have precipitated the resultant
varieties of English.

In order to investigate some basic questions about the nature of Indian English,
we recently completed a fairly extensive study of the English spoken in two Pueblo
Indian reservations in the Rio Grande area of the southwestern United States
(Dozier 1970). Although there are, of course, a number of different locales in
which Indian English might be studied, these locations represent ideal communities
for studying the representative varieties spoken in this region. Both of these
reservation communities are relatively homogeneous in terms of their Native American
populations, with few outsiders living on the reservation. In both cases, they
are also immediately adjacent to larger, non-Indian communities, where the larger
cities serve as the commercial and employment centres. The communities have
their own school systems, operated by the Bureau of Indian Affairs and are staffed,
in part, by persons from the local community. In a number of ways, then, they

377

are quite comparable.   Yet, the communities differ in one way critical to our
concern.   The native, or ancestral languages, typically learned as a first language by the generation over 30 years of age, are genetically unaffiliated.   In
the one case, the ancestral language belongs to the Kiowa-Tanoan family, whereas
in the other case it is a member of a linguistic isolate.

In the context of these two Pueblo communities, labelled simply Pueblo A and
Pueblo B in this study, language samples were collected from a range of community
residents.   Members of the communities conducted tape-recorded interviews with
over 100 speakers from the two communities, representing four different age
categories (10-20, 20-40, 40-60, 60 and above).   The language data from these
interviews is the basis for our descriptive analysis.

Given the descriptive base provided by the language data from these communities,
two questions have dominated our interest in the dynamic dimension of American
Indian English: (1) what are the contributing sources to the varieties of English
identified as "Indian English", and (2) how similar or different are the varieties
of English spoken in different native American communities in a given region e.g.
the Southwest United States?   Answers to these questions can give important insight into the underlying social and psychological dynamics which have brought
these varieties about.   Sorting out the influences is, however, not a simple
matter, and essential theoretical and methodological problems must be addressed
in approaching this task.   For the sake of organisational convenience, we shall
first set forth the kinds of potential sources that might have contributed to the
contemporary codes of English.   Then, we shall present the potential explanations
for apparent similarities in the English used by Native American Indians in
different communities.   Finally, we shall look at several illustrative linguistic
structures which show the dynamic balance found in the resultant varieties of
American Indian English.   Hopefully, these considerations will lead us to some
conclusions which have a valid linguistic and social basis.

Sources of influence

Given the language situation which existed historically in many American Indian
communities, it is reasonable to consider first the possibility that structures
in these varieties of English are directly influenced by the ancestral languages
of the community.   That is, structures in the variety may reflect the imposition
of the native language system which was used in the communities historically and,
in many cases, is used concurrently.   That source language transfer should play
a role in the formation of a distinct variety of English is not surprising, and
there are many known cases of such influences which have contributed directly to
the development of distinct dialects of English (e.g. Marckwardt 1958).   Perhaps
a more important question in this regard is how we formally justify the attribution of this source influence.   The most likely basis for such a determination is
an appeal to the so-called "contrastive analysis hypothesis".   In this approach,
the rules for Ll and L2 are placed side by side and, where there is a conflict,
a form from Ll may be predicted to occur in L2 at this point of conflict.

The basic problem with this perspective lies in the insistence on predictability.
As it turns out, there are many cases where predicted influence simply does not
take place for one reason or another.   Studies of divergence in L2 language
situations (e.g. Corder 1967;   Richards 1971) clearly indicate the failure of the
predictive claim based on the contrastive analysis.   Given such evidence, the
predictive base must be qualified or abandoned.   A weaker version of the contrastive language hypothesis as set forth by Wardhaugh (1970) does not maintain a predictive base.   Instead, it starts with evidence of divergence in L2 and examines
it in the light of the rules of Ll.   If divergence in L2 matches a rule of Ll
where it is in conflict with Ll, then it might be a candidate for attribution to
Ll influence.   The emphasis here is on observed forms rather than the predicted

forms.   It should be noted however that just because there is a similarity in
the divergence of L2 which conforms to a rule in Ll, this does not make Ll the
only source from which it might be derived.   As we shall see, there are alternative explanations which legitimately may have led to the same structure.   These
explanations may compete or converge with the evidence from contrasting Ll and L2.

A further complication in attributing divergence in L2 to transfer from Ll relates
to the nature of transfer processes.   Not all transfer processes are unilateral
and isomorphic.   Selected parts of particular rules or forms may transfer without
the entire rule being realised (i.e. a type of caulking) or rules from the source
language may be extended in the transfer process (cf Weinreich 1964:40-41).   In
either case, the transfer process is not isomorphic.   Furthermore, the dynamics
of the transfer process may result in hyperforms which are not traceable in any
direct way to either Ll or L2 grammars.   These are a by-product of the dynamic
interaction of two systems and cannot be seen in terms of a simple Ll influence;
they involve the creation of new rules based on the conflict of Ll and L2 rather
than a direct transfer of a rule (cf Wolfram 1974:209).   Aspects of "selective",
"extended", and "hyper-transfer" influence are not exceptional, and have been documented in numerous studies of language transfer from quite different perspectives.

Even if we could overcome all the theoretical and practical problems associated
with contrastive analysis, we would not be able to attribute all aspects of divergence in Indian English varieties to source language transfer.   Other alternatives must be considered as legitimate sources of influence.   One alternative
explanation is related to the acquisition of English as a second language historically as described above, but it is not dependent upon the relationship between
Ll and L2, as in the case of source language trasnfer.   Instead, it is the particular structure of L2, in this case English, as it is subjected to general
language learning strategies that accounts for the divergence.   Recent research
on second language acquisition has revealed that there are aspects of divergence
from the target language system which will be found regardless of the structure of
Ll (e.g. Selinker 1974; Burt and Kiparsky 1972; Hatch 1974).   These particular
modifications of the L2 system result from the application of general principles
of language acquisition to particular aspects of L2's structure.

One type of strategy which might account for such modification is rule generalization (or "overgeneralization" as termed by some) of one type or another.   When
the target language has a rule relating to a particular set of items within a
wider set, the rule might be extended to cover the wider set.   An instance of
this involves lexical exceptions such as some of the plural forms of English.
These involve an extensive regular pattern of formation, but also some irregular
plural forms.   The predominant and regular pattern is learned and applied to
those noun forms which are exceptions to the rule, resulting in the "regulariza-
tion" of "irregular" forms (e.g. oxes for oxen, mans for men).

Another instance of generalization might extend a rule beyond its constraints for
application or non-application as found in L2.   This would not involve regulari-
zing lexical exceptions or irregular forms, but expanding the structural limitations of rules' application.   The important aspect of such modifications is their
relationship to the target language system as approached by any learner of the
language.   In a situation of this type, it is quite possible that structures derived from such a process might become "fossilized", that is, the modified forms
may be maintained long after the speaker has gone through the transitional process
of learning the L2 system.   Given the historical language learning situation in
many American Indian communities, it is quite possible that aspects of target
language modification exist along with aspects of language transfer as an essential
part of the contemporary variety.

In order to account for forms on the basis of general second language acquisition strategies, several types of arguments are relevant.   First of all, divergence of this type should be predictable based on our knowledge of the target language system.   Based on the principle of generalization (or over-generalization) mentioned above, certain aspects of the system should be predisposed for modification. Rules with marked lexical exceptions and rules with marked structural restrictions should be subject to such modification, so that we would predict that irregular plural forms or irregular verb forms would be "regularized", or that the marked exception of third person present tense /-z/ might be eliminated by analogy with the lack of marking on other present tense forms.

A second argument comes from data indicating similar modifications in these target languages despite typologically quite diverse source languages.   This, of course, is an empirically-based argument which is dependent on the representativeness of the data.   Although the investigation of second language acquisition from the viewpoint of general acquisitional strategies is relatively recent, there does exist an inventory of divergent forms which have been collected from speakers of English as a second language.   (An example of a collection of this sort is Burt and Kiparsky's The Gooficon, 1972.)   The emergence of the same type of divergence from learners of English whose source languages are typologically quite diverse must be considered as a strong argument for maintaining a target language source, as opposed to native language transfer.

A supportive argument comes from the observation that some of the divergent forms have parallels in first language acquisition.   As mentioned earlier, strategies such as generalization appear to be operative in both first and second language acquisition.   Based on the assumption that such strategies are typical of acquisition regardless of when it takes place, similarity of divergence in first and second language acquisition can be supportive evidence for the attribution of a form to target language adaptation.

An additional argument might be made on the basis of how the forms are distributed among speakers in the community.   This is particularly relevant when the role of bilingualism or the order of first and second language acquisition might differ among community members.   In the case of communities such as those studied here, we have such differences represented among speakers.   For most middle-aged and older community residents the Native American language was the first language learned, whereas many of the younger generation residents are learning English simultaneously or as the first language.   Given this kind of distribution, we might expect that aspects of the varieties related to these general principles would be more prominent among those speakers for whom English was acquired following the acquisition of the Indian language.   Thus, supportive evidence comes from the generational differences found in the distribution of divergent forms as found in some Indian communities.

One more source explanation must be considered for the structures of American Indian English varieties, particularly as we describe their divergence from standard varieties of English.   This is the possible influence of other non-mainstream varieties of English.   Given the dynamics of cultural contact in American society in which ethnic minorities are relegated to roles which may lead to more contact with other non-mainstream groups than with mainstream groups, it would not be surprising for this kind of diffusion to take place.   Studies of such situations have indicated that the influence of surrounding non-mainstream groups can be quite significant (e.g. Wolfram 1974) and that non-English speaking communities will often take on the characteristics of non-mainstream varieties as English becomes a more prominent language within the community (Biondi 1975). Leap's discussion of Isletan English (1974:83) specifically recognises this potential source of influence in American Indian communities.

The basis for identifying a particular form as derived from another non-mainstream variety of English must go beyond the simple attestation of parallel forms in an Indian English variety and some other non-mainstream variety.   Ultimately, that must be a reasonable social basis for expecting that a form might have been incorporated from the other variety.   While diffusion can certainly be selective and several different non-mainstream varieties might lend their influence, we would expect some historical social situation to support a linguistic parallel.

In cases where a structure is attributed to diffusion vis-à-vis other sources, we would expect forms to show a continuous distribution of isoglosses instead of a discontinuous pattern.   As Kiparsky put it:

> An interesting consequence of this (i.e. borrowing items) is that isoglosses formed by the spread of rules over a speech territory should form large, coherent dialect areas, whereas those formed by simplification should be characteristically discontinuous because of independent development of the same change in several speech communities. (1968:195)

Indian English influence from other non-mainstream varieties should show the continuous nature of the isoglossal distribution socially and/or regionally.

It should be mentioned here that some researchers have suggested that some aspects of English variation can be explained, not on the basis of surrounding non-mainstream varieties of English, but on the basis of vestigial influence from a general American Indian English pidgin or creole.   Attestations for a general American Indian Pidgin English were presented some time ago by Leechman and Hall (1955), and further attestations have been advanced by Miller (1967), and especially Dillard (1972, 1975).   Without disputing the possibility of the existence of such a language situation historically in other regions of the United States (cf. Silverstein 1973), we must conclude that it is highly unlikely that it would have existed in the context of the Southwestern United States.   While certain structures are indeed similar to those which might be derived from such a source, there are also structures that might be derived through the kinds of source influences we mentioned above, such as general second language acquisition strategies (cf. Schumann 1974).   Essentially, we have to reconstruct a social milieu amenable to the emergence of such a system and document its widespread usage by Indian and non-Indian groups in the area historically.   Based on our understanding of the contact situation in the Rio Grande region such does not seem plausible, although we might not be able to dismiss this possible source categorically.

As we have seen, there are several different sources which might have been tapped by the emerging variety of English used in some Indian communities in the Southwest Rio Grande area.   Sorting out the actual influences requires both linguistic and social considerations.

Sources of similarity

As we mentioned earlier, one of the important questions concerning the English of Indian communities is how similar or different these varieties may be in different communities.   This was our rationale for studying the English in two different communities with different language backgrounds.   In looking for similarity in the English across different communities, however, we must be careful not to adopt simplistic explanations for the existence of similarities.   As with, and related to our discussion of the original influences of American Indian English varieties, we must recognise that similarities among communities may have several difference explanatory bases.

One possible explanation for similarities between varieties is related to how the

ancestral codes may have influenced these varieties.   It is certainly possible
that these indigenous language systems are imposing their structure on the English
of these communities in quite similar ways.   In order to justify a similarity on
this basis, the ancestral languages must be typologically similar at a point of
conflict with the English structure.   (We have already noted that the ancestral
languages of Pueblo A and B are genetically unrelated.)   Similarity between varieties of English spoken in different Indian communities, then, might be due to
identical structural transfer.

A second possible explanation is related to the inherent structure of the English
system as a target language in second language acquisition.   As mentioned in the
previous section, shared structures in such cases would be maintained regardless
of the first language background.   In this regard, speakers of English as a
second language in Indian communities would not only be akin to each other, but
they would share these characteristics with other learners of English as a second
language in non-Indian communities.   Thus, some similarities might be due to the
identical structural modification of English based on the organisation of the
English system.

A third possible explanation for similarity is exposure to identical non-mainstream models.   Using an idealised mainstream variety of English as a reference
point for describing divergence in Indian English, it is certainly possible to
find structures shared with other non-mainstream varieties of English.   If we can
show that a particular form exists in a contact non-mainstream variety of English,
the possibility of non-mainstream dialect diffusion must be considered as a viable
explanation for shared features.   In such a case, the similarity of structures
might be due to diffusion from a common external source.   If the contact source
is not common to both varieties, then it must at least be identical with respect
to the structure in question.   In such cases of apparent diffusion, we have an
identical non-mainstream English model.

It should be noted that none of the explanations for similarity cited thus far
assumes contact between the communities as a basis for their similar structures.
Similarities found in varieties of English are not prima facie evidence for a
common historical base of English.   There are, however, aspects of contact that
must be considered with respect to the possible explanation of similarities between varieties of English.   Two possibilities exist in the case of the Southwest Rio Grande Pueblos under consideration here.   Although the two communities
considered here are relatively self-contained and are not immediately adjacent to
each other (they are approximately 100 miles apart), a network of Pueblo
communities extends along this region of the Rio Grande area.   Thus, a limited
amount of direct contact between communities may be reinforced through other
adjacent communities in the network.   Diffusion within the network must thus be
considered as a possible explanation for similarities.

It is also possible that other factors unique to the history of Indian communities
could be responsible for the spread of structures common across different Indian
communities.   For example, the operative boarding schools which educated the
previous generations of speakers of English could have provided an environment for
uniting various structures used by this population in a given region.   There is
some evidence that these schools, with their historical policy of English-only for
native speakers of Indian languages, had a levelling effect on the varieties of
English spoken by different groups of Indians (Malancon and Malancon 1976).   In
many cases, these schools serviced students from quite different ancestral language backgrounds, and students were forced to use a variety of English almost
exclusively.   This type of situation would naturally lead to a certain amount of
commonality in the structures.   The role of contact between speakers from
different communities both historically and presently must be placed in perspec-

tive, along with the other types of explanations mentioned above in considering the basis for some similarities in the variety of English.

Some illustrative structures

Based on the preceding discussion, we can now examine some actual language structures which demonstrate the dynamic balance between the various sources as they have influenced the current varieties of Indian English.   These structures reveal some of the different strains of influence, and the ways in which different varieties of Indian English may relate to each other.   For illustrative purposes, we shall consider briefly (1) word-final consonant clusters, (2) unmarked tense usage, and (3) negative concord.

<u>Consonant cluster reduction</u>   In the study of non-mainstream varieties of English, word-final consonant clusters have received more attention than practically any other phonological structure.   When we speak of these clusters, we are referring to those clusters which end in a stop consonant and share the feature of voicing between the members of the cluster (e.g. <u>west</u>, <u>find</u>, <u>desk</u>, <u>act</u>, etc.).   Although reduction occurs in a range of phonological environments, dialect differences are most readily detected when the following item begins with a vowel (e.g. <u>west end</u>, <u>find out</u>, etc.).   Details of reduction have been outlined in many different papers (e.g. Labov 1972; Wolfram 1969; Wolfram and Fasold 1974), and the observed facts seem to be fairly clear.   With this background, then, we can consider the incidence of cluster reduction in the English of Pueblo A and B. Before doing this, however, an important difference in the ancestral languages of these communities must be pointed out.   In the ancestral language of Pueblo A, the words do not end in consonant clusters.   The ancestral language of Pueblo B, on the other hand, does form items with word-final consonant clusters.   With this difference in mind, we can examine Figure 1 below, which details the relative frequency of cluster reduction in the English of the two communities as it is distributed across four different age groups of speakers.

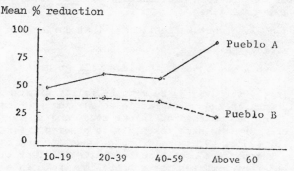

Fig. 1   Distribution of Cluster Reduction in monomorphemic
items followed by a vowel for four age groups of
speakers in two Rio Grande Indian communities.

The differences revealed in the figure seem obvious.   For the older generation of speakers, who learned their English after first learning the ancestral language, the influence of the native language systems is obvious.   Speakers from Pueblo A reveal a much greater incidence of cluster reduction than those in Pueblo B, no doubt a direct reflection of the differences in the phonological structure of

their ancestral language backgrounds.   For the middle-aged speakers, who are more
realistically bilingual, there is some convergence between the groups, but ves-
tiges of the language transfer process are still evident.   The younger speakers
in the two Puebloan communities are even more like each other, indicating a levelling effect of the differences.   So, it seems that source language transfer is
clearly at work in how consonant cluster reduction is revealed in the English of
speakers from these two representative communities.

Unmarked tense usage   Among the characteristic features cited for Indian English,
so-called "unmarked tense" has probably drawn the most attention.   This characteristic has been documented both historically and currently.   Unfortunately,
the bulk of attestations has been anecdotal, and some of the cited examples are
not clear-cut examples of a difference in grammatical structure.   For this
reason, we have given considerable analytical attention to this structure (Wolfram,
Christian, Potter and Leap, 1978).   Our concern is with those cases where the
grammatical marking of tense is not present, whether tense is marked in the main
verb (1), be functioning as a copula (2a), or progressive (2b), or other auxiliaries such as have + en (3a), do support (3b) and modals which carry tense marking
in standard varieties of English.

(1) a. Remember the time they fight for Unge, well, it was because
       there were some mens that could use their strength and they
       knew where the Indian from the pueblo belong.

    b. They all speak in Indian when we first started school we had
       to learn it, the English, in school.

(2) a. Well, now they are, but before they aren't.

    b. We would stay out there the whole day and then the train is
       coming, we useta run over to the railroad tracks.

(3) a. She left and went to work over there; she has never been
       away from home until then.

    b. Kids now go bowling, but we don't have that during our time.

    c. There was a lady that we can see her butt.

    d. And when we useta get in bed, the legs will go under.

Most of the examples in (1) through (3) seem to be fairly straight-forward cases
of a grammatical difference in the rules for tense marking as found among some
speakers from the two Pueblos focussed on in our study and those found in standard English varieties.   By the same token, it is observed (for example, compare sentences (1) a, b, (2) b, (3) a, c, d, that tense marking is a variable
phenomenon.   That is, sometimes tense is marked while at other times it is left
unmarked.   This variable usage raises the possibility that tense is being used
in a systematically different manner in these varieties.   In order to investigate this possibility, we have looked at a number of grammatical-semantic contexts in which unmarked tense occurs in order to uncover any systematic patterns
that might exist.   One of the patterns which emerged from this investigation was
the distinction between "habitual" and "non-habitual".   Habitual refers to those
activities or situations which extended over a period of time while non-habitual
typically refers to those activities which occurred at some specific point in the
past.   In Table 1, the relative incidence of unmarked past tense for the four
age groups of speakers in Pueblos A and B is given in terms of the habitual distinction.

TABLE 1   Comparison of unmarked tense in non-habitual and
habitual past tense contexts for four age groups
of speakers in two Rio Grande Puebloan communities

	Non-habitual unmarked Past/Total	%	Habitual unmarked Past/Total	%
		10-19 year old		
Pueblo A	0/602	0.0	5/73	6.8
Pueblo B	11/534	2.1	8/54	14.8
		20-39 year old		
Pueblo A	0/104	0.0	6/46	13.0
Pueblo B	2/123	1.6	6/83	7.2
		40-59 year old		
Pueblo A	17/473	3.6	72/155	46.5
Pueblo B	8/314	2.5	47/233	20.2
		Over 60		
Pueblo A	7/99	7.1	13/47	27.7
Pueblo B	9/139	6.5	46/104	44.2

Table 1 indicates that unmarked tense is clearly favoured in habitual contexts in
both communities, although this is a variable rather than a categorical constraint.
With an understanding of this semantic constraint on tense unmarking, several observations can be made concerning the source of such a characteristic.   At first
glance, we might be tempted to attribute tense unmarking to a general second
language learning strategy since this modification is fairly well attested (cf.
Hatch 1974, Frith 1977) in studies of second language acquisition regardless of
the native language background.

Before concluding that unmarked tense is simply a product of general second
language learning strategies, however, we must consider the role of the habitual
constraint in the English variety.   Both ancestral languages maintain a distinct
aspectual category marking actions that occur habitually or customarily over a
period of time, and this relationship takes precedence over temporal relationships
such as simple past and non-past.   Although the native languages of the two Pue-
beloan communities are genetically unrelated, they are typologically similar in
this regard.   Thus, it appears that we may have the restructuring of a modification from general language learning strategy in terms of the particular grammatical functions of the source languages.   Tense unmarking, in itself, may not be
the result of language transfer, but the particular aspects of habituality indicated may show the integration of language transfer into a more general language
learning strategy of modification.

Negative concord   Negative concord presents a somewhat different picture from
that of unmarked tense.   For one, there is evidence that negative concord is
quite widespread in a range of non-mainstream varieties of English.   Structures
such as He won't do nothing or There's not hardly no rides like that are documented in virtually all non-mainstream varieties of English.   Negative concord
of this type, however, is also documented as a general characteristic of language
acquisition, since it involves a generalisation of the negative marker.   Thus,

we might attribute its incidence in Puebloan English to at least two different
sources.   With alternative explanations in mind, consider levels of negative concord among speakers from the two Puebloan communities in relation to each other
and in relation to other non-mainstream varieties for which this pattern has been
tabulated.   These figures are given in Table 2, with the percentages reflecting
the actual cases of negative concord, e.g. He won't do nothing, in relation to the
potential number of cases in which it might be permitted structurally, e.g. He
won't do anything.

TABLE 2   Comparison of the extent of post verbal negative
concord for representative non-mainstream
varieties of English

Varieties of English	% Multiple Negation	Varieties of English	% Multiple Negation
Puerto Rican English East Harlem (NYC, 10–20 years old)	87.4	Appalachian English (10–20) (20–40) (above 40)	65.7 68.2 53.1
Vernacular Black English Jets (NYC, 10–20) East Harlem (NYC, 10–20) Detroit (10–20) (above 30)	97.9 97.8 74.5 49.8	Pueblo English A (10–20) (above 30)	74.5 42.9
White Northern Nonstandard English Inwood (NYC, 10–20) Detroit (10–20)	81.0 47.6	Pueblo English B (10–20) (above 20)	66.5 20.9

Table 2 reveals a pattern quite distinct from those indicated in the structures we
discussed previously.   In the case of negative concord, it is the younger speakers (10–20) rather than the older speakers who reveal the highest incidence of
negative concord in some other non-mainstream varieties.   The role of diffusion
in accounting for negative concord in these Indian varieties of English thus
appears to figure prominently.   While we must admit that language learning strategies (or even source language transfer to a limited extent) may have played a
role in how negation is used by older speakers, this does not appear to be the
primary source for the maintenance of this pattern.   If this were the case, we
would expect lower figures of usage by the younger generation, based on the
structures we examined above.   But the dynamic relationship with respect to
negative concord shows that diffusion is figuring prominently in the maintenance
of negative concord.

Other evidence can be cited to support the pattern of distribution we find with
negative concord.   For example, one of the most prominent stereotypes of non-
mainstream English usage, the use of the lexical item ain't, is found only among
the younger speakers in these communities.   Older speakers in these communities
may depart rather drastically from standard English in some aspects, but they
generally avoid the most stigmatised and stereotypical features of nonstandard
speech.   In a sense, we may describe the situation we find in these communities
as a type of "selective prescriptivism", in which certain stigmatised stereotypes of nonstandard speech are avoided at the same time other structures depart-
ing significantly from standard English are employed.   Several observations may
explain this apparent irony in how speakers relate to the standard variety.   It
must first be noted that many of the older speakers were first exposed to English

when they were sent to boarding school.   In some cases, the use of English was
strictly limited to the school and some limited non-Pueblo contact situations.
In this context for learning English we might expect to find that a certain amount
of prescriptivism would have its impact on the emerging variety of English in the
Pueblo.

The realisation of this prescriptivism in these speakers may also be reinforced by
some indigenous values concerning linguistic purism.   Dozier (1956:512), for
example, points out that linguistic purism typified some of the Rio Grande Pueblo
Indians in their use of the native language.   In Dozier's study, this was exemplified in their resistance to loanwords.   In a somewhat analogous situation,
Kroskrity (1977:241) indicates that prescriptivism in a puebloan community in
Arizona is manifested in speakers' concerns for the "correct" form of the ancestral language and the appeal to certain archaisms in particular situations.   The
prescriptive value found in the indigenous culture, then, might be adopted in
English, even at the most incipient stages of learning.   Shibboleths of English
prescriptivism such as ain't might then functionally coincide with an analogous
traditional value.   The overlay of an indigenous cultural value together with the
prescriptivism fostered in the learning context of English might explain why older
speakers appear to reveal more prescriptive items of English than some other non-
native English speaking groups which have been exposed to English initially in the
classroom.   From this perspective, the relative infrequency of ain't usage might
be symbolic on a much deeper level of value orientation.

We would certainly expect that any incidence of ain't, where found, would be most
likely among the younger speakers.   For these speakers, the traditional indigenous value on prescriptivism would not be as prominent and they would be much more
subject to diffusion from other non-mainstream varieties as they are exposed to
the wider range of options among the varieties of English.

CONCLUSION

The study of varieties of English spoken in some Indian communities shows some intriguing configurations in the formation of varieties of English.   Several
sources have obviously been operative in the formation of these varieties, and no
simplistic explanation for their emergence can be offered.   At the same time that
unique aspects of English structure may exist in different communities, the structures found in a given region may unite American Indian English in opposition to
other non-mainstream varieties of English.   There is much yet to be understood
about these varieties in terms of the balance of source influences which have
brought them about.   There is even more to learn about the social and psychological dynamics that have led to development and maintenance of these unique varieties.

REFERENCES

Bickerton, D. Dynamics of a Creole system.   Cambridge: Cambridge University
     Press, 1975
Biondi, L. The Italian-American child: his sociolinguistic acculturation.
     Washington, D.C.: Georgetown University Press, 1975
Burt, M. K. and Kiparsky, C.   The Gooficon: a repair manual for English.
     Rowley, Mass.: Newbury House, 1972
Corder, S. P. The significance of learners' errors.   International Review of
     Applied Linguistics, 1967, 4, 161-169
DeCamp, D. and Hancock, I. F. (Eds.) Pidgins and Creoles: current trends and
     prospects. Washington, D. C.: Georgetown University Press, 1974
Dillard, J. L. Black English: its history and usage in the United States.
     New York: Random House, 1972

Dillard, J. L. *All-American English*. New York: Random House, 1975

Dozier, E. P. Two examples of linguistics acculturation: the Yaqui of Sonora
    Arizona and the Tewa of New Mexico. *Language*, 1956, 32, 146-157

Dozier, E. P. *The Pueblo Indians of North America*. New York: Holt, Rinehart
    and Winston, Inc., 1970

Frith, M. B. *A study of form and function at two stages of developing inter-
    language*. Bloomington: Indiana University Linguistics Club, 1977

Hall, R. A. *Pidgin and Creole Language*. Ithaca, New York: Cornell University
    Press, 1966

Hatch, E. Second language learning - universals?. *Working Papers on Bilingua-
    lism*, 1974, No. 3, 1-17

Hymes, D. (Ed.) *Pidginization and Creolization of language*. Cambridge: Cambridge
    University Press, 1971

Kiparsky, P. Linguistic universals and language change, in E. Bach and R. T.
    Harms (Eds.) *Universals in linguistic theory*. New York: Holt, Rinehart
    and Winston, 1968

Kroskrity, P. V. Aspects of Arizona Tewa language structure and language use.
    Unpublished doctoral dissertation, Department of Anthropology, Indiana
    University, 1977

Labov, W. *Language in the inner city: studies in the Black English vernacular*.
    Philadelphia: University of Pennsylvania Press, 1972

Leap, W. L. On grammaticality in native American English: the evidence from
    Isleta. *International Journal of the Sociology of Language*, 1974, 2, 79-99

Leap, W. L. 'To be' in Isletan English: a study in accountability. Paper
    presented at the International Conference on Pidgins and Creoles. Honolulu,
    1975

Leap, W. L. *Studies in Southwestern Indian English*. San Antonio, Texas:
    Trinity University, 1977

Leechman, D. and Hall, R. A. American Indian Pidgin English: attestations and
    grammatical peculiarities. *American Speech*, 1955, 30, 163-171

Malancon, R. and Malancon, M. J. Indian English at Haskell Institute, 1915, in
    W. Leap (Ed.) *Studies in Southwestern Indian English*. San Antonio, Texas:
    Trinity University, 1977

Marckwardt, A. H. *American English*. New York: Oxford University Press, 1958

Miller, M. R. Attestations of American Indian Pidgin English in fiction and non-
    fiction. *American Speech*, 1967, 42, 142-147

Richards, J. C. Error analysis and second language strategies. *Language Sciences*,
    1971, No. 17, 12-22

Schumann, J. H. Implications of pidginization and creolization for the study of
    adult second language acquisition, in J. Schumann and N. Stenson (Eds.)
    New frontiers in second language learning. Rowley: Newbury House, 1974

Selinker, L. Interlanguage, in J. Schumann and N. Stenson (Eds.) *New frontiers
    in second language learning*. Rowley: Newbury House, 1974

Silverstein, M. Dynamics of recent linguistic contact, in I. Goddard (Ed.)
    Handbook of North American Indians, Vol. 16. Washington, D.C.: Smithsonian
    Institute, 1973

Wardhaugh, R. The contrastive analysis hypothesis, *TESOL Quarterly*, 1970, 4,
    123-129

Weinreich, U. *Languages in contact*. The Hague: Mouton and Co. 1964

Wolfram, W. *A sociolinguistic description of Detroit negro speech*. Washington,
    D.C.: Center for Applied Linguistics, 1969

Wolfram, W. *Sociolinguistic aspects of assimilation: Puerto Rican English in
    New York City*. Arlington: Center for Applied Linguistics, 1974

Wolfram, W. and Fasold, R. W. *The study of social dialects in American English*.
    Englewood Cliffs, New Jersey: Prentice-Hall, 1974

Wolfram, W. Christian, D., Potter, L. and Leap, W. L. *Variability in the English
    of two Indian communities and its education implications*. Final Report
    No. 77-0006 National Institute of Education, 1979

Speech Acts, Social Meaning and Social Learning

S. Ervin-Tripp

*Institute of Human Learning, University of California, Berkeley,
California 94720, U.S.A.*

There are many large issues which could be studied by a union of linguists and
social psychologists such as the issues surrounding language identities of the
large immigrant groups here in Britain, conditions affecting diversity or uniform-
ation of language and of dialect in a country still rich in dialect variation, the
role of language prejudices in the judgments of employers, juries and teachers and
the role of mass media in altering those prejudices.

But it seems that a major gap still exists among researchers. The gap is between
those for whom talk itself is the main data and those for whom talk about talk is
primary. Surely authentic conversation must be at the centre of our field.
Yet it is not, except in a minority of studies.

What I would like to do here is to report some work I have been doing with authentic interaction and then discuss the relation of this work to concerns expressed
by others.

Some 15 years ago I became interested in the possibility that the kind of directives people give each other might reflect the social system. At that time
Roger Brown's (1965) work on address had suggested two major dimensions. It had
also shown that address choices could be seen as a kind of tree structure (Ervin-
Tripp 1968). It seemed that directives might be a good place to find an even
richer system of variation. They might also show us how we use context.

My first approach was to collect many instances from samples of particular settings
where socially diverse people could be found, like hospitals, the armed services
and schools. A strong system emerged, showing the same social variables that
kept appearing: these were familiarity, rank, age, territory, difficulty of task
and role-suitability or predictability of task. But these did not form as good
a structure as did address and what we could not do was to predict the form of
directives without knowing more about continuous interaction - about context.

So now I have 80 or so videotaped natural interaction home scenes in five families
with two or three children between two and eight. I want to find out how social
control is managed by language in these families. So we identified episodes in
which verbal control moves occurred - moves to alter the actions of the others.

How could we identify and classify these in a way that could lead to rules for
control act forms?

Actually psychologists have a long history of paying attention to language.
Content analysis, interaction analysis, various coding systems for the measurement
of interaction have existed for decades.

The level of attention by psychologists has been at an inferential level.   For
instance, we code commands, or we code dominance.   Both of these categories are
natural categories from everyday vocabulary.   A command is an old form in English,
even in Latin.   Dominance is a kind of judgment of overall relationship, which
people make rather easily.   Indeed D'Andrade (Wish, D'Andrade and Goodnow, 1978)
recently showed that is one of the kinds of impressions people take away from an
interaction even if they cannot recall the relative number of commands.

The process of developing a content or interaction analysis code is a kind of
mini-cultural process.   We collect a group, socialise them to our meanings,
identify discrepancies, judge reliability by the extent of agreement, and put
pressure on deviants to raise the reliability of their coding!   High reliability
testifies to a good group process, but it may not tell us very much about what we
really need to have, which is translatability, indeed reversibility, between
mapping levels.   For example, if I code form classes in English for at least
some classes such as articles, and prepositions, and conjunctions, a coder can
supply a finite list.   Along with a knowledge of sequential rules of English it
is possible then to reconstruct possible sentences, to go from the abstract
level to the particular case again.   Unless we can do that, unless we know enough
about the rules of choice in performance, we have lost a lot of information when
we code.   We have lumped, rather than shifted levels and in a system with claims
to psychological reality of levels.

I do not know if the analysis of speech acts will help us with this problem or
not.   Work on the analysis of speech acts has been divided into two camps which
have not much to do with each other.   On the one hand are linguists and philosophers who have been puzzled by the fact that the same utterance can mean different
things depending on the context (Searle 1969, Gordon and Lakoff 1975).   They
would like to devise rules of interpretation so that they can find out what
speakers mean.   In another group are people such as anthropologists (Brown and
Levinson 1978) who are interested in such social meanings as deference, condescension, solidarity, distance, anger and affection.   They have noticed that the
same purpose in terms of instrumental transactions can be achieved by quite different means, the means conveying various social implications.   Clearly these
concerns must be merged.

Let me begin with some examples.   Suppose you walk into a friend's house and see
a three year old cutting up carrots with a very large knife.   You might say to
the child: (1) "Can I help you?"

What are you doing?   Are you making an offer to help, which the child could refuse?   Are you stating your intention to help with or without the child's
acceptance, perhaps at the same time moving in to take over the process?   The
action in your plans is the same: you are doing the cutting.   The difference
between an offer and a statement of intent is in the social relationship, in the
extent to which the child is a beneficiary in control of what happens.

Now suppose you are cutting carrots yourself and the same little child says to
you "Can I help you?".   I think you will not hear it as an offer, but as a request, even a plea, for permission to do something the child wants more than you.
You would certainly be unlikely to consider yourself the beneficiary of an offer,
unless the child was a certified Montessori-trained carrot slicer.

Yet the difference between these situations is not in the actions.   In each case
the speaker wants to do the cutting.   The difference lies in assumptions about the
relative skills of the speaker and hearer.   There are in fact grounds for some
disagreement.   That speakers do not always agree is certainly not surprising.
I think that when children given an offer say "O.K." they seem to imply that offers
are like requests.   Indeed, "Do you want to play outside?" could be either an
offer or request.

Notice that people could be very clear about whether they meant offers, commands
or permission requests.   They could say "Cut the carrots", or "Can I cut the
carrots?" or "I'll cut the carrots", or "I'll help you if you want".   But they do
not.   They choose instead to employ unclear language which jointly signals a
desired action and a social relationship.

Turn to another example.   Picture an elderly landlady and her student in conversation.   The landlady says "Can we move the trash can (dustbin) over here?" The
student will hear the request to move the trash can.   How can this be when the we
pronoun occurs?   Note that the conventional request for unexpected services would
be "Can you move the trash can over here?"   The landlady said can we move the
trash can.   How can the student hear this as implying action for him?   In English
superiors often use we to subordinates asked to do tasks for the common good.
Doctors say "We'll take his temperature at midnight", even when they will not be on
duty.   Teachers say,"We'll get ready for our naps now", though they do not intend
to nap.   Hence if the student regarded himself as subordinate he would hear the
landlady's request clearly.

Suppose he says to the landlady "Can we move the trash can over here?"   The landlady will hear him asking permission to move the bin.   So, in the first example
it is the hearer, in the second it is the speaker who is to do the action.   How
delicately tuned this system is to nuances!   A Turkish student who actually said
to her landlady, "Can we move the dust bin over here?" intending a polite request,
was misunderstood.   The landlady replied, "I didn't know you had a room mate".
She heard a permission request which would have been appropriate from a student.

In this case an understanding of who is to move the dust bin requires recognition
of social rank.   I have tried to show in these examples that we cannot know
whether we are hearing a request for permission or an offer in the first case unless we know who is more skilfull.   We cannot know who is to act unless we know
relative rank.

Each of these examples conveys two potential messages: you move the dustbins +
you are inferior or I move the dust bin if you allow it + you are superior.
How can we as observers tell which is meant?   We have an equation with two un-
knowns, $x + y = b$.

In each of these examples there is also a further social message.   In the first
case, an adult who says, "Can I help you?" to a small child while intending to act
anyway seems to imply social distance.   This is a typical form to superiors or to
inferiors but not to intimates.   The notion of distance, applying both to inferiors and superiors, is apparent in office interaction and in speech to children,
especially when under observation.   Children themselves have quite clear rank
asymmetries, rather than distance as a major factor, and so a subordinate would
not be given such a form by a child except perhaps in role play.

If we had clear messages about the action wanted we would have imperatives like
"Carry the dust bin" or "Let me help you".   If we had clear messages about social
relationships they might be statements like "I can do that better", or "You're
the boss".   We do of course have all of these sometimes.   There is a group in

California that thinks we ought to foreground social meanings explicitly all the
time instead of confounding social messages with other transactions.   The point
is that we have a system which allows us to attend focally either to social relationships or to the actions desired, and let the other dimension remain in the
background.   In this system we jointly signal both what we want and many social
features at all times.   We cannot help indicating adult/youth, inferior/superior,
woman/man, stranger/kin at all times, through our choice of means to convey speech
acts.

In addition, our choices can convey anger, affection or sarcasm.   "Could you
please give me the stapler?" to a near peer is sarcastic or funny.   This perspective helps us to see why there can be chronic communication problems in some
cases.   For instance, a particular speaker may use forms which convey greater
distance or deference than hearers expect, e.g. "I should have thought the
Regent Street Post Office is closer".   The result will be that her control acts
will not be heard as she means them.   Her hints will not be heard as directives.
Her directives will be heard as questions.   Her statements of intent will be
heard as permission requests.   These differences are chronic and regular.   So,
for example, Tannen (1979) has shown that Greek Americans continue the Greek
practice of making their directives less explicit than others in this country.

We see sex differences too.   Women use more distancing or deferential forms to
children than men do, but mothers receive them less often from children than
fathers do, at least in some middle-class American samples.   We are not sure how
general this is.

The net effect is this.   In the course of our everyday transactions we do not say
focally what we mean, but we conflate or collapse several dimensions of meaning at
once.   If we take the perspective of instrumental interaction, in which we use
other people to act, we find that we cannot tell what action is wanted, in some
instances, without making assumptions about rank, distance, normal social roles
and so on.   The natural categories we talk about these interactions with, such
as requesting, ordering, offering, all rely for differentiation on social features such as the right to refuse, degrees of control or levels of assumed relative skill.   And then, because these acts threaten the fact of others and incon-
venience them, we build repayments and hedges into the moves we make.   These
also, no matter how explicit the act indicated, make clear our social calibration
with the partner.   From the other perspective of signalling social relationships
focally, this system makes it possible to convey changes in two ways.   One is
through the selection of acts themselves.   The other is through the verbal
realizations.   The deviation of these from the listener's expectations identifies anger, deference and so on.   For such a system to be learned, and to allow
interpretation, there has to be predictability or redundancy in one of the two
dimensions, the dimension of acts or the dimension of social relationships.

Now I would like to show you some of the work we have been doing on social
learning in respect of this system, and then to tie these concerns to others
expressed in this volume.

We have been using four methods to study these processes.   We began with observations of critical settings and social relationships between adults.   We segregated one set of speech acts only, the requests or commands or hints which
elicited goods or services from others.   There were systematic differences in
their form.   These differences in form were regularly related to social properties like relative rank, age, normal responsibilities, and the cost or importance
of the demand.   The dimensions appeared to correspond to those we had seen so
often in systems of address.

Next we moved to videotaping naturalistic conversations in families. Our purpose
was to identify the contribution of <u>non-verbal</u> communication and, preceding <u>con-
text</u> to the form, during control acts. We wanted families so that we should be
able to follow the development of the complexity of the system at different ages.
Also, we thought there might be enough diversity of age and role within the family.

This work confirmed our less systematic observations that by the middle of the
third year children can already differentiate equals, subordinates and superiors.
They do not make requests the same way to all of them. They are also sensitive
to insiders and outsiders, that is to social familiarity. This differentiation
primarily takes the form of explicit elaboration to superiors and outsiders, not
hinting. They are also capable by four of strategic manipulation of these features for persuasion. My favourite example is not my own but from Catherine
Garvey (1975): "Pretend that's my car". "No. Pretend that's our car."
"O.K.". "Can I drive your car?"

This illustrates a rather extreme deftness in shifting both the pronouns and the
form so that it becomes a subservient permission form with a tribute to possession
by the addressee.

We also observed that the normal, unmarked form for directives by parents was
different from family to family. One must know what this form is to identify
when family members are marking special emphatic moves.

In trying to identify the purposes of the actors in each activity, we began to
realise that exactly the same action could be the target of different types of
speech acts. So if I want you to eat, I can order you to do it, permit you to
do it, offer food and so on. Our decision as to which was being done had to
depend on what the social assumptions expressed in the relationship were. Because these social assumptions themselves are important to people, the acts themselves might then be means to other goals. For example, offering is a frequent
way for small children to establish conversational interaction, to compel attention. We found that usually it was difficult for the youngest children in the
family to find a way to enter and attract the focus of others. Adults too, of
course, differ in their preferred entrée strategies.

A large part of our effort has been in developing situated comprehension and subjective reaction studies. If it is the case that forms speakers use are sensitive to the norms for the rank, age and so on, then whether people hear a speaker
as domineering will depend on whether she <u>exceeds some expectation</u> for the frequency of some acts, and the form the acts take. This would make sense of Wish and
colleagues' finding that the number of directives <u>per se</u> is not important. For
instance, workmen collaborating on a job may give each other a lot of directives
without being judged domineering. And indeed between peers imperatives might be
expected and suitable if the acts to be carried out must be specified. A more
elaborate form would be marked, insulting.

We tried also to find out if children heard as directives statements and questions
such as "Are you fighting?" or "Is the checker there?" which made no action explicit. What we found was that very early the children made practical interpretations of what the situation demanded. Such interpretations are possible because
family life is highly predictable. Their actions depended on their ability to
make such interpretations, and their willingness to cooperate. They rarely referred to the intent of parties to the interaction. In fact what people said in
asking questions or making statements was interpreted literally. Yet the information was enough to get them to change their actions when no act was mentioned.

So if someone was looking for a checker, and said "Is the checker there?" children
would return the checker because they said the speaker needed it, not because they

thought the question implied a request.   We have had to conclude that a large
part of interaction moves smoothly because cooperative partners are affected by
changes in information without making active efforts to infer intent.

So what does it gain us to have moved from using <u>only</u> a social set of categories
to using these categories in conjunction with the level of verbal expression?
First, we gain the possibility of developing clearly specified expression rules or
strategies.   The social entries into these rules or strategies will help us
clarify what the fundamental dimensions of social interaction might be.   We
already have some good clues about these from the work on address rules.   They
clearly have to include, from the earliest ages, dimensions of rank and familiarity, for example.   Second, we gain the advantage of being able to identify what
is <u>different</u> between two systems with precision.   These might be differences between children at different ages, or differences between speakers from different
social communities.   Third, we may be able to gain from this analysis more
understanding of the natural structure of action.   By that I mean that those
social acts which can be realised through the same verbal system constitute a
natural family.   A good example is offering and ordering, which overlap considerably.   For instance, you can say "Do you want to have your juice?"   Whether
this is heard as an offer or directive varies according to power relations, juice
as a benefit versus a requirement of the institution, and the usual use of this
type of form for directives.   All of these are continua, so offer versus request
seems not to be a sharp, discrete distinction.   Others may be.

I would like to take a little time to consider the relation of these speech acts
and social meaning studies to other research.

1. It now appears that many of the structural peculiarities of baby talk are a
result of the different interactional goals of adults interacting with children.
Control acts reflect adult managerial and protective roles, naming reflects
teaching, confirmation checks and repetition reflect concerns with intelligibility.
Controlling function in such register comparisons would isolate differences due to
other processes such as spreading out semantic information, simplifying semantic
choices, and choosing special syntax.   Many of these choices are extremely sensitive to audience effects and are heightened by the presence of observers before
whom, "good parenting" functions are displayed, or speech choices which imply
affection or teaching maturity, whichever the parent thinks is appropriate.

We have noticed that the social factors in the realization of control acts of the
sort we have been studying are so strong they override other factors.   For instance, an adult who says to a 20 month old "Where do you think this goes?" or
"Do you wanna help me?" is not making syntactic simplification primarily.

2. We expect that analysis of speech differences between speakers should extend
now to studies of language functions and to realization of function in language.
By defining clearly what these realizations are we can help accelerate character-
ization of differences.   The observations of R. Lakoff (1975) and P. Brown
(Brown and Levinson 1978) about sex differences provide good examples.   It might
be the case, for example, that when undertaking what Brown and Levinson call
"face-threatening acts" more women than men rank themselves low.   The result
would be a higher incidence of forms which arise from a stance of deference,
more embeddings like "Can you?" "Could you?" "Would you mind?", more use of naming,
more implicit requests which do not name what is desired.   That is, the most common
hypothesis is that the primary difference is just rank or power and that within-sex
comparisons controlling that feature would show the same effects.   O'Barr and
Atkins' (1980) courtroom studies suggest that this might be true, since high-status
women spoke more like men.   Current changes in the occupational experience of
women provide ample opportunity for controlling factors of experience independently

of sex.   But we need also to examine identity-marking functions of gender differences in language and see if they are heightened in particular conditions, e.g.
courtship or gender-solidarity situations such as boys' clubs.

3. It has been demonstrated that the deeper realization patterns as well as the
politeness formulae may be quite different in different communities.   What
happens when new learners must shift from one to the other?   Do they take the
same stance as they seem to in language learning and initially do their mapping at
a fairly surface level?

Native speakers appear to realise and interpret the acts we have been studying
through a combination of idiomatic forms and more systematic analysis schemes.
We would expect to find chronic misunderstandings and misperceptions of social
attributes arising from the differences in the customary ways of accomplishing
these acts.   The problem becomes more acute in scenes where what is necessary is
not situationally cued, since we have found the very quick understanding of
situationally cued needs across language.   Many of the perceived attributes of
foreigners may be explicable through an analysis of these features.   These
differences, we all know, are not just matters of language forms but sociolinguistic rules.   While grammatical or pronunciation differences are considered
linguistic, sociolinguistic differences are not.

We have made a point of separating the actions or goal-states which underlie
people's plans from the speech acts through which they use others as instruments,
and the realizations of those acts through language and its analogues.   Differences between groups can exist at any of these levels.

Attention has been directed already at group differences, at assimilation and
pluralism, at identity monitoring through speech features, at accommodation.
What I have drawn attention to is that language also does social acts, and systematically relies on social features to do so.   The mapping rules between
social acts and their verbal realization - how we do things with words - can show
us how people code their social world.   Indeed, learning to do these acts
properly compels the learner to attend to particular social dimensions.   So this
is a major form of social instruction.   In examining authentic interaction we
see the principle means by which the social system is learned and reaffirmed.

REFERENCES

Brown, R. Social psychology. Glencoe, Illinois: Free Press, 1965
Brown, P. and Levinson, S. Universals in language usage: politeness formula, in
    E. Goody (Ed.) Questions and politeness: strategies in social interaction.
    Cambridge Papers in Social Anthropology, 1978, 8, Cambridge, Cambridge
    University Press.
Ervin-Tripp, S. Sociolinguistics, in L. Berkowitz (Ed.) Advances in experimental
    social psychology. New York: Academic Press, 1968, 4, 91-165
Garvey, C. Requests and responses in children's speech. Journal of Child
    Language, 1975, 2, 41-63
Gordon, D. and Lakoff, G. Conversational postulates, in P. Cole and J. Morgan
    (Eds.) Syntax and semantics: speech acts. New York: Academic Press, 1975
Lakoff, R. Language and women's place. New York: Harper Colophon, 1975
O'Barr, W. and Atkins, B. Women's language or powerless language, in S. McCon-
    nell-Ginet, R. Borker and N. Furman (Eds.) Women and language in literature
    and society. New York: Praeger, 1980
Searle, J. Speech acts, an essay in the philosophy of language. London: Cam-
    bridge University Press, 1969

Tannen, D. Ethnicity as conversational style. <u>Working Papers in Sociolinguistics</u>
     Austin, Texas: Southwest Educational Development Laboratory, 1979, <u>55</u>
Wish, M., D'Andrade, R. G. and Goodnow, J. E. Dimensions of interpersonal communi-
     cation: correspondence between structures for speech acts and bipolar scales.
     Bell Laboratories Report, Murray Hill, New Jersey, 1978

Language and Social Interaction

M. Argyle

*Department of Experimental Psychology, University of Oxford,
South Parks Road, Oxford, U.K.*

The social psychology of language could be defined as "the study of the use of
language and sequences of utterances in social situations". It is partly in
social psychology, and is studied more or less scientifically by experiments,
using statistics, and trying to predict and explain. Only certain aspects of
verbal behaviour have been amenable to this kind of treatment so far, amount of
speech and categories of utterance for example, but not the contents of speech.
The social psychology of language also falls into the field of linguistics and
language study, which are Arts subjects; they look for grammatical and other
rules, study how people have used language in the past, emphasise the originality
of utterances and conversation, and do not try to predict or explain things.
Most social psychologists are on the scientific side of this fence, most ethno-
methodologists are on the arts side in my opinion. Instead of finding empirical
generalisations, they offer interpretations of particular instances. This can
be regarded as the early natural history stage of a scientific endeavour, but I
do not see much sign of movement in that direction.

I want to pursue this dilemma, this conflict of approaches, in three areas of the
social psychology of language.

1. Language as a function of situation

Social psychologists have become aware of the extent to which social behaviour
varies between different situations, and a number of linguists have recognised
the ways in which language varies with situation. Several writers have assumed
a kind of functional hypothesis, to the effect that the language system varies and
is functional in relation to situational goals. I would like to develop this
idea a little further.

The clearest case of language varying with the situation is perhaps multilingualism, where different languages are used at home, at work, and so on.
Diglossia, where there are high and low forms of the language, shows a clear
relation between properties of situation and properties of language – the high
version being used in more formal situations. As Brown and Fraser (1979) and
others have shown, high forms of language have more elaborate syntax and lexicon,
greater phonological precision, more subordinate clauses, more nouns and adjectives, and fewer verbs. This can be given a functional interpretation: formal
situations, where the high version is used, require detailed and impersonal information about tasks; hence more nouns, adjectives, subordinate clauses; in in-

formal situations there is more concern with interpersonal relations, hence there
are more verbs and pronouns, simpler utterances.

Turning to one of the best-known findings in sociolinguistics, Labov (1966) and
others found that the formal-informal, high-low variations in speech are similar
to the differences between the speech of upper-middle and working class people.
This is usually interpreted in terms of self- presentation, the clearest case
being hyper-correction of LMC people in Labov's samples. Similar differences
have been found in this country; Lawton (1968) found a considerable degree of
code-switching, in terms of the Bernstein categories between different verbal
tasks, using a more elaborated code for the more abstract task, suggesting that
code-switching may be due to the task being different.   It is usually assumed
that working class people are at a disadvantage, through using an apparently
imprecise form of speech.   However Collett, Lamb and Fenlow (pers. comm.) appear
to have found that while middle and working class children differed in the usual
way in speech style while doing a laboratory task, there were no class differences
at all in efficiency of communication.

There is more accurate syntax and more elaborate sentence-construction in formal
speech.   In some situations however there is hardly any syntax at all, as when
somebody says, "Orange juice, porridge, kippers, toast and coffee".   (There is
a kind of syntax here - one could not say "Orange juice on toast", or "Quickly,
juice, lightly toast and fried".)   The setting may be needed to decode the
syntax, as in the famous non-question, "Would you be kind enough to pass the salt"
and the form very common in the U.S.A. "Would you like to ...".   In these cases
I suppose that it is functional to use an abbreviated version which discards the
syntax, or a politer version which has a misleading syntax.

If we compare behaviour and communication in different situations, we find that
the repertoires of social acts vary greatly, just as chess, draughts, and tennis
have different sets of moves.   The non-verbal repertoire does not vary, but the
verbal contents do, and the categories of utterance types vary;   for example
the Bales (1950) categories need further sub-divisions for the analysis of psychotherapy interviews, or for management-union bargaining.   Situations require and
create special repertoires of moves (Argyle, Furnham and Graham, 1980).   This is
also true of vocabularies.

Verbal communication requires a shared vocabulary, which may be very large, as in
botanical gardens, or very small, as in a café which only serves tea or coffee.
The actual vocabulary differs enormously between people engaged in sewing, psychology, garages or surgery (Gregory and Carroll, 1978).   These vocabularies are
obviously functional in relation to the job being done.   Vocabularies are also
functional in other ways: technical words may be coined which are freed of emotive association, as in some of the words used in medicine and nursing;   technical
terms may be used to prevent outsiders from understanding, as in criminal argots;
words may vanish since they are no longer useful, as in extended kinship terms
which no longer determined position in society after the Russian revolution.

The meanings of utterances depend on the situation in a number of ways.   Rommetveit (1974) describes a game of battleships where players ask questions like,
"Is it in the 3rd row down?"   At each point in the game questions and answers
assume a body of shared information, onto which new answers are nested.   He offers
this as an example of the building up of a temporarily shared world.   The shared
setting enables speakers to take a great deal for granted, abbreviations and pronouns can be used and ambiguous utterances cease to be so.   Meaning is also
related to goals; "Did you do it?" requires the situation to indicate what "it"
was; however the fuller meaning of this utterance depends on the consequences of

a 'Yes' or 'No' answer, which may involve rewards and punishments.   Meaning depends on the class of objects referred to, and those with which it is contrasted. Thus dog may be contrasted with cat (in the home), or with bitch (at the dog show), or with lion, giraffe, etc. (at the zoo).   Meaning has emotional components, which vary with the situation.   Rips, Shoben and Smith (1973) found that animals are classified in terms of two dimensions: size and ferocity.   It seems very likely that such emotional dimensions might vary with the situation and its goals and that sometimes animals might be classified as good to eat, or entertaining, rather than ferocious.   We carried out a study, using multi-dimensional scaling, which showed that the dimensions used to classify people vary with the setting (Forgas et al. in press).   Meaning depends on the relations between different concepts, and different situations activate different relational meaning systems, so that 'ball', 'over', 'out', 'declare' are linked in one familiar setting (Clark and Clark, 1977).

One of the most obvious ways in which language, or rather speech, varies between situations is in the physical dimensions of sound.   People speak louder if they are further apart, if there is background music, at parties and football matches, and they speak softly in churches, even when there is no service in progress, and at concerts.   They speak loudly if trying to persuade or entertain, softly if they are conducting a meditation.   There are similar variations in speech and pitch.

Wittgenstein (1950) described language as a game that is played in a context for a purpose.   I and my colleagues have been trying to analyse situations in terms of game-like concepts like rules, repertoire, roles and so on.   Some of these factors affect the use of language.

We have carried out two studies of situational repertoires.   In one we asked informants to rate the likelihood of occurrence of a large number of suggested items in four situations, and followed this with cluster analysis of replaceability ratings.   This yielded 65 to 91 elements for the different situations. The main variation was in task activity (e.g. at the doctors) and in the contents of conversation (Graham, Argyle, Clarke & Maxwell, in press).   The second study compared hierarchical cluster analyses of the same items in different situations. It was found that there was a much greater separation and contrasting of work and personal or social issues, in a work situation, as compared with a date, e.g. questions about work and private life (Argyle, Graham & Kreckel, 1980).

As well as having different repertoires, situations have different rules, some of which govern verbal behaviour.   Some rules appear to be universal; in our study these were "be polite", "be friendly", "don't embarrass people", "don't make other people feel small".   Other rules vary between situations, and can be interpreted as functional in relation to situational goals.   For example: "don't pretend you understand when you don't" (at a tutorial), and "make sure your body is clean" (at the doctor's) (Argyle, Graham & Kreckel, 1980).

These rules are rather different from linguistic rules, since they have not yet been stated in a way which specifies the point at which they apply.   After all, behaviour does vary throughout an encounter, so presumably different rules are being brought into play.

2. Sequences of utterances

My second topic takes us to the heart of the interface between arts and science, interpretation and prediction.   The earliest work in this field was very definitely scientific, using transitional probabilities, and first order Markov chains, like Bales (1950).   It is possible to find longer chains than 2, using Dawkins' 'chain analysis' (1976) where the most common pair is defined as a new element, and the analysis is repeated until the data is exhausted. However it must be admitted that this has not increased our understanding of conversations.

Two-step sequences, though short, may be important building blocks, but they do turn out to be quite tricky. What is usually found is that an element of behaviour has a high probability of leading to a second element. A stronger definition would be that an adjacency pair exists when there is a rule to the effect that the second element should follow from the first. David Clarke (in press) at Oxford found a number of common types: question-answer, joke-laugh, accuse-deny, praise-minimise, request-comply or refuse, complain-sympathise, greet-greet, apologise-pardon, and offer-accept or reject; he also found a number of pro-active pairs, i.e. where the same person produces both, e.g. joke-laugh, and accept-thank.   There is some cross-cultural variation here; the adjacency pair most familiar to us, question-answer, does not hold among the Gonja unless the speaker has power to extract an answer (Goody, 1978).   When a social psychologist looks at adjacency pairs, it is evident that several different principles are involved. (1) The speech-act types are related in terms of rules of discourse, whereby a question leads to an answer rather than another question, and a joke leads to a laugh rather than an apology – though a very bad joke could perhaps lead to a farewell or sympathy;   (2) the meanings of successive utterances are linked – as described by Grice's (1975) maxim of relevance;   (3) some 2-step links are based on principles of social behaviour, like reinforcement, response-matching or equilibrium maintenance;   these are not rules, but are more like empirical generalisations or laws;   (4) some 2-step links are based on the rules of particular situations, like auction sales, card games, committee meetings, etc.

I now turn to sequences of utterances longer than 2.   Longer sequences can be constructed out of 2-step units, but there is plenty of evidence for embedding and phrase structure, for utterances as well as words.   Clarke (1975) asked subjects to contribute to artificial dialogues, like the method of statistical approximation to sentences, where 1, 2, 3 etc. previous utterances were supplied. The rated realism of these dialogues increased up to the fourth order, i.e. where three previous utterances were provided, and these were judged as slightly more realistic than real dialogue.

What we need is a conceptual model to unravel these longer chains, and I turn to an old favourite of mine, the motor skill model of social performance (Argyle, 1969).

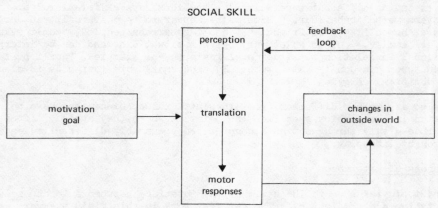

Fig. 1. Motor skill model

The model fits best situations like interviewing and teaching where one person is in charge. It suggests a basic type of 4-step sequence, which can be illustrated from the survey interview, as analysed by Brenner (in press), e.g. 1. Interviewer asks question; 2. Respondent gives inadequate reply; 3. Interviewer re-phrases question; 4. Respondent gives good reply.

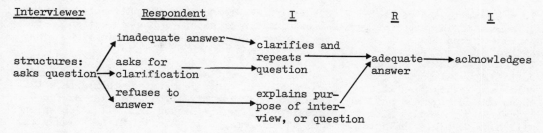

Fig. 2.   Sequences in the survey interview (from Brenner in press)

The model can incorporate situations where each person is pursuing independent goals, as in the following example of a selection interview:

```
Int-1 :  how did you do at physics?
C - 1 :  didn't find it very interesting
Int-2 :  what were your A level results?
C - 2 :  C, but A in Chemistry
Int-2 :  that's very good
```

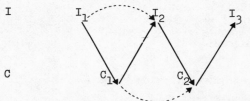

Fig. 3.   Two interlocking 4-step sequences

Another kind of longer sequence is the ritualised routine like greetings, partings, and Goffman's "remedial sequence" (1971). These do not fit a Markovian model, or the social skills model either. They are cases of Jones and Gerard's "pseudo-contingency" (1967), and of Schank and Abelson's "scripts", of which more later.

An important kind of longer sequence is the repeated cycle. Interviewers ask open-ended questions followed by a series of follow-up questions as shown above. Teachers use various cycles, e.g. (1) Teacher lectures, (2) Teacher asks question, (3) Pupil replies. Longer cycles can be introduced if the teacher encourages pupils to initiate ideas, or the teacher comments on the pupils' reply. A repeated cycle, with a build-up of contents towards an educational goal, forms a larger natural unit of discourse, called a "venture" by Smith, Meux, Gombs, Nuthall and Precians (1967).

In teaching, as elsewhere, the sequence of conversation is directed towards situational goals. Take buying and selling: it seems obvious that certain moves will occur in a certain order: 1. Salesperson(S) asks customer(C) what she wants, or is asked by C: 2. S asks for further details of C's needs, or C asks what is

available;   3. S produces objects or information;   4. C asks question, tries goods
out, etc.;   5. C decides to buy, pays;   6. S wraps up object and hands it over.

Take visiting the doctor.   According to Byrne and Long (1976) there are six
phases, some of which may be omitted, but the order cannot change:-

1. relating to the patient;   2. discussing the reason for the patient's attendance;
3. conducting a verbal or physical examination or both;   4. consideration of the
patient's condition;   5. detailing treatment or further investigation;   6. termi-
nating.

Quite different forms of social behaviour occur at a committee meeting, an auction
sale, and for couples kissing on park benches.   Studies of repertoires show that
these can be regarded not only as varying with the situation, but also as functional in relation to situational goals.   Moves are needed in a situation which
will make possible the attainment of situational goals which might be persuasion,
buying things, or making love.   This is particularly true of categories of verbal behaviour: the repertoires for teaching, management-union negotiation, and
psychotherapy for example are quite different.   In addition technical vocabularies are quite different as we have already mentioned.

Furthermore the sequence depends on the nature of the situation.   Schank and
Abelson (1977) suggested that there are scripts for situations, which enable
people to go through the right sequence at for example a restaurant:- finding a
table;   ordering food;   eating courses in the right order;   paying;   leaving a
tip;   and leaving.   Those who go to restaurants need to understand this sequence,
and also the roles, rules and concepts involved.   This is somewhat similar to our
own form of analysis of situations, though it does not go into the goal structure,
the NVC, or the social skills involved.

A provisional conclusion is that the sequence of phases is more rule-governed
than the order of utterances.   I would like to suggest that all encounters have
a basic 5-phase structure, as follows:

    1. greeting
    2. establishing the relationship, clarifying roles
    3. the task
    4. re-establishing the relationship
    5. parting.

The task, episode 3, in turn often has several episodes, which come in a fixed
order, depending on the task.   Each in turn has repeated cycles, which are built
out of 2-step adjacency pairs, and 4-step social skill sequences.

Mention should be made of the "linguistic model" of social behaviour, first introduced by Birdwhistell (1970) for the analysis of non-verbal communication.   However neither he nor anyone else has succeeded in finding the equivalent of grammar
or parts of speech for NVC.   Can the sequence of utterances be analysed on the
model of the sequence of words in sentences?   Clarke has carried out a number of
studies inspired by this idea.   He found for example that people could put back
scrambled conversations into more or less the right order;   they had an intuitive
understanding of order.   And he found that a question and answer pair embedded
within another Q-A-sequence was acceptable, whereas a crossed structure such as
$Q_1 \ Q_2 \ A_1 \ A_2$ was not.

We are now using another idea from the linguistic model and are parsing conversations from top to bottom.   The beginnings of a number of situations were
briefly introduced, and subjects asked to write a sketch of how the situation

might develop.   They were then asked to parse their scripts into the main episodes, and then to parse the episodes into sub-episodes.   There was considerable
agreement on the main episodes;   these were described in fewer words than the sub-
episodes, and the episodes fitted the 5-part schema above.   In the case of purely
social encounters it is not clear whether the task is omitted, or whether the
"task" consists of eating and drinking, or of information exchange.   There was
considerable agreement on the phase sequence for each situation.   For example,
when a wife calls on a new neighbour, it was agreed that the following episodes
would occur: (1) greeting, (2) visitor admires house, (3) other provides coffee
etc., (4) exchange of information about jobs, husbands, interests, etc. (5)
arrange to meet again, introduce husbands, (6) parting.   In our scheme the "work"
can be identified as phase (4) information exchange, though it could be argued
that hospitality (3) the provision of food and drink, is an equivalent of work on
social occasions.   We are trying to produce a set of rules which would generate
the whole set of sequences which we have for each situation.

3. Language and social skill

My third topic is also not represented in this conference.   The issue of social
competence offers a way out of an earlier problem - the goal is to obtain knowledge or understanding which would enable us to instruct someone in how to perform effectively in various situations involving speech.

A socially skilled person is someone who is able to realise his goals in social
situations.   A skilled teacher teaches his pupils more, a skilled therapist's
patients recover, and so on.   For such professional social skills the goals are
fairly obvious, though there may be more than one goal present.   In everyday
situations it is less clear what the goals are.   We have recently studied the
goals and the goal structure (i.e. the relations between goals) for a number of
common situations.   Samples of nurses and occupational therapists rated the
relevance of a list of possible goals in each situation, factor analysis was
carried out for each role in each situation, and later samples rated the degree
and nature of intra-personal and interpersonal conflicts.   For a nurse-patient
encounter the goal structure is shown in Fig.4.:   the only conflict is between
the physical well-being of nurse and of patient.   For a complaint situation
(e.g. about noise at night) there is a great deal of conflict, as shown in Figure
5.

This kind of analysis can act as a map, suggesting the way to move effectively in
each situation.   In a complaint situation, the findings suggest avoid trying to
dominate the other, and concentrate on persuasion.

There is considerable skill in the construction of single utterances.   Bates (1976)
found that Italian children aged 2 would say the equivalent of "I want a sweet",
but by 6, could say "please", rephrase it as a request, with question intonation,
as a conditional ("I would like"), and use formal pronouns in addressing the other.
Adult polite speech goes a long way beyond this, as in "If you're passing the
letter box, could you post this letter for me?" for which it would be hard to provide grammatical rules.   Being polite cannot entirely be reduced to grammar however;   how polite is "Please could you tell me why you gave us such a terrible
lecture this evening?"   Giving orders or instructions needs skill: "do X" does
not get things done, in most settings, even when the speaker has the power to
command.   Orders are usually disguised as suggestions, or even questions.

There is an important non-verbal component in skilled utterances.   The amount of
warmth, directiveness, or questioning is shown by the tone of voice and pitch
pattern.   Elaboration and comments on utterances are provided by special ways of
delivering words or phrases - in special accents, volume, pitch, etc. which Fonagy
(1971) has called "double-coding".

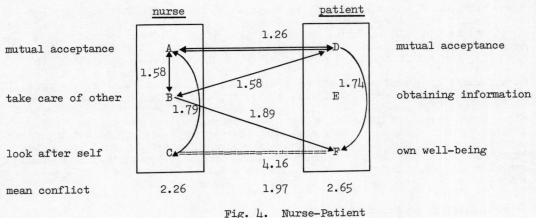

Fig. 4.   Nurse-Patient

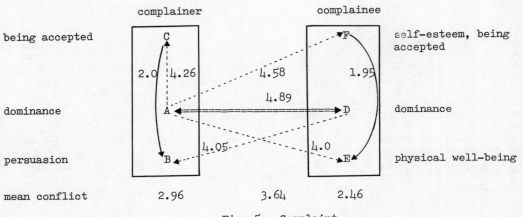

Fig. 5.   Complaint

What is usually regarded as "tact" requires more social skill.   Tact could be defined as the production of socially effective utterances in difficult situations;
these are usually utterances which influence others in a desired way, without up-
setting them or others present.   How do you congratulate the winner without up-
setting the loser?   What do you say to a child who has just been expelled from
school?   This is clearly an area of social skills, where the skill consists in
finding the right verbal message;   again it seems to have little to do with grammar.   McPhail (1967) presented teenagers with written descriptions of a variety
of difficult social situations and asked them what they would say.   The younger
ones opted for boldly direct, often aggressive utterances, but the older ones
preferred more skilled, indeed "tactful" remarks (Figure 6).

Similar considerations apply to professional social skills.   A selection interviewer may want to assess candidates in terms of adjustment, authoritarianism,
judgment, motivation, social competence, etc.   He needs to ask the best questions
to produce useful information in these areas.   Asking "Are you neurotic?" for
example would not be very useful.   The usual approach is to explore the candi··

date's performance in past situations which called for judgment, hard work, sta-
bility, etc.   Tactful skills are required to explore areas of failure, or to find
out the truth where a candidate is concealing it.   A skilled interviewer can control the length of the other's replies by using open-ended or closed questions, by
the amount of head-nodding and other reinforcement given while the other answers,
and by the use of interruptions.

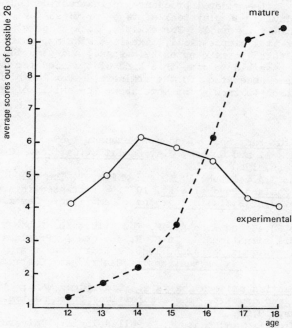

Fig. 6.   Acquisition of social skills in adolescence (McPhail, 1967)

Schools of psychotherapy differ, not in the grammatical constructions used, nor in
different use of categories of interaction of the Bales kind.   They differ rather
in degree of interpretation made by the therapist, and in the amount of direction
given (Mintz, Luborsky and Auerbach, 1971).

I turn now to skilled sequences of utterances.   A selection interviewer starts
each topic with an open-ended question, followed by a series of more closed questions.   The topics also come in a certain order, often following the candidate's
career historically, but leaving difficult topics until later.   Teachers, also,
make use of repeated cycles as described above.

In our social skills training for neurotic mental patients, we have found that
socially inadequate patients are often very bad conversationalists (Trower et al.
1978).   Their conversational failures take several characteristic forms, all of
which can be classified as failures of sequence.

(1) Failure to make non-verbal responses and feedback (head-nods, smiles, uh-huh
    noises) as a listener.

(2) Failure to pursue any persistent plan, producing only passive responses.

(3) Attempts to make conversation by producing unwanted information ("I went to Weston-super-Mare last year").

(4) Failure to make proactive move after replying to a question ("Where do you come from?"   "Swansea ..." end of conversation).

We have given social skills training for verbal as well as non-verbal failure of social performance.   The general procedure is instruction and demonstration followed by role-playing and play back of tape- or video-tape recordings.   Sometimes special exercises are used.   For example, lack of persistent planning can be tackled by practice at a simple skill, like interviewing, where the performer is in charge.   He is asked to make notes beforehand, and plan the whole session. However it is only possible to give this kind of training for deficits which can be recognised and are understood by the trainers.   For the higher reaches of SST in particular, we need to know a lot more about the skills of verbal behaviour.

REFERENCES

Argyle, M. Social interaction.   London: Methuen, 1969
Argyle, M., Furnham, A. and Graham, J.A. Social situations.   Cambridge: Cambridge University Press, 1980
Argyle, M., Graham, J.A., Campbell, A. and White, P. The rules of different situations.   New Zealand Psychologist, 1979.   Reprinted in Argyle, M., Furnham, A. and Graham, J.A. Social situations.   Cambridge: Cambridge University Press, 1980
Argyle, M., Graham, J.A. and Kreckel, M. The structure of behavioural elements in social and work situations.   In M. R. Key and D. Preziosi Nonverbal communication today: current research. 1980.   Reprinted in Argyle, M., Furnham, A. and Graham, J.A. Social situations.   Cambridge: Cambridge University Press, 1980.
Bales, R. F. Interaction process analysis. Cambridge, Mass: Addison-Wesley, 1950
Bates, E. Language and context: the acquisition of pragmatics.   New York: Academic Press, 1976
Birdwhistell, R. Kinesics and context.   Philadelphia: University of Pennsylvania Press, 1970
Brenner, M. Patterns of social structure in the research interview (in press)
Brown, P. and Fraser, C. Speech as a marker of situation, in K. Scherer and H. Giles (Eds.) Social markers in speech.   Cambridge: Cambridge University Press 1979
Byrne, P. S. and Long, B. E. L. Doctors talking to patients.   London: H.M.S.O. 1976
Clark, H. H. and Clark, E. Psychology and language.   New York: Harcourt Brace, 1977
Clarke, D. D. The use and recognition of sequential structure in dialogue. British Journal of Social and Clinical Psychology, 1975, 14, 333-339
Clarke, D. D. The structural analysis of verbal interaction.   Oxford: Blackwell (in press)
Dawkins, R. Hierarchical organisation: a candidate principle for zoology, in P. P. G. Bateson and R. A. Hinde (Eds.) Growing points in ethology. Cambridge: Cambridge University Press, 1976
Fonagy, I. Double coding in speech. Semiotica, 1971, 3, 189-222
Forgas, J., Argyle, M. and Ginsburg, G. J. Person perception as a function of the interaction episode: the fluctuating structure of an academic group. Journal of Social Psychology (in press). Reprinted in Argyle, M., Furnham, A. and Graham, J. A. Social situations. Cambridge: Cambridge University Press, 1980
Goffman, E. Relations in public. London: Allen Lane: The Penguin Press, 1971
Goody, E. N. Towards a theory of question, in E. N. Goody (Ed.) Questions and politeness. Cambridge: Cambridge University Press, 1978

Graham, J. A., Argyle, M., Clarke, D. D. and Maxwell, G. The salience, equiva-
     lence and sequential structure of behavioural elements in different social
     situations. Semiotica (in press)
Gregory, M. and Carroll. S. Language and situation. London: Routledge and
     Kegan Paul, 1978
Grice, H. P. Logic and conversation, in P. Cole and J. L. Morgan (Eds.) Syntax
     and semantics III: speech acts. New York: Academic Press, 1975
Jones, E. E. and Gerard, H. B. Foundations of social psychology. New York:
     Wiley, 1967
Labov, W. The social structure of New York City. Washington, D.C.: Center for
     Applied Linguistics, 1966
Lawton, D. Social class, language and education. London: Routledge and Kegan
     Paul, 1968
McPhail, P. The development of social skill. Paper presented at British Psycho-
     logical Society Conference, 1967, cited in Argyle, M. Social interaction.
     London: Methuen, 1969
Mintz, J., Luborsky, L. and Auerbach, A. H. Dimensions of psychotherapy: a
     factor-analytic study of ratings of psychotherapy sessions. Journal of
     Consulting and Clinical Psychology, 1971, 36, 106-120
Rips, L. J., Shoben, E. J. and Smith, E. E. Semantic distance and the verifi-
     cation of semantic relations. Journal of Verbal Learning and Verbal
     Behaviour, 1973, 12, 1-20
Rommetveit, R. On message structure: a conceptual framework for the study of
     language and communication. London: Wiley, 1974
Schank, R. C. and Abelson, R. P. Scripts, plans, goals and understanding.
     Hillsdale, New Jersey: Erlbaum, 1977
Smith, B. O., Meux, M. O., Coombs, J., Nuthall, G. A. and Precians, R. A study
     of the strategies of teaching. Urbana, Illinois: University of Illinois
     Press, 1967
Trower, P., Bryant, B. and Argyle, M. Social skills and mental health. London:
     Methuen, 1978
Wittgenstein, L. Philosophical investigations. Oxford: Blackwell, 1953

Homo Loquens in Social Psychological Perspective

R. M. Farr*

Department of Psychology, University College, London, U.K.

I was much influenced, in devising a title for my contribution, by the appearance
of Dennis Fry's little volume <u>Homo Loquens: Man as a talking animal</u> (Fry, 1977).
Fry neatly highlights man's most distinctive characteristic as a species.   It is
more important, I shall argue, to set this human characteristic in social psychological perspective than it is to develop a separate "social psychology of
language".   Language already <u>is</u> an inherently social phenomenon.   It is a mistake, in my opinion, to separate socio-linguistics from psycho-linguistics and to
see the former, but not the latter, as being the special preserve of the social
psychologist.   To the extent that they accord to language a role of less than
central significance in their research then psychologists have failed to devise
an adequate science of man.   Rather than awaiting the advent of some future
Messiah who might establish a social psychology of language, time might be better
spent in the interim by taking stock of those social psychologies in which
language did or does, play a significant and unique role.   I propose to confine
myself to (a) Wundt's "folk psychology" and (b) Mead's "social behaviourism".

(a) <u>Wundt's "folk psychology"</u>[1].

Whilst Wundt is widely acknowledged to have been the "Founding Father" of psychology as an experimental laboratory science his voluminous writings in the area
of "folk psychology" remain largely unread and unappraised by the official
historians of psychology(e.g. by Boring).   Wundt's quite considerable influence
on the development of social science now needs to be traced in the histories of
social sciences other than psychology e.g. in British and American anthropology;
in American and French sociology etc. (for a fuller exposition see Farr, 1978).
Malinowski, Boaz, Durkheim, Thomas and Mead were then at, or visited, Leipzig
and were influenced by Wundt's studies in "folk psychology" (as was also Freud
when he read them - see "Totem and Taboo").   By a strange coincidence the
foundations of modern linguistics were also being established at Leipzig at about
the same time though the links between Wundt and de Saussure are indirect, rather
than direct, ones (i.e. via Boaz and Sapir).[2]

---

1. It should be noted that Wundt's title was "Völkerpsychologie".   The associa-
   tive meanings of "folk" and "Völker" are not identical for speakers of English
   and German.
2. I am grateful to Glendon Drake for drawing my attention to these indirect links.

* Now at Department of Psychology, University of Glasgow, Glasgow

Wundt believed that it was not possible to study man's higher cognitive functions in the laboratory by means of introspection.   "It is true that the attempt has frequently been made to investigate the complex functions of thought on the basis of mere introspection.   These attempts, however, have always been unsuccessful. Individual consciousness is wholly incapable of giving us a history of human thought, for it is conditioned by an earlier history concerning which it cannot of itself give us any knowledge" (Wundt, 1916, p.3).   The study of man's higher cognitive processes formed part of Wundt's "folk psychology".   Whilst one could study the "contents" of consciousness in the laboratory by means of introspection it was not possible to use the same technique in order to explore either thinking or the nature of consciousness itself.   Wundt debated whether to call his supplementary psychology either "social" of "folk" psychology.   His prefer-ence for the latter adjective highlights the central significance, for Wundt, of language in the history of human development.   Folk psychology was concerned with the study of language, customs, magic and cognate phenomena.   These were mental phenomena, which could not be accounted for satisfactorily in terms of a psych-ology of individual consciousness.   Folk psychology "relates to those mental products which are created by a community of human life and are, therefore, inex-plicable in terms merely of individual consciousness, since they presuppose the reciprocal action of many" (op.cit., p.3).   The choice of the folk community as a distinct unit of analysis for the development of a new psychology is significant in the context of the present volume.   "Language, for example, is not the accidental discovery of an individual; it is the product of peoples, and, generally speaking, there are as many different languages as there are originally distinct peoples.   The same is true of the beginning of art, of mythology, and of custom" (Wundt, op.cit., p.2).   Wundt's point is that language and religion were in origin the creation of a folk community even though by his day most of them had become universal having long since transcended the limits of a single people.

Durkheim's "social facts" and "collective representations" were similar to those collective mental phenomena which Wundt had made focal in his folk psychology. For Durkheim, as for Wundt, these were phenomena which could not be understood in terms of the psychology of individuals.   Wundt's original distinction between his "folk" and his "individual" psychology now became the basis for distinguishing between sociology and psychology.   We are, today, in danger of perpetuating this originally false distinction if we continue to insist that sociolinguistics and psycholinguistics are distinctly different fields of study.

In his attempts to understand the thought of "primitive man" Wundt depended heav-ily upon linguistic analysis.   He thought that it was the language of primitive man which had led to the differentiation of the horde from the herd.   He noted how thinking was an activity closely bound up with language.   He observed how primitive forms of thought could be preserved linguistically when other aspects of the culture had advanced far beyond the primitive stage.   Wundt sought for the origins of language in the development of the human gesture.   In gesture language "... it is not sounds, but expressive movements, imitative and pantomimic, that form the means by which man communicates his thoughts to man.   ...   This mode of communication is not the result of intellectual reflections or conscious pur-poses, but of emotion and the involuntary expressive movements that accompany emotion.   Indeed it is simply a natural development of those expressive movements of human beings that also occur where the intention of communicating is obviously absent" (Wundt, op.cit., pp. 58,60).   Intentionality is, thus, not a necessary pre-requisite for the development of a language, either in the individual or in the folk community.   Wundt analysed various aspects of the gesture languages of deaf-mutes.   For Wundt, and hence also for Mead, there is thus both a phylogenet-ic and an ontogenetic continuum between non-verbal and verbal aspects of communi-cation.   Wundt points to the purely behavioural origins of language as a mode of

communication.   He noted how gesture languages were often restricted to indicating aspects of the visibly present world.   His various discussions of the
psychology of the sentence sound refreshingly modern.

Social psychologists themselves may have contributed to the continued neglect of
Wundt's "folk psychology".   Psychologies which centred on the study of "folk"
were subsequently adopted and adapted by National Socialist Governments in
Germany.   This may have engendered caution amongst a whole generation of social
psychologists concerning the value of such studies.   Studies of "national
character" (a closely related field to folk psychology) have long been out of
fashion in social psychology.   It is a matter of regret that subsequent political
events may have helped to obscure Wundt's distinctive contribution to the development of a social psychology based on the study of language.

(b) Mead's social behaviourism

Two very different psychologies emerge as a consequence of whether one stresses
either the continuity or the discontinuity between man and other species.   Mead's
social behaviourism was based on a very close reading both of Darwin and of
Wundt's "folk psychology".   In his bio-social approach Mead stressed those emergent evolutionary properties which set man apart from other species e.g. the
relationship between the hand and the development of the human brain and, above
all else, the development of language from the vocal gesture.   Mind emerges, for
Mead, in the course of each individual's ontogenetic and social development.
It arises from interacting within a community of others who share a common
language (a folk community in Wundt's sense of the term).   Meaning is "negotiated"
in social interaction with self and others and so reality (even physical reality)
is socially constructed.

The stress in Watsonian behaviourism was on the continuity between man and other
species.   The behaviour of animals and of young children had been successfully
studied without employing introspection.   Why should not the same methods be
used in the study of adult behaviour?   Watson was reacting against the experimental laboratory tradition of research established by Wundt.   He sought to
dispense with introspection as the privileged mode of investigation in psychology.
It is important to appreciate, in the context of a volume on language, that it
was verbal reports of experience which were being discredited.   In the brave new
science of behaviourism the observer was expected to confine his report to behaviour which he had actually observed.   The potential availability of the "data"
to public scrutiny became an important hall-mark of the new science.   There was,
thus, a rather dramatic change in the status of verbal reports within laboratory
contexts as a direct consequence of Watson's successful challenge.   The doubting
Thomases, who distrusted oral tradition and preferred instead the evidence of
their own senses, were now in the ascendency.   Speech now became verbal behaviour -
something to be recorded, rather than something to be listened to and understood.
Concern with the meaning of behaviour was highly peripheral for Watson.   It was
central to the social behaviourism of Mead.

There was a close affinity between Wundt's "folk psychology" and the social psychology of Mead.   Wundt's notion of the "human gesture" is an important development
of Darwin's notion of motor "attitudes".   Wundt singled out the vocal gestures
which underlay the development of human speech as being of special significance
to an understanding of human evolution.   Mead developed his social behaviourism
from Wundt's concept of the human gesture.   Mead considered Darwin's book The
Expression of the Emotions in Man and Animals (Darwin, 1872) to be the single
most important document for any psychology of language.   Unlike Darwin, Wundt
placed the gesture in its social context.   Mead discusses the "conversation of
gestures" involved in the typical dog or cat fight which Darwin had described so

graphically in his book.   Animals engaging in such "conversations" strike postures and adopt attitudes towards each other.   "Attitude" for Darwin (and hence
also for Wundt and Mead) referred to the often full-bodied orientation of one
organism with respect to another.   This purely behavioural meaning of attitude
has regrettably fallen into disuse within psychology (Fleming, 1967).   A gesture
was a part action which others completed.   It was, thus, for Mead a social action.
Hence his behaviourism, unlike that of either Watson or Skinner, is an inherently
social one.

The distinctiveness of Mead's approach is to be found in the way in which he defines the "meaning" of a gesture or action in terms of the response which it
evokes in others.   As a consequence of interacting with others an individual's
conduct comes to acquire the same significance for himself which it has for those
others.   This comes about through the human capacity to "assume the role of the
other" with respect to oneself.   It is interesting that Morris, who edited and
interpreted Mead's social psychology, went on to develop the foundations of a
science of semiotics (Morris, 1938).

Mead showed how mind and self are social emergents "... and that language, in the
form of the vocal gesture, provides the mechanism for their emergence" (Morris,
p.xiv, in Mead, 1934).   "The self does not exist except in relation to something
else.   The word 'itself', you will recognise, belongs to the reflexive mode.   It
is that grammatical form which we use under conditions in which the individual is
both subject and object.   He addresses himself. He sees himself as others see
him.   The very usage of the word implies an individual who is occupying the
position of both subject and object.   In a mode which is not reflexive, the object is distinguished from the subject.   The subject, the self, sees a tree.
The latter is something that is different from himself.   In the use of the term
'itself', on the contrary, the subject and object are found in the same entity"
(Mead, 1936, p.74).   The self is thus intimately related to the very structure
of language.   Perhaps a heightened awareness of self both as object and agent
might co-vary with a rich repertoire of reflexive verbs e.g. in modern French (in
contrast to modern English).   I am now convinced that man is more truly reflexive
in the autitory than he is in the visual modality (Farr, 1979).   Man rarely appears as an object in his own visual field but he can and does hear himself talk.
Much of experimental psychology is still dominated by the visual mode of exploration.   The extent to which this is the case is often under-estimated.   If experimental psychologists were to take Mead seriously then the study of language could
become much more central than it currently is to the concerns of psychology.

There is an important theoretical affinity between Mead and Vygotsky though both
men developed their systems of thought quite independently of each other.   Both
were concerned with the social communicative functions of language and with the
intimate relation in man as a species between language and thought.   Both men
saw in the symbolic nature of language the key to transcending the obvious limitations of Pavlov's first signalling system (in the case of Vygotsky) and of
Watsonian behaviourism (in the case of Mead).   The understanding of man's higher
cognitive functions only becomes possible when one grasps the central significance of language.   It is significant, I believe, that Thurstone's book on The
Nature of Intelligence (Thurstone, 1924) arose out of his experience at Chicago of
attending Mead's course of lectures on social psychology.   Here we are concerned
with the role of language in those cognitive functions·which set man apart from
other species.   This is much more central to the concerns of psychology than the
development of any separate "social psychology of language".

It is easy to overlook the highly symbolic nature of the environment in which man
lives as this is not visible to the naked eye.   This was Watson's great mistake.
This social reality is no less "real" than the physical reality which is the ob-

ject of study in the natural sciences.   Wundt was at least aware of its significance though he could not study it within the confines of his laboratory.   The
decision to base the science of psychology on what was publicly observable (i.e.
potentially available to visual inspection) was a deliberate and fully conscious
one.   This initial bias can now be corrected by assigning a more important role
to language.   Psychologists have not yet faced up to the challenges and excite-
ments of integrating what they know about behaviour through visual exploration
(scientific observation) with other evidence of an auditory nature which they may
possess about these same behavioural events.   The exciting prospect of integrating different kinds of information about the same events lies in the future.   I
refer here, of course, to cross-modal integration in the mind of the research
scientist rather than to the already well-established field of cross-modal integration in the research subject.

REFERENCES

Darwin, C. The expression of the emotions in man and animals.   London: Appleton
     & Co. 1872. 1965 edition: Chicago: University of Chicago Press
Farr, R. M. On the varieties of social psychology: an essay on the relationship
     between psychology and other social sciences.   Social Science Information,
     1978, 17, 4/5, 503-525
Farr, R. M. Homo socio-psychologicus.   In A. Chapman (Ed.), Models of Man.
     Leicester: British Psychological Society, 1979
Fleming, D. Attitude: the history of a concept.   Perspectives in American History
     1967, I, 287-365
Fry, D. Homo loquens: man as a talking animal.   Cambridge: Cambridge University
     Press, 1977
Mead, G. H. Mind, self and society: from the standpoint of a social behaviorist
     Edited and introduced by C. W. Morris. Chicago: University of Chicago Press
     1934
Mead, G. H. Movements of thought in the nineteenth century.   Edited and intro-
     duced by M. H. Moore.   Chicago: University of Chicago Press, 1936
Morris, C. W. Foundation of the theory of signs.   In O. Neurath (Ed.) Inter-
     national Encyclopedia of Unified Science, 1938, I, ii, 1-59. Chicago:
     University of Chicago Press
Thurstone, L. L. The nature of intelligence.   London: Routledge & Kegan Paul
     1924
Wundt, W. Elements of folk psychology: outlines of a psychological history of the
     development of mankind.   Authorised translation by L. Schaub, London:
     George Allen & Unwin, 1916

The Social Psychology of Language:
A Perspective for the 1980's[1]

W. E. Lambert

*Department of Psychology, McGill University, P.O. Box 6070 Station A,
Montreal P.Q., Canada*

Since the early 50's, I have watched the formation of a fraternity of men and women who have in common a serious interest in the social psychology of language.
What on the surface seems to unite this diversified, international group of people
is an amazement and fascination with language and the powerful influence it has in
social life.   At a deeper level, however, I notice another more basic common interest, namely an amazement and concern that the processes of prejudice, discrimination and other unattractive aspects of social life so often get associated with
language.   It is this deeper level of unification that shapes my perspective on
what directions our subfield will likely take in the future.

From the start of the movement in the 50's, those involved have made substantial
contributions and helped give life and structure to a promising new discipline.
In this short time span, language and its social accompaniments have been explored
from various vantage points so that now we have a healthy store of facts;   theories
have moved from the home-spun, hunch-testing stage to respectable levels of sophistication;   and an impressive number of methodologies, as good as anything in the
hard sciences, has been carefully and systematically developed.   Ingenuity,
vitality and concern have become the hallmarks of the field.

My main argument in this paper is that the practitioners of this new field of inquiry, with their particular perspective, are now well prepared to apply their
accumulated skills to stubborn social problems, and I am convinced that this particular perspective, shaped as it is by a focus on language, is invaluable for the
solution of these problems.   My hope is that the problems we address in the 1980's
will reflect the more general concerns of behavioural scientists - prejudice, discrimination and societal unfairness, that is, the issues that helped unite the
fraternity members in the first place.   What I propose to do here is direct your
attention to a selection of these old and stubborn social problems which I feel
our group is now ready to re-examine profitably because of the new and powerful
social psychology of language that has evolved.   The selection, of course, is a
personal one, presented more as illustrations than as crystal-ball readings for the
field as a whole.   As you will see, the examples range from individual issues,
like attitudes, to broader social issues involving schools, the community, and the
whole society.   In each case, language is a critical factor.   The sixty-four

---

1   I am greatly indebted to N. Sidoti and D. M. Taylor for advice and suggestions
    about the substance of this paper.

dollar questions, however, are: will we have the courage to confront these problems seriously, equipped as we now are? Will we have the persistence to carry
through to practical solutions?

Attitudes as Input and Outcome Features of Language Study

First of all, it seems to me that we are now in a good position to take a more
comprehensive view of the roles that attitudes play both as determiners or predictors of the rate of skill amassment in a second or foreign language and as outcome effects attributable to the degree of skill or lack of skill attained in the
study of the other language. So far, we have two separate streams of research on
this important issue, one on the determiner or "input" side, the other on the outcome or "output" side, with only the beginnings of an attempt at integrating the
two (Gardner, 1979). Meanwhile, important policy decisions about bilingual
education programmes and educational attempts to improve second language competence require that this integration take place soon so that, with the help of such
an integration, guidelines and limits can be suggested to policy makers about what
can be realistically expected. We need to know, for example, if hostile attitudes toward another ethnolinguistic group hamper acquisition of that group's
language, and if successful acquisition actually promotes more friendly attitudes.

Let me briefly review a sample of the research we can build on in this domain.
The need for a social psychology of language learning became apparent to me when
O. H. Mowrer in the 50's began to examine the emotions involved in the interaction
between talking birds and their trainers, and the effects such interaction had on
the birds' skill at talk development. At about the same time, Susan Ervin (1954)
started her work on the role of emotions and attitudes in the child's first- and
second-language development, and Robert Gardner and I began to look at bilingual
skill development from the same perspective (Gardner and Lambert, 1972). My
work with Gardner, exploratory and factor analytic as it was, convinced us that
negative, prejudiced attitudes and stereotypes about the other ethnolinguistic
group, quite independent of language learning abilities or verbal intelligence,
can upset and disturb the motivation needed to learn the other group's language,
just as open, inquisitive and friendly attitudes can enhance and enliven the
language learning process. We also saw that parental attitudes, positive or
negative, are picked up by children, so that the pupils bring a family complex of
attitudes to the language class with them. Gardner and Smythe (1975) have gone
further in exploring these aspects of attitudes and have found that persistence
in language study also hinges in large part on the attitudes the pupil brings to
school.

But there is much more to be done in this domain, and we will continue to rely on
Gardner and others for more information. For instance, Genesee and Hamayan (1979)
working with grade 1 Anglo-Canadian pupils did not find any neat simple relationship between attitudes and second language achievement, indicating that we need to
explore the whole developmental course of attitudes as applied to language learning.
Furthermore, Clément, Gardner and Smythe (1977) and Taylor et al (1977) extended
the domain by studying Francophone Canadians, showing us that attitudes affect
language learning in interestingly different ways when considered from the ethnolinguistic minority group's perspective. For example, Taylor, Meynard and
Rheault (1977) find that for French Canadian university students, the learning of
English can pose a threat to personal and cultural identity, and this can hamper
the progress made in learning that language. What is important here is that
threats of this sort can lead to suspicion and distrust. Other studies have
shown that parents' suspicions and prejudices about outgroups as well as own
group can determine the academic route their children will follow, e.g. French
Canadian parents who see little value in being French in the North American scene
are prone to route their child into an entirely Anglo educational system whereas

if they have hope in the French fact in Canada and pride in being French, they, without hesitation, keep their children in French academic settings and create for them a comfortable French social environment (Frasure-Smith, Lambert and Taylor, 1975).

On the outcome side, the research pace is just as lively, and in this case too the relationship with prejudiced thinking is just as clear. On the outcome side, one would expect that as skill with the other language evolves, attitudes toward the other ethnolinguistic group should become less suspicious and hostile. This is essentially what Richard Tucker and I found when we studied Anglophone Canadian youngsters who had followed a programme of immersion-in-French schooling for 4 or 5 years and compared them with control groups who had had conventional English language schooling only (Lambert and Tucker, 1972). In this case we knew that for both groups the parents' attitudes towards French Canadians were basically the same as of the kindergarten year. By grade 5, however, the "early immersion" pupils relative to the controls "liked" French people more, were much more prone to say that they would be "just as happy" had they been born into a French family, and they saw themselves as becoming both English and French Canadian in their makeup, much more so than the comparison children. Apparently, through their language learning experience, much of the foreignness of the other group was dispelled and they began to appreciate the distinctive and the shared characteristics of the other ethnolinguistic group. But other follow-up studies (cf Cziko, Lambert and Gutter, 1978) using different probing techniques and different age levels sometimes replicated and sometimes did not replicate these favourable attitude outcomes, although in no case were the immersion children less favourable to the other group than the controls.

Thus there is unexplained variability here, and this has prompted us to try out various new measures of attitudes, such as multi-dimensional scaling. In this case we find, as of the end of elementary school, that the early immersion language experience, relative to conventional schooling seems to reduce the perceived social distance between self and French Canadians (Cziko, Lambert and Gutter, 1979). In another study using an open-ended questionnaire procedure, we find that the immersion pupils at grade 6 see English and French Canadians as being less different at the psychological level than do the control pupils (Blake, Lambert, Sidoti and Wolfe, 1979). Then we have surveyed in detail students' and parents' views of the whole immersion experience by asking graduating high school students, some with immersion schooling experience and some without, to look back and evaluate it all for us (Cziko, Lambert, Sidoti and Tucker, 1978). Our conclusions from that survey are important here because they lead us to a level of understanding that prompts many new questions about the relation of language learning and attitudes. What we found is that immersion is an extremely effective means of developing high degrees of skill in the French language for Anglo Canadians, and it leaves these young people with a feeling of confidence, for example, that after high school they could work, study and live effectively in a French environment; that, if given simple opportunities to use French more meaningfully in social situations, they could become fully bilingual. They also expressed a strong willingness and desire to meet and integrate with French-speaking Canadians. Conventional means of teaching the other language do not reach such standards of competence and confidence. At the same time, however, the analysis brought to light various hurdles that these well prepared and motivated young people face if they try to penetrate the French world around them in Quebec. Some of these hurdles are very likely rooted in the English-speaking society itself which does not seem to provide models and examples for making contact with French-speaking people. Some of the hurdles are also very likely attributable to the French-speaking society of Quebec which also does not seem to provide models for encouraging gestures of personal interest coming from English-speaking Canadians. In fact, one begins to wonder how English or French Canadian young people can

learn to live cooperatively as Canadians when, for example, the schools they have
attended have been segregated along religious and linguistic lines for generations.
In such conditions, Canadian young people can reasonably ask why it is that their
society apparently does not want them to learn the other language or to get to
know members of the other ethnolinguistic group.   Incidentally, in an important
large scale investigation with French Canadian secondary school students, Gagnon
(1972) found that the vast majority thought that it was only natural for both
French and English Canadians to learn each other's language, and that, in their
views, the language would best be learned through schooling plus personal contacts.
Over 70% of Gagnon's sample said they would be very appreciative of occasions to
visit English language settings.   Thus in today's Quebec, young people from both
Francophone and Anglophone backgrounds might wonder why society makes it so
difficult for them to learn the other language or make social contacts with the
other group.

Because hurdles of this sort are very likely a major source of frustration, it is
important that educators and policy makers give thought to helping these young
people understand their society and letting them have a hand in improving it.
From our survey, there are apparently few ways these students can use French outside of school;   they would like to be more involved in basically French activities
but usually are not invited;   friendships with French-speaking young people are not
common or easy to establish;   and the majority of both immersion and control
students are thinking of moving out of Quebec in the next four years.   In spite of
current political policies in Quebec that limit the chances of French-speaking
Canadian students becoming as competent in English as these immersion students are
in French, still there are likely numbers of French Canadians who have similar
desires for social contacts but who face comparable societal hurdles in their
attempts to make contact with the English Canadian society (cf Gagnon, 1972).
From the perspective of both groups, then, we begin to understand how easily ethnic
and linguistic segregation can isolate subgroups within a society.   In fact, some
argue that this is to be expected in complex, ethnically-plural nations (see
Rabushka and Shepsle, 1972).   I have argued in another paper that this subgroup
wariness of social contacts across ethnolinguistic boundaries represents a search
for the peace and comfort which comes from being in a setting with one's "own kind"
(see Lambert, 1978).   If this is true, then overly enthusiastic attempts to penetrate these boundaries may be disturbing for both groups.   Applied to the Canadian
scene, this would mean that young people who have mastered the other group's language must test cautiously how far and how quickly they can make social contacts
that will be acceptable to the other group.

Perhaps the most important conclusion to be drawn from this investigation of the
early immersion experience is that we have been forced to place this innovative
form of language training in a broader societal context, leading us to the realisation that we must now seek out solutions for the complex but intriguing problems
associated with social segregation and cleavage within modern societies.   The beginnings of a solution seem to stem naturally from the early immersion experience
itself, especially from what the immersion students are asking of their society,
namely, opportunities to put their competence in the other language to meaningful
use.   French Canadian students may be asking the same, that is, similar opportunities for social contact across the common ethnolinguistic boundary.   As parents,
educators or political leaders, we must listen and try to understand what these
young people are asking.   The solutions needed are likely to be found in the
questions being asked.   It is our opinion that Canada, and especially Quebec,
provides us with a wonderful field station for finding solutions, and in our research we can draw on the goodwill of these two streams of young people.   This is
not to say that Canada is all that special, because each nation offers equally exciting opportunities.

So look where we end up after probing just one little facet of language.   We now
have a series of new questions to contend with.   In what ways do ethnocentric
attitudes hold students back in their attempts to master another language, and how
and in what contexts do open and friendly attitudes help?   Does getting to know
about another group and its language improve attitudes or must one get to really
know the other group?   Do we automatically get to like others through knowing them
or knowing about them?   Perhaps we should reconsider what effects social contact
actually has on attitudes.   If people want to be with "their own kind" thereby
contributing to subgroup "solitudes" within society, what can we expect from
attempts at integration?   How can we prepare people for integration in pluralistic
societies?   When are people ready for integration, ready in the sense that they
will be able to follow through with the respect of others that is called for?
Maybe integration is not the answer?

Language and Education

In educational systems there is more unintentional and intentional unfairness and
prejudice than most of us want to believe.   In many cases, language is involved
in this unfairness and often its role is so subtle that we never notice it, as
Howard Giles and his colleagues have so splendidly shown (Giles and Powesland,
1975).   In Montreal we have also explored some aspects of it.   For instance, we
now know that the ways students use language, including their accents and styles,
elicit biases from teachers that can be devastating.   In a study with grade school
youngsters (Frender, Brown and Lambert, 1970; Frender and Lambert, 1972), we found
that teachers judge and grade pupils with reference to their styles of language
usage, grading down those whose speech contains those features that are usually
found among children from lower social class background, and grading up those who
display stereotyped "proper" features.   We were convinced that these were biases
because we had objective measures of ability and knowledge of subject matter on
these pupils that told a different story.   And a teacher can really upset a
child's schooling and career by giving poor grades, especially unfair and unfounded
poor grades, just as she/he can distort the child's reality by assigning inflated
grades.   In another study (Seligman, Tucker and Lambert, 1972) we also found that
styles of language usage play a more important role in teachers' evaluations of
pupils than does actual written productions of the child, so that a "nice talking"
child is given exaggerated credit that overrides a composition or an artistic
piece that is independently judged to be only average or poor.   At the same time
"poor talking" children who present excellent compositions and art work are likely
to lose credit.   What is more, these biases of the teacher are apparently picked
up by other pupils in the class (cf S. M. Lambert, 1973).   The point I am trying
to make here, then, is that it is high time we explored seriously the impact these
language-based biases have on the academic and social careers of young people.

We have some good leads to go on.   For instance, take the role of language in
tests of ability and intelligence.   The more I study the path analyses of Duncan,
Featherman and Duncan (1972), the more convinced I am that academic achievement and
ultimately occupational achievement are determined as much, if not more, by social-
class factors as by intelligence or ability factors.   David McClelland (1973) has
recently presented a strong case against these biases that haunt the less advantaged youngster whenever language-related tests are brought into consideration.
Over and above the "advantaged" versus the "disadvantaged" speech styles just
referred to, we must take into consideration as well the influences of home background that can enhance or suppress skills in verbalization and expression because
they carry so much weight in assessments of academic achievement.   Furthermore,
family "contacts" play important roles in the biases, as when a young person of
questionable native ability and/or poor motivation is given summer experiences,
through personal contacts, in a lawyer's office or in a medical laboratory making
it almost impossible for him/her not to get into and out of a law school or a

medical programme, because he/she has learned the "lingo" of the lawyer or the doctor.   Versed as we are in the ways of language, we have the responsibility to challenge these forms of unfairness.

Another fascinating lead comes from the current work of Elizabeth Cohen (1979). She finds that a pupil's status among his/her peers within a classroom is determined in large part by an "ability to read": the better the reader, the more status and promise is attributed to him/her.   Of course, ability to read is traceable to social class factors, and again the disadvantaged child suffers in these comparisons.   Furthermore, in mixed-ethnic schools, pupils' perceptions of which group has power reflects the extent to which school authorities involve minority-group adults in administrative and teaching posts.   It turns out then that pupils' perceptions of power are indirectly linked to their perceptions of status which in turn are linked to simple judgments of "reading ability".   Cohen has devised some valuable ways of combatting these debilitating aspects of being disadvantaged.   She refers to these as "status-equiliberating" procedures, for example, having a good reader take on a teaching role to help others improve their reading skills while a poor reader is asked to teach in some other domain of individual expertise (be it needle point, basket ball dribbling, or making a crystal radio).   Thus, through the teacher, these other skills are seen as meriting equal status and appreciation.   Similarly, Elizabeth Cohen is also studying ways of improving minority group children's perceptions of their potential power and status by experimentally varying the proportions of minority group adults to be found in the administrative and teaching staff of public schools.   The main point here is that we too can play decisive roles in following such leads and devising our own modes of combatting these language-related biases in schools.

Language and the Community

In the North American setting, I see two independent movements under way that could be profitably merged.   Each is language-related and each touches on prejudices and discrimination.   One is the marked decline in interest in the study of foreign languages, and the other is the large number of foreign language users who continually come to North America as immigrants and wonder how far they can go in their attempts to keep "old country" languages alive in their families and their communities.   I am of the opinion that the decline in language study reflects mainly the feeling that traditional methods of teaching/learning a foreign language are inefficient and wasteful.   I do not believe it reflects a lack of interest in foreign languages and foreign peoples, since in the Canadian and the American communities where "real life" language learning experiences, like immersion schooling, are offered, large proportions of parents eagerly sign their children up for complete elementary school experiences with a foreign or second language.

Here is my half-baked scheme for bringing these two trends together, thereby offering possible solutions for each of the groups involved.   I have referred to this as "an alternative to the foreign language teaching profession", starting with the proposition that foreign or second language teaching might be better served if taken out of schools, colleges and universities and placed in the hands of the community "language resource persons" who would be asked to establish programmes of "language exchange" in which community members of all ages and all walks of life might serve both as language teachers and language learners.   Thus, one person would stand ready to teach English for 3 hours a week, under the supervision of a master teacher, in exchange for 3 hours a week of Italian, Greek, French, or whatever, taught by another person offering his home language skills, say Greek in exchange for English, or whatever the other language might be.   The point here is that some such community based "alternative" to the foreign language teaching profession might be worth trying, and the social psychology of establishing and overseeing such a programme could be exciting.

Briefly, this alternative should take the following form. (1) It should set its
sights on cultural and linguistic diversity at home, for example, on hyphenated-
Americans or -Canadians, rather than exclusively on peoples and languages in far
away countries.   (2) It should be designed for a broad base of students representing all walks of life, not exclusively for the college-oriented elite.   (3) It
should be geared for children from the earliest grades on.   (4) It should provide
a high degree of competence in the languages taught, for instance the attainment of
functional bilinguality, literary as well as audio-lingual.   (5) It should make
the learning of languages no more important than the learning about other peoples
and their ways of life.   (6) The master teachers and administrators of the alternative should become fully trained in the behavioural sciences so that they can
effectively teach about people's ways of life along with the language.   (7) In
the alternative, language maintenance and bilinguality should be presented as the
maintenance of precious national resources so that the immigrants turning to the
centre can feel free to be as Portuguese, Japanese, Spanish or whatever as they
want to be, at the same time as they can become as American or Canadian as they
want to be.   My guess is that if they are in contact with Americans or Canadians
wanting to become Portuguese or Japanese through their interest in these languages,
then they in turn will want to be American or Canadian, too, as well as Portuguese
or Japanese, or whatever.

There is already a fascinating example of a closely related project underway in
New England under the supervision of Susan Thomas and Rosa Diaz (1977).   They
refer to their programme as "language sharing" wherein teenagers from Italian,
Greek, Spanish or Japanese homes in and around Boston are asked to take a special
course in language arts.   There they are introduced to the idea that they are to
share their home language with groups of children a few years younger than themselves, under the supervision of a master teacher whose task it is to teach them
how to teach and to work out with them a programme in Italian or Greek that will be
interesting to the younger pupils.   The course runs all year and the adolescent
"junior teachers" are provided with materials that give a structure, but the details are worked out individually.   Often gross inadequacies in adolescent's
Italian or Greek have to be worked out at home or with the help of specialists.
The pilot testing of the idea is underway and the results are heartening, for not
only do the adolescents learn to respect and appreciate a home language that typically had been neglected, but they seem to get thoroughly caught up in the teaching
role and school in general.   The younger pupils also seem to accept enthusiasti-
cally the foreign language that is being shared with them.   There is no end to
what the psychologists of language could do with such an idea.

Language and Society

Finally, at a broader societal level there is an important phenomenon running its
course that is also based on feelings of injustice and social neglect, namely the
widespread demand of social subgroups, as in Scotland, Wales, Brittany, French-
Canada, Puerto Rico, for political and social "independence" or "separation" from
the larger nations with which they have been associated.   The contributions that
we can make in this case can take many forms.   For instance, we could explore in
detail the sentiments and feelings of those who opt for separation and search for
the motivational roots of such sentiments.   My guess is that separatist feelings
are an exaggeration of the all-too-human belief that one's own cultural and/or
linguistic group is distinctive and unique, the difference being that in this instance the separatist is worried, often justifiably so, that this distinctiveness
is being threatened.   In my experience, there typically is a marked degree of
ethnocentrism, coupled with a certain amount of xenophobia and paranoia, associated
with separatist feelings.   Because these sentiments seem to depend so much on
beliefs in the distinctiveness of one's culture and language, one might be tempted
to challenge these beliefs on logical and empirical grounds so that an alternative

view could at least be considered - that cultures may not be as unique as most
people think and that neither culture nor language may in fact have all that much
impact on either personality styles or thought (see Lambert, 1979).   On these
matters, emotions tend to cloud thinking so that language and dialect distinctiveness, which are real enough, often carry with them all the excess meaning associated with "culture".   Thus, the claim that "We must fight for the maintenance of
our language and culture" may be no more than a demand for language rights, since
so much or so little may be implied by "culture".

But the world is not ready for logic of this sort, especially since the empirical
facts about culture similarities are, so far, few and far between.   Instead we
have to take seriously the common belief that language and culture shape unique
styles of thought and personality, and we must study how such beliefs become exaggerated in the direction of moves for separation.   In fact, I have been amazed,
in my survey of recent research, to find just how important a role language plays
in personal identity, in intergroup relations and in group-to-society relations.
Because of the importance attached to language, we should not be surprised to find
wide-spread fears among various groups about the possibilities of losing their
"language and culture" in this modern, English-dominated world.   These types of
fears seem to be as common among recent immigrants as among ethnolinguistic groups
of long-term residency (see Lambert, 1979; Taylor, Meynard and Rheault, 1977).
Thinking along these lines has prompted a group of us at McGill to make a distinction between a "subtractive" form of bilingualism wherein an ethnolinguistic
minority group, in attempting to master a prestigious national or international
language, may actually set aside or "subtract out" for good the home language, and
an "additive" form wherein members of a high prestige linguistic community can easily, and with no fear of jeopardising home language competence, "add" one or more
other languages to their repertoire of skills, reaping benefits of various sorts
from their bilinguality.   Since the subtractive route typically leads to the
neglect of the home language, sometimes to "semi-lingualism" (Skutnegg-Kangas and
Toukomaa, 1976), and often to poor chances of success in academic pursuits, a
great deal of attention must be directed to attempts to convert or transform subtractive linguistic experiences to additive ones.   So far we have few examples of
how such a transformation can be carried out (see Lambert, 1979), but for a Franco-
American community in northern Maine and a Hispanic-American community in the San
Diego area, the possibilities of circumventing the debilitating aspects of being an
ethnolinguistic minority are promising.   Essentially, these attempts at transformation provide children of ethnolinguistic minority groups with an opportunity
to be schooled through their home language for a substantial part of the curriculum
in the early school years.   Apparently because instruction is conducted in a relatively comfortable language, the "experimental" classes were better able to keep up
with course content than were the "controls" who had the conventional all-English
curriculum, and they also fared better in English language skill development and,
of course, in French language mastery.   It was also true that the experimental pupils developed a deeper appreciation of the home language, and a deeper pride in
being Franco-American which is not reflected in control children who did not have
the opportunity for home-language instruction.   As a consequence of this pilot study
what we propose is that as signs appear that the home language is being thoroughly
mastered, then a separate programme of English "language arts", in the form of immersion instruction given by native speakers of English, be introduced as early as
possible.   In this plan the important goal of bilingual development would be met
through separate monolingual routes wherein preference in time and order would be
given to the likely-to-be-neglected home language.   The assumption underlying this
approach is that minority group members will be more prompted to embrace and identify with the prestigious national language and the associated society once it is
clear that children with other-than-English home backgrounds are given a programme
that (a) keeps them up with national norms on the all-important content matter, and
that (b) reflects a respect for the foreign language as a valuable national resource

worth protecting, and a respect for the ethnic group itself permits members to be themselves through the maintenance of their language and their "distinctive" style of life. To the extent that Anglo youngsters in the community take the opportunity to "add" French or Spanish or whatever to their repertoires, then the possibilities for developing a genuine bilingual society open up. It is at this point that viable bilingual education programmes can be planned and organised.

The main point of this example is that an educational programme that speaks to the feelings of neglect, to the fears of language and culture loss, and to the marginality that so often characterises ethnolinguistic minority groups may also speak to many of the underlying concerns of separatists. A question remains, however, as to the adequacy of such programmes, because the roots of separatism and independentism may be much deeper than we think. We end up therefore with the need for those of us involved with the psychology of language to turn our attention to broad socio-political issues that impinge on language in society. Whether or not we think of these issues as within our field of expertise, they apparently are becoming part of our field. Thus, we must begin to contend with questions of a new sort. If we become champions of minority languages, whether from a Leninist or a liberalist political position, may we not be running the risk of marking and isolating ethnolinguistic minority groups and thereby exposing them to exploitation and segregation? And how are we to respond to the assimilationism involved in statements like: "If my ancestors came here and gave up the old-country language, that's the way it should be!" or "How can we ever have unity in this country with all these different languages going strong?" For my part, I am finding help in the writings of two important theorists, Jean-François Revel (1972) and Karl Popper (1966). Revel is a modern-day revolutionist who argues very convincingly that any social movement which is directed toward greater freedom and justice automatically engenders conflict and tension, including conflicts between and within ethnolinguistic groups, but that by working through conflicts, new and fairer forms of society can be forged. Revel believes that only in America has history provided all the right conditions for this new society to emerge. Popper provides me with a philosophy of the "open society" and of its enemies who flame defeatist attitudes and separatist sentiments by promises of conflict-free utopias, set aside from the real world, where things will be like they were "in the good old days". My point here is that we have to learn to handle change and conflict as we proceed in our work, and learn to fight against the enemies of open societies.

REFERENCES

Blake, L., Lambert, W. E., Sidoti, N. and Wolfe, D. Students' views of English Canadian, French Canadian tensions in Canada: The influence of immersion schooling. McGill University, mimeo, 1979

Clément, R., Gardner, R. C. and Smythe, P. C. Motivational variables in second language acquisition: A study of Francophones learning English. Canadian Journal of Behavioral Sciences, 1977, 9, 123-133.

Cohen, E. Design and redesign of the desegrated school: Problems of status, power and conflict, in E. Aronson (Ed.) Desegregation, past, present and future, New York: Plenum Publishing Company, 1979

Cziko, G. A., Lambert, W. E. and Gutter, R. The impact of programs of immersion-in-a-foreign-language on pupils' social attitudes. McGill University, mimeo, 1979

Cziko, G. A., Lambert, W. E., Sidoti, N. and Tucker, G. R. Graduates of early immersion: Retrospective views of grade II students and their parents. McGill University, mimeo, 1978

Duncan, O. D., Featherman, D. L. and Duncan, B. Socioeconomic background and achievement. New York: Seminar Press, 1972

Ervin, S. Identification and bilingualism. Harvard University, mimeo, 1954

Frasure-Smith, N., Lambert, W. E. and Taylor, D. M. Choosing the language of in-
    struction for one's children: A Quebec study. Journal of Cross-Cultural
    Psychology, 1975, 6, 131-155
Frender, R., Brown, B. and Lambert, W. E. The role of speech characteristics in
    scholastic success. Canadian Journal of Behavioral Science, 1970, 2, 299-306
Frender, R. and Lambert, W. E. Speech style and scholastic success. Georgetown
    Monographs on Language and Linguistics, 1972, 25, 237-271
Gagnon, M. Quelques facteurs déterminant l'attitude vis-à-vis l'anglais, langue
    seconde, in R. Darnell (Ed.) Linguistic diversity in Canadian society, Vol.2,
    Edmonton: Linguistic Research Inc. 1974
Gardner, R. C. Social psychological aspects of second language acquisition, in
    H. Giles and R. St. Clair (Eds.) Language and Social Psychology, Oxford:
    Blackwell, 1979
Gardner, R. C. and Lambert, W. E. Attitudes and motivation in second language
    learning. Rowley, Mass: Newbury House, 1972
Gardner, R. C. and Smythe, P. C. Second language acquisition: a social psycho-
    logical approach. Research Bulletin No. 232, University of Western Ontario,
    1975
Genesee, F. and Hamayan, E. Individual differences in young second language
    learners. McGill University, Psychology Department, mimeo, 1979
Giles, H. and Powesland, P. F. Speech style and social evaluation. London:
    Academic Press, 1975
Lambert, S. M. The role of speech in forming evaluations: a study of children
    and teachers. Unpublished M.A. Thesis, Tufts University, 1973
Lambert, W. E. Language as a factor in intergroup relations, in H. Giles and
    R. St. Clair (Eds.) Language and Social Psychology. Oxford: Basil Blackwell
    1979
Lambert, W. E. Some cognitive and sociocultural consequences of being bilingual,
    in J. E. Alatis (Ed.) International dimensions of bilingual education.
    Washington, D.C.: Georgetown University Press, 1978
Lambert, W. E. and Tucker, G. R. Bilingual education of children: the St.
    Lambert study. Rowley, Mass: Newbury House, 1972
McClelland, D. C. Testing for competence rather than for "intelligence".
    American Psychologist, 1973, 28, 1-14
Popper, K. R. The open society and its enemies, Volumes 1 and 2, London:
    Routledge & Kegan Paul, 1966
Rabushka, A. and Shepsle, K. A. Politics in plural societies: a theory of
    democratic instability. Columbus, Ohio: C. E. Merrill, 1972
Revel, J. F. Without Marx or Jesus: the new American revolution has begun.
    New York: Dell Publishing Company, 1972
Seligman, C. F., Tucker, G. R. and Lambert, W. E. The effects of speech style and
    other attributes on teachers' attitudes toward pupils. Language and Society,
    1972, 1, 131-142
Skutnegg-Kangas, T. and Toukomaa, P. Teaching migrant children's mother tongue and
    and learning the language of the host country in the context of socio-cultural
    situation of the migrant family. Helsinki: The Finnish National Commission
    for UNESCO, 1976
Taylor, D. M., Meynard, R. and Rheault, E. Threat to ethnic identity and second-
    language learning, in H. Giles (Ed.) Language, ethnicity and intergroup
    relations. London: Academic Press, 1977
Thomas, S. and Diaz, R. A language to share/un lenguaje para compartir. Newton,
    Mass: Educational Development Center, Inc., 1977

Epilogue

W. P. Robinson*, H. Giles** and P. M. Smith**

*School of Education, University of Bristol, 35 Berkeley Square, Bristol BS8 1JA, U.K.
**Department of Psychology, University of Bristol, 8-10 Berkeley Square, Bristol BS8
1HH, U.K.

It would be difficult to construct a taxonomic framework that would capture all
the similarities and differences among the papers in this volume, given their
diversity of perspectives, methodology, topics and techniques. We can nevertheless note with satisfaction the harmonious coexistence and articulation of contributions from a variety of disciplines. While some papers are mainly devoted to
the pursuit of theory, others have been concerned to discover the facts, and yet
others seek to relate the two. Topics vary from dying Amerindian languages to
fighting languages in Wales and to emergent pidgins in Europe. Societal implications of different bases of language structure contrast with small children
beginning to learn to be polite. As topics, courtroom talk and slang are new
recruits whereas sex, ethnicity, attitudes and acquisition are mature veterans of
social psychology conferences. The differences in the current state of knowledge
about these topics require that the questions posed and procedures judged most
appropriate for advancing knowledge should also be different. However, rather
than develop this contrastive analysis ad infinitum, and it might not be that useful
pragmatically, we prefer to return to two of the issues introduced in our Prologue
which we think provide a common basis for our understanding of social psychological
perspectives on language and its use. We refer here to the traditional experimental method and to the role of theories in advancing knowledge, in particular the
concepts and theories of cognitive organization. Each of these concerns poses
major dilemmas and challenges which need to be squarely met by all researchers if
the initial, exciting development of a social psychology of language is to remain
healthy at the end of this decade.

Experimental methodology

In our Prologue we referred to the fact that the experimental method is - and this
has been reflected in this volume - a hallmark of social psychological perspectives
on language and its use. Other methods of inquiry are also well represented.
Have all a legitimate place or are some methods better than others? At least two
conflicts are currently extant, one concerned with the relative merits of experiments and unobtrusive observation, the other an argument about the inappropriate-
ness of the experimental method as such.

Let us begin by asking a basic question: what can be wrong with experiments? One
criticism that seems to us to be entirely justified, is directed against the unnecessary and perhaps misleading uses of materials, subjects and instructions.
Experimental conditions ought to sample and reproduce the outside world in the lab-

oratory but under conditions of greater control than the outside affords.   Nevertheless, many of our designs neglect this maxim and fall too readily into the trap
of using readily-available student informants to complete paper and pencil tests.
We ask them to _imagine_ that they are personnel officers, teachers, etc. when perhaps we should be asking real personnel officers.   We are also prone to ask them
for general reports of what people think they might do rather than provide them
with examples that might expose what they are likely to do.   We seldom both obtain
retrospective or prospective self-reports and make observations of actual performance and then integrate the two.   We do not always stop to ask how the characteristics of interviewers or experimenters, as well as the situation, may be relevant
to the subjects' language behaviour.

Each of these risks can be instantiated in studies of speech markers of personal
and social identity.   For instance, Seligman, Tucker and Lambert (1972) used only
student teachers for their study of the relative weights assigned to vocal, written/
drawing, photographic information in ascribing characteristics to pupils.   Likewise, Fielding and Evered (1980) used trainee rather than experienced doctors when
investigating the effects of supposed patients' accents on medical diagnoses.
(In each case, however, it was at least trainees rather than introductory psychology
students who participated.)   Macaulay and Trevelyan (1973) asked 28 real employers
whether they took accent into account when selecting employees, but did not observe
their practice.   This may have been an important omission: Shuy (1970) obtained
comparable verbal accounts from employers on this issue, but showed that in practice the judgments they had made of speech assigned to Black professionals was
categorically similar to that assigned to Black, skilled manual workers.   Finally,
the large samples of speech analysed by Labov (1966) and Trudgill (1974) were, perhaps necessarily, collected mainly by the authors themselves, i.e. male interviewers.   Are any of the sex differences in pronunciation exposed in these studies
a function of the sex of the interviewer and situation of data collection as well as
of ethnicity, SES, topic, and formality of materials (Giles 1973)?   Evidence that
this might be so is indicated by Brouwer, Gerritsen and De Haan (1979) in their work
on sex of participants and speech.   These criticisms apply only as limits to the
generalisations that can be made to the data.   They do not invalidate them, and they
certainly do not invalidate either experimental or survey methods as such.

Objections might also be lodged against particular experiments on the grounds they
are premature.   It can be argued that experimental methods should not be exploited
until such time as our observations of natural behaviour have enabled us to chart
lists of possible and probable determinants and consequents of the speech in question;   we should have first reached a stage where hypotheses formulated can be
grounded on some naturally-derived empirical foundations and some theoretical explanatory ideas associated with these (as exemplified in Berko-Gleason's paper).
We must admit that social psychologists have often rushed into experimentation,
perhaps because this is the only kind of training they have encountered in their
undergraduate psychology.   Perhaps we should pay more attention to training in
other methods of idea and data generation and learn to stand and stare more at the
phenomena we claim to be studying.   We should not be afraid to do the preliminary
fieldwork that an ecologist or anthropologist would see as essential.   This would
at least provide us with first hand experience of what our experiments are supposed
to be examining.

Such observational contemplation can be applied to approaches at either a macroscopic or microscopic level.   By considering experimental results and their interpretations against a broader background of natural observation, we can sometimes notice
anomalies.   At one time work on the operation of direction of gaze and proxemics
in interpersonal communication was in danger of assigning such critical roles to
cues offered through these systems that we nearly persuaded ourselves that telephone conversations were impossible!   Observation of the real world can save us

from over-estimating the importance of our variables and making them do too much work.   Uninterfering observation which hopes to offer accounts of the most general through the exposure of the minutiae of single cases (Kendon 1967; Sacks, Schegloff and Jefferson 1974) can also lead to error.   In this case we run the risk of developing categories at a level of fineness beyond which human operators either do not or even could not use.   Fineness of measurement is not a virtue that can be left unqualified; it should correspond to what is socially significant.   Hence investigators who adopt five categories of accent are misguided if the participants in certain contexts use only two.   Detectives working in case studies with minute analysis may well succeed in offering a highly detailed, but in some ways arbitrary, description of a unique event, and may not be able to show that their fine scoring has either concurrent or predictive validity; science is concerned with the general represented in the particular and the abstract realised in the concrete.   However, the evaluation of the success of such activities can only be made after they have been conducted and in the light of consequential related studied.   Hence we have no reason to discourage high risk research strategies which offer high gains if validated; indeed, Piaget's early work could be viewed in this light.

If one is instantiating limitations of design and practice, it is kinder to take such examples as those offered above, since, over and above their limitations, each provides positive results, and each can be defended as a pioneering attempt to pin down some covariation.   Other examples might have been chosen which make no such positive contribution.   Experiments can be so bad that their results tell us nothing.   They can be so weak that we cannot understand why stronger manipulations or controls were not introduced from the outset.   The existence of bad or trivial experiments is irrelevant however to the value of the experimental method as such. Indeed, there seems to be no genuine case or principle for rejecting experiments in general; to so do would be to deny the value of an important means of obtaining evidence.   What we ought to be looking forward to are problems where the results generated by natural observation, participant and controlled observations are the same, problems where case studies illustrate what analytical statistics applied to samples of data support, and problems for which the descriptive and explanatory propositions that represent them are supported in each and every conceivable way. Overly liberal and permissive as this may sound, "each and every" is correct, "either/or" is an unnecessary constraint.

Theory

In order to set the scene for this final section, we can use a contrast made by Popper (1976, p.21) (See Figure 1).   Scientifically both columns are arguably important and cannot sensibly be considered without reference to each other, and neither is of significance if not considered in relation to the phenomenological and objective world to which its constituents are intended to refer.   In our theorising, we should not sacrifice the pursuit of one column for the other.   We raise the question only because we are worried that we perhaps spend too much time on concepts and too little on explanatory propositions, particularly as these relate to the mediating processes of cognitive organisation.   Concepts are inventions and recommendations about how to categorise phenomena and no more.   We can invent categories but we cannot discover whether they are true.   It is only when they are entered into propositions whose truth can be checked in some way that we can begin to assess whether they are useful or not, and it is the discovered relations between propositions and the phenomena they attempt to represent that provide the grounds for assessing their usefulness.

The papers in this volume have utilised many concepts: ethnicity, sex, conversation speech act, slang, pidgin, hesitation, attitude, SES, vitality, accommodation e pui. To what extent can these be successfully turned into propositions that can be integrated into explanations?   They are beginning to and will continue to do so, but

IDEAS
that is

TERMS/CONCEPTS   STATEMENTS/THEORIES
                    may be formulated in

WORDS   ASSERTIONS
                    which may be

MEANINGFUL   TRUE
                    and their

MEANING   TRUTH
                    may be reduced by way of

DEFINITIONS   DERIVATIONS
                    to that of

UNDEFINED CONCEPTS   PRIMITIVE PROPOSITIONS

        the attempt to establish (rather than reduce)
              by these means their
MEANING   TRUTH
        leads to an infinite regress

Fig. 1

let us reiterate that it is the explanations and theories into which they enter
that test their use and herald their significance and value. We must of course
defer to those aspects of phenomenology that are pertinent to our activities and we
must be imaginative in our creation of concepts and propositions. We are free to
construct propositions in terms of categories and relations that we invent, but
once we turn to check the correspondence between these and the reality they are intended to represent we can only discover whether or not they are true or false; we
cannot assimilate the world to our theories, the latter have to accommodate the
real world. The data already collected and yet to be collected will set limits to
the theories devised to explain them. Some times we can expect that the data
available will exceed the power of the explanations extant; at other times we can
expect that the theories will be rich enough to generate arrays of propositions
waiting to be tested. And both can be true at the same time. The theories of
cognitive organisation mentioned in this volume all have untapped empirical potential. However many factual findings about language in social psychology stand
isolated and unexplained. In the long run we can hope for a dialectical relation
between theory and data, each facilitating and inhibiting the other, each acting as
a brake on the excessive proliferation of the other as well as inspiring their con-
joint growth.

And what are the qualities of good theories and explanations? We can presumably
still endorse the virtues of a clear presentation of primitive concepts, defined os-
tensively, verbally and operationally, set down in terms of the similarities and
differences they have with each other. These concepts and those derived from them
have to be combined into propositions whose truth or falsity can be checked, prefer-
ably through a variety of testing procedures in as wide a range of contextual reali-
sations as possible. Those who use the theories as bases for collecting data have
to remain on watch for ways of improving the accuracy, precision, simplicity and
elegance of all the components and their manner of articulation, systematically
accumulating what fits and noting what does not. Their replacement can then assimilate the old as well as accommodate to the new. Alas social psychologists have as
yet been rather lax generally in their adherence to such principles. Our concepts
and theories seem to come and go for reasons that have little to do with the advancement of knowledge; fashionable fields wax and wane without bringing forward and integrating what went before. It will be instructive in twenty years time to look
back to see whether, if social psychologists remain interested in language, it is
possible to trace continuities from work reported through to descendants. If we
can, so much the better.

And what priorities do we see for the content of future theories and explanations? In line with our own perspective on the social psychology of language set down in the Prologue, we would like to see more use made of dynamic processes rather than static concepts of cognitive organisation as they mediate language use.   Two can be highlighted as illustrations. First, bridge-building operations between levels of analysis have been one characteristic of a number of papers herein, and several of these were couched in terms of Tajfel's theory of intergroup relations (Tajfel 1978; Tajfel and Turner 1979).   What appeals to us about this theory is that it seeks to specify which aspects of personal or social identity will emerge as significant determinants of behaviour in particular situations.   Sociologically- and situationally-oriented psychologists who see no place for personality-based individual differences in the explanation of any human behaviour are a dying breed, as are those psychologists who view invariant personality traits as the only significant determinants of behaviour.   The compromising interactionists who argue for a joint appreciation of personality disposition and situation are alive and well (Furnham and Argyle, in press), but may be over optimistic about the strength of their analysis.   The Tajfel theory is not inconsistent with one version of the interactionist view in the immediate situation; however, it does in addition endeavour to point out when the identities of a person will be important.   Its major contrast has been between personal and social group identities, specifying when X will behave as an individual and when as a member of a social category (father, Christian, darts player, foreigner, etc.).   If the theory is sound, its significance for language and social behaviour will grow rather than diminish partly because it enables movement from the sociological to the psychological and back and because it can be exploited to view users of language as either victims or agents of social reality, or as both.

Second, the issue of self-consciousness raised in Berger's introduction to the interpersonal communication symposium (as well as less explicitly in a number of other papers) deserves a further airing and comment,   because the implications of his analysis extend across the whole domain of the intersect between language and behaviour.   The issues raised range from considerations of the technical details as to what it is possible and sensible to ask respondents to say and do in data gathering situations to theories about the measure of cognitive discretion available to social groups in developing, establishing and maintaining their identities.   A view of Man as a victim rather than as an agent is, we suspect, bound up with issues of self-consciousness.   Hence, we need to find out (a) what people normally monitor and do not monitor and when; (b) what people can be enabled to monitor and when; and (c) how this monitoring can relate to manifest behaviour.

In work by Robinson and Robinson (Robinson 1980) we are beginning to think in terms of a developmental model of phases.   Within the limited scope of our inquiries children seem to learn to exercise verbal referential communication skills, unaware of problems of ambiguity.   They encode and decode with sufficient skill for verbal interaction to be generally successful.   At some point however they come to realise that messages can be ambiguous; they learn to diagnose the sources of ambiguity and by then have developed a potential for control over the explicitness of their speech that they did not have earlier.   Subsequently, they semi-automate their speech once more, monitoring and checking its referential quality only in problematic circumstances or when they believe communication has failed.   This too simple model of a three-phase development – ignorant general success, followed by awareness of conditions of success and failure, followed eventually by generally unmonitored successful skilled performance with a provision for analysis in specific circumstances – may well be more generally applicable to many other aspects of behaviour in general and communicative behaviour in particular.   Berger (1979) has himself asked questions about monitoring in conversation and has begun to chart possible strategies for use and circumstances of engagement.   He has been facing up to the agent-victim polarization and appears to be avoiding both rabid free-willed individualism and social determinism; however, more generally in sociolinguistics the determinists probably have the upper hand at the present time, particularly as one moves towards the sociological and linguistic poles.   The bias can be justified, yet throughout this book we have seen that people are not always mere victims of their heritage; they can also work for change.

In conclusion, we see at least two major directions in which future studies of language and social psychology are likely to move.   One will centre upon descriptions and explanations of the ways in which language use has the potential to act simultaneously as a dependent and independent variable of cognitive organisation (cf Giles, Hewstone and St. Clair, in press).   The other will explore how conscious and unconscious behaviour relate to phases in and types of language behaviour and the significance that these have for the control and development of speech-associated activities.

REFERENCES

Berger, C. R. Beyond initial interaction, in H. Giles and R. N. St. Clair (Eds.) Language and social psychology. Oxford: Blackwell, 1979

Brouwer, D., Gerritsen, M. and De Haan, D. Speech differences between women and men: on the wrong track? Language in sociology, 1979, 8, 33-50

Fielding, R. G. and Evered, C. The influence of patients' speech on doctors: the diagnostic interview, in R. St. Clair and H. Giles (Eds.) Social and psychological contexts of language. Hillsdale, New Jersey: Erlbaum, 1980

Furnham, A. and Argyle, M. The psychology of social situations. Oxford: Pergamon (in press)

Giles, H. Accent mobility: a model and some data. Anthropological Linguistics, 1973, 15, 87-105

Giles, H., Hewstone, M. and St. Clair, R.   Cognitive structures and the social psychology of language, in H. Giles and R. St. Clair (Eds.) The social psychological significance of communication. Hillsdale, New Jersey: Erlbaum (in press)

Kendon, A. Some functions of gaze direction in social interaction. Acta Psychologica, 1967, 26, 22-63

Labov, W. The social stratification of English in New York City. Washington, D.C.: Center for Applied Linguistics, 1966

Macaulay, R. K. S. and Trevelyan, G. D. Language, education and employment in Glasgow. Social Science Research Report (HR2311), 1973

Popper, K. Unended quest. London: Collins/Fontana, 1976

Robinson, E. J. The child's understanding of inadequate messages and communication failure, in W. P. Dickson (Ed.) Children's oral communication skills. New York: Academic Press, 1980

Sacks, H., Schegloff, E. and Jefferson, G.   A simplest systematics for the organisation of turn-taking in conversation. Language, 1974, 50, 696-735

Seligman, C. R., Tucker, G. R. and Lambert, W. E. The effects of speech style and other attributes on teachers' attitudes towards pupils. Language in Society, 1972, 1, 131-142

Shuy, R. W. Language and success: who are the judges? in R. W. Bailey and J. L. Robinson (Eds.) Varieties of present-day English. New York: Macmillan, 1970

Tajfel, H. Differentiation between social groups. London: Academic Press, 1978

Tajfel, H. and Turner, J. C. An integrative theory of intergroup conflict, in W. G. Austin and H. Worchel (Eds.) The social psychology of intergroup relations. Monterey: Brooks/Cole, 1979

Trudgill, P. The social differentiation of English in Norwich. Cambridge: Cambridge University Press, 1974

Author Index*

Abel, R. L. 368-9, 374
Abelson, R. P. 51, 53
Aboud, F. 133, 139, 148, 154, 169
Addington, D. W. 122, 125
Aebi-Hungerbülher, E. 325
Agar, M. 167-8
Agheyisi, R. N. 363, 365
Alberti, L. 284-6, 325
Allen, V. L. 134,139
Allport, G. W. 2, 6, 143-5, 234-5
Alve, S. 111-4
Amir, Y. 143, 145, 151, 153
Apple, W. 237, 245, 280, 282, 294-7, 300
Ardener, S. 85, 87
Argyle, M. 2-6, 275, 278, 288, 292, 302, 305, 397-407, 429
Arney, W. R. 302, 306
Aronson, E. 268, 273
Atkins, B. 394-5
Atkinson, J. M. 369, 372-3, 374
Aubert, V. 368, 374
Auerbach, J. S. 368, 374
Bailey, G. H. 4, 194, 209-215
Bakeman, R. 302, 306, 318-9
Baldwin, J. 368, 373-4
Bales, R. F. 398-9, 406
Bandura, A. 305
Bankowski, Z. 368, 374
Bardwick, J. M. 127, 131
Barker, R. G. 77, 80
Barnes, R. D. 50, 53, 116, 118-9
Bassili, J. 133, 139, 148, 154
Bate, B. A. 90, 95-6
Bates, E. 403, 406

Bateson, G. 56, 60
Bem, S. L. 90, 96, 115, 117, 119
Ben Debba, M. 284, 286, 325
Berger, C. R. 3, 5-6, 49-53, 72, 75, 429
Berger, P. L. 56, 60
Berlyne, D. E. 305
Berry, J. W. 149, 153, 198, 201
Bialystok, H. 152-3
Bickerton, D. 179, 184, 332, 334, 377, 387
Billig, M. 186, 191
Biondi, D. 377, 387
Birdwhistell, R. 402, 406
Bishin, W. R. 367, 374
Blakar, R. M. 105-9, 111-4
Blake, L. 417, 423
Blanchard, I. 248, 253
Blaubergs, M. 86, 92
Blom, J. P. 346, 351
Bloom, L. 17, 19
Bloomfield, M. 143, 145
Blumberg, A. S. 373-4
Boardman, S. K. 111, 114
Bochner, A. P. 59-60
Bogoch, B. 367, 369, 371, 373-4
Bohannon, J. N. 78, 80
Bolinger, D. 369, 374
Borgatta, E. F. 56, 60
Bouma, G. D. 284, 286
Bourdieu, P. 232
Bourhis, R. Y. 3-5, 66-7, 69, 122, 125, 133, 139, 148, 154, 161, 164, 167-8, 174, 177, 180, 184, 186, 190-1, 208, 229, 230, 232, 335, 343, 360, 362, 364
Bowers, J. W. 4, 194-5, 210, 215, 217-21

---

* Although comprehensive, only the first two authors are indexed if the actual
reference includes more than two, unless the complete citation or junior authors
appear often elsewhere.

Subject Index